Women's Journey to Empowerment

in the 21st Century

INTERPERSONAL VIOLENCE SERIES

SERIES EDITORS

Claire Renzetti, PhD
Jeffrey L. Edleson, PhD

Women's Journey to Empowerment in the 21st Century

A Transnational Feminist Analysis of Women's Lives in Modern Times

EDITED BY KRISTEN ZALESKI

ANNALISA ENRILE

EUGENIA L. WEISS

XIYING WANG

OXFORD
UNIVERSITY PRESS

Oxford University Press is a department of the University of Oxford. It furthers
the University's objective of excellence in research, scholarship, and education
by publishing worldwide. Oxford is a registered trade mark of Oxford University
Press in the UK and certain other countries.

Published in the United States of America by Oxford University Press
198 Madison Avenue, New York, NY 10016, United States of America.

© Oxford University Press 2020

CIP data is on file at the Library of Congress
ISBN 978–0–19–092709–7

9 8 7 6 5 4 3 2 1

Printed by Sheridan Books, Inc., United States of America

CONTENTS

Across the globe the gains that women have made have been championed by feminists who have been at the forefront of women's struggles and mobilization demanding those gains.

—Carty and Mohanty (2015, p. 86)

FROM TABLE DISCUSSION TO GLOBAL COLLABORATION

It was a warm fall evening in Beijing when the idea for this book was born. Around the table of a Beijing-style hot pot, three social work academics, one Chinese and two Americans, discussed the state of the world for women in the 21st century and the longing for a text that could describe the struggles and the successes of women in the fight for equity and safety throughout the world.

As professors and feminist researchers, three of us share some similar but different research interests: Kristen's work is extensively on sexual violence in the United States; Annalisa, as a Philippine American scholar, has been working on sex trafficking issues in the Philippines and throughout the world; and Xiying, as a Chinese scholar with overseas training, has focused on dating violence, domestic violence, and school bullying. Through the discussion, we found that although our research topics are different, the underlying issues of gender inequality and the surrounding social structures are similar, no matter the place on earth. A short time later, we invited Eugenia, whose expertise on feminist global issues and her being of mixed heritage and from Latin America, as well as her vast editorial experience, could help us make this book everything we knew it needed to be for maximum impact.

We felt a compelling need to create a book in a collaborative spirit to include expert contributors that would provide a global lens to survey areas of the world—not just one region, one race, one voice—and study the intersectional issues of gender, race, class, culture, and politics that arise in gender-based violence and the advocacy efforts to fight injustice and promote equality for women and girls throughout the world.

In a way, the collaboration of editing this book over the Pacific Ocean is an act of feminist practice. Mohanty (2004) argues that feminist practice operates at a number of levels: at the level of daily life through the everyday acts that constitute our identities and relational communities; at the level of collective action in groups, networks, and movements constituted around feminist vision of social transformation; and at the levels of theory, pedagogy, and textual creativity in the scholarly and writing practices of feminists engaged in the production of knowledge (p. 5). For us, editing the book was part and parcel of our constructing feminist identities, writing a feminist manifesto, and disseminating women's knowledge along with promoting social justice and transformation. In addition, each chapter embodies the three parts of Mohanty's feminist practice: scholarly overview, advocacy efforts, and a linkage to how each reader can be involved in the march for equality throughout the world.

This book is the result of not only the collaboration of the four editors but also a collective solidarity among feminists covering issues that occur in 14 countries, on five continents, of varying academic, frontline agency, and nongovernmental organization affiliations. This international, multilingual (written in the English language), interdisciplinary collaboration brings forth a rich discussion of feminism and globalization in the 21st century.

TRANSNATIONAL FEMINISM AS THEORETICAL FRAMEWORK

A global perspective is not enough. Mohanty (2004) offers a sustained critique of globalization and urges a reorientation of transnational feminist practices toward anticapitalist struggles. Mohanty defines solidarity in terms of mutuality, accountability, and empowerment. The danger that transnational feminists confront is being able to balance a distinct perspective of nationhood and gender while respecting the various intersectionalities of the broader women's movement. The Fourth World Conference on Women, held in Beijing in 1995, began a new era of collaboration and sisterhood that started to blur the lines of borders. Thus, feminism across and within borders took shape, forming a transnational ideology that was more dependent on intersectionality, politics of difference, and solidarity instead of a local focus. It is through this transnational lens that we are able to fully understand the depth and complexity of women's lives and the sisterhoods and movements that are built from these foundational pillars.

THE CURRENT BACKLASH AND THE IMPORTANCE OF ACTIVISM

Throughout the world, women's voices are needed more than ever. For many countries, the political climate is stripping away women's rights and silencing women's voices while at the same time violence against women is at an all-time high. A moment of reckoning for Western feminists was in 2016, when Donald Trump was elected President of the United States, beating out a woman candidate. Trump ran a campaign that was patriarchal in its beliefs and borderline misogynist (if not entirely misogynist) in its actions. Rather than standing by idly watching the patriarchy in America take hold of its electorate, during his inauguration, millions of women throughout the United States marched in protest. Throughout the world, millions of additional women marched in solidarity. The Women's March, as it came to be known, brought together women and allies from all backgrounds who unified under basic principles of ending violence against women and girls, supporting reproductive rights, empowering communities (LGBTQ, immigrants, disabled, and workers), upholding civil rights, and working for environmental justice (https://womensmarch.com/mission-and-principles). However, the movement has been criticized by feminists who believe it narrowly defines the female agenda, advancing the agenda of "white" feminists but leaving behind feminists of color, LGBT, and marginalized females whose vaginas are of one color as portrayed by the pink vagina hats worn by protestors—in other words, pussy is not pink (Shamus, 2018). This conversation is an example of the importance of inclusive resistance that this book works toward unifying.

Globally, Vladimir Putin (Russia), Xi Jinping (China), Recep Erdogan (Turkey), and Duterte (the Philippines) have given rise to the type of sexist, competitive, and egotistical leadership that has tried to reverse women's rights (Solomon, 2016). Despite the current sociopolitical and economic trends determined to undermine women's agency around the world, the opposition has started to rise. Women have marched, organized, innovated, and run for and won political offices. The personal and the political have become interchangeable in a concrete way, from the advocacy that women have unified around to the justice that they champion. From the boardroom to the classroom, from the parliament of the streets to the capital buildings, women are challenging the system and, in many cases, triumphing. The 21st-century woman does not take oppression and exploitation as a given; she fights against them. The chapters in this book are a testament to that.

ORGANIZATION OF THE BOOK

We have divided the 23 chapters of this text into the four domains we believe are most pressing for the international resistance: institutional neglect of women and girls, social media and free choice, political gender equity, and the 21st century's shape of interpersonal violence. Within each section are personal stories of survivorship and heroism, pictures and art from the front lines, and an academic conversation about how transnational feminism intersects each topic.

Most chapters begin with a story of peril and end with a call to action of advocacy and hope. The goal is to provide readers not only with information but also with immediate next steps they can take to join the fight for justice and equality. With that in mind, this book is an invitation to join the action. There are many opportunities for action no matter where you are located in the world today.

Finally, this book represents the urgency of transnational feminism reaching every corner of the planet to transform the majority of societal institutions toward creating respectful spaces for women and girls. This is a collective journey that we must all embark upon toward ensuring an equitable world that is safe and a place in which women and girls not only survive but also thrive and thus by doing so we will be promoting the future sustainability of our planet and humankind. We, as editors, challenge you to act and not remain a passive bystander in the face of injustices in each moment of your life. As a global community, change is within our reach.

REFERENCES

Carty, L. E., & Mohanty, C. T. (2015). Mapping transnational feminist engagements. In R. Baksh & W. Harcourt (Eds.), *The Oxford handbook of transnational feminist movements* (pp. 82–115). New York: Oxford University Press.

Mohanty, C. T. (2004). *Feminism without Borders: Decolonizing theory, practicing solidarity.* Durham, NC: Duke University Press.

Shamus, K. J. (2018, January 10). *Pink pussy hats: The reason feminists are ditching them.* Detroit Free Press. Retrieved from https://www.freep.com/story/news/2018/01/10/pink-pussyhats-feminists-hats-womens-march/1013630001

Solomon, E. (2016, November 23). *The Dawn of the Strongmen Era is Here.* Macleans. Retrieved from: https://www.macleans.ca/news/canada/the-dawn-of-the-strongman-era-is-here/

Annalisa Enrile is a Clinical Professor at the University of Southern California Suzanne Dworak-Peck School of Social Work, turning classrooms into brave spaces to train the next generation of change-makers. She traces her roots back to the Philippines, where she became a human rights defender and anti-trafficking warrior. She continues to work on both sides of the Pacific and across other oceans fighting to end modern-day slavery. She believes in the transformative power of stories, the strength of community, and the promise of innovation and design.

Eugenia L. Weiss is Clinical Professor at the University of Southern California Suzanne Dworak-Peck School of Social Work. She believes in empowering women and girls in the pursuit of higher education and leadership. She promotes social justice and gender equity through scholarship and advocacy.

Xiying Wang is a Professor of Faculty of Education at Beijing Normal University. She has been working in the area of gender-based violence for more than 15 years. Her articles address the issues of dating violence, sexual coercion, child sexual abuse, domestic violence, school bullying, and other forms of gender-based violence.

Kristen Zaleski is a Clinical Associate Professor at the University of Southern California Suzanne Dworak-Peck School of Social Work and is an expert on issues related to sexual trauma and psychotherapy.

ABOUT THE CONTRIBUTORS

Sarah Ahmed is a PhD Candidate of Sociology (ABD) at the University of Oregon and is working on her dissertation titled "Women's Empowerment Through Polio Eradication: Agency and Representation of Lady Health Workers in Pakistan." She holds an MS in Sociology from the University of Oregon and an MA in International Studies (South Asia) from the University of Washington.

Kimberley Anderson is a PhD student at the University of Leipzig, Germany, with a research focus on refugee and asylum-seeker mothers who have children born of sexual violence. She holds an MS in Child & Adolescent Mental Health from University College London.

Elizabeth M. Aparicio, PhD, MSW, is trained as a clinical social worker and is Assistant Professor of Behavioral and Community Health at the University of Maryland, College Park. A seasoned clinician with a decade of clinical experience with trauma-affected children, youth, and families, she informs and tests community-engaged approaches to reducing intergenerational patterns of family violence through research–practice partnerships with her community partners.

Peter Averkiou is a board-certified pediatrician who was in private practice for 20 years. He currently serves as an Assistant Professor of Integrated Medical Science at the Charles E. Schmidt College of Medicine at Florida Atlantic University.

Claudia M. Bermúdez, PhD, is an adjunct faculty member and coordinator in the Teacher Education Program at Claremont Graduate University. Her research interests include critical social justice, emergent bilingualism, and the intersection of class/race and social/cultural capital within kindergarten through 12th grade education.

Audrey Brammer is the CEO of Upswing Group, a firm that helps nonprofits achieve greater community outcomes. She holds a Master of Social Work degree from the University of Southern California.

Rachel R. Camacho is Director of Student Engagement at Claremont Graduate University. An educational access, completion, and higher education scholar, her research lies at the intersection of education, race, class, and gender, with a focus on increasing access to an equitable education for historically marginalized students and communities.

Saltanat Childress, PhD, MSW, is an Assistant Professor at the University of Texas–Arlington School of Social Work. Her research is focused on women's and child well-being and prevention of family violence in the international context. She is dedicated to improving long-term health outcomes and empowering survivors of domestic violence through developing, adapting, and evaluating interventions focusing on healthy family functioning, economic empowerment, and improving responses of criminal justice, public health, and social service systems.

Tuen Yi Chiu (Jenny) is Assistant Professor at the Department of Sociology and Social Policy, Lingnan University. She obtained her PhD in Sociology from The Chinese University of Hong Kong and was Visiting Fellow at Harvard University. Her research interests include intimate partner violence, gender, marriage and family, migration, transnationalism and aging.

Debra L. Clark, PhD, is an Associate Professor in Cultural Foundations of Education at Kent University. Her research interests are multiculturalism and teacher preparation.

Tyan Parker Dominguez, PhD, MPH, MSW is a Clinical Professor in the USC Suzanne Dworak-Peck School of Social Work. Her research focuses on racial disparities in adverse birth outcomes and infant mortality, with an emphasis on racism-related stress and other social determinants of health.

Stephanie Gopie, MD, MBS, is a surgical resident in Boca Raton, Florida. She is a first-generation American of Guyanese descent.

Michelle Greene is a hospital social worker in Orange County, California. She received her BA in Sociology from California State University, Fullerton, in 2016 and her MSW from the University of Southern California in 2018.

Adrineh Gregorian has degrees from the University of California, Los Angeles, and The Fletcher School of Law and Diplomacy at Tufts University. In 2008, she was awarded a US Fulbright Grant to research reproductive health in Armenia. She is currently pursuing a PhD in Cultural Studies at Claremont Graduate University. Her research focuses on media's role in democratization and social impact.

Toni Handboy (Lakota), MSW, recently graduated with her Master of Social Work from the University of South Dakota. She has worked for 7 years in the field of behavioral health as an integrated care case manager.

Dawn Joosten-Hagye is an Associate Professor of Social Work at the University of Southern California Suzanne Dworak-Peck School of Social Work, where she teaches practice courses and engages in interprofessional education and research. As a licensed clinical social worker, she specializes in evidence-based practice with adults, older adults, and their families in health and behavioral health settings.

Anne Katz is a Clinical Professor of Social Work at the University of Southern California Suzanne Dworak-Peck School of Social Work. Her research interests include women's issues and aging, caregiver stress, interprofessional education, aging in prison, expressive arts and education, and counseling older adults.

Gayle Kimball, PhD, is the author of 20 books, including *Brave: Young Women's Global Revolution, Volume 1: Global Themes* and *Volume 2: Regional Activism*. Comment on her blog globalyouthbook.wordpress.com.

Arianna King is a doctoral candidate in the City, Culture, and Community Program at Tulane University with an MS in Urban Studies from the University of New Orleans. Her current areas of exploration lie at the intersection of urban studies, public markets, and space in West Africa, employing both qualitative and quantitative methodologies.

Jessica Klein is a Licensed Clinical Social Worker and Lecturer of Social Work at the University of Southern California Suzanne Dworak-Peck School of Social Work. She has a private psychotherapy practice in the Los Angeles area where she specializes in the treatment of trauma.

Cary Klemmer is a social worker and PhD Candidate in Social Work at the University of Southern California, Los Angeles. She hopes to improve the lives of lesbian, gay, bisexual, and transgender youth, adolescents, and adults through social work practice, teaching, and research.

Yu Li is a lecturer at Chongqing University of Science and Technology. Her research interests are girl's schooling empowerment and English language education.

Ana Lopez, MSW, ACSW, is the founder of inPhormed, a review platform that creates transparency for migrants searching for work abroad. She has clinical experience working with survivors of domestic violence and human trafficking.

Ming Luo is Postdoctoral Fellow at the Department of Sociology, Peking University. She obtained her PhD in Sociology from the Chinese University of Hong Kong. Her research interests include sexuality, gender, family, and migration.

Kate Majewski is an attorney and social worker who currently works in a collaborative court for justice-involved veterans in Orange County, California.

Liza L. Maza is a Filipina activist for women's emancipation and social liberation. She was a legislator from 2001 to 2010 representing Gabriela Women's Party to the Philippine Congress and became a member of the Cabinet as lead convener of the National Anti-Poverty Commission in July 2016. She resigned in 2018 to pursue the path of real change through participation in organizing and mobilizing mass movements in the Philippines and abroad.

Laura McKinney is an Associate Professor of Sociology at Tulane University. Her research falls at the intersection of gender, international development, and the environment.

Dorotea Mendoza (https://doroteamendoza.com) is a writer and activist who in 1998 co-founded the Purple Rose Campaign against trafficking of women and girls. Since the early 1990s, she has served on executive committees of various direct service, grassroots, and educational women's organizations, such as BABAE, GABNet, and Sari-Sari Women of Color Arts Coup.

Jill T. Messing, PhD, MSW, is an Associate Professor in the School of Social Work and the Director of the Office of Gender-Based Violence at Arizona State University. She specializes in the development and testing of intimate partner violence risk assessments and is particularly interested in the use of risk assessment in collaborative and innovative interventions for survivors of abuse.

Terri Minniear, MSW, serves as a hospital social worker in Orange County, California. She received her BA in Psychology from Chapman University in 2016 and her MSW from the University of Southern California in 2018.

Ya Na, a Mongolian ethnic minority in China, is a PhD Candidate of Cultural Foundations of Education at Kent State University. Her current research interests focus on marginalized girls' education and empowerment in western China.

Wanda Nowicka is a human and women's rights activist, bioethicist, writer, co-founder and President of the Polish Federation for Women and Family Planning (1991–2011), and Member of Parliament of Poland and Deputy Speaker (2011–2015). She was awarded the University-in-Exile Award by the New School in recognition of engagement in the struggle for women's reproductive rights, both in Poland and in the international arena (2008).

Annalise Oatman is a Licensed Clinical Social Worker with an Oxbridge Masters in Philosophy. Her work experience spans outpatient mental health settings treating various traumatized populations. She is a therapist in private practice in San Francisco specializing in creative women and trauma.

Natasha Post Rosow, MSW, graduated from the University of Southern California Suzanne Dvorak-Peck School of Social Work in 2017 after a successful 15-year career as a writer and screenwriter. She holds a BA from Harvard University and an MFA from the University of Texas, Austin.

Nirmala Prakash is an Assistant Professor of Integrated Medical Science and Director in the Office for Diversity and Inclusion at Florida Atlantic University's College of Medicine. Her research interests include violence, LGBTQ health, educational outreach, and community health.

Jennifer Prevot is a first year Internal Medicine Resident at Emory University. She received her MD from Florida Atlantic University and BA from the University of Florida in Food Science and Human Nutrition.

Joanna Regulska is a Vice Provost and Associate Chancellor, Global Affairs, and Professor of Gender, Sexuality and Women's Studies at the University of California, Davis. Her research concentrates on women's agency and political activism by women in central and eastern Europe and Caucasus. She is the author/co-author of eight books and more than 100 articles and chapters. In 2011, she was awarded Doctor Honoris Causa from the Tbilisi State University, Georgia.

Fraidy Reiss is an American forced marriage survivor turned advocate. She's the founder and executive director of Unchained At Last, the only nonprofit dedicated to ending forced and child marriage in the United States through direct services and advocacy.

Vilma Seeberg is Associate Professor for International/Multicultural Education at Kent State University. She teaches graduate courses; directs dissertations; and publishes on education in development, girls' schooling empowerment, and mass education in China.

Melissa Indera Singh is a Licensed Clinical Social Worker with experience in medical social work and crisis response. She is a Clinical Associate Professor at the University of

Southern California Suzanne Dworak-Peck School of Social Work in the Department of Social Change and Innovation.

Claradina Soto (Navajo/Jemez Pueblo), PhD, MPH, is a full-time Assistant Clinical Professor at the University of Southern California Keck School of Medicine in the Institute for Health Promotion and Disease Prevention Research. She has more than 20 years of experience working with American Indian and Alaska Native populations in public health, collaborating with urban and tribal communities in California to reduce and prevent mental health disparities, commercial tobacco use, and substance use and opioid use disorders.

Ruth Supranovich, EDD, LCSW, is a Clinical Associate Professor at the University of Southern California Suzanne Dworak-Peck School of Social Work. She is course lead and co-instructor of a community immersion course in which students travel to the Cheyenne River Sioux Tribe Reservation to learn first-hand about Lakota history and culture as well as engage in decolonizing social work practice.

Elisa van Ee is a clinical psychologist and senior researcher at Psychotraumacentrum Zuid-Nederland, Reinier van Arkel and Behavioural Science Institute, Radboud University, the Netherlands. She has extensive clinical experience with war trauma and organized violence. She is using her combined clinical and research experience to develop research into the effects of complex trauma on families, especially families in challenging circumstances.

Jade Vorster is a medical student at Florida Atlantic University with a passion for public health and social justice. She plans to pursue a career in internal medicine.

Aditi Wahi-Singh, MPH, MSW, is a public health researcher and social worker. Her clinical and research interests include working with children and vulnerable populations, most recently within oncology and early/forced child marriage.

Doni Whitsett, PhD, LCSW, is a Fulbright Scholar and Clinical Professor at the University of Southern California Suzanne Dworak-Peck School of Social Work, where she has taught for more than 25 years. She has been working with cult survivors for three decades, publishes articles on this topic, conducts workshops to educate mental health professionals, and presents at conferences both nationally and internationally.

Ying Xin (Iron) is the executive director of the Beijing LGBT Center in China, where she started the LGBT affirmed psychologists' training and initiated the first national survey on social attitudes towards sexual orientation, gender identity and gender expression. She also initiated China's first trans gender hotline and LGBT affirming psychologists network.

Antigone Davis As Facebook's Global Head of Safety, Antigone works with internal teams, external safety organizations, and government bodies to ensure that Facebook is a world leader in online safety. Antigone serves on the International Advisory Board for WePROTECT and the boards of the Family Online Safety Institute, the National Center for Missing and Exploited Children, the National Center for Victims of Crime, and the National Network to End Domestic Violence.

Women's Journey to Empowerment

in the 21st Century

PART I

Institutional Neglect of Women and Girls

Introduction: Confronting the Global Challenges of the 21st Century

LIZA L. MAZA■

W omen have achieved wins through relentless struggles for equality and empowerment. Despite this, globally, poor and marginalized women still suffer many and varied forms of exploitation and oppression. As a Filipina activist for women's emancipation and social liberation for more than 40 years and having journeyed from the parliament of the streets to the parliament of the state, as representative of the Gabriela Women's Party in the Lower House of the Philippine Congress, and even on to the President's Palace as a member of the Cabinet, I realized that engaging with existing political structures may only achieve piecemeal results, but they are nevertheless necessary to effect reforms. More important, these political structures are sites that can support the work of consciousness raising and organizing of women in massive numbers, thereby strengthening the women's mass movement that will push forward women's strug-gles for equity and social liberation on many more fronts.

In this section, you will read about the marginalization of women's work, edu-cation, and basic health care and how these are ignored by state institutions. In Chapter 1, it is noted that despite the fact that 87% of Ghana's food is created by women, political forces in Ghana have overlooked the devastating impact of climate change on their country's food sources because women's work, or plainly women's struggles, is unseen by the political and social leaders of the country. The authors make a strong argument that only through climate change initiatives can gender equality be manifested. In Chapter 2, you will read how the United States, despite being a leader in the world's economy and having one of the most techno-logically advanced health care systems, continues to fail African American women solely because of the color of their skin. This is not written in the policy of the United States, but the author shows how institutional neglect is created and per-petuated along racial lines. Chapter 3 describes rural Mongolian girls' struggle to obtain education in their quest for empowerment and equality among the Han, who dominate China. These issues are what politicians and activists must fight for in state houses throughout the world. Chapters 4 and 6 tell a story of institutional neglect within the US system and how sexual assault and racial bias can become a normal everyday experience for women. Stories of transnational women's issues are reflected in the Sioux River Tribe discussed in Chapter 5, in which the reader will meet a woman who, despite historical trauma and marginalization, strives to overcome adversity and create empowerment among the women in her tribe.

Across the globe, governments have abandoned, neglected or fell short in their role as primary duty bearers in the recognition, respect, promotion and protection of women's rights. Thus it is important that women continue to study their condi-tion, organize their own movement and mobilize to engage government and attain substantial equality as well as realize full empowerment and social liberation.

Through my work, what I know to be true is that any achievement I had as a congressperson and a cabinet member became relevant to the greater number of women when I ground my work on the grassroots women's movement of peasants, workers, urban poor, indigenous, and youth who comprise the majority of Filipino women. Thus, the successes I achieved were not mine alone but, rather, the gains of the women's movement and, indeed, the entire country. My experience as a legislator also showed me that however difficult gender-specific measures were to pass, economic measures to address women's poverty and political marginalization were met with even more roadblocks. For example, laws that would implement a genuine land reform program that seeks to break the monopoly of landlords as well as legislation on wage increase and benefits of workers, in addition to mea-sures to end informalization of labor through contractual arrangements, have been very difficult to pass. Reforms in the existing political structures aimed to democ-ratize these institutions, such as the anti-political dynasty measures, are watered down or stalled because those in power, who have dominated mainstream politics for so long—the oligarchs, bureaucrat capitalists, and elites—will not do anything against their interests; they are unwilling to give up their privileged position in the status quo.

Thus, it is necessary to also engage outside government and carry out a resistance movement that advocates for real structural change that will realize the demands for substantial equity between women and men in a society in which poverty is eliminated and social justice and development are attained. This resistance movement is all the more necessary and urgent as we witness the erosion of the basic freedoms and democratic rights that women already won during more than a century of struggles worldwide.

The neoliberal globalization underpinned by the ideology of neoconservatism has launched a direct attack on the poor, including women. Neoliberal globalization opened neocolonies and poor countries of the South to unbridled exploitation of the cheap labor of workers and the plunder of their natural resources by capitalist countries and corporate interests. This has intensified the displacement, commodification, and modern-day slavery of women. In the North, women are confronted with problems of joblessness, homelessness, and cutbacks in social services. Neoconservatism espouses militarism, white supremacy, xenophobia, and the traditional view of women and family. This wave of conservative thinking peddles war and siphons off the necessary money for social services, including those that cater to women's health and reproductive rights and centers for victims of rape and sexual abuse, in favor of spending for the military industrial complex and war.

Faced with these challenges, women have acquired a sharper analysis on the necessity not only to ground the movement to the grassroots but also to link it globally. Likewise, there is a deeper understanding that the substantial content of women's advocacy should be framed along the comprehensive view of the women's question that does not fragment but, rather, integrates the issues of class, race, nationality, and gender. In the era of neoliberal globalization, the vision of a society free from exploitation and oppression of women necessitates confronting imperialism and its client states.

The recent history of Filipino women's resistance is replete with examples that we can share to the world as our contribution to the global advance of the women's movement. The founding of my organization, GABRIELA Women's Alliance, in 1984 at the height of the anti-dictatorship struggle provided a platform for women's participation in the uprising that ousted the dictatorship in 1986. Again in 1998, the Alliance actively participated in another People Power movement that ousted a macho-fascist president. In 1992, as part of the anti-bases movement, we also actively campaigned for the non- extension of the US–Philippine bases treaty that eventually pressured the Philippine senate to vote for non-extension and the eventual dismantling of the two largest US bases outside the US territory.

Makibaka Upang Mabuhay! (Struggle to Survive) and Makibaka Huwag Matakot! (Struggle Be Not Afraid) are both slogans and calls that have defined the Filipino women's struggles through the years. At no other time than now are these calls more relevant and profound as women confront the global challenges of the 21st century. We have to strengthen the international women's movement by creating deep roots with the basic masses, uniting with other social movements, linking globally, and engaging in resistance in order to achieve the vision of a society free from all forms of abuse, exploitation and oppression, for ourselves and our children's future.

1

Women and Climate Change

LAURA MCKINNEY AND ARIANNA KING ∎

PHOTOGRAPHIC CASE STUDY

Figure 1.1 A small-scale gravity-fed irrigation system helps villagers grow food despite drought conditions.

Figure 1.2 A dry season irrigation system that yields crops in a rural village of Ghana.

OVERVIEW

The central role of women in sustaining local population needs for sustenance is well documented (Boserup, 1970). Ghanaian women are no exception. Their engagement in subsistence agriculture plays a significant role in the country's economy via contributions to the national food basket. The Social Watch Coalition (2010) estimates that 87% of food crop production in Ghana is attributable to women. Increasingly erratic weather conditions associated with global climate change dynamics complicate the ability of Ghanaian women to fulfill their roles as subsistence providers, many of whom are charged with providing adequate nutrition not only for their own children but also for orphaned children of relatives, the elderly, and those who are sick or otherwise unable to support themselves. The poverty faced by Ghanaian women engaged in agriculture results in their heightened dependence on weather patterns for crop production; in the absence of capital-intensive irrigation systems, they rely on the rainy season to provide the water inputs needed to cultivate crops during the growing season.

As reported by Glazebrook (2011), the 2007–2008 growing season was especially egregious in this regard because the region suffered drought conditions during the rainy season followed by sudden, heavy rains that flooded the area. Flooding was exacerbated in Ghana's northernmost regions by Burkina Faso's (the country bordering Ghana to the north) inability to contain floodwaters, which were released by opening dams that intensified flood conditions downstream. Crop losses have immediate effects on food security in addition to lifelong consequences of malnutrition on children's development. Also, they undermine educational attainment among youth because the loss in yields negates women's ability to generate income that could pay for necessities to attend school, such as uniforms and books. Despite the critical role of women's agricultural activities that undergird the health and well-being of local communities, their voices are consistently left out of discussions, policies, and initiatives aimed at improving the collective lot of individuals residing in poor nations who face disproportionate threats to their livelihoods as a result of climate change.

This chapter provides a case study of the ways in which women are especially vulnerable to climate change dynamics (i.e., women as victims) and particularly well-suited to provide traditional ecological knowledge to navigate the ever-changing environmental conditions associated with climate change (i.e., women as saviors). We focus on women in Ghana for the purposes of our case study, but first we provide a general overview of the intersection of climate change, development, and gender to situate current events within the historical tableau.

Perhaps the most daunting ecological calamity we collectively face is the impending doom of climate change resulting from human alterations to the atmosphere via greenhouse gas emissions, which scientists assure us is an empirical reality (Intergovernmental Panel on Climate Change [IPCC], 2014). There is broad scientific consensus that anthropogenic climate change worsens myriad ecological disruptions with undeniable ripple effects on society, the full scope of which cannot be understated or entirely forecast at present. However, there is great confidence that erratic changes in growing conditions, seasonality, and weather patterns such as intense floods and severe droughts are just a few examples of the dangers associated with climate change that threaten our very existence. Climate change represents an especially critical concern for social and environmental justice advocates because those who have contributed the least in terms of greenhouse gas emissions tend to suffer the most (Roberts & Parks, 2007). The disproportionate concentration of adverse effects among vulnerable populations is commonly cited as constituting a "North–South" divide at the global level.[1] The general view is that wealthy, developed countries such as the United States, Canada, and much of Western Europe in the Global North are overwhelmingly responsible for (and accrue vast benefits from) generating greenhouse gas emissions, yet remain relatively unscathed by the consequences, whereas predominately poor nations of South America, Southeast Asia, and Africa in the Global South neither contribute to nor benefit from climate change but remain the most vulnerable to its consequences.

An emerging area of emphasis within the climate change literature centers on the role of women as unique sufferers of and potential saviors from ecological demise. This discussion, treated by environmental scholars and development practitioners alike, emphasizes the ways in which gender (alongside race and class) intersects with broader social formations to produce asymmetrical consequences of climate change that disproportionately burden women. For example, women and other traditionally marginalized groups will be the hardest hit by food shortages, vulnerability, and disaster devastation, all of which are potentiated by climate change dynamics. In addition, research shows that empowered women leverage their status to enact policies and practices that boost local, regional, and national sustainability. These trends have led to the creation of robust literatures to explore the prevailing social forces that connect gender to environmental degradation and resilience at micro and macro levels of abstraction (Gaard, 2015; Mies & Shiva, 1993; Resurrección, 2013; Rocheleau, Thomas-Slayter, & Wangari, 1996; Terry, 2009).

This chapter provides a general framework for understanding the intersection of gender with climate change as well as nation-specific data to give a sense of how these concepts are experienced on the ground. We underscore the importance of bringing gender into discussions surrounding climate change because its impacts are not gender neutral and, in fact, tend to exacerbate existing gender inequalities (Dankelman et al., 2008). As such, climate change offers a unique analysis of gender inequality as compounded by environmental strife. We begin by reviewing past research on gender and climate change, highlighting myriad connections that link the economic, political, and social status of women to the environment (Kaijser & Kronsell, 2014). We then shift focus to the nation of Ghana, giving a brief survey of social, political, and cultural elements that influence contemporary decision-making in the country as well as Ghanaians' experiences with and responses to climate change. The third section assesses gender equality inclusion and sensitivity within Ghana's recent climate change policymaking initiatives, supplementing this information with prior case studies of Ghana to substantiate our claims of the gendered dimensions of climate change politics in the country. We conclude that gender equality is a critical component for mobilizing just policies and wise decisions surrounding the global climate change crisis.

HISTORICAL TRENDS

Researchers examining issues related to gender and development have, since the 1970s, increasingly indicted globalization and the spread of neoliberalism as exacerbating gaps and further entrenching existing inequalities across nations. Neoliberal policies and ideologies seek to abolish public safety nets, privatize social welfare, restrict government autonomy, and instill "free" markets (McMichael, 2011). The latter serves to trap poor countries in unfavorable production patterns in which a narrow set of primary commodities are produced and sold to an extremely circumscribed set of exchange partners. Moreover, neoliberal interventions overwhelmingly concentrate the most environmentally damaging and least profitable sectors (extraction, mining, and agriculture) in less developed locales. Critically, research confirms the co-occurrence of environmental degradation with gender inequality, supporting that "when women suffer, so does the environment" (McKinney & Fulkerson, 2015, p. 310). These dynamics collectively underscore the importance of incorporating gender as a critical dimension of environmental justice.

Within the cross-national literature, scholars have begun to advance transnational, comparative approaches to analyze the complex social relations in an increasingly globalized economy that condition individual experiences with the environment. Ecofeminist and feminist political ecology scholars (Buckingham, 2010; Mies, 1998; Mies & Shiva, 1993; Rocheleau et al., 1996; Salleh, 1997; Terry, 2009; Warren, 1990) articulate the ways in which women are uniquely positioned in society as an acute sufferer of—and potential savior from—ecological destruction (Gaard, 2015; Resurrección, 2013). These perspectives embrace an intersectional[2] approach to understanding the myriad ways in which individuals experience and interact with the environment, as shaped by the constellation of inequities across racial, gender, class, and colonial divides as well as unequal development trajectories at the local, national, and global levels. Intersectionality is a powerful addition to the ecofeminist

Figure 1.3 Fetching water from the Langbensi Dam.

framework that explicitly theorizes the interconnectedness of power structures that link the domination of women to the domination of nature while acknowledging the differential effects generated at the intersection of gender with multiple axes of inequality discussed previously.

Ecofeminist frameworks offer that women differ from men in their relation to the environment in numerous ways; there is accruing evidence that women are uniquely affected by, concerned about, and motivated to act against environmental degradation (Bell & Braun, 2010; McCright, 2010). Women's relatively greater concern for environmental issues stems from the historical forces and cultural contexts that position them as caregivers, subsistence providers, and collectors of resources needed by the household (Warren, 1990). Concomitantly, the structure and logic of the world economic regime are such that large portions of costs associated with production are absorbed by both women and the environment, resulting in their interconnected domination and exploitation (Mies & Shiva, 1993).

Taking a social constructivist approach, ecofeminists indict the household division of labor and companion sociocultural ideologies as indelibly influencing women's experiences with environmental change. Specifically, the activities allocated to women are directly linked to the health of the environment, a dynamic that is especially pronounced in less developed countries (Mies & Shiva, 1993). For example, gathering food and water is complicated by changing climates, erratic weather, and decreased soil fertility. In light of resource scarcity, women must travel longer distances over increasingly perilous terrain to secure food, fiber, and fuel (Dunaway & Macabuac, 2007). The tendency of women to "eat last" potentiates health risks posed by resource scarcities that impinge on the quality and quantity of available food, amplifying malnutrition and susceptibility to disease among women. Circumstances such as these impede women's ability to nurture the health and well-being of children and the elderly—responsibilities disproportionately assumed by women. Thus, the status of women has ripple effects on local, national, and global well-being.

Ecological losses restrict women's ability to prosper because they are forced to work harder and longer to complete essential tasks for their households and communities. Women are further disadvantaged by ecological degradation insofar as their livelihood strategies (cottage industries and producing handicrafts) that rely on natural resource inputs are imperiled (Dunaway & Macabuac, 2007), exacerbating their already precarious positions in the labor force (Terry, 2009). As such, declines in environmental quality correspond to declines in the status of women, which jeopardize their ability to fulfill traditional roles as caretakers, subsistence providers, and community caregivers. For these reasons, the effects extend beyond women's lives to household well-being, community resilience, and overall sustainability.

In addition to the pernicious effects of environmental degradation on women relative to men, ecofeminist and feminist political ecology scholars equally emphasize the ways in which these dynamics make women especially well-suited to advance sustainability. Ecofeminist perspectives offer that women, when afforded positions of power in society, tend to promote environmental stewardship (Mies, 1998; Norgaard & York, 2005; Roucheleau et al., 1996; Shandra, Shandra, & London, 2008). To the degree that women experience greater economic security and control over economic resources, their ability to address environmental crises is enhanced (Enarson, 2000). Women with access to credit can use funds to protect land and property against disasters, such as investing in irrigation systems to address drought cycles or investing in structural improvements to homes that can withstand heavy wind and better tolerate downpours. Providing women with basic economic rights reduces poverty by allowing women the opportunity to gain control over household finances and increasing their capacity to make decisions about how money is spent (Agarwal, 1994; Gummerson & Schneider, 2012). Indeed, a growing body of literature emphasizes that revenues earned by women are more often used to meet basic needs that improve public health conditions, such as education fees, health care costs, clean water and sanitation services, and clothing for children, in comparison to wages earned by men (Agarwal, 1994; Gummerson & Schneider, 2012; Taj, Akmal, Shah, Ahmad, & Saddozai, 2008). Research also shows women who reside in communities with greater gender equality in formal access to economic resources tend to use their bargaining power to promote community development projects that benefit

Figure 1.4 The Langbensi Dam.

the health and well-being of their community and region (Agarwal, 1997; Kristof & WuDunn, 2009).

The deep connection between women and the environment that has the potential to tip the scales in favor of ecosystem conservation is particularly evident when women are afforded political legitimacy and representation in governing bodies (Buckingham, 2010). There is accumulating empirical evidence of beneficial associations between female representation in governing bodies and positive environmental outcomes (Ergas & York, 2012; McKinney, 2014; McKinney & Fulkerson, 2015). Thirty percent representation by women is often cited as a critical mass or the point at which women gain power to influence decision-making, including with regard to environmental issues, policies, and directives. Unfortunately, less than 25% of nations currently meet this target (World Bank, 2015). This gap is meaningful because excluding women from decision-making processes does not bode well for altering policies to prevent or curtail ecological destruction. Thus, increasing political participation and representation among women represents a critical pathway for resilience.

Of particular importance is recognizing environmental degradation as both a cause and an effect of women's status. Empirical evidence supports that ecological destruction compromises the health, longevity, and status of women (McKinney & Austin, 2015), which reciprocally deepens vulnerability across nations (Austin & McKinney, 2016). Other research shows that empowering women has the potential to boost overall sustainability (McKinney, 2014), alleviate disaster vulnerability (Austin & McKinney, 2016), and check greenhouse gas emissions (McKinney & Fulkerson, 2015). Thus, women are directly affected by—and have the potential to influence—ecological conditions.

Worldwide, women comprise 17% and 14% of parliament and ministerial positions, respectively. This is unfortunate given the accumulating empirical evidence demonstrating the beneficial associations between female representation and positive environmental outcomes (Ergas & York, 2012; McKinney, 2014; McKinney & Fulkerson, 2015). Therefore, increasing political participation and representation among women represents a critical pathway for resilience. One barrier to their participation is perceived incompatibilities of holding public office with traditional caregiver obligations that are disproportionately allocated to women. Through the lens of intersectionality, some social, cultural, and religious beliefs are especially disdainful of women's entry into public spaces, particularly when doing so conflicts with their household labor. Abolishing these cultural, political, and social forces that prevent women's participation in the public sphere, then, represents another key avenue for addressing environmental crises.

In their review of the literature on gender and development, Carr and Thompson (2014) highlight several recurrent observations, including persistent exclusion of women from agricultural decision-making, growing gender inequality in access to arable land, and gender divisions in agricultural practices. Understanding these baseline dynamics—particularly with regard to women in the Global South and their ability to access social and political power—provides inroads for carefully examining how climate change intensifies existing inequalities for women and the environment, including women's increased vulnerability to climate change (Moosa & Tuana, 2014). Empirical research confirms that in the context of climate change, women are becoming further removed from decision-making opportunities with regard to agriculture and the environment, forcing many to rely more heavily on adaptation alone (Arku, 2013; Terry, 2009).

Mukoni (2013) classifies the exclusion of women from climate change decisions and their eventual relegation to adaptation strategies as a contrast between *practical gender needs* and *strategic gender needs*, distinguishing the former as material short-term needs distinct from the latter, which are characterized as invisible long-term needs to challenge and change power relations (Mukoni, 2013, p. 1334). In the context of climate change, existing scholarship documents impressive ingenuity and creativity in meeting short-term needs of women (Arku, 2013; Solomon et al., 2016) but notes a lack of access to decision-making power among women that severely restricts their capacity to challenge power inequalities across gender lines. In summary, the systemic neglect of strategic gender needs in climate change policy compounds gender inequality across environmental, social, political, and economic dimensions. Next, we offer a few key examples taken from our focal nation, Ghana, to substantiate and further delineate the exact mechanisms propagating gender inequality.

RECENT DEVELOPMENTS OF NOTE

In line with ecofeminist theory, we recognize the importance of understanding transnational environmental connections and the value of place-based analyses to parse out the particularities of climate change experiences. Doing so avoids universalizing across geographic locations, enabling researchers to scrutinize the unique social, political, and economic forces influencing modern conditions. It is with this general caveat of relative differences in vulnerabilities to climate change, globally, that we apply ecofeminist frameworks to analyze Ghanaian's experiences with, beliefs about, and responses to climate change.

We focus on Ghana[3] for several reasons: (1) It is a low-income nation in the Global South, a categorical demographic that is disproportionately vulnerable to climate change and its effects (Austin & McKinney, 2016; Roberts & Parks, 2007); (2) Ghana has been the focus of a broad body of climate change research (Antwi-Agyei, Dougill, Fraser, & Stringer, 2013; Arku, 2013; Carr, 2008a, 2008b; Codjoe, Atidoh, & Burkett, 2012; Glazebrook, 2011; Solomon et al., 2016; Westerhoff & Smit, 2009); and (3) since gaining independence from British colonial rule in 1957, the nation has in many ways become a barometer of progress in the region of West Africa. We view Ghana as representative of the substantial challenges facing impoverished nations and the people in them and, as such, a careful analysis in this context may bring light to similar circumstances across other nations in the region or continent. Following ecofeminist perspectives, we emphasize the social, political, economic, and cultural dynamics to elucidate how these factors condition vulnerability and regional adaptation strategies. In focusing on Ghana, we offer concrete examples of the social dimensions of climate change, shifts in women's relationship with the environment over time, and opportunities for the future.

Ghana evidences stark and distinctly spatialized inequalities, with clear concentrations of social, political, and economic power in the Southern region. The capital city, Accra, resides on the southern coastal border and is undergoing rapid expansion as an international trade hub that has begun to engulf the nearby shipping port of Tema. Access to these ports, coupled with inadequate intranational infrastructure, has contributed to the concentration of wealth in southern Ghana and poverty in the north. As expected, various markers of maternal health, education, and income levels (Ghana Statistical Service, Ghana Health Service, & ICF International, 2015) are consistently higher for the Southern region. Although gender inequalities are marked in the Northern region, the gender gap is broadly demonstrated for the nation as a whole, as Ghanaian women tend to have a longer workday, perform twice as much domestic labor, are less likely to complete formal education, have lower literacy rates, and have limited access to credit and agricultural services as well as weaker land-tenure rights compared to their male counterparts (Glazebrook, 2011).

Ghana is home to vast amounts of diversity, not only in terms of its human population, represented by more than eight major ethnic groups who speak dozens of linguistic dialects, but also in terms of its natural and environmental characteristics. Whereas coastal terrain and dense tropical forests typify the physical environment of southern regions of Ghana, the northern regions tend to be dry and savannah-like, presenting a multitude of challenges to cultivation. The range of climatic conditions and geographical features catalyzed a highly specialized agricultural economy across regions. To be sure, the gaps in quality of life in Ghana have important historical underpinnings and are closely tied to ethnic and cultural differences. As early as the 19th century, wealthy and powerful ethnic groups such as the Ga-Dangme and Akan trafficked northern Ghanaians with different ethnicities through the Atlantic slave trade (Getz & Clarke, 2012; Ward, 1948), resulting in substantial social and economic imbalances. The religious and ethnic differences between northern and southern regions of Ghana have stoked intranational conflicts and worsened educational access across regions, with extremely restricted educational opportunities in the predominately Muslim northern regions.

Despite the concentration of social and economic power in the south, both regions have experienced extreme climate change events in recent years. Northern environmental shocks such as droughts and severe dust storms have ravaged the agricultural economy and spurred rural flight to urban centers throughout the country. Several scholars identify rural–urban migration as a primary adaptation strategy for northern Ghanaian farmers who can no longer earn sufficient income from farm work alone (Arku, 2013; Glazebrook, 2011). This regional out-migration has obvious repercussions for women who are left behind to support the household and secure subsistence in an increasingly challenging environmental context. Furthermore, many of these northerners migrate into southern cities, where they encounter excessive rains, sea-level rise, and severe flooding, all of which are part and parcel of changing climates (Amoako & Frimpong Boamah, 2015). In June 2015, torrential rains flooded the central commercial area of Accra, resulting in the loss of nearly 200 lives, many of whom were street vendors and informal laborers. Although events such as the 2015 floods give the impression of greater imminent danger for the southern region, the effect of environmental shifts on the agricultural economy in the northern regions jeopardizes food security and stimulates urban migration, exemplifying the shared burden of climate change throughout the nation.

Two critical moments in Ghana's history are central to understanding the gendered dimensions of climate change in the nation. The first is the introduction of cocoa in 1878 by Tetteh Quarshie. Ghanaian women's productive and reproductive labor were pivotal in the successful development of the cocoa industry as well as the resultant power and wealth, despite frequent exclusion from historical accounts (Allman

& Tashjian, 2000). During the rise of the cocoa industry, marriage evolved from a fluid, family-driven exchange to an increasingly monetized one in which the value of women's labor centers on the extraction of items with high exchange (e.g., cocoa, gold, and kola); this shift galvanized women's dependence on men to take goods to the large foreign markets. Ultimately emerging from these dynamics was a forced separation of family finances as women dove into the cash economy growing surplus agricultural products for local sale. In doing so, some women began earning their own income, which increased their autonomy to the degree that they were freed from labor demands of men in the household (Allman & Tashjian, 2000). Buried in this gendered history of labor is a social and cultural relationship, which offers a helpful framework to understand the relationship between Ghanaian women and the environment today that is constantly under negotiation.

The second critical moment shaping gender relations in Ghana was the implementation of structural adjustment programs (SAPs)[4] of the 1980s and 1990s. Throughout the 20th century and the early 21st century, Ghanaian women reclaimed some social and economic power resulting from their work as traders in the marketplace (Allman & Tashjian, 2000; Chamlee-Wright, 1997; Clark, 1994; Getz & Clarke, 2012; Robertson, 1984), with informal income opportunities playing a central role in determining the socioeconomic status of women (Clark, 2010; King, 2016). However, the system whereby women earned income through the integration of domestic work (e.g., food preparation, hairdressing, and fabric work) into the public marketplace was compromised during SAPs. In an effort to stimulate economic growth according to the principles of SAPs, the Government of Ghana (GOG) eliminated more than 300,000 public sector jobs, occupied mostly by men (Brown, 2006). Desperate for work, unemployed men sought refuge in the informal economy, effectively displacing female vendors and jeopardizing women's access to the social and economic opportunities granted by informal labor (Overå, 2007). Although empirical research from throughout the world reflects on the negative impacts of SAPs on the status of women (Cagatay & Ozler, 1995), the particular way in which this played out in Ghana is telling of gender inequalities in the cultural context. SAPs reified the underlying belief that the labor and economic contributions of women are subordinate to those of men, particularly in times of flux (Konadu-Agyemang, 2000; Overå, 2007). This gender dynamic and the cultural values regarding the household division of labor have obvious repercussions, ultimately decreasing opportunities for women to participate in critical policymaking and decision-making processes.

Case study evidence from the Central Region of Ghana documents distinct gender segregation in terms of crop production, which corresponds to varying sensitivities to climate change. For instance, Carr (2008b) observes that men tend to grow primarily commodity crops (e.g., acacia, cassava, cocoa, coconut, and palm) for regional and global markets that are often part of a diverse livelihood strategy. Women in the community produce crops primarily for local and household consumption (p. 905), often selling any surplus to bolster household income. Although a superficial analysis of this difference might lead some to conclude that men in this community are more vulnerable to climate events, shifting focus to the intersection of gender and livelihood strategies shows that the scale of agriculture and significantly circumscribed livelihood opportunities leaves women more vulnerable than their male counterparts.

This dynamic takes on added importance when examining the application of gender mainstreaming strategies in policymaking efforts to address climate change and development. Evidence from the Eastern region of Ghana highlights the flaws of such approaches that can, in fact, completely disrupt efforts to instill environmental justice (Adusei-Asante, Hancock, & Oliveira, 2015). In this social and cultural context, water provisioning is the work of the women in the community, whereas the male members of the community hold local knowledge of the physical environment, including details about the water table needed for a functional community borehole. Research examining the planning and implementation of a community water project in Tikpe, Ghana, revealed that framing it under the guise of "women's empowerment" alienated men in the community with the disastrous consequence of installing the borehole in a location with a very low water table, a snafu that torpedoed the intention to enhance access to clean water. As climate change challenges create added barriers to clean water, these cultural and gendered dynamics become exceedingly significant and consequential factors to consider.

Glazebrook (2011) adds to this discussion with research from the Upper East region of Ghana, confirming that access to credit for increasingly critical agricultural inputs, such as climate-sensitive seeds and fertilizers, is yet another source of growing inequality across gender and class lines. This study documents incredible feats of creativity and resourcefulness among women farmers, who demonstrate particular expertise on soil arability despite near-constant environmental flux. In summary, there is a bevy of support that women's role as primary producers of food for the household results in a disproportionate burden of climate change because they must leverage myriad strategies to adapt to changing conditions (Arku, 2013; Glazebrook, 2011; Solomon et al., 2016).

Against this backdrop, it is critical that initiatives to address climate change integrate consideration for the gendered nature of environmental degradation and resilience. To explore the efficacy of such efforts, we now turn to a discussion of climate change policies in Ghana, with emphasis on their relative strengths and weaknesses in accounting for the critical links connecting women to the environment.

CURRENT CONDITIONS

The GOG has made strides in addressing gender in the development of recent environmental and climate change policy. In line with the United Nations' advocacy of Millennium Development Goals and strategies to attain them, Ghana has invested time and resources to advance understanding of the social, economic, and developmental issues thwarting progress to achieving these goals and the way in which purported "progress" is connected to ecological degradation. In 2013, the GOG implemented the National Climate Change Policy (NCCP; National Climate Change Committee [NCCC] & Ministry of Environment, Science, Technology, and Innovation [MESTI], 2013) in response to the need for progressive climate change policy. The results reflect an understanding of the spectrum of experiences and consequences that occur across social, economic, ethnic, and geographical lines.

The NCCP was produced collaboratively by governmental ministries and nongovernmental agencies, and gender plays a prominent role in their analysis. The NCCP makes recurrent mention of the importance of recognizing and planning for the disproportionate burden of climate change on Ghanaian women while recognizing their burden stems from persistent systemic inequalities in "social and economic roles that manifest themselves in unequal access to resources and to decision-making processes, reduced access to information, ineffective property rights and reduced mobility" (NCCC/MESTI, 2013, p. 2-6). A multitude of social changes, political actions, and economic objectives are offered to cope with environmental degradation and climate change throughout the nation, including developing climate-resilient agriculture and food security systems by building capacity for farmers in climate-smart agricultural practices on both large- and small-scale farms, the latter of which are associated with the majority of rural women. Given their extremely precarious positions, this move marks a momentous sea change in accounting for the needs of those on the absolute fringes of society. These action items also encourage devoting governmental resources to collecting and sharing "appropriate indigenous knowledge and best practices" (p. 4-2), as well as improving "farming practices through secure land tenure, effective pricing policies, and access to credit" (p. 4-3)—areas ripe with potential for addressing some of the systemic gender inequalities among farmers.

The NCCP also advocates community-based ecostewardship as part of a climate-smart natural resource management system. As the inextricable connections between women and the environment are increasingly accepted as fertile ground for the growth of progressive climate change policy, the GOG's promotion of locally based, community-involved resource management systems is encouraging. These systems— including community-based rainwater harvesting and management plans, alternative solutions to sourcing household cooking fuel, and community reforestation projects for carbon sequestration—present powerful possibilities for incorporating women into critical decision-making processes about the use of natural resources in their communities. Explicit support for protecting national resources to sustain and grow resilience at the local level represents clear progress toward embedding the gendered dimensions of climate change into national policies.

In addition to the inclusion of gender-sensitive attitudes into climate-smart policies, the NCCP directly addresses existing gender inequality in the context of climate change (NCCC/MESTI, 2013, p. 4-18). The document outlines seven key challenge areas for women: the overdependence on natural resources due to insufficient alternative livelihood opportunities, discriminatory land tenure systems, low rates of female literacy, lack of quality data to measure the details of women's disproportionate burden, lack of access to credit and technology to aid in climate adaptation strategy development, and exclusion from local and national decision-making practices. The policy conveys a progressive understanding of the reality that

> women are not just helpless victims of climate change, they are also powerful agents of change and their knowledge and leadership is critical. There is a need, therefore, to ensure that climate change and disaster risk reduction measures are gender responsive, sensitive to local knowledge systems and respect human rights. Women's right to participate at all levels of decision-making must also be guaranteed in climate change policies and programmes. (p. 4-18)

Emphasizing the connections between women's representation in decision-making and the development of successful climate change policy is a notable step in the right direction; we are hopeful Ghana gains momentum as a leader in gender-equal climate change policy in the rapidly developing region of West Africa.

LOOKING TO THE FUTURE

Despite recognition and inclusion of both strategic and practical gender needs to address climate change, women remain largely on the margins of Ghana's formal decision-making processes. According to a recent study, women's representation in local and national governance has not increased substantially since the gender mainstreaming policies enacted in 2000 (Ocran, 2014). The relative lack of representation in the political sphere is echoed in civil society as well, with women displaying low levels of decision-making power in trade and labor unions, nongovernmental organizations, as well as community-based organizations (Dankelman et al., 2008). These realities remind us there is still much work to be done to empower women with the (financial, social, and political) resources needed to legitimate and solidify further their role in the development of national mitigation and adaptation strategies for climate change.

Advocacy

Like most development work, organizations working in the area change fairly rapidly with funding trends and so directing readers to a specific organization may prove a short-sighted approach. However, we encourage readers to familiarize themselves with programs and organizations that use human-centered design (https://www. usaid.gov/cii/human-centered-design). These programs consider those affected by climate change and development challenges as key stakeholders in the creation and implementation of all initiatives. One excellent example of these programs is the Ghana Resiliency in Northern Ghana (RING) program (https://www.globalcommunities.org/node/38365). RING is funded through a partnership between the US Agency for International Development and the GOG with help from Global Communities: Partners for Good. The program offers an innovative à la carte development model allowing communities to pick and choose from a list of possible initiatives, resources, and programs that will work for their individual needs to improve the lives and livelihoods of those within their communities. Options include targeting nutritional deficits that grow with climate change, supporting farming climate resilient crops, and expanding community education. To be sure, there are no silver bullet solutions to these issues; as such, the real advocacy efforts need to come in the form of handing over decision-making power to those most affected.

CONCLUSION

Climate change science has rapidly formalized into a burgeoning area of scientific inquiry (IPCC, 2014). However, leading publications continue to focus more on sustaining earth systems than on inequalities in human development and pathways of modernity between, within, and across nations. Our current challenge, then, is to understand the complex inequalities surrounding global environmental change (International Social Science Council [ISSC], Institute of Development Studies [IDS], & United Nations Educational, Scientific and Cultural Organization [UNESCO], 2016). Consequently, efforts to instill sustainability are unlikely to succeed without greater integration of knowledge regarding social structure, societal dynamics, and human behavior. Macrosociological approaches enable researchers to contextualize individual experiences with, beliefs about, and responses to global environmental change within large, structural systems and broad social forces. We highlight the benefits gained from approaching the nexus of climate change, ecosystem destruction, and persistent inequality by exploring their social, cultural, economic, and political underpinnings.

There is widespread agreement that the challenges of global environmental change require comprehensive assessments of interactions among economic, social, and environmental systems and their intersection with uneven human development and persistent inequality (ISSC, IDS, & UNESCO, 2016; UN, 2016). We contribute to this endeavor by interjecting ecofeminist thought into classical theories of global political economy to build a framework for analyzing the complex structures that connect women to the environment. The chapter argues that current approaches to addressing climate change will benefit from incorporation of frameworks that highlight the role of conflict and inequality in shaping global power relations, wealth differentials, economic systems, political regimes, international policies, human development, production patterns, and value formation. Adopting a broader array of theoretical approaches to scrutinize global environmental change widens the scope of knowledge that can be used to shift toward more inclusive and equitable societies.

The social forces that connect women to the environment are wide-ranging, resulting in unique consequences for women and their heightened potential to promote resilience. These dynamics are particularly crucial in the context of climate change, which is arguably the single most daunting challenge facing society. A central conclusion of our research is that gender inequality is a fundamental hurdle to addressing climate change in an effective and just manner. We wholeheartedly agree that the road to sustainability is paved with equality; realizing sustainability hinges on expanding political, economic, and social equality to women (ISSC, IDS, & UNESCO, 2016; UN, 2016). Consonant with newly established Sustainable Development Goals for 2030 (UN, 2016), we hold that gender equality is desperately needed to mobilize just policies and wise decisions surrounding the crisis of global climate change. Fortunately, the international community of scholars, practitioners, and activists concerned with climate change is coming to embrace the invaluable insights women can bring to bear on such pivotal topics as climate change, environmental degradation, and community resilience. We hope there is still time for the efficacious inclusion of women in climate change discussions, if expansively and urgently enacted in communities the world over.

DISCUSSION QUESTIONS

1. How can transnational feminist approaches that transcend geopolitical boundaries inform strategies to curtail climate change?
2. How is our understanding of women's experiences with their environment in various social/geographic locations worldwide enriched by transnational feminist approaches?
3. How important is gender equality to strategies seeking to advance sustainability?

4. How is our understanding of gender as a relationship between the sexes important to developing more sustainable environmental approaches?

5. What characteristics would environmental interventions that center on the experience of women share across geopolitical boundaries?

NOTES

1. This is not a clear-cut distinction because there are some impoverished areas in the Global North and some relatively wealthy regions in the Global South. However, we use this geographical framing in accordance with the many scholars and activists who bring attention to the vast inequality that characterizes these locational divides, generally (Mies & Shiva, 1993; Roberts & Parks, 2006).

2. Intersectionality approaches (Crenshaw, 1991) highlight the interconnectedness of myriad identities of difference (e.g., race, class, gender, sexuality, ethnicity, nationality, disability, religion, and age) and situate these intersections within diverse forms of exploitation and oppression. Within the ecofeminist framework, intersectional approaches integrate the wide-ranging categories that constitute differences among women, recognizing the complexity of discrimination and identity and exploring the myriad effects on marginalized groups and their relationship to the environment.

3. We acknowledge co-author King brings a wealth of knowledge to the current analysis, having spent years living and conducting research in Ghana, which also motivated our choice.

4. SAPs comprise a wide range of political and economic interventions to reallocate economic resources in less developed nations, typically under the auspices of Bretton Woods institutions (e.g., World Bank, International Monetary Fund, and World Trade Organization). SAPs purport to maximize efficiency of the global economy by adhering to free market principles, including the reduction of wages and government expenditures, removal of investment and trade barriers, and devaluing the national currency. With regard to agriculture, SAPs tend to center on the increased industrialization, mechanization, and chemicalization of production for cash crops; thus, small-scale, low-technology subsistence crop production characteristically undertaken by women is incompatible with the implementation of the vast bulk of SAPs. Moreover, SAPs privilege a small public sector while adding to the precariousness of informal laborers, who are not protected by labor laws or other rights such as minimum wage or health care. Importantly, the majority of Ghanaian women operate in the informal (unprotected) labor force (Dankelman et al., 2008). See McMichael (2011) for further elaboration on how SAPs and other global institutions have shaped, sustained, and reinforced various forms of inequality in the era of globalization.

REFERENCES

Adusei-Asante, K., Hancock, P., & Oliveira, M. (2015). Gender mainstreaming and women's roles in development projects: A research case study from Ghana. In V. Demos & M. Texler Segal (Eds.), *At the center: Feminism, social science and knowledge* (Vol. 20, pp. 175–198). Bingley, UK: Emerald Group.

Agarwal, B. (1994). Gender and command over property: A critical gap in economic analysis and policy in South Asia. *World Development, 22*(10), 1455–1478.

Agarwal, B. (1997). "Bargaining" and gender relations: Within and beyond the household. *Feminist Economics, 3*(1), 1–51.

Allman, J. M., & Tashjian, V. B. (2000). *"I will not eat stone": A women's history of colonial Asante.* Portsmouth, NH: Heinemann.

Amoako, C., & Frimpong Boamah, E. (2015). The three-dimensional causes of flooding in Accra, Ghana. *International Journal of Urban Sustainable Development, 7*(1), 109–129.

Antwi-Agyei, P., Dougill, A. J., Fraser, E. D. G., & Stringer, L. C. (2013). Characterising the nature of household vulnerability to climate variability: Empirical evidence from two regions of Ghana. *Environment, Development and Sustainability, 15*(4), 903–926.

Arku, F. S. (2013). Local creativity for adapting to climate change among rural farmers in the semi-arid region of Ghana. *International Journal of Climate Change Strategies and Management, 5*(4), 418–430.

Austin, K. F., & McKinney, L. A. (2016). Disaster devastation in poor nations: The direct and indirect effects of gender equality, ecological losses, and development. *Social Forces, 95,* 355–380.

Bell, S. E., & Braun, Y. A. (2010). Coal, identity, and the gendering of environmental justice activism in central Appalachia. *Gender & Society, 24*(6), 794–813.

Boserup, E. (1970). *Woman's role in economic development.* London, UK: Allen & Unwin.

Brown, A. (2006). Setting the context: Social, economic, and political influences on the informal sector in Ghana, Lesotho, Nepal, and Tanzania. In A. Brown (Ed.), *Contested space: Street trading, public space, and livelihoods in developing cities* (pp. 58–77). Rugby, UK: ITDG.

Buckingham, S. (2010). Call in the women. *Nature, 468*(7323), 502.

Cagatay, N., & Ozler, S. (1995). Feminization of the labor force: The effects of long-term development and structural adjustment [Special issue]. *World Development, 23*(11), 1883.

Carr, E. R. (2008a). Between structure and agency: Livelihoods and adaptation in Ghana's Central Region. *Global Environmental Change, 18*(4), 689–699.

Carr, E. R. (2008b). Men's crops and women's crops: The importance of gender to the understanding of agricultural and development outcomes in Ghana's Central Region. *World Development, 36*(5), 900–915.

Carr, E. R., & Thompson, M. C. (2014). Gender and climate change adaptation in agrarian settings: Current thinking, new directions, and research frontiers. *Geography Compass, 8*(3), 182–197.

Chamlee-Wright, E. (1997). *The cultural foundations of economic development: Urban female entrepreneurship in Ghana.* New York, NY: Routledge.

Clark, G. (1994). *Onions are my husband: Survival and accumulation by West African market women.* Chicago, IL: University of Chicago Press.

Clark, G. (2010). *African market women: Seven life stories from Ghana.* Bloomington, IN: Indiana University Press.

Codjoe, S., Atidoh, L., & Burkett, V. (2012). Gender and occupational perspectives on adaptation to climate extremes in the Afram Plains of Ghana. *Climatic Change, 110*(1), 431–454.

Crenshaw, K. (1991). Mapping the margins: Identity politics, intersectionality, and violence against women. *Stanford Law Review, 43*(6), 1241–1299.

Dankelman, I., Alam, K., Ahmed, W. B., Gueye, Y. D., Fatema, N., & Mensah-Kutin, R. (2008). *Gender, climate change, and human security: Lessons from Bangladesh, Ghana, and Senegal*. New York, NY: Women's Environment & Development Organization.

Dunaway, W. A., & Macabuac, M. C. (2007). "The shrimp eat better than we do": Philippine subsistence fishing households sacrificed for the global food chain. *Review (Fernand Braudel Center)*, 313–337.

Enarson, E. P. (2000). *Gender and natural disasters*. Geneva: ILO.

Ergas, C., & York, R. (2012). Women's status and carbon dioxide emissions: A quantitative cross-national analysis. *Social Science Research, 41*(4), 965–976.

Gaard, G. (2015, March). Ecofeminism and climate change. In *Women's studies international forum* (Vol. 49, pp. 20–33). New York, NY: Pergamon.

Getz, T. R., & Clarke, L. (2012). *Abina and the important men: A graphic history*. New York, NY: Oxford University Press.

Ghana Statistical Service, Ghana Health Service, & ICF International. (2015). *Ghana Demographic and Health Survey 2014*. Rockville, MD: Author.

Glazebrook, T. (2011). Women and climate change: A case-study from northeast Ghana. *Hypatia, 26*(4), 762–782.

Gummerson, E., & Schneider, D. (2012). Eat, drink, man, woman: Gender, income share and household expenditure in South Africa. *Social Forces, 91*(3), 813–836.

Intergovernmental Panel on Climate Change. (2014). *Climate change 2014—Impacts, adaptation, and vulnerability: Part B. Regional aspects*. Cambridge, UK: Cambridge University Press.

International Social Science Council, Institute of Development Studies, & United Nations Educational, Scientific and Cultural Organization. (2016). *World social science report 2016—Challenging inequalities: Pathways to a Just World*. Paris, France: UNESCO.

Kaijser, A., & Kronsell, A. (2014). Climate change through the lens of intersectionality. *Environmental Politics, 23*(3), 417–433.

King, A. (2016). Access to opportunity: A case study of street food vendors in Ghana's urban informal economy. In V. Demos & M. T. Segal (Eds.), *Gender and food* (Vol. 22, pp. 65–86). Bingley, UK: Emerald.

Konadu-Agyemang, K. (2000). The best of times and the worst of times: Structural adjustment programs and uneven development in Africa: The case of Ghana. *The Professional Geographer, 52*(3), 469–483.

Kristof, N. D., & WuDunn, S. (2010). *Half the sky: Turning oppression into opportunity for women worldwide*. New York, NY: Vintage.

McCright, A. M. (2010). The effects of gender on climate change knowledge and concern in the American public. *Population and Environment, 32*(1), 66–87.

McKinney, L. (2014). Gender, democracy, development, and overshoot: A cross-national analysis. *Population and Environment, 36*(2), 193–218.

McKinney, L., & Austin, K. (2015). Ecological losses are harming women: A structural analysis of female HIV prevalence and life expectancy in less developed countries. *Social Problems, 62*(4), 529–549.

McKinney, L., & Fulkerson, G. M. (2015). Gender equality and climate justice: A cross-national analysis. *Social Justice Research, 28*(3), 293–317.

McMichael, P. (2011). *Development and social change: A global perspective*. Thousand Oaks, CA: Sage.

Mies, M. (1998). *Patriarchy & accumulation on a world scale: Women in the international division of labor*. New York, NY: Zed Books.

Mies, M., & Shiva, V. (1993). *Ecofeminism*. New York, NY: Zed Books.

Moosa, C. S., & Tuana, N. (2014). Mapping a research agenda concerning gender and climate change: A review of the literature. *Hypatia, 29*(3), 677–694.

Mukoni, M. (2013). Rethinking women empowerment at the crossroads of climate change and sustainable development. *International Journal of Development and Sustainability, 2*(2), 1334–1345.

National Climate Change Committee (NCCC) & Ministry of Environment, Science, Technology, and Innovation (MESTI). (2013). Ghana national climate change policy (Government policy). Retrieved from www.un-page.org/files/public/ghanaclimat-echangepolicy.pdf

Norgaard, K., & York, R. (2005). Gender equality and state environmentalism. *Gender & Society, 19*(4), 506–522.

Ocran, R. K. (2014). *Women's political participation: A comparative study on Ghana and Tanzania.* Kuopio, Finland: University of Eastern Finland.

Overå, R. (2007). When men do women's work: Structural adjustment, unemployment and changing gender relations in the informal economy of Accra, Ghana. *Journal of Modern African Studies, 45*(4), 539–563.

Resurrección, B. P. (2013). Persistent women and environmental linkages in climate change and sustainable development agendas. *Women's Studies International Forum, 40,* 33–43.

Roberts, J. T., & Parks, B. C. (2007). *A climate of injustice: Global inequality, North–South politics, and climate policy.* Cambridge, MA: MIT Press.

Robertson, C. (1984). *Sharing the same bowl: A socioeconomic history of women and class in Accra, Ghana.* Bloomington, IN: Indiana University Press.

Rocheleau, D., Thomas-Slayter, B., & Wangari, E. (1996). *Political ecology: Global issues and local experiences.* New York, NY: Routledge.

Salleh, A. (1997). *Ecofeminism as politics: Nature, Marx, and the postmodern.* New York, NY: Zed Books.

Shandra, J. M., Shandra, C. L., & London, B. (2008). Women, non-governmental organizations, and deforestation: A cross-national study. *Population and Environment, 30*(1–2), 48–72.

Social Watch Coalition. (2010). MDGs remain elusive: Eradication and gender justice. Retrieved June 5, 2018, from http://www.socialwatch.org/node/12082

Solomon, D., Lehmann, J., Fraser, J. A., Leach, M., Amanor, K., Frausin, V., . . . Fairhead, J. (2016). Indigenous African soil enrichment as a climate-smart sustainable agriculture alternative. *Frontiers in Ecology and the Environment, 14*(2), 71–76.

Taj, S., Akmal, N., Shah, N. A., Ahmad, S., & Saddozai, K. N. (2008). Gender involvement in small enterprises through micro-credit in rainfed Pothwar. *Sarhad Journal of Agriculture, 24*(4), 779–784.

Terry, G. (2009). No climate justice without gender justice: An overview of the issues. *Gender & Development, 17*(1), 5–18.

United Nations. (2016). *Global sustainable development report 2016.* New York, NY: United Nations, Department of Economic and Social Affairs.

Ward, W. E. F. (1948). *A history of the Gold Coast.* London, UK: Allen & Unwin.

Warren, K. J. (1990). The power and the promise of ecological feminism. *Environmental Ethics, 12*(2), 125–146.

Westerhoff, L., & Smit, B. (2009). The rains are disappointing us: Dynamic vulnerability and adaptation to multiple stressors in the Afram Plains, Ghana. *Mitigation and Adaptation Strategies for Global Change, 14*(4), 317–337.

World Bank. (2015). *World Development Indicators.* "Proportion of parliamentarian seats held by women, 2015." Accessed online: worldbank.org.

2

Inequity Embodied

Race, Gender, and Class in African American Pregnancy

TYAN PARKER DOMINGUEZ ∎

Figure 2.1 "I am a Woman Phenomenally. Phenomenal Woman, that's me."
—Maya Angelou, *Phenomenal Woman*, poem (1978).

We carry our history in our bodies. How can we not?
—Krieger (2008)

CASE STUDY: THE NEELY SISTERS

She didn't cry like I thought she would. I'd asked my sister, Nicole, to talk about the babies she lost. . . . She only made it to four months when her body started to go into labor the first time.

"I think I remember hearing [him make] a sound," she said, "but he was so small."

He didn't make it. She made it to five months the second time.

"He lived for a week, which actually is kind of worse than the other one," she said. "Because you have more attachment. You think he's going to be okay."

Here's what you need to know about my sister: She cries all the time. . . . The heartbreak she'd suffered was part of a national narrative that has hurt Black families in America for decades.

"I don't really talk about it at all, ever," she said.

I told her that Black babies in the United States are two times more likely to die before their first birthday than White babies. . . . Like so many other Black women who are part of this statistic, my sister had no idea of the scope of the issue.

"Now that I know that this is an issue, and I was part of a statistic in this sense," she said, "if I can help someone and prevent that, then I am more than happy to share my story."

"I'm just thinking that it's just me, and it is— it was my body—but the care that I was given in that process could have . . . maybe if it was in a different situation, it would have been a different outcome. I'm just not sure that we're aware that this is an issue beyond just our bodies."

Most people are not aware.

When I found out about this alarming statistic last year, it hit me hard. I was at a conference on maternal health and was drawn to a session about trauma and birth outcomes for Black women. I was in a room with other Black women— some health advocates, some medical professionals. Many of us were learning about the unusually high mortality rate for Black babies for the first time. Some of the women, like my sister, had their own stories.

In the room that day, I immediately thought of the experiences of not just my sister, Nicole, but also my sister, LaKisha. LaKisha, a married woman with a master's degree, developed preeclampsia with her first pregnancy. The complication, which includes high blood pressure, is one of the leading triggers of premature births. . . . My nephew, Isaiah, was born two months early, and weighed just two and a half pounds. He's seen the pictures of himself with the breathing and feeding tubes taped to his skin in the neonatal intensive care unit incubator that he called home for six weeks.

"I could fit in my mom or my dad's hand," he said.

Since learning about these statistics and how my family fits into the broader story, I've been asking myself these questions on repeat: How has this been going on for so long? (Neely, 2018)

This family's story is part of an enduring, though little-known public health crisis. Of all major racial/ethnic groups in the country, African American women are more likely to deliver babies too early or too small; to bury them before their first birth-day; and to die in pregnancy, during delivery, or in the postpartum year (Centers for Disease Control and Prevention [CDC], 1999; Heron, 2017). This phenomenon is not naturally occurring; African American women are not simply "wired" this way. Rather, their pattern of adverse childbearing outcomes is a physical consequence of pervasive and enduring social inequity. The threefold bind of race, gender, and class oppression prematurely "weathers" the body, increasing health risk in childbearing and across the life course.

OVERVIEW

Infant and maternal mortality are internationally recognized barometers of popu-lation health and social well-being.[1] Despite the United States spending more than any other nation on health care, American mothers and babies die at much higher rates than in other wealthy countries. Nearly 6 of every 1,000 infants born alive in the United States die in the first year of life (Kochanek, Murphy, Xu, & Arias, 2017). This rate is 76% higher than the average rate among other major industrialized nations (Thakrar, Forrest, Maltenfort, & Forrest, 2018), ranking the United States behind 55 other countries worldwide (Central Intelligence Agency [CIA], n.d.). For every 100,000 live births in the United States, 24 women die from pregnancy-related com-plications within 1 year of the delivery (MacDorman, Declercq, Cabral, & Morton, 2016). Relative to peer nations, this rate is three or four times higher than average (Kassebaum, 2016; MacDorman, Declercq, & Thoma, 2017), placing the United States at the bottom of the list of major industrialized countries in terms of maternal health (MacDorman et al., 2016). Although rates of adverse childbearing outcomes in the majority population, non-Hispanic Whites, exceed rates among comparable nations (CDC, 2016; Organization for Economic Cooperation and Development, 2017), the United States ranks so low in international comparisons because its racial divide runs so deep (Chen, Oster, & Williams, 2016; MacDorman et al., 2017).

The United States has tracked health statistics by race/ethnicity for well over a cen-tury. During that time, African Americans have posted the highest infant mortality rates of all major racial/ethnic groups in the country, particularly for deaths related to low birth weight (<2500 g or 5 lbs, 8 oz.) and preterm delivery (<37 weeks of gestation), from which they are three or four times more likely to die (CDC, 1999; Heron, 2017; Rossen & Schoendorf, 2014). American Indians/Alaska Natives and Pacific Islanders have the next highest rates of infant mortality, Asians have the lowest, and Hispanics have rates comparable to those of non-Hispanic Whites (CDC, 2016). Rates also vary within racial/ethnic categories (e.g., Cubans and Japanese have better infant outcomes compared with Puerto Ricans and Filipinos), by state (outcomes are best in Massachusetts and worst in Mississippi), and by immigrant status (immigrants have better birth outcomes compared with US-born women) (CDC, 2016).

The high proportion of births to immigrant women likely accounts for Hispanics' and Asians' more favorable pregnancy outcomes. Foreign-born women delivering in the United States tend to be healthier than domestically born women, having fewer sociodemographic, medical, and behavioral risk factors for adverse birth outcomes, and they may benefit from a constitutional hardiness that enables them to leave their homelands and set out to a foreign land in hopeful expectation of new opportunities to improve their life circumstances (Hummer et al., 1999). In addition to this so-called "healthy immigrant effect," cultural protections, such as highly favorable attitudes toward childbearing and strong religiosity and family support, promote better outcomes in immigrants, even among groups that are more economically disadvantaged, such as Mexicans and Southeast Asians (Landale et al., 1999; Sherraden & Barrera, 1996).

When differences in risk (e.g., sociodemographic, medical, behavioral, and psychosocial) are taken into account, childbearing outcomes are still worse in African Americans (Culhane & Goldenberg, 2011; Dominguez, Dunkel Schetter, Glynn, Hobel, & Sandman, 2008; Goldenberg et al., 1996; Saftlas, Koonin, & Atrash, 2000; Shiono, Rauh, Park, Lederman, & Zuskar, 1997). In some instances, African American pregnant women experience somewhat comparable (e.g., prenatal care utilization; Alexander, Kogan, & Nabukera, 2002) or even lower levels of risk (e.g., smoking; Curtin & Mathews, 2016) than those experienced by non-Hispanic Whites. Even more surprising, the racial gap persists among women with extremely low likelihood of adverse outcomes (Alexander, Kogan, Himes, Mor, & Goldenberg, 1999; Saftlas et al., 2000), and it is widest at the highest levels of education and income (Braveman et al., 2015; McGrady, Sung, Rowley, & Hogue, 1992; Schoendorf, Hogue, Kleinman, & Rowley, 1992).

Given this puzzling, and sometimes paradoxical, pattern of risk, some argue that genes tied to African ancestry must somehow compromise reproductive health. This argument is problematic for a number of reasons. If African genes endanger childbearing, then, as sordid as it sounds, slavery should have afforded African Americans some degree of genetic protection. White male rape of African slave women was a regular practice (P. Collins, 1990; Roberts, 1990). It was so common that from 1850 to 1920 (1900 excepted), the US census classified the "Black" population by degree of African ancestry (e.g., Blacks, Mulattos, Quadroons, and Octoroons), in keeping with a "one drop rule" for maintaining White racial purity (Brown, 2015; Pew Research Center, 2015). Interracial sex introduced a not-so-insignificant level of European genetic admixture into the African American population (Baharian et al., 2016). Modern-day admixture patterns in the genomes of African Americans reveal a clear European male–African female bias, with European genetic contributions three times as likely to originate from males than females (Lind et al., 2007). This admixture pattern is not due to the consistent growth in intermarriage in the post-civil rights era: Only 11% of Whites and 18% of Blacks marry outside their racial group, only 11% of White intermarriage involves a Black spouse, only 12% of Black females (compared to 24% of Black males) intermarry, and only 3% of intermarriage involves White male–Black female couples (Livingston & Brown, 2017).

Contrary to the genetic argument for African Americans' poorer childbearing health, Black immigrants' birth outcomes are comparable to those of non-Hispanic Whites (David & Collins, 1997), and their reproductive advantage holds even when accounting for the healthy immigrant effect (David & Collins, 1997; Pallotto, Collins, & David, 2000). As of 2016, there were 4.2 million Black immigrants in the United States (18% of the Black population in the country), hailing primarily from the Caribbean (49%; Jamaicans are the largest subgroup) and Africa (39%; Nigerians are the largest subgroup) (Anderson & Lopez, 2018). Although the infant and maternal mortality rates in those regions are substantially worse than in the United States, especially given the AIDS epidemic (CIA, n.d.), foreign-born Black women delivering in the United States experience better childbearing health compared with American-born Black women (CDC, 2016). Black immigrants' self-reported health varies with the proportion of Blacks in their countries of origin: Africans self-report better health than West Indians, who report better health than Black Europeans (Read & Emerson, 2005). African immigrant pregnant women also perceive significantly less racial bias against themselves personally and their group as a whole than do Caribbean and African American pregnant women (Dominguez, Strong, Krieger, Gillman, & Rich-Edwards, 2009). When one is part of the majority group, the social context tends to naturally cultivate a greater sense of personal agency and cultural esteem, which supports overall well-being (Link & Phelan, 1995; Waters, 1999). Also important is the very different circumstance under which contemporary Black immigrants arrive to and settle in the United States. Voluntary immigration of Blacks en masse to the United States in search of greater opportunity dates back only to the 1920s for Caribbeans and the late 1960s for Africans (Dodoo, 1997), compared to four centuries of forced migration and slave labor before Jim Crow and the struggle for civil rights from which African Americans are descended. The longer immigrants of color reside in the United States, however, and the more acculturated they become, the more racism they perceive (Dominguez et al., 2009) and the worse their health becomes (Callister & Birkhead, 2002; Landale et al., 1999). Indeed, it takes just one generation for Black immigrants' reproductive advantage to erode, as their better childbearing health does not appear to carry over to subsequent generations of daughters born and raised in the United States (J. Collins, Wu, & David, 2002).

What the genetic position also seems to miss is that the genomic roots of the entire human population trace back to Africa (Tishkoff & Kidd, 2004); there is greater genetic variation within racial groups than between them (Rosenberg et al., 2002); and the biological conceptualization of so-called "race" is, at best, scientifically problematic and, at worse, scientifically groundless (Fine, Ibrahim, & Thomas, 2003; Krieger, 2003). Genes operate based on specificity, but African Americans experience excess mortality not only in childbearing but also across a broad spectrum of health indicators at each stage of the life course (Heron, 2017). Overwhelmingly, scientists agree that "race" is a socially meaningful construct but not very useful for dividing the human population into genetically distinct subgroups (Fine et al., 2003; Krieger, 2003; Vo, 2016). Since the first US census in 1790, racial group classifications have changed with every census, as sociopolitical and scientific notions of who is "White" and who is not have shifted over time (Demby, 2014; Painter, 2015). All things considered, racial disparities in adverse perinatal outcomes are more likely the biological consequence of deleterious social conditions rather than the biological expression of "race" genes (David & Collins, 2007; Krieger, 2003; Link & Phelan, 1995).

SOCIAL DETERMINANTS OF HEALTH: RACE, GENDER, AND CLASS

Infant mortality is the most sensitive index we possess of social welfare.
—Newsholme (1910)

Social determinants of health are the social conditions in which people are born, grow, live, work, play, and age. They shape the context within which life happens, and they are by far the largest contributors to population health—more influential than health care, health behavior, and genetics (Jones, Jones, Perry, Barclay, & Jones, 2009; Tarlov, 1999).

Racism is a fundamental social determinant of racial disparities in health (S. James, 2003). It is a system of "race"-based power, rooted in notions of inherent racial group superiority and inferiority, that systematically, pervasively, and unjustly privileges "Whites" and oppresses "non-Whites" (Dominguez, 2008). It manifests at multiple levels (i.e., internal, interpersonal, institutional, and structural) and involves direct, indirect, and group-based exposures across the life course (Jones, 2000; Nuru-Jeter et al., 2009). Whether blatant or subtle in nature, racism is a particularly visceral threat to well-being because it denigrates a core aspect of identity that is ever-visible and unchanging. Racism is linked to a host of negative health behaviors and poor mental and physical health outcomes (Paradies, 2006), including lower infant birthweight (Dominguez et al., 2008), preterm delivery (Giscombe & Lobel, 2005), and infant death (Polednak, 1996; E. Roberts, 1997). Even chronic worry about potential racism threats increases risk of early delivery (Braveman et al., 2017). Health may be further compromised by pervasive racial bias in access to and quality of health care services (Smedley, Stith, & Nelson, 2002). African American pregnant women receive less information and advice, and fewer routine prenatal treatments, than do White pregnant women (Paul et al., 2006). They also are less likely to feel respected and to trust that their medical providers are acting in their best interest, which is not surprising given contemporary experiences of racial bias and a legacy of medical maltreatment dating back two centuries (e.g., the Tuskegee Syphilis Study, medical experimentation on slaves, and exhumation of Black bodies for dissection and medical training) (Gamble, 1997).

Although racism is critical for understanding African Americans' reproductive disadvantage, gender is another factor in a matrix of oppression that can potentially compromise African American women's childbearing health. Gendered racism involves intersectional burdens that African American women experience simply because they are African American women (Jackson, Phillips, Hogue, & Curry-Owens, 2001). Historically, African slave women were subjected to forced breeding, sterilization, rape, and gynecological experimentation (P. Collins, 1990; D. Roberts, 1998). Today, African American pregnant women commonly report disrespectful treatment and assumptions by medical personnel about their marital status, health habits, sexual history, age, economic stability, and insurance status (Murrell, Smith, Gill, & Oxley, 1996; Rosenthal & Lobel, 2011). They also contend with gendered racism across other domains of their lives, such as having their competence questioned at work, being followed by store personnel while shopping, receiving poor service at restaurants, and being compared unfavorably to European standards of beauty (Nuru-Jeter et al., 2009).

As the traditional center of the family, African American women's roles and obligations include nurturing, protecting, and supporting "the village," especially children. Unlike White mothers, Black mothers experience additional intersectional burden as a function of their caregiving roles, as Audre Lorde, a Black lesbian feminist mother and poet (1984, p. 119, as cited in Ehrenreich, 1993), explains:

> Some problems we share as women, some we do not. You fear your children will grow up to join the patriarchy and testify against you. We fear our children will be dragged from a car and shot down in the street, and you will turn your backs upon the reasons they are dying. (p. 492)

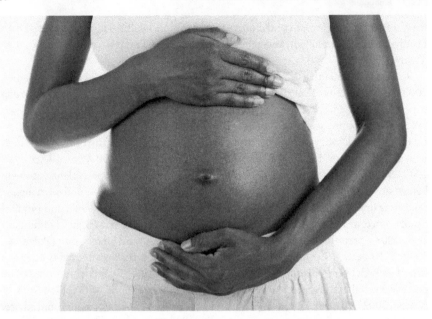

Figure 2.2 "One isn't necessarily born with courage, but one is born with potential. Without courage, we cannot practice any other virtue with consistency. We can't be kind, true, merciful, generous, or honest."

—Maya Angelou, March 5, 1988, *USA Today*

African American women can feel ambivalent about becoming pregnant, guilty if they are pregnant, and quietly distressed once they deliver, as they ponder the gravity of raising their Black child in White America (Jackson et al., 2001; Nuru-Jeter et al., 2009; Rosenthal & Lobel, 2011). To arm their children against racism, many African American parents cultivate ethnic pride and socialize children to the realities of the social world (Hughes et al., 2006). They work to ensure that their children and those of others in "the village" are afforded equitable opportunities to learn, grow, and thrive in safe and supportive environments (Jackson et al., 2001).

Class is another determinant of health that is essential for understanding the role of the social environment in health disparities. It affects health in a stepwise manner, such that each step up or down the economic ladder corresponds to similar shifts in health status (Adler et al., 1994). Class, race, and gender are strongly associated in the United States with women earning less than men, African Americans and Hispanics earning less than Whites, and African American and Hispanic women earning the least. Even at similar levels of education, African American and Hispanic women earn only approximately 70% of what White men earn (Patten, 2016). African Americans also have the lowest net worth, ranking lowest in accumulated wealth, the basis of economic stability and upward mobility (Hanks, Solomon, & Weller, 2018). At every level of education, African Americans earn less, have more people to support with those earnings, have less accumulated wealth, and face higher average costs for basic necessities.

Coined the Sojourner syndrome, the constellation of systematic class, race, and gender oppression that Black women experience intensifies their psychosocial burden and risk for adverse health outcomes (Lekan, 2009). Named for Sojourner Truth, the famous 19th-century former slave turned evangelist, abolitionist, and women's rights activist, Sojourner syndrome also recognizes the tremendous resilience that Black women historically have demonstrated in multiple ways in multiple roles as leaders in their families and communities. However, this extraordinary resilience, captured in the archetype of the "strong Black woman" who keeps on keeping on, making a way out of no way, exacts a heavy mental and physical toll.

> It's what Black women have passed on and collectively reinforced, generation after generation., Black women are taught to push through, keep going, and endure difficult times without protest. Asking for help—or even believing that we're deserving of it—is a sign of weakness and vulnerability that we've been taught we cannot afford. . . . We are paying for this myth we've bought into with our lives. (Ricks, 2018)

Stress: How Social Inequity Gets Under the Skin

> Stress is hemmed into our dresses, pressed into our hair, mixed into our perfume and painted on our fingers. Stress from the deferred dreams, the dreams not voiced; stress from the broken promises, the blatant lies; stress from always being at the bottom, from never being thought beautiful, from always being taken for granted, taken advantage of. Stress from being a black woman in white America. Much of this stress is caused by how the world outside us relates to us. We cannot control that world . . . but we can assert agency in our own lives so that the outside world cannot over-determine our responses.
> —Adisa (1994, pp. 13-14)

African Americans' long-standing pattern of poor childbearing health results from the physical toll of race, gender, and class oppression. Stress is the mechanism by which this trifold burden of social inequity gets under the skin. Subordinate positions in social hierarchies adversely affect physiologic function through chronic engagement of the body's fight-or-flight system (Brunner, 1997; Link & Phelan, 1995). The resulting wear and tear, known as allostatic load, erodes the body's ability to regulate key biologic systems efficiently, thereby increasing health risk (McEwen, 1998). Weathering (Geronimus, 1996; Geronimus, Hicken, Keene, & Bound, 2006) and stress age (Hogue & Bremner, 2005) refer specifically to premature physiologic aging in African American women, given how quickly their reproductive risk increases with age. This phenomenon reflects the physiologic cost of lifelong social disadvantage. The sum total of a woman's life experience affects her pregnancy. Healthy women typically enjoy healthy pregnancies and deliver healthy babies. Given pervasive social inequity, African American women accrue more risks and fewer protections across the life course, compromising their childbearing health well before they ever conceive (Lu & Halfon, 2003).

HISTORICAL TRENDS

Historical approaches to addressing the Black–White gap emanated from a medical model focused on individual health risks and protections based on what little was known about the causes of adverse outcomes, such as preterm delivery (e.g., infection, placental abruption, preeclampsia, smoking, and drug use). Interventions centered on health education, health behavior, and prenatal care, particularly among the poor. The primary focus was on what women did or did not do to facilitate healthy pregnancy and birth. Research demonstrating lower incidence of some behaviors, such as smoking, among African Americans, persistent disparity at similar levels of behavioral, sociodemographic, and medical risk, and higher rates of adverse outcome even among highly educated African American women led scientists at the CDC, the National Institutes of Health, and the Kaiser Foundation to call for a paradigm shift: To understand the childbearing health of African American women, the psychosocial context of their lives—characterized by racism, sexism, and classism—needed specific consideration (Krieger, Rowley, Herman, Avery, & Phillips, 1993; Rowley et al., 1993). The importance of life course experiences for pregnancy outcomes gained traction (Lu & Halfon, 2003), as did biopsychosocial models of racial disparities based on theories of stress and health (Hogan & Ferre, 2001; Landrine & Klonoff, 1996; Myers, Lewis, & Dominguez, 2003; Zambrana, Dunkel-Schetter, Collins, & Scrimshaw, 1999). Recognizing the limits of traditional prenatal care, the field began to emphasize preconception and interconception health, group-based prenatal care (e.g., the centering pregnancy model), and more holistic and community-based approaches to promoting healthy African American pregnancy informed by social determinants thinking (e.g., the Healthy Start program and Best Babies Zones).

The Black–White gap in childbearing health is not static. It varies across time, narrowing during more socially progressive periods and widening during more socially conservative ones (Cohen, 2016; A. James, 2017). It varies across place, with infant mortality disparities ranging from a low of 1.57 in Arkansas to a high of 3.15 in New Jersey (MacDorman & Mathews, 2013), and, for example, from 3.3 per 1,000 Black infant deaths on the west side of Houston to 28.1 in the city's central core (Nehme et al., 2018). Such wide variation indicates that the racial gap is not naturally occurring, the result of some inherent genetic predisposition linked to a "race" gene; rather, it is sensitive to social conditions and, thus, malleable to change.

To put things into perspective, people of African descent have been in the United States for 400 years, the vast majority of them descended from slaves forcibly relocated to build the foundations of what has become one the most powerful countries in all of human history. Legal slavery ended just 150 years ago with the signing of the 13th Amendment, and it took another 100 years for legal discrimination based on race (and color, sex, religion, or national origin) to end. Thus, the post-civil rights era consists of only 50 years since full citizenship rights of the descendants of slaves were legally codified in the United States (A. James, 2017). Since signing of that historic legislation, social parity has continued to remain elusive, with deep, wide, and growing inequality across racial, gender, and class lines, despite the American cultural ethos of rugged individualism. One cannot pull themselves up by their own bootstraps if they do not have bootstraps, let alone boots. A one-size-fits-all approach to addressing disparities is not going to close the racial gap. Nothing less than a full commitment to equity that ensures fair and just opportunities for attaining the highest possible level of health, wherein everyone has access to what they need to be healthy, will work to eliminate disparities (Braveman et al., 2011).

RECENT DEVELOPMENTS OF NOTE

Fueled by social movements, such as Black Lives Matter, and more recent media attention on disparities in infant and maternal mortality, especially in the wake of funding cuts and policy initiatives that threaten essential reproductive and maternal and child health services, several mobilization efforts are underway to address the health of mothers and babies. On the intervention side, these include comprehensive birthing centers; faith-based prenatal support; culturally tailored perinatal programs; home-based care and support through community health workers and public health nurses; and doula and midwifery support during pregnancy, delivery, and postpartum (Simmons, 2017; Villarosa, 2018). Advocacy includes work to improve early and consistent access to quality reproductive and maternal health care, gain legal recognition of and fair reimbursement for doulas and certified midwives (especially direct-entry midwives without nursing degrees), establish infant and maternal mortality review committees in state public health departments, encourage more Black and Brown students to go into the health professions, incorporate social determinants and health equity training into medical school curricula, start a national conversation on racism, promote adoption of an equity lens and "health in all policies" approach in the policymaking process, and foster cross-sector collaborations for collective impact. In addition, notable developments at the national level are the Secretary of Health and Human Services Advisory Committee's (2013) recommendations for a national strategy on infant mortality focusing on promoting health equity to eliminate disparities; the Robert Wood Johnson Foundation's launch of the Culture of Health initiative to set a national agenda and guide action on social determinants of health to promote health equity and improved population health; the US Department of Health and Human Services' launch of Healthy People 2020, the nation's public health plan, with a strong emphasis on social determinants of health and health equity; and the Patient Protection and Affordable Care Act (ACA) signed into law by President Barack Obama in 2010 as the most comprehensive reform of the US health care system since President Lyndon Johnson signed an amendment to the Social Security Act in 1965 authorizing Medicare and Medicaid.

CURRENT CONDITIONS

The National Center for Health Statistics reports that although infant mortality rates have declined for all groups during the past decade, the racial gap has not appreciably closed (Mathews & Driscoll, 2017). African American infants are still twice as likely to die before their first birthday compared to White infants. The news for maternal mortality is even worse. While other wealthy nations have decreased their maternal mortality rates, the US rate has increased nearly 27% during the past decade (MacDorman et al., 2016). African American women are more than three times as likely to die during childbearing as the majority population. The United States does not have the best data systems in place for tracking trends to inform timely solutions. Better data are needed to inform better policies to ensure better health care and greater health equity to eliminate health disparities.

LOOKING TO THE FUTURE

In 1966, in the wake of the passage of the Civil Rights Act, the United States signed the United Nations Declaration on the Elimination of All Forms of Racial Discrimination, thereby solemnly affirming "the necessity of speedily eliminating racial discrimination throughout the world in all its forms and manifestations, and of securing understanding of and respect for the dignity of the human person" (United Nations, 1963, p. 2). The United States ratified the Declaration in 1994, and progress toward achieving the goals of the Declaration was most recently reviewed by the United Nations in 2014. The United Nations Committee on the Elimination of Racial Discrimination (CERD) took approximately half a page to note six positive developments in terms of the United States' progress. It took 12 pages to note its concerns and recommendations for improvement (CERD, 2014). Since that time, former president of the American Public Health Association, Dr. Camara Jones, has called for a national conversation on race, and the National Academies of Medicine has released a report on framing a national dialogue on race and ethnicity to advance health equity. Also since that time, the United States has witnessed one of the most dramatic presidential elections and endured one of the most divisive presidential agendas to "make America great again" by dismantling much of what makes America great. Grassroots movements, campaigns of resistance, marches of protest, and hashtag rebellions, sparked by popular discontent and fueled by social media, are hopeful reminders that democracy is government of the people, by the people, and for the people.

CONCLUSION

The African American reproductive disadvantage is not solely a public health concern for "those people." It is a concern for all people. A thriving and productive society is rooted in a healthy populace in which all members are inherently valued and their potential contributions are actively cultivated (Lu, Verbeist, & Dominguez, 2018). More equitable societies simply do better—they are physically, socially, economically, psychologically, politically, and environmentally healthier (Wilkinson & Pickett, 2010). Healthy People 2020, the United States' current public health plan, envisions a society in which all people live long and healthy lives. To achieve this, health disparities must be eliminated. To eliminate health disparities, all people must have fair and just opportunities to be healthy. This is health equity. To achieve health equity, all people must have fair and just opportunities. This is social equity, and America's future depends on it.

DISCUSSION QUESTIONS

1. Better health is strongly associated with greater socioeconomic resources, such as income and education. However, the Black–White gap in adverse birth outcomes widens with increasing socioeconomic resources. What factors might help explain this apparent paradox?
2. The life course perspective holds that improved pregnancy outcomes will result from prioritizing women's health at each stage of their lives, starting in the womb and extending through childhood, adolescence, and throughout

adulthood. What might a life course approach to closing the Black–White gap in adverse birth outcomes and maternal mortality entail across these different developmental stages?

3. Healthy People is the nation's 10-year public health plan for improving population health. If you were a member of the Secretary of Health's advisory committee to develop the next Healthy People plan, what actions would you recommend to promote greater health equity?

NOTE

1.   Portions of this chapter are adapted from the author's previous work.

REFERENCES

Adisa, O. P. (1994). Rocking in the sunlight: Stress and Black women. In E. C. White (Ed.), *The Black women's health book: Speaking for ourselves* (2nd ed., pp. 11–14). Seattle, WA: Seal Press.

Adler, N. E., Boyce, T., Chesney, M. A., Cohen, S., Folkman, S., Kahn, R. L., & Syme, S. L. (1994). Socioeconomic status and health: The challenge of the gradient. *American Psychologist, 49*, 15–24.

Alexander, G. R., Kogan, M. D., Himes, J. H., Mor, J. M., & Goldenberg, R. (1999). Racial differences in birthweight for gestational age and infant mortality in extremely-low-risk U.S. populations. *Paediatric & Perinatal Epidemiology, 13*, 205–217.

Alexander, G. R., Kogan, M. D., & Nabukera, S. (2002). Racial difference in prenatal care use in the United States: Are disparities decreasing? *American Journal of Public Health, 92*(12), 1970–1975.

Anderson, M., & Lopez, G. (2018, January 24). Key facts about Black immigrants in the U.S. *FactTank: News in the numbers.* Washington, DC: Pew Research Center. Retrieved from https://www.pewresearch.org/fact-tank/2018/01/24/key-facts-about-black-immigrants- in-the-u-s

Baharian, S., Barakatt, M., Gignoux, C. R., Shringarpure, S., Errington, J., Blot, W. J., . . . Gravel, S. (2016). The Great Migration and African-American genomic diversity. *PLOS Genetics, 12*(5), e1006059. https://doi.org/10.1371/journal.pgen.1006059

Braveman, P. A., Heck, K., Egerter, S., Dominguez, T. P., Rinki, C., Marchi, K. S., & Curtis, M. (2017). Worry about racial discrimination: A missing piece of the puzzle of Black–White disparities in preterm birth? *PLoS One, 12*(10), e0186151. Retrieved from https://doi.org/10.1371/journal.pone.0186151

Braveman, P. A., Heck, K., Egerter, S., Marchi, K., Dominguez, T. P., Cubbin, C., . . . Curtis, M. (2015). The role of socioeconomic factors in Black–White disparities in preterm birth. *American Journal of Public Health, 105*, 694–702.

Braveman, P. A., Kumanyika, S., Fielding, J., LaVeist, T., Borrell, L. N., Manderscheid, R., & Troutman, A. (2011). Health disparities and health equity: The issue is justice. *American Journal of Public Health, 101*, S149–S155.

Brown, A. (2015, June). The changing categories the U.S. has used to measure race. *FactTank: News in the numbers.* Washington, DC: Pew Research Center. Retrieved from http://www.pewresearch.org/fact-tank/2015/06/12/the-changing-categories-the-u-s-has-used-to-measure-race

Brunner, E. (1997). Socioeconomic determinants of health: Stress and the biology of inequality. *British Medical Journal, 314*, 1472–1476.

Callister, L. C., & Birkhead, A. (2002). Acculturation and perinatal outcomes in Mexican immigrant childbearing women: An integrative review. *Journal of Perinatal and Neonatal Nursing, 16*, 22–38.

Centers for Disease Control and Prevention. (1999). Achievements in public health, 1900–1999: Healthier mothers and babies. *MMWR Morbidity & Mortality Weekly Report, 48*, 849–858.

Centers for Disease Control and Prevention. (2016). *User guide to the 2016 period linked birth/infant death public use file* (Table 1). Retrieved from ftp://ftp.cdc.gov/pub/Health_Statistics/NCHS/Dataset_Documentation/DVS/periodlinked/LinkPE16Guide.pdf

Central Intelligence Agency. (n.d.). The world factbook: Country comparison: Infant mortality rate (2017 estimates). Retrieved from https://www.cia.gov/library/publications/the-world-factbook/rankorder/2091rank.html

Chen, A., Oster, E., & Williams, H. (2016). Why is infant mortality higher in the United States than in Europe? *American Economic Journal: Economic Policy, 8*(2), 89–124.

Cohen, P. N. (2016). Maternal age and infant mortality for White, Black, and Mexican mothers in the United States. *Sociological Science, 3*, 32–38.

Collins, J. W., Jr., Wu, S., & David, R. J. (2002). Differing intergenerational birth weights among the descendants of U.S.-born and foreign-born Whites and African Americans in Illinois. *America Journal of Epidemiology, 155*, 210–216.

Collins, P. H. (1990). *Black feminist thought: Knowledge, consciousness, and the politics of empowerment.* Boston, MA: Unwin Hyman.

Committee on the Elimination of Racial Discrimination. (2014, September 25). *Concluding observations on the combined seventh to ninth periodic reports of the United States of America.* Geneva, Switzerland: United Nations. Retrieved from https://tbinternet.ohchr.org/_layouts/treatybodyexternal/Download.aspx?symbolno=CERD/C/USA/CO/7-9&Lang=En

Culhane, J. F., & Goldenberg, R. L. (2011). Racial disparities in preterm birth. *Seminars in Perinatology, 35*(4), 234–239.

Curtin, S. C., & Mathews, T. J. (2016). Smoking prevalence and cessation before and during pregnancy: Data from the birth certificate, 2014. *National Vital Statistics Reports, 65*(1), 1–14.

David, R. J., & Collins, J.W., Jr. (1997). Differing birth weight among infants of U.S.-born Blacks, African-born Blacks, and U.S. born Whites. *New England Journal of Medicine, 337*, 1209–1214.

David, R., & Collins, J. Jr. (2007). Disparities in infant mortality: What's genetics got to do with it? *Am J Public Health, 97*, 1191–1197.

Demby, G. (2014, June). *What is your race? For many Americans, a shifting answer.* NPR. Retrieved from https://www.npr.org/sections/codeswitch/2014/06/09/319584793/what-is-your-race-for-millions-of-americans-a-shifting-answer

Dodoo, F. N. (1997). Assimilation differences among African in America. *Social Forces, 76*, 527–546.

Dominguez, T. P. (2008). Race, racism, and racial disparities in adverse birth outcomes. *Clinical Obstetrics & Gynecology, 51*(2), 360–370.

Dominguez, T. P., Strong, E. S., Krieger, N., Gillman, M. W., & Rich-Edwards, J. W. (2009). Differences in the self-reported racism experiences of U.S.-born and foreign-born Black pregnant women. *Social Science & Medicine, 69*, 258–265.

Ehrenreich, N. (1993). The colonization of the womb. *Duke Law Journal, 43*(3), 492–587.

Fine, M. J., Ibrahim, S. A., & Thomas, S. A. (2003). The role of race and genetics in health disparities research. *American Journal of Public Health, 95,* 2125–2128.

Gamble, V. N. (1997). Under the shadow of Tuskegee: African Americans and health care. *American Journal of Public Health, 87,* 1773–1778.

Geronimus, A. T. (1996). Black/White differences in the relationship of maternal age to birthweight: A population-based test of the weathering hypothesis. *Social Science & Medicine, 42* (4), 589–97.

Geronimus, A. T., Hicken, M., Keene, D., & Bound, J. (2006). "Weathering" and age patterns of allostatic load scores among Blacks and Whites in the United States. *American Journal of Public Health, 96* (5), 826–833.

Giscombe, C. L., & Lobel, M. (2005). Explaining disproportionately high rates of adverse birth outcomes among African Americans: The impact of stress, racism, and related factors in pregnancy. *Psychological Bulletin, 131,* 662–683.

Goldenberg, R. L., Cliver, S. P., Mulvihill, F. X., Hickey, C. A., Hoffman, H. J., Klerman, L. V., & Johnson, M. J. (1996). Medical, psychosocial, and behavioral risk factors do not explain the increased risk for low birth weight among Black women. *American Journal of Obstetrics & Gynecology, 175,* 1317–1324.

Hanks, A., Solomon, D., & Weller, C. E. (2018, February 21). *Systematic inequality: How American's structural racism helped create the Black–White wealth gap.* Washington, DC: Center for American Progress. Retrieved from https://www.americanprogress.org/issues/race/reports/2018/02/21/447051/systematic-inequality

Heron, M. (2017, November). Deaths: Leading causes for 2015—Table 2. *National Vital Statistics Reports, 66*(5), 62–72.

Hogan, V. K., & Ferre, C. D. (2001). The social context of pregnancy for African American women: Implications for the study and prevention of adverse perinatal outcomes. *Maternal and Child Health Journal, 5,* 67–69.

Hogue, C. J. R., & Bremner, J. D. (2005). Stress model for research into preterm delivery among black women. *American Journal of Obstetrics & Gynecology, 192*(suppl), S47–S55.

Hughes, D., Rodriguez, J., Smith, E. P., Johnson, D. J., Stevenson, H. C., & Spicer, P. (2006). Parents' ethnic–racial socialization practices: A review of research and directions for future study. *Developmental Psychology, 42,* 747–770.

Hummer, R. A., Biegler, M., DeTurk, P. B., Forbes, D., Frisbie, W. P., Hong, Y., & Pullum, S. G. (1999). Race/ethnicity, nativity, and infant mortality in the United States. *Social Forces, 77,* 1083–1118.

Jackson, F. M., Phillips, M. T., Hogue, C. J., & Curry-Owens, T. Y. (2001). Examining the burdens of gendered racism: Implications for pregnancy outcomes. *Maternal & Child Health Journal, 5,* 95–108.

James, A. R. (2017, February 9). *March of Dimes equity retreat* [PowerPoint slides]. March of Dimes Prematurity Campaign Collaborative: Health Equity Workgroup Meeting, Arlington, VA.

James, S. A. (2003). Confronting the moral economy of U.S. racial/ethnic health disparities. *American Journal of Public Health, 93,* 189.

Jones, C. P. (2000). Levels of racism: A theoretic framework and gardener's tale. *American Journal of Public Health, 90,* 1212–1215.

Jones, C. P., Jones, C. Y., Perry, G. S., Barclay, G., & Jones, C. A. (2009). Addressing the social determinants of children's health: A cliff analogy. *Journal of Health Care for the Poor and Underserved, 20*(4 Suppl.), 1–12.

Kassebaum, N. J. (2016). Global, regional, and national levels of maternal mortality, 1990–2015: A systematic analysis for the Global Burden of Disease Study 2015. *Lancet, 388*(10053), 1775–1812.

Kochanek, K. D., Murphy, S. L., Xu, J., & Arias, E. (2017). *Mortality in the United States, 2016.* NCHS Data Brief No. 293. Hyattsville, MD: National Center for Health Statistics.

Krieger, N. (2003). Does racism harm health? Did child abuse exist before 1962? On explicit questions, critical science, and current controversies: An ecosocial perspective. *American Journal of Public Health, 93,* 194–199.

Krieger, N. (2008). In sickness and in wealth [Documentary series episode]. In L. Adelman & L. Smith (Executive Producers), *Unnatural causes: Is inequality making us sick?* San Francisco, CA: California Newsreel with Vital Pictures.

Krieger, N., Rowley, D. L., Herman, A. A., Avery, B., & Phillips, M. T. (1993). Racism, sexism, and social class: Implications for studies of health, disease and well-being. *American Journal of Preventive Medicine, 9*(6 Suppl.), 82–122.

Landale, N. S., Oropesa, R. S., Llanes, D., & Gorman, B. K. (1999). Does Americanization have adverse effects on health? Stress, health habits, and infant health outcomes among Puerto Ricans. *Social Forces, 78,* 613–641.

Landrine, H., & Klonoff, E. A. (1996). The Schedule of Racist Events: A measure of racial discrimination and a study of its negative physical and mental health consequences. *Journal of Black Psychology, 22,* 144–168.

Lekan, D. (2009). Sojourner syndrome and health disparities in African American women. *Advances in Nursing Science, 32*(4), 307–321.

Lind, J. M., Hutcheson-Dilks, H. B., Williams, S. M., Moore, J. H., Essex, M., Ruiz-Pesini, E., . . . Smith, M. W. (2007). Elevated male European and female African contributions to the genomes of African American individuals. *Human Genetics, 120*(5), 713–722.

Link, B. G., & Phelan, J. (1995). Social conditions as fundamental causes of disease. *Journal of Health & Social Behavior, 35*(Suppl.), 80–94.

Livingston, G., & Brown, A. (2017, May 18). Trends and patterns in intermarriage. In *Intermarriage in the U.S. 50 years after Loving v. Virginia.* Pew Research Center. Retrieved from http://www.pewsocialtrends.org/2017/05/18/1-trends-and-patterns-in-intermarriage

Lorde, A. (1984). Age, race, class, and sex: Women redefining difference. In *Sister outsider: Essays and speeches* (pp. 114–123). Berkeley: Crossing Press.

Lu, M. C., & Halfon, N. (2003). Racial and ethnic disparities in birth outcomes: A life-course perspective. *Maternal and Child Health Journal, 7,* 13–30.

Lu, M. C., Verbeist, S., & Dominguez, T. P. (2018). Life course theory: An overview. In S. Verbeist (Ed.), *Moving life course theory into action: Making change happen* (pp. 1–40). Washington, DC: APHA Press.

MacDorman, M. F., Declercq, E., Cabral, H., & Morton, C. (2016). Is the United States maternal mortality rate increasing? Disentangling trends from measurement issues. *Obstetrics & Gynecology, 128*(3), 447–455.

MacDorman, M. F., Declercq, E., & Thoma, M. E. (2017). Trends in maternal mortality by sociodemographic characteristics and cause of death in 27 states and the District of Columbia. *Obstetrics & Gynecology, 129*(5), 811–818.

MacDorman, M. F., & Mathews, T. J. (2013). Infant mortality in the United States, 2005–2008. *Morbidity and Mortality Weekly Report Supplements, 62*(3), 171–175.

Mathews, T. J., & Driscoll, A. K. (2017). *Trends in infant mortality in the United States, 2005–2014.* NCHS Data Brief 279. Retrieved from https://www.cdc.gov/nchs/products/databriefs/db279.htm

McEwen, B. S. (1998). Stress adaptation and disease: Allostasis and allostatic load. *Annals of the New York Academy of Sciences, 840,* 33–44.

McGrady, G. A., Sung, J. F., Rowley, D. L., & Hogue, C. J. (1992). Preterm delivery and low birth weight among first-born infants of Black and White college graduates. *American Journal of Epidemiology, 136,* 266–276.

Murrell, N. L., Smith, R., Gill, G., & Oxley, G. (1996). Racism and health care access: A dialogue with childbearing women. *Health Care for Women International, 17,* 149–159.

Myers, H. F., Lewis, T. T., & Dominguez, T. P. (2003). Stress, coping, and minority health: Biopsychosocial perspectives on ethnic health disparities. In G. Bernal, J. Trimble, K. Burlew, & F. T. L. Leong (Eds), *Handbook of racial and ethnic minority psychology* (pp. 377–400). Thousand Oaks, CA: Sage.

Neely, P. (June, 2018). *Black babies die at twice the rate of White babies: My family is part of this statistic.* LAist independent news and KPCC public radio. Retrieved from http://www.laist.com/2018/06/21/black_babies_die_at_twice_the_rate.php

Nehme, E., Mandell, D., Oppenheimer, D., Karimifar, M., Elerian, N., & Lakey, D. (2018). *Infant mortality in communities across Texas.* Austin, TX: University of Texas Health Science Center at Tyler/University of Texas System. Retrieved from http://www.utsystempophealth.org/imr-texas

Newsholme, A. (1910). Report by the medical officer on infant and child mortality. In *39th annual report of the Local Government Board* (Suppl.). Local Government Board: London, UK.

Nuru-Jeter, A., Dominguez, T. P., Hammond, W. P., Leu, J., Skaff, M., Egerter, S., . . . Braveman, P. (2009). "It's the skin you're in": African-American women talk about their experiences of racism: An exploratory study to develop measures of racism for birth outcome studies. *Maternal and Child Health Journal, 13*(1), 29–39.

Organization for Economic Cooperation and Development. (2017, October). *CO1.1 Infant mortality.* Retrieved from https://www.oecd.org/els/family/CO_1_1_Infant_mortality.pdf

Painter, N. I. (2015, June). What is whiteness? *The New York Times.* Retrieved from https://www.nytimes.com/2015/06/21/opinion/sunday/what-is-whiteness.html

Pallotto, E. K., Collins, J. W., & David, R. J. (2000). Enigma of maternal race and infant birth weight: A population-based study of U.S.-born Black and Caribbean-born Black women. *American Journal of Epidemiology, 151,* 1080–1085.

Paradies Y. (2006). A systematic review of empirical research on self-reported racism and health. *International Journal of Epidemiology, 35*(4), 888–901.

Patten, E. (2016). Racial, gender wage gaps persist in U.S. despite some progress. *FactTank: News in the numbers.* Washington, DC: Pew Research Center. Retrieved from http://www.pewresearch.org/fact-tank/2016/07/01/racial-gender-wage-gaps-persist-in-u-s-despite-some-progress

Paul, D. A., Locke, R., Zook, K., Leef, K. H., Stefano, J. L., & Colmorgen, G. (2006). Racial differences in prenatal care of mothers delivering very low birthweight infants. *Journal of Perinatology, 26,* 74–78.

Pew Research Center. (2015, June). *What census calls us: A historical timeline.* Retrieved from http://www.pewsocialtrends.org/interactives/multiracial-timeline

Polednak, A. P. (1996). Trends in US urban Black infant mortality by degree of residential segregation. *American Journal of Public Health, 86,* 723–726.

Read, J. G., & Emerson, M. O. (2005). Racial context, Black immigration and the U.S. Black/White health disparity. *Social Forces, 84,* 181–199.

Ricks, S. (2018, August). I stopped playing the "Strong Black Woman" [commentary]. *Yes! Magazine, Fall 2018.* Retrieved from https://www.yesmagazine.org/issues/mental-health/i-stopped-playing-the-strong-black-woman-20180815.

Roberts, D. (1998). *Killing the Black body: Race, reproduction, and the meanings of liberty.* New York, NY: Vintage.

Roberts, D. E. (1990). The future of reproductive choice for poor women and women of color. *Women's Rights Law Reporter, 12*(2), 59–67.

Roberts, E. M. (1997). Neighborhood social environments and the distribution of low birthweight in Chicago. *American Journal of Public Health, 87*, 597–603.

Rosenberg, N. A., Pritchard, J. K., Weber, J. L., Cann, H. M., Kidd, K. K., Zhivotovsky, L. A., & Feldman, M. W. (1992). Genetic structure in human populations. *Science, 298*, 2381–2385.

Rosenthal, L., & Lobel, M. (2011). Explaining racial disparities in adverse birth outcomes: Unique sources of stress for Black America women. *Social Science & Medicine, 72*(6), 977–983.

Rossen, L. M., & Schoendorf, K. C. (2014). Trends in racial and ethnic disparities in infant mortality rates in the United States, 1989–2006. *American Journal of Public Health, 104*(8), 1549–1556.

Rowley, D. L., Hogue, C. J. R., Blackmore, C. A., Ferre, C. D., Hatfield-Timajchy, K., Branch, P., & Atrash, H. (1993). Preterm delivery among African American women: A research strategy. *American Journal of Preventive Medicine, 9*(6 Suppl.), 1–6.

Saftlas, A. F., Koonin, L. M., & Atrash, H. K. (2000). Racial disparity in pregnancy-related mortality associated with live birth: Can established risk factors explain it? *American Journal of Epidemiology, 152*(5), 413–419.

Schoendorf, K. C., Hogue, C. J., Kleinman, J. C., & Rowley, D. (1992). Mortality among infants of Black as compared with White college-educated parents. *New England Journal of Medicine, 326*, 1522–1526.

Secretary's Advisory Committee on Infant Mortality (2013, January). Report of the Secretary's Advisory Committee on Infant Mortality: Recommendations for Department of Health and Human Services (HHS) action and framework for a national strategy. Washington, DC.: Health Resources and Services Administration, US Department of Health and Human Services.

Sherraden, M. S., & Barrera, R. E. (1996). Poverty, family support, and well-being of infants: Mexican immigrant women and childbearing. *Journal of Sociology and Social Welfare, LXXIII*, 27–51.

Shiono, P. H., Rauh, V. A., Park, M., Lederman, S. A., & Zuskar, D. (1997). Ethnic differences in birthweight: The role of lifestyle and other factors. *American Journal of Public Health, 87*, 787–793.

Simmons, A. M. (2017, October 26). Black doulas, midwives, and reproductive health advocates step up in response to rising Black maternal deaths. *Los Angeles Times.* Retrieved from http://www.latimes.com/nation/la-na-global-black-midwives-20171026-story.html

Smedley, B. D., Stith, A. Y., & Nelson, A. R. (Eds.). (2002). *Unequal treatment: Confronting racial and ethnic disparities in health care.* Washington, DC: Institute of Medicine, National Academies Press.

Tarlov, A. R. (1999). Public policy frameworks for improving population health. *Annals of the New York Academy of Sciences, 896*, 281–293.

Thakrar, A. P., Forrest, A. D., Maltenfort, M. G., & Forrest, C. B. (2018). Child mortality in the U.S. and 19 OECD comparator nations: A 50-year time-trend analysis. *Health Affairs, 37*(1), 140–149.

Tishkoff, S.A., & Kidd, K.K. (2004). Implications of biogeography of human populations for 'race' and medicine. *Nature Genetics, 36,* S21–S27.

United Nations. (1963, September 20). *1904 (XVIII): United Nations declaration on the elimination of all forms of racial discrimination.* Retrieved from http://www.un-documents.net/a18r1904.htm

Villarosa, L. (2018, April 11). Why America's Black women and babies are in a life-or-death crisis. *New York Times Magazine.* Retrieved from https://www.nytimes.com/2018/04/11/magazine/black-mothers-babies-death-maternal-mortality.html

Vo, L. T. (2016, August). 220 years of census data proves race is a social construct. *Vox.* Retrieved from https://www.vox.com/2016/8/18/12404688/census-race-history-intersectionality

Waters, M. C. (1999). *Black identities: West Indian immigrant dreams and American realities.* Cambridge, MA: Harvard University Press.

Wilkinson, R., & Pickett, K. (2010). *The spirit level: Why greater equality makes societies stronger.* New York, NY: Bloomsbury Press.

Zambrana, R. E., Dunkel-Schetter, C., Collins, N. L., & Scrimshaw, S. C. (1999). Mediators of ethnic-associated differences in infant birthweight. *Journal of Urban Health, 76,* 102–116.

3

Rural Girls' Educational Empowerment in Urbanizing China

Comparing Han Majority and Mongolian Minority Girls

VILMA SEEBERG, YA NA, YU LI, AND DEBRA L. CLARK ■

CASE STUDY

At age 6 years, Wang Yuanyuan, left her home on the grasslands to attend a school that was a 2-hour drive away from her mother's home on the prairie. In Inner Mongolia, schools are located only in the cities. On the pasture lands, Mongolian people live a nomadic Mongolian lifestyle (follow the herds) and speak only Mongolian. Yuanyuan's mother was single, tending a herd of sheep by herself while raising two daughters. Their life was very difficult, but her mother still managed to send Yuanyuan, the eldest daughter, far away to public boarding school. For the next 12 years, Yuanyuan only rarely saw her family.

In the city, Yuanyuan attended a Mongolian-language public school. Outside the school, however, almost everyone spoke Han Chinese. The cities of Inner Mongolia have long been dominated by Han Chinese culture, economy, and social arrangements (commonly referred to as "hanhua," Han Chinese assimilation in English), which the Mongolians often reluctantly tolerate.

Yuanyuan excelled in school and was admitted to a respected public community college, where she majored in broadcasting to become a bilingual TV personality. By the time she entered college, her Chinese was flawless. Every summer and winter break from school, she worked as a cashier in restaurants or bookstores. Like other Mongolian girls, she was active in sports, especially basketball and soccer. Her biggest dream after graduation was to return to the city close to her home village and work as a Mongolian-speaking TV host. Settled in the city, she would have her mother and sister join her there for a better life.

OVERVIEW

Today, the empowerment journey of most young girls—*if* they have been able to get some secondary schooling—will shape their future, what they hope for, and how they take action. In two regions of China that are located on the edges of the explosive growth of the world's manufacturing zone, only a minority of girls have access to secondary schooling.

In this chapter, we tell the empowerment stories of some girls who survived into the upper grades of secondary school and further.[1] The participants in our study (we use the term "our" to refer to participants henceforth) are girls between the ages of 19 and 22 years from a remote mountain village in Shaanxi, a province in western China, and from Inner Mongolia, a huge autonomous ethnic minority province in northern China. What unites them is their rural background in the "hinterland" and the national umbrella policy on education; what distinguishes them is their ethnicity and the socioeconomic and political contexts of the regions in which they live. Both sets of girls are triply disadvantaged by the underdevelopment of their regions and hence their relative poverty, their gender, and their minority religion and ethnicity. We expected that these different positionalities would impact their life trajectories, but how they would do so was not clear to us. To discern how they envision their hopes, possibilities, and actions as they embark on their adult lives, we conducted interviews and fieldwork in both locales. To interpret the empowerment within those visions, we relied on the conceptual framework of the capability approach and specifically the educational empowerment capabilities framework developed by Seeberg (2014). Empowerment consists of aspirations, agency, and opportunities, or capabilities. To situate the empowering capabilities in these two case scenarios, we delve briefly into the global context of girls' education, the cultural position of the female in both ethnic groups, and the major relevant demographics which altogether constitute the structural opportunity environment. Then, we present the voices of "our" young women on how they see their empowerment path, followed by drawing conclusions and implications for policy and advocacy recommendations.

GLOBAL CONTEXT OF GIRLS' EDUCATION FOR EMPOWERMENT

In 1995 at the United Nations (UN) World Conference on Women in Beijing, Hilary Clinton, at the time the First Lady of the United States, declared, "Human rights are women's rights and women's rights are human rights" (Clinton, 1996). In 2000, UN Secretary-General Kofi Annan, launching a 10-year initiative on girls' education at the opening of the World Education Forum in Dakar, Senegal, put it broad policy terms,

> Educating girls is a social development policy that works. It has immediate benefits for nutrition, health, savings and reinvestment at the family, community and ultimately country level. . . . It is a long-term investment that yields an exceptionally high return. It is also, I would venture, a tool for preventing conflict and building peace. From generation to generation, women have passed on the culture of peace.

In the Millennium Development Goals in 2000 and the Sustainable Development Goals (SDG) in 2015, the UN enshrined a gender goal. SDG Goal 5 seeks to achieve equality and to empower all women and girls through legislative changes to be undertaken by its 195 member countries.

Stark realities of women's position in the world lag far behind the lofty rhetoric, and they affect our girls as well. Worldwide, in 2018, one in three women had experienced physical or sexual abuse; women earned 76% of men's earnings and constituted only 22% of all national parliaments (UN, "Global Issues: Women," n.d.). In addition, 218 million children between ages 5 and 17 years worldwide, 42% of whom were girls, were engaged in child labor not including domestic labor mostly borne by girls and women (International Labour Organization, 2018).

On the education front, however, improvements have been remarkably positive. In 1948, the Universal Declaration of Human Rights declared that every person— regardless of gender—has the right to education (UN General Assembly, 1948). Since the the Millennium Development Goals in 2000, schooling provision has skyrocketed, such that in developing countries 91% of school-age children were reportedly enrolled in primary education in 2015 (UN, 2015). Among the 63 million (9%) who remained out of school in 2016, 53% were girls (World Bank Group, n.d.). At the upper secondary level in 2016, more than twice as many—139 million (36%)— school-age children were out of school, among whom only 48% were female (UN, 2015) which is explained by the phenomenon that in some areas of the world, boys are sent out to work earlier than girls whereas girls is work in the home.

Internationally, a persuasive body of evidence backs up Kofi Anan's claim on the socially beneficial and transgenerational effects of girls' schooling, such as delayed marriage, reduced number of children, improved family health care, and their children's improved well-being (for a summary, see Seeberg & Ross, 2007; Sperling & Winthrop, 2015). Due to the work of prominent scholars with feminist perspectives, such as Nelly Stromquist (1995), Srilatha Batliwala (1994), and Naila Kabeer (1999), attention shifted away from a focus on economic growth of the nation, measured by the gross domestic product (GDP) divided by the number of people, which incorrectly assumed that "a rising tide lifts all boats" and which, unfortunately, does not apply equally to girls and women and ethnically or otherwise marginalized peoples. Feminists alerted the world that the kind of lives that girls and women could lead were worth considering and including in national policy. Scholars showed how girls and women could become empowered and improve their own lives and those of their families. After studying the lives of poor women in India, Kabeer (1999) wrote that empowerment is a "process by which those who have been denied the ability to make strategic life choices acquire such ability" (p. 435). Nussbaum (2000) and other feminists emphasized that empowerment is a dynamic, locally specific process of converting resources into capabilities and valued achievements. They asserted that women's improved confidence, sense of well-being, status in the family, and delayed marriage (United Nations International Children's Fund, 2005) create sociopolitical change for the community, nation, and next generation (Annan, 2000; Save the Children, 2005). The report titled "The Power and Promise of Girls' Education," the annual report by Save the Children, in 2005 was published under the banner, "Educate girls today and it will create lasting change for the next generation. . . . Where mothers do well, so do their children." Girls in school are transforming themselves into stakeholders in their birth families and local communities. At the micro level, critical psychosocial empowerment enables them to develop skills to express their creative energies, exercise new responsibilities, exert more control over their own affairs, and ultimately help find appropriate solutions to local problems. At the macro level, girls' and women's empowerment changes social norms and promotes socioeconomic empowerment, the "mastery that people, organizations and communities acquire over their own affairs and the control that they are able to exercise on their environment" (Easton, 2005, p. 3).

Save the Children (2005) pointed to the social improvements generated by educating girls to "enhance the well-being of children, reduce fertility in the midterm, and improve prospects for future generations" (p. 17). Benefits of education are that girls marry later and have fewer children; infant mortality rates are reduced; girls' earning power is increased; family hygiene, nutrition, overall health care, and children's well-being are improved; and their daughters' chances of enrolling in school are increased by 40% or greater (Caldwell, 1979; Cochrane, 1979; King & Hill, 1991).

Educating girls living in marginalized communities surprisingly quickly reshapes how parents, communities, and school administrators think about girls and their potential (Seeberg, 2011; Seeberg & Luo, 2018; Seeberg et al., 2017); strikes at the crux of so-called intractable poverty; and has the potential to initiate transgenerational, sustainable development—particularly in declining regions. The communities in China's "left-behind" regions—those not benefiting from the booming economic growth in the country's manufacturing centers—have been on the wrong side of severely unbalanced development policy for many decades. In these communities, structural conditions, such as lack of social services, transportation, and energy infrastructure, erosion, soil depletion, and population density, have combined to create excessive poverty and barriers to development. Yet, in just such locations, we have found girls pressing for schooling so that they can take on unexpected responsibilities, such as saving for elder care, for their birth families, and for their communities (Seeberg & Ross, 2007).

China reported a phenomenal increase in enrollment and survival rates for girls at the primary school level due to expansion of 9-year compulsory education in the 1990s (United Nations Educational, Scientific and Cultural Organization [UNESCO] Education for All, 2002). According to the 2017 national census (National Bureau of Statistics, 2017, Table 2-15), of the national population aged 15 years or older, 5.28% are illiterate; 2.74% of males and 7.89% of females are illiterate. In Shaanxi, 3.13% of males and 7.32% of females are illiterate, and in Inner Mongolia 2.71% of males and 6.65% of females are illiterate. Educational disparity between different regions and between rural and urban areas" has been increasing (Zhang, Li, & Xue, 2015). Families with higher income tend to invest much more in children's early education and quality shadow education (private tutoring) compared with low-income families (Yang & Qiu, 2016; Zhang & Bray, 2018), which further widens the educational gap between different regions and between rural and urban areas in China.

As discussed later in this chapter, in China, where primary education is compulsory and only technically free, families living in poverty are burdened by constant charging of school fees. As a result, the traditional preferences for sons to go to school and daughters in their mid-teens to be sold for a bride price (based on field observations) often mitigate against girls' schooling. Thus, for girls, the challenge of getting an education also frequently requires rejection of family norms and actions.

It is this normative concept of empowerment that we investigate among our girls with respect to their education in this chapter.

NATIONAL UMBRELLA POLICY AND CONTEXT OF GIRLS' EDUCATION IN CHINA

China, officially called the People's Republic of China (PRC), is slightly smaller in size than the United States, but it has a population of more than 1.4 billion versus the United States' mere 317 million (UN Population Division, 2018). Thus, the United States has times more room per person compared with China (authors' calculation). China's climate is extremely diverse—tropical in the south and subarctic in the north. Its terrain is not as favorable to human habitation as in the United States, consisting mostly of mountains, high plateaus, and a huge desert in the west and northwest. As a result, most of its people, the Han Chinese comprising 91.6% of the population, are crowded in the ancient farming lands of central and eastern coastal regions (CIA, U.S.A., n.d., n.p.).

Inner Mongolia is a plateau that stretches across the northern area of China. Most of Inner Mongolia is a plateau averaging approximately 1,200 meters (3,940 feet) in

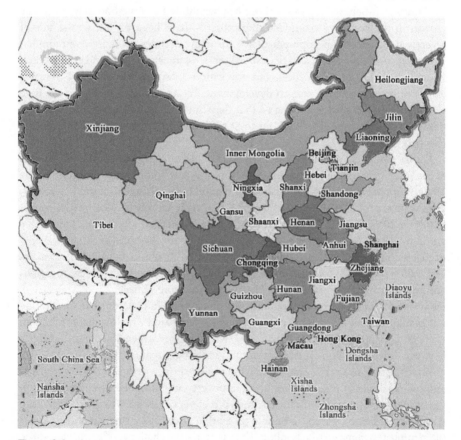

Figure 3.1

altitude and covered by extensive cold arid grassland steppe, the Ordos Desert, and, in the northern plains, discontinuous permafrost. Traditionally, large-scale herding of sheep and horses served as the mainstay of the economy, but due to vast ecological degradation and desertification, a rapid economic transition is underway. Inner Mongolia also possesses large reserves of coal, iron ore, and rare-earth minerals, which have made it a major mining and industrial region, accompanied by pollution. The official languages are Han Chinese and Mongolian, the latter of which is written in the traditional Mongolian script.

Shaanxi lies south of Inner Mongolia and is considered the eastern terminus of the Silk Road. It forms the cradle of Han Chinese agricultural civilization, and Xi'an, its modern capital, comprises the sites of the former capitals of the first to late feudal dynasties for more than 1,100 years, including the famous Terracotta Army funerary project of Emperor Qin Shi Huang (259–210 BC), the first emperor of the first unified dynasty of imperial China. Shaanxi has a variety of climates, from cold and arid near the Ordos Desert in the north to subtropical on the southern exposure of the rugged Qinling Mountains. Shaanxi is considered part of the northwest, a region beyond most industrial development policies of modern China.

China joined the World Trade Organization in 2001, signifying its entrance into the modern globalizing economy. By that time, it had developed an alarming gap in every dimension of life between the booming east coast manufacturing regions and the underdeveloped rest of the country. The left-behind regions, including central China and the borderlands in the north where Inner Mongolia is located, the west where Shaanxi lies, and the southwest, provided the undereducated labor force for the factories in the East.

The centralized education system shows the same gap in quality and quantity of schooling. In the poorest regions, the predictable gender gap inherited from its cultural traditions was striking. Gender inequality intersects with inequalities of income, opportunity, access to services, and participation in political and civic life.

CURRENT CONDITIONS

Typically, official statistics do not capture the range of inequalities, nor do they show the pockets of extreme deprivation. In the context of globalization and the hyper growth of manufacturing, China shows fast growth in the proportion of school-age girls with access to primary school, increasing from 96.3% in 1995 (State Council of the People's Republic of China, 2005) to 99.93% in 2015. The drop off in enrollment in post-compulsory senior secondary school shows the fragility of the system; the gross enrolment rate for all youth, including the overage, was reported as 87% (no gender breakdowns available; Ministry of Education [MoE], 2016). However, girls were reported to constitute a slight majority (50.3%) of those in senior secondary school in 2015 (MoE, 2016). Globalization affects regions, ethnicities, genders, and social classes inequitably. Our two regions showed telling variation that would predict wide-ranging findings. In Shaanxi, girls constituted only 48.7%, but in Inner Mongolia, girls represented slightly more than the majority of students with a relatively high 52.3% (MoE, 2015). In 2017, based on our fieldwork observations, we were surprised by the preponderance of girls in Mongolian junior secondary school classrooms and in higher education levels.

Throughout China, compulsory public education (grades 1–9) is technically free, although fee burdens rise with the scale of deprivation. In the region of Shaanxi, where illiteracy has always been higher than the national average, fees were prohibitive for many families (field observations 2000–2016). Senior secondary school is costly everywhere and out of range for many rural families even in 2018. Central education policy intentionally discriminates in many ways, prioritizing schooling in certain key regions along the coastal manufacturing belt.[2] In 2017, the central government pledged to increase secondary education coverage (schools) nationwide from 87.5% to 90% or more by 2020 (Xinhua, 2017), while admitting that there were shortages in central and western China, especially in vocational technical education. This is particularly important to our participants, who represent a select group already but are more likely to be able to access vocational technical senior secondary schools. Until 2012, China had not been spending as much on education as is generally accepted as a world standard, 4% of the GDP, by UNESCO (Xinhua, 2013). China's educational funding also shows major differences by province: Per pupil public funding in primary school was RMB (Renminbi) 9,558 ($1,529) nationally in 2016, higher in Shaanxi at RMB 11,172 ($1,787), and higher yet in Inner Mongolian Autonomous Region (IMAR) at RMB 13,109 ($2,097),[3] whereas in the major metropolitan centers of Beijing and Shanghai, per student spending was much higher at RMB 25,793 ($4,37) and RMB 22,125 ($3,463), respectively (MoE, 2016, Table 2(1)).

In contrast, the United States spends approximately 7% of GDP on education and approximately $12,000 per student. European countries such as France and England spend 5.5% and 5.6% of GDP, respectively, amounting to $10,000–$12,100 per student (National Center for Education Statistics, 2018; UNESCO, 2018).

The Chinese government has promulgated additional special policy for ethnic nationalities in specially designated autonomous counties, regions, and provinces. The Constitution of the PRC states that "each nationality (ethnic group) has the freedom to use and develop their own spoken and written language" (Dong, Gou, Wang, & Qiu, 2015, p. 26). The most populous but not all ethnic minority autonomous regions and people enjoy several privileges. In Inner Mongolia, the educational system offers instruction in two languages from early childhood through higher education— Han Chinese and Mongolian, their mother tongue (Mongolian Nationality Schools). Students are given preferential admission to institutions of higher education by means of a separate acceptance rate and 10 bonus points on entrance examinations. Recently, students educated in the Mongolian language system have managed to blend into the mainstream Chinese-language educational system at the college level.

SHAANXI AND INNER MONGOLIA: DEMOGRAPHICS AND SCHOOLING

Shaanxi is one of the poorest inland provinces crisscrossed by the vast Qinling mountain range. Globalization reached the village via a one-lane road in 2008. It opened the way for fathers and, later, mothers to leave for low-skilled, often temporary employment in nearby towns and further afield. The first family members who left to find work in the cash economy were able to earn enough money to enable some younger siblings to attend school. To attend the nearest village primary school, children had to walk on goat paths through all types of weather for 1 hour and 40 minutes and make

Figure 3.2

the same journey home after school. To get to the junior secondary school in the near-est market town, because there was no transportation, children walked 4 hours at the beginning of the week and made the return trip on most weekends.

The Chinese government reported per capita net income of rural households in Inner Mongolia in 2013 as RMB 8,595.73 ($1,268. 26) and that of Shaanxi as RMB 6,502.60 ($959.43) (National Bureau of Statistics, 2013). We cannot deduce what this means for the participants in our study or for any household in either location because variation within rural areas of a province are great and not estimated.

The IMAR was the first minority autonomous region founded by the Communist Party of China in May 1947. It lies on the northern border of China with the country of Mongolia, formerly a republic of the Soviet Union and now independent. Since 1949, the Chinese communist government has enforced, as did previous govern-ments, extensive controls on the country's borderlands with its non-Chinese ethnic populations. In many borderland provinces, the Chinese government enticed and compelled settlement of Han populations, so that currently only 20% of the popula-tion in IMAR is ethnically Mongolian (a.k.a. Meng). During the miserable Cultural Revolution, IMAR suffered severe violence as its ethnic religion, a version of Tibetan Buddhism, was driven underground, as were all religions in Han but especially in other ethnic and religious minority regions. Tibetan Buddhism was strongly rooted among Mongolians; hence, most of its temples were destroyed, its Buddhist clerics were imprisoned, and open religious practices were forbidden ("Inner Mongolia," 2017). Although central government policy on the practice of indigenous religions has loosened somewhat since the end of the Cultural Revolution in 1979, the Chinese government's Committee on the Elimination of Racial Discrimination in 1996 reiter-ated "no religion is allowed to disrupt education" (MoE, 1996, p. 22).

Figure 3.3

Mongolians, the proud descendants of Genghis Khan, live on the remote, vast pas-turelands as pastoral farmers and herders as they watch their way of life and grasslands diminish and disappear due to overgrazing and climate change. Although we heard that the remaining farming and semi-herding families were considered relatively well-off, rapid desertification and ecological damage from massive mining operations put this in doubt. As government policy and investment are converting land use, elders are settling, and their children are sent to board in nearby towns and cities (旗 县, Qi, Banner, a.k.a. county) for school. Since 2001, as part of national school consolidation policy, elemen-tary schools in villages or grassland areas (*su mu*) have been closed. For the pastoral farmers' and herders' families in Inner Mongolia, there is little to do but send children at an early age to live in town to attend school while they remain behind (Ma, 2007).

The extent, quality, and level of education have all increased dramatically in the past 10 years, and first-language Mongolian schools are well resourced. Yet Mongolian monolingual graduates are markedly constrained by a language barrier (Ma, 2007) in IMAR, where Han Chinese constitute the most numerous and more prosperous pop-ulation, and certainly within the larger Chinese territory. In IMAR, there are only 13 post-secondary institutions offering Mongolian language programs.

HISTORY: THE CULTURAL POSITION OF THE FEMALE IN BOTH ETHNIC GROUPS

The position of women in Han China has long been guarded by a strict system of patri-archy. Today, China has one of the highest female suicide rates in the world (Cabral,

2003, as cited in UN Commission on Human Rights, 2003, p. 11). Son preference in Han Chinese culture is most strikingly evidenced by the highly skewed, still deteriorating sex ratio of 114:100 boys to girls at birth in 2015.[4] Many second and third Han daughters under the one-child policy (1980–2016) have not been registered at birth and are not entitled to any public services, including school. In 1992, the National People's Congress promulgated the "Women's Law" to stop practices victimizing women, such as "drowning or abandoning female babies, maltreatment of women who give birth to female babies or are sterile, and abandonment of aged women" (National People's Congress, 1992, p. 11).

In Shaanxi, the tradition of preferring sons to go to school and marrying off daughters in their mid-teens for a bride price was still being practiced during the years 2000–2016 per our field observations. In the villages of the Shaanxi Han girls, it was customary to start arranging marriage for the girls at least by age 16 years to be consummated at age 18 or 19 years (fieldwork observations, 2001–2016). If a girl dropped out of junior secondary school, she was targeted by matchmakers and village families with single sons. "In a normal year, there are five to six young men in our small village who reach marriage age but cannot find a wife" (Pang Xuxu's mother, personal communication, 2010).[5] Seeberg (2014) notes that "only the girls who showed good scores on tests in school, and only if their parents supported their schooling, evaded the matchmakers and suitor families" (p. 689).

These modern dilemmas originate in the ancient Han people's cosmological order in which heaven (yang, male) dominates earth (yin, female), which later became inscribed in the Confucian tenets that confine women to the "inner" (*nei*) or domestic sphere (Herr, 2012, p. 330) and reduce their status to that of an attachment, without a name of their own, to their fathers' and later their husbands' lines of descent (Sung, 1975, p.194). "Thus, to ensure herself a modicum of status in this world and a secure resting place in the next . . . it was imperative that a woman marry and produce a son" (Greenhalgh, 1985, p. 267). Our young women were not in a rush to carry on the tradition (Seeberg & Luo, 2012). In the birth cohort (1976–1983), by age 30 years almost all women had married, and the median age for rural women was 22 years nationally (Yeung, 2016).

History told a very different story about Mongolian women; their social status was substantially higher than that of Han women. The woman's role in the pastoral nomadic life was set down in the traditional Oriat Law Code (Chen, 2011) as no less than a man's role. Women were in charge of household chores and livestock production; however, they also participated in military action. Male superiority was recognized in conducting the more dangerous, nomadic, wide-ranging herding work. According to the Oriat Law Code of 1640, women had inheritance rights and wives could get a divorce or could veto a divorce. Husbands were severely punished for abusing their wives, especially during pregnancy, during which time they also could not divorce. Unlike under Confucian ideology that considered women engaged in politics immoral (Lian, 2006; Zhang, 2014), ancient Mongolian women's political powers were well recognized, particularly among ancient Mongolian aristocratic women.

When the Mongols ruled China in the Yuan dynasty (1279–1368), the patriarchal ideology of the Han Chinese majority infused Mongolian society as well so that by the subsequent dynasties, the Ming (1368–1644) to the Qing (1964–1912), the notion of male superiority gradually restricted women's status in family and society (Lian, 2006 Zhang, 2014). Contemporary Mongolian women's status has improved again since the open-door policy (*gaige kaifang*) in 1990. Women are well represented in political leadership (Wuyuann, 2005; authors' personal observation, 2017).

TODAY'S GIRLS BECOMING YOUNG WOMEN IN SHAANXI AND INNER MONGOLIA — CASE STUDY

The Han girls in this study include girls[6] from a remote mountain village in Shaanxi, whose families were poor farming/migrant worker families, and girls living in IMAR. The Mongolian girls (hereafter referred to by the Chinese name Meng) were from more well-off families even though they came from poor ethnic minority regions mostly in IMAR but also two other northern provinces. The 11 Han girls from Shaanxi encountered many hardships in attending and boarding at inferior and utterly under-resourced schools; both the 7 Han girls and the 13 Mongolian girls in IMAR had boarded from early ages in comparatively well-equipped, well-supported larger schools and benefited from preferential funding from the central government.

   In the following discussion, the ethnically Han girls from both locations are reported on separately from the ethnic Mongolian girls. Participants are identified with their pseudonym, ethnicity, location, and year of interview.

Our Young Women Talk About Becoming Empowered

In 2006, Chen Linlin, a ninth grader in senior secondary school, expressed the dreams of many girls living in rural China: "How I wish I could step out of the mountain and walk under my own sky. I wish I could someday be in senior secondary school, even college, to receive higher education, fulfill myself, and achieve my own value" (Chen Linlin, personal communication, grade 9, Han, Shaanxi, 2006).[7] Chen Linin describes her hope for pursuing a dream of education and to develop her own identity. Her dream is shared by others in the Han ethnicity. The following section outlines some of the voices recorded on this topic throughout multiple visits to rural villages in China. We examine Han girls' and then Meng girls' capabilities in the dimensions of agency and aspirations first.

The Voices of Han Girls Talking About School and Family

For girls of the Han ethnicity living in rural mountainous Shaanxi, realizing the dream of getting an education and being able to define their own lives presents almost insurmountable challenges and requires many sacrifices. Simply to get to a primary school, they walk for 2 hours on rough goat paths. When they arrive, they are not welcomed or encouraged by their teachers, nor are their school facilities supportive to their learning. Female items such as sanitary pads are not available, nor is there running water or modern toilet facilities; instead, rough latrines of 10 holes in wide-open shelters serve each gender. Regardless, many Han girls value education and persist if not always enthusiastically. For example, Jing Jian (college, Han, Shaanxi, 2016) stated,

   At the beginning when I left home and entered junior secondary school, there was a huge gap between me and other students because I came from a really

Figure 3.4 Village primary school, Shaanxi, before classes.

remote primary school. I was already behind other students because my parents didn't have much education. Teachers in junior secondary school were very young and taught poorly.

Another young girl, Ding Wen (college, Han, IMAR, 2017) noted, "When I was transferred to a new school, the teacher didn't treat me well, and she didn't pay attention to me. The teacher's attitude was very discouraging, so I kind of gave up on myself for a while."

In addition to the hardships of distance, expense, and inexperienced and uncaring teachers, these girls have the additional burden that parents and/or communities traditionally view girls' education as "spilled water." They view schooling as a waste of precious few resources that will be lost to a future husband's family. Once married, girls are no longer considered as part of their family of birth; they are considered to belong to their husband's family. For example, Jiang Xi (college, Han, IMAR, 2017) stated, "In our family, since I am a girl, my parents only ask me to live [at school] on my own and get married. They see no need for me to be a strong woman."

For some girls, these pressures are too difficult to bear, and they drop out of school, which many later regret. Jing Jian (college, Han, Shaanxi, 2016), a new college student, told us,

A lot of girls from my village went out to get a job right after graduating from junior secondary school and were married and had a child two years later. They completely lost themselves; they live just to live . . . in a city . . . rent a room with children, parents, siblings all together . . . in less than 10 square meters.

Figure 3.5 Junior high school class in a rural town, Shaanxi, 2016.

Others of the Han ethnicity prevail and stay in school, and in their stories there is a greater sense of personal agency and aspirations.

What I Can Do—Agency: Han Girls

Han girls, raised to be timid, struggle against too many restrictions insisted on by their parents. They recognize that a generation gap had opened between them and their parents as the images of a better life in the booming factory towns and high-rise cities swept into their remote village and competed with their old ways of living:

> Well, in their generation, they didn't think about going to big cities. But now, the society progressed a lot, and we started to think about living in big cities and changing our lives. (Ding Wen, college, Han, IMAR, 2017)

> I think the future is different, and through my own effort I will be different. (Wang Jie, college, Han, IMAR, 2017)

The girls become more competent as they interact with a greater diversity of people in senior secondary school, college, or when working in a city, forming new kinds of relationships and confronting new kinds of problems:

> Before I got to college, I lived a simple life in the countryside. Here I gradually learned how to deal with problems. (Chen Jiajia, college, Han, Shaanxi, 2016)

Figure 3.6 Han college student in her bedroom in the village, Shaanxi. Awards for outstanding studies serve as wallpaper.

In school, what you learn is secondary. How to get along with people, interpersonal communication is more important. I learned that. (Wang Qian, college, Han, IMAR, 2017)

My Wishes for the Future: Han

Along with new relationships and capabilities, the Han girls learn to dream bigger. Some are content to hope for better work, whereas others dream of a better but, most important, stable future:

For a village kid like me, becoming a certified nursing assistant is a real possibility. (Jing Jian, college, Han, Shaanxi, 2016)

I have been working part-time for a year or so and I have learned how to socialize. I got a lot of experience in one year. . . . So, my future work must be a job where I can show my strengths. (Lin Lin, college, Han, IMAR, 2017)

I've been studying in the city for more than four years. In the future, I want to find a stable job like civil servant work in a government agency. (Wang Yunyun, college, Han, Shaanxi, 2016)

Visions of a "middle-class" life with its benefits epitomize well-being and stability:

I hope I can have my own house and family in Xi'an. All the families are healthy and get together well. (Wang Yunyun, college, Han, Shaanxi, 2014)

I want to be confident. It helps you in communication and spiritually, don't close yourself off. (Jing Jian, college, Han, Shaanxi, 2016)

Traditionally, filial (family) responsibility was placed on the shoulders of sons, who were responsible for taking care of their parents as they aged. This is one of the reasons for the preference to educate sons. A son's education was viewed in many respects as a retirement account for parents. Because once married, girls were no longer part of the family, investing in their education was similar to putting money into a retirement account for someone else. Our Han girls, however, viewed filial responsibility as theirs as well, which is a regendering of norms:

My life later is definitely not the same as my parents' because of the generation gap. After graduation, I will make more money than they do, and later, they will need me to support them. (Lin Lin, college, Han, IMAR, 2017)

I will try my best to have my parents live in a good house in the future. In the city, I see many old people go to a large park to dance, do Taiji [shadow boxing], or practice calligraphy in the morning. . . . I will help my parents enjoy their lives in the city. (Chen Linlin, college, Han, Shaanxi, 2010)

The Han girls in Shaanxi look forward as they build their futures in the cities. They see their generation as progressing beyond their parents.

The Voices of Meng Girls Talking About School and Family

Whereas the Han girls were often pressured to marry instead of continuing with their education, Mongolian girls enjoy much more support from their parents for further education:

As long as I want to, my parent supports me. At first, my parent wants me to study in medical science, but I prefer landscaping major, and they agreed. (Li Mei, Meng, college, IMAR, 2017)

I have thought about quitting school. But my family doesn't allow me to drop out of school. I don't want my parent working that hard to keep me in school, but they insist that I have to be in school. (Bingbing, Meng, college, IMAR, 2017)

What I Can Do—Agency: Meng Girls

We heard similar stories from the Mongolian girls as we heard from the Han girls. They spoke of developing greater capabilities and of living with and making new and different friends—friends who had come from far-away places to the city schools. This made them feel and act with more confidence:

I made a lot of friends in school. And I gained lots of confidence because of my friends. And what we learned in classes is very useful. (Li Bai, college, IMAR, 2017)

Much like the Han girls, they recognize the gap between their and their parents' generation's lives, but they do not convey a sense of tension as did the Han girls:

You know, life at that times is different now. My parents live in a rural area, but I want to live in the city, and not do hard labor anymore. (Li Yue, college, Meng, IMAR, 2017)

Instead, a general sense of welcome support by their parents came through:

My father helped me decide to which school I should go. But I also thought about it a lot by myself. (Li Yue, college, Meng, IMAR, 2017)

They want me to have a stable job first, then think about marriage later. (Li Yue, college, Meng, IMAR, 2017)

The Meng girls also often exhibit an understanding of the relationship between school rules and the rules of society, which makes them feel more secure and self-confident:

I learned how to follow rules in school, and achieve a sense of self-discipline. (Wang Yuan, college, Meng, IMAR, 2017)

Figure 3.7 Mongolian-language junior high school class in the city.

I was very naughty when I was little, but in school I learned how to follow rules. I think that helps me a lot. (Li Ye, college, Meng, IMAR, 2017)

Some classes we took in this school can be very helpful in future. Because the teacher was very strict on assignments and attendance, we had to spend a lot of time on it. Finally, when I passed the class, I felt a sense of achievement. (Li Bai, college, Meng, IMAR, 2017)

My Wishes for a Good Future: Meng

Different from the Han girls in both locations, the Meng girls frequently expressed a desire to "return home," likely, however, to small or larger cities:

After obtaining my undergraduate degree in veterinary science, I want to go back to my hometown to . . . a pet shop. (Guo Jie, college, Meng, IMAR, 2017)

But after a while, I still think I will go back home and I may do some business in the future. In recent years, my hometown developed a lot. (Li Bai, college, Meng, IMAR, 2017)

I want to go back home or go to Shenyang [a major city in Liaoning Province, adjacent to IMAR]. If I don't need to take care of my parent, I may choose to work in other cities. (Li Yue, college, Meng, IMAR, 2017)

The Meng girls also viewed their education as enhancing their aspirations, which included further education as well as vocational opportunities:

After graduation, I want to look for a job and pursue my undergraduate while working. (Ma Yue, college, Meng, IMAR, 2017)

After my internship in vocational senior secondary school, I want to upgrade my educational and get an undergraduate degree. (Guo Jie, college, Meng, IMAR, 2017)

I want to do the internship first, and then try to stay in the same company. After 2 to 3 years, I want to open a pharmacy with my friends. Only after that do I want to find a boyfriend. (Li Bai, college, Meng, IMAR, 2017)

If I cannot find a job, I will choose to join the army. Being a soldier has always been a dream of mine. (Bingbing, college, Meng, IMAR, 2017)

Meng girls also viewed the world of opportunities before them differently than the Han—due to their ethnic status and linguistic knowledge:

If you can speak two languages, you will have more opportunities. (Li Li, college, Meng, IMAR, 2017)

But I can do better than my parent, because I have a degree and I speak better Han. (Fangfang, college, Meng, IMAR, 2017)

My sister went to school taught in Mongolian, and she can speak and write in Mongolian, but I feel her future is a little bit restricted, because she can only stay in Inner Mongolia. (Li Bai, college, Meng, IMAR, 2017)

Summary

Both Mongolian girls and Han girls certainly acted more forcefully on their own behalf (take more agency) due to the secondary schooling they experienced than they would have without it. Compared to Meng girls in Inner Mongolia, Han girls in Shaanxi were more anxious and gained fewer capabilities. We believe that the difference between the more confident Meng and the more apprehensive Shaanxi Han girls may be accounted for by the difference in early life experience. Meng girls traditionally were expected to be independent and seemed to be well-socialized in the school environment. Han girls in Shaanxi on the other hand were strongly attached to their home village and previous research (Seeberg & Luo, 2018) showed that they identify as villagers even as young adults living in the city.

Both Han and Meng girls held vocational and educational aspirations,[8] but Meng girls aspired to higher education goals. With a greater sense of parental support despite their physical distance and more access to higher educational institutions, though limited by language and in location, Meng girls saw better opportunities and more varied entrepreneurial futures to which to aspire.

Han girls' aspirational values, on the other hand, revolved around finding and keeping decent stable jobs. Meng girls projected a sense of greater trust in their futures—apart from some doubts regarding Mongolian language limitations.

Han girls were more expressive about taking on regendered filial duties to their parents. Meng girls do not subscribe as much to the central Confucian concepts of "male superiority over women" and absolute filial devotion, despite the influence of Han Confucian culture since the Qing dynasty in the 18th century.

Yet, Han girls also felt more pressure to fulfill their parents' expectations regarding marriage, evoking the Confucian tradition of the female being but an attachment to the male line. For Meng girls, marrying was a less salient aspiration and caused little or no conflict with their parents, reflecting the greater Mongolian gender equality and greater influence of Buddhism.

Ethnic differences are apparent in the girls' identities, with Meng girls carrying on the Mongolian custom of becoming more independent and capable women and Han girls' greater familial rootedness.

LOOKING TO THE FUTURE

From the perspective of Sen's (1999) argument that what counts for individuals and the communities in which they live is "the actual living that people manage to achieve" (p. 73), we can draw some implications for the future of the two regions. Clearly, our girls' generation will be living and working in cities, and those with greater educational opportunities—in this case, the Meng girls—will be in a better position to make more valuable contributions. Because, as Sen argues, individual freedom is a quintessentially social product, there is "a two-way relation between (1) social arrangements to expand individual freedoms and (2) the use of individual freedoms not only to improve the respective lives but also to make the social arrangements more appropriate and effective" (p. 31)—in other words, to generate more just social change. The Han girls, who are challenged in their pursuit of greater independence with respect to their birth families and their position within them, will bring about gendered social changes in the direction of greater equity. For the Meng girls, who already practice more independent agency, it is through their occupational and professional aspirations that they will contribute to the urban communities.

IMPLICATIONS FOR POLICY ADVOCACY

Cross-cultural and international research has shown convincingly that when girls and women control resources, they improve the well-being of their families—intergenerationally. As the brief discussion of the two provinces on the margins of globalizing China has demonstrated, macro-structural developments and policy set the stage on which adolescent girls act out their agency and enhance their aspirations. Our research indicates that the Shaanxi Han girls could better enhance their capabilities with appropriate, quality short-term and medium-term skills training applicable to their local economic context (see also Seeberg, 2014).

In recognition of the need for short-term and medium-term skill development, the central government MoE announced in 2017 that it will promote secondary vocational education and improve facilities in schools and the education funding mechanism (Xinhua, 2013). This is perhaps due to the alarming 30% decline in the demand for senior secondary vocational–technical schooling during the 5-year period ending in 2016 (MoE, 2016), which is likely due to its unregulated state and often poor quality.

Implications for policy and interventions for the Meng girls so they may follow through on their strategic life choices go beyond school. More opportunities are needed for diverse economic arrangements, support for entrepreneurship, building businesses, and promoting Mongolian culture and language to enrich urban Mongolian communities and facilitate greater social inter-ethnic harmony.

Both policy recommendations would contribute to economic development in medium-sized towns in Shaanxi and IMAR, which is currently the focus of Chinese national urbanization policy.

DISCUSSION QUESTIONS

1. What role does the generation gap between parents and children play in the lives of Meng girls?
2. How does this differ from that of the Shaanxi village (Han) girls?
3. Is there a generation gap between you and your parents? If so, has this impacted your education?
4. What role do expectations specific to being a girl play in the educational and vocation aspirations of Han and Meng girls?
5. How is this different from or similar to expectations of girls in the United States?

NOTES

1. We thank Dr. Shujuan Luo for her indispensable assistance throughout the years on the China Girls' Education research team. I gratefully acknowledge the funding of this research by the Kent State University Research Council; the Gerald Read Center for International Intercultural Education; and the Dean of the College of Education, Health and Human Services.

2. In 2003, the central government (State Council) pledged to extend the coverage of compulsory education to 85% in the poorest areas of the country, but it stipulated lower literacy standards there than in the cities—an openly discriminatory policy (UN Commission on Human Rights, 2003, p. 7).

3. Neither political expediency nor borderland security explains the variation.

4. On January 1, 2016, the central government ended the one-child policy and allowed all parents to have two children.

5. All names that are used for personal communications are pseudonyms.

6. In other publications, they are identified as Nongcun and Xiangcun sisters (village sisters).

7. The following sections report the personal communications of participants in our research. Their pseudonyms, school attainment level, ethnicity, regional location, and the year of interview are given in parentheses. It will be understood that these are personal communications recorded during the fieldwork.

8. In these comparisons, it is important to remember that the Shaanxi Han girls came from an officially designated extreme poverty county in their province, whereas we do not have the same level of economic data for all the IMAR girls. Because we do not have data, we cannot account for any differences that may have been determined by familiar or regional income gaps.

REFERENCES

Annan, K. (2000, April 26). *U.N. press release Secretary-General addresses World Education Forum on theme of "building a partnership for girls' education."* Retrieved from http://www.un.org/press/en/2000/20000426.sgsm7369.doc.html

Batliwala, S. (1994). The meaning of women's empowerment: New concepts from action. In G. Sen, A. Germaine, & L.C. Chen (Eds.), *Population polices reconsidered: Health, empowerment, and rights* (pp. 127–138). Cambridge, MA: Harvard Center for Population and Development Studies.

Cabral, E. (1999). *China's hidden epidemic.* New York, NY: Ford Foundation.

Caldwell, J. C. (1979). Education as a factor in mortality decline: An examination of Nigerian data. *Population Studies, 33,* 395–413.

Central Intelligency Agency, U.S.A. *The World Factbook* (n.d., n.p.). Retrieved 7/10/2019 from https://www.cia.gov/library/publications/the-world-factbook/geos/ch.html

Chen, Z. (2011). *A preliminary study on the legislative ethical thought of Mongolian—Oriat law code [Qianxi Mengu-Weilate fadian lifa lunli sixiang chutan].* Retrieved from http://big.hi138.com/wenhua/lishixue/201105/306679.asp

Clinton, H. (1996). Women's rights are human rights. *Women's Studies Quarterly, 24*(1–2), 98–101. https://www.jstor.org/stable/40004518

Cochrane, S. (1979). *Fertility and education: What do we really know?* Baltimore, MD: Johns Hopkins University Press.

Committee on the Elimination of Racial Discrimination. (1996). *Concluding observations of the committee following the consideration of the fifth, sixth and seventh periodic reports of the People's Republic of China* (UN Document CERD/C/304/Add.15, para. 14). Retrieved from http://www2.ohchr.org

Dong, F., Gou, Y., Wang, X., & Qiu, J. (2015). Four models of Mongolian Nationality Schools in the Inner Mongolian autonomous region. In A. Feng & R. Adamson (Eds.), *Trilingualism in education in China: Models and challenges* (pp. 25–45). Dordrecht, the Netherlands: Springer.

Easton, P. B. (2005). Capsule analysis. In L. Limage (Ed.), *Literacy and empowerment: Background and issues paper.* Paris, France: UNESCO (limited circulation).

Greenhalgh, S. (1985). Social stratification: The other side of "growth equity" in Asia. *Population and Development Review, 11*(2), 265–314.

Herr, R. S. (2012). Confucian Family for a Feminist Future. *Asian Philogophy, 22*(4), 327–346.

Inner Mongolia has become China's model of assimilation, but Chinese Mongolians are still asserting their identity. (2017, June 1). *The Economist.* Retrieved from https://www.economist.com/news/china/21722853-chinese-mongolians-are-still-asserting-their-identity-inner-mongolia-has-become-chinas-model

International Labour Organization. (2018). *Child labour.* Retrieved March 18, 2018, from http://www.ilo.org/global/topics/child-labour/lang—en/index.htm

Kabeer, N. (1999). Resources, agency, achievements: Reflections on the measurement of women's empowerment. *Development and Change, 20,* 4–30.

King, E., & Hill, M. (1991). Women's education in developing countries: Barriers, benefits and policy. Washington, DC: World Bank.

National People's Congress, PRC. (1992). *Law of the People's Republic of China on the Protection of Rights and Interests of Women,* adopted at the Fifth Session of the Seventh National People's Congress on April 3, 1992, Article 35.

Lian, X. (2006). A tentative study on ancient Mongolian women's relationship between subject consciousness and their social status. *Qianyan, 6,* 217–220.

Ma, R. (2007). Schools on the prairie: Changes in Mongolian grassroots education in pastoral areas [Cao yuanshang de xuexiao: muqu Mengguzu jiceng jiaoyu shiye de bianqian]. *Critique of Anthropology [Zhongguo Renleixue Pinglun], 3,* 88–112.

Ministry of Education of China. (2015). Basic statistics on all region population census in 1953, 1964, 1982, 1990, 2000 and 2010. In *Statistical yearbook 2015* (Table 4-1). Retrieved from http://www.moe.gov.cn/s78/A03/moe_560/jytjsj_2015

Ministry of Education of China. (2016). *National education funds implementation statistics report* [Table 2(1)]. Retrieved from http://www.moe.gov.cn/srcsite/A05/s3040/201710/t20171025_317429.html

Ministry of Education of China (MoE). (2016). *Educational Yearly Statistics 2015.* Retrieved 7/09/2019 from http://www.moe.gov.cn/s78/A03/moe_560/jytjsj_2015/.

National Bureau of Statistics, PRC. (2013). *Per capita net income in China: Rural: Shaanxi.* Retrieved from https://www.ceicdata.com/zh-hans/china/net-income-per-capita-rural/net-income-per-capita-rural-household-Shaanxi

National Bureau of Statistics, PRC. (2017). *Illiterate population aged 15 and above by sex and by be region.* Retrieved from http://www.stats.gov.cn/tjsj/ndsj/2017/indexch.htm

National Center for Education Statistics, USA. (2018). *Education expenditures by country.* Retrieved June 6, 2018, from https://nces.ed.gov/programs/coe/indicator_cmd.as

Nussbaum, M. (2000). *Women and human development.* Cambridge, UK: Cambridge University Press.

Save the Children. (2005). *State of the world's mothers 2005: The power and promise of girls' education.* Retrieved from https://resourcecentre.savethechildren.net/library/state-worlds-mothers-2005-power-and-promise-girls-education

Seeberg, V. (2011). Schooling, jobbing, marrying: What's a girl to do to make life better? Empowerment capabilities of girls at the margins of globalization. *Research in Comparative and International Education, 6*(1), 43–61. http://dx.doi.org/10.2304/rcie.2011.6.1.43

Seeberg, V. (2014). Girls' schooling empowerment in rural China: Identifying capabilities and social change in the village. *Comparative Education Review, 58*(4), 678–707.

Seeberg, V., Baily, S., Khan, A., Ross, H., Wang, Y., Shah, P., & Wang, L. (2017). Frictions that activate change: Dynamics of global to local non-governmental organizations for female education and empowerment in China, India, and Pakistan. *Asia Pacific Journal of Education, 37*(2), 232–247.

Seeberg, V., & Luo, S. J. (2012). Do village girls gain empowering capabilities through schooling and what functionings do they value? *Frontiers of Education in China, 7*(3), 347–375.

Seeberg, V., & Luo, S. (2018). Migrating to the city in north west China: Young rural women's empowerment. *Journal of the Human Development and Capabilities, 19*(3), 289–307. http://dx.doi.org/10.1080/19452829.2018.1430752

Seeberg, V., & Ross, H.; with Liu, J., & Tan, G. (2007). Grounds for prioritizing education for girls: The telling case of left-behind rural China. In D. Baker & A. Wiseman (Eds.), *International perspectives on education and society* (Vol. 8, pp. 109–152). Oxford, UK: Elsevier.

Sperling, G. B., & Winthrop, R. (2015). *What works in girls' education: Evidence for the world's best investment.* Washington, DC: Brookings Institution Press.

State Council of the People's Republic of China, Information Office. (2005). *White papers of Chinese Government: Gender equality and women's development in China.* Retrieved May 15, 2006, from http://www.china.org.cn/e-white/20050824/index.htm

Stromquist, Nelly P. (1995). The theoretical and practical bases for empowerment. In C. Medel-Anonuevo (Ed.), *Women, Education and Empowerment: Pathways towards autonomy* (pp. 13–22). UNESCO Institute for Education.

Sung, L. S. (1975). *Inheritance and kinship in North Taiwan (Doctoral Dissertation).* Department of Anthropology, Standford University.

UNICEF (2005). Gender Achievements and Prospects in Education: The Gap Report. New York. http://www.ungei.org/gap/

United Nations. (n.d.). *Global issues: Women.* Retrieved from http://www.un.org/en/sections/issues-depth/women

United Nations. (n.d.). *The sustainable development agenda.* Retrieved from http://www.un.org/sustainabledevelopment/development-agenda

United Nations. (n.d.). *Out-of-school children and youth.* Retrieved March 28, 2018, from http://uis.unesco.org/en/topic/out-school-children-and-youth

United Nations. (2015). *Sustainable development goals fact sheet.* Retrieved March 28, 2018, from http://www.un.org/sustainabledevelopment/wp-content/uploads/2015/08/Factsheet_Summit.pdf

United Nations Commission on Human Rights. (2003). *16th session: Economic, social and cultural rights: The right to an education.* Retrieved from http://www.refworld.org

United Nations Educational, Scientific and Cultural Organization (2002) Education for All – Is the world on track: Global Education Monitoring Report. Permanently available at https://en.unesco.org/gem-report/education-all-world-track

United Nations Educational, Scientific, and Cultural Organization. (2018). *Government expenditure on education, total (% of GDP).* Retrieved June 6, 2018, from https://data.worldbank.org/indicator/SE.XPD.TOTL.GD.ZS

United Nations General Assembly. (1948). *Universal declaration of human rights* (217 [III] A). Paris, France: Author.

United Nations Population Division. (2018). *World population prospects 2017.* Retrieved from https://esa.un.org/unpd/wpp

World Bank Group. (n.d.). *Children out of school, primary, female.* Retrieved March 28, 2018, from https://data.worldbank.org/indicator/SE.PRM.UNER.FE?view=chart

Wuyuann. (2005). Study on the degree of political participation of Mongolian women in Inner Mongolia, cited in Zhang Cui (2010) Study on the Participation of Minority Women in Political Affairs in Contemporary Chinese Ethnic Areas Central University for Nationalities: PhD thesis. Retrieved 7/10/2019 from http://wap.cnki.net/touch/web/Dissertation/Article/10052-2010261055.nh.html

Xinhua. (2013, May 8). China's education expenditure reaches $357b. *China Daily-English.* Retrieved April 5, 2018, from http://www.chinadaily.com.cn/china/2013-05/08/content_16485720.htm

Xinhua. (2017, April 6). China pledges to improve secondary education coverage: Xinhua News Agency report of National Health and Family Planning Commission announcement. *Xinhuanet News.* Retrieved March 10, 2018, from www.xinhuanet.com

Yang, J., & Qiu, M. (2016). The impact of education on income inequality and intergenerational mobility. *China Economic Review, 37,* 110–125.

Yeung, Wei-Jun Jean. (2016). Paradox in marriage values and behavior in contemporary China. *Chinese Journal of Sociology, 2*(3), 447–476.

Zhang, Y. (2014). Competing Representation under Alien Rule: Women of Mongol-Yuan China. *Intersections: Gender and Sexuality in Asia and the Pacific,* 03. Retrieved from http://intersections.anu.edu.au/issue34/zhang.htm

Zhang, D. D., Li, X., & Xue, J. J. (2015). Education Inequality between Rural and Urban Areas of the People's Republic of China, Migrants' Children Education, and Some Implications, *Asian Development Review, 32*(1), 196–224.

Zhang, W., & Bray, M. (2018). Equalising schooling, unequalising private supplementary tutoring: Access and tracking through shadow education in China. *Oxford Review of Education, 44*(2), 221–238.

4

Sexual Assault on College Campuses in the United States

**AUDREY BRAMMER, KRISTEN ZALESKI,
AND CARY KLEMMER** ■

CASE STUDY: TYRONE AND KENDALL

Tyrone first met Kendall when he was a freshman in biology lab. He asked her to be his lab partner, and later during the semester, they began dating. Tyrone also became a pledge in a fraternity that is known for its academics and community service. Soon after the first semester, Tyrone was invited to join the fraternity, and he invited Kendall to the fraternity house to celebrate his success in joining the organization. As with most fraternity parties on campus, there was a bathtub full of a mix of alcohol called "jungle juice," and Tyrone was told it was only for the girls. When they arrived at the party, Tyrone gave Kendall the juice and he drank a beer. He did not anticipate what would happen next.

Soon after Kendall drank her first glass, she began to act very drunk. She wandered away from Tyrone, appeared a bit dazed and sleepy, and his fraternity brother offered to let her sleep in his room in the fraternity house because Tyrone wanted to continue to party and he did not yet have a room of his own. Kendall walked with Tyrone to the bedroom, and Tyrone told her he would be downstairs if she needed anything. She shook her head in what appeared to be agreement to the plan, and she laid down on the bed and closed her eyes to go to sleep.

Tyrone enjoyed the rest of his evening and at approximately 3 a.m. went back to the bedroom to get Kendall and walk her home. He knocked on the door, but no one answered. He quietly opened the door to find Kendall still asleep in the bed along with his fraternity brother next to her. They were both naked from the waist down. Tyrone immediately began to yell, waking up his fraternity brother and Kendall. Kendall became hysterical and accused Tyrone and his fraternity brother of hurting her while she was asleep.

Kendall was escorted to the local sexual assault treatment center by campus police, and she submitted to a urine test to detect the date rape drug Rohypnol (otherwise known by the street name Ruffies). Campus police investigated the crime scene and determined that the bathtub full of jungle juice had been laced with Rohypnol and many other women who attended the party also suffered from similar symptoms as Kendall. The rape kit is awaiting forensic evaluation, and the police are investigating Tyrone for his involvement in the sexual assault. Kendall has not returned his call and is requesting to be transferred from the university to another state school. If Tyrone is convicted, he may face up to 20 years in prison.

OVERVIEW

Sexual assault on college campuses is a global issue, with women's victimization rates ranging from 13.8% in Nigeria (Kullima, Kawuwa, Audu, Mairiga, & Bukar, 2010) to 77.6% in Turkey (Schuster, Krahé, & Toplu-Demirtas, 2016). Although the vast majority of studies on this form of violence against women are conducted in the United States, studies from throughout the world have revealed the epidemic of sexual violence on college campuses. Goldhill and Bingham (2015) reported a *Telegraph* survey that found that one in three women on UK college campuses were victims of sexual violence, and a recent *Guardian* article described UK college sexual assault at "epidemic" levels (Batty, Weale, & Bannock, 2017).

For the purpose of this chapter, sexual assault is described within female violence, although men are assaulted at high rates as well. For example, Turchik (2012) surveyed more than 300 college-aged men and found that slightly more than 50% reported sexual assault victimization since age 16 years. With regard to gender nonbinary and transgender communities (those whose gender identity or internalized sense of gendered self is not in alignment with their sex assigned at birth), research is lacking, although extant literature shows that they also experience heightened rates of gender-based violence, including sexual harassment assault (James et al., 2016; Stotzer, 2017). An international systematic review estimates that the prevalence of sexual violence among the trans population ranges from approximately 11% to as high as 49% (Blondeel et al., 2018). Currently, there are few data regarding sexual assault of transgender and gender nonbinary individuals on college campuses. However, nascent estimates have shown that 20% of transgender students have been sexually touched without their consent and that they have nine times higher odds of reporting forced penetration and six times higher odds of being in an abusive relationship compared with cisgender male counterparts (Griner et al., 2017).

Prevalence

As Table 4.1 shows, sexual assault of college-enrolled women occurs in every nation for which there is publishing research on the issue and, on average, affects nearly one-third of college women. However, the victimization rates vary dramatically between participating institutions. Kullima et al.'s (2010) study of college women's

Table 4.1 GLOBAL COLLEGE STUDENT SEXUAL ASSAULT RATES FROM A SAMPLING
OF PUBLISHED STUDIES

	Victimization (%)		Perpetration (%)			
Country	Men	Women	Men	Women	Reference	Inclusion Factors
Brazil			34.0		D'Abreu, Krahé, & Bazon, (2013)	Since age 14 years
Brazil			38.8		D'Abreu & Krahé (2014)	
Germany	19.4	35.9	13.2	7.6	Krahé & Berger (2013)	
New Zealand	12.0	21.0			Connor, Gray, & Kypri (2010)	Alcohol consumers
Nigeria		13.8			Kullima et al. (2010)	
Poland	26.0	29.0	9.0	8.0	Tomaszewska & Krahé (2018)	Previous 12 months
Portugal			21.7		Carvalho, Quinta-Gomes, & Nobre (2013)	
Portugal			22.4		Sigre-Leirós, Carvalho, & Nobre (2014)	
Turkey	65.5	77.6	28.9	14.2	Schuster, Krahé, & Toplu-Demirtas (2016)	Since age 15 years
Uganda	31.1	31.1			Agardh, Tumwine, Asamoah, & Cantor-Graae (2012)	Since birth
Average	30.8	34.7	24.0	9.9		

victimization rates at a Nigerian university found that 13.8% of women had been sexually assaulted—an international low. By contrast, Schuster et al.'s (2016) survey of college students' sexual assault rates since age 15 years revealed that 77.6% of women at
a Turkish university had been victimized. Overwhelmingly, studies find that men perpetrate sexual assault more than women: 100% of sampled studies found that men's
perpetration rates were higher, and these studies revealed that, on average, men commit sexual assault at a rate 142% higher than that of women (24.0% for men compared
to 9.9% for women). Although studies' methodologies, specific foci, and subpopulations vary (for a systematic review of the literature on sexual violence among sexual
and gender minority groups, see Blondeel et al. (2018), the problem's global ubiquity
is undeniable.

Most studies also find significant discrepancies between the rates of victimization and perpetration, with the total victimization rates often far exceeding perpetration rates. Several factors may contribute to these discrepancies. The scales used to assess prevalence rates could be more effective at garnering self-disclosure of victimization than perpetration simply because of the items' wording (McDermott, Kilmartin, McKelvey, & Kridel, 2015). Alternatively, subjects may be more willing to disclose victimization than perpetration, even in anonymous surveys, because of fear of repercussions from their disclosure or the perceived social undesirability of their behaviors. Finally, studies suggest that men who perpetrate sexual assault typically have multiple victims (Lisak & Miller, 2002), which could explain why more women report victimization than the number of men who report perpetration. Although all of these factors may logically play a role in the disparity between perpetration and victimization rates, researchers have not reached consensus about which factor(s) is responsible.

Characteristics

Few studies (e.g., Kullima et al., 2010) focus exclusively on determining the prevalence rate of college sexual assault. Most researchers narrow their studies to specific student subpopulations within college campuses and/or layer additional research questions onto their studies of the crime. Despite the appeal of comparing prevalence rates, these differences in the research questions and subpopulations problematize direct comparisons between studies and nations. However, the insights gained from the varied research approaches add valuable information to the discourse, including the crime's risk factors, causes, and effects. For example, alcohol consumption generally increases the likelihood of sexual assault victimization and perpetration (Connor, Gray, & Kypri, 2010; Flack et al., 2015; Krahé & Berger, 2013; Schuster et al., 2016), as does—according to a study conducted in Germany—having prior sexual experiences with both males and females (Krahé & Berger, 2013). Surprisingly, sexist attitudes are not always linked to higher levels of sexual aggression (Rojas-Solís & Raimúndez, 2011), but a Ugandan study revealed that women who are physically assaulted are also more likely to be subsequently sexually assaulted (Agardh, Tumwine, Asamoah, & Cantor-Graae, 2012).

A large body of research on sexual assault has attempted to determine individual factors influencing perpetration, including findings suggesting that positive attitudes toward sexual coercion and symptoms of psychopathology are positively correlated with perpetration rates (Sigre-Leirós, Carvalho, & Nobre, 2014; Tomaszewska & Krahé, 2018). Studies have also shown that the belief in rape myths—specifically the belief that victims of sexual violence are at fault for their victimization—is a predictor of perpetrating assaultive violence and is associated with discriminatory attitudes about racial, ethnic, and religious minority groups (Aosved & Long, 2006; George & Martínez, 2002). Therefore, negative and discriminatory evaluations of populations may also correlate with proclivity to engage in sexually assaultive behaviors. Also, a recent report by the US National Academies of Sciences, Engineering, and Medicine (2018) on sexual harassment of women at universities underscored that the nuanced relationships between graduate students and academic mentors, which are characterized by an imbalance of power, may be a contributing factor in the sexual assault of these students.

A somewhat smaller body of research has focused on the effects of the crime. Studies have identified that victimization often results in physical health concerns—including injury from the assault and contraction of sexually transmitted diseases (Agardh et al., 2012)—and can lead to a decline in mental health and the development of post-traumatic stress disorder, depression, and suicidal ideations (Agardh et al., 2012; Chan, Straus, Brownridge, Tiwari, & Leung, 2008). In addition, a Portuguese study found that perpetration has negative consequences as well, with men reporting decreased sexual functioning after committing a sexual assault (Carvalho, Quinta-Gomes, & Nobre, 2013).

Gender Differences by Relationship Type

Although globally sexual assault—broadly defined—is predominately perpetrated by men against women, that is not the case with all forms of sexual violence. A multinational study by Chan et al. (2008) revealed that with regard to college students' dating relationships, many nations' gender differences in victimization and perpetration rates disappear. Although college women are on average victimized more than men when the type of relationship is not considered, college men are victimized by women approximately equally in dating relationships (Chan et al., 2008; Rojas-Solís & Raimúndez, 2011). Furthermore, although college men on average perpetrate the crime significantly more often than women, the difference in perpetration rates between men and women becomes negligible when focusing only on dating relationships (Chan et al., 2008; Rojas-Solís & Raimúndez, 2011).

Discussion

Sexual assault on college campuses occurs in every nation with damaging results for both victims and perpetrators. Women are significantly more likely to be the target of this crime in most countries, and men are overwhelmingly the perpetrators. Additional insights and comparisons between nations will become possible as more studies are conducted that ask similar questions and that garner participation from multiple institutions within nations instead of single sites. For example, it is our hope that more researchers will begin to consistently assess sexual orientation, gender identity, and gender expression so as to develop an accurate global picture of the risk profile for sexual victimization of subpopulations by gender and sexual minority status. Currently, the diversity of research approaches and questions adds breadth to the international discourse but limits the field's ability to understand how national differences affect the issue of college sexual assault.

HISTORICAL TRENDS IN THE UNITED STATES

The prevalence and nature of college sexual assault against women in the United States does not appear to have changed significantly over time, but research into the crime is relatively nascent, beginning in the 1950s. For many reasons—including the crime's low reporting rates, researchers' almost exclusive use of self-report surveys, and studies' convenience sampling—the field lacks consensus about college sexual assault's victimization and perpetration rates and the extent to which it is a gendered crime. Because the field cannot agree on current prevalence rates or on many of the crime's characteristics, no reasonable claim can be made about either's change over time. However, the discourse surrounding the sexual assault of college students has shifted dramatically, and new university and United States federal policies have been created as a result.

Evolving Discourse

Rape Culture

When college sexual assault first became a major area of research in the 1950s (Kirkpatrick & Kanin, 1957), much of the focus was on understanding the psychopathology of men who perpetrate. This trend in the research quickly shifted in the 1960s as feminist theorists entered the discourse. Instead of focusing on individual-level personality traits and behavioral trends, they highlighted the societal factors that socialize men to use sexual violence as a tool of subjugation, thus creating a "rape culture" that perpetuates patriarchal power dynamics (Brownmiller, 1975). Studies assessing men's acceptance of rape-supportive attitudes and beliefs—termed "rape myths"—became commonplace and revealed the high prevalence of rape myth acceptance in the United States and the correlation between rape myth acceptance and sexual assault perpetration (Burt, 1980). For example, a recent notable finding is that college men who consume alcohol heavily are more likely to perpetuate the rape myth—that women are to blame for sexual assault—compared to women who drink alcohol (Hayes, Abbott, & Cook, 2016). The framework of a rape culture had a dramatic effect on the discourse surrounding college sexual assault and remains prevalent in research on college sexual assault today (Forbes, Adams-Curtis, Pakalka, & White, 2006; Hayes et al., 2016). Unfortunately, early research on sexual assault did not acknowledge the role of sexual orientation and gender diversity in influencing the likelihood of experiencing sexual assault. It was only through the US civil rights and feminist movements that this group gained recognition (Messner, Greenberg, & Peretz, 2015), and today, although strong research methodologies to access and assess the needs of this group have not been uniformly achieved, acknowledgment of this group in research endeavors continues to grow (Frohard-Dourlent, Dobson, Clark, Doull, & Saewyc, 2017; Institute of Medicine, 2011).

Universities' Subcultures of Rape

To understand how rape culture norms were being transmitted on college campuses, researchers in the 1980s began examining subcultures within universities with strong ties to traditional masculinity. Fraternities and collegiate sports became the focus of significant research, revealing that men living in fraternity houses and participating in collegiate sports supported rape myths and perpetrated sexual assault more frequently than their non-Greek- and non-athletics-affiliated counterparts (Boeringer, 1999; Crosset, Benedict, & McDonald, 1995; Frintner & Rubinson, 1993; Koss & Gaines, 1993; P. Martin & Hummer, 1998).

Furthermore, Jozkowski and Wiersma-Mosley (2017) argue that the intersection of gender and class on college universities is magnified by Greek subculture and perpetuates rape supportive attitudes among White privileged college students. To curtail the

Figure 4.1 According to a National Institute of Justice report, the first 2 years of college are the highest risk years, and the first few months of the school year are the highest risk time of the year.

epidemic of college sexual assaults, attitudinal, power, and cultural shifts must happen to create equanimity among class and gender. Sharp, Weaver, and Zvonkovic (2017) discuss an array of influences that affect college sexual assault, including power dynamic in college, faculty engagement, and internalized sexual scripts of both male and female students. The National Academies of Sciences, Engineering, and Medicine (2018) acknowledged this endemic problem on college campuses and has made recommendations for universities to create systemic cultural shifts away from this culture of rape.

Preventing Victimization

By the late 1980s, college sexual assault's high perpetration rates and disturbing cultural antecedents had been thoroughly established, and researchers shifted their focus to methods for preventing victimization through the identification of sexual assault's risk factors and the development of prevention programs. Alcohol consumption was quickly identified as the predominant factor increasing the likelihood of both perpetration and victimization (Abbey, Ross, McDuffie, & McAuslan, 1996; Frintner & Rubinson, 1993; Koss & Gaines, 1993; Larimer, Lydum, Anderson, & Turner, 1999). Programs aimed at reducing victimization were designed, implemented, and tested, including programs educating women about risk factors for sexual assault (Anderson & Whiston, 2005), educating men about consent and rape myths (Flores & Hartlaub, 1998), and educating bystanders about sexual assault and how to intervene if it seems imminent (Banyard, Plante, & Moynihan, 2004; Katz, 1994).

DIVERSITY

By the late 1990s, scholars began regularly critiquing college sexual assault research for its heteronormativity and exclusion of marginalized populations and perspectives (Porter & Williams, 2011; Scarce, 1997), such as transgender and gender nonbinary populations whose experiences are still not well covered in extant literature (Coulter & Rankin, 2017). Surveys quantifying sexual assault perpetration and victimization often assumed heterosexual relations (Koss, Gidycz, & Wisniewski, 1987), and few studies acknowledged the effects of ethnic identities on both victimization rates and perpetration risk factors.

Researchers filled the marginalized population/perspective knowledge gap by conducting investigations into same-sex sexual violence on college campuses (S. Martin, Fisher, Warner, Krebs, & Lindquist, 2011; Porter & Williams, 2011; Scarce, 1997), victimization rates of ethnically marginalized women (Krebs et al., 2011; Porter & Williams, 2011), and rape myth acceptance by ethnically marginalized men (Stephens, 2009; Torres-Pryor, 2004). The results have substantiated the crime's ubiquity but have also revealed that people identifying as sexual minorities (i.e., lesbian, gay, bisexual, or queer), transgender, and gender nonbinary and who are ethnic minorities are sexually assaulted at higher rates than those identifying as heterosexual, cisgender, and White (S. Martin et al., 2011; Porter & Williams, 2011). In addition, these studies have revealed the need for a deeper understanding of gender narratives and interactional norms within and between ethnic identities and how those differences mediate sexual assault perpetration.

For example, although women who identify with marginalized ethnicities are sexually assaulted at higher rates than women who do not, women attending historically Black colleges have been found to experience sexual assault victimization at significantly lower rates than women attending non-historically Black colleges (Krebs et al., 2011). Furthermore, some studies have uncovered different rape myth acceptance rates and differences in the types of accepted rape myths between White students and students identifying with marginalized ethnicities (e.g., Stephens, 2009), whereas other studies have found no rape myth differences between ethnic identities (e.g., Hayes et al., 2016).

RETURN TO PERPETRATOR PSYCHOPATHOLOGY

As stated previously, college sexual assault discourse since the 1960s has remained aware of the United States' rape culture and its societal effects on men's propensity to perpetrate. However, the past two decades have seen a shift toward including the original focus of sexual assault research—the psychopathological characteristics of assailants. This shift has been influenced heavily by prevention literature and related studies focused on understanding the psychosocial differences between perpetrators and non-perpetrators with the goal of informing sexual assault prevention programs (DeGue & DeLillo, 2004; Farr, Brown, & Beckett, 2004; Gidycz, Warkentin, & Orchowski, 2007; Voller & Long, 2010).

GENDER SIMILARITIES

Although historically much of the research has supported the idea that college sexual assault is generally perpetrated by men against women, recent methodology critiques and studies have called that belief into question. Scholarly reviews of college sexual assault literature have revealed that many of the frequently used perpetration and victimization surveys assume that men are perpetrators and women are victims, which skews the available data toward the inevitable conclusion that, overwhelmingly, men perpetrate against women. These reviews also point to the fact that few multi-university studies exist that survey both men and women about perpetration and/or victimization and that thus the gender rates found by most existing studies cannot easily be compared (McDermott, Kilmartin, McKevey, & Kridel, 2015). Furthermore, recent studies surveying women about perpetration and men about victimization have found rates for both that are similar to the rates for men's perpetration and women's victimization (Palmer, McMahon, Rounsaville, & Ball, 2010). Consistently, however, the type of sexual assault that is committed appears to be gendered, with men more often assaulting by use of physical force (Larimer et al., 1999). To gain a more holistic and accurate portrait of the gendered differences of sexual assault victimization and perpetration, studies must also take into account gender identity and expression to understand subgroup (cisgender women, transgender women, transgender men, etc.) risk profiles for both sexual violence victimization and perpetration, especially because of an observed preponderance of sexual violence among sexual and gender minority groups within intimate partnerships (Yerke & DeFeo, 2016).

Policy Change

TITLE IX AND THE CLERY ACT
In 1972, the US Congress passed Title IX, prohibiting federally funded institutions from sex-based discrimination. Sexual violence is included in the regulation as a form of sex-based discrimination, and institutions are required by Title IX to quickly and effectively end any acts of sexual violence of which they are aware or should reasonably be aware (20 U.S.C. §1681, 1972). Within a decade of the passage of Title IX, several high-profile cases of violence on college campuses uncovered universities' under-investigation and underreporting of campus sexual assault, and Congress responded in 1990 with the passage of the Jeanne Clery Disclosure of Campus Security Policy and Campus Crime Statistics Act (the "Clery Act"). The Clery Act requires all educational institutions to publicly publish crime statistics and to report crime information to the federal Department of Education annually (20 U.S.C. § 1092, 1990), with the goal of increasing Title IX-related oversight and accountability. Under the Obama administration, Title IX protections were extended to transgender individuals, which was hailed as a major move toward achieving accountability to all victims of sexual violence (this is further discussed later; US Department of Justice & US Department of Education, 2016). These protections, however, have recently been rescinded by the Trump administration (Kreighbaum, 2017).

VIOLENCE AGAINST WOMEN ACT
In response to increasing public awareness of domestic violence, interpersonal violence, and sexual assault—including the high-profile college sexual assault cases covered by the media—Congress passed the Violence Against Women Act (VAWA) in 1994 (Greenberg & Messner, 2014). This act clearly declared sexual assault a crime and increased punishments for perpetration. In addition, acknowledging the poor treatment women often received from law enforcement when reporting a sexual assault, VAWA funds programs to educate police officers and prosecutors on sexual

assault's prevalence and consequences for victims (42 U.S.C. §13925, 1994). VAWA also funds community programs that raise awareness of sexual assault and that support victims. One such program—the Sexual Assault Nurse Examiners program—aims to increase the rates of successful prosecution by training nurses in hospitals and other emergency medical facilities to gather physical evidence of sexual assault when women seek immediate medical attention for victimization.

In 2013, Congress reauthorized VAWA (through the Violence Against Women Reauthorization Act) with an additional section titled the Campus Sexual Violence Elimination (SaVE) Act. The SaVE Act provides further guidance on the Clery Act's reporting requirements, among which is the expectation that colleges' annual crime statistics reports will include details of their sexual violence prevention initiatives. The SaVE Act also mandates that colleges must attempt to prevent sexual violence by providing bystander intervention trainings to all incoming students (20 U.S.C. §S. 128, 2013).

DEAR COLLEAGUE LETTER

By 2011, the federal Department of Education was acutely aware that sexual violence on college campuses remained highly prevalent despite enacted regulations. The Department of Education's Office of Civil Rights issued a statement called the Dear Colleague Letter (DCL) that provided further guidance on the definition and handling of sexual violence. The DCL clarifies—among other items—that neither a sexual assault victim's request that the school not take action nor criminal prosecution of the act relieves universities of their obligation to also act against sexual assault. Moreover, the DCL asks all colleges and universities to prevent sexual assault through educational programs provided to all students. It further establishes that to find an accused perpetrator "responsible" for a sexual assault, educational institutions should use the "preponderance of evidence" legal model found in civil litigation instead of the "clear and convincing" evidence model used by the criminal justice system (Ali, 2011). This shift in evidence models allows institutions to hold accused perpetrators accountable if the evidence suggests that it is more likely that the assault occurred than that it did not instead of requiring institutions to eliminate any reasonable doubt that the crime occurred.

CONDITIONS OF WOMEN IN THE UNITED STATES

Sexual assault of women on college campuses exists in a larger national context of sexism and patriarchy (Greenberg & Messner, 2014), apparent from women's lived experiences as well as from the quantifiable indicators of systemic oppression discussed in the following sections.

Current Conditions of US Campus Sexual Assault Against Women

Sexual assault of college-enrolled women pervades educational institutions throughout the United States. This crime is perpetrated—by most estimates—against at least one in four women college students, and victimization rates do not seem to be decreasing. Despite this societal problem's ubiquity and heavy media coverage during the past two decades, sexual assault crimes remain largely unreported and unpros-ecuted. The silence surrounding the sexual assault of college women is particularly disturbing when coupled with universities' failure to adhere to federal policies man-dating effective intervention and transparent reporting. This and the following sec-tions examine these concerns, summarizes research on the societal and individual factors that increase perpetration and victimization, and discusses the consequences of college sexual assault.

In September 2018, Betsy DeVos, the Education Secretary appointed by President Trump, reversed many policies enacted to support victims of college crimes (Saul & Taylor, 2018). In particular, DeVos argued that the policies were not strict enough to prove a sexual assault had occurred and, as a result, the accused perpetrators were unfairly found guilty more often. This change in policy is very controversial to sexual assault survivor advocates, who believe it will negatively affect justice.

Silence

Most studies indicate that fewer than 20% of victims report the crime to any authority and that an alarmingly small number of reported college sexual assaults—between 1% and 6%—result in any action being taken against the accused perpetrator (DeMatteo, Galloway, Arnold, & Patel, 2015; Seidman & Pokorak, 2011; Wolitzky-Taylor et al., 2011). Researchers largely agree that the crime's low reporting rate results from vic-tims' fear of poor treatment by authorities or others with power over their career development, such as in the case of relationships between graduate students and their academic mentors (National Academies of Sciences, Engineering, and Medicine, 2018), and that these fears are founded in women's actual experiences with victim-blaming and retraumatization (Maier, 2012).

Compounding and supporting the problem of underreporting is universities' non-compliance with federal regulations. Since the passage of Title IX in 1972, the federal government has passed several bills and issued guidance mandating that all colleges and universities intervene immediately and effectively in sexual assaults, take disci-plinary action against perpetrators, transparently report crime statistics, and prevent sexual assault through educational programs. However, investigations on compli-ance of colleges and universities have revealed alarming failures to comply. A particu-larly disturbing example relates to the federal government's practice of occasionally auditing universities' crime reporting for accuracy and compliance with regulations. Yung (2015) found that on average, universities' reporting of sexual violence crimes increases by 44% during audits and then returns to pre-audit levels immediately after the audit period ends, suggesting intentional noncompliance and cover-up. In addi-tion, universities have been found to take disciplinary action against accused perpe-trators in less than 1% of reported cases, and more than 20% of universities fail to investigate any reports of sexual assault (DeMatteo et al., 2015).

Societal and Individual Influences on Perpetration

Rape culture—societally supported norms that perpetuate men's sexual violence against women—and the resulting popular acceptance of rape myths—including the beliefs that men deserve sex, women who say "no" really mean "yes," and women who are sexually assaulted while intoxicated are to blame for the crime—increase perpetration while also discouraging reporting and adjudication. College men who believe common rape myths have been found to perpetrate sexual assault against women at significantly higher rates than men who do not, and behaviors that increase men's interactions with rape myths—including watching violent pornography—also increase sexually assaultive behaviors (Locke & Mahalik, 2005; Sanday, 2007).

On the individual level, behavior patterns such as drinking heavily at bars and parties (Testa & Cleveland, 2017), as well as certain psychosocial characteristics (Mouilso, Calhoun, & Rosenbloom, 2013; Zawacki, Abbey, Buck, McAuslan, & Clinton-Sherrod, 2003), have been linked to increased perpetration. College men who commit sexual assault have higher rates of psychopathy and antisocial personality disorder diagnoses (Hoertel, Le Strat, Schuster, & Limosin, 2012), and they display a reduced capacity for empathy, including the inability to experience compassion when

Figure 4.2 Drug-facilitated sexual assault (DFSA) is when a victim is forced (often unknowingly) to ingest a drug that will incapacitate them and prevent them from having a memory of the assault. In some cases, victims of DFSA will be alert and look very drunk so others at parties or bars will not realize the victims have been given a substance, and they will assume the victims' behavior is voluntary intoxication. In other cases, drugs will incapacitate a victim in a way that leaves them physically unable to resist. When this kind of crime is reported, it is difficult to detect because most drugs metabolize out of the body very quickly and hospitals do not have a standard test to determine the wide array of substances that can have this effect on unsuspecting victims.

witnessing another's suffering (van Langen, Wissink, van Vugt, Van der Stouwe, & Stams, 2014). Abuse histories also play a role in the prevalence of sexually assaultive behavior: Men who were sexually abused as children sexually assault women at higher rates in adolescence and adulthood (Riser, Pegram, & Farley, 2013).

An additional factor in college sexual assault, as described in the case at the beginning of this chapter, is the prominence of drug-facilitated sexual assault (DFSA), in which the perpetrator will drug the victim's beverage to elicit memory loss and passivity on behalf of the victim. Richer et al. (2017) surveyed almost 400 victim cases that were seen at sexual assault treatment centers and found that slightly more than 50% reported DFSA. Furthermore, the authors noted an increase in prevalence of DFSA among men in recent years.

Consequences

Sexual assault can result in significant health and psychosocial consequences, some of which persist throughout victims' lives (Basile & Smith, 2011; Bryant-Davis, Ullman, Tsong, Tillman, & Smith, 2010). Victims often experience worsened physical health, including the contraction of sexually transmitted diseases, moderate to severe mental health symptoms such as post-traumatic stress disorder, and disconnections from previously available support networks (Basile & Smith, 2011; Patterson & Campbell, 2010; Seidman & Pokorak, 2011). Victimization also increases women's likelihood of drug and alcohol use and other risky behaviors (McCauley, Ruggiero, Resnick, Conoscenti, & Kilpatrick, 2009; Turchik & Hassija, 2014). Similarly, negative consequences have been observed for transgender and gender nonbinary populations. Transgender individuals who have experienced sexual assault have increased odds of experiencing negative consequences, particularly later life homelessness, drug or alcohol use, and suicidal ideation or attempt, compared to their peers who have not experienced this type of violence (Grant et al., 2011; Griner et al., 2017).

Due to the far-reaching consequences of sexual assault, it is the crime with the highest societal cost (Basile & Smith, 2011; Seidman & Pokorak, 2011). Because of the physical and psychosocial health consequences of sexual assault, victimization often results for college women in lowered grade point averages and failure to complete their degrees (M. Griffin & Read, 2012; Jordan, Combs, & Smith, 2014), effects that can have long-term negative career and income implications. Moreover, although the majority of these costs stem from victims' physical and mental health services, lesser known costs, such as the vicarious traumatization of health care workers, also contribute: 51% of sexual assault nurse examiners report experiencing vicarious trauma as a result of their work (Maier, 2012), and social workers who treat sexual assault victims experience significantly higher levels of secondary traumatic stress (Choi, 2011).

LOOKING TO THE FUTURE

To respond to this endemic crime, many educational institutions have implemented programs aimed at preventing sexual assault on their campuses. Bystander intervention, the prevention effort required by the aforementioned Dear Colleague Letter, is the program type most commonly offered. Bystander intervention trains all college students—regardless of gender or risk factors—to identify situations in which sexual assault may occur and to intervene to prevent its occurrence (Foubert, Langhinrichsen-Rohling, Brasfield, & Hill, 2010). Although these programs have significantly increased participants' measured intent to intervene and somewhat decreased their acceptance of rape myths (Katz & Moore, 2013), they have not yet resulted in national reductions in prevalence rates.

Another category of commonly offered prevention programs aims to train primarily women on how to avoid being sexually assaulted, such as avoiding heavy drinking and other risky behaviors (Bedera & Nordmeyer, 2015); however, these programs have largely caused no decrease in participants' victimization (Gidycz, Rich, Orchowski, King, & Miller, 2006) and have resulted in participants' increased fear and anxiety, which reduce their academic performance (Bedera & Nordmeyer, 2015). The final, most prevalent type of prevention program trains primarily men on the definition of consent, to identify and discredit rape myths, and to identify and avoid situations in which perpetration is likely to occur (Foubert, Tatum, & Godin, 2010). Although these programs have been proven effective at changing men's attitudes toward sexual assault, studies have revealed that they are most effective at changing the attitudes of men with low risk factors and relatively ineffective at changing attitudes of men with the highest risk factors (Stephens & George, 2009). In addition, changes in attitudes return to baseline within a few weeks (Davis & Liddell, 2002) and do not necessarily result in changed behavior (Foubert, 2000).

Figure 4.3 Take Back the Night (www.takebackthenight.org) is a popular advocacy event that takes place during Sexual Assault Awareness Month and aims to bring awareness to sexual victimization on college campuses.

Advocacy Efforts

In United States, advocacy groups have become part of the yearly fabric within college culture. For example, Take Back the Night (https://TakeBackTheNight.org) is a long-standing event that often takes place in April, which is commonly acknowledged to be sexual assault awareness month. Take Back the Night includes many opportunities for college students to engage in rallies against sexual violence on campus, and often a candlelight vigil is held in the evening to "take back the night" from sexual predators.

Another advocacy movement that often coincides with Take Back the Night is the Clothesline Project (http://www.clotheslineproject.info). This event is organized around a laundry line that is hung from trees, usually in a main thoroughfare to garner the most attention from college students, on which shirts that are individually designed by survivors of sexual assault are hung.

The US Department of Education Office for Civil Rights also has Title IX representation on college campuses. The Title IX coordinator is the representative who facilitates advocacy and legal investigations into reported sexual assault crimes, as well as other forms of sexual discrimination within the educational system.

CONCLUSION

College sexual assault is a persistent problem throughout the world, and it appears to be increasing in prevalence. Efforts in the United States have made some progress to educate college students about the crime, but many policymakers continue to disagree on how best to solve the problem. Tackling rape culture, increasing a victim's ability to report a sexual assault, and restructuring a more targeted prevention program within college institutions are ways in which this epidemic can change and college students can begin to feel safe on campus to pursue an education without being sexually harassed or victimized.

DISCUSSION QUESTIONS

1. What is drug-facilitated sexual assault on college campuses?
2. Do current prevention programs address the issue of perpetration in a satisfactory way? Why or why not?
3. How do you view rape culture on college campuses? What are some ways to change campus culture to develop less victim blame and more victim empathy and support?

REFERENCES

Abbey, A., Ross, L. T., McDuffie, D., & McAuslan, P. (1996). Alcohol and dating risk factors for sexual assault among college women. *Psychology of Women Quarterly, 20,* 147–169.

Agardh, A., Tumwine, G., Asamoah, B. O., & Cantor-Graae, E. (2012). The invisible suffering: Sexual coercion, interpersonal violence, and mental health—A cross-sectional study among university students in south-western Uganda. *PLoS One, 7*(12), 9.

Retrieved from http://libproxy.usc.edu/login?url=http://search.proquest.com.lib-proxy1.usc.edu/docview/1428013676?accountid=14749

Ali, R. (2011, April 4). *Dear colleague letter.* Washington, DC: US Department of Education, Office for Civil Rights.

Anderson, L. A., & Whiston, S. C. (2005). Sexual assault education programs: A meta-analytic examination of their effectiveness. *Psychology of Women Quarterly, 29,* 374–388. http://dx.doi.org/10.1111/j.1471-6402.2005.00237.x

Aosved, A. C., & Long, P. J. (2006). Co-occurrence of rape myth acceptance, sexism, racism, homophobia, ageism, classism, and religious intolerance. *Sex Roles, 55*(7–8), 481–492.

Banyard, V. L., Plante, E. G., & Moynihan, M. M. (2004). Bystander education: Bringing a broader community perspective to sexual violence prevention. *Journal of Community Psychology, 32,* 61–79. doi:10.1002/jcop.10078

Basile, K. C., & Smith, S. G. (2011). Sexual violence victimization of women: Prevalence, characteristics, and the role of public health and prevention. *American Journal of Lifestyle Medicine, 5*(5), 407–417. doi:10.1177/1559827611409512

Batty, D., Weale, S., & Bannock, C. (2017, March 5). Sexual harassment "at epidemic levels" in UK universities. *The Guardian.* Retrieved from https://www.theguardian.com/education/2017/mar/05/students-staff-uk-universities-sexual-harassment-epidemic

Bedera, N., & Nordmeyer, K. (2015). "Never go out alone": An analysis of college rape prevention tips. *Sexuality & Culture: An Interdisciplinary Quarterly, 19*(3), 533–542. Retrieved from http://libproxy.usc.edu/login?url=http://search.proquest.com.lib-proxy2.usc.edu/docview/1703282738?accountid=14749

Blondeel, K., de Vasconcelos, S., García-Moreno, C., Stephenson, R., Temmerman, M., & Toskin, I. (2018). Violence motivated by perception of sexual orientation and gender identity: A systematic review. *Bulletin of the World Health Organization, 96*(1), 29–41L.

Boeringer, S. B. (1999). Associations of rape-supportive attitudes with fraternal and athletic participation. *Violence Against Women, 5,* 81–90.

Brownmiller, S. (1975). *Against our will: Men, women, and rape.* New York, NY: Simon & Schuster.

Bryant-Davis, T., Ullman, S. E., Tsong, Y., Tillman, S., & Smith, K. (2010). Struggling to survive: Sexual assault, poverty, and mental health outcomes of African American women. *American Journal of Orthopsychiatry, 80*(1), 61–70. http://dx.doi.org.lib-proxy2.usc.edu/10.1111/j.1939-0025.2010.01007.x

Burt, M. (1980). Cultural myths and supports for rape. *Journal of Personality and Social Psychology, 38,* 217–230.

Carvalho, J., Quinta-Gomes, A., & Nobre, P. J. (2013). The sexual functioning profile of a nonforensic sample of individuals reporting sexual aggression against women. *Journal of Sexual Medicine, 10*(7), 1744–1754. Retrieved from http://libproxy.usc.edu/login?url=http://search.proquest.com.libproxy2.usc.edu/docview/1400135656?accountid=14749

Chan, K. L., Straus, M. A., Brownridge, D. A., Tiwari, A., & Leung, W. C. (2008). Prevalence of dating partner violence and suicidal ideation among male and female university students worldwide. *Journal of Midwifery & Women's Health, 53,* 529–537. doi:10.1016/j.jmwh.2008.04.016

Choi, G. (2011). Secondary traumatic stress of service providers who practice with survivors of family or sexual violence: A national survey of social workers. *Smith College Studies in Social Work, 81*(1), 101–119. Retrieved from http://libproxy.

usc.edu/login?url=http://search.proquest.com.libproxy1.usc.edu/docview/858290526?accountid=14749

Connor, J., Gray, A., & Kypri, K. (2010). Drinking history, current drinking and problematic sexual experiences among university students. *Australian and New Zealand Journal of Public Health, 34*(5), 487–494. doi:10.1111/j.1753-6405.2010.00595.x

Coulter, R. W. S., & Rankin, S. R. (2017). College sexual assault and campus climate for sexual- and gender-minority undergraduate students. *Journal of Interpersonal Violence.* https://doi.org/10.1177/0886260517696870

Crosset, T. W., Benedict, J. R., & McDonald, M. A. (1995). Male student-athletes reported for sexual assault: A survey of campus police departments and judicial affairs offices. *Journal of Sport and Social Issues, 19*, 126–140.

D'Abreu, L. C. F., & Krahé, B. (2014). Predicting sexual aggression in male college students in Brazil. *Psychology of Men & Masculinity, 15*(2), 152–162. Retrieved from http://libproxy.usc.edu/login?url=http://search.proquest.com.libproxy2.usc.edu/docview/1417863186?accountid=14749

D'Abreu, L. C. F., Krahé, B., & Bazon, M. R. (2013). Sexual aggression among Brazilian college students: Prevalence of victimization and perpetration in men and women. *Journal of Sex Research, 50*(8), 795. Retrieved from http://libproxy.usc.edu/login?url=http://search.proquest.com.libproxy2.usc.edu/docview/1444668538?accountid=14749

Davis, T. L., & Liddell, D. L. (2002). Getting inside the house: The effectiveness of a rape prevention program for college fraternity men. *Journal of College Student Development, 43*(1), 35–50. Retrieved from http://search.proquest.com.libproxy2.usc.edu/docview/619924136?accountid=14749

DeGue, S., & DiLillo, D. (2004). Understanding perpetrators of nonphysical sexual coercion: Characteristics of those who cross the line. *Violence and Victims, 19*, 673–688. doi:10.1891/vivi.19.6.673.66345

DeMatteo, D., Galloway, M., Arnold, S., & Patel, U. (2015). Sexual assault on college campuses: A 50-state survey of criminal sexual assault statutes and their relevance to campus sexual assault. *Psychology, Public Policy, and Law, 21*(3), 227–238. Retrieved from http://libproxy.usc.edu/login?url=http://search.proquest.com.libproxy1.usc.edu/docview/1697762835?accountid=14749

Farr, C., Brown, J., & Beckett, R. (2004). Ability to empathize and masculinity levels: Comparing male adolescent sex offenders with a normative sample of non-offending adolescents. *Psychology, Crime & Law, 10*(2), 155–167. Retrieved from http://dx.doi.org.libproxy2.usc.edu/10.1080/10683160310001597153

Flack, W. F., Jr., Kimble, M. O., Campbell, B. E., Hopper, A. B., Petercă, O., & Heller, E. J. (2015). Sexual assault victimization among female undergraduates during study abroad: A single campus survey study. *Journal of Interpersonal Violence, 30*(20), 3453–3466. Retrieved from http://libproxy.usc.edu/login?url=http://search.proquest.com.libproxy2.usc.edu/docview/1835545907?accountid=14749

Flores, S. A., & Hartlaub, M. G. (1998). Reducing rape-myth acceptance in male college students: A meta-analysis of intervention studies. *Journal of College Student Development, 39*, 438–448.

Forbes, G. B., Adams-Curtis, L. E., Pakalka, A. H., & White, K. B. (2006). Dating aggression, sexual coercion, and aggression-supporting attitudes among college men as a function of participation in aggressive high school sports. *Violence Against Women, 12*, 441–455.

Foubert, J. D. (2000). The longitudinal effects of a rape-prevention program on fraternity men's attitudes, behavioral intent, and behavior. *Journal of American College Health, 48,* 158–163.

Foubert, J. D., Langhinrichsen-Rohling, J., Brasfield, H., & Hill, B. (2010). Effects of a rape awareness program on college women: Increasing bystander efficacy and willingness to intervene. *Journal of Community Psychology, 38*(7), 813–827. Retrieved from http://dx.doi.org.libproxy2.usc.edu/10.1002/jcop.20397

Foubert, J. D., Tatum, J. L., & Godin, E. E. (2010). First-year male students' perceptions of a rape prevention program 7 months after their participation: Attitude and behavior changes. *Journal of College Student Development, 51*(6), 707–715. Retrieved from http://dx.doi.org.libproxy2.usc.edu/10.1353/csd.2010.0021

Frintner, M. P., & Rubinson, L. (1993). Acquaintance rape: The influence of alcohol, fraternity membership, and sports team membership. *Journal of Sex Education and Therapy, 19,* 272–284.

Frohard-Dourlent, H., Dobson, S., Clark, B. A., Doull, M., & Saewyc, E. M. (2017). "I would have preferred more options": Accounting for non-binary youth in health research. *Nursing Inquiry, 24*(1), 1–9.

George, W. H., & Martínez, L. J. (2002). Victim blaming in rape: Effects of victim and perpetrator race, type of rape, and participant racism. *Psychology of Women Quarterly, 26*(2), 110–119.

Gidycz, C. A., Rich, C. L., Orchowski, L., King, C., & Miller, A. K. (2006). The evaluation of a sexual assault self-defense and risk-reduction program for college women: A prospective study. *Psychology of Women Quarterly, 30*(2), 173–186.

Gidycz, C. A., Warkentin, J. B., & Orchowski, L. M. (2007). Predictors of perpetration of verbal, physical, and sexual violence: A prospective analysis of college men. *Psychology of Men & Masculinity, 8,* 79–94. doi:10.1037/1524-9220.8.2.79

Goldhill, O., & Bingham, J. (2015, January 14). One in three UK female students sexually assaulted or abused on campus. Retrieved from http://www.telegraph.co.uk/women/womens-life/11343380/Sexually-assault-1-in-3-UK-female-students-victim-on-campus.html

Grant, J. M., Mottet, L. A., Tanis, J., Harrison, J., Herman, J. L., & Keisling, M. (2011). *Injustice at Every Turn: A Report of the National Transgender Discrimination Survey.* Washington, DC: National Center for Transgender Equality and National Gay and Lesbian Task Force.

Greenberg, M. A., & Messner, M. A. (2014). Before prevention: The trajectory and tensions of feminist antiviolence. *Advances in Gender Research, 18,* 225–248.

Griffin, M. J., & Read, J. P. (2012). Prospective effects of method of coercion in sexual victimization across the first college year. *Journal of Interpersonal Violence, 27*(12), 2503–2524. doi:10.1177/0886260511433518

Griner, S. B., Vamos, C. A., Thompson, E. L., Logan, R., Vázquez-Otero, C., & Daley, E. M. (2017). The intersection of gender identity and violence: Victimization experienced by transgender college students. *Journal of Interpersonal Violence* [Epub ahead of print]. doi:10.1177/0886260517723743

Hayes, R. M., Abbott, R. L., & Cook, S. (2016). It's her fault: Student acceptance of rape myths on two college campuses. *Violence Against Women, 22*(13), 1540–1555. Retrieved from http://libproxy.usc.edu/login?url=http://search.proquest.com.libproxy2.usc.edu/docview/1832754324?accountid=14749

Hoertel, N., Le Strat, Y., Schuster, J., & Limosin, F. (2012). Sexual assaulters in the United States: Prevalence and psychiatric correlates in a national sample. *Archives of Sexual*

Behavior, 41(6), 1379–1387. Retrieved from http://dx.doi.org.libproxy1.usc.edu/10.1007/s10508-012-9943-5

Institute of Medicine. (2011). *The health of lesbian, gay, bisexual, and transgender people: Building a foundation for better understanding.* Washington, DC: National Academies Press.

James, S. E., Herman, J. L., Rankin, S., Keisling, M., Mottet, L., & Anafi, M. (2016). *The report of the 2015 U.S. Transgender Survey.* Washington, DC: National Center for Transgender Equality.

Jordan, C. E., Combs, J. L., & Smith, G. T. (2014). An exploration of sexual victimization and academic performance among college women. *Trauma, Violence, & Abuse, 15*(3), 191–200. doi:10.1177/1524838014520637

Jozkowski, K. N., & Wiersma-Mosley, J. D. (2017). The Greek system: How gender inequality and class privilege perpetuate rape culture. *Family Relations, 66*(1), 89–103. doi:10.1111/fare.12229

Katz, J. (1994). *Mentors in Violence Prevention (MVP) trainer's guide.* Boston, MA: Northeastern University, Center for the Study of Sport in Society.

Katz, J., & Moore, J. (2013). Bystander education training for campus sexual assault prevention: An initial meta-analysis. *Violence and Victims, 28,* 1054–1067. http://dx.doi.org/10.1891/0886-6708.VV-D-12-00113

Kirkpatrick, C., & Kanin, E. (1957). Male sexual aggression on a university campus. *American Sociological Review, 22,* 52–58. http://dx.doi.org/10.2307/2088765

Koss, M. P., & Gaines, J. (1993). The prediction of sexual aggression by alcohol use, athletic participation, and fraternity affiliation. *Journal of Interpersonal Violence, 8,* 94–107.

Koss, M. P., Gidycz, C. A., & Wisniewski, N. (1987). The scope of rape: Incidence and prevalence of sexual aggression and victimization in a national sample of higher education students. *Journal of Consulting and Clinical Psychology, 55,* 162–170. http://dx.doi.org/10.1037/0022-006X.55.2.162

Krahé, B., & Berger, A. (2013). Men and women as perpetrators and victims of sexual aggression in heterosexual and same-sex encounters: A study of first-year college students in Germany. *Aggressive Behavior, 39*(5), 391–404. doi:10.1002/ab.21482

Krebs, C. P., Barrick, K., Lindquist, C. H., Crosby, C. M., Boyd, C., & Bogan, Y. (2011). The sexual assault of undergraduate women at historically Black colleges and universities (HBCUs). *Journal of Interpersonal Violence, 26*(18), 3640–3666. doi:10.1177/0886260511403759

Kreighbaum, A. (2017, February 23). Transgender protections withdrawn. *Inside Higher Ed.* Retrieved March 12, 2018, from https://www.insidehighered.com/news/2017/02/23/trump-administration-reverses-title-ix-guidance-transgender-protections

Kullima, A., Kawuwa, M., Audu, B., Mairiga, A., & Bukar, M. (2010). Sexual assault against female Nigerian students. *African Journal of Reproductive Health, 14*(3), 189–193. Retrieved from http://www.jstor.org.libproxy2.usc.edu/stable/41329739

Larimer, M. E., Lydum, A. R., Anderson, B. K., & Turner, A. P. (1999). Male and female recipients of unwanted sexual contact in a college student sample: Prevalence rates, alcohol use, and depression symptoms. *Sex Roles, 40,* 295–308.

Lisak, D., & Miller, P. M. (2002). Repeat rape and multiple offending among undetected rapists. *Violence and Victims, 17*(1), 73–84. http://dx.doi.org/10.1891/vivi.17.1.73.33638

Locke, B. D., & Mahalik, J. R. (2005). Examining masculinity norms, problem drinking, and athletic involvement as predictors of sexual aggression in college men. *Journal of Counseling Psychology, 52,* 279–283. doi:10.1037/0022-0167.52.3.279

Maier, S. L. (2012). Sexual assault nurse examiners' perceptions of the revictimization of rape victims. *Journal of Interpersonal Violence, 27*(2), 287–315. Retrieved from http://dx.doi.org.libproxy1.usc.edu/10.1177/0886260511416476

Martin, P. Y., & Hummer, R. A. (1998). Fraternities and rape on campus. In R. K. Bergen (Ed.), *Issues in intimate violence* (pp. 157–167). Thousand Oaks, CA: Sage. Retrieved from http://dx.doi.org.libproxy2.usc.edu/10.4135/9781483328348.n10

Martin, S. L., Fisher, B. S., Warner, T. D., Krebs, C. P., & Lindquist, C. H. (2011). Women's sexual orientations and their experiences of sexual assault before and during university. *Women's Health Issues, 21*(3), 199. doi:10.1016/j.whi.2010.12.002

McCauley, J., Ruggiero, K. J., Resnick, H. S., Conoscenti, L. M., & Kilpatrick, D. G. (2009). Forcible, drug-facilitated, and incapacitated rape in relation to substance use problems: Results from a national sample of college women. *Addictive Behaviors, 34*(5), 458–462. Retrieved from http://dx.doi.org.libproxy2.usc.edu/10.1016/j.addbeh.2008.12.004

McDermott, R. C., Kilmartin, C., McKelvey, D. K., & Kridel, M. M. (2015). College male sexual assault of women and the psychology of men: Past, present, and future directions for research. *Psychology of Men & Masculinity, 16*(4), 355–366. Retrieved from http://libproxy.usc.edu/login?url=http://search.proquest.com.libproxy2.usc.edu/docview/1717509333?accountid=14749

Messner, M., Greenberg, M., & Peretz, T. (2015). *Some men: Feminist allies in the movement to end violence against women.* New York, NY: Oxford University Press.

Mouilso, E. R., Calhoun, K. S., & Rosenbloom, T. G. (2013). Impulsivity and sexual assault in college men. *Violence and Victims, 28*(3), 429–442. doi:10.1891/0886-6708.VV-D-12-00025

National Academies of Sciences, Engineering, and Medicine. (2018). *Sexual harassment of women: Climate, culture, and consequences in academic sciences, engineering, and medicine.* Washington, DC: National Academies Press. doi:https://doi.org/10.17226/24994

Palmer, R. S., McMahon, T. J., Rounsaville, B. J., & Ball, S. A. (2010). Coercive sexual experiences, protective behavioral strategies, alcohol expectancies and consumption among male and female college students. *Journal of Interpersonal Violence, 25*(9), 1563–1578. doi:10.1177/0886260509354581

Patterson, D., & Campbell, R. (2010). Why rape survivors participate in the criminal justice system. *Journal of Community Psychology, 38*(2), 191–205. Retrieved from http://dx.doi.org.libproxy2.usc.edu/10.1002/jcop.20359

Porter, J., & Williams, L. M. (2011). Intimate violence among underrepresented groups on a college campus. *Journal of Interpersonal Violence, 26*(16), 3210–3224. doi:10.1177/0886260510393011

Richer, L., Fields, L., Bell, S., Heppner, J., Dodge, J., Boccellari, A., & Shumway, M. (2017). Characterizing drug-facilitated sexual assault subtypes and treatment engagement of victims at a hospital-based rape treatment center. *Journal of Interpersonal Violence, 32*(10), 1524–1542. doi:10.1177/0886260515589567

Riser, D. K., Pegram, S. E., & Farley, J. P. (2013). Adolescent and young adult male sex offenders: Understanding the role of recidivism. *Journal of Child Sexual Abuse, 22*(1), 9–31. Retrieved from http://search.proquest.com.libproxy2.usc.edu/docview/1282276486?accountid=14749

Rojas-Solís, J. L., & Raimúndez, E. C. (2011). Sexism and physical, sexual and verbal–emotional aggression in courtship relationships in university students. *Electronic Journal of Research in Educational Psychology, 9*(2), 541–564. Retrieved from http://

libproxy.usc.edu/login?url=http://search.proquest.com.libproxy1.usc.edu/docview/913454891?accountid=14749

Sanday, P. R. (2007). *Fraternity gang rape: Sex, brotherhood, and privilege on campus* (2nd ed.). New York, NY: New York University Press. Retrieved from http://libproxy.usc.edu/login?url=http://search.proquest.com.libproxy2.usc.edu/docview/621701628?accountid=14749

Saul, S., & Taylor, S. (2018, September 22). Betsy DeVos reverses Obama era policy on campus sexual assault investigations. *The New York Times*. Retrieved from https://www.nytimes.com/2017/09/22/us/devos-colleges-sex-assault.html

Scarce, M. (1997). Same-sex rape of male college students. *Journal of American College Health, 45*(4), 171–173. Retrieved from http://libproxy.usc.edu/login?url=http://search.proquest.com.libproxy2.usc.edu/docview/619069884?accountid=14749

Schuster, I., Krahé, B., & Toplu-Demirtaş, E. (2016). Prevalence of sexual aggression victimization and perpetration in a sample of female and male college students in Turkey. *Journal of Sex Research, 53*(9), 1139–1152. Retrieved from http://libproxy.usc.edu/login?url=http://search.proquest.com.libproxy2.usc.edu/docview/1835547086?accountid=14749

Seidman, I., & Pokorak, J. J. (2011). Justice responses to sexual violence. In M. P. Koss, J. W. White, & A. E. Kazdin (Eds.), *Violence against women and children, Volume 2: Navigating solutions* (pp. 137–157). Washington, DC: American Psychological Association.

Sharp, E. A., Weaver, S. E., & Zvonkovic, A. (2017). Introduction to the special issue: Feminist framings of sexual violence on college campuses. *Family Relations, 66*(1), 7–16. doi:10.1111/fare.12242

Sigre-Leirós, V., Carvalho, J., & Nobre, P. J. (2014). The role of psychopathological symptoms in the relationship between cognitive schemas and sexual aggression: A preliminary study. *Sexologies: European Journal of Sexology and Sexual Health, 23*(2), e25–e29. Retrieved from http://libproxy.usc.edu/login?url=http://search.proquest.com.libproxy2.usc.edu/docview/1559020178?accountid=14749

Stephens, K. A. (2009). *Rape prevention with Asian/Pacific Islander and Caucasian college men: The roles of culture and risk status* (Order No. AAI3328452). Available from PsycINFO (622048686; 2009-99060-319). Retrieved from http://search.proquest.com/docview/622048686?accountid=14749

Stephens, K. A., & George, W. H. (2009). Rape prevention with college men: Evaluating risk status. *Journal of Interpersonal Violence, 24*(6), 996–1013. Retrieved from http://dx.doi.org.libproxy2.usc.edu/10.1177/0886260508319366

Stotzer, R. L. (2017). Data sources hinder our understanding of transgender murders. *American Journal of Public Health, 107*(9), 1362–1363.

Testa, M., & Cleveland, J. (2017). Does alcohol contribute to college men's sexual assault perpetration? Between- and within-person effects over five semesters. *Journal of Studies on Alcohol and Drugs, 78*(1), 5–13.

Tomaszewska, P., & Krahé, B. (2018). Predictors of sexual aggression victimization and perpetration among Polish university students: A longitudinal study. *Archives of Sexual Behavior, 47*(2), 493–505. Retrieved from http://dx.doi.org.libproxy2.usc.edu/10.1007/s10508-016-0823-2

Torres-Pryor, J. (2004). *Relation between gender role beliefs, acculturation, and rape myth acceptance among a sample of Latino/a college students* (Order No. AAI3115671). Available from PsycINFO (620628986; 2004-99012-155). Retrieved from http://libproxy.usc.edu/login?url=http://search.proquest.com.libproxy2.usc.edu/docview/620628986?accountid=14749

Turchik, J. A. (2012). Sexual victimization among male college students: Assault severity, sexual functioning, and health risk behaviors. *Psychology of Men & Masculinity, 13*(3), 243–255. doi:10.1037/a0024605

Turchik, J. A., & Hassija, C. M. (2014). Female sexual victimization among college students: Assault severity, health risk behaviors, and sexual functioning. *Journal of Interpersonal Violence, 29*(13), 2439–2457. doi:10.1177/0886260513520230

US Department of Justice & US Department of Education. (2016). *Dear colleague letter on transgender students.* Washington, DC: Author.

van Langen, M. A. M., Wissink, I. B., van Vugt, E. S., Van der Stouwe, T., & Stams, G. J. J. M. (2014). The relation between empathy and offending: A meta-analysis. *Aggression and Violent Behavior, 19*(2), 179–189. Retrieved from http://dx.doi.org.libproxy2.usc.edu/10.1016/j.avb.2014.02.003

Voller, E. K., & Long, P. J. (2010). Sexual assault and rape perpetration by college men: The role of the Big Five personality traits. *Journal of Interpersonal Violence, 25*(3), 457–480. Retrieved from http://dx.doi.org.libproxy2.usc.edu/10.1177/0886260509334390

Wolitzky-Taylor, K. B., Resnick, H. S., Amstadter, A. B., McCauley, J. L., Ruggiero, K. J., & Kilpatrick, D. G. (2011). Reporting rape in a national sample of college women. *Journal of American College Health, 59*(7), 582–587. doi:10.1080/07448481.2010.515634

Yerke, A. F., & DeFeo, J. (2016). Redefining intimate partner violence beyond the binary to include transgender people. *Journal of Family Violence, 31*(8), 975–979.

Yung, C. R. (2015). Concealing campus sexual assault: An empirical examination. *Psychology, Public Policy, and Law, 21*, 1–9. http://dx.doi.org/10.1037/law0000037

Zawacki, T., Abbey, A., Buck, P. O., McAuslan, P., & Clinton-Sherrod, A. M. (2003). Perpetrators of alcohol-involved sexual assaults: How do they differ from other sexual assault perpetrators and nonperpetrators. *Aggressive Behavior, 29*, 366–380.

5

The Women of the Cheyenne River Sioux Tribe Reservation

Portrayals of Historical Trauma and Healing

CLARADINA SOTO, TONI HANDBOY, RUTH SUPRANOVICH,
AND EUGENIA L. WEISS ■

CASE STUDY: CAROL

"Carol" (a pseudonym) was born in 1975, the third eldest of 11 children born to "Karen." She is a member of a large extended Lakota family from the Cheyenne River Sioux Tribe Reservation in South Dakota. Karen's mother, "Mary," grew up in the boarding school era. At the mission-run boarding school, Mary (Carol's grandmother) was separated from her family and tribe, beaten for speaking her native tongue, and stripped of her Lakota beliefs and practices. The experience was traumatic and abusive, and it significantly impacted family relationships for generations to come. Separated from her mother during a critical time in her development as a woman, Mary was not taught about birth control, the sacredness of children, and the Lakota way of life for women and mothers. She missed out on the ceremonial traditions that introduce Lakota girls to womanhood and the Lakota values that guide family life. The Catholic-run boarding school provided no education on sexuality or birth control, and subsequently Mary had 5 children by five different fathers. Two generations later, Carol describes the family as "lacking attachment" and as having a notable absence of familial intimacy, such as hugs, kisses, and expressions of affection.

Karen was the eldest of Mary's 5 children and was conceived following a brief liaison between Mary and a "combiner" (combiners were White men who came to the area to work on the combines during harvest time). It was not uncommon at that time for local White ranchers or the more seasonal combiners to lure Native women with alcohol, gifts, and money. While the women sought an escape from poverty, the ranchers wanted access to tribal lands to raise cattle, and some of the methods used by these men were not unlike the sex trafficking of Native girls seen on the reservation today.

There is a generation of mixed-race children born in this era, although the children's paternity was often kept secret because mixed-race children were often rejected by the tribe. At that time, having a child with a White man brought great shame to the family. Mary acknowledged Karen's father was a White combiner, but her shame manifested in verbal and physical abuse to Karen. Mary was unable to teach Karen the Lakota rituals for womanhood, and so like her mother, Karen became pregnant as a teenager. At the age of 14 years, Karen was sent to a boarding school to avoid bringing shame to the family, and her mother gave her newborn son to an uncle to raise as his own. The family did not acknowledge Karen as the boy's mother until many years later. Karen never recovered from these early experiences. She drank alcohol heavily her entire life, eventually dying of complications related to alcoholism at the age of 51 years. All 11 of her children, including Carol, were raised either by relatives or in the foster care system. Only 3 of the 11 siblings had the same father, a Lakota man who also drank heavily, beat Karen severely, and was in and out of her and the children's lives until he passed away soon after Karen died. Only one man claimed his child, and that boy was placed with his relatives in another state and Karen was not able to see him again.

Carol lived with her grandparents on the reservation during her early childhood. She has fond memories of a "time of innocence," going to school, playing with friends, participating in traditional dances and rituals, and attending the local Sioux YMCA (the only YMCA located on an Indian reservation). Initially a fun place to play with friends, the YMCA became a refuge and "safe place" for Carol when, at age 9 years, an uncle living in the home began to sexually abuse her. When social workers "began sniffing around" the home, Carol's grandparents moved the entire family off the reservation to Rapid City, South Dakota. Carol's initial sense of relief was short-lived, however, because the uncle moved in with them again only 2 weeks later. She began running away to escape the abuse, and by age 11 years, she was placed in foster care by social services. After moving from group home to group home, she was eventually sent to live with a White foster family in Hot Springs, South Dakota, where she remained until she was 18 years old.

Carol states that this foster family "saved my life." She explains that they taught her "family values, morals and a strong work ethic" and have maintained a supportive role throughout her life—she refers to them as her adopted parents even though there was no formal adoption process. As devout Christians, they exposed her to their faith, and as a young adolescent, Carol connected with her spirituality in this context. As an older adolescent, however, Carol began her search for her identity, which eventually took her back to the reservation. There, she hoped to reconnect with her biological family and her Lakota heritage. Unfortunately, she was not welcomed as she expected. Her family and some community members criticized her for "dressing White, talking White, living White." Rather than rediscovering her identity as a Lakota woman, she became more confused about who she was and where she belonged. Carol began to drink heavily and started using street drugs.

At age 20 years, Carol married a non-Native man and soon after she had her first child, Lily. Despite being a heavy drinker and methamphetamine drug user, Carol abstained from alcohol and drugs while she was pregnant and Lily was born healthy and full-term. However, not long after Lily's birth, Carol resumed her drug and alcohol use, and soon her marriage was over. When Lily was just 2 years old, her father took custody of her and moved away. Carol plunged further into her addiction. Periodically, she entered drug treatment, only to relapse and return to old behaviors when life became challenging. She became involved with Ben, a Lakota man from the reservation, and was soon pregnant for a second time. Again, Carol maintained sobriety throughout the pregnancy, but after her son's birth, despite promises to herself to be a better mother, she began to leave her newborn with his uncle for increasing longer periods of time while she got high on drugs. When her son was 4 years old, his uncle died of cancer, and Carol knew then that she needed to be there for her son. She once again entered drug treatment, and this time it stuck.

Currently, Carol has been sober for 15 years, has obtained an undergraduate degree in social work and criminology, and is close to obtaining her master's degree in social work. A significant aspect of Carol's recovery has been a reclaiming of traditional Lakota practices and beliefs. She has reconnected with her spiritual self through the spirit of the White Buffalo Woman. She embraces Lakota practices and rituals to guide her in life, and she experiences the healing power of the sweat lodge and the Sun Dance. She strives to achieve balance in her physical, emotional, mental, and spiritual well-being and to "walk the path in a way that honors my people." As a recovery coach and case manager at a Behavioral Health Clinic on the reservation where she was born, she works with substance-abusing pregnant and parenting women to help them connect to their children, both in utero and after birth.

Along with a business partner, Carol has created a nonprofit organization whose mission is to offer holistic services for youth and adults to provide balance and alignment of the four aspects of traditional life: spiritual, mental, emotional, and physical. Their vision is to promote healing and wellness for adults and parents through connection with their history, culture, and traditional practices, as well as to promote leadership and cultural literacy for the youth on the reservation.

Carol would like to share a happy ending, but she is still on a journey. She works closely with a cultural mentor to help navigate the confusion she still experiences with regard to spirituality and cultural identity. Her family members both on and off the reservation have aligned more closely with Christianity, and she recalls a time when her grandmother was so immersed in Christianity that she told her that the Lakota traditions were "witchcraft," only to revert to her Lakota name and rituals prior to her death. Meanwhile, Carol's son, who became close to an uncle who was a devout Christian, rarely engages in Lakota ceremonies or spiritual events. Lily returned to live with Carol on the reservation when she was 11 years old and has come and gone since as the two of them strive to develop and maintain a mother–child bond. Carol lives with her 19-year-old son and his father, but Ben (the father) continues to struggle with alcoholism. Carol states, "I stayed with him for many years because my son wanted his father in his life despite our hardship."

During the year before Karen's death, Carol embraced the Lakota values of Wa'onsila (compassion for the aged, the sick, the poor, and less fortunate persons and caring sincerely from the heart) and Waohola (respect for all creatures in the universe, to have and show special respect to elders and women, and to respect yourself and your family) and took a year off school to care for her mother. She went through a process of forgiveness and healing as she learned more about her mother's own story. Karen had thick scars from self-injurious behaviors (repeated cuts and burns on both arms), evidence of self-loathing and attempts at self-destruction. Carol knew from her own experience and from what she had observed growing up that Karen, her mother, had also struggled with her identity as a Native woman. She knew that Karen was traumatized by rejection from her family and the subsequent rejection of her own children, from the rape and domestic violence that accompanied severe alcoholism, and from the guilt and shame of failing as a mother—the most sacred and important role for the Lakota woman. Carol knew that to break the cycle she too had perpetuated, she needed to mend this fissure. She hopes it will pave the way for her children to do the same for her.

Carol's family history illustrates the devastating effects of colonialism on women. It is hoped that the following discussion will help elucidate how colonialism has disrupted the traditional way of life for Native American families and how the enforcement of European patriarchy on Lakota women has resulted in generations of women who have lost connection with their traditional role in transmitting essential lessons on womanhood to their children.

OVERVIEW

Carol's story, and that of many indigenous women throughout the world, is one fraught with the scars of the aftermath of colonialism. To better understand this situation, this chapter begins by defining terms and demographics globally and in the United States, and then it provides a general understanding of the challenges for indigenous women throughout the world. Next, it describes the impact of the attempted physical and cultural genocide of Native Americans in the United States to provide a context for understanding why so many women face similar problems as those faced by Mary, Karen, and Carol. We describe the concept of "historical trauma" as applied to Native Americans (Brave Heart, 1999) and how indigenous practices and traditions can guide the grieving process and promote healing and regeneration. Finally, we share some of the mythical stories of the power of the Lakota woman and the value placed on children in this community to consider how this narrative provides an opportunity for Lakota women to reclaim their role as the bringers of the next generation and the promise for the future.

Key Terms

Although there is no universally agreed upon definition of indigenous peoples, there are characteristics of communities or populations that are often recognized and accepted as indigenous. Indigenous people are descendants of precolonial or presettler societies who experience a strong relationship to the ecosystem of their ancestral home. They have a distinct culture from the dominant postcolonial culture of their country and are often minority populations within the postcolonial nation states. They attempt to maintain a language and belief system and often have their own social, economic, and political systems. They have a desire to maintain or revive their ancestral environment, culture, and identity (United Nations, 2018; World Health Organization, 2007). The term *indigenous* can vary by region and population and is used to describe "First Nations," which are populations indigenous to Canada; "Australian Aboriginal" or "Torres Strait Islanders" for the Australian indigenous; "Tangata Whenua" or "People of the land" for the Maori people of New Zealand; and "Native American" or "American Indian/Alaskan Natives" (AI/AN) for the US indigenous populations.

Global Demographics

According to the United Nations, in 2014 there were an estimated 370 million indigenous peoples living in more than 70 countries throughout the world. The International Work Group for Indigenous Affairs (IWGIA) more generally states that indigenous peoples constitute 5% of the world's population and that in comparison to non-indigenous communities, indigenous peoples overall are poorer, less educated, die younger, are in worse health, and are more likely to commit suicide (IWGIA, 2006).

In 2012, the United Nations Commission on the Status of Women concluded that indigenous women throughout the world are affected by multiple forms of discrimination and are especially vulnerable to poverty and violence. The IWGIA (2018) indigenous world report states, "Indigenous women and girls are more marginalized and vulnerable than the overall Indigenous population" (p. 607). This report chronicles the current status of indigenous people by geographic region and notes the continuing oppression of indigenous women in countries throughout the world, such as Canada (e.g., the National Inquiry into Missing and Murdered Indigenous Women and Girls), Peru (e.g., the forced sterilization of Andean and Amazonian women from 1996 to 2000), Vietnam (e.g., women excluded from land ownership and education, and rampant domestic violence), and India (e.g., rape of indigenous women by police and military). The United Nations Committee on the Elimination of Discrimination against Women has called out the excessive human rights violations against indigenous women and their systematic discrimination in countries such as Costa Rica, Paraguay, and Rwanda (IWGIA, 2018). This is especially concerning when one considers the critical role that women play in keeping indigenous cultures alive and transferring indigenous knowledge and values to the next generation. The IWGIA world report further states that indigenous women have been "the guardians of knowledge since time immemorial" (p. 594) and notes that the empowerment of indigenous women is critical to the economic sustainability and the exercise of indigenous rights. The IWGIA refers to indigenous women as the key to "good living" or "living well" in collective harmony and connection with "Mother Earth," reminiscent of Carol's desire to "walk in a path that honors my people." The empowerment of indigenous women was a primary theme of the 10-year anniversary celebration of the United Nations Declaration on the Rights of Indigenous Peoples, with a focus on the social and economic rights of indigenous women as well as protection from all forms of violence (IWGIA, 2018).

US Demographics

According to the US Census Bureau, in 2016 there were 6.7 million American Indian and Alaska Natives living in the United States, comprising approximately 2% of the population. There are 567 federally recognized Indian tribes and many urban AI/AN—individuals of AI ancestry and diverse tribal affiliation who have moved from their reservation to urban areas to seek employment, education, or housing or by force through federal government relocation policies (Fleming, 1992). The 2016 American Community Survey reported that 26.2% of single-race AI/AN people lived in poverty in 2016, the highest rate of any race group (the poverty rate for the United States as a whole was 14%). Women comprise approximately 50% of the American Indian population, but this percentage increases as the population ages (US Census Bureau, 2017).

With more than 560 distinct federally recognized American Indian tribes in the United States, many straddling the borders with Canada and Mexico, there is no one common language, religion, or value system. Each tribal community has a unique and local history and present-day priorities to sustain their traditional and cultural way of life. Although there are commonalities, it is a mistake to make broad generalizations about Native American culture. This is especially true for the roles of men and women and views about gender and sexuality, with some tribes maintaining a historical matrilineal or patrilineal line of descent. In matriarchal societies, in contrast to patriarchal ones, the mother is the head of the family, clan, or tribe. The status of women varies by tribe.

There are some common experiences for all American Indian and Alaska Natives in the United States, one of the most painful of which is the loss of their children (Weaver, 2005), clearly illustrated by Carol's story. However, even the backdrop of these losses varies from tribe to tribe and region to region, depending on the geographic location and the arrival and movement of the settlers.

HISTORICAL TRENDS OF THE LAKOTA

Prior to the colonization of the United States, the Lakota were a thriving nation. Lakota women were revered as mothers of each new generation, and Lakota men were noble warriors, hunters, and protectors. Children were raised free of violence. *Mitakuye Oyasin* is a Lakota phrase that conveys the Lakota belief that "we are all related." The Lakota people lived by the principle that all Lakota are bound to each other, to all living things, and to the earth. This philosophy helped maintain a strong respect for all humans, animals, and the land on which we all live. Children are considered sacred in the Lakota tradition. *Wakanjeja* translates in the English language to "child," but the word derives from the Lakota words *Waka*, which means sacred, and *Yeja*, meaning gift. The sacredness of children is derived from the traditional and cultural belief that children are pure and a divine means for the Lakota people to connect to their spirituality and are the key for the preservation of future generations (Sarche, Spicer, Farrell, & Fitzgerald, 2011). Traditionally, Lakota children were raised mostly by the elderly in the family because the elders are holders of the cultural wisdom of the people. Elders are responsible for passing down the Lakota values, beliefs, and practices. Culturally, all Lakota children knew the role of the older relatives in the community and would naturally gravitate to them. The Lakota spirituality, language, cultural values, and traditions upheld a strong and healthy people and reverence and respect for the environment. But after more than 200 years of human and cultural devastation due to wars, reservations, boarding schools, introduction of diseases, trauma, and alcohol, the Lakota people have suffered greatly.

Precolonialism, Native societies were not male dominated for the most part, and violence against women and children was rare (Harper & Entrekin, 2006). With colonization came a focus on male-dominated economies, resulting in the devaluation and marginalization of Native women (Smith, 2005). The patriarchy of the European settlers was imposed upon the Native tribes, and Lakota women were stripped of their traditional spiritually and very powerful status in their communities by this settler worldview (Braveheart-Jordan & DeBruyn, 1995). In the Lakota culture, children were not viewed as property, and motherhood and caring for children held an elevated position. The introduction of alcohol, negotiation of treaties only with men, and the reservation system all served to undermine the status of Lakota women. The notion of land ownership and the extermination of buffalo herds undermined the female symbols of earth and buffalo. Boarding schools further robbed women of their important role, and if mothers refused to send their children to the schools, they were punished with sanctions of rations on food, clothing, and education. With the children gone, the woman's role as caretaker of the children was eliminated. Meanwhile, the Lakota man was robbed of his role as hunter, provider, and protector, which negatively impacted his relationship with women and children (Braveheart-Jordan & DeBruyn, 1995). Smith describes today's sexual violence in Native communities as the colonial legacy of boarding schools and evidence of the intertwining of state violence and interpersonal violence. The distortion of traditional gender roles, the destructive influence of alcohol, and the assimilation that has occurred in terms of sex role socialization have together led to the oppression of the less powerful (i.e., women and children) by both Native and non-Native men (Braveheart-Jordan & DeBruyn, 1995).

Another aspect of colonialism that is a common experience for indigenous women throughout the world is the use of rape and sexual assault to wipe out indigenous communities and control Native people (Harper & Entrekin, 2006). In North America, this sexual assault continued in the boarding schools, where both boys and girls were often physically and sexually abused by their non-Native adult caretakers (Braveheart-Jordan & DeBruyn, 1995; Harper & Entrekin, 2006; Weaver, 2009). The legacy is an intergenerational pattern of sexual vulnerability for women and children that continues today. AI/AN women of all ages are significantly more likely to be victims of sexual assault and domestic violence than any other ethnic group in the United States (Fox, Fisher, & Decker, 2018), and most often by non-Native men (Rosay, 2016). Sapra, Jubinski, Tanaka, and Gershon (2014) document the high rates of child abuse and neglect, intimate partner violence, and concerns about elder abuse for AI/AN, and they make the link to both the consequences and risk factors prevalent in AI/AN communities, such as poverty, lack of education, and substance abuse, as well as the role of historical trauma and ongoing oppression. This cycle can be seen in Carol's family, in which drug and alcohol use by both her and her mother was used to cope with prior trauma and loss but then exposed them to further trauma and loss in a continuous loop that began long ago, first with the loss of traditional family roles and then with the severing of family bonds when Mary was sent to the boarding schools.

Historical Trauma

There are many negative outcomes facing indigenous populations globally that are linked to historical trauma and intergenerational trauma. *Historical trauma* describes a complex and collective experience of traumatic events that occur over time and across generations by a group of people (Brave Heart, 2003). Although historical trauma was introduced to describe the experience of Holocaust survivors, this term can be applied to other oppressed populations globally, such as Armenian refugees, Japanese survivors of internment camps, Canadian First Nations with a family history of forced boarding school, Swedish immigrant children, and family and community survivors of large and significant group traumas such as major wars and natural disasters (Mohatt, Thompson, Thai, & Tebes, 2014). Among oppressed and victimized American Indians, historical trauma has caused much soul wound. Soul wound occurs when the soul or culture of a person is repressed or maltreated, and healing is necessary to bring balance to the individual (Duran, 2006; Duran & Duran, 1995). Among the US Northern Plains tribes, if severe abuse or trauma is experienced by an individual, it is believed that the soul or spirit may leave the body, allowing another spirit to enter (i.e., sadness). In order to heal the individual, a set of healing ceremonies are vital to bring the natural spirit back to the person (Duran, Firehammer, & Gonzalez, 2008).

American Indian and Alaska Natives have experienced genocidal policies, pandemics, forced relocation, removal of children from their families and into boarding schools, and government bans against ceremonies (Brave Heart, 1998a, 1998b; Duran & Duran, 1995; Walls & Whitbeck, 2011). Historical trauma refers to the cumulative effect of these collective experiences as a contributing factor to the destruction of many tribal communities and their cultural way of life (Brave Heart, 2000). According to Mary Yellow Horse Brave Heart (2003), historical trauma is the "cumulative emotional and psychological wounding over the lifespan and across generations emanating from massive group experience" (p. 5). Daily reminders of historical trauma still exist today: impoverished living conditions on reservations, loss of language, loss and confusion regarding traditional beliefs and practices, and loss of traditional family systems (Evans-Campbell, 2008; Whitbeck, Adams, Hoyt, & Chen, 2004).

Although many AI/ANs are generations removed from the direct historical trauma events, the trauma associated with such events can remain in their families and their emotional lives (Danieli, 1998; Whitbeck, McMorris, Hoyt, Stubben, & LaFromboise, 2002). It is possible for the transmission of parents' traumatic experience to be passed to their children. The emotional consequences of historical trauma are transmitted to subsequent generations through physiological, environmental, and social pathways (Brave Heart, 2003; Danieli, 1998; Duran & Duran, 1995; Sotero, 2006), also known as *intergenerational trauma*. A study by Whitbeck et al. (2004) found that American Indians who have not directly experienced the historical traumatic events have frequently (at least once a day) thought about loss of indigenous lands, loss of indigenous language, loss of culture, and loss associated with boarding schools. These frequent thoughts could also stem from the high rates of contemporary lifetime trauma and interpersonal violence, as well as daily discriminatory events (Walters et al., 2011). It has been suggested that historical trauma contributes to AI/AN family violence. Many AI/ANs grew up in a boarding school during the 19th and 20th centuries, when the US government attempted to kill, remove, or assimilate AI/ANs. AI/AN children were removed from their homes at a very young age to attend boarding schools, where they were not allowed to speak their traditional language, wear their clothing, or practice any of their traditional cultural ways. These experiences interrupted the intergenerational transmission of healthy parenting practices and instead created violent behaviors by parents, raised in a boarding school, who anguished and carried much anger and grief inside (Evans-Campbell, 2008). The role of the boarding schools in the disintegration of Carol's family robbed the women of the traditional pathways to transmit cultural knowledge and practices, and in its place addiction and violence became a way of life, piling trauma upon trauma.

RECENT DEVELOPMENTS OF NOTE

The Cheyenne River Sioux Tribe (CRST) reservation is the fourth largest reservation in the United States at 4,267 square miles, and it spans both Dewey County and Ziebach County in South Dakota. Ziebach County consistently rates as one of the poorest counties in the United States, with a median income significantly less than that of most other counties in South Dakota and in the United States (Data USA, 2016). According to the 2016 American Community Survey (US Census Bureau, 2017), the total population on the reservation is 8,459, with 4,291 female residents and approximately 3,000 residents younger than age 18 years. This large reservation is made up of 16 communities, the largest being Eagle Butte. Several of these communities are small and remote from one another, yet they are connected by a common tribal governance and a shared Lakota heritage. The dispersed nature of the CRST communities poses many risks to the residents, especially related to access to health and social services.

In 2016, there were 858 children younger than age 5 years, 1,670 children aged 5–14 years, and 731 youth aged 15–19 years living on the CRST reservation. Thirty-three percent of families with children younger than age 18 years in the home lived below the poverty level (US Census Bureau, 2017). Like Carol and her family, these children are witness to the many struggles and challenges of their parents, relatives, and communities. Although there are several elders on the reservation who continue to practice Lakota spiritual and cultural traditions, many youth do not have access to these individuals. Too many youth predominantly observe adults who have abandoned traditional ways due to the influence of drugs and alcohol use to dull the pain of the loss and trauma of current and historical abuses. The result is that many Lakota youth struggle to see a positive future for themselves, become hopeless, and engage in these same destructive behaviors.

Suicide is the ultimate expression of hopelessness, and according to the Great Plains Area Indian Health Service Division of Behavioral Health, aggregate suicide data from January to December 2017 on the CRST reservation indicate there were 6completed suicides, 118 attempts, and 171 individuals reporting ideation with a plan and intent to carry it out. Although women were less likely to be successful in their attempts, they attempted suicide at much higher rates than men; of all children and youth younger than age 18 years with reported suicidal behavior documented by the Indian Health Service on the CRST reservation, 75% were listed as female. When youth feel hopeless and helpless, they act outward (e.g., violence toward others and related crimes), act inward (e.g., engage in substance abuse, self-harm, and suicide), or sometimes both. Carol's mother evidenced scars of her attempts at self-destruction, and in addition to the self-annihilating intent of alcoholism and addiction, Carol also made more direct attempts on her life beginning in adolescence.

Although no specific data are available, Carol is not only an example but also can provide testimony to the prevalence of drug-exposed infants both in utero and after birth on the CRST reservation. Driving around Eagle Butte, there is the visual reminder of the boarded-up houses (the US Department of Housing and Urban Development condemns any home in which there is evidence of methamphetamine use) of the scourge of methamphetamine manufacturing and use in the community.

CURRENT CONDITIONS

The present-day impact of the past can be observed at the individual level and the population level. For AI/ANs, historical trauma and intergenerational trauma are associated with impaired family communication (Evans-Campbell, 2008), symptoms of post-traumatic stress disorder, survivor guilt, anxiety, depression, suicidality, cultural identity, and substance use (Ehlers, Gizer, Gilder, Ellingson, & Yehuda, 2013; Whitbeck et al., 2004). At the community level, the historical and ongoing experiences of trauma and oppression for AI/ANs have manifested in the highest poverty rate of any race in the United States (US Census Bureau, 2017), unemployment rates far above the national average (US Bureau of Labor Statistics, 2017), suicide rates significantly and consistently higher than those for the general population (National Center for Health Statistics, n.d.), disproportionately high rates of substance abuse disorders (SAMHSA, 2012), high rates of physical and sexual violence against women (Rosay, 2016), disproportionate rates of chronic physical and mental illnesses (Roh et al., 2015), and an overrepresentation of Native American children in both the child welfare system and in the juvenile justice system (US Department of Health & Human Services, 2015).

During a recent visit to the CRST reservation, two of the authors asked various community members and leaders about their primary concern for the young people, and they immediately referenced the high rates of methamphetamine use and associated violence and crime. Tribal leaders have explored unusual means to try to stem the flow of the drug, such as recent laws banning from the reservation tribal members who are found to be selling and trafficking methamphetamine on the reservation.

Carol's story illustrates the intergenerational impact of her grandmother's boarding school experience across three generations of women. Their cultural identity, the essence of their being, was assaulted repeatedly, leaving them vulnerable to new and continued assaults from poverty, addiction, mental illness, and violence. From a transnational and postcolonial feminist perspective, we can appreciate the critical and intersectional (multiple identities such as race [e.g., Native American] and gender [e.g., female]) aspects of indigenous women's loss of power not only in a local context but also in a global sense. The introduction of European patriarchy impacted indigenous women's participation in political, economic, and religious domains within their tribes and represented a loss of social status (Rojas, 2009).

Although the previous description paints a dismal picture of the legacy of colonialism on indigenous people worldwide, in the United States, and on the Lakota people in particular, there is hope for healing and regeneration. Carol is among many indigenous women throughout the world who recognize and embrace the traditions and practices of their original ancestors who thrived successfully for millennia. A visit to the CRST reservation will undoubtedly impress visitors with the obvious poverty and associated travails, but once they meet and interact with some of the tribal members and meet some of the youth, the overwhelming take away is one of hope and resilience. The Dakota Pipeline (DPL) protests of 2017 gave the world an example of the tenacity of the Lakota people. Communicating the Lakota value of *Mitakuye Oyasin*, a resident of the CRST reservation who had been at the protest site with many local youth stated, "We protest for the water, for the land, for all of us—not just for the Lakota, but for all humans and all living things because we all need the Mother Earth to survive" (anonymous resident, personal communication, March 2017).

Jasilyn Charger, a 19-year-old member of the CRST reservation, was profiled in *The New York Times Magazine* for her efforts to bring together Lakota youth to form the One Mind Youth Movement. Initially a group of youth on the reservation who wanted to do something about youth suicide, they became a political movement joining daily protests at the DPL protest site. The Indigenous Environmental Network (IEN) also joined this protest and identified the potential of the One Mind Youth as community leaders. IEN paid for Jasilyn to travel to Washington, DC, to learn about community organizing and for another One Mind group member to travel to Australia to network with Aboriginal climate activists. The young people from CRST now make the connection between the DPL and the larger struggles of indigenous people throughout the world. The prophecy of the black snake from Lakota mythology is no longer just a reference to the oil pipeline for the Lakota people; rather, it symbolizes a more malevolent force infecting indigenous communities throughout the world with dysfunction, addiction, loss, and trauma (Elbien, 2017).

LOOKING TO THE FUTURE

There are several areas in behavioral health treatment, education, and youth leadership programs that are representative of changing times. For instance, in the helping professions, there has been a push to move beyond general cross-cultural competence when working with AI/AN communities (Baltra-Ulloa, 2013) to a more specific focus on recruiting and training of AI/AN mental health practitioners (Goforth, Brown, Machek, & Swaney, 2016), an encouragement to consider cultural adaptations of typical helping strategies and interventions (Bigfoot & Schmidt, 2010), as well as tribe-specific interventions such as Maria Yellow Horse Brave Heart's (1999a) *Oyate Ptayela* parenting program for Lakota families and the "Cherokee Talking Circles" developed for use with United Keetoowah Band of Cherokee Indians youth with substance abuse problems (Lowe, Liang, Riggs, & Henson, 2012). In post-secondary education, some undergraduate and graduate educational program texts, such as *Decolonizing Social Work* (Gray, Coates, Yellow Bird, & Hetherington, 2013) and *The Psychologies of Liberation* (Watkins & Shulman, 2008), are beginning to be required readings.

Among AI/AN communities, youth leadership programs have become an important aspect of community development for many tribes. The United National Indian Tribal Youth (UNITY) formed more than 40 years ago to bring together AI/AN youth leaders and now has members from 160 youth councils representing 35 states and Canada (UNITY, n.d.). UNITY's mission is to "foster the spiritual, mental, physical and social development of American Indian and Alaska Native youth, and to help build a strong, unified and self-reliant Native America through involvement of its youth" (UNITY, 2010, para. 1). In 1980, youth leaders wrote a "Declaration for Independence" in order to take charge of their future through participation in government and economic development (UNITY, 2010). A key aspect of AI/AN youth councils is the preparation of Native youth for leadership positions in their communities and as future leaders of their sovereign nations as well as leaders in US government and politics if they choose. The role of traditional practices and values is forefront. The One Mind Youth Group described previously has grown into an international effort called the International Indigenous Youth Council with a goal to create a more positive future for everyone (Elbein, 2017).

On the CRST reservation, both the Sioux YMCA and the Cheyenne River Youth Project (CRYP) offer opportunities for youth to connect with their culture and language and to develop healthy coping skills such as job training at CRYP and social skills training at the YMCA. At the Wolves Den Boxing Club, young boys struggling to express their traditional role as warrior and protector are steered toward the healthy expression of feelings and physical fitness through organized boxing events. An essential requirement of being a boxing club member is joining elders and adults familiar with traditional practices at regular cultural events, such as Sun Dance, Days of Mourning, Kettle dance, and Welcoming Thunder of New Moons of Spring (Joe Brings Plenty, personal communication, June 6, 2018). Carol hopes to create a similar program for young women and pregnant and parenting mothers so they can reconnect with their traditional role as creators and caretakers of the next generation. This can bring hope not only to mothers currently struggling with addiction and parenting issues but also to future mothers who can embrace the revered responsibility of Lakota women to bare and raise children well so that the Lakota people can thrive and grow and fulfill their commitment to *Mitakuye Oyasin*.

Advocacy

To counter the impact of colonialism, and to dismantle neocolonialist systems of oppression that exist despite declarations of independence and sovereignty, many professions have explored the notion of decolonizing their practices—for example, in education (Battiste, Bell, & Findlay, 2002), psychology (Duran & Duran, 1995), and social work (Gray et al., 2013). This process includes learning the history of indigenous people where you live and work and, importantly, learning from the indigenous people themselves. Non-indigenous do-gooders have historically done more harm than good by imposing their ideas of what "help" the indigenous group needs and receives. History books are full of well-meaning missionaries, politicians, and advocates who have all played a role in decimating indigenous communities and exterminating indigenous cultures. Decolonizing practices are bottom-up and enable interventions and education that are locally relevant and requested. As an advocate for indigenous people, one of the primary things a person can do to decolonize is educate others about the real history of genocide and destruction of indigenous populations to deconstruct colonial myths and make the invisible visible. Watkins and Shulman (2008) note the negative impact on everyone when one group is oppressed and marginalized. They provide guidance on how to move from being a perpetrator of or bystander to oppression to a person who bears witness, reframes the narrative, and supports communities of resistance.

Changing the narrative is an especially powerful action to which people can personally commit and encourage others to do the same. Recent research found that when non-Natives are provided with an accurate narrative about Native American history and current conditions, their perceptions of Native Americans change significantly for the better (Campisteguy, Heilbronner, & Nakamura-Rybak, 2018). This 2-year research project employed multiple methods of data gathering across broad groups of people in the United States and found that individuals and groups with limited exposure to Native Americans and limited knowledge about Native American history were more likely to buy into negative narratives and stereotypes. The research groups found that when the history was accurately presented, it opened the door to critical conversations about current conditions. Conversations uncovered deep respect for Native values and many shared values, such as fairness, connection, unity, and patriotism. This speaks powerfully to the potential for education and conversation to change the narrative and promote healing and hope.

Internationally, support and advocacy for the United Nations Declaration on the Rights of Indigenous Peoples is needed. Charters and Stavenhagen (2009) produced a document to educate about the Declaration and what individuals, groups, and countries can do to make this aspirational document become a reality. A transnational feminist perspective also renders great potential for multiple and global social movements of resistance (Foster, 2018). According to Chandra Mohanty (2003),

> A transnational feminist practice depends on building feminist solidarity across the divisions of place, identity, class, work, belief and so on. In these very fragmented times it is both very difficult to build these alliances ["communities of resistance"] and also never more important to do so. (p. 250)

Those drawn more to the arts can engage in the "liberation arts"; those more inclined toward the sciences and research can consider approaches such as "critical participatory action research" (Watkins & Shulman, 2008). Furthermore, as stated by Strega and Brown (2015), engagement in research must encompass a social justice perspective and be anti-oppressive; the authors suggest that "investigating the strengths and strategies that allow communities and individuals to survive marginalization might make a better contribution" (p. 5) rather than focusing only on deficit-based perspectives. The researcher has to acknowledge his or her social location or position (i.e., privilege) (Potts & Brown, 2015). Gaudry (2015) adds the following principles with regard to research with indigenous populations that engages the community:

1. Research is grounded in, respects and validates Indigenous worldviews.
2. Research output is intended for use by Indigenous communities.
3. Researchers are responsible to Indigenous communities for the decisions that they make, and communities are the final judges of the validity and effectiveness of research projects.
4. Research is action oriented and inspires direct action in Indigenous communities. (p. 248)

On the other hand, supporting indigenous advocacy groups should be done care-fully, ensuring that the groups include indigenous people in leadership positions in their organizations. Non-Native advocates are cautioned to vet a group's credibility with other indigenous people or allies familiar with the cause before committing money, time, and resources. Non-Natives are advised to always engage respectfully with indigenous people and focus not only on the community concerns but also on its strengths.

CONCLUSION

This chapter provides a glimpse into the experiences of indigenous women at vari-ous levels of analysis in terms of history, culture, interpersonal violence, and even internalized oppression. The intersectional aspects of being both Native American and female present further complexities associated with multiple social identities and how to navigate a sense of womanhood, motherhood, and an indigenous iden-tity within postcolonial structures and patriarchal institutions. The ripple effects of historical trauma and intergenerational trauma have served to maintain the status quo. However, by giving voice through this chapter to the Lakota and specifically to the women of the CRST reservation, we hope to make the invisible (and excluded) into the visible (and included). The journey of Carol as depicted in the opening case study is only one individual's example of strength and triumph in overcom-ing adversity through service to the community. It represents the shared hope of many who are empowered despite the challenges of marginalization through domi-nant boundaries and discourses that have failed to reflect the actual power, beauty, wisdom, and resistance of Native Americans in the United States and indigenous people throughout the world. We need to continue to nurture future generations and realize that as a human race, we are all in it together to create a better and more just world.

Update: Since writing the first draft of this chapter, Carol has made some sig-nificant changes in her life. She is no longer living with her son's father, and she has resumed her social work education that had been on hold. She has also begun to focus on her personal well-being and has lost weight through diet and exercise, which has positively impacted her mood and energy level. Sharing her story has inspired her to reinvest in her journey toward healing for herself, her family, and her community.

DISCUSSION QUESTIONS

1. What is the legacy of colonialism on indigenous communities, specifically the effects on women?
2. What is meant by decolonizing practices? Provide examples.
3. What are some ways that you can advocate for indigenous communities and get involved in activism?

NARRATIVES FROM THE FRONT LINES

Letter from Carol to Her Mother Karen[1]

March 10, 2011

Dear Mother:

I want to let you know I love you. I always wanted to know where you were when I needed you the most. When I needed to talk or just laugh. All the times I was so faraway I always thought of you. I would hope and pray that one day you would just say I'm sorry for not being there in your time of need my girl. Well I forgot to tell you all things I wanted to say to you. Now that I have a chance I will.

Thank you for having me and bringing me into this world. You gave me a special gift of life. I have been given an opportunity to bring two more beautiful lives into this world. Thank you for being there for me when I was sick in Sioux Falls. Thank you being there for me when my son was born. Thank you for being at my graduation in Hot Springs. Thank you for thinking of me and searching for me throughout the night when I was a troubled teenager. Most of all thank you for being you.

I thought I knew what is was to be you. What I do know is that you are a beautiful woman, you had a very strong heart and were also a hard worker with a passionate heart. Every time I would see you, there you were worried about someone else, cooking, cleaning and doing everything you could do to keep yourself busy.

Now I know why, it was something we both shared an addiction. I never really understood why you were not there for me, now I know why. Well I know I love you as your daughter and the journey God has taken you. Thank You mom for teaching me that my addiction, is that, just an addiction. I am here and I will be there for my kids in any time of need.

I never really knew, now I do and I understand. What and who you are is what makes you uniquely you. You always was so strong and that is unique. The many times God came to take you home you stayed. It was all for a specific reason, maybe you couldn't say or speak it at the end, but I believe it was because you wanted us to know your love. Above it all we know mom . . . I love you now today and always your daughter . . .

"Carol" (dedicated to all those who've lost loved ones to alcoholism)

[1] Reprinted with permission from Carol.

REFERENCES

Baltra-Ulloa, A. J. (2013). Why decolonized social work is more than cross-culturalism. In M. Gray, J. Coates, M. Yellow Bird & T. Hetherington (Eds.), Decolonizing Social Work (pp. 87–104). New York, NY: Routledge.

Battiste, M., Bell, L., & Findlay, L. M. (2002). Decolonizing education in Canadian universities: An interdisciplinary, international, Indigenous research project. *Canadian Journal of Native Education, 26*, 82–95.

Bigfoot, D. S., & Schmidt, S. R. (2010). Honoring children, mending the circle: cultural adaptation of trauma-focused cognitive-behavioral therapy for American Indian and Alaska Native children. *Journal of Clinical Psychology, 66*(8), 847–856.

Brave Heart, M. Y. H. (1998a). The American Indian holocaust: Healing historical unresolved grief. *American Indian and Alaska Native Mental Health Research, 8*(2), 56.

Brave Heart, M. Y. H. (1998b). The return to the sacred path: Healing the historical trauma and historical unresolved grief response among the Lakota through a psychoeducational group intervention. *Smith College Studies in Social Work, 68*(3), 287–305. doi:10.1080/00377319809517532

Brave Heart, M. Y. H. (1999). Oyate Ptayela: Rebuilding the Lakota Nation through addressing historical trauma among Lakota parents. *Journal of Human Behavior in the Social Environment, 2*(1–2), 109–126.

Brave Heart, M. Y. H. (2000). Wakiksuyapi: Carrying the historical trauma of the Lakota. *Tulane Studies in Social Welfare, 245*–253. Retrieved from http://discoveringour story. wisdomoftheelders.org/ht_and_grief/WakiksuyapiHT.pdf

Brave Heart, M. Y. H. (2003). The historical trauma response among Natives and its relationship with substance abuse: A Lakota illustration. *Journal of Psychoactive Drugs, 35*(1), 7–13.

Braveheart-Jordan, M., & DeBruyn, L. (1995). *Racism in the lives of women: Testimony, theory and guides to antiracist practice.* New York, NY: Haworth.

Campisteguy, M. E., Heilbronner, J. M., & Nakamura-Rybak, C. (2018). *Research findings: Complication of all research.* Reclaiming Native Truth. Retrieved from https://firstnations.org/

Charters, C., & Stavenhagen, R. (Eds.). (2009). *Making the declaration: The United Nations Declaration on the Rights of Indigenous Peoples.* Copenhagen, Denmark: United Nations.

Danieli, Y. (1998). *International handbook of multigenerational legacies of trauma.* New York, NY: Plenum Press.

Duran, E. (2006). *Healing the soul wound: Counseling with American Indians and other Native peoples.* New York, NY: Teachers College Press.

Duran, E., & Duran, B. (1995). *Native American postcolonial psychology.* New York, NY: State University of New York Press.

Duran, E., Firehammer, J., & Gonzalez, J. (2008). Liberation psychology as the path toward healing cultural soul wounds. *Journal of Counseling & Development, 86*(3), 288–295.

Ehlers, C. L., Gizer, I. R., Gilder, D. A., Ellingson, J. M., & Yehuda, R. (2013). Measuring historical trauma in an American Indian community sample: Contributions of substance dependence, affective disorder, conduct disorder and PTSD. *Drug and Alcohol Dependence, 133*(1), 180–187.

Elbein, S. (2017). The youth group that launched a movement at standing rock. *The New York Times Magazine, 31.*

Evans-Campbell, T. (2008). Historical trauma in American Indian/Native Alaska communities: A multilevel framework for exploring impacts on individuals, families, and communities. *Journal of Interpersonal Violence, 23*(3), 316–338.

Fleming, C. M. (1992). American Indians and Alaska Natives: Changing societies past and present. In M. A. Orlandi (Ed.), *Cultural competence for evaluators: A guide for alcohol and other drug abuse prevention practitioners working with ethnic/racial communities* (pp. 147–161). Rockville, MD: Alcohol, Drug Abuse, and Mental Health Administration.

Foster, J. (2018). Key feminist theoretical orientations in contemporary feminist practice. In S. Butler-Mokoro & L. Grant (Eds.), *Feminist perspectives on social work practice: The intersecting lives of women in the 21st century* (pp. 35–58). New York, NY: Oxford University Press.

Fox, K. A., Fisher, B. S., & Decker, S. H. (2018). Identifying the needs of American Indian women who sought shelter: A practitioner–researcher partnership. *Journal of Family Violence, 33*(4), 251–256.

Gaudry, A. (2015). Researching the resurgence: Insurgent research and community-engaged methodologies the 21st-century academic inquiry. In S. Strega & L. Brown (Eds.), *Research as resistance: Revisiting critical, indigenous, and anti-oppressive approaches* (2nd ed., pp. 243–265). Toronto, Ontario, Canada: Canadian Scholars Press.

Gray, M., Coates, J., Yellow Bird, M., & Hetherington, T. (Eds.). (2013). *Decolonizing Social Work.* New York, NY: Routledge.

Harper, S. S., & Entrekin, C. M. (2006). *Violence against Native women: A guide for practitioner action (GrantNo. 96-VF-GX-K005).* Washington, DC: Oceon Violence Against Women and the National Center on Full Faith and Credit.

International Work Group for Indigenous Affairs. (2006). *IWGIA annual report, 2005.* Retrieved from https://www.iwgia.org/images/publications/0549_annual_report_05.pdf

International Work Group for Indigenous Affairs. (2018, April). *The Indigenous world.* Retrieved from https://www.iwgia.org/images/documents/indigenous-world/indigenous-world-2018.pdf

Lowe, J., Liang, H., Riggs, C., Henson, J., & Elder, T. (2012). Community partnership to affect substance abuse among Native American adolescents. *The American Journal of Drug and Alcohol Abuse, 38*(5), 450–455.

Mohanty, C. T. (2003). *Feminism without borders: Decolonizing theory, practicing solidarity.* Durham, NC: Duke University Press.

Mohatt, N. V., Thompson, A. B., Thai, N. D., & Tebes, J. K. (2014). Historical trauma as public narrative: A conceptual review of how history impacts present-day health. *Social Science & Medicine, 106,* 128–136.

National Center for Health Statistics. (n.d.). Suicide rates for females and males by race and ethnicity: United States 1999 & 2017. Retrieved from: https://www.cdc.gov/nchs/data/hestat/suicide/rates_1999_2017.pdf

Potts, K. L., & Brown, L. (2015). Becoming an anti-oppressive researcher. In S. Strega & L. Brown (Eds.), *Research as resistance: Revisiting critical, indigenous, and anti-oppressive approaches* (2nd ed., pp. 17–41). Toronto, Ontario, Canada: Canadian Scholars Press.

Roh, S., Brown-Rice, K. A., Lee, K. H., Lee, Y. S., Yee-Melichar, D., & Talbot, E. P. (2015). Attitudes toward mental health services among American Indians by two age groups. *Community Mental Health Journal, 51*(8), 970–977.

Rojas, M. (2009). *Women of color and feminism.* Berkeley, CA: Seal Press.

Rosay, A. B. (2016). *Violence against American Indian and Alaska Native women and men: 2010 findings from the National Intimate Partner and Sexual Violence Survey.* Retrieved from https://nij.gov/journals/277/Pages/violence-against-american-indians-alaska-natives.aspx

Sapra, K., Jubinski, J., Tanaka, S., & Gershon, M. (2014). Family and partner interpersonal violence among American Indians/Alaska Natives. *Injury Epidemiology, 1*(1), 1–14.

Sarche, M. C., Spicer, P., Farrell, P., & Fitzgerald, H. E. (2011). *American Indian and Alaska Native children and mental health: development, context, prevention, and treatment.* Santa Barbara, CA: ABC-CLIO.

Smith, A. (2005). Native American feminism, sovereignty, and social change. *Feminist Studies, 31*(1), 116–132.

Sotero, M. (2006). A conceptual model of historical trauma: Implications for public health practice and research. *Journal of Health Disparities Research and Practice, 1*(1), 93–108.

Strega, S., & Brown, L. (2015). From resistance to resurgence. In S. Strega & L. Brown (Eds.), *Research as resistance: Revisiting critical, indigenous, and anti-oppressive approaches* (2nd ed., pp. 1–16). Toronto, Ontario, Canada: Canadian Scholars Press.

Substance Abuse and Mental Health Services Admininstration. (2012). Need for and receipt of substance use treatment among American Indians or Alaska Natives. The National Survey on Drug Use and Health. Retrieved from: https://www.samhsa.gov/data/sites/default/files/NSDUH120/NSDUH120/SR120-treatment-need-AIAN.htm

US Bureau of Labor Statistics. (n.d.). Labor statistics 2017. Retrieved from: https://www.bls.gov/

United Nations. (2018). *Fact sheet: Who are indigenous peoples?* Retrieved from https://www.un.org/esa/socdev/unpfii/documents/5session_factsheet1.pdf

United National Indian Tribal Youth (UNITY). (2010). Unity origin and development. Retrieved from: https://unityinc.org/unity-history/#more-8

United National Indian Tribal Youth (UNITY). (n.d.). About UNITY. Retrieved from: https://unityinc.org/about/about-unity/

US Census Bureau. (2017). *Profile America: Facts for features.* Retrieved from https://www.census.gov/newsroom/releases/archives/facts_for_features_special_editions/cb12-ff22.html

US Department of Health and Human Services; Administration for Children and Families; Administration on Children, Youth and Families; & Children's Bureau. (2015). *Adoption and Foster Care Analysis and Reporting System* (Report No. 22). Washington, DC: Author.

Walls, M. L., & Whitbeck, L. (2011). Distress among indigenous North Americans: generalized and culturally relevant stressors. *Society and Mental Health, 1*, 124–136.

Walters, K., Mohammed, S., Evans-Campbell, T., Beltran, R., Chae, D., & Duran, B. (2011). Bodies don't just tell stories, they tell histories: Embodiment of historical trauma among American Indians and Alaska Natives. *Du Bois Review, 8*(1), 179–189.

Watkins, M., & Shulman, H. (2008). *Toward psychologies of liberation.* New York, NY: Palgrave Macmillan.

Weaver, H. N. (2005). *Explorations in cultural competence: Journeys to the four directions.* Belmont, CA: Thomson Brooks/Cole.

Weaver, H. N. (2009). The colonial context of violence: Reflections on violence in the lives of Native American women. *Journal of Interpersonal Violence, 24*, 1552–1563.

Whitbeck, L. B., Adams, G. W., Hoyt, D. R., & Chen, X. (2004). Conceptualizing and measuring historical trauma among American Indian people. *American Journal of Community Psychology, 33*(3–4), 119–130.

World Health Organization. (2007, October). *Health of indigenous people* (Fact sheet No. 326). Retrieved from http://www.who.int/mediacentre/factsheets/fs326/en

6

Women of Color in Academia

Self-Preservation in the Face of White Fragility and Hegemonic Masculinity

CLAUDIA M. BERMÚDEZ AND RACHEL R. CAMACHO ■

CASE STUDY: DAVID AND ANA

Recently, we were asked to teach a qualitative methods class at the same private university where Claudia had earned her doctorate and Rachel was in the process of earning hers. As women of color, we were thrilled at the opportunity to co-teach the course that one of our colleagues (also a woman of color) had developed but had become unavailable to teach. Despite never having met prior to teaching together, we quickly developed a rapport. We met weekly and emailed daily about our class. At our institution, more than half of the faculties are women. Of the women that are faculties in our department, 75% are women of color. Two women of color co-teaching a methodology course, in this department, in many ways reflected the values of the school's commitment to developing educational environments that are just, relevant, and rigorous. It is also an example of a program that lives out its commitment to producing scholars and educators committed to equity, excellence, and social justice in every area of education.

In revising the original syllabus for this introductory seminar course in qualitative methodologies, we were intentional in our focus on decolonizing qualitative methodologies and using seminal works in education that employed qualitative methods and the work of being an educational scholar and researcher. The goal of the course was for each student to produce a research project proposal that would qualify as a research tool, a requirement of the doctoral program. In preparation for this class deliverable, the students were paced through assignments that would enable them to create a viable proposal by the end of the semester. To ensure that each student adhered to academic rigor and ethical standards, the syllabus clearly outlined student learning outcomes, professional ethics, course expectations, and guidelines regarding attendance and participation.

However, by the first few weeks of the 16-week course, we realized we were navigating the treacherous waters familiar to many women of color in academia: hegemonic masculinity and White fragility. Connell (1995) defines the term *hegemonic masculinity* as "the configuration of gendered practice which embodies the currently accepted answer to the problem of the legitimacy of patriarchy, which guarantees the dominant position of men and the subordination of women" (p. 77). One-third of the students in the class were male, but one male student enacted hegemonic masculinity to the degree that Campus Safety became involved. DiAngelo (2011) defines *White fragility* as "a state in which even a minimum amount of racial stress becomes intolerable, triggering a range of defensive moves . . . [including] outward display of emotions such as anger, fear, and guilt, and behaviors such as argumentation, silence, and leaving the stress-inducing situation" (p. 57). Only 20% of students in our class were White (compared to 44% university wide), but one White woman enacted her White privilege to such a degree that her covert and overt acts of hostility led one of the authors to question her role as an authority figure and her investment in asking students to engage and use their authentic voices in an agentic context. Both the students in question chose to attend an institution committed to social justice. Both described their commitment to exploring issues that impact underrepresented students and women in academia. However, when we held them to high academic standards and were vocal about our expectations that they engage in the work of being scholars and situate themselves in the context of the discussions around race and gender that we facilitated in class, they pushed back in racialized and gendered manners.

In a class that reflected diversity, both in demographics and in professional and lived experiences, Claudia and I looked forward to the challenge of co-teaching a methodology course and were equally excited to learn from the students in the seminar. As the semester progressed, one male student in particular, David (a pseudonym), would reveal a pattern of hegemonic masculine behaviors that would attempt to undermine the expertise of my faculty colleague, challenge her expectations of academic rigor, and question her competence.

These behaviors appeared when his performance in the course began to reflect a lack of preparation; a lack of adherence to the deliverables outlined in the course assignments, including academic ethics; and his unwillingness to actively participate in class activities. When Claudia and I observed early in the semester that David might need additional assistance and advisement, we reached out to him via email to offer assistance, recommend support services on campus that he should seek out, and offered to meet with him to discuss revisions to assignments. A pattern of behavior became apparent: The more he struggled in the class, the more support that was extended, the more hostile he became. David's behavior in class escalated—culminating in an incident in which he raised his voice and postured in an aggressive manner as Claudia and I led two separate small group discussions in the same large classroom. This resulted in my decision to end the discussion I was leading because I was concerned that he might continue to verbally accost her. When Claudia communicated this incident and the prior patterns of behavior to the dean, he directed his office to request monitoring and an escort from Campus Safety. Admittedly, I was surprised to hear of the response to our concerns and yet relieved for the support. As I entered the building in which the seminar was held, I walked in at the same time as David. We entered the elevator and rode to the second floor together. We exchanged small talk, and as the doors to the elevator opened, the police escort was visibly at the entrance of the class. David turned to me and questioned the presence of the police officer, to which I replied that Campus Safety frequently patrolled all areas of campus. Once David entered the class-room, I lingered outside of the door and introduced myself to our designated police escort. He assured me that he would be outside of the classroom for the duration of the class and at any point, if he was needed, to let him know. In this class session, sur-prisingly, David's behavior and disposition toward my colleague were more subdued. Upon his departure, the police escort walked us to our cars, and in our conversation with him, he shared that the need for police escorts on college campuses is more com-mon than people realize in response to male student hostility toward their female fac-ulty instructors.

In this course, the reading selections and discussions were grounded in understand-ing epistemologies, methods, and methodologies that counter oppressive approaches to conducting research. The importance of agency, voice, diversity, and the exposure to anti-oppressive methodologies was paramount in this seminar. As such, in conduct-ing qualitative research, students learned of Chicana epistemologies, queer ethnogra-phy, critical race theory, LatCrit, feminist theory, and an intersectional lens. Although David was exposed to the literature and required to engage in critical conversation in the class, it became apparent during the semester that he did not engage in the read-ings nor did he feel an obligation to actively participate in class discussions. Based on our frequent contact with him and a careful analysis of his verbal and nonverbal cues, we concluded that his actions appeared to be grounded in gendered stereotypes and perpetuated patriarchal norms.

Connell and Messerschmidt (2005) elaborated on the definition of hegemonic masculinity, indicating that it is a pattern of practices that enables men's continued dominance over women. Wagner (2011) highlighted two critical points in Connell and Messerschmidt's definition of hegemonic masculinity: "There is a constellation of attitudes, behaviors and expressions that is considered 'masculine' [and] masculinity, while a performance, is socially contingent and thus malleable" (p. 213). In David's performance of hegemonic masculinity, he did not recognize his own oppressive prac-tices in relation to his espoused desire to work with at-risk Latino youth.

Ana (a pseudonym) was a White student who worked as a lecturer in a different institution in a discipline unrelated to education. As early as her first assignment, we realized she had a great deal of difficulty with academic writing and even greater difficulty identifying why she was pursuing a PhD in education. Each time either of us asked her to discuss that issue, she would become very flustered. Her writing was stilted, and she consistently failed to address the basic parameters of class assignments. Both of us corresponded with her weekly via email, offering guidance and support. At the midpoint of the semester, I (Claudia) emailed Ana to inform her about her prog-ress in the course and told her that her participation in class was important and that her voice was valuable. She responded that by asking her to participate in class, I was making her "uncomfortable" and that I was in essence conducting "oral testing" on the material, which caused her a great deal of stress.

Despite her resistance, we continued to give Ana constructive, actionable written and oral feedback, checking with each other to ensure our communication was con-structive and professional (we usually copied each other on email conversations with Ana). Nevertheless, her behavior became more overtly hostile, and it culminated in not obtaining my permission to conduct a pilot interview as part of her final research proposal. This expectation was clearly delineated in the syllabus, reiterated in class sessions, and repeated in two emails I sent directly to her. As Rachel facilitated a coding exercise in class, I asked Ana to step out into a public seating area between classrooms and asked her to explain her rationale for not obtaining my permission to conduct her pilot interview. She became irate and accused me of being inept, having "negative energy," being "militaristic," wanting to discourage her from learning, and questioning how I had ever succeeded as a principal. I calmly assured her that I had been quite successful as an administrator, considered it my job to help her succeed as a graduate student as documented in all my email interactions with her, and steered the conversation back to her failure to follow the guidelines. In notes that I made following that exchange, I wrote, "I am physically and emotionally exhausted from working with [Ana], who is unwilling and unprepared to engage as a scholar."

In my closing lecture to the class, I addressed my belief that teaching is a co-learning experience (Robson & Turner, 2007). I reiterated a theme that Rachel and I had addressed throughout the course: student agency. We had spoken repeatedly in class of the need for students to enact agentic perspectives and agentic actions (O'Meara, 2013). I discussed the idea that part of being a scholar requires that you sit in the vulnerability of your learning and work from the premise that "regardless of what personality traits you might have, if you can't try to continue to improve, that doesn't bode well for your eventual practice or your research career" (Wiltsey Stirman, 2012, p. 42).

During this presentation, Ana sat with arms crossed, pointedly looking away and tapping her foot until I was finished. For her final presentation, she arrived half an hour late with an incomplete PowerPoint and went significantly over time, despite being told her time was up. When she received her final grade in the class, she emailed the program coordinator asking that her grade be changed because I had (incompetently) miscalculated her points. When the coordinator forwarded that email to me, I replied to both of them, informing Ana that her final grade had been correctly calculated, was a very accurate representation of her performance throughout the semester, and would stand.

OVERVIEW

The nature and scope of hegemonic masculinity and White fragility throughout the world is a problem with which women of color in academia frequently contend. What gave Ana the confidence to ignore parameters and expectations established for all students and be verbally abusive toward her professor? Ana was enacting White fragility wherein many White people "believe [they] are superior at a deeply internalized level and act on this belief in the practice of [their] lives, but [they] must deny this belief to fit into society and maintain [their] self-identity as good, moral people" (DiAngelo, 2018, p. 47). Why would David think it was appropriate to raise his voice and use his physical stature to attempt to intimidate his professor? David was enacting hegemonic masculinity wherein "any man that aspires to embody [hegemonic] masculinity must display aggressive and violent behaviour whilst restraining the flow of vulnerable emotions. He should also exhibit strength and toughness, and be competitive and successful" (Morettini, 2016, para. 3). Furthermore, according to Morettini,

Hegemonic masculinity is arguably a global phenomenon that takes place across various social levels in different societies. Hegemonic masculinity affects international relations, domestic politics, military practices; education and sport; corporate governance and the emergence of transnational business masculinities, just to give a few examples. It operates on three levels: the local (family, community, and local culture); the regional (the nation state and the culture embedded in it) and the global (influencing the transnational areas of politics, business and media). Efforts to promote gender equality and a de-hierarchisation of the gender system need to take this into account, and operate on these three levels. (para. 7)

Likewise, White fragility is a transnational issue in academia in which the vast majority of professors are White males (World Bank, 2018). In South Africa, the Minister of Higher Education and Training, Blade Nzimande (as cited in Ramoupi, 2017), stated in an open session of Parliament that it was critical to "address the paucity of black South African academics in our institutions, which manifests in 66% [in 2015] of all university professors still being white."

HISTORICAL TRENDS

In the United States, the pipeline myth contributes to women's inability to access social mobility in specific professions, especially in higher education. This myth is the dogged notion that there are not enough qualified women (i.e., degree holding) available for leadership positions in higher education (Johnson, 2017). According to the National Center for Education Statistics (2016), since 2006, women have earned more than 50% of all doctoral degrees, yet as of 2015, women held 32% of the full professor positions at degree-granting post-secondary institutions. In academia, the higher the academic rank, the fewer women found in these positions.

When the graduate degree attainment rates for women are disaggregated by race, a different story is revealed. Latinas have the lowest attainment rate of graduate degrees compared to all women. In 2003, less than 2% of Latinas held a graduate degree. In 2013, 4% of Latinas held a master's degree or higher (Gándara & the White House Initiative on Educational Excellence for Hispanic Americans, 2015). Finally, men of color hold full professor positions more often than do women of color, whereas women of color outnumber men of color in lower ranking faculty positions. In fall 2015, of the faculty of color who held a full professor rank, 57% were men of color and 43% were women of color (US Department of Education, 2016). Conversely, during the same period of time, 59% of the faculty of color who held an instructor or lecturer position were women of color and 41% were men of color (US Department of Education, 2016). Appropriately, the phrase "the higher the fewer" was coined to acknowledge that even though women have achieved higher educational attainment levels than men in the past decade, the number of women holding high faculty rank positions and receiving comparable salary and recognition has yet to increase (Johnson, 2017). Furthermore, the pay gap between men and women with the same faculty rank is an indication that the glass ceiling is maintained. To be clear, regardless of academic rank, men earn more than women and are more likely to hold a tenure track position and get tenured. In the 2015–2016 academic year, female faculty members earned an average of $73,782, whereas male faculty members earned an average of $89,190—representing an approximately $15,000 difference in salary (National Center for Education Statistics, 2016). Speaking truth to power regarding patterns of pervasive bias experienced by women in higher education is imperative for transformation to occur.

RECENT DEVELOPMENTS OF NOTE

In recent years, women in the United States have mobilized, marched, and leveraged their voices to organize, protest, challenge patriarchy, and use their collective voices to fight for women's rights. From political advocacy to the #MeToo movement, women in the United States continue to illuminate the injustices experienced by women at all levels, from service workers to elected officials and women across all levels of professional industry. In 2017, there was an unprecedented advancement of movement for women's rights. Equally important is that women continue to shine a light on racial, gender, economic, and political inequality in the United States. Although a part of the Global North, the United States continues to be one of the most socially stratified countries in the world (Castilla, 2008; Massey, 2008). And although race, class, and gender are often viewed as separate social constructions, they are lived at the personal level (Collins, 2009; Crenshaw, 1991). These intersections of social identities can facilitate opportunities and/or impede access to social mobility (Baca Zinn & Dill, 1996).

According to the American Association of University Women's publication titled *The Simple Truth About the Gender Pay Gap* (2018), using the rate of change experienced between 1960 and 2016, women are estimated to reach pay equity with men in 2119. In 2016, women working full-time in the United States experienced a pay gap of 20%. This is alarming given that families today increasingly rely on women's wages to support the entire family. Moreover, women's earnings as a percentage of White men's earnings differ by race/ethnicity. In 2016, White women earned 79 cents for every dollar their White male counterparts earned. For women of color, the earnings are less. Latina women earn 54 cents per every dollar earned by a White male. According to the US Census Bureau (2017), among full-time workers in 2016, Latina, American Indian or Alaska Native, African American, and Native Hawaiian or Pacific Islander women had lower median annual earnings compared with those of White and Asian women.

CURRENT CONDITIONS

Chakravarty (2015) defines transnational feminism as a "multi-connotative subfield within women's/gender/sexuality/feminist studies ... featuring anti-hegemonic (anti-racist, anti-colonial, anti-capitalist, etc.) writings ... [that] ... uphold the importance of praxis and interrupt a dominant notion of global sisterhood, multicultural solidarity, and conventional knowledge-making" (p. 25). From this foundational understanding, we propose that the issues of hegemonic masculinity and White fragility resonate on a transnational level where embodied, epistemic, structural racism and sexism are still the norm. Transnational feminists in academia contend with these issues as they continue to work toward the decolonization of feminist theory and praxis.

In her article on gender, race, and place in transnational academic mobility, Mählck (2016) notes that women of color in academia are tasked with crossing racialized and gendered status boundaries. David and the hegemonic masculinity he embodied bristled at two women of color upholding high standards and rebuffed our attempts to help him improve his capacity as a scholar. He responded with derision and exaggerated bravado when he perceived that his instructors were crossing status boundaries that dictate Latinas act in a subservient or care-taking capacity. According to Harris, Medine, and Rhee (2016), classrooms in higher education serve as microcosms of both the academy and society writ large, and therefore reflect long-accepted forms of racism and sexism.

Lazos (2012) posits that the psychological and sociological literature

> establishes with robust empiricism that gender and race influence the way women and minorities are viewed in the classroom . . . [and] . . . [u]nconscious bias, stereotypes, and assumptions about role appropriateness are the subjective parameters that students unconsciously carry in their heads and use to shape the way they perceive their women and minority professors. (p. 166)

The overt and covert replication of racist and sexist norms of behavior was prevalent in our case study. Ana's socialization as a White woman allowed her to repeatedly demonstrate an unwillingness to listen that served to protect her (privileged) worldview (DiAngelo, 2018). Scholars of White privilege note that the tendency for many White people to assume their experiences are normative and neutral is continuously reinforced and rewarded by institutional mechanisms (Ahmed, 2007; Applebaum, 2016; Sullivan, 2006). Furthermore, when these assumptions are challenged, White fragility is triggered, and the entire cycle of White supremacy is perpetuated while constructive, albeit uncomfortable, dialogue is avoided (DiAngelo, 2018). In academia, our White students come to us often aware or unaccepting of their power, privilege, and positionality. Having difficult conversations about these issues and standing in our power as women of color who have earned their place at the table of academia is a critical way to represent our communities by bringing our whole, authentic selves to our work.

LOOKING TO THE FUTURE

First, we propose that women of color in academia form community with other women of color to specifically address hegemonic masculinity and White fragility as issues that impact their professional and personal well-being. The theory of "lift as we climb" to which many of us subscribe cannot be enacted if we allow ourselves to become psychologically, emotionally, intellectually, and spiritually depleted. Self-preservation (i.e., caring for every aspect of one's well-being in order to enhance and strengthen the whole) for women of color in academia is essential. As Hua (2018) observes, "The upshot of the constant demands on our time, our patience, and our professionalism without regard to our welfare is that the health and success of women of color in the academy suffers" (p. 78). As an active self-preservation practice, Rachel and I had a running dialogue about the interactions we had with Ana and David that helped keep us grounded. This dialogue enabled us to identify that the disrespectful and disruptive behaviors the students exhibited were in fact manifestations of larger, systemic issues. At the institutional level, these dialogues need to become part of the norm in order to effect large-scale change. These personal dialogues are a starting point to decoloniz-ing epistemology by foregrounding the "complex relational connections" (Mohanty, 2003, p. 238) among the lived experiences that connect (and divide) women of color in academia in the Global South and the Global North.

In addition, as feminist, queer, and transgender scholarship expands, the critical lens of gender is gaining momentum. This centering of gender studies is broaden-ing our understanding of the structures of power that perpetuate oppressive gender roles and values. To this end, introducing scholarship and research that explore how men are shaped by these hegemonic forces and how they react and respond to them is essential to realizing liberatory practices in and outside the classroom.

Next, we propose that students of color weigh in on this issue as well. Silva (2012) makes the case for academic blogging for minority scholars. She notes in her blog,

> For minority scholars, such as myself, blogging is not just a bullet point on a CV; it is an intrinsic part of what my research is about: a commitment to making the struggles, achievements and contradictions of African Americans, Puerto Ricans or women visible to the broader population. I cannot afford silence. Blogging allows me a platform to talk about issues that may go unnoticed, or issues where the point of view of a person of colour or of a woman have been left in the cold. Because it happens. A lot.... Minority academics who blog must, now more than ever, be aware of how important it is to articulate their ideas and their knowl-edge outside of our departments, our journals, and our conferences. Blogging is a space in which we can do that. Many are already doing it, but that does not mean we do not need more voices participating in the conversations. We must make our voices heard, especially when others do not want to hear us.

Students and academics of color alike can impact policy/social/economic condi-tions by giving voice to issues that have gone unacknowledged and unaddressed for far too long.

CONCLUSION

How do we proceed as women of color in academia when students enact hegemonic masculinity and White fragility? How do we navigate racialized and gendered stereo-types that position us as less intelligent, less capable, and less able to facilitate scholarly discussions? In our experience, having each other to process the situations as they developed affirmed that what we were experiencing was real, significant, and unac-ceptable. We were able to mitigate the sociopsychological costs involved with being the targets of overt and covert hostility from students in ways that allowed us to practice self-preservation, echoed in the words of Lorde, Omolade, Hill Collins, and Anzaldúa—

> Caring for myself is not self-indulgence, it is self-preservation, and that is an act of political warfare.
>
> —Audre Lorde (1988, p. 131)

Women of color warriors are constant warriors. . . . No soldier fights harder than a woman warrior for she fights for total change, for a new order in a world in which she can finally rest and love.

—Barbara Omolade (1994, p. 220)

To maintain their power, dominant groups create and maintain a popular system of "commonsense" ideas that support their right to rule. In the United States, hegemonic ideologies concerning race, class, gender, sexuality, and nation are often so pervasive that it is difficult to conceptualize alternatives to them, let alone ways of resisting the social practices that they justify.

—Patricia Hill Collins (2000, p. 284)

Why am I compelled to write? . . . Because the world I create in the writing compensates for what the real world does not give me. By writing I put order in the world, give it a handle so I can grasp it. I write . . . to become more intimate with myself and you. To discover myself, to preserve myself, to make myself, to achieve self-autonomy.

—Gloria E. Anzaldúa (1987, p. 319)

—and emerge stronger from the fray, ready to add our voices to the vital conversations that need to take place around these issues.

DISCUSSION QUESTIONS

1. How do women of color in academia address hegemonic masculinity and White fragility as they happen in the academy?
2. How can women of color in academia address overt racism and sexism so that it becomes a teachable moment for all involved?
3. When hegemonic masculinity and White fragility are enacted in a public space, how do women of color in academia (a) respond publicly and (b) exercise self-preservation privately?
4. What is the responsibility of higher education institutions to generate supportive spaces for women of color to thrive in academia?
5. What role do institutional diversity and equity officers have in working with women of color in academia as they strive toward inclusivity?

REFERENCES

Ahmed, S. (2007). A phenomenology of whiteness. *Feminist Studies, 8*(2), 150.

American Association of University Women. (2018). *The simple truth about the gender pay gap.* Washington, DC: Author.

Anzaldúa, G. (1987). *Borderlands/la frontera: The new mestiza.* San Francisco, CA: Spinsters/Aunt Lute.

Applebaum, B. (2016). *Critical whiteness studies* (Oxford Research Encyclopedias: Education). Retrieved from http://education.oxfordre.com/view/10.1093/acrefore/9780190264093.001.0001/acrefore-9780190264093-e-5

Baca Zinn, M., & Dill, B. T. (1996). Theorizing difference from multiracial feminism. *Feminist Studies, 22*(2), 321–331.

Castilla, E. (2008). Gender, race, and meritocracy in organizational careers. *American Journal of Sociology, 113,* 1479–1526.

Chakravarty, D. (2015). On being and providing "data": Politics of transnational feminist collaboration and academic division of labor. *Frontiers: A Journal of Women Studies, 36*(3), 25–50.

Collins, P. H. (2009). *Black feminist thought: Knowledge, consciousness, and the politics of empowerment.* New York, NY: Routledge.

Connell, R. (1995). *Masculinities.* Berkeley, CA: University of California Press.

Connell, R., & Messerschmidt, J. (2005). Hegemonic masculinity: Rethinking the concept. *Gender and Society, 19*(6), 829–859.

Crenshaw, K. W. (1991). Mapping the margins: Intersectionality, identity politics, and violence against women of color. *Stanford Law Review, 43*(6), 1241–1299.

DiAngelo, R. (2011). White fragility. *International Journal of Critical Pedagogy, 3*(3), 54–70.

DiAngelo, R. (2018). *White fragility: Why it's so hard for White people to talk about racism.* Boston, MA: Beacon.

Gándara, P., & the White House Initiative on Educational Excellence for Hispanic Americans. (2015). *Fulfilling America's future: Latinas in the U.S., 2015.* Washington, DC: White House Initiative on Educational Excellence for Hispanics.

Harris, M., Medine, C., & Rhee, H. (2016). Silent scripts and contested spaces. *Journal of Feminist Studies in Religion, 32*(1), 101–114.

Hua, L. U. (2018, Spring). Slow feeling and quiet being: Women of color teaching in urgent times. *Teaching and Emotion, 2018*(153), 77–86.

Johnson, H. L. (2017). *Pipelines, pathways, and institutional leadership: An update on the status of women in higher education.* Washington, DC: American Council on Education.

Lazo, S. R. (2012). Are student teaching evaluations holding back women and minorities? In G. Gutiérrez y Muhs, Y. Flores Niemann, C. G. Gonzalez, & A. P. Harris (Eds.), *Presumed incompetent: The intersections of race and class for women in academia* (pp. 164–185). Boulder, CO: University Press of Colorado.

Lorde, A. (1988). *A burst of light: Essays.* London, UK: Sheba Feminist Publishers.

Mählck, P. (2016). Academics on the move? Gender, race and place in transnational academic mobility. *Nordic Journal of Studies in Educational Policy, 2016*(2–3), 1–12.

Massey, D. S. (2008). *Categorically unequal: The American stratification system.* New York, NY: Russell Sage Foundation.

Mohanty, C. (2003). *Feminism without borders.* Durham, NC: Duke University Press.

Morettini, F. M. (2016, October 27). Hegemonic masculinity: How the dominant man subjugates other men, women and society. *Global Policy Journal.* Retrieved from https://www.globalpolicyjournal.com/blog/27/10/2016/hegemonic-masculinity-how-dominant-man-subjugates-other-men-women-and-society

National Center for Education Statistics, IPEDS Data Center. (2016). *Full-time instructional staff, by faculty and tenure status, academic rank, race/ethnicity, and gender (degree-granting institutions): Fall 2015.* Fall staff survey.

O'Meara, K. (2013). Advancing graduate student agency. *Higher Education in Review, 10,* 1–10.

Omolade, B. (1994). *The rising song of African American women.* New York, NY: Routledge.

Ramoupi, N. L. I. (2017, June 15). Why are there so few Black professors? *Mail & Guardian.* Retrieved from https://mg.co.za/article/2017-06-15-00-why-are-there-so-few-black-professors

Robson, S., & Turner, Y. (2007). Teaching is a co-learning experience: Academics reflecting on learning and teaching in an "internationalized" faculty. *Teaching in Higher Education,* 12(1), 41–54.

Silva, L. (2012, July 12). Academic blogging: Minority scholars cannot afford to be silent. *The Guardian* [Higher Education Network Blog]. Retrieved from https://www.theguardian.com/higher-education-network/blog/2012/jul/12/blogging-for-minority-subjects-and-academics

Sullivan, S. (2006). *Revealing whiteness: The unconscious habits of racial privilege.* Bloomington, IN: Indiana University Press.

US Census Bureau. (2017). *American community survey 1-year estimates.* Retrieved from https://factfinder.census.gov

US Department of Education. (2016). *Digest of education statistics 2016* (Table 315.20). Washington, DC: US Department of Education, National Center for Education Statistics.

Wagner, R. (2011). Embracing liberatory practice: Promoting men's development as a feminist act. In J. A Laker & T. Davis (Eds.), *Masculinities in higher education: Theoretical and practical considerations* (pp. 210–223). New York, NY: Routledge.

Wiltsey Stirman, S. (2012). *What predicts grad school success? Intelligence, emotional intelligence, curiosity and conscientiousness may be keys to getting your degree, research suggests* [as cited in N. Swaminathan, American Psychological Association blog]. Retrieved from http://www.apa.org/gradpsych/2012/09/cover-success.aspx

World Bank. (2018). *Data bank: Education statistics—All indicators.* Retrieved from http://databank.worldbank.org/data/source/education-statistics-%5E-all-indicators

PART II

New Media and Free Choice

Introduction: Seizing the Opportunity of Social Media and Not Letting Go

ANTIGONE DAVIS ■

As the Global Head of Safety at Facebook, my job has allowed me to travel the world to hear from organizations focused on growing women's participation in public and political life as well as breaking down barriers to full and equal participation in their communities. No matter where I go, the women with whom I speak view Facebook as invaluable to these efforts; and no matter where I go, ensuring women's safety offline and online is core to their work. Everyone deserves to feel safe on Facebook, and it is important that the employees of Facebook help people who encounter abuse and harassment online. We recognize how important it is for Facebook to be a place where women feel empowered to communicate. We take our role of keeping abuse off of our service seriously, and that means doing what we can to avoid replicating the offline barriers to community participation, such as sexual intimidation and abuse.

This section discusses how Facebook and other similar social media platforms have been used to empower women and elevate their voices to be heard in a way that creates change. Unfortunately, social media has also been harnessed as a new way to facilitate violence against women. Old themes of intimate violence, honor killings, and sexual assault have become repackaged and used in new ways through the internet and mobile devices. Chapter 8 discusses social media star Qandeel Baloch, who demonstrated how women can harness social media to become leaders of ideas, and the irony of her death as a result of her social media presence brining shame to her Pakistani family. Chapter 9 details the fetish industry in Japan and how the internet has empowered men to inflict abuse seen online come to life in a modern culture. Chapter 10 presents the striking story of the Egyptian revolution of 2011, which was spawned by a social media uprising. The chapter discusses how social media both connected women and was used to silence them during the revolution.

Perhaps the most relevant chapter that showcases how Facebook is shaping the platform to protect the rights of women is Chapter 7. During my travels, I have heard incredible stories of women using Facebook to do everything from build family businesses to lobby for government funding for period products so girls do not have to miss school when menstruating. I also have heard stories about the abuse women face online. For example, a city official in India tried to publicly shame a local woman by sharing a photo of her in a pool with her male colleagues; the woman and the men were fully clothed, but she was still in violation of accepted norms. Another example is a sex video of a European teenager that was shared virally throughout her school and beyond to bully and humiliate her. From Kenya to Canada, women have shared their painful experiences about having their most intimate moments exposed without permission. This violation of privacy can be devastating: It can lead to anxiety or depression or even the loss of personal relationships or a job, and its emotional impact is akin to that of a sexual assault. Although these images harm people of all genders, ages, and sexual orientations, women are nearly twice as likely as men to be targeted. At Facebook, we are committed to doing everything we can to prevent this abuse and to support survivors. The non-consensual sharing of intimate images has always violated Facebook's community standards. Facebook removes these images when reported to it and even disables the accounts of individuals who non-consensually share intimate images. Since 2017, Facebook has also used technology to prevent further sharing of the content across Facebook, Instagram, and Messenger. When this content is reported to Facebook, we not only remove each image or video but also create a unique digital fingerprint known as a hash to prevent further sharing. We are also developing classifiers to proactively identify and thwart the sharing of policy-violating content. We have challenges to solve and areas in which we hope to do better. An example is differing cultural global norms: What is considered an intimate image in one area of the world may not be considered intimate in another area. This, too, has implications for us that we need to address. Another challenge is breaking down the stigma that prevents people from reaching out for help. One way we are addressing this is by building a network of partner organizations throughout the world that provide social supports for survivors and do invaluable work to reduce the stigma so that victims will reach out for help. Also, we have supported legislation that makes it a crime to share someone's intimate images without their consent for the purpose of causing emotional distress. We also believe we can do more to help people in crisis prevent images from being shared on our services in the first place. In 2018, we announced a pilot partnership developed with an international working group of women's safety organizations, survivors, and victim advocates, including the Cyber Civil Rights Initiative and the National Network to End Domestic Violence in the United States, the UK Revenge Porn Helpline, the Australian Office of the eSafety Commissioner, and YWCA Canada. Working with these partners, people who worry that someone might try to harm them by sharing an intimate image of them can proactively upload the image via a secure, single-use link so we can create a digital fingerprint of the image and block anyone from sharing it on Facebook. We are aware of the extraordinary challenges that come with sharing an intimate image in this way, so we only offer this pilot through our expert partners, who can support the individual throughout the process. We have also built in extra security to protect the victim's privacy and ensure images are auto-destroyed within 1 week. We look forward to learning from this pilot program, continuing to work with experts on this issue, collaborating with other technology companies, further improving our tools for people in devastating situations, and building more support services directly into the product experience. Also, because my travels have made it abundantly clear that what we see online is intimately connected to what we see offline, we plan to do more programming with experts to build education around healthy offline and online relationships. It can be difficult to watch the sexual abuse that has occurred for centuries offline play out online, especially when current technologies can be a powerful tool for women to achieve full and equal participation in their communities. But this challenge also presents an opportunity. It is not as easy to turn away from this issue as it once was. What we have seen online has helped shine a bright and powerful light on the issue of sexual abuse, galvanized efforts to thwart it offline and online, and brought unprecedented global focus. Now, it is our job to seize this opportunity and not let go.

7

Non-Consensual Image Sharing

Revenge Pornography and Acts of Sexual Assault Online

JESSICA KLEIN AND KRISTEN ZALESKI ■

CASE STUDY: HADDIE

Haddie met Josh through a free dating site, and they immediately began to have lengthy text conversations, which soon resulted in lengthy phone conversations. Josh lived more than 500 miles away, and Haddie's college schedule was too busy for her to take time off to visit him. One afternoon, upon returning to her dormitory after class, she was surprised to find Josh waiting for her outside. Haddie and Josh spent the weekend together, and just before he left to return home, they declared their love for one another. The following day, perhaps because Haddie was missing Josh and feeling a bit rebellious, she took naked photos in bed and sent them to Josh. When he received them, he took some of himself and sent them to her, and an intense couple of weeks followed, during which sensual and sexual texts and photos were exchanged as a replacement for the face-to-face romance they craved.

By the end of the school year, Haddie had noticed that Josh was less available by text. He asked, from time to time, for more sensual photos, but she realized the lack of seeing one another was taking a toll on her, and she did not want to expose her heart anymore to the long-distance relationship. Haddie called Josh to break it off, and they cried together, promising to stay connected and perhaps try again when life was less hectic.

By the time summer arrived, Haddie was having difficulty forgetting Josh and decided to cut off all communication so she could heal her heart. Josh protested at first and then began to be aggressive with hourly calls and texts, demanding to speak to her. Out of desperation to get some relief from his harassment, Haddie blocked him. That was when it happened. Haddie logged onto her social media account and saw

Figure 7.1 Online sexual violence, harassment, and bullying are forms of domestic or sexual violence, and the abuse is often by a current or ex-intimate partner.

that Josh had tagged her friends and family on the naked photos she sent him. Even worse, she saw it was a public post, and the pictures had been shared multiple times. Haddie's mom called, angry and confused. There was nothing Haddie could do to stop the exposure.

Buried under her blankets, curled in a ball on the bed, Haddie listened as her friends crowded around a desktop screen, describing the sites that Haddie's naked photos were on. "I felt disgusting, like a million showers couldn't wash off what I felt. It took a while for me to get mad. I just felt the strongest shame and guilt." Haddie's biggest fear was disappointing or embarrassing her family. "I didn't know how to deal with the feelings that hit me like a truck that day."

OVERVIEW

Non-consensual image sharing (NCIS)—also known as non-consensual pornography, technology-facilitated violence, image-based sexual exploitation, intimate image exploitation, image-based sexual abuse, or, the most popular term, revenge porn — is "when someone shows, sends, or posts nude or nearly nude photos or videos of someone else without the consent of the person pictured" (Lenhart, Ybarra, & Price-Feeney, 2016, para. 1). NCIS sharing is part of a broader concern of cyber harassment and often co-occurs with other forms of cyber harassment, including online privacy breaches, technology attacks, threats of violence, and provocations of strangers to physically harm victims (Citron & Franks, 2014). Non-consensual explicit images that become shared can initially be created consensually—that is, the photo can be taken with the consent of the person photographed—or the images can be obtained without consent, such as surreptitious filming of nudity or a sex act. The literature supports that much of NCIS is obtained in the context of an initially consensual inti-mate relationship and then distributed without the consent of the individual (Bloom, 2014; Dawkins, 2015). However, many naked photographs are obtained through hacking, and sometimes, non-romantic friends or even strangers may expose naked pictures of others whose data they have illegally accessed. For instance, a recent survey found that 43% of those who responded as victims of NCIS also reported that their personal accounts were hacked and personal information was stolen (Lenhart et al., 2016). Other forms of this violence include "upskirting," in which a non-consensual picture of an individual's genitals is posted online without the individual's permission (McGlynn, Rackley, & Houghton, 2017), and sexual assaults that are videotaped and posted online, creating what can only be described as a double violation of personal and virtual sexual boundaries.

NCIS may often be coupled with other devious and evasive behaviors, including the posting of identifying information such as contact information and addresses on social media sites. As a result, victims are additionally exposed to stalking, physi-cal and verbal harassment, blackmail, and threats (Bates, 2017; Citron & Franks, 2014; Walker & Sleath, 2017). In one study of 1,244 victims of NCIS, 50% of the victims had their entire name and identifying social media information appear with the explicit image, and 20% of the victims' email addresses and phone numbers were also shared with the image (Citron & Franks, 2014). When images are posted with identifying information, the shame and embarrassment of the public exposure can become compounded by a sense of feeling unsafe, thus amplifying the nature of the trauma.

The far-reaching impact of technology coupled with continued high rates of sexual violence, stalking, and harassment make NCIS a problem that creates a lifetime of terror for many victims because erasing images is often difficult to do. For example, in New Zealand, a group referred to as Roast Busters bragged about gang raping underage girls on Facebook with the assistance of images and videos, and despite the Facebook page being reported to police, the posts remained up for 2 years after the crimes. Once the Facebook posts were removed from the platform, the videos and images were still found online through internet caches and screen shots of websites (Hunt, 2015; Powell & Henry, 2014). As the Roast Busters case illustrates, once sexu-ally explicit images have been released, it is ultimately outside the control of the victim in how they will be used, where they will be posted, and who will view them. Inherent to the crime is public shame, total loss of control, and violation of bodily integrity and ownership.

Lenhart et al. (2016) found that 1 in 25 Americans reported being a victim of threats or posts of nude photos without their permission, and lesbian, gay, and transgender individuals had the highest incidences—15% of respondents reported being threat-ened with the sharing of naked photos without permission. Women are at greater risk of having non-consensual intimate images shared compared with men; specifically, women are 1.7 times more likely to be victimized through threats or exposure of non-consensual explicit images in the public sphere (Eaton, Jacobs, & Ruvalcaba, 2017). According to Bloom (2014), an increased burden of pressure is placed on women to share sexually explicit images compared with men. Women of color are most vulner-able, followed closely by White women (Citron & Franks, 2014). Young women and adolescents are at an increased risk, and young women between ages 15 and 29 years experience a likelihood of 1 in 10 that they will be victims of NCIS (Lenhart et al.,

2016). Men are also at risk of NCIS victimization; however, men are twice as likely to perpetrate NCIS than women (Eaton et al., 2017).

CYBERFEMINISM

Technology-specific forms of gender-based violence have gained increased attention from and have been researched by so-called *cyberfeminists*, who argue that the anonymity of the internet does not prevent the lived experiences and emotional repercussions of cyber-directed violence (sexism, racism, homophobia, etc.) (Brophy, 2010). That is, despite popular belief that cyberspace can be a place of disembodied experiences for everyone, it is still a place where a woman's subjectivity can be violated despite not having her body physically present for the violence. A woman's body is harmed through its public exposure without her awareness or consent, and she becomes further violated through the resulting humiliation from people she knows seeing her vulnerable images or the violent words often expressed in comment forums about her body in the photographs.

The concept of bodily integrity, as articulated by Patella-Rey (2018), is apt in understanding how victims of NCIS often experience it as tantamount to sexual assault. Bodily integrity posits that women often do not distinguish between "digital representations of their body and the body itself" (p. 786). As such, victims do not simply experience the distress of having a representation of their body shared but, rather, experience the unsanctioned image as a violation of their very body and as a loss of bodily integrity (Patella-Rey, 2018).

MENTAL HEALTH AND BEING A VICTIM OF NON-CONSENSUAL IMAGE SHARING

The concepts derived from cyberfeminism are helpful in understanding and validating the mental health impact of technology-facilitated sexual violence, such as NCIS, rather than victim blame. Survivors of sexual trauma are often confronted with perceived judgments and scrutiny regarding their actions associated with the trauma that suggest they were complicit, or *deserving*, of the violation. This scrutiny is certainly true of survivors of non-consensual explicit image sharing, and whereas male- and female-initiated sexting and explicit image sharing are reported to occur at similar rates, women often experience greater slut shaming (Webb, 2015) and victim blaming following non-consensual sharing of explicit images on the internet.

Historically, survivors of non-sexual violence are not blamed for their assaults and have increased levels of supportive sympathy (DeCou, Cole, Lynch, Wong, & Matthews, 2017), especially when the variables often involved in certain types of sexual assaults, such as consensual flirting or drinking, that lead to victim blaming are not involved. However, comments such as "She took the picture" create the same type of blame that many survivors of sexual assault experience, and some people have further difficulty conceptualizing non-consensual sharing of intimate images as negatively impactful because a woman's physical person was not harmed. These behaviors can lead to the same response in victims of non-consensual sexually explicit image sharing as in victims of other sexual traumas.

There is a link among the negative judgments against a sexual crime victim, increased levels of shame, and consequent high levels of post-trauma symptoms. Shame and fear of judgment also often lead to sexual crimes being underreported (Cohn, Zinzow, Resnick, & Kilpatrick, 2013). In fact, Rennison (2002) reported that in a survey of survivors from 1992 to 2000, 36% of rapes were not reported to law enforcement, nor were 34% of attempted rapes and 26% of sexual assaults generally. Because the factors surrounding the personal and social responses of victims of image sharing and victims of physical sexual assault are similar, acknowledging that survivors of NCIS are at risk for similar psychologically damaging negative impacts is important.

Currently, there is a gap in the literature regarding the damaging impact of NCIS on the mental health of victims, with only one mental health study published on the topic of revenge porn (Bates, 2017). Despite the dearth in research, preliminary evidence suggests that NCIS has profound, deleterious effects on victims. The qualitative analysis by Bates of 18 women in Canada who were victimized by online postings of their sexually explicit images found that being a victim of NCIS created sequelae, including post-traumatic stress disorder, anxiety, depression, suicidal thoughts, and trust concerns. Similarly, Citron and Franks (2014) noted that victims of NCIS often experience debilitating levels of shame and humiliation and reduced self-esteem.

According to the Cyber Civil Rights Initiative (2014), 93% of revenge pornography victims suffer significant emotional distress, 51% experience suicidal thoughts, and 82% experience social or occupational impairment. In addition, Citron and Franks (2014) noted that social and occupational consequences can often follow the posting of NCIS because victims may believe that their reputations in all domains of their lives have been besmirched. Survivors have reported significant life disruptions, such as job loss or difficulties with employment and hardship in engaging in new romantic relationships, following victimization by non-consensual explicit image sharing (Citron & Franks, 2014).

Figure 7.2 Sexting is becoming more common among adolescents and young adults. However, unsolicited pictures, such as the dick pic phenomenon, are viewed as bullying and harassment. Recently, research has found that perpetrators who send unsolicited pictures of their genitalia also test highly on narcissism and sexism scales.

Non-consensual sharing of intimate images lies within the realm of cyberbullying, which in itself is harmful to victims. Those who experience cyberbullying are at increased risk of experiencing low self-esteem, social impairment, anxiety or depression, and maladaptive coping with drugs or alcohol (Castle, 2009; Walker & Sleath, 2017). Furthermore, NCIS has many similarities with other forms of sexual trauma, such as a loss of control, sense of violation of bodily integrity, and evocation of fear and shame.

In summary, it appears that victims of cyber-related sexual violence and bullying experience similar mental health consequences that face-to-face sexual assault victims also report. These findings support cyberfeminist assertions about the cyberworld and its ability to impact the physical and emotional world.

HISTORICAL TRENDS

In mid-2006 a group of teenage boys in the Australian town of Werribee filmed the sexual assault of a teenage girl. The "Werribee DVD," as it became known in the media was initially sold in suburban Melbourne schools for $5 and later on internet sites for up to $60 AUD under the name "Cunt: The Movie," with excerpts made freely available on YouTube. It shows the boys urinating on the girl, setting her hair on fire, throwing her clothes into a river, and forcing her to participate in sex acts. Eight of the youth were charged with assault, manufacturing child pornography, and procuring sexual penetration by intimidation in the Melbourne Children's Court in 2007.
                                                    —Henry and Powell (2015, p. 758)

As technology has become more central to everyday life, sexual assault and harassment through online platforms, or what Henry and Powell (2015) termed "technology-facilitated sexual violence and harassment," have grown significantly each year. According to Clarke-Billings (2016), the United States was the first country in which technology-facilitated sexual violence came to public awareness, and as a result, 38 of the 50 states, as well as the District of Columbia, passed legislation outlawing distribution of revenge porn. Generally, the laws specify that the person distributing the material, including images of the genitals, anus, or female breast or those depicting another in a sexual act without their permission to do so, has the intent to harass or annoy another.

As early as 2013, Australia enacted legal restrictions against sharing sexual images of another person without consent (Clarke-Billings, 2016). Furthermore, Canada and Japan enacted laws in 2014, and between 2014 and 2016, European countries began to introduce legislation against sharing intimate or sexual images without consent, including Germany in 2014, the United Kingdom in 2015, and Scotland in 2016 (Clarke-Billings, 2016).

As legal conversations create laws, law enforcement has begun to take reports at alarming rates. After a law in the United Kingdom was passed against the crime, 200 cases involving children as young as 12 years were reported to authorities in a 6-month period (Halliday, 2015). However, legal reporting has not slowed the creation of websites designed to target victims of this crime; as of 2016, there were believed to be as many as 3,000 websites online (Kamal & Newman, 2016) that promoted the posting and sharing of NCSIs. Hunter Moore, who founded a well-known revenge pornography site, asserted that his and other sites help punish women who take explicit photos of themselves. Camille Dordero (as cited in Roy, 2014, p. 401) reported that Moore stated, "We've all masturbated to you or laughed at you, and it's done. It can't get any worse."

Advocates have attempted to target public sharing websites of non-consensual images through legal enforcement. However, website administrators believe they are protected by the First Amendment, which protects freedom of speech. Currently, no federal ban in the United States exists for NCIS. Writing language for such a bill has been difficult because of the First Amendment and other constitutional mandates; however, on November 28, 2017, Congresswoman Jackie Speier and US Senators Kamala Harris, Richard Burr, and Amy Klobuchar introduced the Ending Non-consensual Online User Graphic Harassment (ENOUGH) Act of 2017. The bill has been referred to the subcommittee on crime, terrorism, homeland security and investigations and has not been passed at the time of this writing.

In summary, free will, choice, and consent in all matters related to sexual expression are the fulcrum that tips the scale from a healthy sexual experience to sexual exploitation and abuse. Laws related to consensual sex are clear. In the United States and many other countries, one must be able to consent to sex by virtue of age, mental status, and simple desire to engage. However, legislation has been slow to extend the same consent laws online that many countries uphold for face-to-face crimes.

RECENT DEVELOPMENTS

> Public policy and media debate on this topic usually begins with the activity labelled as "revenge porn." This typically involves an ex-partner (usually a man) posting consensually created private sexual pictures or videos of their former partners (usually a woman) online and without consent, and in order to exact "revenge" following the break-up of their relationship. The images are routinely reposted across the internet, via social media, and or pornography websites including those specially dedicated to "revenge porn."
> —McGlynn et al. (2017, p. 29)

Sebastian (2017) criticized the use of revenge porn to describe this phenomenon, stating that it is misleading because many people may not be engaging in revenge but, rather, they stole the images through cyber hacking. Privacy, not revenge, is the issue at hand when discussing the phenomenon of NCIS. McGlynn et al. (2017) also argued that the term revenge porn does not fully describe the motivation, intent, extent, or nature of how these images are used against victims. For instance, in 2014, naked images of celebrities were retrieved from various iCloud accounts and shared online, yet this crime is not revenge because it was an unknown assailant who perpetrated it. Thus, the term revenge porn is too narrow of a definition to include the various forms of image-based violence that occurs without consent.

Legal circles are also debating whether to include NCIS as part of the general sexual violence criminalization statutes within the United States. Walker and Sleath (2017) noted "significant challenges that arise when attempting to criticize these behaviors" (p. 22) because there has not been a legal link or acknowledgment that online violations of this crime are akin to the crime of sexual assault. McGlynn et al. (2017) described legislative responses to revenge porn as "piecemeal" (p. 25) and mainly focusing on the actions of ex-partners who engage in vindictive and revengeful acts of cybercrime. McGlynn et al. argued for legal scholars to conceptualize these crimes on a continuum with other forms of sexual violence.

A similar argument has been made against the use of the term "non-consensual pornography." McGlynn et al. (2017) argued that "pornography wrongly focuses attention on the perceived actions of the victims rather than the perpetrator" (p. 38) and that the court system bases its criminal determination on the image being pornographic rather than sexually explicit. As a result, the term continues to be debated, along with terms such as image-based sexual exploitation, intimate image exploitation, and image-based sexual abuse.

Henry and Powell (2015) asserted that cybertechnology is simply a new way to perpetrate old crimes of stalking, intimidation, and sexual violence. In this way, non-consensual pornography should be considered part of the spectrum of aggressive and assaultive behaviors that effectively harm the victims.

CURRENT CONDITIONS

Sexting, or the act of sending sexual images via text message, and other forms of mutually agreed-upon sharing of sexually explicit images are growing in practice and can be viewed as healthy forms of sexual expression (Walker & Sleath, 2017). Walker and Sleath found that "sharing of images and videos within the context of a healthy relationship was not perceived to be problematic and for some was considered a positive 'normal' part of a dating relationship" (p. 20). NCIS, like sexual trauma, exists in a context in which couples may have previously engaged in agreeable, consensual sexual behavior. A majority (70%) of sexual assaults are committed by acquaintances (Bureau of Justice Statistics, 2016), and most instances of NCIS likewise occur because of a dissolution of a relationship (Bloom, 2014; Dawkins, 2015; Larkin, 2014). Not all relationships in which explicit imagery was shared end with digital violence. Those who perpetrate non-consensual sharing of intimate images are outliers in the population, and some researchers believe that perpetrators of NCIS are associated with "higher levels of rape supportive beliefs, peer approval of forced sex, number of sexual partners and exposure to pornography" (Walker & Sleath, 2017, p. 20).

With the advent of camera phones, social media, and the seemingly pervasive use of the internet, the trading of sexually explicit images has increased. Dir and Cyders (2015) reported international estimates of 18%–68% of young adults engaging in the sharing of sexually explicit imagery. In a 2014 Pew Research Center study, Lenhart, Duggan, and Smith found that in the United States, 9% of adult cell phone users sent a sexually explicit image on their phone, and 20% had received such images. Multiple sources corroborated that those in committed relationships are most likely to send sexually explicit imagery (Dir, Coskunpinar, Steiner, & Cyders, 2013; Samimi & Alderson, 2014). Ninety percent of Americans who send explicit images believe they are safe doing so with their current partner (Bloom, 2014).

For many young people, a central aspect of their identities is rooted in the cyber realm. Among adolescents today, technology plays a greater role in their daily lives than ever before. Taking or distributing sexual images of children are crimes in the United States; however, as with adult forms of sexual image sharing, enforcing the crime has become difficult because of the initial intentional creation of the image. Adolescent sexting is an area that warrants greater study and directly links to the high incidence of NCIS. A systematic review of adolescents who sext found that the primary motivations for sexting were flirting to gain romantic attention or enhance a current romantic relationship, experimenting during a phase, or complying with a partner who influenced the person to send them a photograph (Cooper, Quayle, Jonsson, & Svedin, 2016).

Adolescent girls are more likely to send pictures, and adolescent males are more likely to receive them (Gordon-Messer, Bauermeister, Grodzinski, & Zimmerman, 2012). In fact, Englander (2015) found that girls were twice as likely to be coerced to send sexually explicit images than their male peers. Overall, the issues of adolescence, access to technology, sexual experimentation, and neurobiological changes that can increase impulsivity, as well as drug and alcohol experimentation that can increase risk-taking, need to be further studied within this population to understand what kind of personality is more susceptible than others to victimization through this crime.

LOOKING TO THE FUTURE

The research on NCIS is in its infancy (Walker & Sleath, 2017), and much more needs to be done to advocate for victims of this violence. O'Connor, Drouin, Yergens, and Newsham (2017) advocated for uniform laws throughout the United States and globally that consider cyberbullying, sexting, and revenge porn as criminal acts and part of the wider definition of sexual violence. The authors also argued for stricter penalties when no consent is given in the taking of the images and "strict prohibition" (p. 240) against transmitting images to third parties, such as websites that profit from revenge porn. Powell and Henry (2014) agreed that harsher penalties are required and emphasized that the legal climate and prevention education programming should shy away from the victim-blaming practices of female stupidity and naiveté and support a conversation about consent that is subject to civil and criminal sanctions.

Advocacy

Research on the impact of cyber sexual exploitation on victims is needed, as well as initiatives that integrate victim resources, tools for law enforcement, and technical resources to identify and remove content. Created by a victim of NCIS, The Civil Rights Initiative is an advocacy organization that collects formal reports on the crime and finds mental health services and legal advocacy for victims who need it (https://www.cybercivilrights.org). The initiative also has a helpline that victims can call for further information, support, and referral. In addition, the nonprofit Without My Consent is a full-access advocacy site with information for victims on how to report and prosecute against predators who have posted their images.

Some individual vigilantes against revenge pornography have been using their own technological hacking knowledge to fight against predators, with some success in shutting down websites and legal prosecution (Thompson, 2016). In addition, the notorious

Figure 7.3 August 2018 advocates and researchers from throughout the world come together for a roundtable at Facebook headquarters in Menlo Park, California, to discuss image-based abuse prevention.

hacking group Anonymous has also become involved in the identification of sexual perpetrators online who post sexually explicit images of youth and adults (Thompson, 2016). Social media sites, such as Facebook and Reddit, have also begun to create regulations on their platforms that prohibit users from posting sexually explicit photos; however, identifying such photos remains a difficult task. In a failed attempt to advocate for victims, Facebook asked anyone who was afraid they could be a victim of revenge pornography to send Facebook their naked photos so Facebook could notify them if the photos were posted. The lack of awareness of how this request violates the privacy of victims was only recognized after the press release was issued (Romano, 2018). Facebook is continuing to search for other ways to identify these photos, but the fact remains that if a victim is never aware of her photos being posted online, they can remain there for eternity.

In the meantime, victims of any cybercrime, be it identity theft, online bullying, or online sexual exploitation, should be provided with non-victim-blaming support. Regarding NCIS, despite the intention of the person when a photo was originally taken, the distribution of it in a public forum was not with the consent of the user, making it a crime. The context of life continues to change with rapidly evolving technology, and the more empathy the general population can demonstrate for victims of cybercrimes, the sooner those victimized will recover from post-assault psychological reactions, thus helping fight against sexual predators online.

CONCLUSION

Non-consensual image sharing is such a new phenomenon in the 21st century that researchers and scholars on the topic have not agreed on the specific terminology to use to describe it. In this chapter, we termed the abuse non-consensual image sharing, with revenge porn as a subcategory However, the term technology-facilitated sexual violence may better describe the various acts in which a person's image, or other personal information, may be used in a way that results in a sexual assault. Cyberfeminism has begun to argue for the linkage of sexual assault crimes in the physical world with the same emotional and psychological reactions that happen when a crime has been committed in the virtual world. However, because the internet involves the world's governments and is not owned by one country in particular, the prosecution of these technology-facilitated crimes is not easy.

As the chapter has outlined, some advocates argue for a global response to this crime, rather than country by country. As more victims find a voice and legal scholar activists bring these technology-facilitated violations out of the shadows, there is an increasing awareness and urgency to effect change. Research is just beginning to help people understand the psychological impacts of this crime, yet what has been gleaned thus far is a strong connection between NCIS and acutely negative impacts on victims.

More research and policy analysis need to done to determine the best method to prevent and prosecute the perpetrators of this crime. In the meantime, psychological research must begin to understand how to help victims of this crime and facilitate healing from a new kind of sexual trauma taking shape in the 21st century.

DISCUSSION QUESTIONS

1. Through the lens of cyberfeminism, how is non-consensual image sharing a physical violation, even when the victim has never met the assailant in person?
2. What are the arguments for and against the term *revenge porn*. The chapter discussed various terms for this crime. What do you think is the best terminology for this type of sexual violation and why?
3. How does consent become central to the conversation of non-consensual image sharing? How does it impact victim blame?

REFERENCES

Bates, S. (2017). Revenge porn and mental health: A qualitative analysis of the mental health effects of revenge porn on female survivors. *Feminist Criminology, 12*(1), 22–42.

Bloom, S. (2014). No vengeance for "revenge porn" victims: Unraveling why this latest female-centric, intimate-partner offense is still legal, and why we should criminalize it. *Fordham Urban Law Journal, 42*, 233–289.

Brophy, J. (2010). Developing a corporeal cyberfeminism: Beyond cyberutopia. *New Media & Society, 12*(6), 929–945.

Bureau of Justice Statistics. (2016). *National Crime Victimization Survey (NCVS) 2010–2015*. Retrieved from https://www.bjs.gov/index.cfm?ty=dcdetail&iid=245

Castle, S. (2009). Cyberbullying on trial: The Computer Fraud and Abuse Act and United States v. Drew. *Journal of Law and Policy, 17*(2), 579–607.

Citron, D. K., & Franks, M. A. (2014). Criminalizing revenge porn. *Wake Forest Law Review, 49*, 345–391.

Clarke-Billings, L. (2016, November 28). Revenge porn laws in Europe, U.S. and beyond. *Newsweek*. Retrieved from https://www.newsweek.com/revenge-porn-laws-europe-us-and-beyond-499303

Cohn, A., Zinzow, H., Resnick, H., & Kilpatrick, D. G. (2013). Correlates of reasons for not reporting rape to police: Results from a national telephone household probability sample of women with forcible or drug or alcohol facilitated/incapacitated rape. *Journal of Interpersonal Violence, 28*(3), 455–473.

Cooper, K., Quayle, E., Jonsson, L., & Svedin, C. G. (2016). Adolescents and self-taken sexual images: A review of the literature. *Computers in Human Behavior, 55*, 706–716.

Cyber Civil Rights Initiative. (2014). *Revenge porn statistics*. Retrieved from https://www.cybercivilrights.org

Dawkins, J. T. (2015). A dish served cold: The case for criminalizing revenge pornography. *Cumberland Law Review, 45*, 395–447.

DeCou, C. R., Cole, T. T., Lynch, S. M., Wong, M. M., & Matthews, K. C. (2017). Assault-related shame mediates the association between negative social reactions to disclosure of sexual assault and psychological distress. *Psychological Trauma: Theory, Research, Practice, and Policy, 9*(2), 166–172.

Dir, A. L., Coskunpinar, A., Steiner, J. L., & Cyders, M. A. (2013). Understanding differences in sexting behaviors across gender, relationship status, and sexual identity, and the role of expectancies in sexting. *Cyberpsychology, Behavior, and Social Networking, 16*, 568–574.

Dir, A. L., & Cyders, M. A. (2015). Risks, risk factors, and outcomes associated with phone and internet sexting among university students in the United States. *Archives of Sexual Behavior, 44*, 1675–1684. http://dx.doi.org/10.1007/s10508-014-0370-7

Eaton, A., Jacobs, H., & Ruvalcaba, Y. (2017). *2017 nationwide online study of nonconsensual porn victimization and perpetration: A summary report*. Civil Rights Initiative. Retrieved from https://www.cybercivilrights.org/wp-content/uploads/2017/06/CCRI-2017-Research-Report.pdf

Englander, E. (2015, March/April). Coerced sexting and revenge porn among teens. *Bullying, Teen Aggression & Social Media*, 19–21.

Gordon-Messer, D., Bauermeister, J. A., Grodzinski, A., & Zimmerman, M. (2012). Sexting among young adults. *Journal of Adolescent Health, 52*(3), 301–306.

Halliday, J. (2015, October 11). Revenge porn: 175 cases reported to police in six months. *The Guardian.* Retrieved from https://www.theguardian.com/uk-news/2015/oct/11/revenge-porn-175-cases-reported-to-police-in-six-months

Henry, N., & Powell, A. (2015). Embodied harms: Gender, shame, and technology-facilitated sexual violence. *Violence Against Women, 21*(6), 758–779.

Hunt, E. (2015, March 19). New Zealand police apologize to Roast Busters victims. *The Guardian.* Retrieved from https://www.theguardian.com/world/2015/mar/19/new-zealand-police-apologise-to-roast-busters-victims

Kamal, M., & Newman, W. (2016). Revenge pornography: Mental health implications and related legislation. *Journal of the American Academy of Psychiatry and the Law, 44,* 359–367.

Larkin, P. J. (2014). Revenge porn, state law, and free speech. *Loyola of Los Angeles Law Review, 48,* 57–118.

Lenhart, A., Duggan, M., & Smith, A. (2014, February 11). *Couples, the internet, and social media.* Pew Research Center. Retrieved from http://pewinternet.org/Reports/2014/Couples-and-the-internet.aspx

Lenhart, A., Ybarra, M., & Price-Feeney, M. (2016). *Non-consensual image sharing: One in 25 Americans has been a victim of "revenge porn."* Data and Society Research Institute and Center for Innovative Public Health Research. Retrieved from https://datasociety.net/pubs/oh/Nonconsensual_Image_Sharing_2016.pdf

McGlynn, C., Rackley, E., & Houghton, R. (2017). Beyond "revenge porn": The continuum of image-based sexual abuse. *Feminist Legal Studies, 25*(1), 25–46.

O'Connor, K., Drouin, M., Yergens, N., & Newsham, G. (2017). Sexting legislation in the United States and abroad: A call for uniformity. *International Journal of Cyber Criminology, 11*(2), 218–245.

Patella-Rey, P. (2018). Beyond privacy: Bodily integrity as an alternative framework for understanding non-consensual pornography. *Information, Communication & Society, 21*(5), 786–791.

Powell, A., & Henry, N. (2014). Blurred lines? Responding to "sexting" and gender-based violence among young people. *Children Australia, 39*(2), 119–124.

Rennison, C. M. (2002). Rape and sexual assault: Reporting to police and medical attention, 1992–2000: US Department of Justice, Office of Justice Programs. Retrieved from https://www.bjs.gov/content/pub/pdf/rsarp00.pdf

Romano, A. (2018, May 24). Facebook's plan to stop revenge porn may be even creepier than revenge porn. *Vox.* Retrieved from https://www.vox.com/2018/5/23/17382024/facebook-revenge-porn-prevention

Roy, J. (2014, January 23). Revenge-porn king Hunter Moore indicted on federal charges. *TIME.* Retrieved from http://time.com/1703/revenge-porn-kinghunter-moore-indicted-by-fbi

Samimi, P., & Alderson, K. (2014). Sexting among undergraduate students. *Computers in Human Behavior, 31,* 230–241.

Sebastian, M. (2017). Privacy and consent: The trouble with the label of "revenge porn." *Feminist Media Studies, 17*(6), 1107–1111. doi:10.1080/14680777.2017.1380428

Thompson, N. (2016, February 25). The digital vigilante taking on revenge porn. *Wired Magazine*. Retrieved from https://www.wired.co.uk/article/james-mcgibney-troll-hunter

Walker, K., & Sleath, E. (2017). A systematic review of the current knowledge regarding revenge pornography and non-consensual sharing of sexually explicit media. *Aggression and Violent Behavior, 36*, 9–24.

Webb, L. (2015). Shame transfigured: Slut-shaming from Rome to cyberspace. *First Monday, 20*(4). http://dx.doi.org/10.5210/fm.v20i4.5464

8

The Honor Killing
of Qandeel Baloch

Visibility Through Social Media and Its Repercussions

SARAH AHMED ■

CASE STUDY: QANDEEL BALOCH

In June 2016, Qandeel Baloch, a woman who rose to fame through social media, was found murdered in her parents' home in Multan, Pakistan. Soon after, Qandeel's brother confessed to murdering his sister to preserve his family's honor. Honor killings are committed in the name of "honor" against female family members who are found complicit in activities deemed dishonorable by the family (Eisner & Ghuneim, 2013). These crimes are usually committed by the girl's or woman's own family members. Acts of dishonor can range from getting married to a person of one's choice to speaking to someone of the opposite sex and singing or dancing in front of the opposite sex. Honor killings occur primarily in the Middle East and South Asia.

Qandeel was born into a working-class Muslim family in one of the more patriarchal areas of Pakistan's Punjab province. A documentary on Qandeel created by *The Guardian* ("Qandeel," 2017) outlines the difficulties she had to endure before she became a controversial social media star. Yet, despite the odds she faced, Qandeel's use of social media as a platform to find space for her voice and her sexuality was arguably groundbreaking in a culture bound between religion and customs, especially for women from less privileged backgrounds.

Qandeel grew up in a home in which she was not allowed to pursue education like her brother. Instead, when she came of age, her father decided to marry her off in an arranged marriage. In interviews about the marriage, Qandeel confessed to having been harassed by her husband. She later ran away with her son to a women's shelter called Shirkat Gah. Eventually, she had to give up custody of her son to her husband as a price for her freedom from him. Determined to become self-reliant, Qandeel taught herself English and began her career as an attendant on intercity buses owned by Daewoo. In an interview, Qandeel stated (as cited in Chaudhry, 2017),

> [My husband at the time] tried to throw acid on me. He said "I'll burn your face because you're so beautiful." And today the media isn't giving me any credit for speaking about empowerment of women, girl power.
>
> They don't recognize that this girl fought. Today I am capable of taking on the burden of an entire household. But no one gives me credit for that. (para. 15–16)

Qandeel wanted to appear on television and gained attention by auditioning for a program similar to *American Idol*. The judges mocked her for her voice, her fashion sense, and her English accent. The latter can be arguably viewed as the judges mocking for her lower socioeconomic status that could not be hidden despite her attempts to appear more educated and upper class than she was in reality. An American or British English accent is coveted in Pakistan, and attaining it is not accessible for many people due to the associated costs of living abroad, attending a private school, and/or taking private accent coaching lessons.

Qandeel shot to fame when her audition video and the post-exit interview from the show became viral. Later, Qandeel began using Facebook to share videos of her talking candidly to the camera, often lying in bed in a way that sexualized her and the image she crafted. Through Facebook, Qandeel controlled the platform she used to put forth content that would have been too risqué to share in Pakistan through mainstream media. These videos attracted attention from conservative Pakistani audiences who seemed delighted, shocked, and appalled by them. Interestingly, a significant portion of the hate comments regarding Qandeel's videos were posted by Pakistani women, who were uncomfortable with the sexualized nature of the videos. Due to the many complaints Qandeel's page received because of "profanity" and "immorality," Facebook took down her page multiple times, following which she would put it up again. After her death, her page was removed by Facebook. The exact reason for this is not known.

Qandeel's dispute with a local Muslim cleric arguably became the reason for her death. A prominent Muslim scholar appeared on a television show to remind Qandeel of piety that she seemed to have forgotten as a Muslim woman. In response, Qandeel later took pictures and videos of the same Muslim cleric sharing a cigarette with her in a hotel room where he had invited himself to help her reconnect with her faith.

Qandeel held a press conference explaining how she had exposed the so-called pious cleric, claiming she is a Muslim and a daughter of the (Pakistan) nation (Amber, 2016). She also claimed receiving death threats for slandering the cleric and demanded security from the Federal Interior Minister (Amber, 2016). Eventually, she went to her family home to escape the frenzy, where her younger brother drugged her and his family and then killed Qandeel. Qandeel's brother was arrested and confessed to killing his sister for bringing dishonor to the family (Perry, 2016). Qandeel was 26 years old when she was killed.

Qandeel's honor killing was treated differently than most honor killings because it was classified as a crime against the state instead of her family being given the option of pardoning the murderer, which is more frequently the case. Soon after Qandeel's death, the cleric was arrested in connection with the murder but was later released.

Would Qandeel have faced the same kind of controversies had she had the privilege of being born into a wealthy Pakistani family with connections? If she had gone abroad and spoke English with an accent as Pakistani elites do, would she have incurred the same ridicule and shame? And if she came from an influential family, would she have been protected from the stigma of being a self-made woman without a male figure responsible for her success? In her interview, Qandeel stated (as cited in Chaudhry, 2017),

> What about my self-worth? My identity? I am a social media sensation, I am a fashion icon. I don't know HOW many girls have felt support through my persona. I'm a girl power. So many girls tell me I'm a girl power, and yes, I am. (para. 5)

Social media played a major role in giving Qandeel the space and visibility she was denied initially when she appeared on television. Her Facebook page thus gave her space and agency that her socioeconomic background could not have afforded her. Without online space, her videos and later news of her death would not have had the global outreach that they achieved. It was also this platform that Qandeel used to mock the Muslim cleric for his hypocrisy.

Qandeel's story demonstrates how social media has made accessible spaces for marginalized communities, including transgender individuals, religious minorities, and women, to have a voice and be seen. Research on social media needs to document and analyze the use of this platform as a powerful tool for marginalized communities, as well as the efforts being made to protect these spaces and the people using them.

Figure 8.1 Family member of Qandeel Baloch holds photos of her.

OVERVIEW

Killings in the name of honor, or honor killings, are not a new phenomenon in South Asia. In 2015, Pakistan's independent Human Rights Commission published a report citing that 1,100 women were killed in Pakistan in honor-based violence, an increase from 1,000 women in 2014 and 869 in 2013 (Human Rights Commission of Pakistan, 2015). Although honor killings are often misunderstood as being a problem associated with Islam, scholars argue that they are more of an issue with regard to culture, given the prevalence of honor-based violence incidences across South Asia among non-Muslims as well.

According to the United Nations (2014), 5,000 women are killed every year in honor-based violence. The prevalence of honor killings is high in South Asia and in the Middle East, where public opinions on the matter are varied. A 2013 study conducted in Jordan's capital of Amman revealed that one-third of respondents found honor killings to be justified in the defense of the family's honor (Eisner & Ghuneim, 2013). A 2009 survey conducted by the United Nations Population Fund found that 68% of young Iraqi men considered honor killings to be justified (Gharib, 2016).

Honor-based violence occurs in developed nations as well, although in smaller numbers. A research study commissioned by the US Department of Justice found that annually, 23–27 honor killings occur in the United States, 13 occur in the Netherlands, and 10 or 11 occur in the United Kingdom (Helba, Bernstein, Leonard, & Baeur, 2014). Most of the honor killings happen in the homes of migrant families who deem the female family member's actions to be dishonorable to the family and traditions. These actions may include having romantic relations before marriage and speaking with someone of the opposite sex. In 2008, two sisters, Sarah Said (aged 18 years) and Amina Said (aged 17 years), were killed in the name of "honor" in Texas by their father of Egyptian origin (Chesler, 2009). The sisters had previously told their friends that their father was controlling and abusive and subsequently kept their boyfriends a secret from their father.

Social media plays a crucial role in creating awareness of honor killings but also has proved a necessary platform for marginalized individuals to find agency and visibility. Qandeel's rise to fame through provocative videos on her Facebook page provoked much criticism online, particularly by Pakistani women, who condemned Qandeel for not abiding by a more modest and conservative image, citing that she is Muslim and her conduct was not appropriate given that she lives in a Muslim country. However, Qandeel's death opened up a larger conversation on women's status in Pakistan, both online and offline, such that most of her online critics agreed that her death was unjustified and cruel, even though they disagreed with her social media activities.

Social media has opened up new avenues for the marginalized and invisible to become seen and heard, particularly those who may not have the connections or "acceptable" physical characteristics to appear on television. In Pakistan, the rise of a few social media personalities, including Qandeel Baloch, have challenged the hegemony of television as the sole pathway of visibility and fame. However, as Qandeel Baloch's honor killing demonstrates, the visibility of marginalized people, including women and effeminate men and/or transgender individuals, is also met with horrific policing and control that pose life-threatening consequences.

The following sections provide an overview of historic trends, recent developments, and current conditions to gain a better understanding of honor killings throughout the world, particularly in Pakistan, the site of Qandeel Baloch's death. Interwoven in this analysis is the use of social media as a means of creating visibility as well as a form of policing of marginalized individuals.

HISTORICAL TRENDS

Honor killings warrant a larger conversation about control over a woman's visibility and agency by a male family member. Most cases of honor killings stem from male family members curtailing the rights of women in their family. Honor killing is thus used as a disciplinary mechanism to keep women's mobility and agency in check. Chesler (2010) finds that victims of honor killings can be classified into two groups based on their age. In one group, the average age of victims is 17 years. These women are not yet married and are prone to violence from family members, including their fathers. The other group comprises victims whose average age is 36 years. These women are most likely married and susceptible to violence from their in-laws, in addition to their husbands. This stark difference in age indicates that women are still vulnerable to be controlled and to have their freedoms curtailed even after marriage and motherhood.

Awwad (2001) explains the importance of family in the Middle Eastern culture that is often patriarchal, patrilineal, and patrilocal. In such an orientation, Awwad describes men as having the role of defending the honor of their family by policing the actions of women, which can have negative social implications on the status of the family (i.e., bringing shame to the family). The prevalence of honor killings in the Middle East can be traced back to the pre-Islamic era, when honor killings were aimed to protect a family's power structure and reproductive power, not women's sexual behavior (Ruggi, 1998; cited in Awwad, 2001). Awwad warns readers to not conflate Islam with honor killings, instead calling this practice cultural rather than religious. This is supported by a historiographical account indicating that honor killings occurred before Islam and also after colonialism and industrialization. Linking honor killings to Islam may be reducing the complexities of honor killings—why they happen, where they happen, and how to stop them. It also may make invisible honor-based violence that occurs in non-Muslim households.

Countries in the Middle East have a checkered relationship in holding family members responsible for honor killings. Both the 1999 Syrian penal code and the 1960 Jordan penal code give reduced sentences to men for honor-based violence on a female family member (Awwad, 2001). Article 340 of the Jordanian penal code has since faced much backlash from female lawyers and women's rights groups. Under this article, a man can receive a reduced penalty for killing his wife or other female relatives in the name of honor if he does so because they are committing adultery (Human Rights Watch, 2004). In 2017, a judge doubled the sentences of two brothers who killed their sister for fleeing their house after she fell in love. Following this landmark ruling, the Iftaa Department of Jordan, responsible for issuing religious edicts, issued a *fatwa* (a ruling or decision made by an Islamic scholar) declaring honor killing un-Islamic (Maayeh, 2016). Despite these developments, the article still remains in Jordan's penal code. In 2009, Syria introduced a law to prosecute perpetrators of honor-based violence with a prison sentence of 2–7 years (Human Rights Watch, 2009).

Chesler (2010) argues that most honor-based violence is rarely classified as such or reported. When it is reported, it is treated with light punishment because families are less inclined to prosecute, especially if they were complicit in the honor-based violence themselves and/or found it justified because it restored the family's "honor." Chesler further explains that when honor-based violence occurs in the West, many people, including the authorities, do not label it as such.

The advent of social media has allowed the internet to become a new platform for marginalized people to find space and agency online. Odine (2013) shows the importance of women's access to social media especially in countries such as Saudi Arabia, where women do not have much input with regard to national development. Odine uses the example of Saudi Arabia's Hanna Hajjer, whose portraits depict women heartbroken when informed by their husbands that they are bringing home a second or third wife. Through social media, women also have access to participate in digital activism and advocacy issues in countries where women's visibility and/or mobility is controlled. Sara (2015) depicts different hashtag campaigns transnationally to increase awareness of challenges women face, such as the social media campaign to challenge Saudi Arabia's ban on women driving and the campaign against women being forcibly married to their rapists, as in the case of Morocco's Amina Filali.

Although few cases of honor-based violence occur in the United States, mostly in migrant families, beyond these cases, women's mobility and visibility are not challenged like they are in the Middle East. For example, the #MeToo movement is an important social media campaign that enables women to take control of the narrative on sexual harassment.

RECENT DEVELOPMENTS IN PAKISTAN

In Pakistan, the status of women, and women's rights, has had a nonlinear trajectory, which at times has taken steps backward after achieving progress. This in many ways is a reflection of the sociopolitical history of Pakistan. In 2006, Pakistan passed the Protection of Women Act (Criminal Laws Amendment). In 2016, following Qandeel's death, the Parliament passed the Anti-Honor Killing Bill. In this section, the merits of these two bills are discussed, along with critiques of these bills from those who argue these measures are not enough.

Military intervention has been a long and important part of Pakistan's political history featuring military dictators who have taken over democratically elected governments under martial law. To be sure, more than half of Pakistan's history has been under such military leadership. Women's rights in Pakistan were severely compromised under General Zia's mission to Islamize Pakistani society. Women's agency became especially regulated under his reign, both on the streets and on television.

Zia's legacy in marginalizing women is seen through the institution of legislature called the Hudood Ordinances of 1979, wherein zina (extramarital sex) and rape were combined. Hence, under the Hudood Ordinances, a rape victim could be arrested for slandering the character of her alleged rapist if she did not have witnesses and proof of rape. These ordinances were not reversed until 2006, under the Protection of Women Act, notably under another military ruler, General Musharraf.

Additional laws that undermine women's testimonies and allow perpetrators of honor-based violence to receive reduced sentences still exist today. The qisas (retribution) and diyat (blood money) passed under Nawaz Sharif's government in 1990 prioritized the relationship of the offender to the victim over the intensity of the crime.

Subsequently, Sections 309 and 310 gave legal guardians of the victim the right to waive *qisas* and pardon the offender or to accept *diyat* (Sattar, 2015, p. 21). This is problematic because the offender is usually a male family member who can be pardoned by another family member of the victim. Under such arrangements, honor killings become a private family affair instead of a crime against the state. Subsequently, the 2006 Protection of Women Act authorized courts to punish an offender in honor killing cases only when *qisa* had been waived or compounded (Sattar, 2015).

Impinging upon prosecution of honor-based violence is the plea of "grave and sudden" provocation, which was used during British colonialism in some tribal areas. Using this, the perpetrator can claim to deny killing the victim for honor, thereby allowing him to escape the 2016 Anti-Honor Killing Bill, which is one of the criticisms of the bill by feminists. Courts have issued conflicting responses to this plea: Some courts have granted the plea, and others have not (Sattar, 2015).

CURRENT CONDITIONS

Cybercrime laws have recently been introduced in Pakistan, along with a hotline for women to receive help when harassed online (AFP, 2017). The cybercrime laws were met with controversy from critics who claimed the language of the laws was ambiguous and could be misused to curtail freedom of online speech (Khan, 2016).

In addition to judicial reforms, societal norms need to change to hold perpetrators of honor-based violence accountable. Consequently, gender norms and representation of women need to reflect women's agency and rights to tackle the institutionalized patriarchy that cannot be dismantled by judicial reforms alone. Customary laws that continue to marginalize women through tribal courts need to be scrutinized, and women in these areas need increased access to state courts. Given customary laws and entrenched patriarchy, especially in rural areas of Pakistan, it is not surprising, as Sattar (2015) notes, that "Islam in Pakistan's legal system is not the only relevant variable in understanding women's experience of law" (p. 18).

As mentioned previously, Qandeel Baloch's case set a precedent, wherein the state became a complainant, causing a woman's family to no longer have the right to pardon her killer, as is frequently done. Because honor-based violence (including honor killings) is done by a family member, the killer is rarely held accountable by the family of the victim (and, by extension, the family of the killer). Although additional policies need to be put in place to secure women's rights, enforcing current rules must be given priority to hold perpetuators of violence accountable.

One of the challenges of transnational feminism in confronting honor-based violence lies in how culture and faith are taken into account and addressed. For many women in Pakistan, "feminism" has a negative connotation, and they distance themselves from this term. Although this is seen in the United States as well, wherein some female celebrities shy away from being called feminists, Pakistan's colonial past and Islamic identity forge a complicated relationship with Western feminism—one that cannot be overlooked. Mohanty (1991) reminds us of the ways some feminist scholars based in the West might have reduced women in developing countries in the past to be a singular category of "oppressed," which is highly problematic. Hence, Mitra (2011) notes that nongovernmental organization (NGO) workers in India distance themselves from being called "feminist," despite performing work that can be defined as such. Bhavnani, Foran, Kurian, and Munshi's (2016) approach to examining gender and development in developing countries with a focus on culture creates the necessary lens that must be adopted that does not alienate women on the basis of their religion or culture and has the capacity to understand on-the-ground nuances in order to help women find solutions without making them pariahs in their communities.

LOOKING TO THE FUTURE

Tackling honor killings requires a two-pronged approach. Changing the attitudes at the societal level is necessary to decry acts of violence perpetuated by family members. This transformation can only occur with necessary strict measures taken by the state to punish perpetuators of honor-based violence.

Increased protections against stalking and harassment for social media personalities, especially those who cannot afford security measures on their own, must be provided by the state. Qandeel held a conference to publicly share that she was receiving death threats and ask the authorities for protection. Eventually, Qandeel returned to her family home to seek shelter and protection that she believed she did not have living on her own in a larger city. Sattar (2015) recommends that the state act as a *wali* (legal guardian) so that honor-based violence becomes an act against the government instead of a private matter. In addition, Sattar advises creating a law to prevent perpetrators of honor-based violence from using the "grave and sudden" provocation. Under the Pakistan Penal Code, 1860, use of this provocation can result in honor killings not being ruled murder because the perpetrator states he had no self-control due to the grave and sudden provocation invoked by the victim (Sattar, 2015).

Figure 8.2 Women in Pakistan at a rally protesting against violence on women.

Holding conferences, such as the Convention on the Elimination of All Forms of Discrimination Against Women, of which Pakistan is a signatory, can centralize resources and create alliances among advocacy groups transnationally to tackle honor-based violence. Finally, Sattar (2015) adds that unified crime reports and data on honor killing need to be documented.

For transnational feminists, particularly those located in the West, it might be useful to adopt a cultural-sensitive lens when addressing honor-based violence and to not conflate honor-based violence with Islam. Mohanty's (1991) critique of earlier Western feminist accounts of women in developing countries is an important reminder of the dangers of creating blanket statements that may reify sociopolitical pressures on women instead of empowering them.

Honor-based violence is prevalent in areas of the Middle East and South Asia due to socioeconomic, cultural, and political factors that create differences in the way women are treated compared to women in developed countries. Advocacy, especially for activists and advocates in the West, against honor-based violence must be inclusive and culturally sensitive to ensure victims and advocates in countries in which honor-based violence occurs do not feel alienated. Bhavnani et al.'s (2016) approach to introducing a women, culture, and development (WCD) model is similar to incorporating culture within development studies. By including culture in the lens of understanding gender, gender relations, and development, WCD factors how certain customs and cultural norms can create situations in which women are marginalized. A call to action under WCD would thus be finding solutions while addressing customs and the culture in a way that does not alienate women from their community or culture. Writing off honor-based violence as exclusively situated in Islam can also alienate women from non-Islamic backgrounds who are victims but are denied visibility or agency to claim victim status.

Advocacy

Several organizations in Pakistan help women and advocate for women's rights in various capacities. Shirkat Gah (Urdu translation: a place to come together) is a women's resource center from which Qandeel sought help when she left her husband's house. The Aurat Foundation (Urdu translation: Women's Foundation), established in 1986, advocates on women's rights issues through public-awareness programs, demonstrations, and lobbying.

In addition, women such as the late lawyer Asma Jahangir and the late human rights activist and NGO worker Sabeen Mahmud have created important spaces for women to seek help and for discussions on how to combat violence.

Globally, Amnesty International has been vocal in condemning honor killings throughout the world, including Pakistan. Oxfam, too, launched a local movement from 2005 to 2011 to create awareness of honor killings in Pakistan (IRIN News, 2004).

Qandeel's story is not unique. Women are continually marginalized on social media. In July 2018, an Iranian woman, Maeda, was arrested for posting an Instagram video of her dancing. Women's presence continues to be policed and silenced. Supporting local and international organizations that aim to protect women's voices and presence both on social media and offline is thus necessary.

CONCLUSION

This chapter examined the case of Qandeel Baloch, a social media star who catapulted to fame with Facebook videos that were deemed controversial and immoral by many Pakistanis. Her case represents a global example of honor-based violence. Qandeel's death brought to light many paradoxes in Pakistani society regarding the silencing of women deemed too un-Islamic as well as the invisibility of women of lower socio-economic status in Pakistani society who aspire to compete with those with more privilege.

Social media became central for Qandeel to reclaim space, visibility, and, most important, agency. However, the social capital and prominence Qandeel acquired through social media was not enough to protect her from being publicly humiliated and discredited on social media as well as on television talk shows. Furthermore, Qandeel did not have the necessary political connections or capital to hire security for herself or convince authorities to take the death threats she received seriously. Given the lack of strict prosecution and penal code for honor-based violence, especially outside of metropolitan areas, Qandeel's brother viewed his "responsibility" of keeping his family's honor to be more important than the punishment he would receive for murdering his own sister.

In order for honor-based violence to be taken seriously, a drastic shift needs to occur at the state and societal level. The protection of a woman's visibility and agency must be upheld by both the community and the state through social norms and penal codes. Subsequently, transnational alliances forged to increase awareness and solidarity with victims need to be culturally sensitive to allow victims to feel welcome without being reduced to a single category of "victim" or "oppressed." Discussions on honor killings must be vibrant and complex to reflect and encompass the complexities and diversities of the victims.

DISCUSSION QUESTIONS

1. What are some of the socioeconomic challenges Qandeel had to face to become famous?
2. How has social media given more visibility and agency to women who are otherwise marginalized in their society because of cultural, religious, and/or class factors?
3. How does the increased visibility of marginalized people challenge social norms and social control? How can the state become more involved to ensure the safety of the people who use social media as a platform to speak?

REFERENCES

AFP. (2017, April 7). *Pakistan hotline offers safe space for women harassed online.* Retrieved February 14, 2018, from https://tribune.com.pk/story/1377056/pakistan-hotline-offers-safe-space-women-harassed-online

Amber, S. (2016, June 28). *"Daughter of nation" Qandeel Baloch opens up about her encounter with Mufti Qavi.* Retrieved from https://dailytimes.com.pk/73179/daughter-of-nation-qandeel-baloch-opens-up-about-her-encounter-with-mufti-qavi

Awwad, A. (2001). Gossip, scandal, shame and honor killing: A case for social constructionism and hegemonic discourse. *Social Thought & Research, 24*(1–2), 39–52.

Bhavnani, K., Foran, J., Kurian, P. A., & Munshi, D. (2016). *Feminist futures: Reimagining women, culture and development* (2nd ed.). London, UK: Zed Books.

Chaudhry, H. (2017, July 15). *No one gives me any credit for speaking about girl power: Qandeel Baloch.* Retrieved February 14, 2018, from https://images.dawn.com/news/1175807

Chesler, P. (2009). Are honor killings simply domestic violence? *Middle East Quarterly, 16*(2), G1–G11.

Chesler, P. (2010). Worldwide trends in honor killings. *Middle East Quarterly, 17*(2), 3–11.

Eisner, M., & Ghuneim, L. (2013). Honor killing attitudes amongst adolescents in Amman, Jordan. *Aggressive Behavior, 39*(5), 405–417.

Gharib, M. (2016, July 19). *"Honor killings" are a global problem—and often invisible.* Retrieved February 13, 2018, from https://www.npr.org/sections/goatsandsoda/2016/07/19/486607329/honor-killings-are-a-global-problem-and-often-invisible

Helba, C., Bernstein, M., Leonard, M., & Baeur, E. (2014, November 26). *Report on exploratory study into honor violence measurement methods.* Retrieved February 13, 2018, from https://www.ncjrs.gov/pdffiles1/bjs/grants/248879.pdf

Human Rights Commission of Pakistan. (2015). *Annual report 2015.* Retrieved February 13, 2018, from http://hrcp-web.org/hrcpweb/hrcp-annual-report-2015

Human Rights Watch. (2004, April). *Honoring the killers: Justice denied for "honor" crimes in Jordan: IV. Honor crimes under Jordanian law.* Retrieved from https://www.hrw.org/reports/2004/jordan0404/4.htm

Human Rights Watch. (2009, April 17). *Syria: No exceptions for "honor killings."* Retrieved from https://www.hrw.org/news/2009/07/28/syria-no-exceptions-honor-killings

IRIN News. (2004, November 8). *Oxfam to launch campaign against honour killing.* Retrieved from http://www.irinnews.org/news/2004/11/08/oxfam-launch-campaign-against-honour-killing

Khan, R. (2016, August 11). *Cyber crime bill passed by NA: 13 reasons Pakistanis should be worried.* Retrieved February 14, 2018, from https://www.dawn.com/news/1276662

Maayeh, S. (2016, December 3). *Jordan says "honour killing" is against Islam.* Retrieved February 13, 2018, from https://www.thenational.ae/world/jordan-says-honour-killing-is-against-islam-1.203182

Mitra, A. (2011). To be or not to be a feminist in India. *Affilia, 26*(2), 182–200.

Mohanty, C. (1991). Under Western eyes—feminist scholarship and colonial discourse. In C. T. Mohanty, A. Russo, & L. Torres (Eds.), *Third World women and the politics of feminism* (pp. 51–80). Bloomington, IN: Indiana University Press.

Odine, M. (2013). Role of social media in the empowerment of Arab women. *Global Media Journal, 12*(22), 1–30.

Perry, J. (2016, July 19). *Brother "proud" of killing Pakistan social media star.* Retrieved February 14, 2018, from https://www.cnn.com/2016/07/18/asia/pakistan-qandeel-baloch-brother-confession/index.html

Qandeel. (2017, September 22). *The Guardian.* Retrieved February 13, 2018, from https://www.youtube.com/watch?v=jUVyz2OQjbc

Sara, A. (2015). Digital activism for women's rights in the Arab World. In *Upholding Gendered Peace at a Time of War* conference. Beirut, Lebanon. Retrieved February 14, 2018, from http://womeninwar.org/wordpress/wp-content/uploads/2015/08/

Beirut/8/Aline%20Sara_Digital%20Activism%20for%20women's%20rights%20 in%20the%20Arab%20World.pdf

Sattar, A. (2015). *The laws of honour killing and rape in Pakistan: Current status and future prospects.* Retrieved February 14, 2018, from https://aawaz.org.pk/cms/lib/down-loadfiles/1448430520v2%20Final%20AS%20Laws.pdf

United Nations. (2014, February 17). *Global violence against women in the name of "honour."* Retrieved February 13, 2018, from http://iheu.org/wp-content/uploads/2014/ 03/433_A_HRC_25_NGO_Sub_En_IHEU_Honour.pdf

9

Public Meets Private

Fetishing Japanese Women

ANA LOPEZ, MICHELLE GREENE, TERRI MINNIEAR,
AND ANNALISA ENRILE ■

CASE STUDY: TAKAKO TANOOKA

Takako Tanooka was groped on Japan's busy trains on her first day of high school (Ito, 2016). Takako Tanooka is an alias adopted in order to maintain anonymity (Ekin, 2017). The sexual assaults continued almost daily on her way home from school (Ito, 2016). When the assaults happened, bystanders did nothing, even when Tanooka yelled for help (Matsunaga, 2017). Tanooka found that trying to catch her assailant was difficult on the congested trains (Ito, 2016). Her attackers included young teenage males and older businessmen, known as salarymen in Japan (Ito, 2016).

In the mornings, Tanooka avoided the groping by riding Japan's women's only train cars; however, this solution was not available to her on her way home, when she would be groped regularly (Ito, 2016). Tanooka and her mother went to the police, who told her to change her behavior by standing in different areas of the train and to take different routes home (Ito, 2016). Tanooka tried self-defense, and with her mother, she practiced publicly speaking out to assailants (Ito, 2016). Inspired by Tanooka, her friend's mother Yayoi Matsunaga began a campaign through the Groping Prevention Activities Centre and crowdsourced images for pins that schoolgirls could wear on their clothing while on the trains to help deter groping (Ekin, 2017). To capture one of Tanooka's assailants, she had to chase him off the train until police intervened on the platform (Matsunaga, 2017).

In Japan, groping (*chikan* in Japanese) on public trains has been problematic since the 1990s, and police have adopted the following slogan to deter the problem: "Groping is a crime" (Ito, 2016). Men who grope women are known as chikan (Ito, 2016). Some assailants force women to touch their genitals, some cut the skirts

Figure 9.1 Some reports state that Japan is one of the most busy transit centers in the world. Trains in Tokyo are reported to be at 200% capacity at rush hour, making close contact with others unavoidable.

of women, and some masturbate publicly (Ito, 2016). Many women do not report these crimes. Japan is a collectivist shame-based society, and individuals prefer to not report private incidents to prevent embarrassment to their families. Chikan reportedly stops occurring when girls grow older and no longer wear their school uniforms (Ekin, 2017). The girl's school uniform, known as the "sailor suit," was introduced in the 1920s (Kinsell, 2002). The school uniform's design is based on the Japanese navy uniform, which was constructed under foreign gaze and later became eroticized.

OVERVIEW

In the United States, women historically have had to fight against societal norms that place them inferior to men. The history of feminism is categorized by different waves in the United States and throughout the world. In Western culture, the first wave of feminism is marked by the movement that began in the late 19th century and early 20th century when women fought for suffrage and to create more opportunities for women. During this time, a radical uproar was sparked by anti-war protests, women working while men were fighting in wars, and the civil rights movement. The second wave is commonly considered to span from approximately 1960 through the 1990s (Rampton, 2015). A women's ability to be anything other than a housewife, a woman's sexuality, and reproductive rights were being brought to the surface by advocates, and other minority groups started being recognized (Rampant, 2015). Differing from the first wave of feminism that was populated mainly by White, heterosexual, affluent women, the second wave dealt with the struggles that people of all races, genders, and classes faced. The current wave of feminism focuses on opening opportunities for women, and women and other minority groups are able to be heard when discussing their oppression (Dixon, 2011). The three waves of feminism are placed in the context of Western culture and show the progress that women have made toward equality and fighting patriarchal standards. Although these messages foster positivity, they contradict and conflict with Western culture's media messages when projected to Third World and developing countries (Dixon, 2011).

Japan is a constitutional monarchy with an emperor whose powers have shifted primarily to ceremonial duties (Masumoto & Latz, 2018). Japan's first female in the Diet (the Japanese government's legislative branch) was feminist Kato Shidzue, elected in 1946 (Gelb, 1997). Japan's average household size is 2.39 persons, and the average monthly income is 457,376 yen (4,220 USD) ((Statistics Bureau, n.d.). The average age of marriage for men is 30.9 years and for women 29.3 years (Statistics Bureau, n.d.). Japan has a population of 126.7 million. The Japan Railway, one of the country's largest train lines, has a ridership of almost 300,000 per day. The percentage of females molested by chikan varies widely from 24% to 78% (Horii & Burgess, 2012). The number of women groped by chikan is underreported, and it is believed to be much higher.

In the United Kingdom, it is estimated that 10% of women are groped on trains but that 90% go unreported (Newman, 2016). Other cities that have reported incidents of groping on mass transit include New York City and Hong Kong (Horii & Burgess, 2012). In response to groping, women-only train cars now exist in Japan, Egypt, South Korea, Russia, Indonesia, Taiwan, and South Africa, where the economy has spurred a growth in women commuting to jobs (Horii & Burgess, 2012, p. 44).

HISTORICAL TRENDS

In Japan, marriage rates began dropping since 1980 along with the desire for romantic relationships (Yamada, 2017). Statistics indicate that interest in relationships, pair bonding, sex, and love has been on a steady decline since the 1980s and will likely not increase. A survey from 1987 found that 86% of 15-year-old males reported the desire for sexual relations; in 2001, this rate had declined to 50%, and it was 25.7% in 2014 (Yamada, 2017). This relationship degradation is replicated in high school, where in 1982, 54% of students reported having intimate feelings for another individual, but that percentage had dropped to 31% in 2012 (Yamada, 2017). A 2015 survey showed that 40% of single individuals did not want lovers (Yamada, 2017).

Japan is a conservative, shame-based collectivist culture. Abuse of girls has been overt since the 1980s. Adams (2007) describes the social family structure, sexless marriages, and the high frequency of co-sleeping children and parents that lead to the obsession with young girls. Horii and Burgess (2012) suggest that salarymen are often perpetrators due to their loss of status as powerful wage earner and their new status symbolizing economic collapse, which causes them to want to regain power by dominating young women in the public sphere. There has also been an increase in consumption and materialization with "a greater emphasis on pleasure and recreation" (Lin, 2008, p. 33).

The Private Sphere

CHILD ABUSE AND INCEST

Children in Japan are viewed as extensions of the family rather than as beings, and interference in family issues is off limits to outsiders (Adams, 2007). Incest was not criminalized until two decades ago; however, mutual relationships are not outlawed (Adams, 2007). Historical creation myths of Japan include incestuous relationships, and geneticists have found this to be practiced as recently as 1959 (Adams, 2007). In rural areas, it was common and praiseworthy for widowed fathers to marry their own daughters (Adams, 2017).

Research conducted of women in universities found that 48% of the students had been victimized in childhood (Adams, 2007). Women in prisons report childhood victimization rates as high as 82% (Adams, 2007). In one area of Japan, it was found that of 162 girls who were sexually abused, in 40% of the cases the abuse was committed by the father and that 20% of girls older than age 16 years still shared a bed with their fathers (Adams, 2007). Currently, when police investigate sexual abuse in the home, they must get permission from the parents before they can see the home and acquire evidence; therefore, it is still unusual for police to make arrests (Adams, 2007).

Child pornography was not outlawed until 2014, but loopholes have been exploited through *chaku ero* or "erotically clothed" soft pornography and lolicon manga comics (Varley, 2017). Chaku ero is considered legal because it does not display nudity but only highly suggestive poses, and profits can be as high as 5 million yen (46,154.00 USD), whereas profits for high school girl videos are approximately 1 million yen (9,230.00 USD) (Varley, 2017). Lolicon is the manga version that includes graphic images of sexual violence, including incest, which remains completely uncensored due to the free speech rights of artists (Varley, 2017). Sales of manga were more than 261 billion yen (2.4 billion USD) for 2015 (Varley, 2017). Some individuals in favor of maintaining free speech for artists argue that lolicon is useful for pedophiles to satisfy their urges without harming real children (Varley, 2017).

VIRTUAL REALITY GIRLFRIENDS AND DATING SIMS

With a loss of interest in relationships, the Japanese population is on the decline and individuals are engaging with virtual reality to satisfy their emotional needs. Games and home assistance tools have been designed with an affective capacity to simulate romantic partners. In 2016, Gatebox released Azumi Hikari, an artificially intelligent virtual assistant similar to Amazon's Alexa (Boxall, 2017). Azumi is a small anime hologram inside a cylindrical tube with sensors for temperature and motion. Azumi can control smart home devices and can also send reminders encouraging owners to return early and simulate enthusiasm upon notification of an early arrival (Morris, 2016).

Dating simulation games create a space for the gamer to pursue a relationship with a virtual avatar by selecting preset options through predetermined love maps (Gn, 2014). LovePlus is a game released in 2009 that simulates dating in high school. The gamer chooses one of three girls to friend and eventually date (Bennet, 2011). LovePlus has become well known because an otaku married one of the avatars in the same year of its release (Gn, 2014). Otaku are young collectors and consumers of pop culture who are experts in media and technology (Niu, Chiang, & Tsai, 2012).

Victims of chikan, such as Tanooka, have also identified otaku as their assailants. Mystic Messenger is a female-oriented dating simulation that also allows the player to pursue a relationship with a male avatar (Moore, 2016). Although there has been controversy surrounding dating simulations, Gn argues that the games simply reinforce the structure and values of romantic relationships for those who cannot attain them but wish to do so.

The Public Sphere

LOVE HOTELS CATERING TO EVERY FETISH

As the age of marriage increases, Japan's focus on sex for reproduction has shifted to sex for gratification (Lin, 2008). It is important to note that single and couple households have grown, and birth rates and intergenerational households have decreased (Lin, 2008). Love hotels have filled the gap in a place where sex in an intergenerational home is not private. Love hotels became popular when the expectation was to remain in the parents' home until marriage and when decisions were traditionally made based on the benefits for the family unit and not individuals. In 2005, love hotels were utilized more than half a billion times (Lin, 2008). These hotels became popular because they represented a sensible way to deal with basic physical needs (Lin, 2008).

Love hotels are private, and most only accept cash. In most love hotels, if food is ordered, the staff place it in a box built into a wall so the client can open the box without encountering anyone, thus guaranteeing the client's privacy (Japanese Journey, 2017). In the 1970s, these hotels were primarily associated with crime and prostitution (Lin, 2008). Love hotels have been cleaned up, and now videos populate YouTube explaining how to use one and how to find the one that suits one's personal pleasure (Broad, 2016). These hotels have themed rooms, including medical-style rooms, shame rooms, school classrooms, bondage rooms, gagged Hello Kitty rooms, and Jurassic Park rooms (Broad, 2016). In one hotel, a room has been designed to look like the inside of a train carriage and the floors are made of mirrors (Broad, 2016). Costumes are also available in many of these hotels, including schoolgirl uniforms and other subservient-based costumes, along with sex dolls (Broad, 2016). Men can pay for as little as 1 hour in a hotel room and simulate attacks on schoolgirls.

BURUSERA SHOPS

Burusera shops became popular in Japan during the 1990s. Burusera shops allowed schoolgirls to sell their used schoolgirl uniforms and used underwear for pocket change (Nakano, 2014). As part of the process, a girl would travel to the shop, be photographed from the waist down in her underwear, and then remove the underwear for sale (Nakano, 2014). However, this practice eventually evolved to become a performance in front of the man who was purchasing the used underwear (Nakano, 2014). The sale of used underwear eventually became part of Japan's huge vending machine economy (Nakano, 2014). In 2004, the public became concerned about the sale of used underwear from minors, and legislation was passed criminalizing the sale and facilitation of sale of minors' used underwear; however, it remained legal for women older than age 17 years to sell their used clothing (Nakano, 2014). With the crackdown on fetishes that affect minors, this market has shifted to the internet, with sales remaining similar to previous sales at brick-and-mortar shops (Nakano, 2014).

Figure 9.2 The Japanese porn industry is estimated to be worth more than $20 billion. Sex tourists can partake in experiences that include virtual-reality sexual encounters, and many collect "baseball cards" of their favorite pornography actresses (male Japanese porn actors are not common).

FETISH CAFES AND SHOPS

Japan has many themed cafes that cater to otaku. Several internet articles and review sites advise otaku and tourists on which maid cafes, schoolgirl cafes, robot cafes, cosplay cafes, and train cafes to visit. In one cafe, the second floor is designed to look like the inside of a local train car that only has one food and one drink item on the menu (Kozuka, 2013). Another cafe looks like a long commuter train car, and inside young women dressed like maids serve customers by letting them know they "can board [their] train" (Kozuka, 2013).

JOSHI KOSEI, THE HIGH SCHOOL GIRL FETISH

In the 1990s, clients who wanted physical contact with girls selling used underwear in the burusera began to seek services from *joshi kosei* (JK) in the form of *enjo kosai* (compensated dating) (Nakano, 2015). JK is how Japan identifies schoolgirl culture specific to high school girls (Vicenews, 2015). Lolita culture, the obsession with young girls in Japan, is rampant because of the existing patriarchal sexist society (Vicenews, 2015). Japan has approximately 300 JK cafes staffed by approximately 5,000 authentic schoolgirls (Varley, 2017). JK cafes are places where men can pay to "innocently" spend time with minors through enjo kosai, which reached its peak in the 1990s (Vicenews, 2015). Men could go for walks away from the establishments with the girls without prying eyes, they could fall asleep in a girl's lap, or they could drink coffee and talk to the girls (Varley, 2017).

In addition to JK cafes, there are JK shops with services such as compensated/walking dates, massage, face slaps, ear cleaning, fortune telling, naps, and bedsharing as therapy. The state department noted in a white paper report, an annual report on human trafficking in Japan, that walking dates often lead to prostitution (Vicenews, 2015). Laws have recently been passed aiming to change JK businesses by no longer allowing girls younger than age 17 years to work at these establishments (Kuroki & Iwahashi, 2017). With this change, there was a shift from JK services being overt on the streets to being arranged through the internet so that the girls now make house calls, thus making it more difficult to stop (Kuroki & Iwahashi, 2017).

CURRENT CONDITIONS

Transnational Feminism

Feminism in the context of American and Western culture is limited and is not applicable to all women globally because of the limitation of rights that women may have in their own countries. Outside of Western culture, people internationally have their own interpretations of feminism and views of the waves of feminism (Dixon, 2011). Women of color have identified the first wave of feminism as being focused on "challenging white feminist assumptions on the primacy of 'sex'" (p. 86). The second wave of feminism is known to be the period of time between 1975 and 1985, coinciding with the United Nations Decade for Women, which had the goal of pursuing equal rights for women throughout the world (Dixon, 2015). Although the Decade for Women had hopes of unifying individuals internationally, it actually further expressed the divide between Western and non-Western feminist ideals (Gurel, 2009). A third wave of feminism has been driven by Third World countries that have disagreed with the perceived Western notion that identifying as female is enough to unify all women globally (Dixon, 2011). Following the acknowledgment by women from Third World countries that there are cultural and socioeconomic divides between them and the women of Western culture, transnationalism feminism was developed (Dixon, 2011). Transnational feminism aims to view the complexities of the intersectionality of gender, sexuality, and the diversity of women's cultures in order to note the importance of individual experience rather than a universal woman experience (Gurel, 2009). It is also important to note that countries may have different social norms and expectations of what it means to be either male or female, which may affect the issues that the countries face (Dixon, 2011). It is imperative to acknowledge that a third wave of feminism has developed that supports the feminism that occurs in developing countries for women who may not share the same experiences and goals that coincide with Western feminist ideals (Dixon, 2011).

Japan, along with other countries, emerged from World War II with a new perspective on society and politics. The women's movement experienced a resurgence perhaps due to the role of Japan in the war, especially the Japanese military's use of sexual slavery, euphemistically referred to as "comfort women" (Takeshita, 2016). The effort for redress and reparation has been an international effort for justice, with women from many countries coming together in solidarity to effect change (Chou, 2003). Another aspect of transnational practice may also be due to the high rate of intermarriage (to other races and ethnicities) in Japan and the diaspora (Takeshita, 2016). The dispersion of Japanese women throughout the world supports and encourages a transnational lens, and the presence of a universal injustice of sexual slavery creates a need for international solidarity.

Sexism

The literature has provided differing definitions of sexism, but it can be best defined as a form of prejudice and acts of discrimination against someone primarily on the basis of the person's gender. "Traditional" and "modern" sexism differentiate between different ideologies of sexism. Traditional sexism involves individuals believing that traditional gender roles should continue to exist (Swim, Aikin, Hall, & Hunter, 1995). Modern sexism, on the other hand, involves the belief that gender equality has been achieved.

Due to sexism and other cultural factors, women still struggle to earn the same amount as men in the workplace, women represent less than 20% of US representatives and senators, women in professional sports are not valued as much as their male peers, and men still dominate in the highest paid professional fields.

There is also still a global issue of inequality for women, in which women are not granted access to basic necessities and basic education, and they are victims of murder and rape simply because they are female. Internationally, women still face limitations that are imposed by sexism on aspects of their lives, such as the jobs that they can perform, not being able to vote for the laws that govern them, the clothing they can wear, the education they can obtain, and the right to control what happens to their bodies (Dixon, 2011). Women throughout the world have made strides toward fighting against the patriarchal customs and norms that have been endorsed and continued generation after generation (Dixon, 2011).

Chikan, Private Meets Public

High rates of sexual abuse in households, failing masculine status, and a prevalence of shame have led to unwanted sexual abuses of women in the public sphere in Japan. Friend of Takako Tanooka and a grassroots leader in chikan awareness, made it clear that groping is so common that it can happen to one victim multiple times. A strong economy has led to more women using the train (Horii & Burgess, 2012). The media began extensively covering stories of women being groped in public in the late 1990s (Adams, 2007). Documents tales of women being molested by their medical doctor, groped by their bosses, having the undersides of their skirts photographed and cut with scissors, and the story of a woman who had a bare penis smacked on her face on a congested commute. Ekin (2017) reports stories of men's hands in girls' underwear, penetration, and ejaculation on clothing all while on the train.

In 2009, men began using online chat rooms in order to facilitate groping women in public (Horii & Burgess, 2012). The profile of the chikan is often an oyaji, a middle-aged unhygienic failed businessman (Horii & Burgess, 2012). According to interviews, oyaji were the primary purchasers at burusera shops, and the image most often used by police to warn women of chikan is that of oyaji (Horii & Burgess, 2012). However, a study conducted in 2000 showed that most chikan were men younger than age 34 years and that groping was committed primarily by males aged

15–25 years and seemed to decline as men age (Horii & Burgess, 2012). The salary-man was the symbol of success in the economic boom of Japan's 1950s and 1960s, and when the economy collapsed in the 1990s, that symbol for success became the symbol for the downfall of the nation, thus effecting the ideal of a patriarchal econ-omy (Horii & Burgess, 2012).

LOOKING TO THE FUTURE

Due to the technological advances during the past 20 years, people are now able to voice their opinions through a multitude of platforms. As discussed previously, hostil-ity and negativity can fester on the internet and social networking sites, but they can also be a place for activism to occur. Social networking sites provide a highly visible platform for activists and feminists to share their experiences and forward links to each another, in addition to providing an opportunity to be empathic toward others. For those who struggle with truly feeling capable of advocating for themselves or oth-ers, social media can help them learn more about feminist issues and events for advo-cacy. Social media is inclusive in the fact that anyone who has access to a smart device can use it, but it is exclusive in the sense that people who do not have access are not able to participate in the multitude of discussions.

Education is also an avenue that many individuals who want to take action can utilize to have their voices heard. Sexism is a convoluted and complex subject to understand, and learning more about the different types of sexism, such as hostile and benevolent sexism, can help one identify the possible sexist prejudice or discrimina-tion that a person has experienced.

In addition to education, involving oneself in advocacy by joining organizations that focus on women's rights and equal rights for all may help one obtain informa-tion that would otherwise not be available. These organizations are often a gateway to opportunities to contact local representatives, lobbying, and other political activ-ism. This may be a primary option for women in the United States and other modern countries that have laws which provide women the opportunity to be involved with these types of activities.

Due to the disconnect that is apparent among feminists in different countries because of their differing experiences, the internet may be the driving force that brings women from throughout the world together in a mutually shared space (Dixon, 2011). Utilizing online networking transnationally through nongovernmental organizations may provide women with an opportunity to meet one another and may be a positive step toward global feminism (Dixon, 2011).

Stop Chikan Campaign

The Japanese government has attempted to stop chikan by posting awareness post-ers in and around train stations. In addition, grassroots awareness campaigns sell pins for young girls to wear on their clothing or backpacks. Matsunaga Yayoi, a grassroots organizer, has taken her campaign directly to train stations, where girls can purchase pins immediately before utilizing public transportation. Matsunaga notes that many young women who appear to look well-behaved and obedient are targeted by chikan.

Often, onlookers witness this act and do nothing. Even when the victim cries for help, bystanders often do nothing (Yayoi, 2017). Matsunaga often tells Tanooka's story of experiencing multiple groping attacks, yelling for help, and eventually chasing down her own abuser before receiving help.

In discussing the chikan issue further with Matsunaga (2017), she explained that lobbying for the removal of school uniforms would do nothing for the adult victims. Matsunaga also mentioned that women-only train cars would not resolve the issue because there are not enough of these cars available for all the women who take public transportation in Japan. Horii and Burgess (2012) argue that women-only train cars maintain male dominance in the public sphere, but they can empower women to take control of their commute. Matsunaga's campaign is currently working to spread awareness and education about this problem. Matsunaga holds contests and selects winning pin designs from crowdsourced drawings from girls and boys. Her intent is to reduce stigma to victims of chikan by raising awareness, educating participants, and teaching them to speak against what has traditionally been kept silent.

Gender-Segregated Train Cars

Almost two decades ago, women-only train cars were introduced for the late evening hours in Tokyo (Horii & Burgess, 2012). Many women who approve of these train cars are not always able to use them because the cars are not always available or because it is too inconvenient to do so (Horii & Burgess, 2012). Some argue that women-only train cars do nothing to change the current patriarchal system that makes

Figure 9.3 In Japan, in order to protect female passengers from unwanted attention while traveling, railway companies have created women-only cars on their trains.

women feel unsafe in public (Horii & Burgess, 2012). Rather, this solution simply allows this hegemonic masculinity to stay in place.

In response to women-only train cars, a recent study and petition have garnered attention pushing for men-only cars (Simmonds, 2017). Reasons for segregation include fear of false accusations and, although uncommon, fear of women gropers (Simmonds, 2017). More than 50% of both men and women support the idea of gender-segregated train cars (Baseel, 2017). In 2017, a surge in false groping claims were made to a Japanese insurer (Persio, 2017).

Teaching Confidence

Train advertisements state that girls should be "brave and speak up," encouraging them to be confident. Matsunaga's (2017) friend's daughter, Tanooka, initially felt embarrassed wearing a pin, so Matsunaga opened the conversation to the community to reduce the stigma by hosting crowdsourced contests for pin designs. Her campaign held a contest in which more than 1,000 participants, both girls and boys, submitted new pin designs. Surveys have shown a 60% decline in groping by pin wearers (Ekin, 2017). This has also paved the way for train police to discuss this problem in high schools so that girls no longer feel shame talking about this problem and society can stop normalizing this crime (Ekin, 2017). By bringing attention to this problem, Matsunaga hopes to change the shame and stigma the victims feel so that society will be more involved in stopping this violent act.

CONCLUSION

The schoolgirl obsession plagues Japan. Incest and child pornography were only criminalized in the past two decades. Japan has a history of incest, close family structures, and few home interventions for abuse. Japan is also a masculine and patriarchal society in which men recently saw their status change during the last recession. Despite the conservative and formal relationships, sexual taboos are normalized and ignored in the public domain. Groping has become so rampant in Japan that offenders now have their own name—chikan. The police and government present awareness and confidence-building discussions in schools, and grassroots organizing has also mobilized the conversation on this problem. Perhaps the next generation of boys will grow up understanding that groping strangers is not normal.

DISCUSSION QUESTIONS

1. How are the fetishes discussed in this chapter supported by Japanese culture and societal rule?
2. Select an issue described in this chapter. How would you construct a solution using a transnational feminist lens?
3. How will current developments in technology affect the fetishes in Japan?

REFERENCES

Adams, K. A. (2007). The sexual abuse of children in contemporary Japanese families. *Journal of Psychohistory, 34*, 178–195.

Baseel, C. (2017, June 29). *Majority of Japanese women in poll support idea of men-only train cars.* Retrieved October 23, 2017, from https://en.rocketnews24.com/2017/06/29/majority-of-japanese-women-in-poll-support-idea-of-men-only-train-cars

Bennet, C. (2011, December 9). *My girlfriend is virtual: An American's experience with "LovePlus."* Retrieved from http://geekout.blogs.cnn.com/2011/12/09/my-girlfriend-is-virtual-an-americans-experience-with-loveplus

Boxall, A. (2017, December 21). *A holographic virtual girlfriend lives inside Japan's answer to the Amazon Echo.* Retrieved from https://www.digitaltrends.com/home/gatebox-azuma-hikari-virtual-assistant-news

Broad, C. (2016, July 19). *Inside a Japanese love hotel.* Retrieved October 19, 2017, from https://www.youtube.com/watch?v=IXgX_r-x-XE

Chou, C. C. (2003). An emerging transnational movement in women's human rights: Campaign of nongovernmental organizations on "comfort women" issue in East Asia. *Journal of Economic & Social Research, 4*(2), 153–181.

Ekin, A. (2017, March 8). *Sexual assault in Japan: "Every girl was a victim."* Retrieved October 24, 2017, from http://www.aljazeera.com/indepth/features/2017/03/sexual-assault-japan-girl-victim-170307101413024.html

Gelb, J. (1997). A "new woman" of Japan: A political biography of kato shidzue. *Journal of Asian Studies, 56*(1), 208–209. Retrieved from http://libproxy.usc.edu/login?url=https://search-proquest-com.libproxy2.usc.edu/docview/230381009?accountid=14749

Gn, J. (2014, October 20). Cute technics in the love machine. *InVisible Culture: An Electronic Journal for Visible Culture.*

Horii, M., & Burgess, A. (2012). Constructing sexual risk: "Chikan," collapsing male authority and the emergence of women-only train carriages in Japan. *Health, Risk & Society, 14*(1), 41–55. doi:10.1080/13698575.2011.641523

Ito, M. (2016, July 30). Commuters fight back against groping. *The Japan Times.* Retrieved from https://www.japantimes.co.jp/news/2016/07/30/national/social-issues/commuters-fight-back-groping/#.W2AYT-hlBxA

Japanese Journey. (2017, April 17). *How to use a Japanese love hotel.* Retrieved October 22, 2017, from https://www.youtube.com/watch?v=1z6Zam73rSU

Kozuka, J. (2013, April 23). *5 Tokyo bars for train nerds (yes, they exist).* Retrieved October 19, 2017, from http://travel.cnn.com/make-tracks-tokyos-train-bars-086761

Kuroki, K., & Iwahashi, Y. (2017, July 6). Tokyo's new "JK" ordinance takes aim at schoolgirl exploitation. *The Japan Times.* Retrieved October 24, 2017, from https://www.japantimes.co.jp/news/2017/07/06/national/crime-legal/tokyos-new-jk-ordinance-takes-aim-schoolgirl-exploitation

Lin, H. S. (2008). Private love in public space: Love hotels and the transformation of intimacy in contemporary Japan. *Asian Studies Review, 32*(1), 31–56. doi:10.1080/10357820701872094

Masumoto, K., & Latz, G. (2018, July 26). Japan. *Encyclopaedia Britannica.* Retrieved from https://www.britannica.com/place/Japan/Government-and-society

Matsunaga, Y. (2017, September 22). Stop chikan badge campaign [Skype interview].

Moore, E. (2016, November 1). Category: "Cute technics in the love machine." Retrieved from https://courses.digitaldavidson.net/fms321/category/cute-technics-in-the-love-machine

Morris, D. Z. (2016, December 18). The creepy virtual assistant that embodies Japan's biggest problems. *Fortune.* Retrieved from http://fortune.com/2016/12/18/gatebox-virtual-assistant-japan

Nakano, K. (2014, December 3). Hitting the skids: The demise of Japan's used underwear trade. *Tokyo Reporter.* Retrieved October 24, 2017, from http://www.tokyoreporter.com/2014/12/03/hitting-the-skids-the-demise-of-japans-used-underwear-trade

Nakano, K. (2015, January 27). Tokyo police targeting the school girl "Holy Land" of Takadanobaba. *Tokyo Reporter.* Retrieved from http://www.tokyoreporter.com/2015/01/27/tokyo-police-targeting-school-girl-holy-land-takadanobaba

Newman, C. (2016, April 21). The secrets of men who grope women on public transport—and how to spot them. *The Telegraph.* Retrieved from https://www.telegraph.co.uk/women/life/the-secrets-of-men-who-grope-women-on-public-transport---and-how

Niu, H., Chiang, Y., & Tsai, H. (2012). An exploratory study of the Otaku adolescent consumer. *Psychology & Marketing, 29*(10), 712–725. doi:10.1002/mar.20558

Persio, L. (2017, June 07). Japanese commuters are taking out insurance in case they are falsely accused of groping other passengers. *Newsweek.* Retrieved from https://www.newsweek.com/demand-insurance-against-false-groping-claims-surges-japan-619625

Simmonds, R. (2017, August 23). *Petition gathers support for men-only train carriages in Japan.* Retrieved October 23, 2017, from https://en.rocketnews24.com/2017/08/24/petition-gathers-support-for-men-only-train-carriages-in-japan

Statistics Bureau. (n.d.). *Summary of the latest month on family income and expenditure survey.* Retrieved August 30, 2017, from http://www.stat.go.jp/english/data/kakei/156.htm

Takeshita, S. (2016). Intermarriage and Japanese identity. In E. Healy, D. Arunachalam, & T. Mizukami (Eds.), *Creating social cohesion in an interdependent world* (pp. 175–187). New York, NY: Palgrave Macmillan.

Varley, C. (2017, March 8). *Is Japan turning a blind eye to paedophilia?* BBC Three. Retrieved October 20, 2017, from https://www.bbc.co.uk/bbcthree/article/57eaaf23-0cef-48c8-961f-41f2563b38aa

Vicenews. (2015, July 20). *Schoolgirls for sale in Japan.* Retrieved October 18, 2017, from https://www.youtube.com/watch?v=0NcIGBKXMOE

Yamada, M. (2017). Decline of real love and rise of virtual love: Love in Asia. *International Journal of Japanese Sociology, 26*(1), 6–12. doi:10.1111/ijjs.12066

10

Women's Voices in Egypt and Globally

GAYLE KIMBALL ■

CASE STUDY: YARA

Feminist standpoint theory maintains that social research should begin from the bottom up, with marginalized people's lived experiences (Harding, 2003). In Marxist theory, a standpoint is a collective identity or voice gained through collective political struggle. This approach suggests that marginalized and oppressed people know the most about their situation, and it is touted as "one of the most influential and debated theories to emerge from second-wave feminist thinking" (Bowell, n.d.). For this reason, we listen to the voice of our first grassroots activist, a high school student who communicated with me on Skype and email.

Yara was in Cairo's Tahrir Square on January 25, the first day of the 2011 revolution, after she took an exam in her high school. She celebrated her 15th birthday during the protest. She was involved previously with political groups such as the April 6 Youth Movement and had some connections with the administrators of the popular "We Are All Khaled Said" Facebook page. Her group of activists believed that approximately 200 people would show up in Tahrir Square on the first day, but by approximately 3:00 p.m., they heard the ground shaking and were shocked that more than 80,000 people had come to the square.

Yara slept in a tent in Tahrir Square, where the largest demonstrations took place, despite the fact that Egyptian girls are not allowed to sleep in mixed-sex gatherings. She knew martial arts; the last man who tried to sexually harass her ended up with a broken arm. She saw people killed by police gunfire, including one of her friends. Their deaths made her want to complete the goals of the protesters even if it meant she too would be killed. Yara and many of her middle-class peers throughout the world

Figure 10.1 High school student demonstrating in Tahrir Square, July 2011. (Her mother was present in the Square doing childcare).

rebel against the traditional cycle they are taught to follow: Go to school, get into a good college, do a boring job, and marry and have kids. They are ambitious and give each other courage to rebel through their global social networks. When detested President Hosni Mubarak announced he was stepping down on February 11, Tahrir Square exploded with joy. Yara said, "In that instant all the barriers between my imaginary utopia and the real world faded. I couldn't tell them apart. Ah yes! That's why I do this."

However, her joy didn't last. Two years later, during the huge July 2013 demonstrations that gave the military the excuse to oust Muslim Brotherhood President Mohammed Morsi, sexual harassment was worse than ever. Sexual harassment lessened during the January demonstrations, but it resumed afterwards. The United Nations Entity for Gender Equality and the Empowerment of Women reported that 99% of Egyptian women have experienced sexual harassment, mostly in the form of touching (El-Dabh, 2013). After General Abdel Fattah el-Sisi was elected president in 2014, Yara decided that the people wanted a pharaoh rather than democracy. In sadness, she left Egypt to attend university abroad, as many other young people try to do as a result of Egypt's struggling economy and political climate of fear and repression (Ismil, 2016).

Fearlessness characterizes young activists such as Yara, who went to the front lines of battle where almost 1,000 protesters were killed and many more were wounded, as discussed in my book, *Brave: Young Women's Global Revolution* (2017). One of the influences on these middle-class youth is that they grew up reading about fictional rebels, played violent video games, and were desensitized by violent movies. Yara was inspired by the *Harry Potter* books and film series (2001–2011), in which Harry, Hermione, and Ron defy authority—in the most widely read book series in history. The Parkland, Florida, teenage leaders of #NeverAgain also referred to the series, nicknaming Governor Scott the Dark Lord Voldemort. Yara's intelligence, school success, and encouraging father gave her confidence and courage to speak up against injustice, as did support from her generation of global internet friends who refused to accept the status quo.

Social movement theory can be used to understand Yara's activism and the success of the youth-led revolution in ousting Mubarak. A movement succeeds when it makes better use of its resources than does the opposition (usually an autocratic ruler). The oppressive government utilizes resources such as security forces and media propaganda to portray youth activists as hooligans or terrorists. The resources of young middle-class rebels include having the time, energy, and electronic connections to organize with many others without much police interference. In a study of Asian student movements, Weiss and Aspinall (2012) reported that student power is strengthen by self-identity as an activist, the university system, the government, other social movements and allies, and the stage of national economic development.

OVERVIEW

International Women's Day on March 8 has been observed globally since the early 1900s, leading a reasonable person to believe that inequality caused by sexism would no longer be so common.[1] Many think of the United States as an advanced nation at the forefront of equality efforts, but a 2015 United Nations (UN) fact-finding mission reported a shocking gap between rhetoric and the facts of "women's missing rights" (Grobe, 2015). It was concluded that "in global context, US women do not take their rightful place as citizens." The report specifically pointed to the increasing barriers to abortion and other reproductive health care, low numbers of women legislators (the US ranks 103 globally [Women in National Parliaments, 2018]), a 21% gender wage gap, and cuts to social safety net programs. Many of President Donald Trump's cabinet appointees voted against the Violence Against Women Act and the Fair Pay Act when they were members of Congress and are anti-reproductive choice and climate change deniers (Chira, 2016). In an era in which the Canadian and French cabinets are half female (albeit not in the top positions), Trump's cabinet is composed of the most white males since President Ronald Reagan's cabinet.

Although women comprise half the world's population, men dominate in power positions and often ignore women's voices and concerns. Women held less than one-fourth of global parliamentary seats in 2017 (15% in Egypt), and only 18 countries had an elected woman as head of government in 2018 (Women in International Politics, 2018). These leaders are shown in a slide show (Van Oot, 2017). Nine national legislative bodies lack any women at all, and 32 countries do not have constitutional guarantees for gender equality, including the United States, which has not passed the Equal Rights Amendment (ERA) proposed in 1923 (more states are currently ratifying the ERA). At the current rate of progress, it will take 40 years to reach gender parity in the world's national legislatures (Clark, 2014). Yet the Inter-Parliamentary Union reports that women's presence in parliaments and ministerial positions results in significant increases in investments in social welfare and legal protection, as well as honesty in government and business (Devlin & Elgie, 2008).

The lack of equal representation of women in governments is not due to deficits in female ambition or ability, or not "leaning in" enough, as advocated by Facebook COO Sheryl Sandberg, but "arises from men choosing men," explains Margot Wallström (2011), former Swedish Prime Minister and head of the Council of Women World Leaders. She suggests that women need to support each other and publicize gender discrimination because "I have lost count of how many times I have experienced or witnessed men ridicule or ignore women at meetings or in public, and exclude them for the decision-making process." Wallström says we need laws to stop discrimination—such as quotas for female candidates—and to enable a better work–life balance with parental leave, childcare, and other family programs exemplified by Scandinavian governments.

Businesses also are more productive when they include women in leadership to provide diverse insights about how to succeed. When women do paid work, poverty decreases and the gross domestic product (GDP) increases. In influential Hollywood and Bollywood films, men do most of the speaking and have more freedom to be older and not conventionally attractive. In 2017, only 24% of protagonists in the 100 highest grossing Hollywood films were women, and only 34% of these films included 10 or more female characters who spoke, compared to 79% of the films that included 10 or more men with speaking parts (Center for the Study of Women in Television and Film, 2017). In Indian films, only 25% of the characters in 2014 were women. The United Kingdom had the most female characters with 38%, whereas the United States had only 29% (Statista, 2018).

Women's voices are silenced early in their lives by illiteracy. Girls comprise the majority of the world's illiterates and children not attending school, although the World Bank's "Voice and Agency" report on the multiplier effect found that education for girls increases their earning ability and inhibits child marriage and early childbirth (Klugman et al., 2014). The World Economic Forum (WEF, 2014) found a clear correlation between gender equality—measured by access to employment, education, participation in government, and health care—and GDP. Educating girls is linked to increased prosperity and healthier children. However, the WEF reported only a small improvement in the gender pay gap during the 9 years it collected data—an increase of only 4% from 2006 to 2014. Globally, the pay gap was 32% in 2017, an increase from 31.7% the previous year (Smith, 2018).

Despite lip service by development experts about the importance of including "girl power" and women in development programs, programs funded by the UN, various nongovernmental organizations (NGOs), and governments spend only a small percentage of funds on gender equality. "Girl power" is a popular concept, but Australian scholar Anita Harris (2004) believes that girls are used by Western commercial interests to symbolize the self-made "can-do" girl of the future, mixing feminism and the concept of "grrrl power" with neoliberal capitalist individualism. She adds that girls are portrayed as the "poster girls for success in neoliberal times" and "the ideal citizens of the future," so long as they are compliant entrepreneurs and consumers (pp. 147–148). An equal voice for the talents and perspectives of women is still missing from government, corporate leadership, media, development programs, and more. Wallström blames the patriarchy.

HISTORICAL TRENDS

Some colonized countries included women's movements as part of their nationalist move-ments for independence. Feminists rejected the Orientalist portrayal of Arab women as backward and submissive victims (Ridouani, 2011). Hoda Shaarawi and colleagues, part of the educated elite, were active in the 1919 "Ladies' Protests" against British occupa-tion. Women demonstrators (some wearing *niqab* face veils as I saw in Tahrir Square in a contrast of tradition and subversion, along with the more common *hijab* hair scarf) helped achieve independence in 1922. A year later, Shaarawi co-founded the first formal feminist organization, the Egyptian Union for Women, which is still active.

Despite decades of feminist activity, extended family remained more important than the husband and wife relationship, youth were expected to obey parents, and sons were valued over daughters, as revealed in the autobiographies of an exceptional woman, physician Nawal El Saadawi (a documentary about her and other Egyptian women is *Hidden Faces* [Longinotto & Hunt, 1990]). She was born in a village near Cairo in 1931 when the British ruled Egypt, as she explains in her books about her rebellion against tradition. Although her relatives were disappointed about the birth of a girl, her parents were loving and supportive of her and her education, as her father was an educator and she was a bright student. Yet when she was 6 years old, without warning, a midwife grabbed her and cut off her "impure" clitoris with a razor, saying it was God's will.

Her parents bowed to family pressure to search for a husband for her, starting when she was only 10 years old. She found ways to scare off suitors, such as blackening her teeth and smiling to show them off to one unappealing man. She also spilled coffee in his lap while deliberately tripping in her new high heels. This tactic earned her a "sound thrashing" but kept her single. She later chose her own husbands, three of them over time, with two divorces. Starting at age 11 years, she was no longer allowed to go out of the house to play with other children in the fields, safely kept inside to perform domestic tasks and preserve her all-important virginity. Her parents did allow her to live with her aunt to go to school in Cairo. She joined other girls in her high school to break down the metal door to their boarding school to join a protest march against the British. With her mother's support, Nawal continued attending school rather than get-ting married. She became one of the few women doctors, receiving her medical degree in 1955, and became director of public health education for the government until she was fired in 1972 due to the publication of her book, *Women and Sex*, which included criticism of female genital mutilation (FGM).

The most striking theme of El Saadawi's autobiographies is the cruelty with which girls and women are treated by both sexes. She explained in *A Daughter of Isis* (El Saadawi, 1999, p. 47), "Everything in a woman's life was seen as shameful, even her face" (similar to Manal al-Sharif's girlhood, the Saudi woman driver who wrote about her transformation to feminism in *Daring to Drive: A Saudi Woman's Awakening* [2017].) El Saadawi slept in Tahrir Square during the January 2011 revolution, said she was changed by the revolution, and opposed the counter-revolution that occurred afterwards, stating (as cited in Al Yfai, 2012), "We are still facing a system based on power and no justice, in Egypt and in the world." She observed that more education is necessary in a country with so many illiterate people who can be brainwashed. Two months after the revolution, El Saadawi founded the Egyptian Union for Women. She explained that her age makes her more angry, not less.

The Egyptian Revolutionaries

Protests occurred in all the major Egyptian cities in January 2011, not just Cairo. Rana Allam was in Tahrir Square; she believes that the revolution succeeded because the whole country came to a standstill, with businesses and schools shut down in every city (Del Panta, 2016). Egyptian activist Jawad Nalbusi reported that the women who demonstrated against President Hosni Mubarak in Cairo's Tahrir Square were amazingly brave: "If there is to be a renaissance in this part of the world, it will be from women, not men. The women will lead" (as cited in Schiffrin & Kircher-Allen, 2012, p. 33). Mona Prince described her experiences in *Revolution Is My Name: An Egyptian Woman's Diary from Eighteen Days in Tahrir* (2014). She described being beaten and molested by police and her mother sitting in a chair to block the door so Prince could not join the demonstrators. She said the revolution was about hope, as revealed in a sign she made: "Now I can get married and have children. There is hope in the future" (p. 143).

Amal Abdel Hadi, a founding member of the New Women Association, reported that the revolution catapulted Egyptian women into the public sphere. Hadi observed (as cited in Mahfouz, 2011),

> The mainstream media only seeks the images and voices of men, but I am an eyewitness and I can tell you that women, especially young women, are omnipresent in this revolution. They are doing amazing arts activities. Their creative graffiti, pictures, workshops, et cetera . . . are mindblowing. What is most amazing is that these young women are literally living in Midan al Tahrir [in tents near men like Yara did]. This would have been unheard of before!

Figure 10.2 Egyptian members of the Young Egyptian Feminists League founded by Meena Mosbah.

Hadi added (as cited in Mahfouz, 2011), "We are seizing this opportunity to push boundaries—to dare to talk about taboo issues related to women" such as female circumcision. Women bloggers and artists contributed to the success of the revolution. Aya Tarek is known as one of the youngest (born in 1989 in Alexandria) and most talented street artists; her artwork is shown online along with the creations of other women graffiti artists (Graffiti Artists, 2013, 2016).

Asmaa Mahfouz, aged 26 years, is called the leader of the Revolution because of her famous video appealing to men's honor to come to Cairo's Tahrir Square on January 25, 2011. Her parents forbade her to demonstrate on the street or use the internet, so she used her phone to organize from her bedroom. This illustrates the importance of electronic media in enabling women to be powerful activists throughout the world from the safety of their homes. In a viral Facebook video, Mahfouz called on Egyptians to come to Tahrir Square for their human rights, their honor, and their dignity (Mahfouz, 2011). Wearing hijab and speaking from home, she said, "If you think yourself a man, come with me on January 25th." Mahfouz reported that Mubarak's officials threatened her if she left her home, but "women participated, no different from men, in all aspects of the revolution. Women fought with police in Tahrir Square throughout the 18-day rebellion, and have continued to take part in street activism into the post-Mubarak era" (Morrow & Moussa al-Omrani, 2012). Women participated from the first day on the front lines, in the streets, and as planners and organizers, as seen in videos and reports ("Videos: Egyptian Women Activists, 2011 Revolution," 2011).

Whereas only approximately 10% of the people on the streets in previous protests were women, women comprised approximately one-third to one-half of the demonstrators in Tahrir Square, including women aligned with the Muslim Brotherhood, who led chants in a radical shift from their past (Raddsch, 2012). They smuggled food and medical supplies to Tahrir Square under their black robes, and they ripped up pavement rocks to throw at police (Aziz, 2012). Women and girls were the first to bring blankets to sleep in the square, they nursed the injured, they opened their homes to activists, and they sat in leadership circles discussing actions in Tahrir Square, as shown in my photos on Facebook, which also include some interviewees (Kimball, 2014). Israa Abdel Fattah appeared frequently on television to announce Mubarak had to go before the protesters would negotiate with the government.

A demonstrator, Saydael, is a divorced nurse who, like many others, relied on Facebook pages such as "We Are All Khaled Said," along with her cell phone, to receive news. Before Saydael felt very alone, but she told me in Tahrir Square in July 2011, "Everyone is together like one hand." She said men and women support each other, but traditional attitudes die hard. Some of the men still want women to be subordinate and think their place is in the home. Saydael suggested men want women to look down at men's feet, not up at their faces, to try to break women's spirit. Maybe men fear being controlled, she said.

With a university student translating, I interviewed a blue-collar woman from Upper Egypt who worked in a clothing factory. She was not able to receive an good education from poor-quality government schools, so she paid for tutoring to become literate. She is not married but would like to be so she can have her own home. She said that she, rather than her parents, will choose her own husband. She came to Tahrir Square by herself, a courageous act, to demonstrate for democracy because she wants a secure country in which women can walk freely in the streets anytime, without unpleasant touching and words. She had been harassed recently on the streets outside the square, so she wants police to help protect women; currently, they do not care. The revolution opened her eyes to new ways of thinking. Before, she did not think about anything but work. Now she believes that women have the same abilities as men to protest.

Two women activists are featured in the 2014 documentary, *The Square*: Ragia Omran fights for the rights of imprisoned activists, and filmmaker Aida El Kashef set up the first tent in Tahrir and co-founded a citizen journalism group. She was one of the women who fought on the front lines; women bloggers like her played an important role in the revolution. Video blogger Sarrah Abdelrahman, aged 23 years, said her life changed on January 25: "It gave me life, it gave me a sense of ownership over the physical and figurative space my body occupies. I learned that day the importance of their principles; freedom, bread and social justice" (as cited in Alhassen & Shihab-Eldin, 2012).

Sally Zohney worked for UN Women Egypt and is a storyteller with the women-led group BuSSy, founded in 2006 at the American University in Cairo to encourage people to "break the silence" about issues such as being unmarried or domestic violence. She reported that everyday feminism blossomed in the wake of the revolution. The topic was no longer elitist and exclusive to closed-door events (O'Regan, 2015). In February 2011, the Coalition of Feminist Organizations in Egypt coordinated 16 groups, including Nazra for Feminist Studies and the New Woman Foundation. A list of women's groups, along with more history of Egyptian feminism, is available on the global youth web page (Kimball, 2014). Hibaaq Osman, the founder of the women's rights NGO Karama (dignity), concluded (as cited in Metzker, 2014), "The revolutions in the Arab world have opened up many new possibilities for women," as governments change and Arab women NGOs work together.

Figure 10.3 Factory worker from lower Egypt demonstrating on her own in Tahrir Square, July 2011.

El-Sisi became the next freely elected president after President Muhammed Morsi was ousted in a coup, although as head of the Armed Forces, El-Sisi defended the invasive "virginity tests" of women demonstrators that he said protected soldiers from accusations of rape (while soldiers watching, doctors performed gynecological exams to determine if the hymen was intact). Samira Ibrahim was the only victim who had the courage to take her case to court, resulting in an order in December 2011 to stop the virginity tests, although a military court exonerated the military doctor who performed the invasive test (Mohsen, 2012). Also in December 2011, the photo of the famous "blue bra" protester kicked by police and her robe torn went viral. Journalist Rana Allam explained in a Skype interview that women supported el-Sisi because they were afraid of Morsi's Islamic government: "The first thing Islamists do is to oppress women. Women have to be covered, not work, etc. El-Sisi spoke nicely, promised to rid them of the oppressor." However, she views him as the most repressive leader ever.

In one of the worst killings of demonstrators in recent history, el-Sisi's security forces killed approximately 1,000 pro-President Morsi demonstrators occupying Rabaa al-Adawiya Square on August 14, 2013, and thousands more were wounded (Ketchley & Biggs, 2015). His regime allows for no criticism, jails and tortures thousands of political prisoners, and shuts down feminist and other civil rights NGOs. Using the pretense of security measures, by 2018, the government had shut down independent media except for a few online news outlets and blocked more than 48 news sites, including the Human Rights Watch website (Amnesty International, 2017), and almost 500 websites (El-Taher, 2018). Allam said that as the government shuts down feminist groups, their leaders become the face of the woman's movement and they continue to speak out on social media. Despite these abuses, President Trump praised el-Sisi for doing a "fantastic job," with no mention of his rollback in civil rights.

CURRENT CONDITIONS

Young women globally exhibit great courage in fighting for their rights. The most well-known is Pakistani Malala Yousafzai's advocacy of education for girls since she was 11 years old. Young women have led recent uprisings in Lebanon, Egypt, Yemen, Morocco, Israel, Chile, and the Never Again movement in the United States; my chronological list is available online (Kimball, 2014). Despite women's leadership, a study of 843 protest movements from 2006 to 2013 reported that only 50 of the protests focused on women's rights and 23 concerned lesbian, gay, bisexual, and transgender rights (Ortiz, Burke, Berrada, & Cortés, 2013). Rather, the main movement themes were economic inequality and real democracy. Leftist and nationalists groups often state that women's issues and class inequality will be addressed after the hypothetical revolution. Kurdish Rojava in northern Syria and the Zapatistas in southern Mexico are current feminist revolutions that actually work to institutionalize the inclusion of women's voices now—not in a tentative future. Despite women's leadership in the Arab Spring that set off a global wave of uprisings for democracy in 2011, their issues were often ignored after the revolution, as in Egypt.

Recent feminist activism is described as "plural, prefigurative, decolonial, ethical, ecological, communal and democratic" (Dinerstein & Amsler, 2017). The British authors maintain that women are the main leaders of prefigurative politics that experiment with creating utopias now, such as organizing child care and health care in occupied public spaces. This feminist effort opposes patriarchal, authoritarian, capitalist, violent, and colonial structures, which is true of the recent uprisings in general and suggests the impact of feminist organizing on the language of current uprisings.

Some activists use distinctly female tactics. During the Yemeni revolution led by journalist Tawakkul Karman in 2011, women used the tribal norm against violence against women in battle by sitting on the ground and reciting the Quran to keep soldiers at bay. Threatening female nudity jump-started Liberian peace talks in the early 2000s, as did women's threat to withhold sex, according to activist Leymah Gbowee. She advises today's activists to stop being polite and take action away from their computers, like the student leaders of the #Never Again gun control movement did (Heydarpour, 2018). In the 2007 international "Panties for Peace" campaign against military rule in Burma/Myanmar, women coordinated by a Thai group sent underpants to Burmese embassies because the generals believe that contact with women's underwear robs them of their power. Women used the tactic of withholding sex in the Ukrainian "Don't Give It to a Russian" T-shirt and Facebook campaign in 2014. Proceeds of the shirts were donated to the Ukrainian army.

Some suggest that girls and women have a distinct organizing style. Jessica Taft (2011) interviewed 75 girls in Vancouver, San Francisco, Mexico City, Caracas, and Buenos Aires. She found that the common pattern in girls' organizing is that they aim for a positive optimistic feeling in their groups and emphasize ongoing learning and discovery with horizontal and consensus decision-making. Their groups often provide girls with a network of friendship and support, especially when their peers think activism is "nerdy" or boring. Social movement theorists note that collective identity generates support for movements such as those of activist girls who identify as politicos (Flesher Fominaya, 2010). The Young Feminist Fund (FRIDA), a funding organization for young feminists globally, observes that the groups it funds are typical of

Figure 10.4 Contrast between traditional and Western garb, demonstrating in Tahrir Square, July 2011.

women's organizations in using co-leadership to share power and moving away from a focus on the individual leader to the collective (Van der Gaag, 2013).

After the Revolution

Youthful activists are blamed for not organizing a plan to fill the vacuum after Mubarak left, but feminist author Rana Allum explained in our interview from exile that there is no democratic infrastructure because they are detained after they speak up: A Facebook post is all it takes. She said, "Every day we hear about a young person who was forcibly disappeared or detained. Sisi has gotten rid of opposition parties and the five most serious candidates who might run against him for reelection." Therefore, he won by 97% in 2018.

After the revolution, sexism returned even stronger due to backlash against women speaking out, and women's issues were put on the back burner. Fear rules everything, reports Rana Allam. Even the youth are afraid to speak out, especially on university campuses, where students are prohibited from political talk. In 2014, a female student at the Suez Canal was arrested just for carrying pictures of former President Morsi in her bag. Professors turn students in to security forces if they try to organize a meeting. "This era is the worst for students," reported Mohamed Nagy, a researcher at the Association for Freedom of Thought and Expression (as cited in Ismail, 2016). He said the security forces specifically target students. El-Sisi gave his government the power to appoint university presidents and deans in 2014 and gave them the power to expel students at will. The government even shut down art galleries and cafes where youth gathered.

The Egyptian rebels fought for bread, freedom, and dignity, but women were not organized as a group to make demands for women's rights. Reem Wael said women were betrayed as soon as the military and the Muslim Brotherhood took over after Mubarak's dethroning, and women were told to return home. She argues that women's liberation has little chance to succeed in a nationalist struggle because "national revolutions are inherently male. Women are allowed to participate but not to feature feminist goals, told their issues will be considered after the revolution, similar to what Nehru and Gandhi told women involved in the Indian liberation struggle" (as cited in Suneri, 2000).

Wael reported the "woman friendly" atmosphere in Tahrir changed the day that Mubarak resigned in February 2011. In reaction, many feminist NGOs sprung up like mushrooms, including Egyptian Women for Change, the Egyptian Center for Women's Rights, Egyptian Youth Association for Development, the New Woman Foundation, socialist and workers' groups, and other progressive organizations. Some of them organized discussion groups in Tahrir during the January demonstrations, and the Coalition of Egyptian Feminist Organizations was founded in 2011.

Ghadeer Ahmed organized Girls Revolution on Facebook and Twitter on the first anniversary of the revolution as "an icon of rebellion" in order for women to share their experiences of sexism and to be able to discuss prohibited topics such as sexuality, sexual violence, and abortion rights (Ahmed, n.d.). Girls Revolution campaigns to enable women's voices to be heard, organizing the "We Will Wear Dresses" campaign in 2012 in response to blaming women for inviting sexual harassment by wearing the wrong clothes. Its campaign the next year was called "We Will Ride Bicycles" (similar to an earlier cycling campaign for women in Turkey). A group of young women from Girls Revolution demonstrated outside the Saudi embassy in Cairo in August 2017 to support the Saudi "Photograph Your Legs" campaign to protest the Saudi police arrest of a young woman wearing "indecent clothing." The Egyptian women said they wanted to confront "patriarchal attempts to dominate women's bodies."

Founder Ghadeer Ahmed told me in an interview in 2018 that she feels safe to talk publically about women's rights because the government "considers women's rights defendants as having leisure time just talk about women, not a threat to the state." She grew up in Mahalla in a nonpolitical family of lower middle-class workers who did not own land. When she was a college student in what she says is a low-quality government school, she was politicized by local demonstrations in her hometown during the January revolution. She took photos and tweeted news of the uprising. She and her two sisters took the train to demonstrate in Tahrir Square, an almost 3-hour train ride, but they were required by their parents to return home the same day. The revolution inspired her to uncover her hair; when her parents pressured her to wear hijab due to criticism from their acquaintances for not raising her to be a moral woman, she moved to Cairo. She became so brave that she chased after a harasser on the street, yelling and hitting him with her shoes in hand. She is currently writing a book about women's tales of abortion tales, which is illegal in Egypt. Like other feminists I interviewed, she does not feel hopeful except for the fact that her younger sister is even braver than she.

The new constitution adopted in 2014 included Article 11, which committed the state to "achievement of equality between women and men." The constitution commits the government to "ensure appropriate representation of women" but not equality. It reserved only 12% of parliamentary seats for women but for the first time set aside 25% of the 15,000 local council seats for women and 25% for people younger than age 35 years (Fracolli, 2017). This was better, however, than the Muslim Brotherhood President Morsi's parliament, with only 1.6% women. In 2018, el-Sisi appointed a record six women to the cabinet of 34 ministers, and he noted that women comprised 15% of parliament members, but activists said that state feminism does not make real changes. Rana Allam stated that the parliament is a joke because the political parties were created by intelligence agencies to create the appearance of democracy; opponents call them "cartoon parties."

The Year of Egyptian Women was declared in 2017 when the first woman governor was appointed. The internet lit up with sarcasm and condolences because the previous Year of the Youth saw detention, jailing, disappearances, torture, and murder of young people; most of the thousands of political prisoners are youth. The regime even detained a group of singers for posting songs critical of the government. On the other side of the political spectrum, Salifist Islamist groups accused el-Sisi of acting against God's will by selecting women ministers to rule over men, and feminists disparaged the revival of state feminism without commitment to equality.

Fault lines came to the surface after the revolution, with attacks on women escalating, including continued virginity checks for women prisoners. This violation is not a new problem, but it was used to publically humiliate women protesters. The reactionary shift meant that feminists have to debate old issues, such as child marriage and girls' education, and that women's "bodies have become part of the battlefield itself, a means to control political action" by women: "It seems that the feminist movement was genuinely unprepared" for this assault from reactionaries (Ghanim, 2017).

However, some see the silver lining of increasing repression as bringing "activism to a new level of intensity," similar to the Trump effect in the United States (Kato, 2017).

Resurgence of State Feminism and Silencing Civil Society

Post revolution, women are "re/making and re/mapping urban Egypt" in a "version of 'revolution' as the continual live-streaming of creative energy" in the cultural and social worlds, observed Margo Badran (as cited in Craig Romano, 2017). When I asked what led her to feminism, a feminist who did not wish to be named explained,

> It wasn't much of a choice really, when you face sexism and discrimination, sometimes by law, since you are a child. The inheritance laws robbed me of my inheritance from my father. Then the laws hit me again as I was trying to leave my ex-husband. I ended up giving up my home and all my financial rights to get my divorce. My marriage itself was a challenge, because most men, including my ex-husband, believe they have a right to "straighten their wives" and "obedience" is the name of the game, or you get beaten. That is not to mention what we face on the streets and at work. It is really hard not to become a feminist and fight for our rights.

I asked her why other women who face abuse do not protest and which groups are most effective in helping women who lack the advantage of a good education:

> The best approach I saw was that of Legal Aid NGOs, those who take the fight to court for these women, free of charge like Azza Soliman and her CEWLA organization. Many civil society organizations worked on awareness, but now that work has stopped since Sisi passed the harsh NGO law. [A similar repressive NGO law was passed in China in January 2017.] These organizations would go to rural communities, talk to women, hold sessions, and tell them about their rights.

Even after the revolution, 99% of Egyptian women still experience sexual harassment, according to UN interviews conducted in 2013 (El-Dabh, 2013). According to a 2017 Thomson Reuters Foundation study, out of 19 cities, Cairo was ranked the most dangerous city for women, its worst ranking since the revolution . In reaction, groups such as Tahrir Bodyguards, the Coalition of Feminist Organizations in Egypt, I Saw Harassment, the Daughters of Egypt Are a Red Line, and Operation Anti-Sexual Harassment (OpAnti-SH) have formed. The latter was organized to extract women from "circles of hell" mobs of violent rapists who sometimes use knives and tasers, to support the victims' recovery from harassment and attacks, and to push for prosecution of attackers. Yasmin El-Rifae is currently writing a book about OpAnti-SH, describing it as a feminist and revolutionary organization. She compared it to the global #MeToo movement: "When narrative is grabbed by the voiceless, it has the ability to grow with a pace and breadth that is startling and exciting and unknowable. Didn't the Arab revolutions themselves show us that?" (El-Rifae, 2018).

In a move against pervasive sexual harassment, el-Sisi's government passed a law to criminalize it in 2014 with up to 5 years in prison and fines. El-Sisi visited a hospitalized assault victim who was attacked in Tahrir during his inauguration celebration. He also revived the government's National Council for Women (NCW) and directed the government to implement the 2030 Women's Empowerment Strategy formulated in 2017. The NCW formally addressed the problem of sexual harassment in its National Strategy for Combating Violence Against Women in 2015, but activists observed that the plan did not have any teeth because police and judges generally support male abusers.

Dalia Abdel Hameed, head of the gender program at the Egyptian Initiative for Personal Rights, stated that "we don't have a functional feminist movement" because human rights organizations that work for women's issues are under attack by the el-Sisi government (Shams El-Din, 2015). She said the movement has, however, created a "certain level of correct political awareness," such as public criticism of sexist statements by prominent people, as more women are speaking up. She thinks real change will require social change so that laws will be enforced. (For a discussion about masculinity and patriarchy, see Ghannam's 2013.)

After listening to many voices throughout the country, Amira Hanafi wrote the *Dictionary of the Revolution* (2016), "which aimed to document the rapid amplification of conversation about politics in public space following 25 January 2011." She suggested that the discussion of words such as "harassment," "virginity test," "ideal girl," and "abaya with snaps" is particularly relevant to women's issues.

Egyptians are also part of the transnational #MeToo movement to voice experiences with sexual harassment, explained in an article about how OpAnti-SH tries to protect women under assault in the streets (El-Rifae, 2018). However, the only university gender studies program is at the American University in Cairo and instruction is in English rather than Arabic. Other universities do offer some graduate courses in women's studies.

In 2016, the "worst law in Egyptian history" was passed, according to Suzan Fayad, the director of el-Nadeem Center, which helps victims of torture and other violence. The NGO law placed government control over civil society groups under the guise of fighting terrorism. The government prohibited public gatherings of more than 10 people without permission from the Interior Ministry. After the feminist leaders were accused of inciting "irresponsible liberation" of women, their organizational and personal assets were frozen, along with those of three other civil rights groups. A court upheld the ruling in January 2017. The government targeted feminist groups Nazra Association for Feminist Studies founded by Mozn Hassan in 2005, Azza Soliman's Center for Egyptian Women's Legal Assistance (its reports about legal discrimination against women are online), and the Nadeem Center for the Rehabilitation of Victims of Violence and Torture co-founded by Aida Seif el-Dawla. The government banned "terrorist spies" Hassan and Soliman from traveling outside the country in what the government called a counter-revolution, and it inhibited their efforts to educate Egyptians about women's rights. (Solliman also co-founded the international Musawah movement to publicize progressive interpretations of Islam.)

Accused of destabilizing the country, Hassan explained (as cited in Ford, 2017), "We're not this nice acceptable women's organization, we're not a development-only [organization]. We think the feminist movement is a political movement. We've always had a human rights perspective. . . . We are not like other feminist organizations." Hassan praised the diversity of the movement with different approaches: radical, cultural, Islamist, and socialist feminists. Human Rights Watch (2018) issued a report on other human rights violations that occurred in 2017. Groups spoke up in opposition in a statement signed by 14 Egyptian women's rights groups, 130 academics (many from the American University in Cairo), and 48 international groups (Nazra, 2016). Many of these groups avoid using the term feminism, which is often denigrated as a harmful Western influence.

LOOKING TO THE FUTURE

Based in Alexandria, I interviewed Menna Mosbah, the founder and CEO of the Young Egyptian Feminists League (YEFL), which began in 2015. At age 27 years, she is in the vanguard of feminism. She already has a decade of experience working for develop- ment and women's groups, including a UN Women youth citizenship program. At age 20 years, she was inspired by what she considers the first and only revolution in Egyptian history: "Everything changed," she said in our 2018 interview. Women like her were free to raise their voices and felt safe in the squares. They believed they were changing their destiny by opposing corruption, but although the people in power changed, the system has not. Her parents are well educated and proud of her achievements, but traveling to conferences outside the country has had the largest impact on her, she said, "The way I'm talking doesn't feel Egyptian" in terms of her independence and outspokenness.

Mosbah notes that most current women's groups have to abide by the government's ability to limit foreign funding; thus, they aim for human rights. In contrast, unfettered feminists aim for "gender equality" with measureable standards, as spelled out in the Organisation for Economic Co-operation and Development's (OECD, n.d.) gender indi- cators (the OECD is the economic association of 35 developed countries). This approach has more depth; is less superficial; and addresses violence against women, including FGM. It aims to empower women and to change the culture, not just inform women about their rights. When I asked Mosbah about the most active current organizing, she highlighted Nazra for Feminist Studies as the most feminist due to its effort to pass a stronger law against sexual harassment and to form a feminist alliance of existing NGOs.

YEFL is also unusual in that it is not based in Cairo like the other women's rights organizations but, rather, also has performed work in Alexandria, Aswan, and Luxor. It has a modern view, in contrast to old-fashioned feminists who view women as vic- tims: Mosbah states, "We're not victims, we can decide our destiny." She thinks that the roles of men and women are not different except for those dictated by physiol- ogy, unlike the women government ministers, who she often hears state that their role as mother or grandmother comes first. (Mosbah reports that the young pop music group, Bnt Elmasrwa, sings about FGM and other women's issues, thus representing another avenue for women's voices in addition to the internet and art.)

Seven years after the revolution, Mosbah noted that the president would like people to forget about the ideals of the revolution and appeals to older women voters by sweet- talking them, making statements such as "Women are the light of my eyes." Egyptians are used to a pharaoh but are unhappy with the poor economy that lacks industrial imports and may "explode." However, she thinks it is even worse in the United States under President Trump, who she believes is racist and sexist. Mosbah said, "Every time I join a program I'm asked why you are keeping doing this since you're not seeing a positive impact on the ground?" Many young people she knows are fed up with poor education and lack of jobs and want to leave Egypt, but she does not. She said what keeps her going is her dream of "Planet 50/50" (a reference to UN Women's goal of gender equality by 2030) and a quote from Eleanor Roosevelt: "The future belongs to those who believe in the beauty of their dreams." It takes time to change culture, so she fears she may not see it in her lifetime but believes eventually "everything will change."

A key factor shaping the global future is the increasing number of women graduates and women workers in the new knowledge economy, many of whom delay marriage and parenting to establish their careers. The World Bank reports that the ratio of university graduates is 93 men to every 100 women, including the majority of Egyptian, Saudi, Iranian, and Nigerian students (Charmie, 2014). Orielle Lake, Salazar, and Twist (2016) state, "Women-led movements arising around the world herald a profound shift that changes everything," like the women leading the Green Energy Revolution in Africa. Barcelona's mayor, Ada Colau, proclaimed (as cited in Conley, 2018), "This is the century of women and of feminism; we've raised our voices and we won't stop. No more violence, discrimination, or pay gap!"

In conversations organized by Amira Hanafi to collect material for her *Dictionary of the Revolution*, one participant said, "We are the youth of Egypt and no ruler can rule us, because we really are pharaohs and no one can stop us" (Hanafi, 2016). Another participant observed that members of the current generation in secondary school do not respect or care about anyone and are fearless because they see their older siblings without a future, so they will be the change makers. The following facts also indicate change will occur: The median age in Egypt is 24 years, women are a majority of university students, and women outscore men on international math and science tests and are the majority of new faculty. Also, 38% of the population is urban and 39% uses the internet. In addition, youth (ages 15–24 years) unemployment rates are high (38% of young women and 29% of men) (Facts, 2017). Education and internet access coupled with high unemployment and an authoritarian government point to future rebellion by both women and men.

A survey that does not offer much hope for the future, the UN Women and Promundo survey of 10,000 people in Egypt, Morocco, Lebanon, and Palestine, reported in 2017 that 87% of Egyptian men and 77% of Egyptian women believed that women's role is to "care for the home," and 90% of men and 58.5% of women believed that men should make the final decisions (El-Behary, 2017). Many more Egyptian women believed that women could be the leaders of political parties—76% compared to 39% of men. Younger men were not more liberal. Additional discussion of the survey findings is provided on my webpage (Kimball, 2017). As long as Egyptians vote for a military "pharaoh," inequality will remain.

Rana Allam reported in our interview that many of the working lower class women she knows have to give their earnings to their husbands the moment they walk in the door or risk being beaten. Although more girls are in school, this does not necessarily translate into a progressive society because the Egyptian education system is one of the worst, so students do not learn about civil and social studies or even sex education. Allam thinks that the globalization of information might bring change; young people gain knowledge through the internet. They know now that a father should not beat his children, whereas in the past this was considered normal.

Offering an optimistic view, in her book *Fifty Million Rising: The New Generation of Working Women Transforming the Muslim World* (2018), Pakistani researcher Saadia Zahidi makes the case that revolution follows the increasing number of educated and employed women, access to smartphones, and the large percentage of young adults in these countries. The tipping point for change is 30%, she reports, and currently women comprise more than 31% of the workforce in the Muslim world, thus "transforming culture" (Zahidi, 2018, p. 237). Zahidi believes that the largely negative view of Muslim women in the West will have to change to fit the new reality. And so will Muslim men: Zahidi found that many Egyptian men do not want their wives to work outside the home, viewing it as a threat to their masculinity.

CONCLUSION

The Egyptian Center of Women's Rights and the UN Women's Fund for Gender Equality held a conference in 2017 titled "A Wave of Women's Voices . . . 1000 and Counting," indicative of more Egyptian women being heard. The Women's Voices Program works to encourage young women leaders, especially in the 15,000 local council seats. Some progress is occurring with regard to respecting women's voices even in a time of great repression.

Iranian Asef Bayat refers to lifestyle rebellions as a "social nonmovement." We may think of social movements with demonstrators in the streets as the driver of political change, but Bayat (2013, 2017) argues that what he calls social nonmovements also make change. They occur with lifestyle changes in daily life by many individuals. They are not united in an organization or by ideology: "Theirs is not a policy of protest, but of practice" as they gradually normalize what was not acceptable. Often, these individuals are women, youth, the urban poor, and immigrants.

This may be the hope for Egypt. For example, Bayat observed that rather than participating in organized campaigns, Iranian women resisted authoritarian regimes through daily practices such as running for political office, attending university, jogging, playing soccer, and being employed. Getting an education and obtaining employment are probably the best hope for women's liberation in Egypt, as it is throughout the world.

DISCUSSION QUESTIONS

1. Girls and women appear to have more egalitarian or horizontal values and ways of organizing compared with boys and men. Because they comprise the majority of university students in Egypt and globally, how do you predict they will change traditional systems as they assume more power and express their voices?
2. Could Egypt's women activists have been as revolutionary without internet access? How important was it that they could organize from home using their cell phones and computers?
3. What do you observe about who speaks and monologs in groups you belong to and in media?

NOTE

1. This chapter uses the first person to report on my field research in Egypt and the experiences of Egyptian women I interviewed from 2011 to 2018 in person or online. Some were videotaped and can be viewed online (Kimball, YouTube), and others are reported on in *Brave: Young Women's Global Revolution* (2017), Volume 2. This chapter reports on their observations of recent feminists' work to empower women's voices.

REFERENCES

Ahmed, G. (n.d.). *Girls' revolution*. Retrieved from https://www.facebook.com/EgyGirlsRev

Al Yfai, F. (2012, May 12). Top Egyptian feminist says "nothing has really changed" since revolution. *The National*. Retrieved from https://www.thenational.ae/arts-culture/books/top-egyptian-feminist-says-nothing-has-really-changed-since-revolution-1.400140

Alhassen, M., & Shihab-Eldin, A. (2012). *Demanding dignity: Young voices from the front line of the Arab revolutions*. Ashland, OR: White Cloud Press.

Al-Sharif, M. (2017). *Daring to drive: A Saudi woman's awakening*. New York, NY: Simon & Schuster.

Amnesty International. (2017, June 13). *Dozens of news sites blocked as Egypt ramps up digital censorship*. Retrieved from https://www.amnesty.org/en/latest/news/2017/06/dozens-of-news-sites-blocked-as-egypt-ramps-up-digital-censorship

Aziz, S. (2012, June 27). What Egypt women want. *The Egypt Monocle*. Retrieved from http://egyptmonocle.com/EMonocle/op-ed-what-egypts-women-want

Bayat, A. (2013). *Life as politics*. Palo Alto, CA: Stanford University Press.

Bowell, T. (n.d.). Feminist standpoint theory. *Internet encyclopedia of philosophy*. Retrieved from http://www.iep.utm.edu/fem-stan

Center for the Study of Women in Television and Film. (2017). *It's a man's (celluloid) world*. Retrieved from https://womenintvfilm.sdsu.edu/research

Charmie, J. (2014, March 6). Women more educated than men but still paid less. *Yale Global*. Retrieved from https://yaleglobal.yale.edu/content/women-more-educated-men-still-paid-less

Chira, S. (2016, December 7). Is Donald Trump's cabinet anti-woman? *The New York Times*. Retrieved from https://www.nytimes.com/2016/12/07/opinion/is-donald-trumps-cabinet-anti-woman.html

Clark, H. (2014, March 6). Retrieved from https://www.undp.org/content/undp/en/home/presscenter/speeches/2010/03/04/helen-clark--international-womens-leadership-conference.html

Conley, J. (2018, March 8). On International Women's Day, women across Spain stop all work in "feminist strike." *Common Dreams*. Retrieved from https://www.common-dreams.org/news/2018/03/08/international-womens-day-women-across-spain-stop-all-work-feminist-strike

Craig Romano, J. (2017, March 8). *Women driving positive change in the Middle East*. Wilson Center. Retrieved from https://www.wilsoncenter.org/publication/women-driving-positive- change-the-middle-east

Del Panta, G. (2016, July 15). The role of the Egyptian working class in Mubarak's ouster. *Open Journal of Sociopolitical Studies*. Retrieved from http://siba-ese.unisalento.it/index.php/paco/article/download/16319/14070

Devlin, C., & Elgie, R. (2008, February 3). The effect of increased women's representation in Parliament: The case of Rwanda. *Parliamentary Affairs*, 61(2), 237–254. Retrieved from http://pa.oxfordjournals.org/content/61/2/237.full

Dinerstein, A., & Amsler, S. (2017, January 24). Women on the verge: The essence of feminist struggle. *ROAR Magazine*. Retrieved from https://roarmag.org/essays/women-on-the-verge

El Saadawi, N. (1999). *A daughter of Isis*. London, UK: Zed Books.

El-Behary, H. (2017, May 8). 87 percent of Egyptian men believe women's basic role is to be housewives. *The Independent*. Retrieved from http://www.egyptindependent.com/87-egyptian-men-believe-women-s-basic-role-be-housewives-study

El-Dabh, B. (2013, April 28). 99.3% of Egyptian women experienced sexual harassment. *Daily News Egypt.* Retrieved from https://www.dailynewsegypt.com/2013/04/28/99-3-of-egyptian-women-experienced-sexual-harassment-report

El-Rifae, Y. (2018, January 22). What the Egyptian revolution can offer #MeToo. *The Nation.* Retrieved from https://www.thenation.com/article/what-the-egyptian-revolution- can-offer-metoo

El-Taher, M. (2018, February 19). *Closing windows . . . censorship of the Internet in Egypt.* AFTE Egypt.org. Retrieved from https://afteegypt.org/digital_freedoms-2/2018/02/19/14655-afteegypt.html?lang=en

Facts: Egypt people 2017. (2017). Some progress is occurring with regard to respecting women's voices even in a time of great repression. Retrieved from https://theodora.com/wfbcurrent/egypt/egypt_people.html

Flesher Fominaya, C. (2010, November 6). Collective identity in social movements. *Sociology Compass, 6*(4), 393–404. Retrieved from https://www.academia.edu/615452/Collective_Identity_in_Social_Movements_Central_Concepts_and_Debates

Ford, L. (2017, January 12). Egypt court ruling upholds decision to freeze assets of women's rights activists. *The Guardian.* Retrieved from https://www.theguardian.com/global-development/2017/jan/12/egypt-court-ruling-upholds-decision-freeze-assets-womens-rights-activists

Fracolli, E. (2017, January 5). *Women and quotas in Egypt's parliament.* The Tahrir Institute for Middle East Policy. Retrieved from https://timep.org/commentary/women-and-quotas-in-egypts-parliament

Ghanim, H. (2017, January 18). *Between trauma and resistance: Feminist engagement with the Arab Spring.* Heinrich Boll Stiftung. Retrieved from https://lb.boell.org/en/2017/01/18/between-trauma-and-resistance-feminist-engagement-arab-spring

Ghannam, F. (2013). *Live and die like a man: Gender dynamics in urban Egypt.* Stanford, CA: Stanford University Press.

Graffiti artists. (2013). *Beauty queen of Fararita.* Retrieved from https://www.facebook.com/beautyqueenofazarita?ref=ts&fref=ts

Graffiti artists. (2016, August 14). *Women in graffiti: A tribute to the women of Egypt.* Retrieved from http://suzeeinthecity.wordpress.com/2013/01/07/women-in-graffiti-a-tribute-to-the-women-of-egypt

Grobe, S. (2015, December 14). UN experts find level of discrimination against women in US "shocking." *Euronews.* Retrieved from http://www.euronews.com/2015/12/14/un-experts-find-level-of-discrimination-against-women-in-us-shocking

Hanafi, Amira. (2016, September 30). *A dictionary of the revolution.* Ibraaz. Retrieved from https://www.ibraaz.org/projects/143   http://qamosalthawra.com/en#aboutarchive.qamosalthawra.com

Harding, S. (2003). *The feminist standpoint theory reader.* New York, NY: Routledge.

Harris, A. (2004). *Future girl: Young women in the twenty-first century.* New York, NY: Routledge.

Heydarpour, R. (April 12, 2018). Nobel Laureate Leymah Gbowee. *Women in the World.* Retrieved from https://womenintheworld.com/2018/04/12/nobel-laureate-leymah-gbowee-says-armchair-activism-isnt-enough

Human Rights Watch. (2018). *Egypt: Events of 2017.* Retrieved from https://www.hrw.org/world-report/2018/country-chapters/egypt

Ismil, A. (2016, June 1). *After university crackdown, Egyptian students fear for their future.* Reuters. Retrieved from https://www.reuters.com/investigates/special-report/egypt-students

Kato, M. (2017, Winter). Women of Egypt. *The Cairo Review of Global Affairs*. Retrieved from https://www.thecairoreview.com/essays/women-of-egypt

Ketchley, N., & Biggs, M. (2015, August 14). *The Washington Post*. Retrieved from https://www.washingtonpost.com/news/monkey-cage/wp/2015/08/14/counting-the-dead-of-egytps-tiananmen

Kimball, G. (2014). Videos retrieved from https://www.youtube.com/user/TheGlobalyouth; https://globalyouthbook.wordpress.com/2014/04/16/youth-led-21st-century-uprisings; https://www.facebook.com/pg/Global-Youth-SpeakOut-160382763986923/photos/?tab=album&album_id=297718913586640; https://wp.me/p47Q76-IU

Kimball, G. (2017). *Brave: Young women's global revolution*. Chico, CA: Equality Press.

Klugman, J., Hanmer, L., Twigg, S., Hasan, T., McCleary-Sills, J., & Santamaria, J. (2014). *Voice and agency: Empowering women and girls for shared prosperity*. World Bank. Retrieved from https://openknowledge.worldbank.org/handle/10986/19036

Longinotto, K., & Hunt, C. (Directors). (1990). *Hidden faces* [film]. 20th Century Vixen.

Mahfouz, A. (2011). Retrieved from www.learningpartnership.org/blog/2011/02/women-protest-egypt

Metzker, J. (2014, June 13). Women's movements in the transitioning Arab states. *Qantara.de*. Retrieved from https://en.qantara.de/content/womens-movements-in-the-transitioning-arab-states-for-dignity-peace-and-equal-rights

Mohsen, H. (2012, March 16). *What made her go there? Samira Ibahim and Egypt's virginity test trial*. AlJazeera.com. Retrieved from https://www.aljazeera.com/indepth/opinion/2012/03/2012316133129201850.html

Morrow, A., & Moussa al-Omrani, K. (2012). *Women fight for rights in new Egypt*. IDN-InDepth News. Retrieved from http://www.indepthnews.info/index.php/global-issues/human-rights/1100-women-fight-for-rights-in-new-egypt

Nazra. (2016). Retrieved from http://nazra.org/en/2016/03/solidarity-statement-egyptian-feminist-organizations-coalition-nazra-feminist-studies; http://nazra.org/en/2016/03/48-organizations-around-world-condemn-escalating-measures-against-mozn-hassan; http://nazra.org/en/2016/03/130-academics-express-their-solidarity-mozn-hassan-and-nazra-feminist-studies

Noujaim, J. (Director). (2014). *The square* [film]. Los Gatos, CA: Netflix.

O'Regan, K. (2015). Egypt's embattled feminism. *Middle East Eye*. Retrieved from http://www.middleeasteye.net/fr/node/55070

Organisation for Economic Co-operation and Development. (n.d.). *Gender development*. Retrieved from http://www.oecd.org/dac/gender-development/43041409.pdf

Orielle Lake, O., Salazar, L., & Twist, L. (2016). *The Sophia century: When women come into co-equal partnership*. Bioneers. Retrieved from http://media.bioneers.org/listing/the-sophia-century-when-women-come-into-co-equal-partnership-osprey-orielle-lake-leila-salazar-and-lynne-twist

Ortiz, I., Burke, S., Berrada, M., & Cortés, H. (2013, September). *World protests 2006–2013*. Washington, DC: Friedrich Ebert Stiftung. Retrieved from http://policydialogue.org/files/publications/World_Protests_2006-2013-Executive_Summary.pdf

Prince, M. (2014). *Revolution is my name: An Egyptian woman's diary from eighteen days in Tahrir*. Cairo, Egypt: American University in Cairo Press.

Raddsch, C. (2012, May 17). *Unveiling the revolutionaries: Cyberactivism and the role of women in the Arab Uprisings*. Rice University Institute for Public Policy Research Paper.

Ridouani, D. (2011). The representation of Arabs and Muslims in Western media. Meknes paper, RUTA, 3. Retrieved from https://www.cnn.com/videos/

politics/2018/06/25/baby-trump-blimp-moos-pkg-ebof.cnn/video/playlists/
wacky-world-of-jeanne-moos/

Schiffrin, A., & Kircher-Allen, E. (2012). *From Cairo to Wall Street: Voices from the global spring.* New York, NY: The New Press, 33.

Shams El-Din, M. (2015, May 27). *Human rights in focus: Dalia Abdel Hameed.* Mada Masr. Retrieved from https://madamasr.com/en/2015/05/27/feature/politics/human-rights-in-focus-dalia-abdel-hameed

Stastista. (2018). *Share of female characters in movies worldwide in 2014.* Retrieved from https://www.statista.com/statistics/412497/share-of-female-characters-in-movies-worldwide-by-country

Smith, R. (2018, April 19). This is where equal pay is considered most important. *WeForum.* Retrieved from https://www.weforum.org/agenda/2018/04/chart-of-the-day-this-is-where-equal-pay-is-considered-most-important

Suneri, L. (2000). Moving beyond the feminism versus nationalism dichotomy. *Canadian Women's Studies, 20,* 143–148.

Taft, J. (2011). *Rebel girls: Youth activism and social change across the Americas.* New York, NY: New York University Press.

Van der Gaag, N. (2013). *Because I am a girl: The state of the world's girls 2013.* Plan International. Retrieved from http://plan-international.org/files/global/publications/campaigns/biag-2013-report-english.pdf

Van Oot, T. (2017, October 19). Who runs the world? *Refinery.com.* Retrieved from https://www.refinery29.com/2016/03/105325/female-world-leaders-2016#slides

Videos: Egyptian women activists, 2011 revolution. (2011). Retrieved from https://wp.me/p47Q76-Jw

Wallström, M. (2011, May 1). A womanly virtue: Female representation as global security strategy. *Harvard International Review, 32*(1), 30–34. Retrieved from http://hir.harvard.edu/print/women-in-power/a-womanly-virtue

Weiss, M., & Aspinall, E. (Eds.). (2012). *Student activism in Asia: Between protest and powerlessness.* Minneapolis, MN: University of Minnesota Press.

Women in International Politics. (2018, February 20). *2018, women and political leadership—female heads of state and heads of government.* Retrieved from https://firstladies.international/2018/02/20/2018-women-and-political-leadership-female-heads-of-state-and-heads-of-government

Women in National Parliaments. (2018, May 1). *World classification.* Retrieved from http://archive.ipu.org/wmn-e/classif.htm

World Economic Forum. (2014). *Global gender gap report.* Retrieved from http://www3.weforum.org/docs/GGGR14/GGGR_CompleteReport_2014.pdf

Zahidi, S. (2018). *Fifty million rising: The new generation of working women transforming the Muslim world.* New York, NY: Nation Books.

PART III

Gender Equity and Politics

Introduction: Advocates Are Not Giving Up in the Fight to End Gender Violence

FRAIDY REISS ■

know a forced marriage can happen at any age. It happened to me at age 19 years.

I grew up in an insular religious community in New York City, where I was groomed from early childhood to expect an arranged marriage as a teenager to a stranger my family would choose for me and a lifetime of caring for him and bearing his children.

I am sure my family had no idea that the stranger they chose as my husband was violent and unstable. But when I later told them what he was doing to me, they declined to help me, and when I finally managed on my own to escape after 12 years in my abusive marriage, my family punished me by shunning me and my two daughters. My family declared me dead.

I rebuilt my life with my two daughters and in 2011 founded Unchained At Last, the only organization dedicated to helping women in the United States resist or escape forced marriages. I helped hundreds of women. I discovered the healing power of turning one's trauma into a force for good. I felt pretty darn proud of myself.

And then.

I started receiving calls from girls younger than age 18 years who begged for the same help Unchained was providing to adults. Except I was nearly powerless to help them before their 18th birthday.

That is how I first realized that child marriage is a significant problem in the United States, particularly for girls.

Although the minimum marriage age in most US states is 18 years, legal loopholes in most states allow those younger than 18 years to marry. When I started researching this in 2015, legal loopholes existed in all 50 states; only after Unchained pushed relentlessly for change did 2 states end child marriage in 2018. As I write this in January 2019, marriage before age 18 years remains legal in 48 states.

Throughout the world, women and men are fighting for equal protections under the law, but not all legislators are listening. Perhaps more important, society is also not listening. Patriarchal values are resistant to change. However, also persistent are those who are fighting for change.

The chapters in this section focus on how politics are failing women and how our sisters are fighting back. Chapter 11 details the refugee crisis and the experience of being nationless. Who do you turn to when your home country is no longer a safe place? How can women save themselves? Chapter 12 discusses the legal loopholes in the United States that allow child marriage to continue despite the United Nations calling it an act of gender-based violence. Chapter 13 details aging Australians and how the mental health of elderly women is largely ignored. Chapter 14 outlines the current politics in Poland on abortion rights and the fighters who are demanding Poland allow women access to their own health care. Chapter 15 presents a story of perseverance and women warriors who are fighting for Filipinas' bodies every day and how they have changed policies with their actions. Chapter 16 details the heartbreaking story of Myanmar and Aung San Suu Kyi. Once praised for her advocacy and fight for freedom of her country that resulted in a Nobel Peace Prize, Aung San Suu Kyi is now being asked to return her prize as she stands blind to the rape, slaughter, and war that are occurring among the Rohingya Muslims in her country.

In each of the chapters in this section, small grassroots movements are emphasized. Often, governments and public officials are searching for the answers, the keepers of legislation with the power to help protect the vulnerable. However, throughout the world, the machinations of government are slow and not always responsive. Furthermore, in many areas, government may be rife with corruption. This section shows that there are alternatives—that social workers, villagers, frontline medical workers, teachers, youth, and others are joining together to bring awareness and action to social injustices that otherwise are ignored. Some countries are combating the violence brought forth against women. In other countries, more needs to be done, but advocates are not giving up in the fight to end gender violence.

Unlike other forms of gender violence, child marriage in the United States has a simple solution. Every state can pass commonsense legislation to eliminate the loopholes that allow marriage before age 18 years. Yet legislators throughout the country—mostly male legislators—have refused to pass the legislation or have watered it down so it still allows marriage before age 18 years in some circumstances. It is worse in other countries, where child marriage is not only condoned but also encouraged. Under the guise of social, cultural, or religious norms, girls' free will is cut short before they even have a chance to begin.

The main reason I am determined to end child marriage is that it can easily be forced marriage. Children who have not yet turned age 18 years and become legal adults face overwhelming legal and practical barriers if they try to leave home, access a domestic violence shelter, retain an attorney, or take legal action. In many US states, children are allowed to be married off—typically by a parent or a judge, not on their own—but are not allowed to file for divorce. Advocates who try to help children escape an unwanted or abusive marriage can be charged criminally for their efforts.

The Unchained team and I are not giving up. We achieved a historic victory in May 2018 in Delaware when it became the first state to end all marriage before age 18 years. We achieved another major victory in June 2018 when New Jersey became the second state to do so (see www.unchainedatlast.org).

There are still 48 US states, and most of the world, that must ban child marriage before we can declare a full victory. Globally, the United Nations has called for an end to child marriage by 2030, and there is work to be done on every continent. Wherever you live, please contact your elected officials and urge them to eliminate a human rights abuse that destroys girls' lives. Urge them to end child marriage.

11

Refugee Mothers Raising Children Born of Sexual Violence in Dutch Society

A Delicate Balance of Parenting, Prejudice, and Psychopathology

KIMBERLEY ANDERSON AND ELISA VAN EE ■

CASE STUDY: MUNASHE

Munashe was born in 1986 and was raised in a village in the Democratic Republic of Congo. Growing up, her father had multiple wives and many children, and they lived together in a family house. Although she did not receive much attention while growing up, Munashe described it as a happy time in her life: "I did not mind helping out and there was always someone around. I was never alone." When she was 16 years old, a man started paying attention to her. She enjoyed this very much because she rarely received attention from her father. After a short time, Munashe and the man married, moved into a house together, and a year later Munashe gave birth to their first child, Amina. Munashe missed her family but was very fond of Amina and dreamed of one day having her own large family.

Several years later, in the middle of the night, rebels attacked her village. Munashe heard them go to each house and the screams of her fellow villagers. Scared to death, she and her child hid in her hut, but when the rebels entered, there was no escape. In front of Amina, they raped Munashe—once, twice, three times—until she fainted. When she woke up, everything was silent. She crawled out of her hut only to see many dead bodies, including that of her husband. Amina was nowhere to be found.

From that moment, Munashe does not clearly recall what happened to her. She remembers her uncle paying money to a man he knew, she remembers a truck, she remembers a plane—but in between there are many blank spaces. She arrived at a place that is nothing like her country. It is cold, and the people she encounters do no hurt her but also do no treat her particularly kind. Never in her life has she felt so lonely. She cries constantly because she worries about the fate of Amina and is over-whelmed by people asking questions; she does not want to think back to what hap-pened. A few days later, when she is interviewed by the immigration services, she tries to explain about the rebels in her village, the fear, the murders, and of course her child. She does not speak about the times she was raped because she is not only ashamed but also overwhelmed with sadness about her husband and worried that Amina is not being cared for. Munashe is sure that the rebels took her but that she is still alive.

Soon after the interview, Munashe is moved to an asylum center where many other asylum seekers of various nationalities live. she is given a room among other women from Africa, including some from Congo. There is not much space and nothing to do. Munashe does not talk to many people, but she begins to notice people whispering about her. The men in the asylum center approach her repeatedly, asking questions and trying to touch her. She is afraid—during the day of these men and at night of the memories of her child. Munashe knows she will have to talk again to immigration officials, and so she is more prepared for her second interview. However, when she faces the male translator from the same ethnic group as her tribe, the ground trem-bles beneath her feet and she turns silent. Months go by waiting in the asylum cen-ter, and Munashe does not notice her belly growing. She becomes increasingly more depressed. It is not until a doctor examines her that she discovers she is pregnant.

Straight away she is referred to the health clinic, where she reveals for the first time that the child was conceived during rape. Munashe is torn; she does not want to believe that there is a baby growing inside her. The doctor tells her she can have an abortion, but Munashe has only ever heard bad things about ending a pregnancy. Back home, she had heard of women in her village taking herbs and seeing the witch doctor, but after listening now about what would happen to her at a hospital in the Netherlands, she feels sick and knows she would never be able to go through with it. She would never be forgiven in the eyes of God.

After the child is born, professionals continue to worry about Munashe's well-being, and she is referred to a specialist trauma institute for mental health treatment and help with her relationship between her with her child. In the meantime, her appli-cation for asylum is denied. In the asylum procedure, it was held against her that she was not "honest" or "complete" in the first and second interviews when asked about her reasons for applying for asylum. Her attorney decides to appeal, but this is rejected as well. Finally, her attorney decides to apply for asylum based on medical grounds. At least this will allow Munashe to stay in the Netherlands during treatment. The Red Cross is asked to trace Munashe's daughter Amina, but after much waiting, it reports that it is not able to locate her.

In therapy, Munashe cannot find words for the evil juxtapositions she faces. On the one hand, her newborn baby is part of her, but on the other hand, the baby is part of the rapist father. The newly born child is innocent but connected to her trauma and grief. The features of the rapist father remind her of the experiences she suppresses, but the features of herself remind her of a lost child in Congo. How can she focus on the present when she is continuously reminded of the past? Munashe questions whether she is to blame for her fate; she was raped, and she did not protect her child. Holding on to her values of family, religion, and tradition means that she believes she should be blamed, but challenging her values means losing part of her identity. How can she feel resilient instead of burdened by what she values so deeply? Therapy will improve her mental health, but improvement means loss of her status and a return to her home country. Therapy targets recovery from trauma symptoms, but recovery also means a return to an unsafe place where she may be re-traumatized. She is conflicted in that she questions whether she should desire a return to Congo, where she can search for her lost child, or whether she should desire to permanently stay in the host country to build a future for her newborn.

Unfortunately, the story of Munashe and her struggle is not unique. Many women who experience sexual violence encounter a complex interplay of difficulties that prevent their recovery. They are victims but yet are held responsible by their cultural beliefs. They experience symptoms but need to function as mothers. They are too ashamed to speak out to immigration services, but when they do, they are not considered trustworthy because they speak "too little, too late." They need to build a future but are threatened with the possibility of being sent back to their country of origin, which represents their traumatized past. These challenges create a vacuum in which it can be nearly impossible for these women to move toward recovery. It is precisely this vacuum where Munashe and other mothers like her need to find their way by seeking professional support.

OVERVIEW

A prominent feature of conflicts today is the use of rape and other forms of sexual violence, most often directed at local civilian populations and perpetrated by armed combatants (Bartels et al., 2010; Clifford, 2008; Rees et al., 2011). Sexual violence is a form of gender-based violence defined by the World Health Organization (WHO, 2002) as "any sexual act, attempt to obtain a sexual act, unwanted sexual comments or advances, acts to traffic, or otherwise directed, against a person's sexuality using coercion, regardless of their relation to the victim, in any setting" (p. 149). According to Rule 156 of International Humanitarian Law, rape, sexual slavery, enforced prostitution, and enforced pregnancy during armed conflict are deemed serious criminal violations, and the case of *The Prosecutor v. Kunarac, Kovac and Vukovic* (Buss, 2002) highlights the first instance in which such acts were treated as crimes against humanity. Sexual violence can also include sexual harassment, being forced to undress, forced marriage, forced abortion, and trafficking of people for the purpose of sexual exploitation (Koshin, Wang, & Rowley, 2007)—all observed in conflicts during this century.

To estimate the number of people affected globally, both directly and indirectly, by sexual violence is a challenging task for two reasons. First, although there is much evidence from locations that are well known to be affected by conflict-related sexual violence, such as Bosnia, the Democratic Republic of Congo, Uganda, and Syria (Apio, 2008; Parker, 2015; Peterman, Palermo, & Bredenkamp, 2011; Wood, 2006), such data collection is often surpassed by journalistic investigation, which may informally tap into wider networks and elicit more representative figures. For example, Human Rights Watch (2002) interviewed survivors of rape in the Democratic Republic of Congo, as well as those who had escaped being raped, their family members, and other people who had witnessed sexual violence. It documented sexual violence carried out by multiple groups of combatants and reported as many as 2,000 incidences of rape in just one location. Second, and perhaps more important, underreporting is known to occur as a result of engrained cultural beliefs and social customs that surround sexuality, gender roles, and the consensual nature of sexual violence in more conservative nations, thus often preventing disclosure of being sexually victimized (Johnson et al., 2010; Kelly, Albutt, Kabanga, Anderson, & VanRooyen, 2017). Consequently, in some cultures, if it becomes public knowledge that a woman has been raped, she is commonly faced with stigmatization and being ostracized from community members. Women in African countries such as the Democratic Republic of Congo (Kohli et al., 2013) and "comfort women" who were taken by the Japanese military during World War II (Jonsson, 2015), for example, are known to be rejected and altogether abandoned by their communities. In many instances, the depth with which sexual violence and related crimes can permeate society is extensive. Sexual violence is often associated with other acts of community violence, such as pillaging, destruction of homes, devastation of crops and livelihoods, and subsequent forced displacement (Harvard Humanitarian Initiative, 2010). Rape is also frequently conducted in public, with family members forced to witness and even participate (Human Rights Watch, 2016). Thus, sexual violence impacts not just the survivors but also the wider community.

Munashe has heard other women in the asylum center talk about rebels who came to their villages too. One or two women are very loud and outspoken—they tell stories of other women they know to have been raped. They say they are glad it was not them because the husbands of these women left them, they are not allowed to attend the local church anymore, and they are thought of as dirty. This worries Munashe. She also feels dirty but hopes that these women will not find out what happened to her.

Furthermore, within many societies, conflict has not been a single event but, rather, has continued in waves of fluctuating severity over many decades—it is frequently accompanied by natural disasters such as drought and famine that lead to poverty in the most extreme forms. It is not uncommon for women in such instances to report multiple crimes of sexual violence over their lifetime, largely coinciding with changing security (Wood, 2006). Compounding this issue is the fragility with which governing parties of some nations are constructed, where conflict is rarely entirely resolved and few perpetrators are brought to justice. Syria is the most recent example of such a situation (for an overview of the complex web of politics and religion in Syria under the Assad regime, see Carpenter [2013]). This means that in some societies that experience conflict, for many people there is often no guarantee of security from central authorities. This lack of safety creates constant fear and drives local people to flee their country in search of a better life.

This chapter attempts to untangle the complexities of sexual violence in conflict, examining recent migration patterns and what these mean for women who conceive children during conflict-related sexual violence. It also considers how these events lead people to become refugees, using the Netherlands as an example of a host country. The chapter concludes with recommendations for how to support mothers and children born of sexual violence in post-conflict and non-conflict settings.

HISTORICAL TRENDS

Forced migration has reached unprecedented numbers in recent decades, as conflicts in Bosnia–Herzegovina, Iraq, Afghanistan, South Sudan, Ethiopia, Eritrea,

Democratic Republic of Congo, Burundi, Colombia, and elsewhere have resulted in vast numbers of persons fleeing their homes in search of safety. Based on data from the United Nations High Commissioner for Refugees (UNHCR, 2017), a total of 68.5 million people were reportedly displaced as of 2016; 12.4 million of these people were newly displaced in 2016, 47% of whom were women.

The year 2014 marked a significant milestone in migration history, with the forced movement of persons out of the Middle East and Africa into Europe, documented as the largest migration since World War II (UNHCR, 2017). The Syrian conflict—the most recent ripple effect of the Arab Spring of 2011—has caused unimaginable human suffering, and there is no indication that this will end soon (Alisic & Letschert, 2016). Furthermore, conflict has continued to rage in countries such as Afghanistan, Iraq, Somalia, South Sudan, and Eritrea, and new or reignited conflicts have erupted in Burundi, Niger, Nigeria, Yemen, and Libya. This has extended the total number of people seeking asylum in Europe and elsewhere, well beyond the increasingly urgently displaced Syrian population. Many countries are unprepared for the arrival of so many refugees and struggle to adequately provide necessities.

In addition to forcing local people to flee, these conflicts feature sexual violence as a commonality. In many communities, in which women are viewed as symbols of caste or ethnic identity, forced impregnation is a method of breaking down family and community structures, defiling social ties and patrilineage, and impacting the prospects of future generations (Dossa et al., 2014). Forced impregnation leaves a mother with a child who not only serves as a living reminder of the trauma of sexual violence but also has genetic links to a conflicting group and may even resemble the rapist father. One mother said, "When I look into his eyes, when I see the shape of his nose, I see his rapist father"; another stated, "My child is like a shadow. A shadow from the past that will forever haunt me" (van Ee & Kleber, 2012, p. 642).

The total number of children worldwide conceived from conflict-related sexual violence is unknown—perhaps "tens of thousands" (Carpenter, 2007, p. 3) or as many as 10,000 in Rwanda alone (Weitsman, 2008). For women who conceive a

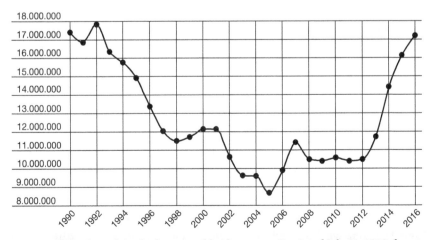

Figure 11.1 Total number of refugees worldwide per year. Retrieved July 11, 2018, from https://www.vluchtelingenwerk.nl/feiten-cijfers/cijfers/wereldwijd

child through sexual violence, the social repercussions are far-reaching and long-lasting. In many cultures, a mother and her child may become the focus of humiliation from the community (Albutt, Kelly, Kabanga, & VanRooyen, 2016). Some historical labels forced upon babies born from rape during wartime include "Russian brat" in Germany after World War II, "dust of life" in Vietnam after the Vietnam War, and "Devil's children" in Rwanda and "children of hate" in Bosnia–Herzegovina after conflicts in these countries during the 1990s (Theidon, 2015). WHO (2002) has declared such children to be at heightened risk of being not only stigmatized but also ostracized and abandoned. Many pregnancies are terminated, but infanticide of these children is also known to occur directly after birth or during childhood (Human Rights Watch, 1996).

In northern Uganda, children born to mothers captured by the Lord's Resistance Army are known to have become the focus of stigma because they bear both the status of an illegitimate child and are assumed to have links to rebels. They are feared, cast into the lowest possible social group, and consequently ostracized from their community (Apio, 2008). In the Democratic Republic of Congo, male relatives of female sexual violence survivors interviewed in focus groups (Kelly et al., 2017) shared the opinion that children born of rape were not only lacking the physical and emotional support from a father as a primary caregiver but also without a place in the traditional Congolese family sense because they were often rejected from their families, along with their mother. One participant stated, "It isn't as easy since the husband accepting the child knows that he is not his." In post-war Bosnia–Herzegovina, following militarized "rape campaigns," children born of sexual violence came to represent a social underclass that prevented them from escaping extreme alienation and poverty. Children known to have since discovered their origins are described as feeling suicidal as a result of bullying and abuse (Carpenter, 2007).

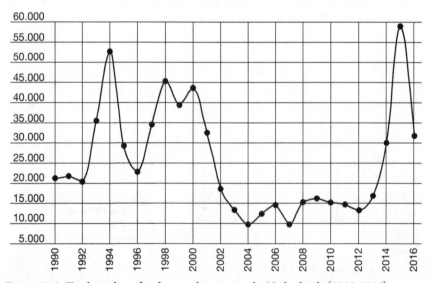

Figure 11.2 Total number of asylum applications in the Netherlands (1990-2016). Retrieved July 11, 2018, from www.statline.cbs.nl/statweb/.

RECENT DEVELOPMENTS OF NOTE IN THE NETHERLANDS

The Netherlands is a relatively small but densely populated country in northwestern Europe, with a population of 17 million. It is famous for its flat terrain, agriculture, and liberal society. The Netherlands is part of the European Union (EU) and has actively participated in the resettlement of refugees during the past several decades. Latest data show that as of 2015, 88,536 refugees had been located and officially recognized in the Netherlands, with the majority from Syria and Eritrea (Vluchtelingenwerk, 2018). The Dutch Immigration and Naturalization Service works on the principle that people can be granted asylum if they "have good reason to fear persecution or inhumane treatment, or because it is unsafe to return to their country due to war" (2016). Upon entry, the Dutch central agency for the reception of asylum seekers (Centraal Orgaan opvang Asielzoekers) provides asylum seekers with basic facilities such as accommodation in an asylum center. They are also given a medical examination and a lawyer to help prepare for the asylum procedure. To allow them time to recover from their journey, asylum seekers are given at least 6 days of rest before the official procedure starts. In the Netherlands, asylum seekers are discouraged from formally working while undergoing asylum procedures, although some may obtain permission to work for several weeks per year.

Munashe is surprised to learn that she will be given her own space in the asylum center. She has a bed and a sink, some small space for her belongings, and she will share a bathroom with four other families. She had never heard of the Netherlands before, and since arriving, she has mixed feelings. She is relieved that she no longer has to fear conflict or rebels, but meeting other women asylum seekers concerns her that they will one day find out what happened to her and that she might be ridiculed. However, she has noticed women of different ethnicities spending time together and their children all playing together; maybe she and her baby will be able to join soon, too.

Health care is provided by the Dutch health care service for asylum seekers (Gezondheidcentrum Aseilzoekers), located at asylum centers for those registered to receive aid. Those with more severe difficulties of a psychological nature can be referred to specialist treatment facilities. If granted a temporary or permanent residence permit, they are considered refugees and different regulations apply. According to the

Figure 11.3 An example of an asylum centre in the Netherlands. From COA, Retrieved July 11, 2018, from www.coa.nl

Dutch government, this permit gives its holder certain rights but also carries obligations. For instance, permit holders are entitled to accommodation but are obliged to learn the Dutch language and take a civic integration examination comprising various components, including writing, reading, speaking, listening, knowledge of Dutch society, and an orientation to the Dutch labor market. Those who pass the examination receive an integration certificate. Refugees can borrow money for the courses and exam, which they do not have to repay if they integrate within 3 years. However, if they do not, or if they fail the exam, they are fined and have to repay the loan. They will also be screened to establish their qualifications and professional experience to foster a rapid integration. The procedure to obtain a residence permit is structured to be as short as possible, but due to appeals it often lasts years. Many asylum seekers live in an asylum center for this duration without the opportunity to work, learn the language, or participate in society.

The Netherlands, as with many European countries, was not prepared for the recent high influx of asylum seekers. With limited reception places, asylum seekers were accommodated in emergency locations with inadequate facilities throughout the country. Informal settlements also began to appear in unused offices, churches, and even parking garages. These were used mainly by undocumented migrants—those who had their asylum request denied. Upon denial, asylum seekers are given 4 weeks to return to their native country, but many remain in cities because returning is too dangerous. To address this issue, "bed, bath and bread" shelters were opened at night so people had a place to sleep (Amnesty International, 2015).

Eventually, the time period in which immigration services must make a decision to grant asylum was extended from 6 to 15 months. As a result, the Dutch government decided to "warn" asylum seekers at its borders of the longer waiting times to start the asylum procedure, the condition of reception facilities, and the required personal contribution toward the costs of their own reception and the reception costs of their family (Dijkhoff, 2016). With the protracted application process for asylum in many countries, the health and well-being of many refugees are often compounded by the uncertainty of their future (Lindert, Carta, Schäfer, & Mollica, 2016). A loss of support networks, a lack of privacy, and feelings of not being useful have been highlighted as barriers to mental well-being (de Jonghe, van Ee, & Dieleman, 2004; van Dijk, Bala, Ory, & Kramer, 2001). A longitudinal study among Iraqi asylum seekers conducted in the Netherlands (Laban, Gernaat, Komproe, Schreuders, & de Jong, 2004; Laban, Komproe, Gernaat, & de Jong, 2008) identified the duration of the asylum procedure as being an important risk factor for common psychiatric disorders (e.g., depression, anxiety, and somatoform disorders), a lower quality of life, higher disability, and poorer overall physical health. Those who remained in the Netherlands for more than 2 years had a significantly higher prevalence of these psychopathologies (66.2%) compared with those who had been in the country for only 6 months (42%). A lack of work and family-related issues were also highlighted as important factors in the mental well-being of asylum seekers.

The recent increase in the number of asylum seekers has polarized Dutch society. On the one hand, many citizens volunteered at asylum seeker centers to teach the language and provide activities for children, they donated clothes and shared meals, universities offered courses, and individuals and organizations offered housing. Many citizens were relieved that they were able to do something about the suffering instead of only watching the refugee crisis unfold on the news. On the other hand, many citizens became scared, and discussions arose regarding a shortage of jobs, housing, and health care. At a time of major cuts to social security in the Netherlands, the inflow of asylum seekers was considered to be overloading an already burdened system. Right-wing politicians readily made use of this anxiety, and xenophobic comments rapidly increased and became more widely accepted. In addition to this polarization, tension has arisen as a result of reports of incidents of sexual violence perpetrated elsewhere in Europe by some asylum seekers toward other asylum seekers (as well as local people). Survivors of sexual violence can remain vulnerable because of the cultural values of other people living in such close proximity within asylum centers. To date, the Netherlands has put in place no safeguarding during the asylum procedure or at accommodation locations to maintain the safety of vulnerable groups, particularly with regard to sexual violence. It is an extreme juxtaposition that victims of war commit acts of violence in countries of refuge. It is, in fact, detrimental to their asylum application to become involved in violence or crime. Partly as a response to the sexual violence by certain asylum seekers, a Participation Agreement was added to the civic integration procedure. The Participation Agreement is legally required to be signed by newcomers and declares that they have been informed of, and will respect, the values and basic rules of Dutch society (Civic Integration Act). This process is a positive step toward integrating refugees and increasing interaction within Dutch society. Clearly, however, this process will not solve the issue of unwanted foreign values, primarily regarding women and sexuality, being brought into Western societies.

CURRENT CONDITIONS

There can be confusion regarding the appropriate terminology to use when referring to people forced to flee their countries and the perception of their needs, due in part to the media and certain right-wing politicians or parties. Ideally, there is a distinction between applicants and those who have received official refugee status in a host country—those whose rights are guaranteed by the Geneva Convention (UNHCR, 1951). However, the distinction between displaced people, asylum seekers, and refugees becomes blurred because many people do not reach their intended destination. The long migration routes may not always go according to plan, and journeys can eventually span years instead of weeks, involve extended stays in makeshift camps such as the "Calais Jungle" (Clare, Nyiri, Yamamoto, & Preston, 2016) and "labor camps" in Libya, or require asylum seekers to take (multiple) perilous trips across the Mediterranean Sea (Carta, Moro, & Bass, 2015). In reality, the combination of the legal framework through which people can apply for asylum and the risk of harm in returning to their own country can force people to remain "underground" or to remain illegal and without official documentation or recognition (Carta et al., 2015). Thus, pursuing a rigid distinction between the terms "refugee" and "asylum seeker" is unfeasible. It does not strengthen a sense of belonging but, rather, incites "otherness" and a lack of community (Olsen, El-Bialy, Mckelvie, Rauman, & Brunger, 2016). This is especially the case since the Dublin Regulation was reinforced in 2015, which grants EU member states the right to deport asylum seekers to the first EU country they entered (European Commission, 2019). This has resulted in some less developed countries on the border of Europe (e.g., Bulgaria and Hungary) struggling to meet the needs of their own people and the influx of refugees, causing tension.

Figure 11.4 An example of an Internally Displaced Persons camp near Duhok in Northern Iraq. By K. Anderson, 2016. Reprinted with permission.

Experiences of sexual violence—in their home country and during migration and stays in camps or asylum seeker centers—are pervasive among female refugees and asylum seekers, and an extensive evidence base highlights the risk of long-lasting effects for victims. The physical effects of rape are widely known: obstetric fistulae (an abnormal opening between the vagina and other organs, including bladder and rectum); sexually transmitted infections, including HIV/AIDS; unwanted pregnancy; and genital injury (Koshin Wang & Rowley, 2007; Mukwege & Nangini, 2009). In addition, survivors of sexual violence are known to suffer protracted psychological and emotional reactions that are equally as intrusive as physical ones. These include sleep problems, flashbacks, aggression, lack of concentration, somatic complaints, anxiety, adjustment disorders, dissociation, personality disorder, and memory loss (Campbell, Dworkin, & Cabral, 2009; de Jong et al., 2001; Kelly et al., 2012; Loncar, Medved, Jovanović, & Hotujac, 2006). Post-traumatic stress disorder (PTSD), in particular, necessitates attention because Breslau et al. (1998) estimated a 49% likelihood of experiencing PTSD as a result of rape. Rothbaum, Foa, Riggs, Murdock, and Walsh (1992) reported in their study of 95 female rape victims that 94% met symptomatic criteria for PTSD within 1 week of the assault. Although these symptoms began to improve after 8 weeks, by 3 months, 47% of their sample still met full criteria for the disorder. Mollica, Caridad, and Massagli (2007) assessed 376 Bosnian refugees over a period of 3 years and found that 45% of people who suffered PTSD in the post-war period as a result of exposure to conflict still presented with symptoms more than 10 years after the exposure to traumatic events. Atkeson, Calhoun, Resick, and Ellis (1982) also found that female victims of rape experienced significantly greater depressive symptoms during the 4 months following the assault. In a sample from Rwanda (Kantengwa, 2014), 14 interview participants shared how they viewed themselves in a strongly negative way post-rape, which for mothers ultimately meant they were less emotionally and physically able to respond to their children. Subsequently, they observed disobedient and aggressive behaviors in their children, which they likened to "bewitching." Carpenter (2007) touches on the concern that the psychological sequelae of rape has been linked to abuse or neglect of children. Often, abuse is reported by women who have raised a child born of rape, either intentionally or because they believed they had no acceptable alternative. van Ee, Mooren, and Kleber (2014) suggest that although parenting abilities of refugees may overall remain stable after traumatic experiences, disturbances that pervade continuously over time may produce the greatest impact on the child—not necessarily an intergenerational transmission of trauma symptoms from mother to child but limitations in parenting that disrupt the development of the child.

Refugee mothers with a child conceived from sexual violence may face ever more complex psychopathology and emotional reactions as a result of raising a child who is unplanned. According to van Ee and Kleber (2013), the perception of the child, the sociocultural attitudes to sexual violence and "fatherless children," as well as post-traumatic and comorbid symptomatology are the major obstacles to secure attachment relationships between mothers and children born of sexual violence. Children born of sexual violence have a compounded trauma, experiencing the negative responses from their community and the complex emotional reactions of their mothers. For example, in a sample of 46 asylum seekers and refugees in the Netherlands, symptoms of PTSD in mothers were linked to psychosocial difficulties in children, with children demonstrating lower levels of responsiveness to their mothers (van Ee, Kleber, & Mooren, 2012). From a social perspective, refugee mothers are also understood to face particular difficulties as a result of language and other social barriers, leading to isolation and a lack of practical support. Abortion is offered to refugee women as an option in the Netherlands, particularly if professionals are aware of the circumstances surrounding the infant's conception. Although no data are available on rates of pregnancy termination for refugee mothers with children born of sexual violence, research suggests that women who conceive children through conflict-related sexual violence do make use of abortion services where they exist (Delić, 2015) or turn to self-induced or clandestine practices (Human Rights Watch, 1996).

Ultimately, as a refugee mother in Dutch society, raising a child born of sexual violence involves a risk and an opportunity. In the country of origin, it is possible that the strict social customs and taboos surrounding sexual violence may ease, but clinical observations show that refugees' conceptions of their own culture can become frozen in time, maintaining the convictions held at the moment they left. They may have little connection to developments in their own culture and remain afflicted by "old voices." Integration into Dutch society could alleviate such difficulties because "Western culture" is often more neutral or accepting of a child conceived in this manner. Furthermore, creating connections with Dutch citizens could lead to exposure to different perceptions of the child and can promote healing for both mother and child. Unfortunately, services that are tailored for these mothers and children are inadequate in most refugee host countries, limited to a selection of diligent professionals who are able to recognize their dyadic victimhood.

LOOKING TO THE FUTURE

For women raising children born of sexual violence in a country that is not their own, difficulties with parenting and psychopathology are compounded by asylum procedures, overcrowded conditions, a limited support network, and relative social isolation. There are often barriers to work or training and to accessing appropriate health services, culture shock, language problems, and even discrimination. Traumatic experiences of the past can afflict for many years those who have experienced exile (Carta et al., 2015).

To date, infant mental health and specialist refugee services in the Netherlands (which are tertiary care providers) largely encompass the small body of professionals with expertise in supporting refugee mothers with children born of sexual violence. Many combine research with practice and operate group programs that put mothers in contact with each other. Services provided at these expert centers are trauma-focused therapy, mother–child therapy, child therapy, and nonverbal therapy (including art, music, and play). Often, a combination of therapies, preferably in individual and group settings, is offered to enable a combination of trauma-focused and attachment work and break the isolation of these mothers. Regarding integration into Dutch society, some local organizations bring together Dutch volunteers and migrants so that they can interact in activities such as sports and migrants can learn the Dutch language and first aid techniques. However, it is also often the initiative of individual people to plan events that bring together local people and refugees.

Despite these efforts, existing services for refugee mothers have gaps in their provisions, specifically regarding psychosocial well-being, and indeed, especially for mothers with children born of sexual violence. Based on recommendations from a review of the literature on similarly vulnerable populations (Anderson & van Ee, 2018), focus group data from male relatives of sexual violence survivors in eastern Democratic Republic of the Congo (Kelly et al., 2017), and a study of subject matter expertise (Anderson & van Ee, 2018), a framework of psychosocial support for mothers and their children born of sexual violence—particularly those who are refugees—can be developed. At an individual level, mothers in the first instance are ideally supported toward stabilization in treatment. This would address the most pressing concerns—whether physical or psychological—and set mothers up for longer holistic intervention programs. This may also involve home visits and psychoeducation or more intensive forms of psychotherapy, such as eye movement desensitization and reprocessing (using eye movement and tactile stimulation across both sides of the brain to release emotional experiences that are trapped in the nervous system) or narrative exposure therapy (reframing one's life story so that it no longer focuses on traumatic experiences, in order to reduce the persistent feeling of distress). In addition, where possible, women will discuss in more detail options for termination and adoption during unwanted pregnancy. Group work may then be used to encourage mothers to focus on post-traumatic growth and personal strength, using the experiences of others as guides. Both verbal and nonverbal modalities should be offered during group treatment, and these should address the biopsychosocial nature of traumatic stress. For children, some specialized support would be best provided in sessions concurrent with their mothers to avoid obstacles in obtaining childcare. It would target aggression and conduct problems in children and focus on making sense of violence they may have witnessed, as well as provide some basic schooling and enhance social capacity.

Programs and treatment that address mothers or children, however, provide only a partial response to these complex relationships. Ultimately, treatment that includes husbands and spouses, as well as extended family members, has a better chance of relieving the burden on women and the repercussions on their families. At this macrosocial level, communities with customary leaders, religious figures, or respected people of influence are ideally engaged in anti-stigma campaigns, setting positive examples, and encouraging social inclusion and interpersonal support. Such cohesion from communities could pave the way for the advocacy of stricter punishment for sexual violence crimes and lobbying governments to bring those responsible to justice. This would require a wider global effort toward improving legislation for particularly vulnerable groups of refugees and would only succeed in a political climate that promotes inclusion and compassion toward migrants and refugees. Simultaneously, greater funding for research on this subject is required to strengthen the evidence

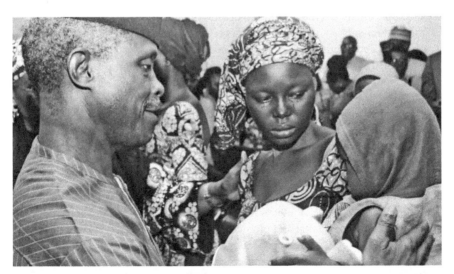

Figure 11.5 Nigerian Vice President holding baby of Chibok girl who was kidnapped by Boko Haram. From France24, by P. Ojisua, 2016. Retrieved July 11, 2018, from www. france24.com/en/20161105-nigerian-troops-schoolgirl-kidnapped-boko-haram-with-baby.

base, particularly the development of specialized treatments and the training of practitioners who can deliver tailored treatment interventions.

Advocacy

Advocacy is important for survivors of sexual violence, for children born of rape, and for refugees with poor mental well-being. Vulnerable groups require not only the attention and support of state-provided services but also the compassion of the wider public. Offering time, skills, and knowledge in voluntary capacities to support refugees can go a long way toward assisting with integration and assimilation. This is likely to have a ripple effect across not only the life of one person but also within communities. Using our voice to speak up on behalf of those afraid to do so can draw the attention of policymakers and state officials.

CONCLUSION

Conflict-related sexual violence is a criminal act that continues to necessitate global attention and resources. Hundreds of thousands of women are persistent targets of armed combatants (and, increasingly, civilian perpetrators), who frequently use rape as a weapon of war. Rape often takes place in circumstances of other forms of extreme violence, and it can result in protracted physical, psychological, and emotional consequences for the victims. Migration is increasingly an option chosen by many people to escape conflict and associated crimes, but this is rarely straightforward or economical. Often, this involves crossing multiple international borders. It can also involve paying vast amounts of money to illegal smuggling operations and negotiating with state officials and individual state laws regarding asylum. In the current climate of forced migration and displaced persons, the spotlight is firmly on Europe and its handling of asylum applications and the integration of refugees into society.

The Netherlands is no exception to this scrutiny, and as of 2018, the Netherlands was hosting approximately 90,000 displaced persons (Vluchtelingenwerk, 2018). Those granted asylum are provided a 5-year residence permit and are offered housing, clothes, food, and a small wage. However, such actions do not always equate to the amelioration of war-related difficulties, and refugees can often find themselves suffering long after the fact. PTSD is commonly observed in survivors of war crimes, and depression, anxiety, and adjustment difficulties are also often attributed to those with complex trauma histories. Women with children conceived of sexual violence have compounded difficulties and require specific care and treatment, as do their children. Boundaries of access to care provisions as a refugee, however, are numerous and complicated; thus, psychopathology can go untreated for long periods of time. Both verbal and nonverbal psychosocial interventions can promote recovery and restore family dynamics to enhance mental and physical well-being. However, it is imperative that treatment extends beyond individualistic, Eurocentric support. The family, the community, and wider society must be engaged in addressing the issue of sexual violence, and survivors must be at the heart of designing and implementing support programs.

DISCUSSION QUESTIONS

1. Considering the information outlined in this chapter regarding the fear of stigma and shame surrounding sexual violence against women, how can immigration interviews be better structured to facilitate the disclosure of such events by asylum seekers?
2. What kind of policies would help newcomers integrate in a country? Should there be particular attention for the position of women in these policies?
3. Care for mothers and their children born of sexual violence requires expert knowledge. What structure can you outline for (mental) health care that attends to the complex needs of these mothers and children?

REFERENCES

Albutt, K., Kelly, J., Kabanga, J., & VanRooyen, M. (2016). Stigmatisation and rejection of survivors of sexual violence in eastern Democratic Republic of the Congo. *Disasters*, *41*(2), 211–227. https://doi.org/10.1111/disa.12202

Alisic, E., & Letschert, R. (2016, April). Fresh eyes on the refugee crisis. *European Journal of Psychotraumatology*, *1*, 1–4.

Amnesty International. (2015). *Mensenrechten op straat: Bed, bad, brood en de menselijke waardigheid in Nederland*. Amsterdam, the Netherlands: Author.

Anderson, K., & van Ee, E. (2018). Mothers with Children Born of Sexual Violence: Perceptions of Global Experts Regarding Support in Social Care Settings. *Healthcare for Women International*, *40*(1), 83–101. doi:10.1080/07399332.2018. 1522319

Apio, E. (2008). *Bearing the burden of blame: The children of the Lord's Resistance Army, northern Uganda*. London, UK: Coalition to Stop the Use of Child Soldiers.

Atkeson, B. M., Calhoun, K. S., Resick, P. A., & Ellis, E. M. (1982). Victims of rape: Repeated assessment of depressive symptoms. *Journal of Consulting and Clinical Psychology*, *50*(1), 96–102. https://doi.org/10.1037/0022-006X.50.1.96

Bartels, S. A., Scott, J. A., Mukwege, D., Lipton, R. I., VanRooyen, M. J., & Leaning, J. (2010). Patterns of sexual violence in eastern Democratic Republic of Congo: Reports from survivors presenting to Panzi Hospital in 2006. *Conflict and Health*, *4*(1), 9. https://doi.org/10.1186/1752-1505-4-9

Breslau, N., Kessler, R., Chilcoat, H., Schultz, L., Davis, G., & Andreski, P. (1998). Trauma and posttraumatic stress disorder in the community. The 1996 Detroit Area Survey of Trauma. *Archives of General Psychiatry*, *55*(7), 626–632.

Buss, D. (2002). Prosecuting mass rape: *Prosecutor v. Dragoliub Kunarac, Radomir Kovac and Zoran Vukovic*. *Feminist Legal Studies*, *10*(1), 91–99.

Campbell, R., Dworkin, E., & Cabral, G. (2009). An ecological model of the impact of sexual assault on women's mental health. *Trauma, Violence & Abuse*, *10*, 225–246. https://doi.org/10.1177/1524838009334456

Carpenter, C. (2007). *War's impact on children born of rape and sexual exploitation: Physical, economic and psychosocial dimensions*. Pittsburgh, PA: University of Pittsburgh.

Carpenter, T. (2013). Tangled web: The Syrian civil war and its implications. *Mediterranean Quarterly*, *24*(1), 1–11. https://doi.org/10.1215/10474552-2018988

Carta, M. G., Moro, M. F., & Bass, J. (2015). War traumas in the Mediterranean area. *The International Journal of Social Psychiatry, 61*(1), 33–38. https://doi.org/10.1177/0020764014535754

Clare, G., Nyiri, P., Yamamoto, C., & Preston, E. (2016). The Calais "jungle." *British Journal of General Practice, 66*(651), 510–510. https://doi.org/10.3399/bjgp16X687193

Clifford, C. (2008). *Rape as a weapon of war and its long-term effects on victims and society.* Paper presented at the 7th Global Conference: Violence and the Contexts of Hostility, May 5–7, Budapest, Hungary. Retrieved from https://www.peacewomen.org/sites/default/files/vaw_rapeasaweaponofwar_stopmodernslavery_may2008_0.pdf

de Jong, J. T., Komproe, I. H., Van Ommeren, M., El Masri, M., Araya, M., Khaled, N., . . . Somasundaram, D. (2001). Lifetime events and posttraumatic stress disorder in 4 postconflict settings. *JAMA, 286*(5), 555–562. https://doi.org/10.1001/jama.286.5.555

de Jonghe, D., van Ee, M., & Dieleman, M. (2004). Living in an asylum seekers centre: Asylum seekers about their health. *Nederlands Tijdschrijft voor Geneeskunde, 82*, 112–117.

Delić, A. (2015). *Kvalitete života i dugoročne psihičke posljedice u žena sa iskustvom ratnog silovanja.* Tuzla, Bosnia and Herzegovina: University of Tuzla.

Dijkhoff, K. (2016). Brief van de staatssecretaris van Veiligheid en Justitie aan asielzoekers aan de grens. Retrieved from: https://www.rijksoverheid.nl/documenten/brieven/2016/02/18/brief-van-de-staatssecretaris-van-veiligheid-en-justitie-aan-asielzoekers-aan-de-grens-engels

Dossa, N. I., Hatem, M., Zunzunegui, M. V., & Fraser, W. (2014). Social consequences of conflict-related rape: the case of survivors in the Eastern Democratic Republic of Congo. *Peace and Conflict: Journal of Peace Psychology, 20*(3), 241–255.

European Commission. (2019). Migration and Home Affairs. Country responsible for asylum application (Dublin). Available at: https://ec.europa.eu/home-affairs/what-we-do/policies/asylum/examination-of-applicants_en. [Date retrieved: 08-07-2019].

Harvard Humanitarian Initiative. (2010, April). *"Now, the world is without me": An investigation of sexual violence in eastern Democratic Republic of Congo.* Harvard Humanitarian Initiative and Oxfam International. Retrieved from https://www.oxfamamerica.org/static/oa3/files/now-the-world-is-without-me-sexual-violence-in-eastern-drc.pdf

Human Rights Watch. (1996). *Shattered lives: Sexual violence during the Rwandan genocide and its aftermath* (Vol. 129). New York, NY: Author.

Human Rights Watch. (2002). *The war within the war: Sexual violence against women and girls in eastern Congo.* New York, NY: Author.

Human Rights Watch. (2016). *"I just sit and wait to die": Reparations for survivors of Kenya's 2007–2008 post election sexual violence.* New York, NY: Author.

Immigration and Naturalisation Service (IND). (2019). Asylum Seeker. Available at: https://ind.nl/en/asylum/Pages/Asylum-seeker.aspx. [Date accessed: 08/07/2019].

Johnson, K., Scott, J., Rughita, B., Kisielewski, M., Asher, J., Ong, R., & Lawry, L. (2010). Association of sexual violence and human rights violations with physical and mental health in territories of the eastern Democratic Republic of the Congo. *JAMA, 304*(5), 553–562. https://doi.org/10.1001/jama.2010.1086

Jonsson, G. (2015). Can the Japan–Korea dispute on "comfort women" be resolved? *Korea Observer, 46*(3), 1–26. Retrieved from https://www.researchgate.net/publication/286626428_Can_the_Japan-Korea_Dispute_on_Comfort_Women_be_Resolved

Kantengwa, O. (2014). How motherhood triumphs over trauma among mothers with children from genocidal rape in Rwanda. *Journal of Social and Political Psychology, 2*(1), 417–434. https://doi.org/10.5964/jspp.v2i1.334

Kelly, J., Albutt, K., Kabanga, J., Anderson, K., & VanRooyen, M. (2017). Rejection, acceptance and the spectrum between: Understanding male attitudes and experiences towards conflict-related sexual violence in eastern Democratic Republic of Congo. *BMC Women's Health, 17*(1), 1–11. https://doi.org/10.1186/s12905-017-0479-7

Kelly, J., Kabanga, J., Cragin, W., Alcayna-Stevens, L., Haider, S., & Vanrooyen, M. (2012). "If your husband doesn't humiliate you, other people won't": Gendered attitudes towards sexual violence in eastern Democratic Republic of Congo. *Global Public Health, 7*(3), 285–298. https://doi.org/10.1080/17441692.2011.585344

Kohli, A., Tosha, M., Ramazani, P., Safari, O., Bachunguye, R., Zahiga, I., . . . Glass, N. (2013). Family and community rejection and a Congolese led mediation intervention to reintegrate rejected survivors of sexual violence in eastern Democratic Republic of Congo. *Health Care for Women International, 34*(9), 736–756. https://doi.org/10.1080/07399332.2012.721418

Koshin Wang, S., & Rowley, E. (2007). *Rape: How women, the community and the health sector respond.* Geneva, Switzerland: Sexual Violence Research Initiative and World Health Organization.

Laban, C. J., Gernaat, H. B. P. E., Komproe, I. H., Schreuders, B. A., & de Jong, J. T. V. M. (2004). Impact of a long asylum procedure on the prevalence of psychiatric disorders in Iraqi asylum seekers in the Netherlands. *Journal of Nervous and Mental Disease, 192*(12), 843–851. https://doi.org/10.1097/01.nmd.0000146739.26187.15

Laban, C. J., Komproe, I. H., Gernaat, H. B. P. E., & de Jong, J. T. V. M. (2008). The impact of a long asylum procedure on quality of life, disability and physical health in Iraqi asylum seekers in the Netherlands. *Social Psychiatry and Psychiatric Epidemiology, 43*(7), 507–515. https://doi.org/10.1007/s00127-008-0333-1

Lindert, J., Carta, M. G., Schäfer, I., & Mollica, R. F. (2016). Refugees mental health— A public mental health challenge. *European Journal of Public Health, 26*(3), 374–375. https://doi.org/10.1093/eurpub/ckw010

Loncar, M., Medved, V., Jovanović, N., & Hotujac, L. (2006). Psychological consequences of rape on women in the 1991–1995 war in Croatia and Bosnia and Herzegovina. *Croatian Medical Journal, 47*(1), 67–75.

Mollica, R. F., Caridad, K. R., & Massagli, M. P. (2007). Longitudinal study of posttraumatic stress disorder, depression, and changes in traumatic memories over time in Bosnian refugees. *Journal of Nervous and Mental Disease, 195*(7), 572–579. https://doi.org/10.1097/NMD.0b013e318093ed2c

Mukwege, D. M., & Nangini, C. (2009). Rape with extreme violence: The new pathology in South Kivu, Democratic Republic of Congo. *PLoS Medicine, 6*(12), 1–5. https://doi.org/10.1371/journal.pmed.1000204

Olsen, C., El-Bialy, R., Mckelvie, M., Rauman, P., & Brunger, F. (2016). "Other" troubles: Deconstructing perceptions and changing responses to refugees in Canada. *Journal of Immigrant and Minority Health, 18*(1), 58–66. https://doi.org/10.1007/s10903-014-9983-0

Parker, S. (2015). Hidden crisis: Violence against Syrian female refugees. *Lancet, 385*(9985), 2341–2342. https://doi.org/10.1016/S0140-6736(15)61091-1

Peterman, A., Palermo, T., & Bredenkamp, C. (2011). Estimates and determinants of sexual violence against women in the Democratic Republic of Congo. *American Journal of Public Health, 101*(6), 1060–1067. https://doi.org/10.2105/AJPH.2010.300070

Rees, S., Silove, D., Chey, T., Ivancic, L., Steel, Z., Creamer, M., . . . Forbes, D. (2011). Lifetime prevalence of gender-based violence in women and the relationship with mental disorders and psychosocial function. *JAMA, 306*(5), 513–521. https://doi.org/10.1001/jama.2011.1098

Rothbaum, B. O., Foa, E. B., Riggs, D. S., Murdock, T., & Walsh, W. (1992). A prospective examination of post-traumatic stress disorder in rape victims. *Journal of Traumatic Stress, 5*(3), 455–475. https://doi.org/10.1007/BF00977239

Theidon, K. (2015). *Hidden in plain sight* [Review]. *Current Anthropology, 56*(12), S191–S200. https://doi.org/10.1353/tam.2004.0163

UNHCR. (1951). Convention and protocol relating to the status of refugees. Geneva: UNHCR.

UNHCR. (2017). Global Trends. Forced Displacement in 2017. Geneva: UNHCR.

van Dijk, R., Bala, J., Ory, F., & Kramer, S. (2001). "Now we have lost everything": Asylum seekers in the Netherlands and their experiences with health care. *Medical Anthropology, 13*, 284–300.

Van Ee, E., & Kleber, R. J. (2012). Child in the shadowlands. *The Lancet, 380*, 642–643. doi:10.1016/S0140-6736(12)61360-9

Van Ee, E., & Kleber, R. J. (2013). Growing up under a shadow. *Child Abuse Review, 22*, 386–397.

Van Ee, E., Kleber, R. J., & Mooren, T. (2012). War trauma lingers on: Associations between maternal posttraumatic stress disorder, parent–child interaction and child development. *Infant Mental Health Journal, 33*(5), 459–468.

Van Ee, E., & Mooren, T. M., & Kleber, R. J. (2014). Broken Mirrors: Shattered relationships in refugee families. In R. Pat-Horenczyk, D. Brom, C. Chemtob & J. Vogel (Eds), Helping children cope with trauma: Individual, family and community perspectives. New York/Oxford: Routledge.

Vluchtelingenwerk. (2018). *Vluchtelingen wereldwijd.* Retrieved November 7, 2018, from https://www.vluchtelingenwerk.nl/feiten-cijfers/cijfers/wereldwijd

Weitsman, P. (2008). The politics of identity and sexual violence: A review of Bosnia and Rwanda. *Human Rights Quarterly, 30*(3), 561–578. https://doi.org/10.1353/hrq.0.0024

Wood, E. J. (2006). Variation in sexual violence during war. *Politics and Society, 34*(3), 307–342. https://doi.org/10.1177/0032329206290426

World Health Organization. (2002). Sexual violence. In *World report on violence and health* (pp. 147–182). Geneva, Switzerland: Author.

12

Child Marriage in the United States

ADITI WAHI-SINGH AND KRISTEN ZALESKI ■

CASE STUDY: TAYA

I was 15 years old when my father arranged my "spiritual" marriage to a man twice my age and a complete stranger. I met him that morning and was married that same night in a religious ceremony. I was 16 and 6 months pregnant when the state of Nevada legally allowed my marriage to a man who had clearly committed statutory rape.

I was born in 1980 in Boulder, Colorado, at the foot of the majestic Rockies. My early childhood was spent in Colorado. My dad was my sole guardian for the majority of my childhood. After my mother left him, my father remarried twice. Shortly after my father remarried for the third time, he moved the family to California. My father was a part of a religious organization that was akin to a cult. This group dictated much of our lives and our understanding of the world. He moved to California to be closer to the leader of this group, and his role within the group meant everything to him. My dad had become extremely abusive toward my brothers and me. We were afraid of him growing up. From a young age, gender roles were ingrained into my life. Girls were meant to serve their family and be obedient to their father and elders.

I was sent to live with my mom when I was 13 years old. My mother was not a part of the group, and for the first time in my life, I felt truly loved and accepted for who I was. However, life with my mother was not easy. She was a working nurse, and during her off hours, she drank heavily. During the time that we were separated from my mother, she had become an alcoholic. She felt that my father had taken her children away from her, and this had deeply affected her. We had spent many years without seeing our mother. I felt truly grateful to be living with her during that time in my life. At 15 years old, I was just finishing my freshman year. Although it had been a rocky year for me at school, I had made some decisions about my life and what I wanted to be. I wanted to join the Air Force Academy so that I could one day attend law school. These were my hopes and dreams at 15. This would all change for me in a blink of an eye. My dad had asked that my brothers and I visit him that summer. He had found out that I was seeing a boy my age and was very upset about it.

When I arrived in California, my father told me that I was going to be married. He said that if I were to have sex outside of marriage that I would go to hell. He told me that the leader of the group would pick someone for me. I met the man who was chosen for me by the leader of our group one morning that summer. I was married that evening by the head leader of our group in a religious ceremony. This spiritual marriage happened in Los Angeles during a religious convention. I was handed over to this stranger after our ceremony. A few weeks after our spiritual marriage ceremony, my new husband took me abroad to his home country. I did not know this man, yet he was legally able to leave the country with me. My mother was not even aware that I had left the country. I was told not to communicate with my mother except to tell her that I was going to live with my dad now.

We returned to the California about 6 months later. In 1996, shortly after I turned 16, I was 6 months pregnant, and we were legally married in Reno, Nevada. Reno was just a short 4-hour trip from the Bay Area where we lived. The state of Nevada only requires a notarized permission slip from one parent to get around the minimum marriage age requirement of 18 years old. I was not yet able to obtain a driver's license, but somehow under the eyes of the law, I was a wife. My mother still did not know I was being given away to a man almost twice my age in legal matrimony. I had no idea what that small piece of paper meant for me. It meant that I was now legally bound to a man, and in order to leave him, I would now have to obtain a divorce. The only thing I remember about that trip was that I got to go sledding, and that was fun because I had not seen snow since I had left Colorado.

Shortly after the birth of my daughter, I fell into a deep depression. I saw girls my age attending high school and asked my family and people in my group why I was not allowed to go to school or have lives like those girls. My questions were met with my community telling me that I would not be able to care properly for my daughter if I returned to school. My place was at home taking care of my family and household. That I should even want to go to school was looked down upon in my group, and I was shunned because of it. It took me all of 7 years to finally leave him.

My struggle continued after I left him. I had little means, yet I was responsible for raising two small children on my own. By the time I realized the extent of what had happened to me and how bad my situation had been, the statute of limitations on statutory rape and child molestation had tolled. I was left with most of the responsibility of raising my kids with no legal recourse against my ex-husband. At times, I struggled to keep a roof over my family's head. I still struggle with depression and anxiety. The effects of childhood marriage have had unending consequences well into my adulthood. However, despite all this, I have managed to move on. I am still in school even after all these years. Now, I am pursuing a master's degree in Public Administration. Both of my children have grown up being able to make their own decisions in life. My children have been my anchor and reason to carry on through all the struggles. I hope that one day, when they start their own families, they do so willingly and lovingly.

Figure 12.1 It is estimated that 90% of child births in developing nations are from children who are married.

OVERVIEW

Child marriage is a legal or cultural marriage involving a child younger than age 18 years (Nour, 2009). Worldwide, approximately 15 million girls younger than age 18 years are married annually (Barr, 2018), and it is estimated that there are 40,000 new child brides each day, especially in developing nations throughout Africa and Asia (United Nations Population Fund, 2012). Child marriage disproportionately affects girls (Koski, Clark, & Nandi, 2017) and has been documented as a human rights abuse that undermines girls' health, education, and economic opportunities and increases their risk of experiencing violence (Mathur, Greene, & Malhotra, 2003).

According to the United Nations, child marriage often is a result of gender bias and discrimination by families that choose boys over girls to pursue education. Advocates argue that early marriage creates a permanent end to a girl's childhood more often than a boy's childhood because of early forced sexual encounters, early pregnancy, and premature exit from school to attend to household chores for the new husband (UNICEF, 2014; Wodon, 2016). The 2018 United Nations Sustainable Development Goals call for an end to child marriage by 2030, and the US State Department (2016) has adopted strategies intended to prevent child marriage abroad.

The marriage of a child has been studied globally in developing nations mostly as a practice of child abuse and dishonor. However, developed nations, such as the United States and European countries, also engage in the practice but do not view it as the same kind of abuse. Globally, reasons for child marriage include financial needs of the families, cultural and religious norms of preserving sexuality (particularly for girls) for marriage, lack of access to education, and rural residence.

Syrett (2016) summarized a century of American census data and reported that between 1880 and 1920, 11% or 12% of girls were married in the United States compared to 6.2% between 2010 and 2014 (Koski & Heymann, 2018). Specifically, Koski and Heymann reported higher American child marriage rates among those who identify their cultural heritage as Chinese or American Indian (10.2%).

Fertility and Health Outcomes

Most research on child brides has been conducted within developing nations, not in the United States. Much of this research finds that child marriages are consistently linked with early, more frequent, and more unwanted pregnancies compared with adult marriages in developing countries (Koski et al., 2017; Santhya, 2011). Mathur et al. (2003) reported a positive correlation between child marriage and early childbirth, defined as giving birth before age 18 years, and postulated that the causes were a lack of knowledge about reproductive health and a girl's inability to influence decision-making related to family planning. Early pregnancy is specifically problematic because childbearing at a young age is often associated with severe health consequences, including higher risk of obstetric complications, obstructed labor, pregnancy-induced hypertension, and maternal mortality (Mathur et al., 2003).

Kim, Longhofer, Boyle, and Brehm (2013) examined marriage laws among 115 poor and middle-income countries throughout the world and found that setting the minimum marriage age to 18 years decreased adolescent fertility, whereas having no restriction or allowing parental consent to bypass the age law resulted in higher rates of adolescent pregnancy. Interestingly, a decrease in child marriage and early childbirth could have promising effects on population overgrowth in the world (Wodon, 2018). For poor nations with high rates of child marriage, a decrease in these marriages and, thereby, a decrease in early childbirth could equate to more fiscal resources to educate their population and provide potential for economic incline (Wodon, 2018). Thus, Wodon suggested that setting clear legal standards requiring married persons to be age 18 years or older is the most efficient way to reduce pregnancy rates.

In addition to negative health outcomes in teen mothers, the literature also suggests that children of teen mothers exhibit similar negative health outcomes. Efevbera, Bhabha, Farmer, and Fink (2017) studied more than 37,000 mothers who had children while they were younger than age 18 years and found what they termed *intergenerational effects*, wherein children of teen mothers showed poorer health outcomes compared with children of mothers who gave birth after the age of 18 years. They also found that child marriage was significantly associated with infant mortality rates in 96 countries. The younger the teen mother, the higher the likelihood her child will not survive, even when controlling for socioeconomic factors (Chen et al., 2007). Even infants who survive past the first year tend to have lower birth weights, inadequate nutrition, and other serious health concerns (Jain & Kurz, 2007).

Furthermore, the less income and education the child bride has, the poorer the health of the child (Efevbera et al., 2017). As children of teen mothers grow older, they tend to experience increased behavioral problems, lower test scores, and higher rates of abuse and neglect compared with children born to adult mothers (Hoffman & Maynard, 2008). In the United States, in particular, children of teen parents are more likely to be placed in foster care and more likely to be incarcerated as adults than are children of adult parents (Hoffman & Maynard, 2008).

Mental health concerns are also a paramount issue within the debate of child marriage. Le Strat, Debertret, and Le Foll (2011) found that women married as children have higher rates of divorce, substance use, and mental illness (specifically persistent depressive disorder, generalized anxiety disorder, and antisocial personality disorder) compared with women married as adults. Furthermore, women married as children often experience significantly greater life stressors and higher rates of suicidal thoughts and attempts than do women married as adults (Gage, 2013). For example, high school-aged girls who had marriage proposals were twice as likely to have suicidal thoughts as those who did not (Gage, 2013).

Abuse

Young girls with minimal education and a lack of resources often lack power within their marriage and households, making them more likely to suffer from domestic violence and sexual abuse (Jensen & Thornton, 2003). Studies have shown that compared with women married as adults, women married before age 18 years report experiencing twice as much physical violence and three times as much sexual abuse (Jain & Kurz, 2007). Furthermore, Raj (2010) found that the odds of experiencing interpersonal violence increased as age at marriage decreased, meaning younger child brides are more susceptible to abuse from a spouse.

Because of lack of education, women married as minors are more apt to accept abuse from their husbands as justifiable (Jensen & Thornton, 2003). In addition, these women are likely to be isolated because they tend to drop out of school once married, resulting in a loss of connection from friends, which makes them more prone to accepting abuse from their spouses, who may be the only people in their lives.

RECENT DEVELOPMENTS OF NOTE

Scant child marriage research has been conducted in the United States. The following discussion is an exhaustive review of the literature available.

During the past three decades, there has been a global decline in the number of girls married before age 15 years; however, high prevalence rates continue to persist for marriages of girls aged 16 and 17 years (Raj, Jackson, & Dunham, 2018). Child marriage affects approximately 900 million children worldwide, 720 million of whom are girls (Raj et al., 2018). Similar to global statistics, child marriage disproportionately impacts girls in the United States because 6.8 of every 1,000 girls are reported to be married as children compared to 5.7 of every 1,000 boys (Koski & Heymann, 2018). Not all US states track data on the age of marriage; however, of the 38 states that do, more than 167,000 children were estimated to be married between 2000 and 2010, with some as young as age 10 years (Reiss, 2017). Given these numbers, the organization Unchained at Last estimated that approximately 248,000 children younger than age 18 years were married between 2000 and 2010 nationwide (Reiss, 2017). More recently, using US census data, Koski and Heymann (2018) estimated that more than 78,000 individuals were married as children in the United States between 2010 and 2014. Child marriage is a significant issue not only globally but also nationally: It impacts a substantial number of children, especially girls, in the United States.

Although the legal age to marry in the United States is 18 years, loopholes in most states allow child marriage to occur with parental consent and a judicial court order. According to Human Rights Watch, in 23 states, children of any age can marry under some circumstances, making US child marriage laws more lax than those in countries such as Afghanistan, Honduras, and Malawi (Barr, 2018). Although several states have introduced bills to ban child marriages, as of May 2018, only Delaware has taken the initiative to completely ban it (Unchained at Last, 2017).

Similarly, Tennessee's governor recently signed a bill to prohibit marriage of minors younger than age 17 years, which, although not a complete ban, is a stricter law compared with those of most other states (Buie, 2018). Legislative efforts in most other states that introduced bills to implement stricter marriage laws for minors were met with strong opposition. For example, the governor of New Jersey, Chris Christie, stated religious freedom as the reason for vetoing the bill to ban child marriage twice in his state. Likewise, in California, the American Civil Liberties Union opposed a comparable bill, stating that a ban on child marriage would "unduly intrude on the fundamental rights of marriage without sufficient cause" (Luna, 2017, para. 3). Thus, those opposing child marriage bills in the United States argue that delaying the marriage age to 18 years is unconstitutional because marriage is a fundamental right.

The other perspective is that children's rights to marry are not being *taken away* but, rather, delayed until age 18 years, much like smoking, voting, and many other fundamental constitutional rights practiced in the United States. By delaying marriage until at least age 18 years, individuals have more rights and access to more resources, such as applying for a credit card or a loan for financial independence, seeking shelter at a domestic violence center in the event of interpersonal abuse, or legally being able to hire an attorney to file for divorce.

In addition to a dearth of resources, children married before age 18 years are likely not adequately equipped with regard to brain development and maturity levels. For example, Wahi, Zaleski, Lampe, Bevan, and Koski (2019) interviewed 21 adults married as children and found that adolescent fantasies and make-believe interfered with their understanding of real-life marriage roles and responsibilities. One participant described his role as a husband as sitting in a lazy chair and drinking soda, whereas another imagined that having a child was akin to playing with dolls (Wahi et al., 2019).

In cases of child marriage, often the power and control are in the hands of the adult spouse. For instance, in some cases, child brides are forced to marry the adult men who raped or impregnated them or both. This scenario, in turn, increases the likelihood of being raped continuously after marriage. Furthermore, as Senator Anthony Delcollo of Delaware stated, child marriage allows for "an exception for circumstances that would otherwise be considered statutory rape" (as cited in Feleke, 2018, para 7). Consequently, delaying the right to marriage until age 18 years has proven to be more beneficial by providing individuals with increased power and control. As a result, under the United Nations Sustainable Development Goals of gender equality and the empowerment of all women and girls, approximately 170 countries throughout the world, including the United States, have set targets to end child marriages by 2030 (Koski et al., 2017).

CURRENT CONDITIONS

Child brides in the United States have minimal rights; consequently, they are often forced to remain in not only unhappy but also abusive marriages. To better understand the reasons for and outcomes of child marriage in the United States, Wahi et al. (2019) conducted a qualitative study of adults who were wed as children and found that more than 85% of the participants reported being physically, sexually, emotionally, or financially abused during their child marriages. One of these women stated that she tried to leave her abusive husband when she was 16 years old and, without the help of her family, went to a domestic violence shelter; however, to her surprise, the domestic violence shelter turned her away because only individuals aged 18 years or older could partake in its services. Stories such as this are not uncommon; other women in the study reported experiencing similar situations and a frequent feeling of being trapped or helpless (Wahi et al., 2019).

As the case of Taya notes, cultural and religious marriages exist outside the laws of the United States and make political and legal interventions more difficult when no gatekeepers are involved. Taya was married at a young age in a religious ceremony, and only when she was pregnant did her husband and father ask for a legal marriage. Anecdotally, in the United States, many citizens romanticize the Romeo and Juliet marriages of young lovers or marriages resulting from teenage pregnancy; thus, these are viewed as culturally acceptable. For example, Koski and Heymann (2018) found that cultural and religious views, especially with regard to pregnancy outside of wedlock, facilitated the approval of "shotgun" child marriages in the United States. However, more research needs to be conducted to determine whether American child marriage actually involves the love-struck teenagers as often as society romanticizes about. For example, in Wahi et al.'s (2019) study, only four women consented to the marriage, seven did not love their husband at all during their marriage, and three were unsure if they were in love.

In the United States, when children are engaged to be married, there seems to be some protections put in place, such as speaking to a judge to ensure the marriage is consensual and not forced. However, those interviews often take place in front of the parent, who might be active in forcing the marriage, and are done without any training on behalf of the judges about the unique issues involved in child marriage. The case of Taya shows that some states have no protections for minors against marriage if a permission slip is presented. The interviewees in Wahi et al.'s (2019) study reported that in cases in which judicial approval is required, judges do not speak to the children alone, and if being coerced, children may not be able to say in front of their parent or guardian that they do not wish to get married. Thus, even when protections are put in place, those responsible for upholding the protections are not safeguarding children from forced marriage.

The causes of child marriages vary; however, themes of coercion and helplessness are common among many child marriage survivors. For example, Sherry Johnson, a well-known advocate for banning child marriage, stated that she was raped, impregnated, and married by age 11 years (Basu, 2018). Her story, as reported by the Cable News Network (CNN), is detailed here (Basu, 2018):

> Each day before school, Johnson sought out her aunt for lunch money because
> Johnson's mother worked as a substitute teacher and could barely make ends

meet. Her aunt lived nearby in the same house as the bishop of their church, and one day, when Johnson was 8, he summoned her into his bedroom.

"I got your lunch money. Come and get it."

He forced her to lie on the bed, used petroleum jelly, and penetrated her. He said nothing and then sent her on her way, blood dripping down her legs. Johnson ran to a bathroom to wash herself, but she was a child in the fourth grade. She could not understand what had happened.

After that, she was raped repeatedly by the bishop and also a church deacon. But when she tried to talk about it, no one believed her, not even her mother. It happened so frequently that Johnson accepted it as a part of growing up.

Her elementary school classmates cruelly told her she smelled like fish.

Several months passed when, one day in class, she was summoned to a room where students received their vaccinations. Johnson was confused. She never got shots; her church forbade them.

She was examined by a nurse and sent back to class. A few minutes later, she heard her name again, blaring through the intercom. She was to collect all her belongings and wait in the office for her mother to pick her up. What had she done wrong?

"You're going to have a baby," her mother blurted out in the car. "Who's been messing with you?"

"I tried to tell you," Johnson replied. "But you said I was lying."

A doctor examined her and gave her the news: She was seven months pregnant. She did the math and knew it was the deacon's baby.

Her mother stood up in church and told everyone her daughter was lying about being raped. She blamed Johnson for bringing shame on the family and sent her away to Miami with the bishop who had raped her. She was dropped off at Jackson Memorial Hospital and left there alone to have her baby.

On a February night in 1970, Johnson, only 10 years old, waited in a hospital hallway. She tried to imagine how a baby would come out of her body; no one had explained it to her. The stares burned through her; she felt like an oddity at an amusement park.

At 1:54 a.m., she gave birth to her first child. When she returned to Tampa, a child welfare worker came by to ask questions. She figure her elementary school must have tipped off the state.

The men who had raped her were adults and if the truth were to surface, they would face statutory rape charges. Instead, Johnson's mother arranged for her daughter to marry one of her rapists, the deacon. She bought a white dress and veil for her daughter and accompanied bride and groom to the Hillsborough County courthouse in Tampa.

Johnson was 11. The man she was marrying was 20.

Johnson remembers sitting at a long table that seemed bigger than her house. She remembers her mother speaking with the judge. The judge refused to marry a girl so young, even though she had a baby.

But a month later, they tried again, this time in neighboring Pinellas County, where Johnson was allowed to sign on the dotted line. The judge was fully aware of her age; the license lists her date of birth.

She had not finished fifth grade yet on March 29, 1971, when she became a wife as well as a mother.

So began a life of burden, a life she was forced to accept. (para. 30–46)

Wahi et al. (2019) identified other reasons for child marriage to be a family-forced action to protect an assailant from a statutory rape charge. Other survivors reported being unsure about the marriage at first but felt pressured from their families because of a pregnancy or inability of the family to take care of them financially or emotionally. Thus, in many cases, a child bride may not have a real choice and may be forced into a marriage because she does not believe that she has the power to say no.

LOOKING TO THE FUTURE

Ending child marriage will help break the intergenerational cycle of poverty by allowing girls and women to participate more fully in society. Empowered and educated girls are better able to nourish and care for their children, leading to healthier, smaller families. When girls are allowed to be girls, everybody wins.
—UNICEF (2014)

Wodon (2016) stated that ending child marriage throughout the world "is the right thing to do ethically" (p. 594). Fortunately, child marriage worldwide seems to be declining slightly each year, especially for girls younger than age 15 years (UNICEF, 2014). Unfortunately, enacting laws against child marriage rarely slows the practice in developing countries. Koski et al. (2017) analyzed data from 31 sub-Saharan African countries and found that despite laws being enacted, the legislation alone was not

Figure 12.2 Girls Not Brides, a global organization fighting to end child marriage, uses awareness and empowerment campaigns that educate communities about the risks of being a young married girl. The organization believes that for change to happen, values and norms that support the practice of child marriage need to shift.

enough to prevent the practice of child marriage in many countries. Some suggest that to stop child marriage, a cultural paradigm shift must occur along with legal action.

To begin this mental transformation, more education can be directed to young girls about the harmful practice, which may help deter it, and to community leaders and families to help them understand the detrimental, rather than protective, effects of the practice and empower them to make changes. In addition, the legal and political climate of setting up protections can be further enhanced (Malhotra, Warner, McGonagle, & Lee-Rife, 2011; Wodon, 2016). Those legal policies can include laws ending the practice of child marriage, but they also must include a decision to pursue education for girls beyond primary school and provide funding to encourage families to seek education for not just sons. For example, Kalamar, Lee-Rife, and Hindin (2016) advocate for cash transfers, school vouchers, free school uniforms, reduced costs related to school, education of teachers to empower girls as much as boys, as well as other measures.

In 2016, the US State Department issued a strategy to empower adolescents throughout the world and identified child marriage as a threat to the well-being of adolescents, stating,

> It produces devastating repercussions for a girl's life, effectively ending her childhood . . . before she is physically and mentally mature . . . depriving her of the chance to reach her full potential, and preventing her from contributing fully to her family and community. (p. 6)

To date, 20 US states have introduced bills to either strengthen current marriage laws to protect minors or completely ban marriage for those younger than age 18 years. Of these states, only 1 has succeeded in completely banning child marriage, and 7 states have passed bills that have added limits to child marriage. The rest of the 30 states have yet to take any stance on improving their existing marriage laws, which allow minors to marry with parental consent and judicial approval. Thus, there is much work to be done to protect minors in the United States.

Furthermore, many advocacy and child welfare agencies, such as the National Association of Social Workers and the National Academy of Pediatrics, have not taken a stance on the issue of child marriage.

Yet, there are notable nonprofit organizations in the United States tackling the issue head on. Fraidy Reiss, the founder of Unchained at Last and a forced marriage survivor, has drafted legislation that aims to close the loopholes that allow children to marry in the United States. Despite a strong advocacy pull in the past few years, many state legislators are unaware that child marriage is an ongoing and prominent social justice problem. Many legislators believe child marriage is a problem of developing countries and are not aware that hundreds of thousands of children are married legally in the United States. Individuals interested in furthering this cause and helping protect children can push this legislation in their state and write to, call, or meet with their state legislators to discuss this topic. Furthermore, the Tahrir Justice Center also advocates throughout the country to protect child marriage in the United States, stating "current laws are failing to protect vulnerable children and teens" (www.tahirih.org).

In addition to furthering legislation efforts, readers can raise awareness about the issue of child marriage by writing op-ed pieces for their local newspapers. Much like elected officials, the general public is often unaware of the existence of child marriage in the United States, and media coverage is an excellent way to increase awareness on this topic. Thus, the important steps to banning child marriage in the United States include increasing awareness and implementing policy change to end these marriages completely.

CONCLUSION

Based on the current literature, it is clear that child marriage often results in countless negative outcomes, including poor physical and mental health; lack of education; increased likelihood of physical, sexual, emotional, and financial abuse; and lack of power and control. Although child marriage occurs for a myriad of reasons globally, it is vital to recognize the long-term impacts on the child rather than focusing on possible short-term gains, such as marrying due to pregnancy or to flee an abusive home. The most disadvantaged of our youth are being pushed into marriages in which they often feel helpless and see a future that is grim. Given that child marriage disproportionately impacts girls and individuals with low socioeconomic status, this social justice issue needs to be addressed by laws established by governments worldwide. Policies need to be implemented that ban child marriages to protect girls and allow them the right to be children, receive an education, and have a chance at a brighter future.

DISCUSSION QUESTIONS

1. What are the public health concerns about child marriage? What are some suggestions in the chapter to buffer these health concerns?
2. For more developed countries such as the United States, in which education beyond primary school is easily attained without much cost, what more can be done to prevent child marriage?
3. What does your culture believe about children who enter marriage? Discuss your cultural, religious, and personal beliefs about love, and also discuss community standards for marriage. Compare with a classmate.

REFERENCES

Barr, H. (2018, May 10). *Delaware ends child marriage: 49 to go and counting—Better protection in Afghanistan than some US states*. Human Rights Watch. Retrieved from https://www.hrw.org/news/2018/05/10/delaware-ends-child-marriage-49-go-and-counting

Basu, M. (2018, January 31). *Sherri Johnson was raped, married, and pregnant by 11: Now she's fighting to end child marriage in America*. CNN. Retrieved from https://www.cnn.com/2018/01/29/health/ending-child-marriage-in-america/index.html

Buie, J. (2018, May 22). Gov. Bill Haslam signs law banning Tennessee marriage of minors under 17. *The Tennessean*. Retrieved from https://www.tennessean.com/story/news/politics/2018/05/22/governor-signs-law-banning-tennessee-child-marriage/632925002

Chen, X. K., Wen, S. W., Fleming, N., Demissie, K., Rhoads, G. G., & Walker, M. (2007). Teenage pregnancy and adverse birth outcomes: A large population based retrospective cohort study. *International Journal of Epidemiology, 36*(2), 368–373.

Efevbera, Y., Bhabha, J., Farmer, P., & Fink, P. (2017). Girl child marriage as a risk factor for early childhood development and stunting. *Social Science & Medicine, 185,* 91–101.

Feleke, B. (2018, May 12). *Delaware becomes first US state to fully ban child marriage.* CNN. Retrieved from https://www.cnn.com/2018/05/12/us/delaware-child-marriage-ban/index.html

Gage, A. J. (2013). Association of child marriage with suicidal thoughts and attempts among adolescent girls in Ethiopia. *Journal of Adolescent Health, 52*(5), 654–656.

Hoffman, S. D., & Maynard, R. A. (2008). *Kids having kids: Economic costs and social consequences of teen pregnancy.* Urban Institute. Retrieved from http://webarchive.urban.org/publications/211515.html

Jain, S., & Kurz, K. (2007). *New insights on preventing child marriage: A global analysis of factors and programs.* Washington, DC: International Center for Research on Women.

Jensen, R., & Thornton, R. (2003). Early female marriage in the developing world. *Gender & Development, 11*(2), 9–19.

Kalamar, A. M., Lee-Rife, S., & Hindin, M. J. (2016). Interventions to prevent child marriage among young people in low- and middle-income countries: A systematic review of the published and gray literature. *Journal of Adolescent Health, 59*(3), S16–S21.

Kim, M., Longhofer, W., Boyle, E. H., & Brehm, H. N. (2013). When do laws matter? National minimum age-of-marriage laws, child rights, and adolescent fertility, 1989–2007. *Law & Society Review, 47*(3), 589–619.

Koski, A., Clark, S., & Nandi, A. (2017). Has child marriage declined in sub-Saharan Africa? An analysis of trends in 31 countries. *Population and Development Review, 43*(1), 7–29.

Koski, A., & Heymann, J. (2018). Child marriage in the United States: How common is the practice, and which children are at greatest risk? *Perspectives on Sexual and Reproductive Health, 50*(2), 59–65.

Le Strat, Y., Dubertret, C., & Le Foll, B. (2011). Child marriage in the United States and its association with mental health in women. *Pediatrics, 128*(3), 524–530.

Luna, T. (2017, May 9). Under-18 marriage ban weakened after ACLU opposes. *The Sacramento Bee.* Retrieved from https://www.sacbee.com/news/politics-government/capitol-alert/article149610849.html

Malhotra, A., Warner, A., McGonagle, A., & Lee-Rife, S. (2011). *Solutions to end child marriage.* Washington, DC: International Center for Research on Women.

Mathur, S., Greene, M., & Malhotra, A. (2003). *Too young to wed: The lives, rights, and health of young married girls.* International Center for Research on Women. Retrieved from http://citeseerx.ist.psu.edu/viewdoc/download?doi=10.1.1.677.8700&rep=rep1&type=pdf

Nour, N. M. (2009). Child marriage: a silent health and human rights issue. *Rev Obstet Gynecol, 2*(1), 51–56.

Raj, A. (2010). When the mother is a child: The impact of child marriage on the health and human rights of girls. *Archives of Disease in Childhood, 95*(11), 931–935.

Raj, A., Jackson, E., & Dunham, S. (2018). Girl child marriage: A persistent global women's health and human rights violation. In S. Choudhury, J. Erausquin Toller, & M. Withers (Eds.), *Global perspectives on women's sexual and reproductive health across the lifecourse* (pp. 3–19). New York, NY: Springer.

Reiss, F. (2017, November 16). *Child marriage is happening at an alarming rate across the US*. CNN. Retrieved from https://www.cnn.com/2017/11/15/opinions/moore-case-spotlights-risk-to-young-girls-reiss/index.html

Santhya, K. G. (2011). Early marriage and sexual and reproductive health vulnerabilities of young women: A synthesis of recent evidence from developing countries. *Current Opinion in Obstetrics and Gynecology, 23*(5), 334–339.

Syrett, N. (2016). *American child bride: A history of minors and marriage in the United States.* Chapel Hill, NC: North Carolina Press.

Unchained at Last. (2017). *Child marriage—Progress.* Retrieved from http://www.unchainedatlast.org/child-marriage-progress

UNICEF. (2014). *Ending child marriage: Progress and prospects.* Retrieved from https://data.unicef.org/wp-content/uploads/2015/12/Child-Marriage-Brochure-HR_164.pdf

United Nations Population Fund. (2012). *Marrying too young: End child marriage.* Retrieved from https://www.unfpa.org/sites/default/files/pub-pdf/MarryingTooYoung.pdf

US State Department. (2016). *U.S. global strategy to empower adolescent girls.* Retrieved from https://2009-2017.state.gov/documents/organization/254904.pdf

Wahi, A., Zaleski, K. L., Lampe, J., Bevan, P., & Koski, A. (2019). The lived experience of child marriage in the United States. *Social Work in Public Health, 34*(3), 201–221.

Wodon, Q. (2016). Early childhood development in the context of the family: The case of child marriage. *Journal of Human Development and Capabilities, 17*(4), 590–598.

Wodon, Q. (2018). Education budget savings from ending child marriage and early child-births: The case of Niger. *Applied Economics Letters, 25*(10), 649–652.

13

Coping with Loneliness

Health and Well-Being Among Older Women in Australia

DAWN JOOSTEN-HAGYE AND ANNE KATZ ■

OVERVIEW

Loneliness can kill. Researchers and practitioners are finding that loneliness is more than just unpleasant—it can be fatal. In recent years, more attention has been given to loneliness and social isolation in older adults. Psychosocial factors intersect and affect the well-being of older adults as well. For example, loneliness may lead to ill health, but ill health may also lead to loss of social contacts and the eventual feelings of loneliness. Solid social connections are essential to people's mental and physical well-being. Considerable research attention has been devoted to investigating these issues, particularly in Europe, the United States, and, more recently, Australia. Most of these studies have focused on older people living in the community, although similar problems have been identified in residential care settings. Risk factors for loneliness include widowhood, separation and divorce, being childless, living alone, deteriorating health, and life events such as loss and bereavement. Other sociodemographic factors include age and low income, particularly for women. Often, lack of money can limit opportunities, as can mobility issues.

The Silver Line Helpline, a 24-hour call center for older adults, received a call from a woman who spoke lightheartedly of spring and of her 81st birthday the previous week (Haffner, 2016). "Who did you celebrate with?" asked the volunteer, "No one, I . . . " (p. 2). And with that, the woman's cheer turned to despair; her voice began to quaver as she acknowledged that she had been alone at home not just on her birthday but for days and days. The telephone conversation was the first time she had spoken in more than a week (Haffner, 2016). Approximately 10,000 similar calls come in weekly, according to Haffner.

Housing can also be an issue. Many older adults want to age in place, but it can be isolating. Of course, one can live alone and not be lonely, or one can live with others and feel very alone. Loneliness can be as destructive as being obese or smoking. Loneliness is becoming so pervasive that some professionals are starting to screen for loneliness. Prevalence rates of loneliness in adult populations ranges from 17% in US adults (Theeke, 2010) to more than 30% in older adults in Australia (Steed, Boldy, Grenade, & Iredell, 2007). Australian census data show that more than one in three women and one in five men aged 65 or older live alone. Aged and Community Services Australia (2015) reviewed a wide body of research and found up to 10% of older Australians suffer from loneliness. The 2017 National Seniors Social Survey found that there was concern regarding longevity and increased loneliness of older Australians, and it revealed that older women are at a disadvantage.

The older adult population is projected to grow from 8% of the global population in 2010 to 16% by 2050, or roughly 16 billion (National Institute on Aging, 2011). The proportion of Australians aged 65 years or older is projected to increase to more than 6.5 million by 2051, with the highest projected growth rate for those aged 80 years or older (Australian Bureau of Statistics, 2006).

Older adults are more likely than adults of other age groups to live with comorbid conditions. Comorbidity refers to an individual living with two or more illnesses or disorders that co-occur simultaneously, with each interacting with and impacting the other illness or disorder (National Institute of Health, 2010). This can include having two or more chronic conditions (i.e., cardiovascular disease and diabetes) and/or two or more conditions including NCDs, substance use, and/or mental health disorders. Comorbid conditions affect the health and well-being of older adults. Comparatively few Australian studies have focused on comorbidity associated with chronic disease. However, these studies show high prevalence of comorbidity across national health priority areas. Following is a case study that is used to illustrate the context of health and well-being as it affects older women in Australia.

CASE STUDY: MRS. M

Mrs. M, an 89-year-old woman diagnosed with clinical depression and loneliness, lived in Melbourne, Australia. Her husband had been deceased for 15 years; they had no children. Fifty years ago, she moved to her current house in an area with a "village atmosphere," but now the once friendly neighborhood was extinct. She had outlived her loved ones and had lost her zest for life. She had a will with friend's names written down as next of kin but had crossed off each one as they had passed away. Her final wish was to die in her own home with dignity. Mrs. M had asthma and suffered with chronic debilitating arthritis, which made it difficult for her to leave the house. Due to her inactivity, she gained weight and was recently diagnosed with obesity and type 1 diabetes. She was unable to participate in regular physical activity, which contributed to her depression. Walking was very difficult and painful for her. She believed that old age was a curse and felt like a "half-dried rug—with all its purpose rung out."

According to the World Health Organization (WHO, 2014), noncommunicable diseases (NCDs), or chronic conditions, accounted for approximately 68% of all deaths globally in 2012 (56 million). The top four NCDs globally are cardiovascular diseases (heart attack and stroke), cancer, chronic respiratory diseases (i.e., asthma and chronic obstructive pulmonary disease), and diabetes (WHO, 2017). Mrs. M had two of these chronic conditions—diabetes and asthma. Cardiovascular disease causes more deaths internationally each year than any other chronic condition, representing 48% of all deaths from NCDs (WHO, 2014). Modifiable risk factors that contribute to NCD deaths globally each year include tobacco (7.2 million), excess sodium intake (4.1 million), alcohol consumption (3.3 million, including cancer), and insufficient physical activity (1.6 million) (WHO, 2017). As is often the case, Mrs. M's physical activity was compromised due to her other chronic conditions. Metabolic risk factors (i.e., hypertension, overweight/obesity, hyperlipidemia, and hyperglycemia) and low socioeconomic status (SES) are also associated with higher rates of NCDs globally (WHO, 2017). The rates of comorbid conditions are higher for adults aged 60 years or older (60%), with a higher percentage of females affected (25%) than males (21%) (Australian Institute of Health and Welfare, 2016). Mrs. M is part of this 25%. She experienced comorbid depression and chronic arthritis that impacted her functional health and ability to leave her home, in addition to obesity.

Internationally, 1 in 5 older adults are living with a neurological or mental health disorder (WHO, 2017). In fact, 1 in 10 older adults have subthreshold depression, or depression among older adults that does not meet diagnosable criteria (WHO, 2017). Mrs. M's clinical depression impacted her daily functioning to the extent that it was difficult for her to leave her house. In 2015 and 2016, a survey of general practitioners in Australia revealed that nearly one in four office visits (24.4%) for adults aged 65 years or older were mental health related, with more females seeking mental health-related services (58.1%, or 3 out of 5) compared with males (Australian Institute of Health and Welfare, 2017b). In 2017, more females than males had a mental health condition and a sedentary lifestyle (Australian Bureau of Statistics, 2017b)—like Mrs. M, who was forced to lead a sedentary lifestyle due to her multiple chronic conditions. Internationally, among adults aged 60 years or older, the most common neurological and mental health disorders include depression (7%), dementia (5%), anxiety disorders (3.8%), and substance use (1%) (WHO, 2017). Mrs. M is among the 7% of older adults living with depression.

Loneliness is also linked to overall morbidity and mortality in older adults as well as a major predictor of psychological problems such as depression and anxiety. The literature suggests that loneliness is linked to multiple chronic health conditions, such as cardiovascular diseases and hypertension, and other common chronic conditions, including stroke, lung disease, obesity, and adult-onset diabetes (Tomaka, Thompson, & Palacios, 2006). This is certainly the case for Mrs. M, whose comorbid arthritis led to reduced physical activity and a subsequent diagnosis of obesity. Combined with the loss of her spouse and the social support network to which she was accustomed, Mrs. M developed depression. She experienced loneliness in her advancing age. The experience of loneliness and how it impacts individuals physically and psychologically has social implications. Although the way people experience loneliness is subjective—for example, what one person might experience as loneliness may feel different to someone else—understanding loneliness is important for the development of a range of social policies. Loneliness is not uniformly distributed throughout the older population; people in the oldest age cohorts, who are more likely to become socially constrained due to caring for a spouse, mobility restriction, or living with dementia, experience more severe loneliness (Warburton & Lui, 2007). Lauder,

Sharkey, and Mummery (2004) reported that loneliness is a common problem, with nearly two-thirds of the community study sample reporting some feeling of loneliness. Furthermore, in central Queensland, they found that 36% of the population was lonely. As early as 1979, Berkman and Syme reported that socially isolated adults have higher rates of mortality.

From the 2017 National Seniors Social Survey, concern regarding longevity and increased loneliness of older Australians surfaced. The survey found that 70% of women older than age 80 years live alone, like Mrs. M, compared to only 25% of men in this age group. "[In addition] people are experiencing more loneliness as they age and women more so than men—many are experiencing depression and no sense of purpose" (Aged Care Guide, 2017). As previously mentioned, Mrs. M felt like a "half-dried rug—with all its purpose rung out." Loneliness is a significant risk factor for a wide range of physical illnesses, including heart disease and the common cold (Cohen, Doyle, Skoner, Rubin, & Gwaltney, 1997). Loneliness is also a predictor of high levels of hospital emergency department use, independent of chronic illness (Geller, Janson, McGovern, & Valdini, 1999). Risk factors include experience of domestic violence in a current relationship, not having recent paid employment, and not being married/partnered (Lauder et al., 2004). Mrs. M is among the 70% of older women in Australia experiencing loneliness.

HISTORICAL TRENDS

In 2013, Australia health expenditures represented 9.4% of the gross domestic product (GDP) at $5,060 per person; in comparison, health expenditures in the United States represented 17.1% of GDP at $10,963 per person (Australian Institute of Health and Welfare, 2016). In 2013–2014, Australia's health expenditures reached $155 billion (Australian Institute of Health and Welfare, 2016). In 1984, Medicare was enacted as Australia's universal public health insurance program to ensure Australians subsidized or free access to health provider treatment and services offered at public hospitals under three coverage areas: pharmacy, hospital, and medical (Australian Institute of Health and Welfare, 2016). Funding for universal health care is divided across the government (local, territory, state, and federal), nongovernmental organizations, those with private health insurance, and out-of-pocket expenses (Australian Institute of Health and Welfare, 2016). Taxpayers pay a 2% levy on their taxable income and surcharges that increase with income to fund Medicare (Australian Institute of Health and Welfare, 2016).

A variety of health services are provided by health providers in the community, primary health care settings, and private and public emergency and hospital-based settings by health professionals and government and nongovernmental agencies (Australian Institute of Health and Welfare, 2016). Territory and state governments, along with the Australian government, fund and deliver community health, community-based health, and home health services; health programs for populations; research in health and medical fields; services for Torres Strait Islanders and Aboriginals; and immunizations, nutrition, safety, physical activity, smoking cessation, health promotion, and public health activities, services, and programs (Australian Institute of Health and Welfare, 2016). In 1992, Australia passed mental health policy that shifted practices of delivering care for those living with mental health conditions in institutions to community-oriented care and called for practices of integrating mental health services with health services (WHO, 2008a). These services would be beneficial for Mrs. M to address her physical and mental health issues. In 2015, 31 primary health networks (PHNs) were created by the Australian government to improve outcomes, efficiency, and effectiveness of health services for individuals living with chronic health and comorbid conditions (Australian Institute of Health and Welfare, 2016). These PHNs emphasize coordination of services between hospital and primary health care systems with clients who meet one of six priority areas: older adults; Torres Strait and Aboriginal; and the workforces of health, eHealth, mental health, and eHealth services (Australian Institute of Health and Welfare, 2016).

RECENT DEVELOPMENTS OF NOTE

Females aged 55–64 years have less pension for retirement on average than their male counterparts ($196,409 and $310,145, respectively; Australian Bureau of Statistics, 2017a). Several factors contribute to this trend of lower pensions pre-retirement for females in comparison to males: There are fewer females than males in the labor force, underemployment rates are higher for females, females have higher rates of part-time employment, females have a lower income ratio of 0.89 of the wage earnings of males, and females are twice as likely to care for someone with a disability (Australian Bureau of Statistics, 2017a). When considering issues of safety and social justice, females in Australia are five times more likely to be sexually assaulted than males, they are underrepresented in government and on boards, female college graduates have a lower starting salary in 16 out of 19 key industries, and fewer females than males hold executive positions for the Australian Public Services (42%) and as Federal Circuit Court Judges (42%) (Australian Bureau of Statistics, 2017a).

For example, Mrs. P is a divorced woman who was abused by her husband. Mrs. P worked part-time while she raised her children as a single mom, also caring for her ill mother. In 2015–2016, females older than age 65 years received fewer Medicare services compared with males (i.e., 29 compared with 35 services, respectively) (Australian Bureau of Statistics, 2017b). In 2014–2015, visits to a primary care physician were reported by 89% of females during a 12-month period; however, 1 in 10 did not get a medication prescribed due to the cost, 1 in 5 reported long wait periods, and 1 in 20 did not see their doctor due to costs of visits (Australian Institute of Health and Welfare, 2017a). Mrs. P is part of this group, often unable to get her medication and/ or see her doctor due to costs.

CURRENT CONDITIONS

There is a growing crisis among aging baby boomer women, especially in regional Australia. According to the Australian Bureau of Statistics (2012), approximately 105,000 people were homeless in 2011. The number of older women (aged 55 years or older) who were homeless increased 12% is based on 2011. People older than age 55 years make up more than 25% of the Australian population, and while they are underrepresented in the homeless data, they are even less likely to receive support from specialist homelessness services. However, statistics show that the number of women aged 55 years or older using homelessness services has increased by 52% from 2011 to 2016 (Australian Institute of Health and Welfare, 2017b).

Mrs. L, a 71-year-old retired nursing aide, found herself living on the streets after the rent on the flat she had lived in for 15 years increased from $280 to $500 in 1 month. Things were so bad that she did not care whether she was alive or dead. She never imagined homelessness was something that would happen to her, but the costs of living on her fixed income were so high, in addition to the costs of her medications for high blood pressure and cholesterol, that she could not afford to pay rent and for food and medication. She did not know where to turn. Unfortunately, this situation is common. For many in this group, a lack of financial resources and assets makes it impossible to sustain their housing, as with Mrs. L. The following reasons have been identified: being forced out of the workforce early, having insufficient superannuation and/or savings to fund the costs of living, discrimination in the housing market, death of an income-earning spouse, poor health or serious illness often resulting from abuse (indirectly or directly), and separation and/or divorce (Homelessness Australia, 2016). Crane and Warnes (2010) highlighted the individual and structural factors mentioned previously as causes of homelessness among older women. Recently, more attention has been paid to gender and homelessness, specifically regarding how disadvantage is experienced by women throughout the life course and may result in later life homelessness. Batterham, Mallet, Yates, Kolar, and Westmore (2013) suggested that financial insecurity in later life may be more the experience of older women, who had lower paid roles and/or more precarious employment. Health crises or age discrimination could put jobs at risk and throw them into a housing crisis (McFerran, 2010).

Transnational Feminism

Improving gender equality, human rights for women, social conditions among women, employment conditions, and reproductive health, as well as "ending the feminization of poverty and resisting violence against women," are uniting objectives adopted by women's groups internationally concerned with addressing issues women experience across national boundaries (Moghadam, 2010, p. 24). Health-related gender equality is a women's issue for adult and older adult women in Australia because many low-income women report barriers to timely, affordable medical care and medications to manage comorbid conditions.

The 2014–2015 National Health Survey conducted in Australia revealed in self-reported data that approximately one in four (23%) Australians were living with two or more of the following eight chronic conditions: arthritis, asthma, back pain, cancer, cardiovascular disease, chronic obstructive pulmonary disease, diabetes, and mental health disorders (Australian Institute of Health and Welfare, 2016). Among adults aged 65 years or older, 85% were living with at least one of the eight chronic conditions in 2014–2015 (Australian Institute of Health and Welfare, 2018). Those with chronic conditions had lower SES (30% with low SES vs. 19% with high SES), and among those in remote regions or locations (28%) in comparison to those living in major cities (21%) (Australian Institute of Health and Welfare, 2016).

The most common comorbid conditions among older adults aged 65 years or older in 2014–2015 were arthritis and cardiovascular disease (32%), arthritis and back pain

(17%), and back problems and cardiovascular disease (16%) (Australian Institute of Health and Welfare, 2016). In 2007, approximately 12% of individuals living with a mental health condition had a comorbid chronic condition, and 5.3% had comorbid mental health (two or more) combined with a chronic condition (one or more) (Australian Institute of Health and Welfare, 2017b). Individuals with a psychotic illness are 3 times more likely to have diabetes and 1.5 times more likely to have a chronic condition related to heart disease (Australian Institute of Health and Welfare, 2017b).

Barriers to medical services have been identified in qualitative data from the Australian Longitudinal Study on Women's Health survey of women of three age cohorts (birth years: 1921–1926, 1946–1951, and 1973–1978; (Walkom, Loxton, & Robertson, 2013). Women with low incomes or whose incomes are slightly higher than the qualifying income for bulk-billed medical services (i.e., no co-payment for services) in Australia experience barriers to accessing medical care and medication to manage their comorbid conditions due to an inability to pay the co-payment (among those not qualified for bulk-billed services), providers being fully booked (for those who qualify for bulk-billed services), and travel-related expenses to utilize medical services (Walkom et al., 2013). This was the case for Mrs. L, who could no longer afford to pay for her medications to treat her high blood pressure and cholesterol. Women in the older age cohort (born 1921–1926) reported greater issues with medication costs (57.6%) compared with women in the younger older adult cohort (born 1946–1951; 28.2%) and those in the adult cohort (born 1973–1978; 20.8%) (Walkom et al., 2013). One participant from the 1921–1926 cohort reported issues with costs of medications to treat her condition: "Having to pay extra for medication because generic brands do not keep severe [condition] under control" (Walkom et al., 2013, p. 5). Daily use of prescribed medications is higher for older women than for males (4.1 vs. 3.5, respectively), and older women are prescribed medications more often than males (70% and 61%, respectively) (Elliot, 2006). Accessing primary care in rural areas is a barrier, as described by one participant from the 1921–1926 cohort: "Small country town medical clinics do not give bulk-billing to aged pensioners and insist on cash the day of the visit. . . . Many pensioners would not seek medical help when needed if at the time no cash was available" (Walkom et al., 2013, p. 4).

A description of an integrated care program highlighting a demonstration project implemented at a community-based level to address comorbid conditions among older adults in the district of St. Vincent's in Sydney follows. With the passage of mental health policy in 1992 promoting integration of mental health services into primary care, in 2008 the city of Sydney implemented an integrated care program in the district of St. Vincent's, an inner-city district with 13,000 residents aged 65 years or older with high risk factors for mortality, disability, and disadvantages due to comorbid health and mental health conditions that include homelessness; residence in a nursing home, hostel, or government housing; survivors of the holocaust; individuals living with HIV/AIDS; Torres Strait Islander or Aboriginal; and non-English speaking (WHO, 2008b). Less than 1% of residents in the district present to hospitals for treatment of comorbid conditions, with care being provided more commonly in primary care settings because such services have an overarching goal of the identification of older adults with comorbid health and mental health conditions and early coordinated and collaborative interventions with other agencies that are evidence-based with relapse prevention, recovery, and rehabilitation through primary care physicians, geriatric psychiatrists, community-based aged care, and geriatricians (WHO, 2008b).

Assessments by geriatric psychiatrists occurred at patients' homes, physicians' offices, and in outpatient community or inpatient hospital settings; however, timeliness of services for comorbid conditions is concerning because it took an average of 5 years from planning to full implementation of the program to meet the needs of 13,000 residents within the district with one part-time psychiatrist, one part-time psychiatry trainee, one full-time clinical psychologist, and one full-time clinical nurse consultant (WHO, 2008b). Key outcomes from the implementation of this project include reduced "revolving door" older adults in specialized mental health, increased skills of primary care physicians in assessing older adults with comorbid health and mental health conditions, and improved continuity of care between primary care physicians and specialized services (WHO, 2008b). Unfortunately, the case study does not provide data on older adult mental health and physical health outcomes for improvements in symptoms and conditions as a result of this integrated care program. Mrs. M could certainly benefit from this type of community-oriented integrated care program.

LOOKING TO THE FUTURE

Advocacy within organizations to address older adult females' comorbid health and mental health conditions should include efforts to ensure that timely assessment, screening, referral to specialized services, and collaborative practices and partnerships are in place with district-level providers of mental health, substance use, and specialized geriatric care enabling access to integrated care services. In response to this need, in 2013, the Agency for Clinical Innovation Aged Health Network Executive Committee developed a framework for integrated care of older adults with complex needs for comorbid conditions. The framework includes design principles; factors regarding older adults (i.e., initial contact, specialized care, care management and treatment planning, crisis intervention for acute needs, and support for end-of-life and palliative care and recovery); components to enable integration (i.e., support to providers of care, engagement with older adults and their families/caregivers, and alignment of policy and resources); and key stakeholders of the Australian aged network to improve outcomes of older adults (i.e., national, regional, state, and district) and promote strategies to reduce health care expenses for older adults, as well as increase satisfaction of older adults' experiences (Agency for Clinical Innovation, 2013). Under the model, best practices for integrated care include care plans for interdisciplinary teams; coordination of care across providers and agencies; initial older adult contact access; management and planning; crisis/acute care; specialized care for older adults; recovery/rehabilitation; supportive care for end-of-life and palliative care; in community care; in community continuity of care; alignment of resources, policy, and performance incentives; and macro, meso, and local implementation strategies (Agency for Clinical Innovation, 2013). One specific case study from this model implemented at Silver Chain in Western Australia in metro Perth for non-emergency home and hospital services demonstrated reduced emergency room visits among older adults, improved access to services for older adults, care in the home rather than in the hospital, no cost to participants, collaboration with primary care physicians, and earlier discharges from acute care if hospitalized (Agency for Clinical Innovation, 2013).

To address current conditions of homelessness among older women, the following strategies are suggested:

1. More attention should be focused on the issue of homelessness among older women.
2. There should be increased collaboration between housing/homelessness services and established aged services in the community.
3. Increase the amount of affordable housing. Some may also need support as they age in place to address changes in functional health and/or comorbid conditions.
4. Policy and service responses need to acknowledge the diverse life experiences of older women in housing crisis.
5. Engagement with older women needs to be linked to current circumstances as well as background.

CONCLUSION

Rather than treat comorbid health and mental health disorders separately, integrated approaches are needed. Specifically, integrated, collaborative multi-agency approaches are needed to address the growing issues for older adult women, such as homelessness and loneliness, as they intersect with comorbid conditions. Chronic conditions are a global issue, accounting for more than two-thirds of all deaths each year. Loneliness is linked with comorbid health conditions as well as depression and anxiety among older adults. As such, integrated approaches are essential. Stakeholders at all levels should collaborate to develop integrated, holistic approaches responsive to the unique needs of older women that address multifactorial issues, such as barriers to services, wages, housing, utilization of resources, as well as the evident gaps in knowledge.

To date, research has identified successful strategies in building social support and fostering social inclusion to decrease loneliness, yet not all older adult women have access to resources and services associated with these strategies. Some successful strategies include direct interventions such as supporting and maintaining existing relationships, supporting new social connections, as well as various psychological approaches. Technology and transportation are other strategies that are used, as well as neighborhood approaches and volunteerism. In 2018, the Australian government announced an inclusion of $46 million toward the "community visitors" scheme, designed to reduce loneliness in adults (Lim, 2018, p. 1). In some areas of Australia, virtual senior centers are available, in which seniors living in their own homes and nursing homes can participate in a variety of virtual events by connecting to the platform using a tablet or computer. Reducing loneliness has health benefits, but the solution is not as simple as connecting lonely people with other people. It is important to establish meaningful connections. A public health campaign in Australia could help play a role in destigmatizing loneliness and addressing health implications, and this is gathering momentum in Australia. With targeted solutions, feelings of loneliness could improve. Future areas to address include loneliness within care settings and the needs of Black and minority ethnic groups, including lesbian, gay, bisexual, and trans older people.

Ensuring equality in access to health, mental health, social services, and economic resources as well as financial opportunities to reduce the feminization of poverty and cumulative disadvantage throughout the life course for women is of global importance. Older women, as key stakeholders, should be involved in planning, delivery, and evaluation of programs, as well as all levels of advocacy and policy formulation, to ensure their voices, perspectives, and unique needs are heard, addressed, and considered.

DISCUSSION QUESTIONS

1. How can gender equality be attained when comorbid physical and mental health disorders of older adult females are aggregated in various reports generated for older adults on integrated care services to date in Australia?
2. A significant body of research has identified successful strategies for building social support and fostering social inclusion to decrease loneliness. Which of these are the most successful?
3. How can the homelessness problem in Australia be redefined from a problem of "the individual" to a systemic issue of unaffordable housing and poverty?

REFERENCES

Aged and Community Services Australia. (2015). *Social isolation and loneliness among older Australians* (Issues paper No. 1). Deakin, Australian Capital Territory, Australia: Author.

Aged Care Guide. (2017). *Longevity and loneliness biggest risks for older Australian women*. Retrieved from https://www.agedcareguide.com.au/talking-aged-care/longevity-and-loneliness-biggest-risks-for-older-australian-women

Agency for Clinical Innovation. (2013). *Strategic framework for integrated care of the older person with complex health needs*. Chatswood, New South Wales, Australia: Author.

Australian Bureau of Statistics. (2006). *Population projections, Australia, 2004–2101*. Retrieved from https://www.abs.gov.au/AUSSTATS/abs@.nsf/Lookup/3222.0Main+Features12004%20to%202101?OpenDocument

Australian Bureau of Statistics. (2012). *Census of population and housing: Estimating homelessness: 2011* (No. 2049.0). Retrieved from https://www.abs.gov.au/AUSSTATS/abs@.nsf/Lookup/2049.0Main+Features12011

Australian Bureau of Statistics. (2017a). *Selected highlights: Differences between Australian men and women*. Retrieved from http://www.abs.gov.au/ausstats/abs@.nsf/Lookup/by%20Subject/4125.0~Sep%202017~Main%20Features~Selected%20Highlights~2

Australian Bureau of Statistics. (2017b). *Health*. Retrieved from http://www.abs.gov.au/ausstats/abs@.nsf/Lookup/by%20Subject/4125.0~Sep%202017~Main%20Features~Health~6

Australian Institute of Health and Welfare. (2016). *Australia's health 2016*. Retrieved from https://www.aihw.gov.au/getmedia/666de2ad-1c92-4db3-9c01-1368ba3c8c98/ah16-3-3-chronic-disease-comorbidities.pdf.aspx

Australian Institute of Health and Welfare. (2017a). *The health of Australia's females*. Retrieved from https://www.aihw.gov.au/reports/men-women/female-health/contents/who-are

Australian Institute of Health and Welfare. (2017b). *Mental health services—In brief 2017.* Retrieved from https://www.aihw.gov.au/getmedia/3ac11554-817d-4563-ad97-46bc6a90bee5/20502.pdf.aspx?inline=true

Australian Institute of Health and Welfare. (2018). *Chronic illnesses.* Retrieved from https://www.aihw.gov.au/reports-statistics/health-conditions-disability-deaths/chronic-disease/overview

Batterham, D., Mallet, S., Yates, E., Kolar, V., & Westmore, T. (2013). *Ageing out of place: The impact of gender and location on older Victorians in homelessness.* Melbourne, Victoria, Australia: Hanover Welfare Services.

Berkman, L. F., & Syme, S. L. (1979). Social networks, host resistance, and mortality: A nine year follow-up study of Alameda County residents. *American Journal of Epidemiology, 109,* 186–204.

Cohen, S., Doyle, W., Skoner, D., Rubin, B., & Gwaltney, J. (1997). Social ties and susceptibility to the common cold. *Journal of the American Medical Association, 277,* 1940–1944.

Crane, M., & Warnes, A. M. (2010). Homelessness among older people and service responses. *Reviews in Clinical Gerontology, 20,* 354–363.

Elliot, R. A. (2006). Problems with medication use in the elderly: An Australian perspective. *Journal of Pharmacy Practice and Research, 36*(1), 58–66.

Geller, J., Janson, P., McGovern, E., & Valdini, A. (1999). Loneliness as a predictor of hospital emergency department use. *Journal of Family Practice, 48*(10), 801–804.

Haffner, K. (2016). Researchers confront an epidemic of loneliness. *The New York Times.* Retrieved from https://www.nytimes.com/2016/09/06/health/lonliness-aging-health-effects.html

Homelessness Australia. (2016). *Homelessness and older people.* Retrieved from https://www.homelessnessaustralia.org.au/sites/homelessnessaus/files/2017-07/Homelessness_and_Older_People.pdf

Lauder, W., Sharkey, S., & Mummery, K. (2004). A community survey of loneliness. *Journal of Advanced Nursing, 46*(1), 88–94.

Lim, M. (2018). Loneliness is a health issue, and needs targeted solutions. *The Conversation.* Retrieved from http://theconversation.com/loneliness-is-a-health-issue-and-needs-targeted-solutions-96262

McFerran, L. (2010). *It could be you: Female, single, older and homeless.* Woolloomooloo, New South Wales, Australia: Homelessness NSW.

Moghadam, V. M. (2010). Transnational feminisms. In J. Lee & S. Shaw (Eds.), *Women worldwide: Transnational feminism perspectives on women* (pp. 15–46). New York, NY: McGraw-Hill.

National Institute on Aging. (2011). *Global health and aging.* Retrieved from http://www.who.int/ageing/publications/global_health.pdf

National Institute on Drug Abuse. (2010). *Comorbidity: Addiction and other mental illnesses.* US Department of Health and Human Services, National Institute on Drug Abuse (NIH Publication No. 10-5771). Retrieved from https://d14rmgtrwzf5a.cloudfront.net/sites/default/files/rrcomorbidity.pdf

National Seniors Australia and Challenger. (2017). *Seniors more savvy about retirement income: A report by National Seniors Australia and Challenger.* Retrieved from https://www.challenger.com.au/-/media/challenger/documents/reports/NSA-Report-2017-Savvy-Seniors.pdf

Steed, L., Boldy, D., Grenade, L., & Iredell, H. (2007). The demographics of loneliness among older people in Perth, Western Australia. *Australasian Journal on Ageing, 26,* 81–86.

Theeke, R. A. (2010). Sociodemographic and health-related risks for loneliness and outcome differences by loneliness status in a sample of U.S. older adults. *Research in Gerontological Nursing, 3,* 113–125.

Tomaka, J., Thompson, S., & Palacios, R. (2006). The relation of social isolation, loneliness, and social support to disease outcomes among the elderly. *Journal of Aging and Health, 18,* 359–384.

Walkom, E. J., Loxton, D., & Robertson, J. (2013). Costs of medicines and health care: A concern for Australian women across the ages. *BMC Health Services Research, 13,* 484.

Warburton, J., & Lui, C. (2007). Social isolation and loneliness in older people: A literature review. Australasian Centre on Ageing. Retrieved from: https://espace.library.uq.edu.au/view/UQ:160390

World Health Organization. (2008a). *Integrating mental health into primary care: A global perspective.* Retrieved from http://www.who.int/mental_health/policy/services/Australia.pdf

World Health Organization. (2008b). *Integrating mental health into primary care: A global perspective.* Retrieved from https://www.who.int/mental_health/resources/mental-health_PHC_2008.pdf

World Health Organization. (2014). *Global status report on noncommunicable diseases 2014.* Retrieved from http://apps.who.int/iris/bitstream/10665/148114/1/9789241564854_eng.pdf?ua=1

World Health Organization. (2017). *Fact sheet: Noncommunicable diseases.* Retrieved from https://www.who.int/news-room/fact-sheets/detail/noncommunicable-diseases

14

Repressive Policies and Women's Reproductive Choices in Poland

The Case of State Violence Against Women

WANDA NOWICKA AND JOANNA REGULSKA ∎

CASE STUDY: "I DON'T STOP FIGHTING"—ALICJA TYSIĄC

Alicja Tysiąc was the first woman to file a complaint with the European Court of Human Rights (ECHR) due to refusal of lawful abortion (ECHR, 2007). She suffered from severe myopia, an eyesight condition with a threat of blindness. When she became pregnant for the third time, three ophthalmologists with whom she consulted confirmed that the continuation of pregnancy could lead to blindness. At the same time, these doctors did not agree to write the necessary referral to authorize legal abortion. A gynecologist from the Warsaw clinic refused to perform an abortion, finding no medical grounds for it. Alicja was forced to give birth, which caused further damage to her eyesight. She raises her children alone, and the social welfare system qualifies her as a disabled person, belonging to the highest category of disability.

Alicja sued the Polish state in the ECHR. The Court agreed with Alicja that the Polish state violated Article 8 of the Convention (the right to respect for private life) and awarded compensation in the amount of 25,000 Euros. This, however, is not the end of Alicja's story; her victory outraged the anti-choice movement. She has been the subject of the most violent hate speech and personal attacks on her and her family. Opponents could not bear that she broke the taboo surrounding abortion and openly and publicly admitted that she wanted an abortion.

The assaults have continued, with accusations that "she took money for wanting to kill her baby" ("Zobacz," 2009). Pro-life groups have been trying to sow conflict in her family relations by falsely pitting Alicja's daughter, Julia, against her mother. Alicja has not surrendered. She filed a complaint with the Polish court against one journalist who compared her behavior to that of fascist leaders of World War II; she won the case. Over the years, Alicja has become an outspoken advocate for women's rights. In a recent interview (Niemczyńska, 2016), she said that her daughter Julia, who is now 16 years old, declared that if she were in Alicja's situation, she would have made the same decision as her mother.

Case Study: "Our Child Will Be Dying in Torment"—Agnieszka and Jacek

Agnieszka and Jacek wanted their first child very much. Unsuccessfully, they tried to have a baby for 13 years. When Agnieszka became pregnant in 2014, their happiness about the pregnancy sharply ended when an ultrasound test indicated lethal malformation of the fetus. They decided to have a legal abortion. Unfortunately, the director of their hospital, famous anti-abortion advocate Professor Bogdan Chazan, refused to allow the pregnancy termination to be performed in his hospital. He also declined to refer Agnieszka to another hospital. He cited the conscience clause (discussion later). This was illegal: He had no right to do so because he was not Agnieszka's doctor but, rather, the manager of the hospital, who by law cannot object on behalf of other doctors. Agnieszka was forced to continue the pregnancy to term. She said in a heartbreaking television interview that "when other mothers planned to buy a cradle for their child-to-come, we planned a funeral. I had to give birth to the child so that he could die." The born baby was drastically damaged; he died after 10 days in pain. As Jacek said in the same interview, "Doctor Chazan forced us to watch our child suffer terrible pain for 10 days" (Górka, 2016).

The case of Agnieszka and Jacek was publicly debated. Professor Chazan was dismissed from the hospital where he worked, but he has become a hero and a martyr for the anti-abortion cause. The couple decided to go to the Polish court and sue Chazan; however, the prosecutor rejected the case before it could be heard by the court on the questionable grounds that the pregnancy did not endanger the woman's life ("Śledztwo," 2015). Anti-abortion groups used the Chazan case to reduce doctors' obligations toward women.

In October 2016, Agnieszka and Jacek decided to tell their story in a television interview (Górka, 2016). They wanted to warn against attempts to further restrict abortion after the leader of the ruling party, Jarosław Kaczyński, confirmed that the government wanted to make sure that even very malformed fetuses would be delivered so that the born child could be named, baptized, and buried (Fishwick, 2016).

Under the rule of restrictive legislation, hundreds of women and their families have suffered physically and emotionally because they could not obtain legal abortions. As the cases of Alicja Tysiąc and Agnieszka and Jacek have shown, women who seek abortion on medical grounds, to which they are legally entitled (when their health is at risk or the fetus is badly deformed), are undergoing hell (Federation for Women and Family Planning, 2005). Few women decide to bring legal charges against hospitals. Many seek support of international institutions when domestic, Polish institutions fail. The three cases won through ECHR give hope to Polish women.

Abortion on criminal grounds—that is, when pregnancy is a result of rape or incest—is also a complete fiction. A government report ("Sprawozdanie Rady Ministrow," 2014) indicated that from 2010 through 2013 in public hospitals, a total of four abortions were performed: No abortions were performed in 2010 and 2011, one abortion was performed in 2012, and three abortions were performed in 2013. These numbers are striking when taking into account the fact that approximately 20% of women report experiencing rape, in most cases by family members (Grzybek & Grabowska, 2016). Indeed, abortions are performed, but not legally and not in secure and healthy environments.

OVERVIEW

The stories of Alicja Tysiąc and Agnieszka and Jacek, and many more untold, exemplify "culture wars" and speak of pain, angst, and the brutality inflicted by the Polish state on women. Polish women do not, however, remain silent. The autumn of 2016 in Poland witnessed unprecedented women's resistance in the 25-year history of the struggle over reproductive rights. The National Strike of Women and Black Protest—street actions organized by women throughout the country and reported by the world media—were prompted by the attempt to ban abortion on any grounds, even to save a woman's life. This latest abortion crisis demonstrates that although reproductive rights in Poland have been the subject of heated political debates that have taken place regularly since the 1989 political transformation, they remain unresolved and are contested by both sides of the confrontation.

Poland is not unique; similar debates and attacks on women's reproductive rights are taking place in many areas of the world, including Central and Eastern Europe (CEE). What is characteristic of the Polish case is, on the one hand, an extreme radical and fanatic approach by conservative politicians and the pro-life movement (still rather unusual in Europe) and, on the other hand, remarkable resilience and engagement of individual Polish women and informal groups that have translated into a mass mobilization. Continuous presentation of extreme legal proposals by anti-choice radicals, such as a full ban on abortion or limitation of access to infertility treatment, as well as the use of fanatical methods in public spaces (e.g., billboards with images of bloody fetuses placed on cars parked in front of hospitals or schools) have led to increased mobilization, radicalization, and more rapid response on the part of the pro-choice movement. The pro-choice movement began to protest not only in front of the Parliament but also in front of religious institutions and churches using quite strong language and visuals as it learned that only drastic slogans and actions have impact on legislators. The aim of the conservatives is to implement one of the most restrictive pieces of legislation that would secure a complete ban on abortion—a ban that demonstrates neither sympathy nor respect for women. In response, women have shown their power of resistance.

This chapter examines the actions of the Polish state with regard to women's reproductive rights. It demonstrates how such state violence instigates and provides encouragement to others to pursue similar behavior. The alliance between state and church has produced a set of legal and moral controls over women's bodies and shifted the power to decide away from women. Indeed, as soon as women become pregnant, they cannot make autonomous decisions about their reproduction and fertility; a doctor, a policeman, a prosecutor, the media, anti-abortion believers, and/or a priest have more to say about a woman's pregnancy and can make decisions regarding it. De facto, the state and church have become women's enemy, standing in opposition to them and participating in furthering women's oppression.

Figure 14.1 Demonstration "No to torturing women" (Nie dla torturowania kobiet) in front of the Polish Parliament in Warsaw on April 3rd 2016 (before Black Monday). Photo Katarzyna Pierzchała.

Furthermore, public and political debates and controversies regarding women's autonomous reproductive choices continue to be the subject of struggle at various scales and are not confined within national borders; they take place in local communities, in national parliaments, and in international courts. These transnational and local battles have resulted in the development of a global community of mutual support and a flow of information and knowledge, as well as strategy and resource sharing. After years of communist isolation, the opening of borders by democratic Poland allowed for transnational flows and mobility to take place; unsurprisingly, both sides of these disputes benefitted from the new political and social context.

This chapter discusses the broader, regional context of reproductive rights in CEE. Next, a brief history of the abortion struggle in Poland is presented, and then the impact of restrictive anti-abortion legislation on women's lives is examined. Finally, we show that despite years of relentless pro-life pressure that has resulted in a change of public attitudes, women continue to resist, organize, and mobilize; thus, the struggle over women's reproductive rights continues (Karwowska, 2018).

HISTORICAL TRENDS

Democratization of Eastern Europe and the Revival of Conservatism

Political transformation and the establishment of new democracies in Poland and in the rest of CEE was not without pain and costs. Chief among these was the revival of new political forces and trends, such as nationalism, xenophobia, radical right-wing

Figure 14.2 "Hangers – symbol od pro-choice movement—left behind after the demonstration No to torturing women" (Nie dla torturowania kobiet) in front of the Polish Parliament in Warsaw on April 3rd 2016. Photo Katarzyna Pierzchała.

ideas, and religious fundamentalism (Meyer Resende, 2015; Pankowski, 2010). The shift from a socialist welfare state guaranteeing relative economic security to neo-liberalism and a free market economy that left many people behind and with fewer resources to live fed radical movements and conservative attitudes and led to the emergence of conservative and populist perspectives. In a time of political and economic transformation and growing insecurity, the Roman Catholic Church used the opportunity to strengthen itself institutionally, reintroduce religion to schools, and prioritize anti-choice teaching. Indeed, in many countries in CEE, such as Poland, Hungary, Lithuania, and Slovakia, or even farther south in Croatia, such ideologies and beliefs have quickly taken strong roots. Anti-choice proponents have argued that legal abortion is an obsolete idea, attributed to communist ideology, and should be abolished as a communist remnant in the new democratic societies. The experience of the region shows that democracy and women's rights do not always go hand in hand.

As Regulska and Grabowska (2013) argue, "Violations of women's human rights, particularly in the areas of women's reproductive rights and violence against women, persist even in the countries of the region where democratic consolidation and economic reforms have advanced" (p. 143).

Poland was the first country in CEE to severely restrict abortion in the early 1990s. Pressure by the Roman Catholic Church, which is powerful in Poland, and personal engagement of the beloved "Sainted Father," or the "Polish Pope," were behind the push to change existing legislation to restrict abortion. John Paul II, who visited his fatherland every other year, warned against the "culture of death" and preached repeatedly that "the nation that kills its own children has no future," alluding to abortion ("John Paul II," 2005). Mishtal (2015) describes the Polish transition as "the central contradiction of postsocialist democratization in Poland—that it is an emerging democracy, on the one hand; and . . . a declining tolerance for reproductive rights, women's rights, and political or religious pluralism, on the other hand" (p. 11). She further observes that reproductive politics and "governance of women's bodies in postsocialist politics is an essential constitutive feature of the Polish democratization process" (p. 11).

Hunter's (1992) concept of "culture war," although applied to the US context when it was created, illustrates well the tensions that emerged in Poland after the transition. Reproductive rights, especially as they relate to abortion, sex education, LGBT rights, the role of the church and its impact on state legislation and policies, tensions around conservative versus modern families, and debates about traditional women's roles and gender equality, are continuously deliberated, disputed, and contested. They are also a frequent subject of political mobilization and demonstrations, media attacks, and family clashes.

The additional dimension that frames these culture wars in Poland and in CEE is a desire to catch up with the West and to become equal. Whereas conservatives want to maintain control over ruled societies, liberals see an opportunity to become a member of Western Europe, something to which Eastern Europeans have long aspired. For conservatives, reproductive issues are fundamental; they envision a society that is controlled and governed by tradition and religious morality. Polish liberals would prefer not to address reproductive health at all, leaving it within the private sphere and maintaining status quo. Therefore, although they oppose any attempt of liberalization of abortion, they disagree with increasing restrictions to reproductive choices.

Since 1989, attempts to restrict abortion have been undertaken in many countries throughout the region, especially those in which the Catholic religion dominates (Lithuania, Croatia, Hungary, Slovakia, and Russia, in addition to Poland). When right-wing parties have returned to power, abortion debates returned to the political agenda. For example, although in Hungary the law still allows for abortion to be performed on social grounds, some restrictions have been introduced in order to inhibit access to health services ("Abortions in Hungary," 2016). Moreover, the protection of life became constitutionally guaranteed in 2012, and this opened the door to further legal restrictions. Similarly, in Russia, anti-abortion campaigns are constantly undertaken by religious anti-choice groups supported by the head of the Russian Orthodox Church, Patriarch Kirill, who has been pushing to ban abortion for more than a decade (Cichowłas, 2016). Since the fall of the Soviet Union, attempts to restrict access to legal abortion have been made on a regular basis; however, to date, only minor procedural restrictions, introduced in 2011, have been implemented (Population Research Institute, 2011). In these discussions, demographic arguments about the nation dying as a result of low birth rates, so compelling in Russia, were used frequently. Many believe, against the evidence, as in Romania or Poland, that if women are forced to give birth due to abortion restrictions, the rate of childbirth will increase ("Półtawska apeluje do Polaków," 2015). Paradoxically, these diverse discriminatory laws have been introduced democratically—fundamentalists have learned how to use democratic systems efficiently to promote an anti-woman agenda; as a result, women in CEE cannot feel safe.

The dynamic situation within the region did not remain unnoticed by outside parties involved in reproductive rights debates. International pro-life movements, especially from the United States, began to support local CEE groups financially and operationally (e.g., Human Life International [https://www.hli.org], Matercare International [n.d.], and Pharmacists for Life International [http://www.pfli.org]). Similarly, women's groups and activists engaged international supporters of women's reproductive rights. As discussed later, they crossed national boundaries into CEE and built transnational networks of support.

HISTORY OF ABORTION STRUGGLES IN POLAND

The history of abortion in Poland is uneven and rather twisted. During the past 100 years, Polish legislation has made a full circle from very restrictive laws of the 1920s and early 1930s to being at the forefront of liberal legislation in the 1950s–1980s and then again losing its progressive stand after 1989. Indeed, during the past two decades (since the 1990s), Poland has become a disgraceful leader of backward repressive policies. One might ask if and when this trend will reverse again and the pendulum will move toward more progressive pro-women policies.

First Liberalization, Before World War II

In 1930, Tadeusz Boy-Żeleński, a famous Polish medical doctor, writer, and social activist, wrote the following in his book, *Women's Hell* (1930/2013):

> To push a poor girl into motherhood, take her job away because of pregnancy, kick her in disdain, throw on her the entire burden of guilt, threaten her with years in prison if she is desperately trying to get rid of this problem beyond her capacity—this is the philosophy of laws obviously written by men. (p. 11)

This sentence is still relevant today, more than 80 years later. Boy-Żeleński and journalist, writer, and social activist Irena Krzywicka were campaigning for liberalization of restrictive anti-abortion laws in the 1920s and 1930s. In numerous articles and essays describing women's reproductive oppression as women's hell and "the greatest crime of the Criminal Code" (p. 8), they worked hard to raise awareness in society about the need for liberalization of anti-abortion legislation.

Their work was not in vain. Because of their and others' tireless efforts, before World War II, Poland became one of the first countries in the world to introduce legal abortion in certain conditions. The state failed, however, to liberalize abortion on social grounds. In 1932 (Criminal Code, 1932), abortion was, in the end, legalized on medical and criminal grounds despite strong opposition from the Roman Catholic Church. Polish abortion regulations of 1932 were second only to those of the Soviet Union in terms of their liberal character at that time. Women in the Soviet Union enjoyed liberal laws between 1920 and 1936, when Joseph Stalin restricted access to abortion for Russian women.

Socialist Era: Abortion on Social Grounds Legalized

A woman cannot be forced to give birth. Abortion has always been a social issue. At that time (in the 1950s of the twentieth century) there was no effective contraception. Women hurt as a result of unsafe, hidden abortions, [they] constituted the majority of patients in gynecological wards of the Polish hospitals.

—Dąbrowska-Szulc (2006)

After World War II, the impoverished Polish society, in a completely demolished country, suffered significant economic and political hardships. The League of Polish Women—the only women's organization allowed under communism—together with doctors, the medical community, and family planning activists, raised the need of liberalizing abortion laws on social grounds because many women were dying as a result of illegal and unsafe abortions. However, resistance to this idea was very strong on the part of policymakers because in the entire Stalin-ruled Soviet Bloc, of which Poland was a part, abortion was illegal. The Roman Catholic Church, although not as powerful under communism as in the past, was nevertheless still very influential, and it also vehemently protested against any changes to anti-abortion legislation.

Liberalization of the right to abortion in Poland, Russia, Bulgaria, Hungary, Czechoslovakia, and other states of the Soviet Bloc was only possible after Stalin's death in 1953. Yet, in order to change the law, a favorable political climate would not be sufficient; what was needed was the mobilization and active engagement of many people—women politicians, medical doctors, social activists, and others. Unfortunately, that period in the history of abortion rights struggles has not been well documented, and it is only known and remembered on the basis of a few oral testimonies by those who participated in these processes.

In 1956, Maria Jaszczuk, a member of Parliament, proposed a law that would legalize abortion on social grounds. After lengthy discussions, the new legislation was approved by the Polish Parliament (Zielińska, 1990). This liberalization basically made abortion available upon request throughout the communist period. In the 1960s, European women, including those from Sweden (Francome, 2015), traveled to Poland for abortions because restrictive anti-abortion laws remained in Western Europe until the early 1970s.

For almost 40 years, the abortion law was neither criticized nor challenged, and it was largely used by women who had very limited access to any other forms of contraception. The controversies regarding abortion were to occur, unexpectedly, soon after the 1989 democratic transformation of Poland.

Restrictive Legislation in Democratized Poland

The process of abolishing the communist political system and introducing a market economy and democratic rule of law started in Poland in 1980 with a general strike in the Gdańsk shipyard. Soon after, the entire country, organized by the Solidarity Trade Union and led by the popular leader Lech Wałęsa, was rising in protest, but also in hope for a change. Unfortunately, the sense of possibilities did not last long; martial law was imposed by the communist regime on December 13, 1981. Eight years of underground resistance undertaken by the political opposition and many civic movements under the Solidarity umbrella prepared fertile ground and built momentum that led to the democratic transformation.

June 4, 1989, is an important date in Polish and European contemporary history. It was a day of semi-democratic parliamentary elections, as a result of which candidates of the democratic opposition were elected to the Polish Parliament, which subsequently led to the formation of the first government having democratic legitimacy. This is also a symbolic date, marking the beginning of the groundbreaking political transformation of Europe that resulted in the establishment of the democratic Republic of Poland, soon followed by the demolition of the Berlin Wall in November 1989. These events led to the fall of the communist and totalitarian regimes of the Soviet Bloc and denoted the end of the Cold War and the collapse of the Soviet Union. Fifteen new states were established, and thus the social, economic, and political geography of Europe was changed.

The euphoria of freedom and liberation was short-lived, however, because these new democratic processes brought about negative effects regarding women's reproductive rights. Although in 1989 the anti-abortion stance was still unexpected and undesired by a majority of society, this was a sentiment and a belief that would shift during the next several years. The Roman Catholic Church, which under the communist regime played a positive role in supporting the democratic opposition, gained unprecedented access to the political arena in the new political context. This sudden security afforded to the Church allowed for the revelation of its conservative face, up to now almost absent in religious teaching and unnoticed by the majority of society (Nowicka, 1996). The Church, nascent anti-choice groups, and Catholic parliamentarians started to push Parliament to introduce a ban on abortion, thus declaring war against women's rights.

Polish society was completely unprepared for the possibility of restrictions on abortion. For almost 40 years, generations of women had lived under the liberalized rule of abortion law; abortion was easily accessible and widely practiced in public and private health care facilities. Only the oldest women remembered the controversies and disputes that occurred in the 1950s. Society, in shock, observed drastic anti-choice propaganda using violent ideological language previously unheard of but increasingly utilized by church, the media, and in Parliament. Social movements, including the women's movement, absent under communism, were in the early stages of development, and there were no organizations that could effectively oppose those threats.

The late 1980s and early 1990s war over women's bodies and autonomy resulted in drastic changes to laws. At that time, the radical right-wing parties began to submit anti-abortion draft laws in Parliament; at least six legislative proposals were submitted, each proposing a full ban on abortion (with some variations) and criminalizing women who underwent abortions. These most repressive drafts were rejected by Parliament one after another due to massive social mobilization. People began to undertake a variety of actions aimed at preventing the imminent ban: The new pro-choice organizations fought back.

The most successful pro-choice campaign was initiated by two former opposition leaders and at that time members of Parliament, Barbara Labuda and Zbigniew Bujak, who established the committee that called for a national referendum on the issue of criminalization of abortion. The committee managed to collect more than 1.5 million signatures in support of a referendum on abortion legislation. At that time, 65% of people were against restricting abortion (Nowicka, 2004). Unfortunately, Parliament, which was much more conservative than society, voted against the referendum. Nevertheless, the widespread mobilization of society did have an impact on the debated legislation, and the anti-abortion law, although finally passed, was less repressive than previous proposals. The anti-abortion law, officially called the Law on Family Planning, Human Embryo Protection, and Conditions of Admissibility of Pregnancy Termination, was finally accepted January 7, 1993. It permitted abortion under three conditions: (1) to save a woman's life and health, (2) in cases in which there is serious fetal malformation, and (3) when pregnancy is a result of crime (rape and incest). The key change introduced was the elimination of legal abortion on socioeconomic grounds, which was the main reason for abortions in Poland during the communist period.

Since the law change, the abortion issue was regularly reintroduced to the political agenda, either by the pro-choice movement—which continued efforts to liberalize restrictions to abortion—or by the increasingly stronger anti-choice movement, which became especially strong at the beginning of the 21st century. In 1994, Parliament, dominated by the left-wing Social Democrats, revised the law and allowed abortion on social grounds. Unfortunately, it could not be implemented because Lech Wałęsa, a devoted Catholic and the former Solidarity leader who had become president of Poland, vetoed the law.

A second attempt at liberalizing anti-abortion legislation was undertaken in 1996, after a new president was sworn in. For a second time, the parliamentary left majority passed a law that liberalized abortion termination on socioeconomic grounds, and this time, President Aleksander Kwaśniewski, of left provenance, signed it. However, the Solidarity trade union, which in the 1990s transformed into a radical conservative anti-choice political force closely connected with the Church, again played a negative role in restricting women's rights. It filed a complaint in the Constitutional Tribunal maintaining that the liberalized law was unconstitutional. In 1997, the Constitutional Tribunal, dominated by conservative justices, adopted the very controversial ruling that abortion on social grounds is unconstitutional. After only 1 year of greater freedom, abortion became restricted again. These years of struggles, but also of anti-abortion propaganda offered by the Church, media, and state institutions such as the Constitutional Tribunal and from the highest political figures who had gained respect among the citizens, such as Lech Wałęsa, began to have a social effect; people were no longer as supportive of legalized abortion as they had been a decade earlier.

Hardening of Anti-Choice Sentiments and the Emergence of Transnational Solidarity

Whereas at the end of the 20th century pro-choice advocates had well-grounded assumptions that anti-abortion laws could be liberalized, at the beginning of the 21st century, the chances for liberalization were diminished greatly, as the case of Alicja Tysiąc and that of Agnieszka and Jacek exemplified. Worse, anti-abortionists continued proposing repressive laws and policies not only against abortion but also against contraception and in vitro fertilization. These unfavorable developments for women's rights occurred as a result of several factors. The weakening of the political left, which ruled for many years but lost power in 2005 and became an opposition party, was clearly a strong deterring force. By 2015, no left parties were elected to Parliament, which meant that there was no party to articulate a women's agenda. Since 2005, the leadership of Poland has alternated between two main right-wing parties—one more centrist, Civic Platform (Platforma Obywatelska), and the radical right-wing Law and Justice (Prawo i Sprawiedliwość [PiS]). Second, the position of the Roman Catholic Church became even stronger than in the past due to numerous legal and financial concessions received from every political ruling force, as a result of which its impact on the state policies related to reproductive health and rights significantly increased (Mishtal, 2015, pp. 1–2). Finally, the anti-choice movement had grown and become very powerful, supported not only by the Catholic Church but also by international anti-choice movements. Three powerful anti-choice proposals were introduced in 2006, 2011, and 2015. The proponents of the first proposal tried unsuccessfully to introduce in the Polish Constitution the protection of life from the moment of conception until natural death. The two other attempts were undertaken through a Civic Legal Initiative and proposed a full ban on abortion. Although none of these initiatives succeeded, they lost only narrowly; the most serious danger was inevitably approaching.

Despite many setbacks within the country, pro-choice organizations continued their struggle for liberalization of abortion, often with the help and support of the international women's movement. One of the largest campaigns in Poland was undertaken in collaboration with Rebecca Gompert, Dutch founder of the Women on Waves (WoW) project (Moore, 2003). The Women's Committee (Komitet Ster–Kobiety Decydują) invited WoW to participate in the campaign. Members of WoW arrived at Władysławowo, a small town located on the coast of the Baltic Sea, and set up the campaign on a boat named *Langenort*. WoW provided legal abortions on board the Dutch ship in extraterritorial waters, but its main focus was to raise awareness about the violation of women's reproductive rights in Poland. The *Langenort* was stationed in the Baltic Sea for almost 2 weeks in 2003. The project generated extensive media coverage throughout the world.

Fanatic opponents arrived in Władysławowo to block women from getting on the boat and receiving abortion services. Although the tensions and protests were visible, the most important outcome in addition to supporting individual women was the fact that public opinion and the media expressed support for women. WoW and a follow-up initiative, Women on Web (n.d.), continued their solidarity actions and engagement in supporting Polish women, and women in other countries with repressive legislation, by providing abortion pills via mail.

The previously discussed events underscore a clear division between women's rights and needs and the beliefs of the Polish state. Throughout the years, the Polish state and its agencies have not only become more responsive to conservative political pressures as exhibited by the Vatican and the Polish Catholic Church but also

Figure 14.3 Black Monday called also National Strike of Women and also Umbrella Revolution—demonstration at Warsaw Castle Square on October 3rd 2016 to protest against parliamentary decision to proceed the draft law aimed at full ban on abortion and to reject liberal legislation. Photo Katarzyna Pierzchała.

Figure 14.4 "Angry women" demonstrating during Black Monday called also National Strike of Women and also Umbrella Revolution (October 3rd 2019) in Warsaw at Nowogrodzka Street in front of the office of Chief Leader of ruling party Law and Justice—Jarosław Kaczyński. Photo Katarzyna Pierzchała.

embraced what Mishtal (2015, pp. 17–22) calls "the politics of morality." That moral stance, as exhibited by state, media, and the Church, as well as by an increasingly larger segment of Polish society, gives power to many—except women, as experienced by Alicja and Agnieszka—to intervene and control women's lives. These interventions have propagated gender-biased policies and regulations in which women are not only controlled but also responsible for the acts of others over which they themselves do not have power. Surveillance, control, and abuse of institutional power by the state and its institutions created the governance environment within which a multiplicity of actors (priests, bishops, and church hierarchy; presidents, prime ministers, elected members of Parliament, political parties, governmental units, and their officers; pro-life international and domestic organizations and nongovernmental organizations; lobbyists, advocates, lawyers, and courts; and doctors, nurses, and ordinary people) are permitted to pursue their anti-women agenda. Government authorities do not even pretend that they are trying to help women, and this was especially evident in the government's appeal to ECHR of the Alicja Tysiąc judgment issued earlier by ECHR. The Polish government explicitly stated that it is not obliged to help women get lawful abortions because this is their own business (the Polish government eventually lost the case because it was rejected by ECHR in September 2007).

RECENT DEVELOPMENTS OF NOTE

The Umbrella Revolution and the National Women's Strike: The Mobilization of 2016

The recent abortion crisis in Poland was fueled by the shocking attempt to introduce a full ban on abortion, which was proposed by radical anti-choice groups supported by the Roman Catholic Church and the right-wing ruling party, PiS. In spring 2016, the extremist organization Pro Foundation announced it would submit to Parliament a Civic Legal Initiative that would criminalize women who underwent abortion and would ban abortion even if a pregnancy threatens a woman's life. Soon after, a pro-choice initiative called Save the Women started to collect signatures to propose a draft law liberalizing abortion (The Law on Women's Rights and Conscious Parenthood) on request until the 12th week of pregnancy. Both civic initiatives collected more than the obligatory 100,000 signatures; the Pro Foundation collected half a million signatures due to the support of Church structures, and the Save the Women committee collected 250,000 signatures. Street protests against the ban of abortion started immediately after the announcement, and they became stronger in fall 2016, when Parliament was due to start proceedings.

On September 23, 2016, the Polish Parliament voted in favor of beginning parliamentary proceedings in support of the repressive draft law and almost simultaneously (a few minutes later) rejected the rather modest pro-choice draft. As a result, women, men, students, workers, old and young demonstrated throughout the country (Centrum Badania Opinii Społecznej [CBOS], 2016). Countless street protests and numerous actions exploded not only in Warsaw, the capital city, but also in other cities throughout the country. The most visible pro-choice demonstration was the Black Protest, lasting approximately 2 weeks, during which ordinary and celebrity women and men wore black clothes. The culmination of all the protests was the National Women's Strike.

Krystyna Janda, a famous Polish actress and theater director, reminded Polish citizens that 40 years ago, women in Iceland organized a general strike, and she called on Polish women to do the same. She did not expect any response; yet the response throughout the country was remarkable. Marta Lempart, a publicly unknown woman, proposed via social media the National Strike of Women for October 3 (Lempart, 2016). Thousands of women and many supporting men declared participation in the strike. Thousands of women did not go to work, and those who could not attend the protest wore black at work. Many employers declared solidarity with the women's strike. Universities and even schools supported their students on that day and did not count their absences against them. Unprecedented rallies spontaneously organized by ordinary women in approximately 150 cities and small localities gathered thousands of people in the streets despite heavy rain, which led to the campaign being called the "umbrella revolution." This massive mobilization terrified the ruling party, which obviously was not expecting such huge opposition and the successful self-organization of the grassroots society in such a short time. Three days later, on October 6, after very short proceedings, the Sejm (the lower chamber of the Polish Parliament) rejected the repressive draft law.

For the first time, the ruling authoritarian regime of the PiS party decided to withdraw one of its unpopular political projects. The political significance of such a move did not escape attention; the importance of such a step goes far beyond women's reproductive rights. There is no question that women showed their power and won. The largest Polish daily, *Gazeta Wyborcza*, announced enthusiastically on the front page, "Polish Women Won Against Law and Justice" (Kondzińska, 2016). A famous Polish social activist and a leader of the largest charity organization in Poland, Jerzy Owsiak (2016), said, "It was the most beautiful civic Monday in a new reality," suggesting the critical significance of the women's victory for other opposition movements and actions. As noted by Kublik (2016), many believed that

women together can do a lot. They have woken up the sense of potency in Poles, citizen's strength versus state authority, which they would rather not give up. The conservative revolution carried out by the ruling party generated resistance, the "umbrella revolution." And it seems today that this rebellious power may be more attractive for society than the power of "good change" [as the Law and Justice Party describes their rule].

As is often the case in such movements, the actual concerns expressed by women are less important than other political considerations. Presumably, the ruling party calculated that it is better not to fight over this particular project, even if some conservative quarters will be upset, than to have thousands of people throughout the country on the streets demonstrating for a long period of time. Thus, the regime voicelessly showed its fear of the public expression of discontent; once that was revealed, people also recognized their power, and the protests continued.

The umbrella revolution showed the strong connection of the Polish women's movement with international movements and a solidarity of global women with struggles for women's reproductive rights everywhere. Support actions and rallies in front of Polish embassies were organized not only in major Western European cities such as London, Paris, and Berlin but also in Nairobi, Kenya, and other cities. Women from Iceland who organized their strike in 1975 sent a very moving and encouraging

YouTube message to Polish activists, connecting all women's struggles together ("Icelandic Women," 2016). Polish women, for their part, acknowledged other struggles taking place abroad; they explicitly expressed solidarity with Irish women fighting repressive anti-abortion legislation in Ireland. The demonstrations generated much interest and widespread coverage by the world media, thus generating publicity for women's struggles in Poland.

The persistent—now more than two decades long—commitment of Polish women nationally and internationally to oppose a ban on abortion and to protect women's rights has been primarily sustained through grassroots mobilizations. Impressively, the driving force behind the protests was not mainstream women's organizations (which of course did join such protests) but, rather, individuals and informal groups who via the internet built networks that resulted in the National Strike. In most cases, these individuals had never before participated in any form of public life, including protest actions. The National Strike and Black Protest resembled a peaceful uprising— a decentralized mass movement that adopted diverse forms of protests, from street actions to the symbolic wearing of black clothes. These strategies allowed for mass mobilization, resembling the mass solidarity mobilizations of the 1970s and 1980s in Poland.

Despite this first victory, the struggle is not over. The ruling party has experienced renewed pressures from the anti-choice movement and the Roman Catholic Church. The 2016 legislation discussed in the following section, milder by their standards, proposed to ban abortions in the case of fetal malformation and especially in cases of Down syndrome genetic disorder. Women's movements have decided not to close their umbrellas and to continue fighting against new restrictions.

CURRENT CONDITIONS

The Force of Anti-Abortion Law: The "Underground Women's State"

The anti-abortion law in effect for almost 25 years had numerous negative effects on women's lives, health, and autonomy (Nowicka, 2008). Most important, it caused much suffering. Eliminating access to abortion on social grounds neither reduced the need for abortion nor stopped the procedure from being performed; the law just pushed abortions to a hidden and risky underground (Snochowska-Gonzalez & Zdrojewska, 2009), endangering thousands of women and limiting their access to safe abortion. What was also unexpected is that the law turned out to be even more restrictive in practice.

The ECHR (2007), which offered the judgment in the case of Alicja Tysiąc, argued that the current law has a chilling effect; women de facto can exercise fewer rights than they actually have de jure. The Court noted,

> The legal prohibition on abortion, taken together with the risk of their incurring criminal responsibility under Article 156 § 1 of the Criminal Code, can well have a chilling effect on doctors when deciding whether the requirements of legal abortion are met in an individual case. (p. 27)

Indeed, the implementation of anti-abortion law goes far beyond what is contained in the law by practically banning almost all abortions and, at the same time, failing to implement its preventive provision. According to the law, the government is obliged to guarantee modern sex education in school curricula and to offer full access to family planning. Yet, such policies have never been implemented. Although contraception is available with a doctor's prescription at pharmacies, public doctors rarely provide such prescriptions to women. On the other hand, condoms are widely available without prescription, in shops and gas stations. As a result, women in need of contraceptives have to visit private doctors, which in turn increases the cost of securing contraceptives on a regular basis, making contraception especially difficult for women with limited economic resources. Currently, there is neither a policy nor plans to improve access to modern family planning that would support disadvantaged and young women and diminish unwanted pregnancies and, subsequently, the need for abortion. Sex education is also not part of school curricula. Schools offer religiously biased, pro-family programs that are meant to promote sex only after marriage, natural contraception, and anti-abortion attitudes among the young; they do not provide basic information on broader sexuality, including how to avoid the consequences of premature sex.

The prolonged anti-abortion drive has had many negative consequences for women and their health and also for the future of the pro-choice movement. At least three consequences require further discussion: (1) the impact of restricted abortion on access, (2) the creation of an underground abortion business, and (3) the increased and very effective use of the conscience clause.

Inaccessibility of Legal Abortion

> Once the legislature decides to allow abortion, it must not structure its legal framework in a way which would limit real possibilities to obtain it.
> —ECHR (2007, p. 27)

Although Polish law allows for abortion on a few grounds, most women are not able to exercise this right in public hospitals. Stigma surrounding abortion, fear of many providers not to be labeled as abortionists and pressure on medical doctors executed by anti-choice and religious movements, combined with opportunistic attitudes aimed at avoiding controversial services, has led to denial of legal abortion services in most hospitals. The Coalition of NGOs' (2016) report to the United Nations Human Rights Committee states,

> [Women's] access to services is effectively curtailed by Poland's maintenance of criminal sanctions for abortions performed outside of the very limited circumstances allowed for by the law and by the highly restrictive nature of the law itself. These combine to generate a punitive and stigmatizing environment that undermines effective implementation of Poland's abortion law and creates a chilling effect for medical professionals.

A Polish government report ("Sprawozdanie Rady Ministrow," 2014) states that almost no legal abortions are being performed in the public health care system, and the numbers are declining yearly (only 752 abortions were performed in 2012, and

744 were performed in 2013). These official numbers are particularly striking considering the fact that women of reproductive age constitute more than 10 million of the Polish population of 38 million. According to the government report, there are voivodeships (the largest administrative unit in Poland) in which almost no abortions were performed in 2013. For example, in Lublin voivodeship, with 2 million inhabitants, only 2 abortions were performed, and in Podkarpacie voivodeship, also with 2 million inhabitants, only 3 abortions were performed. The largest number of pregnancy terminations, 244, took place in Mazovian voivodeship (where Warsaw, the capital of Poland, is located), which is inhabited by more than 5 million people.

This symbolic number of legal abortions is a clear indication that access to abortion services has been dramatically restricted in Poland. Women who need abortions are forced to seek help underground or outside of the Polish health system. The situation is even worse when the fetus is deformed.

In November 2016, the ruling party passed a law ("Ustawa o Wsparciu," 2016) on the support of pregnant women and their families "for life." This law aimed to encourage women to give birth to deformed fetuses by providing a one-time allowance of 4,000 PLN (approximately $1,000). The one-time allowance is equivalent to approximately 2 months' salary and therefore will have only a short-term positive impact on the family budget. It will certainly not change drastically the situation of a family affected by the birth of a child requiring long-term special care and long-term support. This law has been ridiculed by the women's movement as a form of cheap bribery. Rather than supporting women's decisions in cases of fetal malformation, the state pushes women to make the heroic act of having and raising children with numerous health and mental challenges.

Abortion Underground

Most women who cannot continue pregnancy decide to have illegal abortions in a so-called abortion underground, which started operating even before the law was restricted because women already experienced problems with accessing limited legal abortion services. The character of the abortion underground has changed throughout the years, reflecting medical developments, especially increased access to medical abortion. At first, illegal abortion services were offered by gynecologists in small private clinics by surgical methods. Doctors performed illegal abortions purely for financial reasons and treated them as a source of additional, nontaxed income. Currently in Poland, unlike in the 1950s, doctors do not support women in their struggle for reproductive rights; the motivation of sympathy or support is very rare. Therefore, prices for abortions are high, on average approximately $500, which is slightly more than the monthly minimum wage. This means that for the majority of Polish women, obtaining an abortion is extremely expensive and hardly accessible. Although abortion in the underground is relatively safe because it is often performed by medical doctors, there have been cases of women dying due to post-abortion complications.

Traveling abroad for abortion, sometimes called—inadequately and frivolously— "abortion tourism," is another "option" for women seeking abortion. Such practices are already quite developed and are growing. With open borders, Polish women seeking abortions travel to many European countries, primarily Slovakia, the Czech Republic,

Germany, Austria, the Netherlands, and the United Kingdom. In some countries, medical clinics have developed services designed specifically for Polish women. This option is often chosen by well-off women because high service costs prevent many others from being able to use these clinics.

In recent years, the phenomenon of abortion via internet has been exploding. Some international feminist nongovernmental organizations provide abortion pills (i.e., medical abortions) through a medically sound, woman-friendly internet service located outside of Poland ("Potrzebuję Pigułek Aborcyjnych," n.d.). The web page is accessible to women throughout the world and provides online counseling (in Polish and other languages), followed by mail delivery of the pills. The service suggests a reasonable voluntary donation (less than $100) for those who can afford it. However, delivery does not always occur due to mail screening in some regions of Poland, resulting in the confiscation of pill packages.

The climate of crime surrounding abortion leads to situations in which women seeking abortion services outside of health systems are often exposed to crooks who want to make a profit on desperate women; they offer false pills to women, which often are just placebos. Although official statistics regarding illegal abortions are not collected due to their criminal nature, according to estimates provided by the Federation for Women and Family Planning, up to 150,000 abortions may be performed in the underground (Nowicka, 2008).

Conscience Clause

Doctors or even entire hospitals that are denying abortions evoke the conscience clause, which is guaranteed by law. Refusals based on conscience are widespread and constitute a key obstacle to accessing pregnancy termination services. Theoretically, Article 39 of the law obliges a doctor using the conscience clause to refer a patient to another doctor who will provide the service in question ("Ustawa o Zawodzie Lekarza," 1996). However, this obligation was never practiced by doctors–objectors. They did not want to help women even by providing information. Moreover, they believed that this obligation of referral was unacceptable because they would be indirectly participating in abortion. Therefore, the Supreme Medical Chamber sued to void Article 39 in the Constitutional Tribunal. The Tribunal, dominated by conservative justices, agreed with doctors and released them from the duty of providing women information on abortion. This filing was a direct result of Dr. Chazan's behavior in Agnieszka and Jacek's case discussed previously.

At the same time, the ruling did not indicate who should inform women about the clinics performing abortions. Thus, the Constitutional Tribunal (2015) adjudged that doctors' right to refusal prevails over women's right to medical service. The Tribunal's conscience clause judgment went against recommendations of the United Nations Committee on Economic, Social and Cultural Rights (2009), which called on Poland to "take all effective measures to ensure that women enjoy their right to sexual and reproductive health, including by enforcing the legislation on abortion and implementing a mechanism of timely and systematic referral in the event of conscientious objection" (p. 6).

Polish doctors deny women not only abortion but also other reproductive health services, including contraception counseling, in vitro fertilization, and/or prenatal examinations (amniocentesis). Women seeking reproductive health services have been de facto expelled from the health care system. Many of them are not even trying to seek "controversial" services in the public health system, although as insured, they could have access to services free of charge. Instead, they go directly to private clinics inside or outside of the country to avoid humiliating treatment and unnecessary procedures that do not guarantee access to services. Those who cannot afford private health care take a risk and utilize underground services, travel abroad, or have to accept the outcomes.

LOOKING TO THE FUTURE

The Future of Institutionalized State Violence Against Women

The situation of Polish women regarding their reproductive rights confirms that the Polish state, represented by its health and law enforcement institutions, acts violently against women. On numerous occasions, as discussed previously, the state has sided against women's interests, and it is no longer safeguarding the implementation of the few reproductive rights that women still have under the constitution and Polish law. Women seeking lawful abortions can hardly exercise their rights because hospitals refuse to perform them even if pregnancy constitutes a risk to their lives; we can argue, then, that in Poland there is currently almost a full ban on abortion.

There is no effective legal mechanism by which women trying to exercise their rights can complain. Even the weak mechanisms, such as the referral obligations imposed on doctors using the conscience clause, were abolished by the Constitutional Tribunal. If a woman files a complaint in the Polish court for denial of legal services, she usually loses the case, and thus only the international arena remains open to women seeking justice.

For years, no matter who has been in power, Poland has persistently ignored recommendations of several of the United Nations human rights committees that monitor the implementation of the human rights conventions as well as those of the European human rights bodies, including ECHR and the Commissioner for Human Rights of the Council of Europe. These international institutions regularly provide Poland with recommendations on how to improve the law and policies regarding human rights of women in the sphere of reproduction and sexuality. No significant actions have ever been taken by the Polish government to address these concerns. The state policies completely ignore the implications of the anti-abortion law on women's lives, health, and personal circumstances. Such anti-women state policies constitute a form of institutionalized violence that discriminates against women and leads to multiple forms of control, oppression, and bodily harm. In the oppressive state, no woman of reproductive age can be free of fear, stigma, and loneliness.

One significant aspect of the state violence against women is the impact that these repressive policies has had on people's attitudes and opinions. In 2013, the Public Opinion Research Center (CBOS, 2013) published the results of an in-depth study titled "Abortion Experience of Polish Women." CBOS observed that according to its research (which has been carried out regularly since the early 1990s), attitudes and opinions regarding abortion have changed significantly. Paradoxically, acceptance of repressive legislation has increased during the past 20 years. The CBOS analysis argues that this shift is due to the normative role of the law in force and the stigma surrounding the issue of reproductive rights, but also because of submissiveness to existing law rather than to people's real beliefs and convictions.

It seems, however, that decreased support for abortion has also resulted from the continuous, vehement, anti-choice propaganda by the Catholic Church during religious services, on the one hand, and state support of the pro-life movement, on the other hand. The Polish education system, for example, plays a critical role in forming children's attitudes. By allowing anti-abortion religious instruction to be provided in the public schools and simultaneously failing to provide modern sex education or, more commonly, by offering so-called pro-family education guided by religious teaching on reproduction and sexuality, schools shape children's attitudes and instill them in the next generation. Moreover, many state institutions, including government, parliament, health, and law enforcement institutions, instill in women the conviction that abortion is morally wrong and that they should feel guilty if they consider pregnancy termination.

CONCLUSION

Despite the propaganda, women do undergo abortion. Although such propaganda has only limited impact on women's ultimate decision regarding whether or not to have an abortion, it does negatively impact women's well-being. Many women declare anti-abortion attitudes against their self-interest, even if in reality they actually do have an abortion if faced with such a decision. Among adult women, no more than one in four but no less than one in three has had at least one abortion. This, as noted by CBOS (2013), translates to 4.1–5.8 million women. Practicing Catholic women have more abortions than those who do not attend church, which can be attributed to anti-contraception propaganda promulgated by the Church.

It is difficult to predict how the overall situation regarding women's reproductive rights will develop in the near future, especially given the highly unfavorable political climate. One major question is whether the ruling party, PiS, will decide to push for further restrictions to already very restrictive reproductive legislation and policies or will give up, not daring to risk open confrontation with nascent women's movements and umbrella revolutions. Powerful pressures of anti-choice groups will continue and may in fact lead to further restrictions, if not by legislation then by government regulations.

The major question is whether the umbrella revolution was a short-term campaign or is the beginning of a larger, sustainable women's movement that will not only preclude the ruling party from further anti-women legal restrictions but also, in the longer term, soften existing limitations regarding women's rights, including reproductive choices. Although it is too early to predict, current self-mobilization and the determination of women throughout the country give some cause for cautious optimism that this more forceful mobilization of women will have a transformative and empowering effect and will reinforce the past determination with which women resisted states' intrusions into their bodies. Will the National Strike become a turning point, leading to societal change in which women's autonomy and decision-making are universally recognized? It remains to be determined.

DISCUSSION QUESTIONS

1. How have women's rights in Poland been affected by the democratic transition?
2. Why have reproductive rights of women in Poland become subject to restrictive state policies?
3. How have Polish women exercised their agency in their struggle to resist negative changes that limit their rights?

REFERENCES

Abortions in Hungary Fall 22%. (2016, June 16). *Visegrad Post*. Retrieved from http://visegradpost.com/en/2016/06/16/abortions-hungary-fall-22

Boy-Żeleński, T. (2013). *Piekło Kobiet [Women's hell]*. Warsaw, Poland: Jirafa Roja. (Original work published 1930)

Centrum Badania Opinii Społecznej. (2013, May). *Doświadczenia Aborcyjne Polek [Abortion experience of Polish women*; Research Communique BS/60/2013]. Retrieved from http://www.cbos.pl/SPISKOM.POL/2013/K_060_13.PDF

Centrum Badania Opinii Społecznej. (2016, November). *Polacy o prawach kobiet, "czarnych protestach" i prawie aborcyjnym [Poles about women's rights, "black protests," and abortion law*; Research Communique NR/165/2016]. Retrieved from https://www.cbos.pl/SPISKOM.POL/2016/K_165_16.PDF

Cichowłas, O. (2016, September 29). Russia's abortion debate is back. *The Moscow Times*. Retrieved from https://themoscowtimes.com/articles/russias-abortion-debate-is-back-55545

Coalition of NGOs. (2016). Supplemental information on Poland for the Periodic Review by the Human Rights Committee at its 118th session, October 17–November 4, Warsaw, Poland.

Constitutional Tribunal. (2015, October 7). *Wyrok w sprawie prawa do odmowy wykonania świadczenia zdrowotnego niezgodnego z sumieniem [Judgement on the right to refuse medical services inconsistent with conscience]*. Retrieved from http://trybunal.gov.pl/rozprawy-i-ogloszenia-orzeczen/wyroki-i-postanowienia/art/8602-prawo-do-odmowy-wykonania-swiadczenia-zdrowotnego-niezgodnego-z-sumieniem

Criminal Code. (1932). Art. 233, July 15.

Dąbrowska-Szulc, E. (2006) Unpublished notes on conversation with Maria Jaszczuk (1915–2007), Auschwitz prisoner, member of the League of Polish Women, member of Parliament (1947–1956). Private archive.

European Court of Human Rights. (2007, March 20). *Case of Tysiąc v. Poland: Judgment* (Application No. 5410/03). Retrieved from http://hudoc.echr.coe.int/eng?i=001-79812

Federation for Women and Family Planning. (2005). *Contemporary women's hell: Polish women's stories*. Warsaw, Poland: Author.

Fishwick, C. (2016, October 27). Poland's abortion laws: Activists blame grip of "hardline" church. *The Guardian*. Retrieved from https://www.theguardian.com/world/2016/oct/27/polands-abortion-laws-activists-blame-grip-of-hardline-church

Francome, C. (2015). *Unsafe abortion and women's health: Change and liberalization.* Oxford, UK: Routledge.

Górka, D. (2016). *To była świadoma decyzja prof. Chazana, że nasze dziecko będzie umierało w cierpieniach* [*It was a conscientious decision by Prof. Chazan;* video]. TVN24. Retrieved from http://www.tvn24.pl/wiadomosci-z-kraju,3/prof-chazan-odmowil-im-aborcji-dzis-opowiadaja-swoja-historie,685587.html

Grzybek, A., & Grabowska, M. (2016). *Przełamać taboo: Raport o przemocy seksulanej.* [*Breaking taboo: Report on sexual violence*]. Warsaw, Poland: Ster Foundation for Equality and Emancipation.

Human Life International. (n.d.). Retrieved from https://www.hli.org

Hunter, J. D. (1992). *Culture wars: The struggle to define America.* New York, NY: Basic Books.

Icelandic women support #blackprotest [video]. (2016, October 2). Retrieved from https://www.youtube.com/watch?v=Z2bGy2DuUZ0

John Paul II: In his own words. (2005, April). *CBC News Online.* Retrieved from https://www.polsatnews.pl/wideo/narod-ktory-zabija-wlasne-dzieci-jest-narodem-bez-przyszlosci-posel-pis-cytuje-jana-pawla-ii_6677451/

Karwowska, A. (2018, June 30). *"Ten nieludzki projekt ma trafić na śmietnik, na hasiok! To nie żarty, to zamach na prawa kobiet"* [*"This inhuman project should be thrown out, to garbage! This is not a joke, this is attack on women's rights."*] Retrieved from http://www.wysokieobcasy.pl/wysokie-obcasy/7,163229,23615694,lempart-rozczaruje-panow-z-pis-w-poniedzialek-bedziemy-protestowac.html

Kondzińska, A. (2016, October 6). Polki wygrały z PiS. "Drodzy państwo, przestraszyliście się, prawda?" Polish women won against Law and Justice. "Dear All you became frighten."]. *Gazeta Wyborcza Daily.*

Kublik, A. (2016, October 8). Rewolucja Parasolek [Umbrella Revolution; interview with Prof. K. Skarżyńska]. *Gazeta Wyborcza Daily.*

Lempart, M. (2016, September 28). Ludzie Wyjdźcie na Ulice [People, go out to the streets]. *Koduj24.pl.* Retrieved from http://koduj24.pl/marta-lempart-ludzie-wyjdzcie-na-ulice

Matercare International. (n.d.). *Who we are: Mission.* Retrieved from https://www.matercare.org/who-we-are/mission

Meyer Resende, M. (2015). *Catholicism and nationalism: Changing nature of party politics.* New York, NY: Routledge.

Mishtal, J. (2015). *The politics of morality: The Church, the State, and reproductive rights in postsocialist Poland.* Athens, OH: Ohio University Press.

Moore, T. (2003, July 7). On board Poland's abortion ship. *BBC News.* Retrieved from http://news.bbc.co.uk/2/hi/europe/3051436.stm

Niemczyńska, M. (2016, April 21). Nie przestaję walczyć. ["I don't stop fighting"; interview with Alicja Tysiąc]. *Duży Format* (supplement to *Gazeta Wyborcza Daily*). Retrieved from http://wyborcza.pl/duzyformat/1,127290,19950413,alicja-tysiac-nie-przestaje-walczyc.html

Nowicka, W. (1996, November). Roman Catholic fundamentalism against women's reproductive rights in Poland. *Reproductive Health Matters, 4*(8), 21–29.

Nowicka, W. (2004). The struggle for abortion rights in Poland. In R. Parker, R. Petchesky, & R. Sember (Eds.), *Sex politics: Reports from the front lines* (pp. 167–196). Rio de Janeiro, Brazil: Sexuality Policy Watch. http://www.sxpolitics.org/frontlines/book/pdf/sexpolitics.pdf

Nowicka, W. (Ed.). (2008). *Reproductive rights in Poland* [Report]. Warsaw, Poland: Federation for Women and Family Planning.

Owsiak, J. (2016, October 3). Comment on Facebook [Quoted by national media]. Retrieved from https://www.facebook.com/jerzyowsiak/posts/1118436404902017

Pankowski, R. (2010). *The populist radical right in Poland: The patriots*. New York, NY: Routledge.

Pharmacists for Life International. (n.d.) Retrieved from http://www.pfli.org

Półtawska apeluje do Polaków: "Proszę, walczcie o Polskę, ona umiera!" [*Półtawska appeals to Poles: "Please fight for Poland, she is dying!"*]. (2015). *Fronda.pl*. Retrieved from http://www.fronda.pl/a/poltawska-apeluje-do-polakow-prosze-walczcie-o-polske-ona-umiera,50984.html

Population Research Institute. (2011). *Russia: A dying nation*. Retrieved from https://www.lifesitenews.com/news/a-dying-nation-must-see-video-lifts-veil-on-russias-abortion-crisis [https://www.youtube.com/watch?v=d302W7nRycQ&feature=youtu.be]

Potrzebuję pigułek aborcyjnych [*I need abortion pills*]. (n.d.). Women on Web. Retrieved from https://www.womenonweb.org/pl/i-need-an-abortion

Regulska, J., & Grabowska, M. (2013). Social justice, hegemony, and women's mobilizations. In J. Kubik & A. Linch (Eds.), *Postcommunism from within* (pp. 139–190). New York, NY: NYU Press.

Śledztwo w sprawie odmowy aborcji przez prof. Chazana umorzone [Investigation dropped in notorious case of Prof. Chazan's abortion refusal]. (2015, May 4). *Newsweek Polska*. Retrieved from http://www.newsweek.pl/polska/sledztwo-w-sprawie-odmowy-aborcji-przez-prof-chazana-umorzone,artykuly,362521,1.html

Snochowska-Gonzalez, K., & Zdrojewska, A. (2009). *Underground women's state* [Documentary film]. Warsaw, Poland: Entuzjastki Film Group.

Sprawozdanie Rady Ministrow z wykonywania oraz o skutkach stosowania w roku 2012 ustawy z dnia 7 stycznia 1993 o planowaniu rodziny, ochronie płodu ludzkiego i waunkach dopuszczalności przerywania ciąży [*Government report on the implementation and the effects of the 7 January 1993 law on family planning, human life protection and conditions of admissibility of pregnancy termination*]. (2014). Warsaw, Poland.

United Nations Committee on Economic, Social and Cultural Rights. (2009, November). *Concluding observations on Poland*. Retrieved from http://tbinternet.ohchr.org/_layouts/treatybodyexternal/Download.aspx?symbolno=E%2fC.12%2fPOL%2fCO%2f5&Lang=en

Ustawa o wsparciu kobiet w ciąży i rodzin "Za życiem" [*Act on the support of pregnant women and families "for life"*]. (2016, November 4). http://prawo.sejm.gov.pl/isap.nsf/download.xsp/WDU20160001860/T/D20161860L.pdf

Ustawa o zawodzie lekarza [*Law on the medical profession*]. (1996, December 5). Dz.U. 1997 nr 28 poz. 152.

Women on Web. (n.d.). *About Women on Web*. Retrieved from https://www.womenonweb.org/en/page/521/about-women-on-web

Zielińska, E. (1990). *Przerywanie Ciąży: Warunki legalności w Polsce i na świecie* [*Pregnancy: Legal conditions in Poland and the world*]. Warsaw, Poland: Wydawnictwo Prawnicze.

Zobacz, co pisał "Gość Niedzielny" o Alicji Tysiąc [See what "Sunday Visitor" wrote about Alicji Tysiąc]. (2009, September 23). *Gazeta.Pl*. Retrieved from http://wiadomosci.gazeta.pl/wiadomosci/1,114873,7069987,Zobacz__co_pisal__Gosc_Niedzielny__o_Alicji_Tysiac.html

15

Stepping Forward, Standing Strong

Philippine Women Human Rights Defenders

ANNALISA ENRILE AND DOROTEA MENDOZA ■

CASE STUDY: LIZA MAZA

In July 2018, Liza Maza was forced into hiding. Arrest warrants for double murder had been issued against her and three fellow activists and former legislators.

Liza Maza is Chairperson Emerita of GABRIELA, a Philippine-based international women's organization, and Lead Convener of the National Anti-Poverty Commission in the Philippines. As a former congresswoman, she is author and co-author of laws that have served to protect and ensure women's rights and welfare, including the Magna Carta of Women, the Anti-Trafficking of Persons Act of 2003, the Juvenile Justice and Welfare Act of 2006, the Philippine Nursing Act, Anti-Torture Law, the Rent Control Act of 2009, and the Anti-Violence Against Women and Their Children Act of 2004.

The warrant for Liza's arrest was based on murder charges that had already been dismissed in 2006, determined by the court as baseless, with indisputable evidence supporting the innocence of the accused. The lawless climate of the Duterte government has been characterized by the tens of thousands of killings under its so-called "war on drugs" and the assassinations of political opponents. Due to the extreme militarism prevalent in the country, with impunity being the norm, there was no guarantee that the judicial system would or could do its job.

A few days after the issuance of the arrest warrants, on July 30, 2018, the Philippine National Police launched a manhunt. On August 4, a civic society group offered a bounty of P1 million for information leading to the arrest of Maza and the three former congresspersons. Notably, this reward offer was announced by former Philippine president Gloria Macapagal Arroyo's lawyer. This is the same president under whom the original double-murder case, which began in 2004, had been filed. By 2006, the case had been found in the court to be unsubstantiated and was thrown out. Therefore, it was not difficult for Liza's lawyers and supporters to infer that the revival of the case was a well-orchestrated scheme to punish and persecute Liza and her three fellow lawmakers for exposing and challenging extrajudicial killings, enforced disappearances, and other human rights abuses under Macapagal Arroyo's term. Nevertheless, the July 2018 arrest warrant, using a defunct case, was clearly part of the Duterte administration's political persecution campaign against progressive opposition, dissent, and the growing anti-tyranny movement.

The 2018 attempt to silence Liza was not the first of its kind. In the 1990s as an activist, Liza was constantly red-baited in the mainstream media and harassed by law enforcement. In 2005, Liza (as a congresswoman) filed a bill to legalize divorce; she received death threats and faced the ire of the influential Catholic Church.

In March 2006, President Gloria Macapagal Arroyo declared a state of national emergency and charged 48 individuals with rebellion. Among them were Representative Liza Maza of the Gabriela Women's Party and 5 other congressional representatives. She and her colleagues obtained sanctuary at the congress building, in a type of house arrest for nearly 2 months. Among the acts of rebellion that the group was charged with was the 1971 Plaza Miranda bombing, which killed political opponents of then president Ferdinand Marcos. Liza was 14 years old at that time. It was impossible for them to be involved. As a response, women in Thailand, Indonesia, and India held pickets in support. At the Women's International Democratic Federation in Portugal, delegates from 17 countries passed a resolution that called for the immediate revocation of the charges. In the United States, a "drop-the-charges" petition collected 5,000 signatures within hours. The rebellion charges were subsequently dropped.

The same sort of galvanized unity in support of Liza occurred in July and August 2018. The Alliance to Defend Secretary Liza Maza was launched in the Philippines. Simultaneously, Liza's longtime friends and comrades in the United States and Canada formed the North American Alliance in Defense of Secretary Liza Maza. The Women Cross DMZ, for which Liza did peace work, declared its support and issued a statement calling for the Duterte administration to immediately withdraw the arrest warrants and drop the fabricated murder charges. The statement was signed by renowned feminist author and activist Gloria Steinem (United States) and Nobel Peace Laureates Mairead Maguire (Ireland) and Leymah Gbowee (Liberia). On August 14, 2018, Judge Trese Wenceslao dismissed the murder cases and quashed the warrants of arrest.

OVERVIEW

Liza's case exemplifies the vulnerability of human rights defenders to their own violation and exploitation. In many instances, human rights defenders come from the same communities and marginalized contexts. They may have been organizers who gained leadership through their insight, the rapport they built with communities, or even positions in their organizations. There is a fine line between those who defend and those whom they are protecting. Furthermore, cases such as Liza's demonstrate just how symbiotic and important this relationship is as she and others found themselves in need of help and support to ensure their human rights.

The idea of human rights is simple: They are freedoms that every person should be able to have—the right to safety, free speech, education, and to be free (Freeman, 2017). In fact, it is such a simple idea that most people take their everyday rights for granted. They do not realize that throughout the world, millions of people experience human rights abuses or violations that have a variety of contexts, such as summary executions, arbitrary or political arrests and detentions, violence against women, access to basic needs, and labor violations or threats (Freeman, 2017). Human rights violations can affect almost any population, location, or community, but communities that are marginalized, poverty-stricken, or discriminated against are the most vulnerable. For instance, children, indigenous peoples, minorities (including religious, national, and sexual minorities), women, and refugees or other displaced persons will have more exposure to and direct contact with experiences that violate their human rights (United Nations Human Rights Office of the High Commissioner, n.d.). Human rights violations occur in every area of the world, and with globalization, these violations occur across borders. Human Rights Watch's "World Report 2018" investigated the current status of human rights in more than 90 countries. Although Human Rights Watch was clear that each country has its own unique circumstances, it found that in general, there was a lowering of human rights in countries with authoritarian populist movements with leaders who came to power through demonization of marginalized populations and by fueling general divisiveness between communities and distrust of democratic institutions. These countries include the United States, China, and Russia, whose leadership consists of "strongmen" who have publicly declared anti-rights agendas. The Philippines is also included on this list because of the election of Rodrigo Duterte, who became president in 2016. One of his first moves was to condemn the Commission of Human Rights and threaten to close it (Thompson, 2016). His so-called "anti-drug" policies have encouraged vigilantism and resulted in the deaths of hundreds (Thompson, 2016). At the beginning of 2018, at the direction of President Duterte, the Philippines declared hundreds of human rights defenders, activists, and advocates as "terrorists to the state." This list included the United Nations Special Rapporteur on the Rights of Indigenous Peoples and several journalists (Lang, 2018). The United Nations Assistant Secretary-General for Human Rights expressed his worry at the targeting of human rights defenders and that it sent a message that democratic operation and expression are in grave danger (Cabico, 2018).

The term *human rights defenders* was coined after the ratification of the United Nations Declaration of Human Rights in 1998. The term encompasses those who identify and act as advocates, activists, professionals, and workers; those who monitor and take reports; and others who work in the human rights arena. The point of unity that all human rights defenders share is that they seek to promote and protect basic civil rights. They may do this in multiple capacities, including providing legal aid, mental health services, casework, and general protection such as providing shelter or security. Although there are stereotypes of human rights defenders as service providers or relief aid workers, in most of the world, the bulk of human rights defenders are disrupters who aim to shift the status quo and ignite revolution (Bennett, Ingleton, Nah, & Savage, 2015). Women's rights defenders are often subsumed under this more general category, even if the bulk of their work has to do with or is solely focused on women and women-identified populations. Recently, there has been an increase in the number of women right's defenders, which has coincided with an increase in anti-women sentiment throughout the world (some of which is from national leadership). The work of women's rights defenders is mainly in the arena of interpersonal violence, community violence, sexual assault, reproductive rights, and activism. For instance, the Association for Women's Rights in Development notes that the intersection between gender rights and human rights is an obvious one, with the most gains made in the area of gender with regard to human rights defense (Jones, Rosenhek, & Turley, 2014). In the Philippines, President Duterte has indicated that rape is not an important issue; in fact, he continues to joke about it (Villamor, 2018). In areas such as the Middle East, with the existence of honor killings and severe limitations to basic rights, the fight for women's rights is most intense (Abbas, 2015). Even the United States is not immune: The closure of reproductive health clinics that perform abortions, the continued wide pay gaps, and the #MeToo movement highlighting sexual harassment and assault are indicative of a global erosion of women's rights (Fielding, 2017).

The work of human rights defenders is difficult and dangerous—not just for those whom they help but also for themselves. Frontline Defenders reported that in 2017, more than 300 human rights defenders were killed. More than two-thirds of those who were killed were defending land from mega projects that threatened indigenous peoples and would displace communities. Those who were not killed were subjected to death threats or fabricated charges, as in the case of Liza. Activists, journalists, and lawyers are subjected to arrests and being labeled or red-baited as part of smear campaigns (United Nations Human Rights Office of the High Commissioner, n.d.). Although there are protections such as asylum in other countries, emergency relocations, and funding for support, these are not widely offered. Furthermore, most human rights defenders, such as Liza, refuse to leave the country and people they are trying to protect.

The Philippines is riddled with corruption (Batalla, 2015). It has a history of violations in the spheres of labor, politics, and gender rights (Batalla, 2015). For instance, in 2017, there were human rights violations in the form of more than 350,000 displaced persons, more than 4,000 extrajudicial killings, overpopulated prisons, and the trafficking of thousands of women and children (US Department of State, 2017). Harassment of progressive activists and the press was also reported by Karapatan (n.d.), a human rights organization that also serves as a watchdog against government exploitation. There are no specific data regarding the number of human rights defenders in the Philippines, but there are thousands of civic organizations and people's movements (C. Palabay, personal communication, March 8, 2018). According to Karapatan, human rights defenders are subject to harassment, illegal arrest, and extrajudicial killing. The role of women in this arena is especially notable in that women are vulnerable in a patriarchal landscape in which they may be questioned and jailed for their husband's actions as well as subjected to torture such as rape and other sexual assault (C. Palabay, personal communication, March 8, 2018).

This chapter discusses the human rights situation in the Philippines as well as the pivotal role that human rights defenders play in the social, political, and economic context of the country. It also examines recent political developments that have put the lives of human rights defenders in greater peril. Finally, a highlight of the continued work being performed internationally and in the Philippines to safeguard and support human rights defenders is presented.

HISTORICAL TRENDS

The Philippines is known for its turbulent past, beginning as a colonial conquest of Spain, in addition to the current situation with President Duterte, whose vigilante policies have resulted in murder and destruction. It is important to review Philippine colonial history to understand the current state of human rights defenders because many of the robust people's movements and grassroots actions have direct ties to the ideologies of Philippine revolutionaries against the Spanish. That is, the Philippines has always been a country in the midst of struggle. In the 1500s, Spain "discovered" the Philippines, then a country composed of hundreds of tribes with a hierarchy of its own but that fell under Spain's control (Agoncillo & Alfonso, 1960). Throughout the next 400 years of Spanish rule, there were numerous rebellions culminating in the Philippine revolution from 1896 to 1898. The revolution was led by Andres Bonifacio (a peasant leader) and Emilio Aguinaldo (an upper-class son of a municipal governor). Rather than admit defeat to the Filipinos, the Spanish sold the Philippines to the United States as part of the Treaty of Paris. The Philippine–American War ensued from 1899 to 1901, when the Philippines conceded to the United States and became a US territory along with Puerto Rico. From 1942 to 1945, during World War II, the Japanese controlled the Philippines after it was surrendered by the United States. It was not until 1946 that the United States "freed" the Philippines to become its own sovereign state and republic (Francia, 2013). After less than 50 years as a free republic, the Philippines was taken over by martial law and the dictatorship of Ferdinand Marcos from 1972 to 1986.

Throughout the country's turbulent history, ongoing rebellions and guerilla warfare have characterized the response of the people, including the women. In all these instances of rebellion and "people's power," women have figured prominently. The following are examples:

- Gabriela Silang is one of the most famous people in Philippine history. Gabriela was married to Diego Silang, a military general during the rebellion against Spain in the Ilocos region. Diego was killed, and Gabriela continued to lead the fight until she and her troops were captured. She was the last to be hanged in a public square as an example that a woman's place was not in rebellion (Roces, 2012).
- Due to the Hukbalahaps, the Philippines was mostly freed from the Japanese when General Douglas MacArthur staged his triumphant "return to Leyte." In the meantime, women and men fled to the hills to engage in guerilla warfare against the Japanese. Known as the "Huk Amazons," women carried out dangerous courier missions, participated in military missions, and had to handle women's issues such as birth and rape within the context of living in the jungles and forests as they waged war (Lanzona, 2009).
- Martial law dictator, Ferdinand Marcos, who ruled the country from 1972 to 1986 when he was overthrown by the massive "People's Power" movement. Women were instrumental in the events that led to the end of the dictatorship. For instance, women ran radio communications throughout the large rallies to maintain coordination (Libang, personal communication, March 8, 2018). Some of the most famous images of the People's Power movement were of nuns kneeling in front of tanks and praying on rosaries (Katsiaficas, 2013).

Although the ousting of a dictator should have signaled significant changes, the reality was that there were more human rights violations than ever. Some have hypothesized that this is because there has not been a real change in the ruling families of the Philippines (Velasco, 2006). The same families that experienced privilege and were land owners and wealthy in the Spanish era exist today. Because of this, the motivation for change has not permeated into the ruling elite (Simbulan, 2005). This is the case even with changes in the Philippines constitution after martial law and the provisions for rule. The main change was that the president could serve only one 6-year term. Presidents who followed Marcos include Fidel Ramos (the architect of martial law), Gloria Macapagal Arroyo (who had the highest number of human rights violations), and former actor Joseph Estrada (who was impeached in 2001, 4 years into his presidency).

The situation was not without hope for the general population, however, because another change in the constitution offered a way into politics for those who were not of the political elite. The "party-list rule" allowed individuals to run for congress and represent marginalized communities. Those who received 3% of the popular vote got a congressional seat and could serve up to three terms as a congressperson (Rimban, 2015). This is the rule that Liza ran under and was able to gain a congressional seat representing women. As part of the congress, she was able to help pass the first juvenile justice law in the Philippines (Congress of the Philippines, 2006), a violence against women law (Congress of the Philippines, 2004), and an anti-trafficking law (Congress of the Philippines, 2003).

After martial law, the groups and organizations that formed to rid the country of the dictatorship continued in various forms. Thousands of organizations were documented by Rivera and Newkirk (1997), including nonprofit organizations, nongovernmental organizations, advocacy groups, and think tanks. Many of these groups were composed of and led by women who were specifically concerned with human rights. Even mixed gender organizations such as Karapatan were led by women and formed women's committees within the larger group (Gahl, 2017). Expansion of such groups was necessary due to the growing struggles within the country regarding restrictive policies that continued to benefit the privileged elite.

The Human Security Act of 2007 further eroded human rights. Under this law, terrorism is defined as anything that causes "widespread and extraordinary fear and panic among the populace." This law allows the arrest of terror suspects even when there is no initial evidence to substantiate a case, and people can be detained without charges (Pereire, 2007). Critics of the law cite that the ambiguous language creates a system in which anyone can be picked up and jailed and that this law could be misused (Human Rights Watch, 2007). In fact, during the first month after the law was passed, three US citizens—two of Philippine descent—were detained as supposed terrorists even though there was no evidence (Lacsamana, 2015). Known as the GABNet 3, Annalisa Enrile, Judith Mirkinson, and Ninotchka Rosca were barred from leaving the country because their names were on a blacklist/no-fly list due to their participation in leading an all-women delegation for human rights in 2006. International and local pressure from women's organizations caused the US and Philippine governments to reconsider their actions. Liza, then a congresswoman, was instrumental in enabling them to leave the country (Santilla, 2007).

The unique human rights violations based on gender, such as rape and imprisonment/torture while pregnant, continued to occur. In 2010, a group of health workers who were conducting a medical mission in Morong, Rizal, were arrested and accused of being members of the New People's Army. Among the 43 who were arrested, 26 were women, 2 of whom were pregnant. They were placed in detention for 12 weeks before being transferred to a prison in Manila, where the pregnant women gave birth. They reported that they were subject to torture, such as being blindfolded and interrogated for up of 36 hours straight, and the women were subjected to sexual harassment and molestation (Human Rights Watch, 2010; JASS Feminist Movement Building, n.d.). Even more sobering is that the case of the Morong 43 occurred after the Ampatuan massacre, in which 21 women were killed, raped, or mutilated in the crossfire of feuding between political clans (McIndoe, 2009).

Whether formal laws or cultural and social norms, there is an environment of corruption, persecution, and state-influenced violence in the Philippines. Although it would be easy to blame the current administration, this environment has defined the Philippines for decades. Women, whether from elevated or subordinated roles in Philippines society, have been one of the first lines of defense for human rights throughout the history of the country (Roces, 2012).

THE PHILIPPINES AT A GLANCE

The Philippines comprises more than 7,000 islands, with the 3 largest islands—Luzon, Visayas, and Mindanao—comprising its most populated areas. It is a democratic sovereignty, although many would argue that significant foreign influence (especially from the United States) has shaped its policies and government actions. The Philippines adheres to a multiparty system with more than 10 major political parties. The underlying sentiment, however, is that the political party with which one is affiliated is not important; most important are the political legacies of and membership in the long-held ruling political families of the Philippines, such as the Zobel-Ayalas, Conjuancos, and Macapagals families. The divide between ultra-rich and poor is vast and growing. In 2017, Credit Suisse reported in *Entrepreneur Philippines* magazine that only 0.06% of the country's adult population earns $1 million per year, and of this percentage, only 12 families earn more than $1 billion per year (Simbulan, 2005). However, their earnings account for 80% of all resources. In a country with a population of 105 million (July 2017 estimate), that is significant (Statistica, n.d.). The economy of the Philippines is mostly services (56.3%) and agriculture (25.4%). The fastest growing service sector industry is call centers (Central Intelligence Agency, n.d.). Although a boon in the latter has resulted in a burgeoning middle class, the lack of any real basic industry (e.g., oil or steel) means that much of the population remains dependent on remittances sent from migrant workers abroad. The fastest economic growth is within the upper classes. The intersection of the rich and the powerful is expressed in government and politics.

Women were first granted the right to vote in 1937, but they still comprise less than 10% of members of both houses. Although two women have held the highest office of president, both were controversial. Gloria Macapagal Arroyo's presidency has been described as oppressive. She was charged with plunder, and there were attempts to charge her for the Morong 43 case because of the torture that occurred in the prisons (Hutchcroft, 2008). Women also have a high rate of education, numbering above 50% men's achievement rates (United Nations Educational, Scientific and Cultural

Organization, n.d.). This may be because women are expected to earn money and help support their families. The global push for professionals in the nursing industry and domestic help is also a reason for high rates of education. For instance, in 2018, the need for nurses and caregivers in the developed world increased from thousands to millions. Also, the preference for English-speaking nannies throughout the world has resulted in a strong demand for educated Pilipinas (Piller, 2018).

Historically, women held egalitarian, if not more elevated, roles in society. Women who were babaylans were considered the keepers of traditions, healers, and decision-makers about planting and harvest. If men wanted to join the ranks of the babaylans, they had to don the clothing of women. These were the first women persecuted by the Spanish and labeled as witches (Mendoza & Strobel, 2015). Feminism in the Philippines was exemplified as early as the revolutions against the Spanish and well into the period of US control. The first schools for women were established in the early years of US control and offered women the opportunity to learn as well as organize. The suffrage movement was born out of these first universities. While upper- and middle-class women pushed for this, women working in the factories also fought for their rights and gained major concessions from their employers (Basu, 2018). By the beginning of World War II, not only were women working in military hospitals and civic groups offering support but also many were fighting side by side with men against the Japanese occupation. Their work for rights continued after the war and into the martial law period. When martial law was declared, women who were organizing fled to the mountains because all groups had been declared illegal. The most progressive of these organizations, MAKIBAKA (Malayang Kilusan ng Bagong Kababaihan or Movement of New Women) was an alliance of women's organizations that was deemed illegal and communist. It operated from the hills to bring awareness and fight against human rights abuses. In the late 1980s, more civic and people's organizations began to form aboveground, including GABRIELA, an alliance of women's organizations (Enrile & Levid, 2009). These groups were instrumental in the ousting of the dictator, and they continue to fight for women's rights.

CURRENT CONDITIONS

Under President Duterte, the Philippines has experienced the greatest vulnerabilities to human rights and human rights defenders since the martial law era. Liza's experience is exemplary of his administration. The lead convener of the National Anti-Poverty Commission, Liza was considered part of President Duterte's cabinet. Her work was starting to gain traction by providing genuine change in urban poor areas. Despite this, trumped up charges were still leveled on her, and a bounty was put on her head. In the current state of the Philippines in which vigilantism has become the rule of law, the bounty was tantamount to a target on her back. During this entire process, instead of President Duterte stepping in to support or protect Liza from harm or provide her a nonthreatening space to demonstrate her innocence, he further exacerbated the situation and created more danger. It is not surprising that upon the charges being dropped, Liza resigned her post. She stated (as cited in Leonel, 2018),

> Genuine change cannot happen when the old forces of fascism and corruption, and the defenders of elite and foreign interests, are consolidating their position

in government. The problem of poverty cannot be solved if the attacks against those who are fighting poverty are still continuing.

Poverty and human rights violations not only occur in the Philippines at an alarming rate but also occur abroad, making migrant workers vulnerable. Pilipina women comprise a majority of the migrant worker population that sends remittances and accounts for $33 billion, or 10% of the Philippine gross domestic product ("Philippines Is 3rd," 2018). Despite this large amount, research indicates that remittances do not spark real economic growth (Clemens & McKenzie, 2018). Women of Philippine descent in the diaspora truly fit Mohanty's definition of a transnational woman—living in two countries and not fully in one or the other, but building movements in two or more countries (Carty & Mohanty, 2015). This means that the issues that continue to occur in the Philippines are not only relevant but also touch their lives directly. Furthermore, migrant and immigrant women must contend with their own abuse in host countries. Famous cases in Philippine history are Flor Contemplacion, a maid who was executed in Singapore for allegedly murdering two people and was posthumously found innocent, and Sarah Balabagan, a 15-year-old girl working in the United Arab Emirates who was sentenced to 1 year in jail and 100 cane strokes for defending herself against a rapist; these are just two of the hundreds of cases that exist today (San Jose, 2015). Even President Duterte cannot ignore the abuse and has attempted (with little success) to repatriate migrant workers.

Human rights defenders constantly place their lives on the line. They are often attacked, persecuted, and sometimes disappear or are assassinated. Unfortunately, threats to their lives and well-being are common. But also common is the citadel

Figure 15.1 (Left to right) Teddy Casino, Satur O'Campo, Liza Maza, and Rafael Mariano—the first set of progressive PartyList Congresspeople vow to *Tuloy ang laban* ("continue the fight"). The four were red baited in Congress and held under house arrest in their congressional offices under then Philippine president, Gloria Macapagal-Arroyo. Upon release, they renewed their vow to the Filipino people to fight for basic human rights and not be deterred despite their imprisonment.

formed by the communities they serve and by their networks of fellow human rights defenders and activists. In Liza's case, whenever she has been threatened, the response from the international women's community has been swift. Liza, in particular, through many facets of her work and because of her maintenance of a transnational perspective, works through international collaborations and ties. Women Cross the DMZ, the Association for Women's Rights in Development (AWID), the Women's International League for Peace and Freedom (WILPF), the Women's Environment & Development Organization (WEDO), and GATW are examples of organizations that operate beyond borders.

It is important to note that women human rights defenders cannot always count on their male counterparts or mixed gender organizations. Activists and human rights defenders are not immune to having gender-based bias and having that carry through the work. When Liza was charged with rebellion in 2006 and was (in effect) under house arrest in her office in the congressional building, media coverage often failed to mention her, focusing solely on her fellow accused, who were men. In local and international media such as *The New York Times*, she was very rarely mentioned (Mydans, 2006). Yet, it was Liza out of all the accused who was able to test the boundaries of her house arrest, leaving the premises twice and eluding arrest because she was protected by women legislators who supported and shielded her, as well as an international community of women who kept vigil (Rosca, 2006). The historic invisibility of women still occurs even in the most progressive sectors of society (Espinoza, 2001; Pulido, 2006).

LOOKING TO THE FUTURE: A CALL TO ACTION

A critical lesson to be learned from women human rights defenders is that in the current capitalist global system, all rights, no matter how basic, are not a given, nor are they guaranteed. From voting rights to equal pay, reproductive rights, and the most basic rights listed in the Universal Declaration of Human Rights, women have to put in a lifetime of struggle.

The first call to action, then, is to continuously acknowledge, honor, and study the work of all women human rights defenders, past and present, local and global. This allows learning and modeling so that errors and triumphs are incorporated into future work. Then, women must put that learning into practice. This is because change is not primarily effected by governments or their sanctioned institutions but, rather, by ordinary individuals whose extraordinariness comes from the simple yet difficult act of stepping forward and standing up. Stepping forward means being engaged—with one's life, community, and environment. This could take the form of being involved in an organization, protesting detrimental policies, voting, and working across borders. There is a plethora of opportunities for engagement. The important point, as Liza has demonstrated in her more than four decades of work, is that a dogged commitment to a well-discerned path is required, with the knowledge that all paths of struggle and resistance are inherently inseparable.

Change happens in the process of engagement. While Liza's Gabriela Women's Party-list engaged in parliamentary work, the ranks of women involved also actively provided an alternative to what was not working legislatively. For instance, while fighting for health care policy for women and protesting lack of coverage, they also built a mobile health clinic and Liza's office provided medical funds for women in need (http://www.gabrielawomensparty.org). In other words, engagement also means proactively building the community and the world that one wants to see.

CONCLUSION

It is not surprising that when one of their own is under attack, women activists and leaders of grassroots movements and international organizations—even when their ideologies conflict—instantaneously and organically join forces. The same closing of ranks is seen when womankind in general is under attack: The #MeToo movement empowered women to step forward and inspired a resurgence of global sisterhood; the 2004 March for Women's Lives in Washington, DC, gathered more than 1 million women to protest the curtailment of women's reproductive rights; and the 2017 Women's March after the election of Donald Trump started out as a national effort in the United States but spread to all corners of the world, including Antarctica (Peters & Wolper, 2018). The unity of women is the reaction to a collective history of oppression that spans borders and the intersectionality of identity and experience.

DISCUSSION QUESTIONS

1. What are human rights defenders and what are examples of their work?
2. How does international solidarity to support and protect human rights defenders take on a transnational feminist lens? What are specific examples of transnational feminist solidarity?
3. Liza's story is just one of many. Select another woman human rights defender and tell her story through a transnational feminist lens. What are the similarities? What are the differences?

REFERENCES

Abbas, R. (2015). No to oppressing women initiative. *Journal of Middle East Women's Studies, 11*(2), 240.

Agoncillo, T. A., & Alfonso, O. M. (1960). *A short history of the Filipino people.* Quezon City, Philippines: University of the Philippines.

Basu, A. (2018). *The challenge of local feminisms: Women's movements in global perspective.* New York, NY: Routledge.

Batalla, E. V. C. (2015). Treading the straight and righteous path: Curbing corruption in the Philippines. *Asian Education and Development Studies, 4*(1), 51–75.

Bennett, K., Ingleton, D., Nah, A. M., & Savage, J. (2015). Critical perspectives on the security and protection of human rights defenders. *International Journal of Human Rights, 19*(7), 883–895.

Cabico, G. K. (2018, May 17). *UN exec: Human rights defenders in the Philippines under threat.* Retrieved from https://www.philstar.com/headlines/2018/05/17/1816092/un-exec-human-rights-defenders-philippines-under-threat#Xr0mmP3OI2LvD4gp.99

Carty, L., & Mohanty, C. T. (2015). Mapping transnational feminist engagements. In R. Baksh & W. Harcourt (Eds.), *The Oxford handbook of transnational feminist movements* (pp. 82–115). New York, NY: Oxford University Press.

Central Intelligence Agency. (n.d.). *Philippines. The world factbook.* Retrieved from https://www.cia.gov/library/publications/the-world-factbook/geos/rp.html

Clemens, M. A., & McKenzie, D. (2018). Why don't remittances appear to affect growth? *Economic Journal, 128*(612), F179–F209.

Congress of the Philippines. (2003). Twelfth Congress. Second Session. Republic Act No. 9208: Anti-Trafficking in Persons Act of 2003.

Congress of the Philippines. (2004). Twelfth Congress. Third Session. Republic Act No. 9262: Anti-Violence Against Women and Their Children Act of 2004.

Congress of the Philippines. (2006). Thirteenth Congress. Second Session. Republic Act No. 9344: Juvenile Justice Law of 2006.

Enrile, A., & Levid, J. (2009). GAB [riela] Net [work]: A case study of transnational sisterhood and organizing. *Amerasia Journal, 35*(1), 92–108.

Espinoza, D. (2001). Revolutionary sisters. *Aztlán, 26,* 17–58.

Fielding, S. (2017). 7 Statistics about women's equality in America that show the fight is far from over. *Bustle.* Retrieved from https://www.bustle.com/p/7-statistics-about-womens-equality-in-america-that-show-the-fight-is-far-from-over-77336

Francia, L. H. (2013). *History of the Philippines: From Indios Bravos to Filipinos.* New York, NY: Overlook Press.

Freeman, M. (2017). *Human rights* (3rd ed.). Malden, MA: Polity.

Gahl, M. J. (2017). *"Our struggle is not a choice!": Insecurities and protection strategies of women land right defenders. A Philippine case study on Leyte and Sicogon island.* Doctoral dissertation, Global Campus.

Human Rights Watch. (2007). *Philippines: New terrorism law puts rights at risk.* Retrieved from https://www.hrw.org/news/2007/07/17/philippines-new-terrorism-law-puts-rights-risk

Human Rights Watch. (2010). *Philippines: Aquino's order to free "morong 43" a positive step government should investigate allegations of mistreatment.* Retrieved from https://www.hrw.org/news/2010/12/14/philippines-aquinos-order-free-morong-43-positive-step

Human Rights Watch. (2018). *World report 2018: Events of 2017.* Retrieved from https://www.hrw.org/world-report/2018

Hutchcroft, P. D. (2008). The Arroyo imbroglio in the Philippines. *Journal of Democracy, 19*(1), 141–155.

JASS Feminist Movement Building. (n.d.). *Enough! Stop violating women's dignity and basic human rights.* Retrieved from https://justassociates.org/sites/justassociates.org/files/free_the_43_statement.pdf

Jones, R., Rosenhek, S., & Turley, A. (2014). A movement support organization: The experience of the Association for Women's Rights in Development (AWID). *SUR: International Journal on Human Rights, 20,* 399.

Karapatan. (n.d.). *About us.* Retrieved from http://www.karapatan.org

Katsiaficas, G. N. (2013). *Asia's unknown uprisings Volume 2: People power in the Philippines, Burma, Tibet, China, Taiwan, Bangladesh, Nepal, Thailand, and Indonesia, 1947–2009.* Oakland, CA: PM Press.

Lacsamana, A. E. (2015). *Revolutionizing feminism.* New York, NY: Routledge.

Lang, C. (2018, March 13). *Philippine government labels human rights defenders "terrorists."* Retrieved from https://redd-monitor.org/2018/03/13/philippine-government-labels-human-rights-defenders-terrorists

Lanzona, V. A. (2009). *Amazons of the Huk rebellion: Gender, sex, and revolution in the Philippines.* Madison, WI: University of Wisconsin Press.

Leonel, J. N. (2018, August 20). *Liza Maza resigns from Duterte Cabinet.* Retrieved from http://newsinfo.inquirer.net/1023050/liza-maza-resigns-from-duterte-cabinet#ixzz5PmDoPVcs

McIndoe, A. (2009). Behind the Philippines' maguindanao massacre. *Time.* Retrieved from http://content.time.com/time/world/article/0,8599,1943191,00.html

Mendoza, S. L. L., & Strobel, L. M. (Eds.). (2015). *Back from the crocodile's belly: Philippine babaylan studies and the struggle for indigenous memory.* Manila, Philippines: UST Publishing House.

Mydans, S. (2006). Veteran revolutionary trapped in the halls of power. *The New York Times.* Retrieved from https://www.nytimes.com/2006/04/18/world/asia/18filip.html?rref=collection%2Fbyline%2Fseth-mydans&action=click&contentCollection=undefined&region=stream&module=stream_unit&version=search&contentPlacement=45&pgtype=collection

Pereire, K. (2007). Analysis and review of the Philippines Human Security Act 2007. Research Analyst of International Centre for Political Violence and Terrorism Research Philippines Const. Art. XIV. 1987.

Peters, J. S., & Wolper, A. (Eds.). (2018). *Women's rights, human rights: International feminist perspectives.* New York, NY: Routledge.

Philippines is 3rd top remittance receiving country in the world. (2018). *Philstar.* Retrieved from https://www.philstar.com/business/2018/04/23/1808669/philippines-3rd-top-remittance-receiving-country-world

Piller, I. (2018). Scripts of servitude: Language, labor migration and transnational domestic work. *Journal of Sociolinguistics, 22*(2), 250–253.

Pulido, L. (2006). *Black, brown, yellow, and left: Radical activism in Los Angeles.* Berkeley, CA: University of California Press.

Rimban, L. (2015). *Party list: Messing with the party list.* Philippine Center for Investigative Journalism. Retrieved from http://pcij.org/stories/messing-with-the-party-list

Rivera, R., & Newkirk, G. F. (1997). Power from the people: A documentation of non-governmental organizations' experience in community-based coastal resource management in the Philippines. *Ocean & Coastal Management, 36*(1–3), 73–95.

Roces, M. (2012). *Women's movements and the Filipina, 1986–2008.* Honolulu, HI: University of Hawai'i Press.

Rosca, N. (2006). *The invisibility of the Filipina.* Retrieved from http://www.womensmediacenter.com/news-features/the-invisibility-of-the-filipina

San Jose, B. A. (2015). Achieving human security for migrants: The limits of state policies and migration-development initiatives. *Bandung: Journal of the Global South, 2*(1), 21.

Santilla, F. (2007). *GABNET 3 attempts to board planes a success, despite harassment from immigration officials.* Retrieved from http://la.indymedia.org/news/2007/08/204840.php

Simbulan, D. C. (2005). *The modern principalia: The historical evolution of the Philippine ruling oligarchy.* Quezon City, Philippines: University of the Philippines Press.

Statistica. (n.d.). *The Philippines—Statistics & facts.* Retrieved from https://www.statista.com/topics/3914/the-philippines

Thompson, M. (2016). Bloodied democracy: Duterte and the death of liberal reformism in the Philippines. *Journal of Current Southeast Asian Affairs, 35*(3), 39–68.

United Nations Educational, Scientific and Cultural Organization. (n.d.). *Philippines.* Retrieved from http://uis.unesco.org/country/PH

United Nations General Assembly. (1998). *The Universal Declaration of Human Rights, 1948* (217 [III] A). Retrieved from http://www.un.org/en/universal-declaration-human-rights

United Nations Human Rights Office of the High Commissioner. (n.d.). *Who is a defender.* Retrieved from https://www.ohchr.org/en/issues/srhrdefenders/pages/defender.aspx

US Department of State. (2017). *Philippines 2017 human rights report: Country reports on human rights practices.* Retrieved from https://www.state.gov/documents/organization/277355.pdf

Velasco, R. (2006). Parties, elections, and democratization in post-martial law Philippines. In T. S. Encarnacion Tadem & N. M. Morada (Eds.), *Philippine politics and governance: An introduction* (pp. 97–117). Quezon City, Philippines: University of the Philippines.

Villamor, F. (2018, August 31). Duterte jokes about rape: Again Philippine women aren't laughing. *The New York Times.* Retrieved from https://www.nytimes.com/2018/08/31/world/asia/philippines-rodrigo-duterte-rape-joke.html?&moduleDetail=section-news-3&action=click&contentCollection=Asia%20Pacific&region=Footer&module=MoreInSection&version=WhatsNext&contentID=WhatsNext&pgtype=article

Heto ang bagong tulang, "Ang Diskurso ng Pagsuko" tungkol sa hinihinging pagsuko sa Batasan 4 at ang kanilang paninindigan.

ANG DISKURSO NG PAGSUKO

Puting bandila ang iwinawagayway,
bilang simbolo ng pagsuko.
Hinihiling ng panig na natatalo
na itigil na ang putukan,
marahil, para makaligtas sa tiyak na kamatayan.

Itinataas naman ng nasusukol ang dalawang kamay,
para ipakitang wala siyang sandata.
Hudyat sa kung sinong alagad ng batas
na hindi siya banta, kaya hindi dapat mautas.

Pero bakit susuko, kung hindi talunan, o walang kasalanan?
Pahabain ang buhok, na kagaya ni Macario Sakay
kung may ipinaglalabang kasarinlan at kalayaan.
O kaya'y bigkasin ang paulit-ulit na linya
sa teleserye ng mga Bayani alyas Bagani, at magwika:
"Huwag, huwag kang sumuko, Ganda. Lumaban ka, Lakas."
Kahit pa ang teleserye ay malapit nang magwakas.

Ang diskurso ng pagsuko ay naglilihis sa ating lahat
sa higit na mahahalagang tanong:
Ano ang krimeng ibinibintang?
Sino-sino ang naghahabi ng kasinungalingan?
Paanong hindi maaaring maghugas ng kamay
ang lahat ng sangkot sa paglikha ng kulturang tumatanggap
sa mundong ang katarungan ay baligtad:
Pinunong itinatanghal ang berdugo't mandarambong
Samantalang pinapaslang ang lumad at magsasaka,

sa gubat at nayon,
Ipinipiit ang welgista at mamamahayag,
at pulahan ang sumbat sa sino mang mag-aklas.
Ano ang ikinatatakot sa Makabayan?
Sino silang nangangamba, at bakit?
Bakit ang tanong ng walang ninais
kundi ang maglingkod, mag-alay ng buhay,
walang yaman, kundi dangal. Iyon lamang.

Iwagayway ang pulang bandila nang tanggap,
ang kanyang sagisag.
Itaas ang kamao at magpahayag:
Hindi isinusuko ang prinsipyo.
Hindi tayo aatras sa mga duwag na sa atin ay nandarahas.
Tapang ang kalasag, hangarin ay sibat,
Hangga't kabalikat ang masa, walang hindi mahaharap.

—Joi Barrios-Leblanc, Department of South and Southeast
Asian Studies, University of California, Berkeley

16

Rape as a Weapon of War in Myanmar/Burma

ANNALISE OATMAN AND KATE MAJEWSKI ■

Figure 16.1 According to UNICEF, in 2019, an estimated 460,000 children in Myanmar/Burma will be affected by conflicts or natural disasters and will require humanitarian assistance.

CASE STUDY: GALAU DAU YANG

Galau Dau Yang's husband is a farmer who struggles with opium addiction, a common problem in the Kachin region of Myanmar. When men dressed in police uniforms entered Galau Dau Yang's home one evening, stating that they were searching

Figure 16.2 Many communities still struggle to access basic services in health, education, water and sanitation, and child protections. Twenty-five percent of children (more than 4 million) live in households that do not use improved toilet facilities.

for drugs, she told them that her husband had been gone for days. They searched the house anyway and then strip searched her and took turns raping and sodomizing her. When they left, they took her clothes with them, stating that they would use them to frame her and levy drug charges against her if she told anyone about what had happened.

She did, however, speak out about what happened. First she went to the hospital and then to the police. She has remained vocal about her experience and about the experiences of so many other women and girls in the Kachin and other borderland regions of Myanmar. Her courage inspired other women in the region to speak out about similar experiences. Galau Dau Yang also went to the local pastor, Hkun Sun, to discuss what she had experienced. Hkun Sun was instrumental in continuing to publicize Galau Dau Yang's case as an example of the kinds of atrocities that many women in the borderlands of Myanmar have endured (Cengel, 2014).

Unfortunately, Galau Dau Yang is just one of millions of women affected by sexual violence in conflict settings. This chapter explores the nature and scope of sexual violence in conflicts throughout the world, both historically and currently, and describes the present-day conflict setting in Myanmar, where women and girls live under the threat of this kind of violence.

OVERVIEW

According to the International Criminal Court (ICC, 2002), sexual violence includes acts such as rape, sexual slavery, forced prostitution, pregnancy, abortion, and sterilization (Cohen, 2016; Cohen & Nordås, 2014; Meger, 2016). Sexual violence becomes "conflict-related" if it has a connection with armed conflict, such as being committed by actors engaged in war (and related activities) or near a site where it is occurring (United Nations, 2011). Examples include communities under attack or living under occupation, as well as refugee populations fleeing the chaos of battle. Research of wartime experiences has shown a strong correlation between conflict and the number of reported rapes. In addition, women are more likely to be subjected to "extreme war rape" during times of conflict, such as gang rape, torture, or mutilation—crimes that are comparatively rare during peacetime (Cohen, 2016; Farr, 2009).

Statistics on exactly how many women and girls are affected by conflict-related sexual violence are limited, with questionable reliability and validity (Palermo, Bleck, & Peterman, 2014; True, 2015). A cross-sectional study of 24 countries estimated that just 7% of women who had experienced gender-based violence made a formal report of the assault, indicating that most of these crimes go unreported (Palermo et al., 2014). Obtaining accurate data from conflict settings is even more challenging because survivors may fear shame or stigma from their community or reprisals from authority figures (who may have been the perpetrators). In addition, conflict often breaks down traditional institutions such as roads, infrastructure, and courts so that formal reporting may not be possible (Hynes, 2004; Leiby, 2009; True, 2015). Unfortunately, the ubiquity of sexual violence in conflict settings also seems to perpetuate the low report rates, as two common reasons cited by victims for remaining silent were the beliefs that (1) there was no use in reporting and (2) "violence was a normal part of life that women must bear" (Palermo et al., 2014, p. 607).

Despite these challenges, scholars have attempted to calculate the incidence of sexual violence in conflict settings, examining all active conflicts from 1989 to 2009. It was found that although reports of sexual violence did not emerge out of all conflicts, this period experienced 53 violent conflicts with at least one year of "massive" or "numerous" reported rapes of women and girls (Cohen & Nordås, 2014; von Einsiedel, 2014). Both state and non-state actors (e.g., paramilitary or rebel groups) were found to have committed sexual violence; however, state actors represented the majority of reported sexual violence, which is perhaps attributable to rebel groups relying more on the goodwill of civilian populations (and thus relying less on sexual violence as a method of achieving their means) (Cohen, Green, & Wood, 2013). As noted previously, reported assaults likely represent a fraction of actual assaults committed in these conflicts due to a variety of reasons, including shame and a sense that there would be no use reporting (Palermo et al., 2014). Reports of mass sexual violence have come from throughout the world— including countries such as Peru, Indonesia, Columbia, Iraq, Sudan, Cambodia, and Somalia—affecting millions of women (Cohen & Nordås, 2014; Leiby, 2009). In the past few decades alone (Meger, 2016),

estimates suggest as many as 500,000 women [and girls] were raped during the Rwandan genocide, up to 50,000 in Bosnia, some 200,000 women in the Bangladesh liberation war, 250,000 in the Sierra Leonean civil war, and most staggeringly, more than 400,000 women in a single year of the ongoing conflict in eastern Congo. (p. 1)

Also during this same period, approximately 90% of conflicts have been centered in developing countries, meaning the greatest harm has been inflicted on already vulnerable populations (Black, Bouanchaud, Bignall, Simpson, & Gupta, 2014).

In addition to the direct threat of sexual violence by armed combatants, war creates further risk factors that affect the health and safety of women and children. The chaos of war often forces populations to flee their homes and communities. According to the United Nations Children's Fund (UNICEF, 2016), there are currently an estimated 27.4 million refugees globally, with an additional 30 million displaced within their own country. Refugee populations are estimated to comprise 80% women and children, and approximately 20% are women of reproductive age (with 1 in 5 estimated to be pregnant) (Black et al., 2014). The loss of home and community, unfortunately, greatly increases the risk that women will experience sexual violence and be denied access to critical services (e.g., reproductive health services) (Andersson, Kaboru, Adolfsson, & Namegabe, 2015; Black et al., 2014; Hynes, 2004). In addition, scholars have found that conflict not only introduces the risk of assault by armed actors but also increases the risk of sexual violence from civilian perpetrators because rates of intimate partner and intrafamily violence also increase during times of conflict (Wirtz et al., 2014; Wood, 2014).

Although the actual number of women affected by sexual violence in conflict settings is difficult to ascertain, its effects are apparent throughout the world. Sexual violence is both a public health issue and a justice issue that has a major impact on victims at many levels, including increased risk of sexually transmitted disease, traumatic injuries such as fistulas, as well as "depression, post-traumatic stress disorder, anxiety, stigma and social rejection" (Spangaro, Adogo, Zwi, Ranthuugala, & Davies, 2015, p. 2).

HISTORICAL TRENDS

Before describing the conflict in Myanmar, it is important to briefly review the history of sexual violence in wartime. An examination of history indicates that the relationship between war and sexual violence is not a recent phenomenon but, rather, one that has existed for millennia. Mass rapes and sexual assaults against women were recorded in conflicts in Ancient Greece and Rome, by pilgrims and knights during the Crusades, and by soldiers during the American Revolution (Hynes, 2004; Meger, 2016). Unfortunately, although history records that these events happened, until recently very little attention was paid to their scope or consequences. For instance, until the 1990s, victims of war-related sexual violence had no forum under international law to seek justice for the crimes committed against them; thus, most of these crimes have gone unexpiated (Aydelott, 1993; Blair, Gerring, & Karim, 2016; Farwell, 2004). In recent years, feminist scholars have demanded a more thorough accounting of war and its aftermath (Hynes, 2004). These scholars argue that history has ignored sexual violence during war because it often happened to women and was viewed as a natural byproduct of war or simply a domestic issue that did not merit consideration—an omission that these scholars considered to be a reflection of the misogynistic and patriarchal values that they often ascribe as a root cause of such violence (Blair et al., 2016; Hynes, 2004; Meger, 2016; True, 2015). The history of wartime research itself is gendered so that often the important facts, dimensions, and layers of a given conflict do not come to light until decades later, sometimes as the result of powerful state actors (often male) suppressing state-sanctioned policies (Enloe, 2010).

In addition to evaluating the scope of sexual violence in conflict, scholars also debate why sexual violence increases both in frequency and ferocity during times of war (Cohen et al., 2013). Traditionally, leaders and policymakers judged sexual violence by armed combatants to be something that unfortunately happened in the chaos of war—something that led a few "bad apples" (Leiby, 2009, p. 448) to use the mayhem of battleas an excuse to commit sexual crimes against women (Wood, 2006). Feminist scholars later expanded upon this idea, arguing that the sexual violence seen in war was really the manifestation of men's general misogyny toward all women, allowed to be totally expressed in times of war (Brownmiller, 1975; Meger, 2016).

More recent scholarship has criticized both of these theories, asserting that these generalizations do not account for the way that armed actors seem to purposely engage in planned sexual violence in a systemic and organized way to obtain a specific political, military, or economic outcome—in other words, as a weapon of war (Leatherman, 2011; Meger, 2016). The ongoing civil war in the Democratic Republic of Congo provides an example of an economic incentive to use rape in armed conflict, in that armed groups have been accused of purposely using rape to terrorize communities in order to encourage movement away from land rich in natural resources (Meger, 2010). In addition, scholars argue that employing sexual violence can achieve military goals. For instance, the Islamic State in Iraq and Syria (ISIS) has used the promise of sexual slaves as a method to recruit fighters, thus increasing their size and influence (Ahram, 2015). ISIS has also used human trafficking of women and girls as a source of revenue—an example of an additional economic function (Ahram, 2015). Sexual violence can also serve as a way of shaming and demoralizing one's enemies while at the same time creating strong bonds and group cohesion within one's own unit (one particular reason cited for the increased rates of gang rapes during wartime) (Arieff, 2011; Cohen, 2016; Diken & Bagge Lausten, 2005; Farr, 2009). Thus, to these scholars, it is important to examine the various *functions* of sexual violence in conflict zones in order to determine why states and other armed actors directly employ it, or to begin to explain it as a phenomenon at all.

The most recent trend in research on this topic, however, cites flaws in each of the approaches discussed previously, arguing that they present a "homogenized view of sexual violence in conflict [that] obscures the specific social, cultural, political and economic determinants that inform the conflict and give meaning to this violence" (Meger, 2016, p. 2). This theory asserts that citing a broad, philosophical explanation for sexual violence, such as chaos or patriarchal oppression, is inherently flawed because sexual violence does not happen in all conflicts, indicating there are other contributing factors that vary across conflicts. For instance, a review of 48 armed conflicts in Africa between 1989 and 2009—between various types of state, paramilitary, and rebel combatants—found that 64% had no reports of any form of sexual violence, whereas others (e.g., the previously described conflict in Rwanda) had massive numbers of reports (Cohen et al., 2013). However, there are social, political, and logistical factors that may impede on an assult survivor's ability and willingness to report rape or sexual violence, some of which may vary over time during the conflict and these, as previously discussed earlier. There are many factors that might explain a lack of reporting by sexual assault survivors (Wood, 2006).

This more recent body of research and literature also takes issue with labeling conflict-related sexual violence as "a weapon of war." First, it is argued that evidence suggests that conflict-related sexual violence is rarely directly and explicitly ordered by commanders but, rather, is usually a practice that is implicitly tolerated because it is not viewed as worth the cost of its punishment (e.g., the loss of time implicated in the discipline of soldiers and the possible reduction of morale among soldiers) (Cohen et al., 2013; Wood, 2006). Second, it is asserted that focusing on sexual violence as mainly a strategy of war means other, related forms of violence are likewise ignored in policy proposals. Specifically, as mentioned previously, women face increased risks of intimate partner and family violence during times of conflict, an issue that is not addressed in current efforts that depict sexual violence as mainly perpetrated by armed soldiers or rebel forces (Blair et al., 2016; Cohen et al., 2013). As a result, scholars argue, an imperfect understanding of the phenomenon of sexual violence in wartime means current policy interventions cannot adequately address this issue. This text posits that any real change would indeed require policymakers to embrace a viewpoint that accounts for the complex nature of sexual violence across a variety of settings, functions, and actors (Anholt, 2016; Wood, 2006).

MYANMAR (BURMA)

Recent historical trends as they relate to documented wartime sexual violence in Myanmar have roots in the complex ethnic and cultural landscape of this area, which was further complicated by the effects of British colonial rule in relatively recent history. The history of the region now known as Myanmar, prior to British rule (which lasted from 1886 until 1947), was a tale of rising and falling city-states as well as temporarily unifying kingdoms and dynasties set up by the varying ethnic groups that inhabited the Irrawaddy Valley and environs from the time of the earliest human settlements in the region approximately 13,000 years ago (Canadian Friends of Burma, 2016).

When Myanmar emerged as an independent sovereign nation in 1948, it did so in the spirit of the Pang Long Agreement (Women's League of Burma [WLB], 2015b). According to this agreement, Myanmar would exist as a peaceful collective of ethnic states with equal levels of representation and political power (WLB, 2015b). However, soon after obtaining independence, civil war broke out between Myanmar's different ethnic groups as the result of unfair (or, in some cases, nonexistent) representation and political power granted to each of the ethnic minority states on the borderlands (WLB, 2015a). Myanmar currently recognizes 135 different ethnic groups, largely of Rohingya Muslims. The Rohingya are considered and consider themselves to be ethnically Muslim, they speak a Bengali dialect, and they have lived primarily in the northwestern border regions of Myanmar—in or near the Rakhine state. There are additional ethnic minority groups who do not fall under the category of Rohingya, including the Kachin, Shan, Karen, Arakan, Mon, Palaung, Chin, and Karenni (Al Jazeera, 2017a). Civil war mostly took the form of borderland states launching insurgencies in protest against unfair political representation. In order to quell insurgencies launched from the borderlands, the Myanmarese military has maintained a heavy presence in these regions (Saan & Radhakrishnan, 2012).

Amid the fairly continuous presence of the military in the borderlands, complete military junta rule in Myanmar occurred in two sequential episodes between the time that sovereignty was wrested from the United Kingdom in 1947 and the time of Myanmar's first democratic elections in November 2010 (which were organized by the State Peace and Development Council) (Egreteau, 2012). With each rise of the junta, political imprisonment and torture were the consequences that the Myanmarese public faced for participating in any form of protest or demonstration against the junta (Oxford Burma Alliance, 2015). In March 2011, the military junta, which had ruled the country from 1962 to 1974 and again from 1990 to 2008, was formally dissolved (Egreteau, 2012). However, the subsequent election of the heavily military-backed Union Solidarity and Development Party (USDP) added a heavy praetorian element to the new civilian constitutional regime and raised suspicions in Myanmar and within the international arena that the vote was rigged (Egreteau, 2012).

The new civilian constitution of Myanmar was drafted in 2008 and has served as a road map for the sweeping political transitions the country has undergone since the disbandment of the junta (Egreteau, 2012). The civilian constitution set up a decentralized parliament composed of 14 province-based legislatures and made instrumental the military role in governance (Egreteau, 2012). The major political parties of Myanmar are the All Mon Region Democracy Party, the National Democratic Force, the National League for Democracy, the National Unity Party, the Rakhine Nationalities Development Party, the Shan Nationalities Democratic Party, the Shan Nationalities League for Democracy, and the Union Solidarity and Development Party (IndexMundi, 2014a, 2014b). In addition, the new constitution enshrines the eminent position of armed force members in governance by reserving top positions only for those with military experience (effectively barring women from them) and requiring that 25% of parliament be composed of military men (Global Justice Center [GJC], 2013).

RECENT DEVELOPMENTS OF NOTE

Women were only granted the right to vote in Myanmar in 2013 (GJC, 2013). That same year, only 25 of the 440 seats of the lower house (5.7%) and 4 of the 224 seats of the upper house (1.8%) were held by women, for a total of 29 of the 498 elected seats (166 seats are appointed by the military) that make up the Union Parliament (5.8%) (GJC, 2013). These figures placed Myanmar in a tie with Yemen for the lowest percentages of women in upper parliamentary positions in the world (GJC, 2013). As of February 2016, however, the percentage of female members of parliament had more than doubled from 5.8% in 2013 to 13% (International Women's Development Agency, 2016).

However, the women of Myanmar have been institutionally marginalized in the areas of education, political involvement, and religion. The ban against female literacy was lifted in the 1920s when missionaries established coeducational schools (Dassah, 2011). This led to a small but visible increase of women in tertiary education and consequently in medical, legal, political, and journalistic careers (Dassah, 2011). Throughout the turbulent saga of Myanmarese sovereignty, however, women were relegated to a dismally small legislative and political role—a role that was completely wiped out during both phases of military rule (Egreteau, 2012; GJC, 2013). The new civilian constitution more deeply entrenches the institution of political gender inequality by enshrining military dominance in parliament (i.e., male dominance, because women are barred from joining the military) (GJC, 2013). Although the Myanmarese military, as of 2013, has tentatively made it known that women aged 25–30 years are now welcome to enlist (Song, 2013), there will still be a great deal of ground to cover before Myanmarese women come within sight of political parity in Myanmar's deeply praetorian political arena. Last, in the realm of religion, Myanmarese Buddhist women were traditionally barred from being a part of the *sangha* (Buddhist monastery) in any capacity, contributing to their cultural relegation to second-class status as human beings, worthy of significant participation in neither the religious nor the political spheres (Ikeya, 2006).

Despite this, probably the most recognizable face on the international scale in Myanmarese politics is that of Aung San Suu Kyi, the famous female pro-democracy opposition leader, founder of the National League for Democracy Party, and recipient of the Nobel Peace Prize as well as the Mahatma Gandhi Award for Reconciliation and Peace in 2009 (Pillay, 2017). After a decade living as a political prisoner under house arrest, she has now relaxed her position on some fronts in an effort to join forces with Myanmar's leading political players (Pilling, 2011). She was released (and her party authorized) conveniently after the end of Burma's first elections (a time of sweeping political reforms ushered in by the new constitutional regime) so that the National League for Democracy would have no chance of gaining a political foothold (Pilling, 2011).

CURRENT CONDITIONS IN MYANMAR

The conflict in the borderlands of Myanmar has created conditions wherein sexual violence has been employed for a variety of reasons. These border regions have experienced significant conflict for several decades, tracing back to the earliest days of Myanmar's independent sovereignty in the late 1940s, when ethnic minority groups launched insurgencies in the borderlands to protest against their lack of representation (or, in some cases, lack of independent governance) after the first independent governing bodies of Myanmar were formed (Nallu, 2011). Although Burma's military junta was formally dismantled in 2011, the subsequently elected (and heavily military-backed) USDP drafted a new "democratic" constitution that enshrined military dominance in the governing bodies of Burma (Egreteau, 2012). The new "civilian" constitution not only reserves top positions for armed service members (and requires that 25% of the legislature be composed of armed service members) but also places members of the armed forces beyond the purview of the common law (GJC, 2013). While conflicts in Myanmar have created great, and increasing, instability (with hundreds of thousands of internally displaced persons in the Rakhine, Kachin, and Shan states at the time of this writing; Jenssen, 2017), the current political and military situation in the country has increased the power of the military over Myanmarese citizens.

In order to stymie insurrections in the borderlands (which are home to many of Myanmar's ethnic minority groups), the Myanmarese military has maintained a heavy presence in these regions (Saan & Radhakrishnan, 2012). The primary ethnic groups affected are the Kachin, Shan, Karen, Arakan, Mon, Palaung, Chin, Karenni, and Rohingya (Nallu, 2011; Saan & Radhakrishnan, 2012). The communities most affected are the Kachin and the northern Shan states (Cengel, 2014). In the 1990s, human rights groups and Burmese ethnic independence organizations began citing the frequent rapes perpetrated by Myanmarese soldiers against ethnic minority women (Nallu, 2011). Since then, military presence in borderland regions has grown heavier at the same time as people have grown more impoverished due to pipeline, hydroelectric, and mining projects furthering displacement ("Burma's Army," 2014). After rapes began to be documented, one women's rights group documented 81 rapes in 8 months, and in nearly half of these cases the women were also murdered or died from their injuries (Nallu, 2011). The leader of the Shan Women's Action Network recorded 173 episodes of rape or sexual violence involving 625 women just in the Shan state in 2002 (Nallu, 2011). There have been virtually no instances of the rapists facing punitive measures of any kind (Saan & Radhakrishnan, 2012). Leaders of the WLB are convinced that Myanmarese soldiers are not only granted impunity for the rapes of ethnic minority women and girls but also ordered by superior officers to rape (Nallu, 2011). Increasing documentation of these incidences is presenting a clearer picture of the nature of the systematic rapes occurring in the borderlands: Approximately half of the cases are gang rapes, in nearly half of the cases the women are also murdered or die later from their injuries, and the rapes have been happening to girls as young as age 7 years (Kachinland News [KLN], 2014). The majority of these rapes are committed by officers in front of their troops, but all instances are met with impunity (both the rapes committed by officers and those committed by lower ranking men) (Saan & Radhakrishnan, 2012). According to some civilian reports, the soldiers (both officers and lower ranking men) usually enter villages or internally displaced persons camps and inform villagers they have been ordered to rape (Saan & Radhakrishnan, 2012).

Approximately 140,000 Rohingya currently live in internment camps in Myanmar, which they are not allowed to leave without government permission (Al Jazeera, 2017a), and between 600,000 and 700,000 Rohingya refugees (mostly women and children) have fled to overcrowded refugee camps in Bangladesh in order to escape the constant threat of rape and violence (GlobalGiving Foundation, 2018). United Nations (UN) officials state that the situation is beginning to increasingly resemble a full-scale genocide. As of August 2017, nearly 300 villages have been burnt to the ground in the Rakhine state as part of Myanmar's "clearance operations." The exodus of Rohingya and other ethnic minority groups since the fall of 2017 is now being called by the UN the "world's fastest growing crisis" (BBC News, 2018). At the time of this writing, the situation is rapidly evolving and escalating in a number of ways (both in terms of renewed insurgencies sparking brutal Myanmarese military counter-attacks and in terms of the growing scale of the exodus, with the Rohingya and other ethnic groups stateless and not welcome in either country—Bangladesh or Myanmar). The situation currently bears hallmarks of classic ethnic cleansing operations, and it is not possible for the present tract of writing to be entirely up to date at the time of publication due to the ongoing development of the situation. For that reason, the *nature* of the sexual violence that has been (and continues to be) implemented by the junta on a sweeping scale is explored in more depth for the example it provides of the nature of wartime sexual violence in general.

The use of sexual violence in Myanmar likely serves several functions. A primary function is often economic benefit to perpetrators. In some instances, women in the borderlands are drugged, beaten, kidnapped, and forced to live among the Myanmarese army battalions cooking and cleaning during the day, thereby providing a source of free labor, and subjected to gang rapes at night (Saan & Radhakrishnan, 2012). In addition, sex trafficking of refugees in this area has been reported along the Myanmarese–Thai border, another example of an economic motive to sexually exploit women and children (Bastick, Grimm, & Kunz, 2007). The Shan Human Rights Foundation and the Shan Women's Action Network released the first report in 2002 documenting rapes perpetrated by the Myanmarese army against ethnic minority women with a frequency that bespoke systematization, even though rapes of this sort had been documented since 1993 (Saan & Radhakrishnan, 2012).

Sexual violence also serves political and military objectives because rape has been used as a counter-insurgency tool meant to suppress ethnic populations (Bastick et al., 2007). It is thought that systematic rapes are employed as a military strategy to discourage resistance against the government by weakening the cultural fabric of ethnic groups in the borderlands as well as to terrorize them and encourage their removal from the land (Nallu, 2011). When one considers that girls as young as age 7 years have been raped, that soldiers have been reported to enter villages and inform people that they have been ordered to rape, and that the victims of gang rape in these scenarios are often mutilated and brutally murdered (KLN, 2014), one can only imagine the level of constant terror inflicted upon the inhabitants of Myanmar's borderlands.

Furthermore, transnational feminism considers conflict-related mass rapes to inflict collective trauma on the communities in which they occur. The women who have been raped sustain severe psychological trauma and are often socially ostracized as the result of having been raped, which amounts to the removal of the vitality and strength that psychologically healthy women bring to their communities. Men whose wives, sisters, or daughters were raped are humiliated and emasculated by the fact that it occurred and they were unable or unwilling to stop it (men who attempt to intervene in conflict-related rapes of their kin are often killed).

LOOKING TO THE FUTURE

The grassroots movements aimed at shedding more light on the rapes that have been occurring in the borderlands (sparked by brave women such as Galau, mentioned previously) contributed to the rapist of a 7-year-old girl being successfully brought to justice (Cengel, 2014). The victim of the rape immediately told her mother, who then galvanized local community support in bringing the soldier to the local police station. The soldier was transferred into the custody of the military police, and then the case went cold and nothing happened for weeks. The local community responded by stirring pastors, journalists, activists, politicians, and other professionals into action on behalf of the girl. Eventually, a trial was held in civilian court, and the rapist was sentenced to lifetime imprisonment—the first trial and the first conviction of its kind in Myanmar (Cengel, 2014).

In most cases of rape in the ethnic minority territories and in camps for internally displaced persons in the borderlands, however, there are no structures in place for women to report or act as witnesses to rapes and other crimes. Sometimes, women who report or act as witnesses to rapes receive death threats from other community members or run the risk of fomenting a violent response from their own family members (Kelly, 2016). For this reason, many of the cases that have come to light in as much detail as the one described previously are anomalies in the landscape of silence and shame surrounding the vast majority of rapes in the borderlands. The combination of the shame felt by victims and the impunity enjoyed by soldiers creates a legal and cultural vacuum within which rape continues to be used unabated as a weapon of war.

Figure 16.3 Protests against Aung San Suu Kyi and what many perceive to be the ethnic cleansing of the Muslim Rohingya people.

It is unclear exactly why the case of the 7-year-old girl was a success while so many countless others have vanished into obscurity in legal indictment processes and community memory. Perhaps when the brutal rape of women is a constant threat and an imminent local reality and no legal action is taken on behalf of the victims, gender violence becomes normalized and thus accepted by both victim and perpetrator. Marginalized communities of largely internally displaced persons with little economic or political resources also face challenges related to access to courts, attorneys, and lawmakers, and they may be geographically removed from areas where such crimes could even be reported. These challenges may make the task of even beginning to know how to address the issue seem too monumental to undertake. It is unclear if the case of the 7-year-old girl will remain an anomaly, the one citable case wherein the crime of rape (perpetrated by a soldier against a civilian) intersected with the crime of child sexual abuse, such that a compelling case for indictment could finally be made and sufficient community support could be rallied to bring the soldier to justice on both counts. Whatever the variables at play, this was the first instance of a soldier being divested of impunity for sexual crimes against ethnic minority communities in Myanmar.

On the national level in Myanmar, the WLB launched its Women Against Violence Program in 2005 (WLB, 2015). This program brings people together in Myanmar's rural and ethnic communities to have open discussions about issues of violence against women as well as ways that this scourge can be brought to an end (WLB, 2015). Every year, 3000–4000 men and women attend the open forums. For many, it is the first time that issues such as domestic violence are discussed in public (WLB, 2015). The program also connects victims of gender-based violence to practical services that help them overcome the basic physical and psychological repercussions of their victimization (WLB, 2015). It has set up safe houses in New Delhi, India, and in Thailand for domestic violence survivors (WLB, 2015). Another important goal of the program is to raise awareness of patterns of violence against women in Myanmar via visual media and the promotion of Stop Violence Against Women Day and International Women's Day (WLB, 2015). It also promotes the careful documentation of women's rape and violence experiences in Myanmar (including a Convention on the Elimination of All Forms of Discrimination Against Women shadow report in 2008) (WLB, 2015).]

Interestingly, since the fall of 2017, when the level of violence perpetrated by Myanmarese law enforcement and military officials began to escalate in the borderlands (mostly the Rakhine state), national leader Aung San Suu Kyi has been criticized by UN officials and international leaders for her silence on the issue. A UN special envoy on sexual violence in conflict, Pramila Patten, claimed that at a meeting with government officials, Suu Kyi "avoided" discussion on ethnic cleansing of the Rohingya (McPherson, 2017). Furthermore, Gandhi's granddaughter and peace activist, Ela Gandhi, as well as South African Anglican cleric and human rights activist, Archbishop Desmond Tutu, have both implored Suu Kyi to show the same courage in leadership that she has shown in the past by speaking out about ethnic cleansing of the Rohingya and by leveraging all of her power to put an end to the ethnic cleansing (Pillay, 2017). Suu Kyi did make public comments in September 2017 regarding the Rohingya crisis, stating that she "feels deeply" with regard to the suffering of "all people" and that she condemns "all human rights violations" (Al Jazeera, 2017b).

On the international level, the International Campaign to Stop Rape and Gender Violence in Conflict (SRGV) recognizes that rape is systematically used as a means to inflict terror and erode the social fabric of communities (SRGV, 2015). It also recognizes that the perpetrators often enjoy impunity for these acts of sexual violence in conflict, whereas survivors experience stigma within their communities (SRGV, 2015). SRGV proposes a three-pronged approach to addressing and expunging this ongoing international human rights atrocity: protection, prevention, and prosecution.

The *protection* pillar of the campaign seeks to address factors that increase the likelihood of re-victimization (SRGV, 2015). According to this pillar, victims should be referred to basic psychological and medical services in order to avoid being re-victimized, and data should be collected on the impact of protective measures so that improvements are made where necessary and effective protective practices are continued (SRGV, 2015).

Regarding the *prevention* of rape in conflict, SRGV (2015) recognizes that major overhauls are needed within the military cultures of its four target countries. It is the responsibility of the governments of these countries to recognize the severity of the problem and launch initiatives to end it as well as to ensure that their armies are trained at every level to respect and uphold human rights. Because this is not currently taking place, victims are often left vulnerable and are then re-victimized (SRGV, 2015). The organization asserts that if militaries are properly outfitted and trained to do so, they have the power and capacity to stop rape rather than perpetuate it (SRGV, 2015).

The *prosecution* pillar seeks to address the amnesty granted to perpetrators of rape in conflict zones (SRGV, 2015). Although cases of rape in conflict zones have been brought before local and national courts as well as international criminal tribunals in recent years, the legal culture of many of these conflict zones is such that there are many barriers to victims of rape achieving legal redress (SRGV, 2015). Therefore, justice systems need to be reformed to the extent necessary to bring perpetrators of these crimes to justice and to protect civilian women from continuing to be victimized (SRGV, 2015).

In addition to the efforts of the SRGV and the WLB, the GJC, Burma Campaign UK, Women Under Siege Project, and Amnesty International have launched targeted initiatives to document instances of militarized rape in Myanmar and to protect victims and prosecute perpetrators. On the local, grassroots level, the Kachin Independence Organization, the Gender Development Initiative, the Shan Women's Action Network, and the Shan Human Rights Foundation have been formed by concerned Myanmarese citizens to address issues of wartime gender violence and other human rights atrocities in Myanmar.

Because the UN considers international criminal law to override any form of amnesty granted at the national or state level for war crimes, crimes against humanity, genocide, or any other major violations of international humanitarian law, the kind of impunity granted to Myanmarese soldiers for borderland rapes is forbidden by international law (Gaeta, 2014). So, in the case of rape as a military strategy, it appears that the deliverance of justice hinges upon the definitions of "crimes against humanity" and "war crimes." However, the Rome Statute of the ICC (2002) already recognizes rape as a war crime *and* as a crime against humanity. Furthermore, Article 27 of the Fourth Geneva Convention does consider rape to be a "war crime" and a "grave breach" of the clauses contained therein. In addition, there is a growing body of international treaty law requiring that states investigate and offer up for extradition any individuals guilty of a grave breach of any of the four Geneva Conventions of 1949 (Saan & Radhakrishnan, 2012). Despite this growing body of international law, no state has yet been held accountable for the use of rape as a weapon of war (GJC, 2013).

Why is this? It should be the case that rape's constitution of a grave breach of the statutes of the Geneva Convention (when used as a weapon of war) implicates "universal jurisdiction"—that is, it is incumbent upon all nations to do everything within their power to bring the perpetrators of this war crime to justice (Penn & Nardos, 2003). An actual *enactment* of the Rome Statute would go a long way to begin to bring the perpetrators of systematic military rape in Myanmar to justice—this would grant international criminal courts post factum administration of justice dating back to July 1, 2002, when the statute was passed (Saan & Radhakrishnan, 2012).

That rape is being used as a weapon of war is undisputed by international legal experts, military experts, international crime tribunals, global civil society, and governments (GJC, 2012). In 1993, the International Criminal Tribunal for the Former Yugoslavia declared rape directed against a civilian population in armed conflict to be a crime against humanity (along with the crimes of torture and genocide) (UN, 2015). This was also the case with the 1994 International Criminal Tribunal for Rwanda, which included rape as a crime of genocide (UN, 2015). There have also been multiple UN Security Council resolutions throughout the years (namely 1820, 1888, and 1960; GJC, 2012) aimed at protecting girls and women from rape in armed conflict and from sexual exploitation in general (UN, 2015). The consensus of the Security Council is that rape is indeed a tactic of war and that it is a threat to international security (United Nations Human Rights, 2015). Despite international legal recognition of the contemptibility of rape as a weapon of war, for the most part, international legal action remains to be taken (GJC, 2012).

The president of Myanmar, Thein Sein, has publicly pledged his commitment to the advancement and protection of women as well as to a UK-led oath to end militarized rape; however, he has made no moves to back up this pledge, and nothing has changed for Myanmarese women ("Burma's Army," 2014). Penn and Nardos (2003) assert that the *legal culture* of a nation or a people has to change before a proliferation of new laws (or, in this case, public announcements of commitment to new initiatives) can make any difference in the lives of women who are oppressed and/or sexually abused. The same is the case with reference to international laws that condemn rape and other forms of sexual exploitation. The proliferation of these kinds of international laws is a step in the right direction, but real change will not occur until the cultural values underlying the perpetuation of rape are changed. Currently, women are stigmatized and shunned for being raped in most countries, whereas in most cases perpetrators enjoy amnesty from such punitive social sequestration (UN, 2015). If a prescription could possibly be offered for how this state of affairs *should* be rearranged, it would seem to make more sense for things to be the other way around.

Often, a reliable entryway into the collective psychology around a cultural institution (even a tragic cultural institution such as rape) is the subtle way that things are commonly worded. Although the Geneva Convention recognizes rape as an international crime, it is listed as a crime against honor rather than a crime of violence (Penn & Nardos, 2003). There is currently a movement to recognize rape not as a crime of honor but, rather, as a crime of violence and as a form of torture—an important distinction because this would deepen the security of its current placement within the realm of war crime and crime against humanity (Penn & Nardos, 2003). Recognition of the brutal violence, the terror, and the torture that are implicated within the rape experience of women not only in the borderlands of Myanmar but also anywhere rape is wielded as a weapon of war might inspire more urgency on the international legal front to uphold the human rights statutes that have been signed into law. Forensic images and war photography depicting the victims of these crimes are not for the faint of heart but are testament to the worthiness of wartime rape to be elevated to the category of torture in the international mind, especially when victims have no way of knowing how long the rape will last (i.e., how many perpetrators there will be), whether and how they will be injured or mutilated, or whether they will die as the result of the ordeal and in what manner.

Such a distinction would surely further the cause of women's organizations in Myanmar that are attempting to mobilize an international investigation into the practices of the Myanmarese military. Because the Rome Statute of the ICC (2002) recognizes systematic rape as a war crime and a crime against humanity, the WLB is attempting to put launch an international investigation into some of the practices of the Myanmarese military with regard to Myanmar's ethnic minorities—practices such as forced labor and forced removal, as well as the torture, rape, and murder of women (Nallu, 2011). In addition, part of the GJC's platform to eliminate barriers to the true introduction of democracy to Myanmar and the vindication of some of the grave human rights abuses that continue to take place there is to have rape internationally recognized as a weapon of war (GJC, 2012). International treaty law may put it in writing, but until international recognition is achieved and the public consciousness is changed on these issues, international human rights litigation will do nothing to impede the next raid on a borderlands village.

In addition to the role of international consciousness in the perpetuation or elimination of this problem, it could be that the historically institutionalized exclusion of women from political processes in Myanmar contributes to the sustainment of issues of violence against women within its borders. Myanmar consistently has one of the lowest percentages of women in high-ranking government positions among all Southeast Asian countries and the world ("Burma's Army," 2014; GJC, 2013). The paucity of politically powerful women in Myanmar may contribute to the lack of effort to mobilize initiatives on behalf of what might be considered a "women's issue." However, the percentage of female members of parliament in Myanmar has more than doubled (up to 13%) since women were granted the right to vote in 2013. In addition, the Myanmarese female political anomaly, Aung Saan Su Kyi, who was formerly less vocal on the matter, has begun to speak out as an advocate for justice on behalf of Myanmarese ethnic minority victims of militarized rape ("Burma's Army," 2014). Furthermore, despite the culture of silence and shame surrounding rape in Burma, more victims in the Kachin and other borderland states are beginning to speak up about their experiences. The growing decibel of public discourse on this issue continues to fuel community and organizational support for bringing the perpetrators of systematic rape to justice—a trend that appears to have been sparked by the watershed event of the 7-year-old girl's rapist being extradited and sentenced to life imprisonment (Cengel, 2014).

CONCLUSION

Despite the seemingly crushing grip of military rule in Myanmar, the struggle for democracy and human rights continues. The rise of internationally renowned pro-democracy leader, Aung San Suu Kyi, to the political forefront and the pro-democracy demonstrations inspired by her were followed by a violent reassertion of military dominance and mass killings (Pilling, 2011). Although her election to public office in the first democratic elections resulted in her being placed under house arrest for 10 years (Pilling, 2011), she continued to inspire the struggle for democracy and human rights from within the confines of her home. She continues to do so now in the political forum (Pilling, 2011).

The Myanmarese army's noncompliance with Section 1820 of the Security Council Resolution has been recognized on the international front (SRGV, 2015). It is the iron stronghold of the junta that prevents lasting and successful change efforts and/or the complete eradication of rape as a weapon of war in the borderlands. If there is nothing that can be done on the international front to peacefully bring democracy to Myanmar (i.e., to expunge military rule), then something needs to be done to change the military culture of rape with impunity. Perhaps Myanmar's military leaders should be tried before international criminal tribunals and held responsible for internationally recognized war crimes until the military as a whole is forced to recognize and comply with Section 1820, as well as to train armed service members to comply with it.

Additional funding for grassroots organizations (possibly via their connection to larger campaigns such as SRGV), such as the one that succeeded in convicting the rapist of a 7-year-old girl and the ones that first brought systematized military rape in Myanmar to the national and international consciousness via careful documentation of occurrences of rape, could serve as a major injection of power and means for the forces that are already acting on behalf of ethnic minority women in the borderlands of Myanmar. In this situation, as in so many others, there is a general paucity of economic and political motivation for individuals in positions of power to address the issue (Bunch, 2008), and this needs to change.

Perhaps another avenue by which these systematic crimes could be brought to an end would be for a re-emergence of respect for the Pang Long Agreement to take place. This may sound idealistic. But what has been the reason for insurgencies launched by Myanmar's ethnic minority groups? They do not believe they are fairly represented within the governing bodies of the country. Perhaps peace talks and peace agreements can be made with these groups, giving them what they want (political representation) in exchange for an agreement not to launch insurgencies. It is likely that agreements of this sort would only be possible after the victory of Myanmar's current struggle for democracy. So the emergence of democracy in Myanmar would not only play an instrumental role in ending human rights atrocities within the country but also eliminate the factors that inspire insurgencies in the borderlands and, thus, the only political motivation for systematized rape in those regions.

DISCUSSION QUESTIONS

1. How is the resiliency of women both harnessed and targeted (as in the case of mass rapes committed by armed actors in "enemy" communities) in times of war?

2. Consider the difference between an *enactment* of international law and an *implementation* of international law. What impedes the implementation of international law as it relates to war crimes? Consider logistical, cultural, and institutional barriers.

3. How does the political empowerment of women (especially in countries in which women are institutionally disenfranchised and disempowered) impact the issue of sharply increased gender violence in times of war?

REFERENCES

Ahram, A. I. (2015). Sexual violence and the making of ISIS. *Survival, 57*(3), 57–78.

Al Jazeera. (2017a, March 14). *Myanmar: Major ethnic groups and where they live.* Retrieved from aljazeera.com/indepth/interactive/2017/03/myanmar-major-ethnic-groups-live-170309143208539.html" https://www.aljazeera.com/indepth/interactive/2017/03/myanmar-major-ethnic-groups-live-170309143208539.html

Al Jazeera. (2017b, September 19). *Aung San Suu Kyi condemns "all human rights violations."* Retrieved from https://www.aljazeera.com/news/2017/09/aung-san-suu-kyi-condemns-human-rights-violations-170919034711821.html

Andersson, G., Kaboru, B. B., Adolfsson, A., & Namegabe, E. N. (2015). Health workers' assessment of the frequency of and caring for urinary and fecal incontinence among female victims of sexual violence in the eastern Congo: An exploratory study. *Open Journal of Nursing, 5,* 354–360.

Anholt, R. M. (2016). Understanding sexual violence in armed conflict: Cutting ourselves with Occam's razor. *Journal of International Humanitarian Action, 1*(6), 1–10.

Arieff, A. (2011). Sexual violence in African conflicts. *Current Politics and Economics of Africa, 4*(2), 351.

Aydelott, D. (1993). Mass rape during war: Prosecuting Bosnian rapists under international law. *Emory International Law Review, 7*, 585–631.

Bastick, M., Grimm, K., & Kunz, R. (2007). *Sexual violence in armed conflict: Global overview and implications for the security sector.* Geneva, Switzerland: SRO Kundig.

BBC News. (2018, April 24). *Myanmar Rohingya: What you need to know about the crisis.* Retrieved from https://www.google.com/amp/s/www.bloc.com/news/amp/world-asia-41566561

Black, B. O., Bouanchaud, P. A., Bignall, J. K., Simpson, E., & Gupta, M. (2014). Reproductive health during conflict. *The Obstetrician & Gynaecologist, 16*(3), 153–160.

Blair, A. H., Gerring, N., & Karim, S. (2016). *Ending sexual and gender-based violence in war and peace: Recommendations for the next U.S. administration.* Washington, DC: United States Institute of Peace.

Brownmiller, S. (1975). *Against our will: Men, women and rape.* New York, NY: Simon & Schuster.

Bunch, C. (2008). Feminist quandaries on gender and violence: Agency, universality, and human security. In S. Bahun-Radunovic & V. G. J. Rajan (Eds.), *Violence and gender in the globalized world: The intimate and the extimate* (pp. 9–13). Burlington, VT: Ashgate.

Burma's army uses rape to demoralize ethnic minorities, report says. (2014). *The Guardian.* Retrieved from http://www.theguardian.com/global-development/2014/nov/25/burma-army-rape-ethnic-minorities

Canadian Friends of Burma. (2016). *History of Burma.* Retrieved from http://www.cfob.org/history

Cengel, K. (2014). Rape is a weapon in Burma's Kachin state, but the women of Kachin are fighting back. *Time.* Retrieved from http://time.com/6429/burma-rape-in-kachin

Cohen, D. K. (2016). *Rape during civil war.* Ithaca, NY: Cornell University Press.

Cohen, D. K., Green, A. H., & Wood, E. J. (2013). *Wartime sexual violence: Misconceptions, implications, and ways forward.* Washington, DC: United States Institute of Peace.

Cohen, D. K., & Nordås, R. (2014). *Sexual violence in armed conflict dataset.* Retrieved October 16, 2016, from http://www.sexualviolencedata.org

Dassah, M. O. (2011). Refiguring women, colonialism and modernity in Burma. *Journal of International Women's Studies, 12*(4), 148–152. Retrieved from http://vc.bridgew.edu/cgi/viewcontent.cgi?article=1134&context=jiws

Diken, B., & Bagge Lausten, C. (2005). Becoming abject: Rape as a weapon of war. *Body & Society, 11*(1), 111–128.

Egreteau, R. (2012). Burma/Myanmar. *Political Insight, 3*(2), 30–33. doi:10.1111/j.2041-9066.2012.00110.x

Enloe, C. (2010). Eight women, one war. In *Nimo's war, Emma's war* (pp. 1–16). Berkeley, CA: University of California Press.

Farr, K. (2009). Extreme war rape in today's civil-war-torn states: A contextual and comparative analysis. *Gender Issues, 26*, 1–41.

Farwell, N. (2004). War rape: New conceptualizations and responses. *Afillia, 19*(4), 389–403. doi:10.1177/0886109904268868

Gaeta, P. (2014year). War crimes and other international 'core' crimes. In A. Clapham & P. Gaeta (Eds.), *The Oxford handbook of international law in armed conflict* (pp. 737–765). Oxford, United Kingdom: Oxford University Press.

Global Justice Center. (2013). *The gender gap and women's political power in Myanmar/Burma.* Retrieved from http://globaljusticecenter.net/documents/Gender%20Gap%20in%20Burma%20(Timeline).pdf

GlobalGiving Foundation. (2018). *Rescue a Rohingya refugee family.* Retrieved from https://www.globalgiving.org/projects/rescue-a-rohingya-refugee-family

Hynes, H. P. (2004, December). On the battlefield of women's bodies: An overview of the harm of war to women. *Women's Studies International Forum, 27*(5), 431–445.

Ikeya, C. (2006). The "traditional" high status of women in Burma: A historical reconsideration. *Journal of Burma Studies, 10,* 51–81. doi:10.1353/jbs.2005.0003

IndexMundi. (2014a). *Burma demographics profile.* Retrieved from http://www.index-mundi.com/burma/demographics_profile.html

IndexMundi. (2014b). *Burma political parties and leaders.* Retrieved from http://www.indexmundi.com/burma/political_parties_and_leaders.html

International Criminal Court. (2002). *Rome statute.* Retrieved from http://www.icc-cpi.int/nr/rdonlyres/ea9aeff7-5752-4f84-be94-0a655eb30e16/0/rome_statute_english.pdf

International Women's Development Agency. (2016, February 1). *Women MPs doubled in Myanmar's new look parliament.* Retrieved from https://www.iwda.org.au/women-mps-doubled-in-myanmars-new-look-parliament

Jenssen, T. (2017, July 15). *The faces of Myanmar's internally displaced.* Al Jazeera. Retrieved from https://www.aljazeera.com/indepth/features/2017/07/faces-myanmar-internally-displaced-170711090042972.html

Kachinland News. (2014). Burmese army soldiers raping ethnic women with impunity. *Kachinland News.* Retrieved from http://kachinlandnews.com/?p=24092

Kelly, N. (2016). *Kachin's civilians: From violence to hopelessness.* Aljazeera. Retrieved from https://www.aljazeera.com/indepth/features/2016/07/kachin-civilians-violence-hopelessness-160731122826184.html

Leatherman, J. (2011). *Sexual violence and armed conflict.* Malden, MA: Polity Press.

Leiby, M. L. (2009). Wartime sexual violence in Guatemala and Peru. *International Studies Quarterly, 53,* 445–468.

McPherson, P. (2017, December 27). Aung San Suu Kyi "avoided" discussion of Rohingya rape during UN meeting. *The Guardian.* Retrieved from https://www.theguardian.com/world/2017/dec/27/aung-san-suu-kyi-avoided-discussion-of-rohingya-during-un-meeting

Meger, S. (2010). Rape of the Congo: Understanding sexual violence in conflict in the Democratic Republic of Congo. *Journal of Contemporary African Studies, 28*(2), 119–135.

Meger, S. (2016). *Rape loot pillage: The political economy of sexual violence in armed conflict.* New York, NY: Oxford University Press.

Nallu, P. (2011, December 9). *Burma: Rape used as military weapon.* Inter Press Service. Retrieved from http://search.proquest.com.libproxy2.usc.edu/docview/910114771?accountid=14749

Oxford Burma Alliance. (2015). *Education in Burma.* Retrieved from http://www.oxford-burmaalliance.org/education-in-burma.html

Palermo, T., Bleck, J., & Peterman, A. (2014). Tip of the iceberg: Reporting and gender-based violence in developing countries. *American Journal of Epidemiology, 179*(5), 602–612.

Penn, M. L., & Nardos, R. (2003). Culture, traditional practices and gender-based violence. In W. S. Hatcher & M. K. Radpour (Eds.), *Overcoming violence against women and girls: The international campaign to eradicate a worldwide problem* (pp. 87–102). Lanham, MD: Rowman & Littlefield.

Pillay, T. (2017, September 11). Gandhi's granddaughter calls for Myanmar leader to act on genocide. *Times LIVE.* Retrieved from https://www.timeslive.co.za/news/world/

2017-09-11-gandhis-granddaughter-echoes-plea-for-myanmar-leader-to-act-on-ethnic-cleansing

Pilling, D. (2011, January 29). Aung San Suu Kyi. *Financial Times*. Retrieved from http://go.galegroup.com/ps/i.do?id=GALE%7CA247811194&v=2.1&u=usocal_main&it=r&p=AONE&sw=w&asid=8b48ff10ab24c8f29fe6a3c47188adff

Saan, P. P., & Radhakrishnan, A. (2012, March 15). *License to rape: How Burma's military employs systematic sexualized violence.* Women's Media Center. Retrieved from http://www.womensmediacenter.com/women-under-siege/license-to-rape-how-burmas-military-employs-systematic-sexualized-violence

Shan Human Rights Foundation/Shan Women's Action Network. (2002, May 1). *License to rape: The Burmese military regime's use of sexual violence in the ongoing war in Shan State.* Retrieved from https://www.peacewomen.org/node/89660

Song, S. (2013). Myanmar's military now recruiting women for the first time in history. *International Business Times*. Retrieved from http://www.ibtimes.com/myanmars-military-now-recruiting-women-first-time-history-1441700

Spangaro, J., Adogu, C., Zwi, A. B., Ranmuthugala, G., & Davies, G. P. (2015). Mechanisms underpinning interventions to reduce sexual violence in armed conflict: A realist-informed systematic review. *Conflict and Health, 9*(1), 1–14.

The International Campaign to Stop Rape and Gender Violence in Conflict. (2015). *Join now.* Retrieved from http://www.stoprapeinconflict.org

The International Campaign to Stop Rape and Gender Violence in Conflict. (2015d). *Stop rape in conflict.* Retrieved from http://www.stoprapeinconflict.org/learn

The International Campaign to Stop Rape and Gender Violence in Conflict. (2015e). *Stop rape in Burma.* Retrieved from http://www.stoprapeinconflict.org/burma

United Nations. (2011). *UN action against sexual violence in conflict: Analytical & conceptual framing of conflict-related sexual violence.* Retrieved June 15, 2014, from http://www.stoprapenow.org

United Nations. (2015). *Background information on sexual violence used as a tool of war.* Retrieved from https://www.un.org/en/preventgenocide/rwanda/about.shtml

United Nations Children's Fund. (2016, October 27). *Patterns in conflict, civilians are now the target.* Retrieved from http://www.unicef.org/graca/patterns.htm

United Nations Human Rights. (2015). *Rape: Weapon of war.* Retrieved from http://www.ohchr.org/en/newsevents/pages/rapeweaponwar.aspx

Von Einsiedel, S. (2014). *Major recent trends in violent conflict* [Occasional paper]. New York, NY: United Nations University Centre for Policy Research.

World Bank. (2015a). *Labor force, female (% of total labor force).* Retrieved from http://data.worldbank.org/indicator/SL.TLF.TOTL.FE.ZS

World Bank. (2015b). *School enrollment, primary (gross), gender parity index (GPI).* Retrieved from http://data.worldbank.org/indicator/SE.ENR.PRIM.FM.ZS

Women's League of Burma. (2015a). *About us.* Retrieved from https://www.womenofburma.org/background

Women's League of Burma. (2015b). *Women against violence.* Retrieved from http://womenofburma.org

Wood, E. J. (2006). Variation in Sexual Violence during War. *Politics and Society, 34*(3), 307–342.

Wood, E. J. (2014). Conflict-related sexual violence and the policy implications of recent research. *International Review of the Red Cross, 96*(894), 457–478.

PART IV

Intimate Partner Violence

Introduction: To Always Believe in Possibility and to Always Believe in the Power of Change

IRON ■

veryone holds their own secrets; mine began when I hit puberty. My secret made me feel like I was suspended between childhood and adulthood until I turned age 30 years and my secret had to be told. My secret is about my body and gender. I realized I was different from other kids from primary school. I was a people person, I was generous, and I had all kinds of hobbies and friends. Generally, I had a good and happy childhood. But the whole time, I kept a secret that I did not tell anyone. To begin with, I did not accept my identity as a woman. Second, I am a non-hetero. These feelings made me feel "abnormal" or that I would die alone because I would not fit in the narrative that Chinese society writes. In China, a girl's success and future are centered on being able to marry a good man.

In this section, you will read about how women have found themselves stuck between society's norms and their own convictions to fight for their voices. Chapter 17 outlines the fate of girls in Kyrgyzstan and how patriarchal customs are experienced and enforced on women. Chapter 18 details China's slow response to domestic violence and how advocates are beginning to change the cultural views despite the politics that endorse violence within marriages. Chapter 19, also based in Chinese society, describes the lesbian experience and how violence within same sex relationships is a hidden epidemic. Chapter 20 outlines the global issue of cults and the sexual and psychological toll they take on women in the United States. Chapter 21 ethnologically studies Trinidad and Tobago and the prominence of violence against women in society. Chapter 22 is focused on hope and change, showcasing how women can empower themselves and create opportunities for other women. Finally, Chapter 23 outlines prostitution and its close connection to US military bases throughout the world. All of these chapters involve intimate violence, targeted not just at gender but also at sexuality and second-class rights that First World and Third World nations condone. Each chapter also describes the fight against these acts of intimate violent and how women are rising up to change the foundation of the culture.

My own awakening into changing my Chinese cultural legacy was on my first day in college. That day, a professor said, "We can't change the society, we can only change who we are to adapt to it." I strongly disagreed and began to seek out my own knowledge. I often skipped class to read books at the library, such as Li Yinhe's work, *Subculture of Homosexuality* and *Queer Theory*. I sought my own world of identity. I began to see the person I was meant to be: a feminine pansexual being who champions diversity and inclusiveness. I formed a network with left-leaning young scholars, activists and artists, anarchists and Marxists throughout the world. Although I did not fully understand or agree with all of them, it set me on my path to make the world better.

I was cast in a play called *Vagina Monologues* and I was asked to play a lesbian. It was the first time that a lesbian character was ever presented to the public in Wuhan, China. During the show, someone stood up and debated with me, and in that moment I realized the importance of advocacy and sex education. I became involved in the feminist and LGBT movement. In 2010, I orchestrated street advocacy called "Smile 4 Gay" in Wuhan. People contacted me from social media and persuaded me to form a Wuhan-based LGBT group. In August 2010, Wuhan Rainbow was founded. The creation of this organization led to many experiences. It was the first time I met people with different gender identities and sexual orien-tations. It was the first time I found a place to discuss my confusion regarding my own body and gender and the challenges that people with different gender identi-ties and sexual orientations face. For the first time, I felt the existence and power of the community. Within a year, Wuhan Rainbow became a household name within national LGBT organizations.

After all these years, I eventually realized that my lack of self-acceptance of female identity is not about me being a transgender; it is about not knowing that females can choose their own life and start their own career. There are still people out there denied of who they are because of their gender. My job is to be who I am and empower more people to accept and be who they are. To always believe in possibility and to always believe in power of change—that is my philosophy.

This section embodies that philosophy. The stories presented in the chapters in this section are deeply intimate, but all involve rebellion—a woman who will not accept the status quo. Together, women throughout the world must unite to fight for a seat at the patriarchal table. Together, we create our culture of acceptance and opportunity.

17

Domestic Violence in Kyrgyzstan

Finding a Voice of Strength and Empowerment

SALTANAT CHILDRESS, ELIZABETH M. APARICIO,
AND JILL T. MESSING ∎

CASE STUDY: ASEM

> I was rapidly calling my Mom, "Mom, hurry, my husband is going to kill me with an ax!" She didn't have quite the reaction I expected. She had such a tone as if it was my own fault, "Well, men are men, they get angry!"
>
> —Asem

Imagine living in a cultural and social context that expects complete obedience and compliance from a woman once married, regardless of whether or not her husband is abusive. This was Asem's daily reality. One summer several years ago, Asem (aged 37 years) finally sought help in the shelter in Bishkek (the capital of Kyrgyzstan) after a lifetime of abuse in order to get divorced. Not only was she being physically, sexually, and verbally abused by her husband but also both his family and her family refused her pleas for assistance. Soon after she finally escaped him, Asem's husband committed suicide by hanging. His relatives had berated him repeatedly, telling him that because he did not have male children, they would not transfer the family property to his or his daughters' names. He hung himself because he could not stand the psychological pressure and derision of his relatives regarding the lack of male children.

Asem described the series of events that led to her escape from continuous physical and emotional abuse by both her husband and his family and, eventually, to her husband's death. Her story illustrates a set of cultural and social barriers that trap women in abusive circumstances. Asem's story is tragic because she was only able to seek help after decades of physical, emotional, and sexual abuse and bride kidnapping.[1].

Options for exiting abusive family situations, such as escaping to a shelter, are very few in Kyrgyzstan. Women seek help from shelters as a final and extreme solution.

In this chapter, we use Asem's story to illustrate the social and cultural barriers to getting help encountered by many abused women in Kyrgyzstan (Childress, 2018). We explain how domestic violence occurs, is perpetuated, and how it is (or is not) addressed in Kyrgyz society because of the failures of systems at different ecological levels, including families and institutions embodying larger societal values. We add richness and depth to Asem's story by including the stories of 15 other women who participated in a research study while living at a domestic violence shelter in Kyrgyzstan (Childress, 2018). The experiences drawn from in-depth interviews with these Kyrgyz women help us better understand the difficulties and barriers women face when asking for help with an abusive relationship and also the strength and resilience with which they overcome these barriers to seeking help.

Asem was born into an educated family in a village in the south of Kyrgyzstan. She finished high school with straight A's and continued her studies, majoring in art at the local art school. She was a leader among her peers in high school and college. While in college, Asem was a victim of date rape. She did not realize that she was raped because she had no knowledge about sexual violence at that time and, more broadly, neither her parents nor any of her educational institutions ever talked with her about sex. After graduation, Asem returned to her village and was hired as a graphic designer by a gold company. Asem's career at the gold company came to an end after 3 months when she was bride kidnapped by her future husband.

Asem's husband's tribe was known for its abuse of women, and Asem's parents were against her marriage to him. However, she decided to stay with her abductor to avoid bringing shame to the family. On the wedding night, her husband and his relatives became aware that Asem was not a virgin, and thus began many difficulties and accusations. Asem's in-laws blamed her for not being pure, and she believed that the abuse from her husband and in-laws was her fault (even though she lost her virginity as a result of rape). She reported, "I thought it all was my fault and lived with the guilt that I wasn't a virgin. For all the quarrels, I blamed myself, thinking this was something for me to endure, this was my punishment." Asem's husband used information about her rape to blackmail Asem in order to keep her subordinated and under his control. Asem described her husband's threats, "'If you go back to your parents, I will tell them you didn't come as a virgin.' I was ashamed. I lived in fear, didn't say a word against him, and didn't raise my head. I was scared and stayed."

Eventually, despite her husband's threats, Asem went back to her birth family several times due to constant episodes of abuse. Her birth family did not want to give her refuge and pushed her back into the house of the abuser. Asem explained that her mother blamed her, rather than her husband, for the abuse:

> "You know his character as you've lived with him till this moment, so don't you do this and that!" . . . I told my parents, "I am not going back," but they wouldn't listen to me and always sent me back. . . . My parents were worried that they would be gossiped that they made all their daughters divorce [because my sister was divorced]. They thought of their own dignity.

Asem's story of bride kidnapping and the loss of virginity before marriage represents a cultural norm that legitimates men's violence and prevents women from seeking help.

On the one hand, this cultural norm enables bride kidnapping because once a woman has been raped, the man can claim her. On the other hand, if the woman is not a virgin, she is even more devalued, thereby creating more rationalization and justification for abuse. For Asem, and for many other women, this specific devaluation of women based on their virginity conditioned the way domestic violence, and particularly help-seeking, played out.

Asem's story also illustrates the strength of Kyrgyz cultural norms about marriage and divorce and how these norms effectively cut off a venue or path for help-seeking. Asem's parents already experienced the shame of Asem's older sister's divorce and could not tolerate having a repeat of that. Commonly recited Kyrgyz proverbs, such as *chykkan kyz chiyden tyshkary* ("The girl who is married belongs to someone else's family"), reflect the reality that being married in Kyrgyz culture typically equates to a woman leaving her own family and becoming, essentially, the property of her husband's family. Parental help from the women's family is discouraged; women are socialized to focus on their husband's family and to work out any problems internally within that family structure. Thus, women lose protective connections to their family of origin. Such cultural expectations conflict directly with help-seeking and enable isolation. The cultural construct that is enforced is that the birth family does not want to take their daughter back, even when she is being abused, because this brings shame upon them. These cultural norms were prominently evident in all of the interviews, illustrating the particular social construction of marriage in the Kyrgyz culture, which disempowered and penalized women to preserve marital families and maintain the status quo.

Asem feared being stigmatized by her community and never sought help from formal institutions. After her husband beat her severely at her parents' home, her father took her to the police station to file a complaint. At the police station, she was ridiculed by the police, who freed the husband 2 days after his relatives paid them a bribe. Reporting her abuser to the police became a further blaming trope for the abuse and an additional barrier from help-seeking for Asem: "The police made fun of me, 'If you sue him, aren't you gonna have trouble finding another husband?' Since then my entire life he blamed me, 'You and your dad turned me to the police,' and [that] would shut me up."

After having two daughters, Asem underwent an ectopic pregnancy surgery, which led to the removal of her fallopian tubes. This surgery made it impossible for Asem to give birth to a son—a strong hope of Asem's and an important cultural imperative. Her inability to have a son became another reason for her partner to abuse her. Asem explained that she was held responsible and was shamed for not having produced a son: "If I said something to him, he would shut me up, 'You are such a great woman at delivering me male children, aren't you?' I started looking down on myself. I started feeling like a handicap." Asem was thus devalued in the family after failing to produce a son. Her failure became a pretext and blaming trope, resulting in continual violence and abuse: She had failed to enable her husband to continue the family line and therefore deserved all the abuse he could muster. Asem explained, "From the very beginning, I kept acknowledging my faults: First—I wasn't a virgin; second—I turned my husband in for jail. After that—I couldn't deliver a son. . . . I kept submitting myself and enduring all that."

Asem's mother-in-law coached her son on how to control his wife and instigated many household scandals. Her sisters-in-law continually intervened in Asem and her husband's life and even made them follow their rubric on "how to live a happy life." Everyone in his family knew about each scandal endured by Asem and her partner; it was like a live reality show for his relatives. Asem's story exemplified the extreme influence of her mother-in-law, who controlled every aspect of Asem's life. She explained how her mother-in-law actively promoted and even took apparent satisfaction in the abuse: "My mother-in-law controlled everything. She was afraid I would establish my authority. When I had black eyes, she would invite neighbors over for tea as if saying, 'Look how my son rules his wife!' Her mood would be great."

For 17 years, after her husband's beatings, Asem would leave her husband to ask her family for help and then return to her partner when they refused to help. The last time she left him was when her youngest daughter questioned her dignity and threatened to never talk to her again if she returned to her husband. Asem avoided her husband for approximately 1 year, not returning his calls or text messages. She learned about the crisis center from a newspaper article and reached out for counseling to get divorced. In the meantime, her husband's relatives tried to marry him to another woman. He lost his job, property, family, and, eventually, his life to suicide. Asem blamed herself for not going back to him, and she stated regret and feeling that she could have prevented such an unhappy ending. She confessed that she never wanted a divorce but just a time-out or a sincere apology from her partner. She wished for their reconciliation and a marriage free of violence and abuse.

OVERVIEW

In recent years, there has been mounting evidence and widespread acknowledgment of the pervasiveness of domestic violence against women (VAW) in Kyrgyzstan. According to the recent National Demographic and Health Survey, 23%[2] of women aged 15–49 years reported experiencing physical violence at least once since age 15 years, and 13% reported experiencing physical violence within the past 12 months (National Statistical Committee, Ministry of Health, & ICF International, 2013). In addition, a study of 1,600 women throughout the country found that 83% of women had experienced some form of domestic violence[3] (Alternative Report Kyrgyzstan, 2015). The report also revealed that the annual number of appeals to crisis centers and shelters has increased steadily, from 2,236 in 2004 to 5,000 in 2007 and 8,906 in 2011. Even these high numbers are recognized as significant underestimates. However, in 2017, there were only an estimated 14 crisis centers in Kyrgyzstan, of which only 2 were state-funded shelters with minimal capacities (McCormack & Djaparkulova, 2017). International organizations such as Human Rights Watch (2006, 2015) have also documented acceptance of VAW by varied stakeholders, including survivors of domestic violence, government officials, police, and civil society activists.

During the past two decades, the women's movement in Kyrgyzstan has reacted strongly to VAW by demanding legislative action. A group of women's nongovernmental organizations (NGOs) have spearheaded these efforts to shift the issue of VAW out of the shadows of the home and into public policy discussion. These NGOs were instrumental in the drafting of legislation and succeeded in their efforts to ensure its passage in parliament. Taking advantage of a new constitutional provision that allows public participation in the legislative process, a small group of women's NGOs and crisis centers drafted a law and collected the 30,000 public signatures needed to submit the draft bill to parliament (Kangeldieva et al., 2005).

In response to international human rights efforts and years of lobbying by local women's rights groups, the government of Kyrgyzstan has publicly recognized that VAW is a social problem and not just a "family issue," and it has undertaken both policy and legal initiatives to address the problem. The government ratified the Convention on the Elimination of All Forms of Discrimination against Women (CEDAW) in 1997 (Coomaraswamy, 2003; United Nations, 1999). In 2003, the government adopted the Law on Social–Legal Protection from Domestic Violence, which prohibits physical, psychological, and sexual violence (including marital rape) among family members and protects women through restraining orders and other mechanisms (Human Rights Watch, 2006). Despite these advances, domestic violence survivors in Kyrgyzstan face significant hurdles. Before discussing recent developments and current conditions in gender relations in the Kyrgyz society, it is important to understand the gendered historical context of Kyrgyzstan.

HISTORICAL TRENDS IN THE ROLE OF WOMEN AND GENDER RELATIONS IN KYRGYZ SOCIETY

The sociocultural constraints that contribute to trapping Kyrgyz women in violent domestic situations have deep historical roots. Significant background factors affecting Kyrgyz gender relations include traditional nomadic Kyrgyz values; a moderate Islamic background; an influential Soviet period of gender equality; and a return to traditional family norms following the fall of the Soviet Union, including female subordination (Asian Development Bank, 2006; Bauer, Green, & Kuehnast, 1997).

In the pre-Soviet era, Kyrgyz men and women operated independently, and gender norms were much less conservative than in other Muslim countries (Bauer et al., 1997). The nomadic lifestyle required both men and women to ride horses, hunt, and prepare food in order to support their families. Women remained largely responsible for domestic tasks, such as putting up the portable tent called a "yurt," taking care of children, cooking, and housework (Bauer et al., 1997, p. 15). Traditional norms and religious practices prevailed, including subservience to the husband's family, polygamy, bride kidnapping,[4] and payment of *kalym* (bride price).

Soviet times brought a new era, wherein Islam and much of the Kyrgyz cultural identity were suppressed (Light, 2005), resulting in expanded economic roles as well as social and legal protections for women. The Soviets emphasized women's literacy and education, expanding existing opportunities and training (Tabyshalieva, 2000). Following the fall of the Soviet Union in 1991 and the removal of Soviet norms of gender equality, traditional roles for women in Kyrgyzstan reemerged. Such a resurgence in traditional roles made abused women and their children incredibly vulnerable within the larger context of struggling institutions and ineffective social protection of the post-independence and transition periods. Despite government efforts to ensure women's rights and protect gender equality through legislation, women in Kyrgyzstan appear especially vulnerable to economic and social deprivation, taking many steps back from the gender-equality policies of the Soviet era (Dudwick, Gomart, Marc, & Kuehnast, 2003; Kangeldieva et al., 2005; Somach & Rubin, 2010).

Since the country's independence from the Soviet Union, women in Kyrgyzstan have lived in a context characterized by structural inequality, a lack of socioeconomic empowerment, and political instability. Kyrgyzstan is currently ranked in the bottom half of countries (81st out of 144) in terms of gender gap (World Economic Forum, 2016), and just above the bottom third of countries (120th of 188) in terms of human development indicators (United Nations Development Programme, 2016). Unemployment is high, poverty is widespread, and no satisfactory model of economic and political development has fully taken hold. The dissolution of Soviet social control and economic stability has led to unstable social norms, fostering widespread corruption, alcoholism, racial and ethnic resentment, and violence. This context has furthered a patriarchal, violent masculinity across broad segments of society, which has become a major sociocultural force in Kyrgyzstan and the rest of Central Asia[5] (International Crisis Group, 2016). Such social and political circumstances have enabled a return of fundamentalist Islamic religious values and institutions to again take hold of the region, including polygamy, bride price and bride kidnapping, early or forced marriages (United Nations Population Fund, 2016), and the mass subordination of women.

Recent Social Policy Developments

On April 27, 2017, Kyrgyz President Almazbek Atambaev took an important step toward addressing domestic violence against women when he signed a revised Law on Protection from Family Violence and accompanying legislation that includes measures to improve protections for victims of domestic abuse and strengthen police and judicial response (UN Women, 2017). The new law requires police to register a domestic violence complaint from anyone, not just the victim. The law also recognizes not only physical and psychological abuse but also "economic abuse," which in Kyrgyzstan often takes the form of restricting access to food, shelter, and basic financial resources; excluding women from owning property and assets; destroying the tools of labor or claiming its fruits; gambling; and undermining women's professional reputation.

Another important provision of the law is that it allows any victim of domestic violence to be eligible for shelter and medical and mental health services regardless of whether criminal proceedings have been opened. Another significant amendment made to the law of the Kyrgyz Republic on weapons increases safety for women experiencing domestic violence by restricting access to purchasing or possessing weapons by domestic violence offenders (Human Rights Watch, 2017). Furthermore, the law (Article 29-3) makes an important provision for mandatory correction programs (i.e., batterer intervention programs) for batterers whose court-mandated protection order was extended. Efforts to adopt the "Draft Regulations on Standard Correction Programs for Behavior Change of Persons Who Batter" are also underway by the government and civil society to introduce standard batterer treatment programs in Kyrgyzstan. Finally, the governmental decree No. 226 dated March 30, 2018, adopted the action plan on the development of manuals for provision of legal, social, and psychological aid to intervene in cases of early marriages and childrearing, promote healthy lifestyles and gender relations, and educate youth and the general population on violence prevention.

These measures exemplify the efforts of the government under the *National Strategy of the Kyrgyz Republic on Achieving Gender Equality Until 2020* (Government of the Kyrgyz Republic, 2012) to "provide social services for survivors of gender-based violence; improve the justice sector's response; and introduce programs for men who batter based on the state demand" (Items 3.2.2, 3.2.3, and 3.2.4, p. 8). The government has assigned responsibilities for preventing domestic violence and assisting victims to multiple government and nongovernment entities, including the Ministries of Justice, Internal Affairs, Social Development, Labor, Health, and Education and the Office of Ombudsman; however, it has not allocated appropriate resources and funding to target training of frontline police and social work and public health professionals and to ensure meaningful legal, psychological, and social services for women survivors of abuse.

CURRENT CONDITIONS

Women face enormous barriers to help-seeking in Kyrgyzstan. Sociocultural norms, including social sanctions, shame, and stigma, discourage help-seeking behaviors, forcing women to endure abuse from their partners for prolonged periods with minimal support from formal and informal sources. In addition, women experience legal and systemic barriers ranging from ineffectual police and institutional responses to abuse against women, including failure to enforce protection orders, corruption, negligence, and pro forma police attitudes that present significant hurdles for women seeking help to escape abusive relationships (Childress & Hanusa, 2018).

Despite the active discussion of these issues in society, the appearance of various slogans, and calls for action, the government is not active or effective enough to solve gender-based violence problems, particularly sexual violence. Also, despite some progress in raising awareness and sensitization of governmental agencies about gender issues, there have not been serious changes in the approaches of specific sectoral policies to ensure equal access to rights and opportunities for the majority of the population (Aidarbekova et al., 2017). According to the Ministry of Internal Affairs of the Kyrgyz Republic, in 2010–2014, 35,759 crimes were committed against women, including sexual violence, forced marriage, and health injuries as a result of domestic violence (Aidarbekova et al., 2017). The number of women seeking help from aksakal[6] courts and crisis centers and domestic violence shelters was reported to be 8,458 in 2015 (Aidarbekova et al., 2017), whereas the number of women seeking help from medical establishments such as outpatient clinics and family medicine centers, forensics, hospitals, and emergency care registered in the Ministry of Health of the Kyrgyz Republic was 3,607 in 2016 (National Statistical Committee of the Kyrgyz Republic [NSC], 2016). According to the Judicial Branch of the Kyrgyz Republic (NSC, 2016), the number of cases examined by courts for administrative infractions and criminal cases related to domestic violence (Article 66-3[7]) steadily increased from 887 in 2014 to 1,877 in 2016. A significant number of victims do not appeal their domestic violence cases to law enforcement agencies because of societal stigma and negative attitudes associated with victim blaming, thus resulting in a continuing near absence of efforts to effectively and directly address this issue (Aidarbekova et al., 2017; Childress, 2018).

These conditions point to the importance of mobilizing a Kyrgyz feminist social movement and centering the experiences and values of Kyrgyz women to improve the policy atmosphere for combating violence against women, as opposed to focusing only on instrumental measures such as policies or laws. The Kyrgyz feminist social movement can become the driver that changes areas of social work policy and practice, such as service provision and resource allocation. Consistent with the theoretical feminist and ecological frameworks and women's lived experiences, this chapter implies the need for a "Kyrgyz feminism" to push back against the patriarchal norms and traditions and to empower women to seek help. The global feminist critique calls for confrontation with many cultural norms and values such as those in traditional Kyrgyz society, particularly in the context of violence or human rights violations. "Kyrgyz feminism" would be distinct from Western feminism, which has a very different starting point. The Kyrgyz starting point is basic protection, basic dignity, and human rights, whereas Western policy emphasizes economic opportunity and workplace equality.

In the next section, we shift to describing other women's experiences of coping, resiliency, and recovery and the use of services that helped them overcome barriers and increase their agency, self-reliance, and self-esteem. The section provides illustrative quotes from 15 women to describe how they survived and persisted, working toward a future goal that enabled them to break free from an abusive relationship.

STORIES OF EMPOWERMENT AND RESILIENCE, AND SHARING LESSONS LEARNED

To describe her journey of resiliency and empowerment from the sense of complete frustration and annihilation that she experienced from abuse, Natasha compared herself to the "phoenix bird[8] rising from the ashes" and stressed the need to persevere and renew her determination. She observed, "Patience, strong will, stubbornness, you need so much of it! There were moments when I gave up; I had nothing left. I was like that phoenix bird that rises from the ashes . . . over and over again."

For many women, their children were a source of immeasurable strength and determination in the face of adversity, struggle, and ever-present barriers. The women thought beyond their current circumstances and worked to pursue their dreams for a better life for themselves and their children. Sabina looked to her children to inspire the persistence she needed to survive:

My source of willpower is my children. I will never ever give up. My sister says, "I've never seen a woman like you with so much misfortune, neither house nor home, but with so much strength. You are a strong woman!"

Spirituality plays an important role in recovery by giving strength to prevail, revealing the benefits of suffering, and giving lives purpose. Salamat reported using strategies such as praying, attending religious services, and seeking help from religious leaders. Salamat shared the importance of spirituality:

My strength is spirituality. Through prayer I understand many things, fight these barriers. It's good I went through this so to serve other women like me; there are

Figure 17.1 Woman with children.
Source: Photo courtesy of Mika T. Artwork by Jumagulova Erkebu from Bishkek, Kyrgyzstan.

Figure 17.2 Woman on the hourse.
Source: Photo courtesy of Mika T. Artwork by Jumagulova Erkebu from Bishkek, Kyrgyzstan.

millions of them. I gained strengths and stood through everything through these trials.

At the shelter, social support, acceptance, and counseling from staff built the self-confidence and self-esteem of abuse survivors. For many women, the shelter provided the first opportunity for them to speak about their experiences openly with other women in similar circumstances. Gulzinat observed that she had become calmer and more confident during her stay at the shelter; she noted, "This organization helped me gain confidence. I understood, matured, and calmed down more. It is the shelter that gave me practically everything in this life." Gulbara also expressed gratitude that the shelter staff had helped her become calmer and more confident:

> The shelter gave me enormous help. . . . I learned that women are stronger than men. . . . I got ahold of myself, gained freedom, and became more decisive. There is no way back. Only forward. For my child, for the good, for the better life."

Women benefited from the physical shelter, support, and guidance they had received, and some of them used the safety of the shelter to plan for their future. They discussed several goals for their future lives. Many women wanted to obtain additional education or send their children to school. Many of them expressed a profound desire to acquire peace of mind and a sense of stability and hope for themselves and their children. They wanted to lead "normal" lives in which no one would harass or threaten them. Natasha concluded that the best way to help her children avoid abuse in their future lives was to serve as a role model for them. She explained, "Women should never endure. The only way to solve this problem is to leave. If the child sees that Mom respects herself, then she will learn it through her experience. When she grows up, she would follow the same footsteps." Ainura explained why it was so important for women to take rapid and resolute action: "One shouldn't endure violence. Minimal violence will encourage more. This is equal to having a small hole in your shirt: You don't fix it, it gets bigger and tears more. Then you throw it away and get nothing to wear."

The women had many ideas about how to help other women in domestic violence situations. Given the opportunity to give voice to their deep experiences and under-standing of suffering and survival in the face of violence, women offered their perspec-tives and insights on coping and the factors essential to escaping abuse (Childress, Gioia, & Campbell, 2018). Their descriptions focused on several key factors for abused women: being decisive and strong, respecting and appreciating themselves, knowing their rights, and never giving up (Childress, Panchanadeswaran, & Joshi, 2017). Salamat emphasized the need to be decisive: "First of all, decisiveness. You shouldn't hesitate, thinking that he might change. If you don't want to live in such dirt, don't endure it. Pull yourself together, if you can take no more." Natasha reached a similar conclusion; she explained, "Women need to appreciate themselves. We are not born to endure beating. Our role is to give birth to children, to bring them up, to give warmth and comfort. We are not a piece of meat or the punching bag." Another key factor to escaping abuse that the women noted was refusing to ever give up. Gulzinat summarized this viewpoint: "Never give up. Set a goal, go towards it, no matter what. They say, 'Women have to be this or that, must endure.' All this is nonsense. Women are just as equal as men. They must know their own rights."

Kyrgyz youth, much like the rest of world's youth growing up in the digital age, are beginning to reject violence that has been tolerated in past generations. The women interviewed indicated that the younger generation of women was changing and trying to avoid living with the husband's family. Asem observed the emergence of this generational difference:

> Only such brainless women like me would endure all that and stay. Girls nowadays would just say, "Either live with your mother or with me," or leave. But we [women of our generation] are like the people of the past. We try to live in the ways of the past.

Women also discussed ways to help domestic violence victims and what programs or types of assistance from the government and/or NGOs would have been helpful as they sought help to escape their abusers. The numerous ideas offered by survivors are classified into the following key categories: (1) providing practical assistance in areas such as financial aid, childcare, housing, and employment; (2) increasing the number of crisis centers and shelters; and (3) increasing awareness, education, and prevention. Women requested more help in several practical areas, including financial aid, housing, childcare, transportation, counseling, legal aid, education, and finding a job. Gulbara, for example, described how some assistance with these practical matters would allow her to work toward being able to support her family. She commented,

> If there were some support from the government in finding me a job, or an apartment, to get someone to babysit my child, I would work and live there. I would be able to do it. That is what I must become.

Gulzinat focused on job assistance specifically, arguing that such help would allow women to avoid becoming dependent on their husbands. She explained,

> Many women depend on their husbands. Men rule everywhere. Public officials, husbands work earning money; many wives stay home. It's necessary to provide women with jobs. In order to be confident in their future, they need to earn their living by themselves.

Many women emphasized the need for increasing the number of domestic violence services in the country. Marital counseling and support groups for men with mental health issues and behavioral problems such as gambling, substance use, and extramarital affairs were also cited as a way to prevent domestic violence. Salamat described the importance of opening more domestic abuse agencies:

> To give direction and help improve people's thinking, they should open more centers. There are now centers for drug users and prisoners, but they all have reached limits. Many women now sleep in the streets, drink, nevertheless are good women.

Ainura also stressed the importance of opening more centers as well as spreading information about the existence of these shelters. She explained,

We don't have many programs like this; they have to be globalized. When I found out about this shelter, I was shocked. Could it be possible that there is such a thing in Kyrgyzstan? I didn't have any information.

Women identified raising awareness and increasing education as key strategies for helping other women. Specifically, the women discussed intervention efforts that focus on raising awareness of gender-based violence and promoting beliefs about marital relationships based on gender equality and independent relationships. They asserted that this goal could be achieved by mainstreaming the education of families and raising the profile of these issues among governmental actors as matters of national health and development policy. Natasha explained, "We need to raise family violence as number one topic in the country. Violence happens in every second family. It's a closed topic. I haven't seen a single TV program that talked about family violence, particularly, how to help women." Ainura also described the significance of education about domestic violence:

Everyone needs psychological education. When a person grows morally, psychologically, and ethically, he can then go out to the world and get the information he needs. It turns out everything is opposite in our society . . . in the entire humanity.

Many women believed that the government needed to address socioeconomic problems such as poverty and unemployment that resulted in other behavioral problems, such as alcohol abuse, substance abuse, and gambling, which could often lead to family quarrels and violence. Sabina summarized this idea: "Those in power, their main task is to eradicate unemployment, vodka, and casinos. Men want to forget their troubles and avoid listening to their wives' long tongues [nagging for money]. They come drunk and don't give a moment of peace."

This section described women's stories of empowerment and ideas for helping other survivors. The women's ideas demonstrate innovative ways in which communities, service providers, and formal institutions could improve efforts to reduce family violence by outreach, prevention, and intervention. Survivors expressed strong desires for opportunities to help other women and organize themselves and their communities against abuse. Women envisioned organizing more shelters for survivors and providing financial support, childcare, and housing. They also suggested providing greater opportunities for education and employment and for learning skills to build independence and resilience. Women called for greater focus on interventions for abusive men, including batterers' treatment and accountability, and focus on children and their needs related to their education and the teaching of models of healthy relationships.

LOOKING TO THE FUTURE

The experiences narrated by the women emphasize the need for concerted multisectoral efforts to advance the safety and protection of women in Kyrgyzstan. This chapter emphasizes the need for broader, societal-level changes; even if service providers help survivors by mediating or providing temporary services, cultural barriers will still significantly hinder their ability to seek help. At the societal level, interventions should focus on addressing cultural myths and propagating new messages within the society about marriage and families. At a minimum, interventions should help families understand and recognize the dynamic of domestic violence and encourage them to accept abused women when they want to return to their natal households, because shutting the door seems to cut off the most natural and critical refuge for women seeking relief from abuse.

The state of the contemporary transnational feminist movements calls for a more complex understanding and reassessment of their role, dynamics, and strategies in the globalizing world. This chapter calls for critical evaluation of approaches and interventions designed to address gender-based violence in specific cultural contexts. It is important to dismantle power differentials, elitism, co-optation, and ethics of representation that perpetuate tensions within the global feminist movements by constructing the roles of *rescuers* and *victims* (Agustín, 2007; Grewal, 2005; Moghadam, 2005; Mohanty, 2003). To achieve meaningful social change, there is a deep need within transnational feminist networks for equitable redistribution of global resources; defining empowerment, agency, and development from the viewpoint of the marginalized; and the embodiment of authenticity and self-determination (Harcourt, 2009; Hawkesworth, 2006; Petchesky, 2003).

Although NGOs play an important role in the development of the women's movement and the promotion of gender equality in Kyrgyzstan, they have limited resources available to tackle the problem at the societal level (Asian Development Bank, 2005) and lack evidence-driven bases for their approaches to respond to domestic violence service provision. One of the concerns expressed by Initiative for Social Action and Renewal in Eurasia is that although donors often perceive female domination of civil society in Kyrgyzstan as a positive change, the gendered nature of civil society represents a negative trend toward a lack of female access to authentic decision-making (Handrahan, 2001). Women are leading civil society because they are considered to be more socially responsible than men. Civil society work is viewed as a difficult and undesirable social service task that the state is unable or unwilling to provide. Thus, the government encourages women's involvement in this less prestigious sector while simultaneously excluding women from roles in political and economic decision-making.

Another concern expressed in the globalizing gender and development literature is that women leading NGOs have been stereotyped for their dependence on aid and deference to donors and thus lack cooperation and collaboration within the women's movement (Simpson, 2006). The emergence of these organizations has been evident during the past 20 years of the transition era, whereby elite urban NGOs connected to donors and international organizations have asserted considerable power and autonomy over issues and actions to take. They have become the center points for networks, resources, and services characterized as "exclusive, authoritative, and elitist organizations that do not tend to trickle down to women's groups as a whole" (p. 23). Instead, these NGOs "are starting to become like donors: bureaucratic, and not transparent" through the representation in Western discourses in women's conferences as "global theaters" and the North–South divide (p. 25).

These challenges call for reconsidering the notions of civil society, mainstream activism and inclusion, and deconstructing relations of power in order to spread resources more equally worldwide. In addition, these challenges emphasize the importance of more culturally sensitive, bottom-up grassroots approaches whereby local service providers and survivors find voice and lead the development and implementation of interventions informed by a more nuanced understanding of hierarchies and exclusions among diverse development actors and their organizations. Finally, these challenges emphasize the need for attitudinal societal changes and shifts away from patriarchal cultural belief systems that justify and normalize male entitlement and control over women, including economic control, psychological domination, sexual and reproductive control, and gender-based violence. Although an emerging feminist movement can begin to change cultural norms, it is equally important that men embrace equality and nonviolence; without participation of men, domestic abuse will continue. The stories of the women presented in this chapter are instructive for showing how NGOs and transnational feminist networks can be useful in tackling women's issues, whereby positive results will occur only if the global society changes its attitudes toward and beliefs about vulnerable women.

CONCLUSION

Drawing upon the first known social work study in Kyrgyzstan to discuss barriers to help-seeking among women survivors of abuse, we used feminist and grounded theory approaches to bring women's voices to the forefront of the discussion and to put a spotlight on patriarchal values that construct cultural identity and women's roles in the Kyrgyz society. We took a closer look at Asem's case to explain how and why violence against women is justified and normalized through patriarchal norms and also how it is validated and legitimized as a measure of displaced aggression and social control. Although some women's stories shared in this chapter emphasize the role of institutional or structural factors for abuse, Asem's story shows the problem of gender-based violence as a confluence of powerful sociocultural norms that sanction violence and abuse. Asem's story demonstrates how women fear the stigma and shame of seeking help; how men literally beat down their wives believing it is normal and acceptable; and how other women accept it, validate it, and perpetuate it. It shows how women endure the abuse relying on their own internal strengths, cunning, and problem-solving skills in the face of minimal support from family, community, and societal institutions. Finally, it shows how women find new meaning and hope from their experiences and lessons learned. Our work calls for transformational change and tackling the culturally embedded structures of patriarchy to promote universal cosmopolitan norms. This is important because the social structure and constructions of female identity and shame are less accessible to the realm of policy and legislation and, therefore, are deeper and more difficult to change compared with institutions and policies, which are subject to scrutiny, accountability, and law. To make any headway on family violence, we must address it at all these levels to improve social outcomes for women and create social change.

DISCUSSION QUESTIONS

1. How do proverbs about cultural expectation about marriage, status of daughter-in-law, and virginity reinforce family conflict and play a role in discouraging women from seeking help?

2. How can Kyrgyz women change the culture? What would that take?

3. What can social work do at various levels of intervention under these circumstances? Is it simply limited to helping women who are at the final end (fleeing death)? What kinds of individual, family, community, and policy interventions would help prevent violence in the first place?

ACKNOWLEDGMENTS

We thank all women who shared their experiences and stories, although their names must remain anonymous. We hope that their stories can be part of building a broader women's movement toward eliminating violence against women and that the results of this research will be used to improve the lives of many women and families in Kyrgyzstan. Special thanks to the director and the staff of the crisis center and shelter where this research took place. We admire their courage, resilience, and strength.

NOTES

1. Bride-kidnapping (in Kyrgyz: *alakachu*) refers to the Kyrgyz traditional practice of abduction for forced marriage (Kleinbach, Ablezova, & Aitieva, 2005). Bride-kidnapping includes a variety of acts ranging from staged abduction for marriage to violent non-consensual kidnapping and rape. It typically involves a young man (who could be a complete stranger) and his friends taking a young woman by deception or force to the home of his parents or a close relative. The woman is held in a room until the young man's female relatives convince her to put on the marriage scarf. If necessary, she is kept overnight and sometimes raped. "Rape of the abducted women is used to make the marriage irreversible and shame the women into staying. But even in case the woman is not raped, social stigma gives little choice to the woman but to stay with the abductor's family. Social constraints include expectation that women are virgins when they marry. If she escapes, she would face disgrace and become ostracized by her community and family because of the suspicion of having had a sexual intercourse. This will create difficulty for her new life and finding a different husband" (UN Women, 2016, p.10).

2. Government data on violence against women is limited, often referring to registered cases rather than estimating broader prevalence (Human Rights Watch, 2015). In many countries, incl. Kyrgyzstan, such surveys as Demographic and Health Survey and Multiple Indicator Cluster Surveys, provide the first national estimates of the level of acceptance of intimate partner violence.

3. The report states that domestic violence includes physical violence but does not provide a breakdown of the types of violence assessed or a definition of domestic violence.

4. Historically, these bride-kidnapping practices have been used by consenting couples due to financial or social constraints to marrying otherwise (Thomas, 2009). More recently, scholars have emphasized economic factors underlying the increase in bride-kidnapping, including an increase in subsistence farming resulting in need for more extra workers in the family, and more systemic factors such as male domination and power over women's mobility and sexuality resulting from an increasingly destabilized

world (Werner, 2009). Although bride-kidnapping is considered an officially banned criminal act (Article 154-155 of the Criminal Code of the Kyrgyz Republic stipulates that "the abduction of a woman for marriage contrary to her will is punishable by imprisonment for up to 7 years and 10 years where the bride is minor"), it is reported to be one of the most common forms of forced marriages in Kyrgyzstan (Radio Free Liberty, 2014; Thomas, 2009).

5.   The tragic events that occurred in southern Kyrgyzstan as a result of the eth-nic conflict in 2010 were accompanied by large-scale acts of violence against women and other vulnerable groups. Crisis centers recorded 70 cases of sexual violence during the ethnic conflict; rape was used to intimidate and humiliate women and demonstrate the strength and power of men (Alternative Report Kyrgyzstan, 2015).

6.   "The term *aksakal* itself translates into 'white beard' and refers to a respected elder of the community. Aksakals have long been looked to in Kyrgyzstan for advice and leadership, particularly to resolve disputes among community members. In 2002 the role of the *aksakals* was codified in the Law on Aksakal Courts. Aksakal courts, local government structures that operate on the neighborhood or district level, now work in tandem with other government agencies and arbitrating bodies to deal with certain community matters" (Human Rights Watch, 2006, p. 63).

7.   Article 66-3 of the Administrative Code of the KR stipulates that any intentional acts of family violence (physical, sexual, or psychological) of one family member against another family member resulting in the infringement of constitutional rights and freedom, infliction of light harm and suffering to the health, physical or psy-chological development of the family member regardless of his/her age and gender that don't qualify as criminal shall result in administrative fine of up to 10 estimate indicators or administrative arrest for up to 5 days (Association of Crisis Centers of Kyrgyzstan, 2018).

8.   According to Greek mythology, the phoenix is a mythical bird that after a life of five or six centuries immolates itself on a pyre and rises from the ashes to begin a new cycle of years: often an emblem of immortality or of reborn idealism or hope.

REFERENCES

Agustín, L. M. (2007). *Sex at the margins: Migration, labour markets, and the rescue industry.* London, UK: Zed Books.

Aidarbekova, Ch., Boronchieva, G., Duishenbekova, G., Ilibezova, L., Kachikeeva, B., & Tulekova T. (2017). *Report on judicial practices on crimes against women and girls in the Kyrgyz Republic.* Retrieved March 7, 2017, from http://www.kg.undp.org/content/dam/kyrgyzstan/Publications/gender/Analyticheskii_Otchet_po_Gendernomy_Nasiliyu_RU.pdf

Alternative Report Kyrgyzstan. (2015). *Alternative report to the Fourth Periodic Report of the Kyrgyz Republic to the CEDAW Committee.* Bishkek, Kyrgyzstan: Council of NGOs. Retrieved from http://wsc.kg/en/alternative-report-kyrgyzstan-2015

Asian Development Bank. (2005). *The Kyrgyz Republic country gender assessment: A gen-dered transition. Soviet legacies and new risks.* Retrieved from https://www.adb.org/sites/default/files/institutional-document/32233/cga-kyrgyz-republic.pdf

Asian Development Bank. (2006). *Gender assessment synthesis report 2006: Mainstreaming gender in poverty reduction strategies in four Central Asian republics.* Retrieved from https://www.adb.org/sites/default/files/institutional-document/32229/cga-synthesis.pdf

Association of Crisis Centers of Kyrgyzstan. (2018). *Legislation.* Retrieved May 7, 2018, from http://neomak7.wixsite.com/accwebkg/lawskyr

Bauer, A., Green, D., & Kuehnast, K. (1997). *Women and gender relations: The Kyrgyz Republic in transition.* Manila, Philippines: Asian Development Bank.

Childress, S. (2018). "Plates and dishes smash; married couples clash": Cultural and social barriers to help-seeking among women domestic violence survivors in Kyrgyzstan. *Violence Against Women,* 24(7), 775–797. doi:10.177/1077801217722239

Childress, S., Gioia, D., & Campbell, J. (2018, March). Women's strategies for coping with the impacts of domestic violence in Kyrgyzstan: A grounded theory study. *Social Work in Health Care,* 57(3), 164–189. doi:10.1080/00981389.2017.1412379

Childress, S., & Hanusa, D. (2018, February). "All the system is simply a soap bubble": Legal help-seeking for domestic violence among women in Kyrgyzstan. *Journal of Family Violence,* 33(2), 147–160. doi:10.1007/s10896-017-9945-0

Childress, S., Panchanadeswaran, S., & Joshi, M. (2017, November). Leaving and beyond: Voices of survivors of domestic violence from Kyrgyzstan. *Journal of Interpersonal Violence* [Epub ahead of print]. doi:10.1177/0886260517743550

Coomaraswamy, R. (2003). *Violence against women: Report of the Special Rapporteur on violence against women, its causes and consequences.* New York, NY: United Nations, Economic and Social Council.

Dudwick, N., Gomart, E., Marc, A., & Kuehnast, K. (2003). *When things fall apart: Qualitative study of poverty in the former Soviet Union.* Washington, DC: The World Bank.

Government of the Kyrgyz Republic. (2012, November 15). *National strategy of the Kyrgyz Republic on achieving gender equality until 2020* (No. 589). Retrieved June 1, 2017, from http://cbd.minjust.gov.kg/act/view/ru-ru/93343?cl=ru-ru

Grewal, I. (2005). *Transnational America.* Durham, NC: Duke University Press.

Handrahan, L. M. (2001, November). Gendering ethnicity in Kyrgyzstan: Forgotten elements in promoting peace and democracy. *Gender and Development,* 9(3), 70–78.

Harcourt, W. (2009). *Body politics in development: Critical debates in gender and development.* London, UK: Zed Books.

Hawkesworth, M. E. (2006). *Globalization and feminist activism.* Lanham, MD: Rowman & Littlefield.

Human Rights Watch. (2006, September). *Reconciled to violence: State failure to stop domestic abuse and abduction of women in Kyrgyzstan.* New York, NY: Author. Retrieved September 9, 2007, from https://www.hrw.org/report/2006/09/26/reconciled-violence/state-failure-stop-domestic-abuse-and-abduction-women

Human Rights Watch. (2015, October). *"Call me when he tries to kill you": State response to domestic violence in Kyrgyzstan.* New York, NY: Author. Retrieved September 2016 from https://www.hrw.org/report/2015/10/28/call-me-when-he-tries-kill-you/state-response-domestic-violence-kyrgyzstan

Human Rights Watch. (2017, May). *Kyrgyzstan's new domestic violence law: Government moves to improve response to abuse.* Retrieved May 2018 from https://www.hrw.org/news/2017/05/10/kyrgyzstan-new-domestic-violence-law

International Crisis Group. (2016, October). *Kyrgyzstan: State fragility and radicalization* (Briefing 83, Europe & Central Asia). Retrieved October 10, 2016, from https://www.crisisgroup.org/europe-central-asia/central-asia/kyrgyzstan/kyrgyzstan-state-fragility-and-radicalisation

Kangeldieva, A. A., Kudaibergenova, A. Z., Tugelbaeva, B. G., Sydykova, L. C., Ilibezova, E. K., & Ibraeva, G. K. (2005). *Report on the status of women in the Kyrgyz Republic 2000–2005.* Bishkek, Kyrgyzstan: Secretariat National Council on Women, Family, and Gender Development under the President of the Kyrgyz Republic.

Kleinbach, R. L., Ablezova, M., & Aitieva, M. (2005). Kidnapping for marriage (ala kachuu) in a Kyrgyz village. *Central Asian Survey, 24*(2), 191–202.

Light, L. (2005). *Violence against women in Kyrgyzstan: The study in transition.* Paper presented at the World Conference on Prevention on Family Violence 2005, Vancouver, British Columbia, Canada.

McCormack, M., & Djaparkulova, A. (2017). *Report to the UN Special Rapporteur on violence against women.* Retrieved June 2017 from http://www.ohchr.org/Documents/Issues/Women/SR/Shelters/Meghan%20McCormack_Aiymbubu_Djaparkulova_Shelters.pdf

Moghadam, V. M. (2005). *Globalizing women: Transnational feminist networks.* Baltimore, MD: Johns Hopkins University Press.

Mohanty, C. T. (2003). *Feminism without boarders: Decolonizing theory, practicing solidarity.* Durham, NC: Duke University Press.

National Statistical Committee of the Kyrgyz Republic. (2016). *Gender statistics.* Retrieved July 4, 2018, from http://stat.kg/ru/statistics/gendernaya-statistika

National Statistical Committee of the Kyrgyz Republic, Ministry of Health [Kyrgyz Republic], and ICF International. (2013). *Kyrgyz Republic demographic and health survey 2012.* Bishkek, Kyrgyz Republic, and Calverton, MD: Authors. Retrieved September 13, 2013, from https://dhsprogram.com/pubs/pdf/fr283/fr283.pdf

Petchesky, R. P. (2003). *Global prescriptions: Gendering health and human rights.* London, UK: Zed Books.

Radio Free Liberty. (2014, May 29). *Bride-kidnapping in Kyrgyzstan.* Retrieved from https://www.rferl.org/a/bride-kidnapping-in-kyrgyzstan/25403604.html

Simpson, M. (2006). Local strategies in globalizing gender-politics: Women's organizing in Kyrgyzstan and Tajikistan. *Journal of Muslim Minority Affairs, 26*(1), 9–31.

Somach, S., & Rubin, D. (2010). *Gender assessment: USAID/Central Asian Republics* (No. GEW-I-01–02-00019). Retrieved May 19, 2010, from http://www.culturalpractice.com/wp-content/downloads/3-2010-7.pdf

Tabyshalieva, A. (2000). Revival of traditions in post-Soviet Central Asia. In M. Lazreg (Ed.), *Making the transition work for women in Europe and Central Asia* (World Bank Discussion Paper No. 411, Europe and Central Asia Gender and Development Series, pp. 55–57). Washington, DC: World Bank.

Thomas, C. (2009). *Forced and early marriage: A focus on Central and Eastern Europe and former Soviet Union countries with selected laws from other countries.* Geneva, Switzerland: United Nations Division for the Advancement of Women. Retrieved from http://www.un.org/womenwatch/daw/egm/vaw_legislation_2009/Expert%20Paper%20EGMGPLHP%20_Cheryl%20Thomas%20revised_.pdf

UN Women. (2016). *Research report on gender in society perceptions study: Violence against women and girls component.* Bishkek, Kyrgyzstan: UN Women Kyrgyzstan Country Office.

UN Women. (2017). *New progressive law on domestic violence adopted in Kyrgyzstan.* Retrieved June 2017 from http://www.unwomen.org/en/news/stories/2017/5/news-new-progressive-law-on-domestic-violence-adopted-in-kyrgyzstan

United Nations. (1999). *In face of widespread violence against Kyrgyz women, Kyrgyzstan urged to re-evaluate its programs and policies.* Retrieved from https://www.un.org/press/en/1999/19990122.wom1082.html

United Nations Development Programme. (2016). *Human development report 2016.* New York, NY: United Nations. Retrieved June 2017 from http://hdr.undp.org/sites/default/files/2016_human_development_report.pdf

United Nations Population Fund. (2016). *Gender in society perception study 2016.* Bishkek, Kyrgyzstan: Author. Retrieved June 2017 from http://www.stat.kg/media/publicationarchive/f776d502-fec6-454c-ab6c-08d77eadff9f.pdf

Werner, C. (2009). Bride abduction in post-Soviet Central Asia: Marking a shift towards patriarchy through local discourses of shame and tradition. *Journal of the Royal Anthropological Institute, 15*(2), 314–331.

World Economic Forum. (2016). *The global gender gap report 2016.* Retrieved October 2017 from http://reports.weforum.org/global-gender-gap-report-2016/economies/#economy=KGZ

18

Dating Violence in China

XIYING WANG ∎

CASE STUDY: A TRAGIC CASE OF DATE RAPE

In 2003, the Huang Jing case became the first documented date rape case since Deng Xiaoping initiated economic reforms in 1978. Huang Jing was a 21-year-old female primary school teacher in Xiangtan City, Hunan Province, who died February 24, 2003, in her school dormitory naked, with bruises and her boyfriend's sperm on her body. Huang Jing's mother and feminist activists believed that her death was due to date rape by her 26-year-old boyfriend. The local court applied the general public's concept that "only rape by strangers counts as rape," and it found her boyfriend not guilty because they were romantically involved and her hymen remained intact. The court did not take into consideration the injuries to her body, the sperm that was found on her belly, and that fact that she was unwilling to participate in sex. Criticizing the unjust judgment and revealing the patriarchal and sexist ideology associated with this case, Chinese feminist activists Ai Xiaoming and colleagues and students supported Huang Jing's mother's appeal and launched a movement to combat date rape and dating violence. Their actions involved writing articles (Ai, 2004a, 2004b, 2004c), organizing symposiums, establishing a memorial website, filming a documentary about Huang Jing's case titled *Heaven Garden* (*Tiantang Huayuan*), and so on. All these actions sparked a social movement against date rape, and Huang Jing has become a symbol for mobilization against dating violence and sexual assault, making the issue more visible in public discourse. Because date rape and dating violence have not been widely examined in academia, and therefore the general public knows even less about this issue, young women have little understanding of the issue and lack coping skills, and there remain huge barriers for them to acknowledge their pain and suffering that stem from date rape and date violence.

OVERVIEW

This chapter (1) defines dating violence and discusses the prevalence, risk factors, and consequences of dating violence throughout the world; (2) focuses on China to discuss how dating violence is related to historical trends, the current status of women, the women's movement, and Chinese violence research; and (3) reviews the development of dating violence research in China, as well as discusses advocacy strategies and future directions.

Dating violence is defined as aggressive behavior that occurs in intimate dating relationships, involving acts and/or injuries, including attacks and self-defense. As defined by Straus, Hamby, Boney, and Sugarman (1996), it includes physical assault, verbal and psychological aggression, and sexual coercion in both heterosexual and homosexual relationships. Different types of violence include the following behaviors by a perpetrator: verbal aggression that includes insulting or swearing at the partner, sulking or refusing to talk about an issue with the partner, storming out of a room or house, and doing or saying something to spite the partner. Sometimes verbal violence and psychological aggression are cross-linked (Straus et al., 1996). Physical assault includes "minor" and "severe" violence. The former is defined as a perpetrator throwing an object at his or her partner that could physically hurt the partner, or it may involve the perpetrator twisting, pushing, shoving, grabbing, or slapping the victim. The latter includes a perpetrator using a knife or gun, punching or hitting, choking, slamming, beating up, burning, scalding, or kicking a victim (Straus et al., 1996). Psychological aggression includes the following behaviors: insulting, saying things to upset, saying mean things, criticizing, calling names, making the other feel guilty, making the other feel inferior, giving the other the cold shoulder, degrading, and hurting feelings (Stets, 1991). Sexual coercion includes a range of behaviors, such as verbal manipulation (insistent arguing, false pretense, threats to terminate a relationship, or threats of physical force), physical aggression, and rape.

In the United States, sociologist Makepeace (1981) performed the pioneering investigation of dating violence and found that one out of five college students had experienced at least one incident of physical abuse in dating relationships. Dating violence has been examined in thousands of research articles and books throughout multiple disciplines in the United States and the world. Straus (2004) examined the prevalence of dating violence among 8,666 students at 31 colleges and universities in 16 countries: China, India, Israel, Korea, Singapore, Australia, New Zealand, Belgium, France, Germany, the Netherlands, Portugal, Brazil, Mexico, Canada, and the United States. At the median university, 29% of the students had physically assaulted a dating partner in the previous 12 months (range = 17–45%), and 7% had physically injured a partner (range = 2–20%). In this study, the Chinese data were collected in Hong Kong; the overall assault perpetration rate was 28.6% and the severe assault perpetration rate was 9.4% among 220 college students. These results were consistent with findings in the United States by Sugarman and Hotaling (1989) that between one-third and one-half of college students reported that they had experienced or been the initiator of violence in a dating relationship. The three previously discussed studies considered only physical violence; if verbal and psychological aggression were included, then the prevalence rate of dating violence would be much higher (Laner, 1983; Ryan, 1998; Shook, Gerrity, Jurich, & Segrist, 2000).

Jennings and colleagues (2017) performed a systematic review based on 169 studies on dating and intimate partner violence among young persons aged 15–30 years. They found that the prevalence of dating/intimate partner violence among youth and young adults ranged from 6% for boys and 9% for girls (Ackard & Neumark-Sztainer, 2002) to 21.8% for young men and 37.2% for young women (Magdol et al., 1997). Wincentak, Connolly, and Card (2017) conducted a meta-analytic review of prevalence rates of teen dating violence (aged 13–18 years) based on 101 studies and found an overall prevalence of 20% for physical teen dating violence and 9% for sexual teen dating violence. Across 30 lower income countries, a national demographic and health survey found that of ever married/cohabiting females, 28% of girls aged 15–19 years and 29% of women aged 20–24 years reported lifetime experience of physical and sexual intimate partner violence (Decker et al., 2015). All these studies have demonstrated that dating violence is a worldwide social phenomenon.

Most of the aforementioned studies emanate from the discipline of psychology, employing a traditional positivist epistemology and using quantitative methods and the Conflict Tactics Scales 2 (CTS2) to measure the prevalence of dating violence and test hypotheses of risk factors, thus acknowledging that violence in intimate relationships is a significant problem not just among married heterosexual couples but also among both heterosexual and homosexual cohabitating and dating couples (Rhatigan, Moore, & Street, 2005). However, except for a few nationwide surveys (Koss, 1989; Tjaden & Thoennes, 2000), these studies also have some drawbacks. For instance, most studies in the United States involve small convenience sampling, and the participants are predominantly White female college and high school students. Most important, CTS items do not offer the context of violent behavior and cannot compare to the descriptions of torture and abuse detailed in narratives (Dobash & Dobash, 2004).

Vagi and colleagues (2013) reviewed articles published between 2000 and 2010 that reported on adolescent dating violence perpetration using samples from the United States or Canada. In total, 53 risk factors and 6 protective factors were identified from 20 studies. The 53 risk factors were categorized into the following general categories: mental health problems (e.g., depression and anxiety), aggressive thoughts/cognitions (e.g., acceptance of violence in dating relationships), youth violence (e.g., fighting and general antisocial behavior), substance use (e.g., alcohol and marijuana), risky sexual behaviors (e.g., sexually active in eighth grade and a high number of sex partners), poor relationships and friendship quality (e.g., hostile couple interactions, involvement with antisocial peers, and low friendship quality), poor family quality (e.g., parental marital conflict and childhood physical abuse), demographics (e.g., sex and race), and the use of aggressive media. From the 20 articles reviewed, only 3 articles identified protective factors, of which 6 were distinctive. For instance, 4 of these protective factors were identified at the individual level: having high cognitive dissonance about perpetrating dating violence—that is, when adolescents who perpetrated adolescent dating violence realized that what they were doing was wrong (Schumacher & Slep, 2004); high empathy (McCloskey & Lichter, 2003); better grade point average (Cleveland, Herrera, & Stuewig, 2003); and (higher) verbal IQ (Cleveland et al., 2003). Two additional protective factors were found at the relationship level: having a positive relationship with one's mother (Cleveland et al., 2003) and feeling a sense of attachment to school (Cleveland et al., 2003).

FEMINIST THEORY IN TACKLING DATING VIOLENCE

Feminist theory is an important approach to both the advancement of social move-ments and academic research on violence against women. Second-wave feminists have organized consciousness-raising groups to help women "speak out" (Alcoff & Gray, 1993; Naples, 2003) and to analyze dating violence as abuses of male power that occur as a result of a patriarchal society (DeKeseredy, 1989; DeKeseredy & Kelly, 1995). Within this theoretical framework, the almost exclusive focus is on the suf-fering of the "victims" and the application of the trauma paradigm to explore such consequences as depression, anxiety, low self-esteem, feelings of isolation and stig-matization, re-victimization, substance abuse, and sexual difficulties (Armsworth & Stronck, 1999; Denov, 2004). These feminists validate the psychological injury that results from being abused, they empower women politically, and they educate society at large about this dimension of violence against women. However, they also create a dominant, stereotypical, expert institutional discourse of "abusive men and abused women" and, more generally, of "men exercising power over women" (Lamb, 1999). This discourse tends to deprive the "victims" of "authority regarding the complexity of their own experience and may inadvertently reinforce viewing audience presupposi-tions that violence is an event that women cannot prevent, recover from, or explain without expert advocacy" (Hengehold, 2000, p. 194). It also fails to recognize the strengths that "victims" often exhibit "in the face of extreme injury and develop in the process of surviving" (Gilfus, 1999, p. 12).

Transnational feminists tend to use the term "survivor" (Alcoff & Gray, 1993; Gilfus, 1999; Hengehold, 2000; Naples, 2003) in place of "victim" in the abuse situ-ation because "victims are often presented as trapped, and survivors, conversely, are shown as making choices. . . . They are constructed in ways that place them at opposite poles of an agency continuum" (Dunn, 2005, p. 2). Compared to the word "victim," the term "survivor" makes visible the two sides of women's lives: One is a passive picture of their victimization, and the other is an active and positive script in which women resist, cope, and survive. Transnational feminists highlight women's agency and resistance to cope with their experience of being abused, and they shift the research emphasis from attending to the pathology of abused women to theorizing the complicated experiences of women that are embedded and con-structed socially and historically. Transnational feminism emphasizes the similar gender-based suffering throughout the world, sisterhood and solidarity among women globally, while acknowledging the different experiences of women with regard to age, race, class, disability, and so on in their own sociocultural context, especially between the Global North and Global South, the developed and develop-ing countries.

HISTORICAL TRENDS: VIOLENCE RESEARCH IN CHINA

In China, it was not until the early 1990s that the concept of domestic violence was formally introduced as an academic term describing a social problem. It was not until the revised Marriage Law was adopted in 2001 that an actual "domestic violence" wording was included as a legal matter at the national level (Milwertz & Bu, 2009). According to Zhang (2009), "The term violence against women was introduced, through the 1995 Beijing conference, into the Chinese state's policy discourse, forcing the state to recognize the topic as a legitimate 'woman question' and to introduce the issue into public discourse" (p. 68).

Milwertz and Bu (2009) outline the four stages of new knowledge production concerning gender-based violence by Chinese feminists during the 1980s and 1990s:

> They more or less "accidentally" discovered wife-beating (*da laopo*) in the course of addressing other gender inequality issues. They then started investigating the characteristics and extent of wife-beating. This in turn led to their re-interpretation of wife-beating as a women's movement issue and the re-naming of the phenomenon as domestic violence (*jiating baoli*). Finally, some activists defined domestic violence as an issue involving gender relations and as a human rights issue. (p. 136)

Nowadays, domestic violence is a household concept in urban China, and most well-educated women are well informed about the concept and have learned to use it to define their own experiences of abuse in intimate relationships. In the past three decades, much research has been conducted on domestic violence; the following are representative studies:

- According to the All-China Women's Federation (ACWF)'s survey conducted in 2004, among the 0.27 billion families in China, 30% experience domestic violence to different degrees (He & Zuo, 2004). According to the third-wave survey on Chinese women's social status by ACWF and the National Bureau of Statistics of China (ACWF & NBS, 2011), conducted through 125,978 questionnaires, 24.7% women reported suffering different kinds of domestic violence, including physical, psychological, economic, and sexual abuse.
- The Chinese Law Society Domestic Violence Network's random sampling survey on domestic violence carried out from 2000 to 2003, which received 3,543 completed questionnaires distributed in Zhejiang, Hunan, and Gansu provinces, showed that 34.7% of families encounter domestic violence.
- Using a nationally representative sample from the 1999–2000 Chinese Health and Family Life Survey, Parish, Wang, Laumann, Pan, and Luo (2004) found that 34% of women and 18% of men aged 20–64 years had been physically assaulted during their current relationships.
- Wang, Fang, and Li (2013) conducted a quantitative study on men's perpetration and women's experiences of gender-based violence in China that included 1,103 women and 1,017 men aged 18–49 years. Among female respondents who were in intimate relationships, 39% reported experiencing physical and/or sexual intimate partner violence. Men's reporting was higher, with 52% of men reporting their own abusive physical and/or sexually violent behavior toward their intimate partners. Different types of intimate partner violence overlapped: 27% of the men who reported they had perpetrated physical intimate partner violence also reported having perpetrated sexual violence against a partner.

The reported figures consistently suggest that domestic violence continues to be a serious and widespread issue in China. Extant research offers a snapshot of different factors associated with gender-based domestic violence in China, and gender norms associated with hegemonic patriarchal masculinities have been found to lie at the root of the problem. The patriarchal organization of Chinese families and society, which affirms men's dominance over women, is a key issue cited by various authors (Chan, 2012; Tang, Wong, & Cheung, 2002). Within prevalent cultural narratives, men are represented as subject to violent impulses, and women are liable to provoke men through nagging and disobedient conduct, or even simply by being too beautiful.

For a long time, the term "domestic violence" has been used interchangeably with "violence against women and girls" to emphasize men's perpetration and women's victimization within violent marital relationships. However, the concept of domestic violence has been used to emphasize violence between married partners, ignoring different forms of violence within the family and among other family members and violence in other intimate relationships, including dating and cohabitation. Compared to domestic violence, other forms of violence have been ignored, and research is just emerging that includes areas such as dating violence; sexual violence/rape; child sexual abuse; homophobic hate crimes; sexual harassment in the workplace and public life; sex trafficking; school bullying; and violence against men, against LGBTQ individuals, and within homosexual relationships.

The most significant advancement is the enactment of the first national law on anti-domestic violence in March 2016. The law defines domestic violence as violent behavior that occurs among family members, including physical violence and spiritual violence; however, the definition of domestic violence does not include economic control and sexual violence, including marital rape. The anti-domestic violence law for the first time issued the regulations of written warnings and restraining orders, representing a huge step forward. The last article of the anti-domestic violence law stipulates that the law can also be applied to people who cohabitate or live together. Feminists read this as a signal that the law also protects the victims of dating violence, especially if they live together.

RECENT DEVELOPMENTS: WOMEN'S SOCIAL STATUS IN CHINA

China has experienced major changes in the past two decades. In 2010, China became the world's second largest economy; however, the development of gender equality does not seem to be keeping pace with economic development. Measuring countries' achievements in attaining gender equality and empowering women in economic life, education, health, and politics, the World Economic Forum has annually published the *Global Gender Gap Report* (GGGR). Since 2006, China's ranking has decreased almost every year, from 63 in 2006 to 100 in 2017.

The 2017 GGGR estimated that China could experience a $2.5 trillion increase in gross domestic product (GDP) from gender parity and contribute to the global GDP. The 2017 report also shows that China has fully closed its gender gap in professional and technical roles and women's enrollment, while recording a small decrease in wage equality for similar work. However, China was one of the three lowest ranked countries in terms of the Health and Survival sub-index. China was the lowest performing country on the sex ratio at birth indicator in 2017. Normal sex ratio at birth is gener-ally between 103 and 107 male live births per 100 female live births, but the sex ratio at birth in China peaked at 120.5:100 for 2005 (Li, 2007) and declined to 117.8:100 for 2011 (United Nations Population Fund, 2012) and 115.88:100 for 2014 (National Burear of Statistics, 2015). The culture of son preference, the availability of ultrasound scans and selective abortion, and the nearly 40 years of a one-child policy are all fac-tors that contribute to the unbalanced sex ratio in China.

At home, women are still the primary caregivers, and their average leisure time is much less than that of men (ACWF & NBS, 2011). The gender gap for education years narrowed to 0.3 years in 2010 (ACWF & NBS, 2011). According to the Ministry of Education, colleges and universities nationwide recruited 51.35% female students in 2012. Female college students generally do better academically but have much more difficulty finding a job after graduation (Tong & Su, 2010). Women work harder but are paid less than men: The average annual income of women laborers is equal to 67.3% of that of men in urban areas and 56.0% of that of men in rural areas, although the average number of working minutes per person is 574 for women and 537 for men (ACWF & NBS, 2011). These statistics clearly show that a glass ceiling firmly prevents women's development in their career paths. Women's economic and political partici-pation has lagged notably behind that of the most highly ranked countries, especially with regard to high-ranking positions. According to corporate records examined by *The New York Times*, fewer than 1 in 10 board members of China's top 300 companies are women. Women held 1 of 25 positions on the 19th CPC Politburo, and women have never held positions on the Politburo Standing Committee throughout the his-tory of China's reform era.

The women's movement is facing an unprecedented backlash at different levels. The state discourse emphasized women's "unique role" in the family and that women should consciously shoulder the responsibility of taking care of the elderly and edu-cating their children to become useful to the country. Only emphasizing women's family role as mothers, wives, and daughters is a countermarch against the idea that "women hold up half the sky" of the socialist era. Most male elites do not care about gender issues and pay no attention to feminism and gender studies. The "let women go home" proposal that was initiated by two male professors in the 1980s has repeat-edly reappeared, with some sexist congressmen openly declaring that it is best for women not to pursue a PhD. The neoliberal market force not only objectifies women's bodies but also marginalizes women in the social, political, and cultural arenas and reasserts the hegemony of ruling elites. The mass media depicts feminists as some of the most undesirable women in the world, and most established female celebri-ties, writers, and even gender study scholars have distanced themselves from the label of feminist. According to a study by *Ms. Magazine* (Meltzer, 2014), the number of American women calling themselves feminists increased from 50% in 2006 to 68% in 2012. Although no corresponding study can be found in China, I am sure that the percentage would be much lower. The feminist movement in China cannot obtain worldwide women's support and endorsement, and this will be a major barrier to future development. The political discourse echoes with the reviving Confucian tra-ditional gender roles—"'men work outside, women work inside" and "husband leads and wife follows"—and the establishment of a powerful "guideline" for gender roles that represents strong backlash forces. At the same time, throughout the world, there has been a very direct conservative backlash against the values and achievements of feminism—for instance, Christian nationalism, public debates about the rollback of women's rights, and widespread Islamic fundamentalism in the United States and throughout the world.

CURRENT CONDITIONS: THE DEVELOPMENT OF DATING VIOLENCE STUDIES

Dating violence is underresearched in China, compared to studies on dating violence in the West and domestic violence studies in China. Many incidents of violent behavior in dating relationships are reported in newspapers, magazines, and daily television programming and are discussed extensively on the internet, which shows that people have begun to pay attention to the social phenomenon, but in a very gossipy way: Violence is ignored, but romance, jealousy, and extramarital affairs are emphasized.

In 2017, the Jiang Ge case attracted much attention from the media and the general public throughout China. Jiang Ge was a 24-year-old Chinese postgraduate student living in Tokyo, Japan. She had a temporary roommate, Liu Xin, also a fellow Chinese student, living with her so that Liu Xin could avoid harassment and stalking from her ex-boyfriend. Liu Xin broke up with her ex-boyfriend Chen Shifeng after a brief cohabitation; however, Chen did not accept the breakup and harassed, stalked, and threatened Liu Xin. On November 3, 2016, Chen followed Liu Xin to her residence shared with Jiang Ge. When Jiang Ge answered the door and tried to talk Chen back to his senses, she was murdered by Chen with 10 knife stabs while Liu Xin tried to get help from the local police. In December 2017, Chen was found guilty of intentional murder and sentenced to 20 years in prison. Among the attention this case received in China, it was not Chen Shifeng but, rather, Liu Xin who was the recipient of the most public blame. The general public believed that Jiang Ge was a courageous young woman who defended her friend and sacrificed her life while Liu Xin betrayed her and hid in a room to let her friend take the fall for her. Liu Xin was accused of being responsible for Jiang Ge's death, and she suffered from cyberbullying and received many death threats. At the same time, it seemed as though nobody paid much attention to what Chen Shifeng had done, which was brutal, criminal, and unjust. He was the one who should have taken full responsibility for the death of Jiang Ge. It also seemed that the public forgot that Liu Xin was a victim too: She suffered from dating violence, stalking, and was witness to the death of her friend, and later she was the victim of cyberbullying and secondary victimization from the Chinese general public.

Fifteen years after the death of Huang Jing, Chinese society seems to have made very limited progress in understanding dating violence as a social problem and that the victims of dating violence need to be protected. In addition, the media depicted the Jiang Ge case of dating violence as "failed dating and murder." Such bloody violent descriptions in the media resemble horror stories or movies more than reflections of the overall real social phenomenon. They usually attribute murders to failures of love and the abnormal personalities of the criminals, and they regard these as rare and isolated incidents, with no connection to the conflicts and violence that regularly occur in the lives of those who date. This stereotypical depiction of violence makes it difficult to raise people's awareness about the spectrum of violence and to prevent "minor" violence from escalating into "severe" violence.

To date, no nationwide survey of dating violence has been performed in mainland China, and only a few quantitative studies can provide limited information on this topic in China. Tang Can (2005), in her study of sexual harassment in China, found that 6.51% of her sample of 169 women had experienced being forced to have sex in dating relationships. Wang (2009) conducted a survey with convenience sampling of 1,015 college students in Tianjin to understand the prevalence of dating violence. She found that 58.1% of participants reported experiencing psychological violence and 25.6% reported experiencing physical violence, among which 12.3% reported serious physical violence and 3% reported sexual violence. Chan (2012) conducted a survey among 3,388 university students in Beijing, Shanghai, and Hong Kong and found that psychological aggression was the most common type of violence perpetrated (71.6%), more than physical violence (47.7%) or sexual violence (17.5%). Shen, Chiu, and Gao (2012) conducted a questionnaire survey of 976 Chinese adolescents in Taiwan, Hong Kong, and Shanghai and found a perpetration rate of 27.3% and victimization rate of 39%. In 2010, one of China's leading LGBT rights organization, Tongyu (Common Language, 2010), collected 419 questionnaires among lesbians in eight cities: Beijing, Shanghai, Anshan, Chengdu, Kunming, Nanning, Zhuhai, and Guangzhou. It found that 42.2% of participants reported that they had experienced violence and abuse from their girlfriends and that 10% of them had suffered serious violence. Yu, Xiao, and Liu (2013) collected questionnaires from 418 gay men and 330 heterosexual men. They found that 32.8% of gay men had suffered at least one kind of dating violence, and 12.4% of gay men had been threatened with outing by a partner. Among those experiencing abuse, 83.9% of gay men had never told anyone about it; this percentage was far higher than that for heterosexuals who had experienced violence. The previously cited data are evidence that dating violence is a social problem in China, with a similar prevalence rate as that in the United States, and that it exists in different age groups and in both heterosexual and homosexual intimate relationships.

In order to establish a pluralistic, complex, and multilayered picture of young people's dating lives in contemporary China, I have been conducting a qualitative research study since 2002 and have talked with more than 100 young Beijing men and women through individual interviews and focus group. I have published a series of articles (Wang & Ho, 2007, 2011; Wang & Nehring, 2014) and a book titled *Gender, Dating, and Violence in hUrban China* (Wang, 2017). I attempt to understand young people's lived experiences of dating violence and their meaning-making process. Unlike most studies, which use high school and college students as their sample, my study is not limited to students but, rather, includes many types of young people of different family backgrounds, education, socioeconomic classes, household registrations, and jobs. Here, I highlight and challenge the myths that exist in the area of dating violence research.

First, I challenge the traditional approach of researching different types of violence separately and argue that the boundaries of physical, psychological, verbal, and sexual violence are blurred so that sometimes one violent incident may include elements of different types of violence. Note that physical assault is overemphasized and verbal, psychological, and sexual violence are mostly ignored among research.

Second, I challenge the idea that only severe violence counts as violence and argue for the importance of researching the spectrum of violence, including "minor," "trivial," and long-term severe violence. In fact, minor and trivial violence exist extensively in young people's daily lives and have been largely ignored. It is striking that psychological violence is predominant in young dating couples' lives, with "breaking up" and "infidelity" being the two situations in which all kinds of violence are focally embedded, thus diverting the focus of physical violence in current violence studies in China.

Third, I challenge the dichotomy of "abusive men and abused women" and the idea that women are the only victims of dating violence. I have studied the violent behaviors of both men and women, and I argue that the roles of perpetrators and victims sometimes are fluid and interchangeable, especially in circumstances of mutual violence and trivial and minor violence. Young urban women, raised as only children in nuclear families, can be willful, assertive, competitive, professionally ambitious, and even aggressive in their dating relationships. A new dating mode has emerged: women who are assertive, willful, and aggressive and men who are loving, tender, and even fragile. In this mode, "tender" men go to great lengths to accommodate their "spoiled sassy" women, and the traditional pattern of "men being superior to and dominant of women" has shifted. However, this is not the whole picture: Women are aggressive in their everyday lives but seem to be quite submissive with regard to sex. Sexual coercion happens quite commonly in young people's dating lives, and many female participants report that their experience of virginity loss contains some elements of sexual coercion. The concept of "gender-asymmetric mode of mutual violence" was proposed to explain the situation: Women are physically aggressive toward men, whereas men are sexually coercive toward women and may treat women very well in other aspects of their lives; meanwhile, they may or may not be verbally or psychologically violent toward each other. This mode of mutual violence is very common in young Chinese couples' dating lives, and it contributes a new perspective to understanding the escalation of violence in dating relationships.

Finally, I challenge the dichotomy of romantic love and violence and argue that these concepts sometimes coexist in violent dating relationships, although the ideal situation would be living with love and free from violence. In past studies, romantic love and violence have been dichotomized, just as they are in the general public's perception. However, many studies (Borochowitz & Eriskovits, 2002; Chavez, 2002; Fraser, 2003; Jackson, 2001) reveal that romantic love is coexistent with violence in intimate relationships, and sometimes love is used by men and women to justify violence. On the one hand, it is argued that the discourse of romantic love legitimates the jealousy of "people in love," in their desire to possess the other, and their attempts to control their partners' lives in order to feel more secure and loved. On the other hand, it is argued that romantic love discourses may bind women in relationships with abusive men, normalize dominance and superiority for men and deference and dependence for women, regulate women in a variety of ways to remain in the relationship, keep women silent about men's violence, and lead women to attempt to change men. These studies imply that love and violence can be mutually functional, which means that violence results from love and violence even becomes a means of preserving so-called "love."

CREATIVE ADVOCACY AND ACTIVISM

Chinese feminist activists and scholars have employed numerous strategies to raise public awareness of gender-based violence, including media-based information sharing and knowledge building, performance art, training professionals, and public campaigns and events (Wang, Qiao, Yang, & Nehring, 2013). On days such as Valentine's Day, International Women's Day (March 8), Orange Days (25th of every month), and 16 Days of Activism Against Gender-Based Violence (every year from November 25, the International Day for the Elimination of Violence against Women, to December 10, Human Rights Day), Chinese feminists organize many activities, events, and campaigns.

The year 2012 is regarded as a turning point in the Chinese feminist movement because young grassroots feminist activists took action by implementing a series of "performance art style" activities. One of the earliest performance art performances was called "wounded brides." On Valentine's Day, the day on which romantic love is promoted, three young women dressed as "wounded brides," wearing wedding gowns covered with fake blood, and walked up and down Qianmen Street, a popular tourist location in Beijing, to remind the public of the seriousness of gender-based violence. The three characters carried slogan boards and walked on the street the street while other peer colleagues distributed anti-gender-based violence-related flyers to passers-by. The slogans included "Hitting is not compassion, and scolding is not love. No violence, Love better!"; "Violence is nearby, how can you keep silence?"; and "Love is not the excuse of violence."

Funded by UN Women China, I have implemented a 3-year action research program in a private school in Beijing to prevent school-based violence, including dating violence and school bullying. The project involves both boys and girls, aged 13–18 years. It promotes gender equality, healthy masculinities, and fosters peer leadership to promote healthy romantic and peer relationships with teens. We set up a social work internship station, designed a curriculum, adopted interactive participatory

Figure 18.1 "Wounded brides" on Qianmen Street.

workshop styles, and provided training to 218 teenagers on five themes: the power of gender, respecting gender diversity, prevention of gender-based violence, establishing healthy relationship, and taking action (each theme usually lasts 2 hours). Regarding the theme of establishing a healthy relationship, teenagers are taught what is consent in a respectful relationship, how to make decisions, and how to communicate nonviolently. They are taught the concept of "consent" in intimate relationships. Also, to help them with their own romantic relationships, they are taught that "no means no" emphasizes respect for people's will and "yes means yes" is a confirmative consent. In addition to workshops, the program organizes an annual orange campus campaign, guest lectures, study trips, international exchanges, and so on.

After attending the group training, teenagers have a deeper understanding of gender roles, are more willing to break gender stereotypes, and take action to promote gender equality and prevent different kinds of gender-based violence including dating violence. One 11th grade female student wrote,

> After taking part in this activity, I felt that there is a huge responsibility on my shoulder. When I witness gender-based violence, I will not be a passive bystander. I will be a person actively advocate gender equality, and I hope to help everyone believe in gender equality.

A male 11th grade student said,

> Every one of us, is a small drop of water, dropping into a river will cause a small wave. What we need to do is to keep dropping to cause more waves, and later on, more people will response us to change themselves, and change the society.

CONCLUSION

Dating violence in China is an important area of study on its own; at the same time, it is necessary to investigate the phenomenon and its connection to the larger subject of

Figure 18.2 Orange Campus Campaign 2017.

Figure 18.3 Orange the World: 2017 Social Media Campaign.

gender-based violence, women's social status, and the feminist movement and advocacy, both local and global. Through this chapter, I attempt to convey some strong
messages to both young people and helping professionals. First, both need to be more
sensitive to the existence of dating violence, including minor and trivial violence, and
to be more aware of the potential danger of escalation from minor violence to severe
violence. Second, it is important for helping professionals to recognize the agency and
strength of young people temporarily trapped in violent dating relationships and to
remind them that there are choices and ways to disrupt an ongoing, escalating cycle of
violence. Prevention is always better than intervention; helping professionals need to
make an impact on children and teens before violence occurs. Third, young men and
women, but especially young women, need to learn to disrupt the predominant beliefs

Figure 18.4 Self-reflection after Attending the Workshops.

and myths of dating violence and become fully aware of their right to reject any kind of violence, no matter how trivial, in the name of love.

DISCUSSION QUESTIONS

1. Vagi and colleagues (2013) published a review article on risk factors and protective factors of dating violence (pp. 638–639). They listed only six protective factors. How do these factors (dis)appear in your life, and how do they help you avoid dating violence?
2. With your classmates, make a plan to organize a campaign during the 16 Days of Activism Against Gender-Based Violence. What is the plan?
3. In your opinion, what are the similarities and differences between dating violence and domestic violence?

REFERENCES

Ackard, D. M., & Deumark-Sztainer, D. (2002). Date violence and date rape among adolescents: Associations with disordered eating behaviors and psychological health. *Child Abuse & Neglect, 26*, 455–473.

Ai, X. (2004a). Stop phallogocentrism: Review of the case of Huang Jing [In Chinese]. *Feminism in China*, spring, 15–25.

Ai, X. (2004b). Striving for legal justice for Huang Jing: Our arguments and actions [In Chinese]. *Feminism in China*, spring, 2–14.

Ai, X. (2004c). When did the rape stop? Why? [In Chinese]. *Feminism in China*, spring, 26–30.

Alcoff, L., & Gray, L. (1993). Survivor discourse: Transgression or recuperation? *Signs: Journal of Women in Culture and Society, 18*, 260–290.

All-China Women's Federation & National Bureau of Statistics of China. (2011). *Report on major results of the Third Wave Survey on the social status of women in China*. Beijing, China: Author.

Armsworth, M. W., & Stronck, K. (1999). Intergenerational effects of incest on parenting: Skills, abilities, and attitudes. *Journal of Counseling and Development, 77*, 303–314.

Borochowitz, D. Y., & Eriskovits, Z. (2002). To love violently: Strategies for reconciling love and violence. *Violence Against Women, 8*, 476–494.

Chan, K. L. (2012). The role of Chinese face in the perpetration of dating partner violence. *Journal of Interpersonal Violence, 27*, 793–811.

Chavez, V. (2002). Language, gender and violence in qualitative research. *Quarterly of Community Health Education, 21*, 3–18.

Cleveland, H. H., Herrera, V. M., & Stuewig, J. (2003). Abusive males and abused females in adolescent relationships: Risk factor similarity and dissimilarity and the role of relationship seriousness. *Journal of Family Violence, 18*(6), 325–339.

Common Language. (2010). *Report on the situation of domestic violence among lesbians and female bisexuals*. Beijing, China: Author.

Decker, M. R., Latimore, A.D., Yasutake, S., Haviland, M., Ahmed, S., Blum, R.M., Sonenstein, F., & Astone, N. M. (2015), Gender-based violence against adolescent and adult women in lower- and middle-income countries, *Journal of Adolescent Health, 56*(2), 188–196.

Dekeseredy, W. S. (1989). Woman abuse in dating relationships: The role of peer support. *Dissertation Abstracts International, 49,* 3878.

Dekeseredy, W. S., & Kelly, K. (1995). Sexual abuse in Canadian university and college dating relationships: The contribution of male peer support. *Journal of Family Violence, 10,* 41–53.

Denov, M. S. (2004). The longer-term effects of child sexual abuse by female perpetrators: A qualitative study of male and female victims. *Journal of Interpersonal Violence, 19,* 1137–1156.

Dobash, R. P., & Dobash, R. E. (2004). Women's violence to men in intimate relationships. *British Journal of Criminology, 44,* 324–349.

Dunn, J. L. (2005). "Victims" and "survivors": Emerging vocabularies of motive for "battered women who stay." *Sociological Inquiry, 75,* 1–30.

Fraser, H. (2003). Narrating love and abuse in intimate relationships. *British Journal of Social Work, 33,* 273–290.

Gilfus, M. E. (1999). The price of the ticket: A survivor-centered appraisal of trauma theory. *Violence Against Women, 5,* 1238–1257.

He, Y., & Zuo, Z. (2004). *A survey by the All-China Women's Federation shows that 30% of households in China have domestic violence* [In Chinese]. Retrieved June 23, 2014, from http://zqb.cyol.com/content/2004-03/24/content_842543.htm

Hengehold, L. (2000). Remapping the event: Institutional discourses and the trauma of rape. *Signs: Journal of Women in Culture and Society, 26,* 189–214.

Jackson, S. (2001). Happily never after: Young women's stories of abuse in heterosexual love relationships. *Feminism and Psychology, 11,* 305–321.

Jennings, W. G., Okeem, C., Pikuero, A. R., Sellers, C. S., Theobald, D., & Farrington, D. P. (2017). Dating and intimate partner violence among young persons ages 15–30: Evidence from a systematic review. *Aggression and Violent Behavior, 33,* 107–125.

Koss, M. (1989). Hidden rape: Sexual aggression and victimization in a national sample of students in higher education. In M. A. Pirog-Good & J. E. Stets (Eds.), *Violence in dating relationships: Emerging social issues* (pp. 145–168). New York, NY: Praeger.

Lamb, S. (1999). *New versions of victims: Feminists struggle with the concept.* New York, NY: New York University Press.

Laner, M. R. (1983). Courtship abuse and aggression: Contextual aspects. *Sociological Spectrum, 3,* 69–83.

Li, S. (2007). *Imbalanced sex ratio at birth and comprehensive intervention in China.* Hyderabad, India: UNFPA China.

Magdol, L., Moffitt, T. E., Caspi, A., Newman, D. L., Fagan, J., & Silva, P. A. (1997). Gender differences in partner violence in birth cohort of 21-years-olds: Bridging the gap between clinical and epidemiological approaches. *Journal of Consulting and Clinical Psychology, 65*(1), 68–78.

Makepeace, J. M. (1981). Courtship violence among college students. *Family Relations, 32,* 97–102.

McCloskey, L. A., & Lichter, E. L. (2003). The contribution of marital violence to adolescent aggression across different relationships. *Journal of Interpersonal Violence, 18*(4), 390–412.

Meltzer, M. (2014). Who is a feminist now? *The New York Times.* Retrieved from http://www.nytimes.com/2014/05/22/fashion/who-is-a-feminist-now.html

Milwertz, C., & Bu, W. (2009). Non-governmental organising for gender equality in China—Joining a global emancipatory epistemic community. *International Journal of Human Rights, 11*, 131–149.

Naples, N. A. (2003). Deconstructing and locating survivor discourse: Dynamics of narrative, empowerment, and resistance for survivors of childhood sexual abuse. *Signs: Journal of Women in Culture and Society, 28*, 1151–1185.

National Bureau of Statistics. (2015). Population annual statistics. Retrieved from http://data.stats.gov.cn/gwwz.htm

Parish, W. L., Wang, T., Laumann, E. O., Pan, S., & Luo, Y. (2004). Intimate partner violence in China: National prevalence, risk factors and associated health problems. *International Family Planning Perspectives, 30*, 174–181.

Rhatigan, D. L., Moore, T. M., & Street, A. E. (2005). Reflection on partner violence: 20 years of research and beyond. *Journal of Interpersonal Violence, 20*, 82–88.

Ryan, K. M. (1998). The relationship between courtship violence and sexual aggression in college students. *Journal of Family Violence, 13*, 377–394.

Schumacher, J. A., & Slep, A. M. (2004). Attitudes and dating aggression: A cognitive dissonance approach. *Prevention Science, 5*(4), 231–243.

Shen, A. C. T., Chiu, M. Y. L., & Gao, J. (2012). Predictors of dating violence among Chinese adolescents: The role of gender-role beliefs and justification of violence. *Journal of Interpersonal Violence, 27*, 1066–1089.

Shook, N. J., Gerrity, D. A., Jurich, J., & Segrist, A. E. (2000). Courtship violence among college students: A comparison of verbally and physically abusive couples. *Journal of Family Violence, 15*, 1–22.

Stets, J. E. (1991). Psychological aggression in dating relationships: The role of interpersonal control. *Journal of Family Violence, 6*, 97–114.

Straus, M. A. (2004). Prevalence of violence against dating partners by male and female university students worldwide. *Violence Against Women, 10*, 790–811.

Straus, M. A., Hamby, S. L., Boney, M. S., & Sugarman, D. B. (1996). The revised Conflict Tactics Scales (CTS2): Development and preliminary psychometric data. *Journal of Family Issues, 17*(3), 283–316.

Sugarman, D. B., & Hotaling, G. T. (1989). Dating violence: Prevalence, context, and risk markers. In M. A. Pirog-Good & J. E. Stets (Eds.), *Violence in dating relationships: Emerging social issues* (pp. 3–32). New York, NY: Praeger.

Tang, C. (2005). Sexual Harassment in China. In: L. Tan & B. Liu (Eds), *Review on the Chinese women's studies in recent 10 years*. Beijing: Social Science Academic Press.

Tang, C. S. K., Wong, D., & Cheung, F. M. C. (2002). Social construction of women as legitimate victims of violence in Chinese societies. *Violence Against Women, 8*, 968–996.

Tjaden, P., & Thoennes, N. (2000). *Full report of the prevalence, incidence, and consequences of violence against women*. Washington, DC: US Department of Justice, Office of Justice Programs, National Institute of Justice.

Tong, X., & Su, Y. (2010). Gender segregation in the process of college student job seeking: A survey of higher education as a prelabor market factor. *Chinese Education and Society, 43*, 90–107.

United Nations Population Fund. (2012). *Sex imbalance at birth: Current trends, consequences, and policy implications*. Bangkok, Thailand: UNFPA Asia and the Pacific Regional Office.

Vagi, K. J., Rothman, E. F., Latzman, N. E., Tharp, A. T., Hall, D. M., & Breiding, M. J. (2013). Beyond correlates: A review of risk and protective factors for adolescent dating violence perpetration. *Journal of Youth and Adolescence, 42*(4), 633–649.

Wang, X. (2009). *Intimate partner violence: A survey based on 1015 college students.* Tianjin, China: Tianjin Renmin Publishing House.

Wang, X. (2017). *Gender, dating, and violence in urban China.* New York, NY: Routledge.

Wang, X., Fang, G., & Li, H. (2013). *Gender-based violence and masculinities study: Chinese quantitative research report.* Beijing, China: UNFPA China.

Wang, X., & Ho, S. Y. (2007). My sassy girl: A qualitative study of women's aggression in dating relationships in Beijing. *Journal of Interpersonal Violence, 22,* 623–638.

Wang, X., & Ho, S. Y. (2011). 'Female Virginity Complex' Untied: Young Beijing Women's experience of virginity loss and sexual coercion. *Smith College Studies in Social Work, 81,* 184–200.

Wang, X., & Nehring, D. (2014). Individualization as an ambition: Mapping the dating landscape in Beijing. *Modern China, 40,* 578–604.

Wang, X., Qiao, D., Yang, L., & Nehring, D. (2013). *Hard struggles in times of change: A qualitative study on masculinities and gender-based violence in contemporary China.* Beijing, China: UNFPA China.

Wincentak, K., Connolly, J., & Card, N. (2017). Teen Dating Violence: A Meta-Analytic Review of Prevalence Rates. *Psychology of Violence, 7,* 224–241.

World Economic Forum. (2017). *Global gender gap report.* Retrieved from https://www. weforum.org/reports/the-global-gender-gap-report-2017

Yu, Y., Xiao, S., & Liu, K. Q. (2013). Dating violence among gay men in China. *Journal of Interpersonal Violence, 28,* 2491–2504.

Zhang, L. (2009). Chinese women protesting domestic violence: The Beijing conference, international donor agencies, and the making of a Chinese women's NGO. *Meridians: Feminism, Race, Transnationalism, 9,* 66–99.

19

Female Same-Sex Intimate Partner Violence in China

State, Culture, Family, and Gender

MING LUO AND TUEN YI CHIU ■

CASE STUDY: "SOMETHING BAD WILL HAPPEN TO YOU!"

After 2 years in a same-sex relationship, An wanted to break up with Mo because Mo was abusively controlling her in the relationship. With fierce opposition to An's decision, Mo smashed a window glass in their rented apartment in Beijing. She started to send An messages with threats or hints of harm. Mo even told An to "make a will . . . in case something bad will happen to you." Although An was afraid of Mo, she also worried about Mo's psychological and emotional well-being. Because Mo showed signs of hysteria, An worried that Mo would go to extremes, such as inflicting self-harm or committing suicide, to keep An in the relationship. At first, An decided to endure Mo's insults and aggression with the hope that her tolerance would pacify Mo. So again and again, An forgave Mo's violent acts, including sexual abuse and stalking, and satisfied Mo's requests in exchange for a peaceful breakup. Mo, however, did not keep her promises to let An go but repeatedly towed An back to their miserable and abusive relationship. An tried to secretly move out and stay with her mother but failed because Mo threatened to publicly reveal her homosexual identity to shame her family. Out of anger and coercive control, when An returned to their rented apartment one day, Mo seized the chance to lock An in the bedroom. An was confined for 2 days until she managed to call her friends for help. Realizing the danger in staying with Mo, An eventually sought help from a nongovernmental organization (NGO).

OVERVIEW

An's story exemplifies a common scenario in which intimate partner violence (IPV) occurs in a same-sex relationship. IPV refers to "a pattern of behaviour where one intimate partner coerces, dominates, or isolates another intimate partner to maintain power and control over the partner and the relationship" (National Coalition of Anti-Violence Programs, 2016, p. 11). It encompasses an array of physical, emotional, psychological, sexual, and economic abuses (Hattery, 2009), as well as stalking and control of reproductive or sexual health (Black et al., 2011). Although IPV is widely recognized as a type of gender-based violence that originated in women's subordination under men in gender relations (Ellsberg & Heise, 2005), it by no means implies that it does not exist in non-heterosexual intimate relationships. Due to the stereotypical perception that IPV only occurs in heterosexual relationships and that it is perpetrated by men, IPV in same-sex relationships remains a hidden phenomenon. In recent decades, some scholars started to acknowledge that IPV in same-sex relationships is a universal and significant social and public health issue that profoundly affects the physical, emotional, and psychological well-being of men and women in same-sex relationships. Evidence from existing studies suggests that the prevalence of IPV is as high or even higher in same-sex relationships than in heterosexual relationships (Brown & Herman, 2015; Goldberg & Meyer, 2013; Hester & Donovan, 2009; Leonard, Mitchell, Pitts, Patel, & Fox, 2008; Messinger, 2011; Walters, Chen, & Breiding, 2013). Considering that men and women in same-sex relationships do not experience IPV in a similar manner, this chapter specifically focuses on female same-sex intimate partner violence (FSSIPV). A review of the prevalence of FSSIPV reported in existing studies conducted throughout the world is provided next.

Prevalence of FSSIPV

In a recent review of IPV and sexual abuse among lesbian, gay, bisexual, and transgender people (LGBT), Brown and Herman (2015) reported that 25.0–40.4% of lesbians in studies using representative sampling in the United States had experienced IPV in their lifetime, and 10.2% had experienced it in the past 12 months (Goldberg & Meyer, 2013; Messinger, 2011; Walters et al., 2013). Overall, the lifetime prevalence of rape, physical violence, and/or stalking reported by lesbians (43.8%) is statistically higher than that of heterosexual women (35%) (Walters et al., 2013). Outside the United States, approximately 26% of lesbian respondents from Victoria, Australia, reported being sexually abused by their same-sex partners in 2007, which further confirmed that lesbians were more likely to report victimization in intimate relationships compared with other women and men (Leonard et al., 2008). In the United Kingdom, 49.1% of the female respondents in a nonrandomly sampled survey ($N = 800$) conducted in 2007 reported having experienced domestic abuse at some time in their same-sex relationships (Hester & Donovan, 2009). In Asia, five local NGOs in Hong Kong conducted a survey of FSSIPV from December 2006 to February 2007. Using a nonrandom sampling ($N = 219$), the survey revealed that approximately one-third of the respondents reported that they had experienced various forms of IPV in their same-sex relationships; in particular, 16% of the respondents reported being physically abused (Women Coalition of HKSAR, 2007). In 2009, an internet-based survey

($N = 339$) showed that the majority (79.1%) of LGB respondents reported experiencing IPV at least once in their relationships and that no gender differences were found in terms of the prevalence of IPV (Mak, Chong, & Kwong, 2010). A recent survey that included responses from 1,076 young adults at a university in Hong Kong revealed that sexual minority respondents reported significantly more dating violence than did heterosexual respondents (Wong et al., 2017). The mean difference between the two groups was 0.83 at the 95% confidence level after adjusting for sociodemographic factors including age, sex, education, and childhood adversities. A comparable prevalence rate of FSSIPV is also found in mainland China: 42% of lesbian and bisexual women in a survey conducted by an NGO in Beijing reported that they were victims of FSSIPV (Tongyu, 2009).

Common forms of FSSIPV

In general, psychological abuse is the most common form of FSSIPV (Hester & Donovan, 2009; Messinger, 2014; Walters et al., 2013). Turell (2000) found that exposure to verbal threats and using children as tools appear to be common tactics of emotional abuse against lesbians. For example, with regard to suffering emotional abuse, victims have voiced statements such as "She treated me like a servant" and "Played mind games with me" as well as other kinds of psychological abuse that commonly occur in female same-sex relationships (Turell, 2000). Outing—the threat to expose the sexual identity of the victim—is a particularly common form of IPV used by perpetrators to socially isolate and control the victims. Coming out is not a common practice in mainland China (Kam, 2012) because women are under huge pressure from their families to get married and have children and because homosexuality is still largely considered socially unacceptable. In Hong Kong, one in six lesbian and bisexual women have been threatened with exposure of their sexual identity to co-workers or family members by their abusive partners (Women Coalition of HKSAR, 2007). Very often, victims experience multiple forms of violence in an abusive relationship. For example, An, the lesbian victim discussed at the beginning of the chapter, was verbally threatened, stalked, had restricted personal freedom, and was sexually abused by her ex-girlfriend Mo.

Reported rates of FSSIPV

Despite the comparable victimization rates of lesbians worldwide, evidence from the United States and the United Kingdom reveals that FSSIPV is "less likely to be reported by victims to authorities, less likely to be prosecuted within the legal system, and generally disregarded by helping agencies as well as the general public" (Little & Terrance, 2010, p. 430) compared to IPV against women in heterosexual unions (Turell, 2000). It has been estimated that approximately 50% of lesbian victims remain silent throughout their plight (Karmen, 2001). It is especially the case when the victims are caught in a "double closet," such that seeking help would mean disclosing not only their experience of domestic violence but also their sexual orientation (Kaschak, 2001; McClennen, 2005). One reason why An had to return to Mo even after she had moved out to stay with her mother was that she worried that Mo would disclose her lesbian identity to her mother. Staying in the closet was also the reason why An called friends, rather than family members, for help when she was physically confined by Mo.

Although the statistics presented here provide a general picture of the phenomenon of FSSIPV worldwide, the majority of the existing research has been conducted in the West (for reviews, see Messinger, 2011, 2014). Systematic research on the prevalence and contextual mechanisms of FSSIPV in the non-Western context, especially in Chinese societies, remains limited. Given the salient impacts of Confucianism, collectivism, patriarchy, familism (an ideology that places priority on family over self), filial piety, and the distinct institutional and state setting on sexuality and intimate relationships in the Chinese context, theories developed in the West may not be applicable. Further examination of the mechanisms of FSSIPV in a non-Western context is warranted. Employing a transnational feminist approach of intersectionality, this chapter uses China as a case in point to discuss how systems of the state, culture, family, and gender intersect to structure, reinforce, and sustain the hegemonic system of heteronormativity in China. It discusses how such intersection has fundamentally influenced legislation and policy of anti-FSSIPV, which has subsequently shaped the victimization and entrapment of lesbians in abusive same-sex relationships. By unraveling the cultural and institutional heterogeneity within the broader category of FSSIPV, this chapter demonstrates how a feminist approach of intersectionality developed in the West can be applied in a non-Western context to inform future studies, service providers, policymakers, and advocacy to design and/or implement appropriate measures to identify, intervene, and prevent FSSIPV by incorporating an LGBT cultural-sensitive framework. Such a framework has implications for advocacy groups with regard to delineating strategies to advance the rights of LGBT people in a cultural context in which the family plays an important role and coming out is not an option for some FSSIPV victims. Before discussing the case of FSSIPV in China, the next section provides an overview of the historical trends of policies regarding FSSIPV worldwide.

HISTORICAL TRENDS

Despite worldwide evidence of LGBT's vulnerability to FSSIPV, policy changes to legally protect and support victims of FSSIPV often lag behind. In the United States, the Violence Against Women Act, a federal law passed in 1994, did not include protections for women in same-sex relationships. It expired in 2011 and immediately entered a 2-year legislative battle before reauthorization. Extending the legal protection for women in same-sex relationship was included in one version of the legislation passed along party lines in the Senate and House, which was opposed by conservative Republicans. In 2013, the House finally passed an all-inclusive version of the bill to expand federal protections to LGBT people, native Americans, and immigrants (Cannon, 2015). Despite this legislative revision and policies designed to help LGBTs, female victims in same-sex relationships were found to keep reticence about their violent experiences (Briones-Robinson, Powers, & Socia, 2016). Recent studies have linked victims' reticence or reluctance to seek help with the way government officers are trained and police response to same-sex IPV versus heterosexual IPV (Cannon, 2015; Pattavina, Hirschel, Buzawa, Faggiani, & Bentley, 2007; Russell & Sturgeon, 2019). For example, police were found to be less likely to use their arrest authority in FSSIPV cases, especially when minority women were involved (Pattavina et al., 2007). Moreover, many agencies that provide training on IPV for police officers and social workers have been found to continue to employ their long-standing agenda focusing on the heterosexual "female victimization and male perpetration" model and have failed to provide sufficient training on same-sex dynamics (Hamel & Russell, 2013). Sensitization training in terms of same-sex IPV is critical because police officers with less experience tend to use non-arrest options in instances of same-sex IPV cases (Russell & Sturgeon, 2019), which might leave the victim in even greater danger because the perpetrator might retaliate against the victim for reporting the abuse.

In Hong Kong, the Domestic and Cohabitation Relationships Violence Ordinance was passed and launched in 1986, yet it only provided protection and support for people in heterosexual marriages. Local feminist organizations (e.g., The Association for the Advancement of Feminism) continuously criticized the implementation of the ordinance, which was inclined to keep family integrity rather than to protect female victims. In 2004, after several appalling tragedies of domestic violence occurred, the Legislative Council of Hong Kong decided to revise the ordinance and extended the legal protection to ex-spouse, ex-cohabitant, and members of the extended family. Revisions that entailed protection of same-sex cohabitants encountered objections by Christian churches and conservative members of the Legislative Council. In order to counterbalance objections and pass the revision in 2008, the Secretary for Labour and Welfare promised to include same-sex cohabitants in the next revision, which left the issue for public debate and campaign for another year. Finally in December 2009, the third revision of the ordinance included protection for same-sex cohabitants, which resulted in protests from Christian groups. These groups argued that same-sex cohabitation should not be addressed in the scope of the family and that it should not be encouraged and thus not be protected under the law.

On July 6, 2006, the United Nations issued the "In-Depth Study on All Forms of Violence Against Women," which stated,

> Forms and manifestations of violence against women are shaped by social and cultural norms as well as the dynamics of each social, economic and political system. Factors such as women's race, ethnicity, caste, class, migrant or refugee status, age, religion, sexual orientation, marital status, disability or HIV status will influence what forms of violence they suffer and how they experience it. (p. 70)

However, to date, only several countries or regions (e.g., the United States, United Kingdom, European Union, Hong Kong, and Brazil) have explicitly acknowledged same-sex partners as the target of protection in their anti-domestic laws or ordinances.

THE CASE OF CHINA

China is still largely regarded as a patriarchal society. Due to the one-child policy and son preference, the sex ratio at birth in China in 2004 was 121 males to 100 females, although it declined to 117 males to 100 females in 2011 (National Bureau of Statistics of China, 2012). Women in China are expected to conform to traditional gender norms—to get married and become social and biological reproducers. In 2012, the average age of marriage for women was 22.8 years, and 2.1% of women older than age 15 years entered early marriage (marry between ages 15 and 19 years) (National Bureau of Statistics of China, 2012). Gender inequality is still significant in China. Although 45.9% of females aged 16 years or older are engaged in paid employment, only 25.1% of heads of government institutions, parties, civil societies, enterprises, and public institutions are women (National Bureau of Statistics of China, 2012). There is no official statistic about female homosexuals in China, but Li Yinhe, the first scholar to research LGBT issues in China, estimated that the number may be as high as 6.5 million (Li, 1998). This estimation is based on the percentage of LGBT population in Kinsey's work (Kinsey, Gebhard, Martin, & Pomeroy, 1953; Kinsey, Martin, & Wardell, 1948) and the Chinese population. In mainland China, lesbians commonly refer to themselves as *lala*. Survey data collected from 505 students at three universities in Beijing in 2002 indicated that the majority of these young Chinese were opposed to homosexuality (Higgins, Zheng, Liu, & Sun, 2002). Homosexuality is considered a failure and a disgrace of the family because it is believed to be against procreation and family formation. Given the stigmatization and conservative gender ideology in Chinese society, female homosexuals remain largely invisible. As a sexual minority, lala are marginalized and rendered "second class" in society. However, pressure for female homosexuals comes not only from society but also from their families of origin. Most parents do not accept that their children are homosexual (Engebretsen, 2009; Kam, 2012). Coming out by a homosexual may trigger verbal and/or psychological violence from their family of birth (Tongyu, 2009). In a survey conducted by a grass-roots NGO in mainland China in 2007, 48% of the respondents indicated that they had experienced domestic violence in their family of birth, and their "coming out" was significantly correlated with the burst of violence from parents. Victims believed that their sexual identity was the root cause of their victimization in the family of birth (Tongyu, 2009). As a result, staying hidden or in the closet is not only a strategy to protect themselves from discrimination in the workplace but also a way to protect their family from being harassed and stigmatized by others. Against this backdrop, female homosexuals who experience IPV become "the minority within the minority."

Voices of female victims in same-sex relationships are rarely heard in mainstream, anti-domestic violence movements in mainland China. To date, there is no official publication or research on FSSIPV in China. The only available data were collected in 2007 by the grassroots NGO Tongyu, sponsored by the Anti-domestic Violence Network of China Law Society. Using nonrandom sampling, a total of 428 valid questionnaires were collected from female respondents in eight cities of China: Beijing, Shanghai, Guangzhou, Zhuhai, Nanning, Kunming, Chengdu, and Anshan. The majority of respondents were young (aged 26 years on average), highly educated (66.5% had a college degree), single (92%), in a dual-parent household (78.5%), identified themselves as lesbian (74.8%), and had not yet come out to parents (83.2%). The report showed that 48% of the respondents had experienced domestic violence in their family of birth, and 42% were victims of FSSIPV; these rates are comparable to the prevalence rates reported in the studies reviewed previously in this chapter. Psychological abuse was the most common form of IPV reported by the respondents: 38.7% of them reported being psychologically abused, whereas 26.5% of the respondents experienced physical violence and 5.7% reported having been sexually abused. However, only 55% of victims sought help. Among them, 82.3% sought help from the lesbian community, such as lesbian friends or lesbian support groups. Twenty-one percent of them approached family members, and only 10% contacted the police or the Women's Federation (the most influential organization supported by the Chinese government that deals with women's issues). Although no scientific studies that systematically compare women's IPV experiences in same-sex and heterosexual relationships have been performed, an internet-based survey ($N = 2,177$) in 2015 showed that there were no significant differences in the prevalence rates and forms of IPV experienced by heterosexual and non-heterosexual couples; however, homosexual victims were more likely to experience severe psychological abuse in violent intimate relationships compared to their heterosexual counterparts, and bisexual victims were more likely to experience forced sex compared to their heterosexual and homosexual counterparts (Wang, Wang, Chiu, & Jiao, 2015).

In the case study presented at the beginning of this chapter, An never thought to seek help from the police. Although Mo threatened to harm her and perpetrated physical and sexual violence against her, she considered IPV as a private matter that should be kept behind closed doors. The report by Tongyu (2009) indicated that due to social discrimination against homosexuals and the lack of legal protection in China, it is extremely difficult for lesbian victims to obtain social support. Although there is a demand for social services for homosexuals who experience violence, to date, there is only one NGO in Beijing, the Rainbow Anti-Gender Based Violence Service Center, which provides services to victims of FSSIPV. In addition to the lack of social recognition and legal protection, the lack of relevant training and knowledge about homosexuals in China also impedes the development of services for homosexuals. The next section discusses how an unfavorable political atmosphere, a deep-rooted collectivist culture, institutionalized familism, and gender structure in contemporary China constitute an interlocking "closet" that has not only increased the vulnerability of Chinese female homosexuals but also entrapped them in abusive same-sex relationships.

CURRENT CONDITIONS: FSSIPV IN CHINA

China has its distinct institutions of state, culture, family, and gender. This section focuses on how these systems intersect to structure, reinforce, and sustain the hegemonic system of heteronormativity in China, which has subsequently shaped the victimization and entrapment of lesbians in abusive same-sex relationships.

Sexuality and the State

Although the Chinese government does not recognize same-sex marriage or civil union, it has gradually relaxed its repressive laws and policies against LGBT people and same-sex couples. In 1997, the reference that criminalized and identified male anal sex as "hooliganism" was deleted in the Revised Criminal Law (Jeffreys, 2006). In 2000, the Ministry of Public Security announced that "members of the Chinese public have the right to choose their own sexuality" (Jeffreys, 2006, p. 10). Finally, in 2001, the Ministry of Health removed homosexuality from the list of mental illnesses in the *Chinese Classification and Diagnostic Criteria of Mental Disorders* (Davis & Friedman, 2014). In the late 1990s, state and local media began to report news about LGBT issues and produced television programs and published articles about homosexuals in China, which showed the state's increased tolerance toward homosexuals. Since then, homosexuals have become increasingly more visible in the public sphere. Civil society in China has flourished, and LGBT organizations have been actively advancing the rights of sexual minorities throughout the country (Rofel, 2013). In particular, since 2001, sociologist Li Yinhe has repeatedly proposed the Chinese Same-Sex Marriage Bill to the National People's Congress and to the Chinese Political Consultative Conference, which has generated nationwide news reports and caused heated debates, thereby bringing the cases of the LGBT community to light. In 2009, two gay and lesbian couples publicly campaigned for the right of same-sex marriage by taking wedding photos on the streets of Beijing and being interviewed by both domestic and international media ("Beijing's 'Happy Couples,'" 2009). Following this, a number of public wedding ceremonies of homosexual couples have been performed (Davis & Friedman, 2014), even though same-sex marriage has yet to be legalized.

Notwithstanding the seemingly gradual loosening of state regulation on homosexuality and the increased visibility of LGBT people in the country, censorship from the state and discrimination from the public against same-sex relationships have not vanished. In 2016, the Chinese government released a new set of regulations for content on television shows after it forcefully canceled a popular gay-themed drama called "Addicted" (*shàng yǐn*). The new guidelines state that "no television drama shall show abnormal sexual relationships and behaviors, such as incest, same-sex relationships, sexual perversion, sexual assault, sexual abuse, sexual violence, and so on" ("China Bans Depictions," 2016). By banning homosexual content, the government specified portrayals of homosexuals as "vulgar, immoral and unhealthy content" ("China Bans Depictions," 2016). Similar censorship was carried out in 2015 when a documentary about young gay Chinese titled "Mama Rainbow" ("China Bans Depictions," 2016) and a gay-themed episode of the online talk show "U Can U Bibi" (Lin & Chen, 2016) were pulled offline. State censorship of homosexual media content represents not only overt stigmatization of homosexuals but also a reassertion of the heteronormative system in China. Even with the inclusion of violence among "people living together" in the newly passed law on anti-domestic violence in 2016, same-sex couples are not included and thus not legally protected. When asked whether same-sex cohabiting couples were included in the new law, Guo Linmao, a member of the legislative affairs commission of the parliament's standing committee, confirmed the exclusion of homosexuals by denying the existence of violence among homosexuals in the country: "Our law does not cover homosexuals, and there is no such thing.... We have not yet discovered this form of violence [between same-sex partners], so to give you a certain answer, it can be said that people who cohabit do not include homosexuals" (French Centre for Research on Contemporary China, 2016). Although the law was said to have deliberated on the extent to which state authorities should intervene in intimate and family relations (French Centre for Research on Contemporary China, 2016), the statement given by the state authority has nonetheless (1) reinforced the myth that violence does not exist between same-sex partners, (2) institutionally marginalized homosexuals as a group, and (3) risked the safety of those who are in abusive same-sex relationships. Even today, there is no law protecting homosexuals from discrimination directed at their sexual orientation (Human Rights Watch, 2016), and assistance from the police, shelters, or authorities is not available for LGBT victims, making them exceedingly helpless when they experience IPV. Because they are not entitled to the public benefits that are provided for heterosexual married couples,

FSSIPV victims who do not have adequate economic and housing resources might be trapped in an abusive relationship.

In summary, despite the seeming loosening of legal regulation on homosexual behaviors, the interventions, censorship, and reluctance of the state to legalize same-sex marriage and protect homosexuals from violence have institutionalized heterosexual unions as the only form of intimacy, which has provided solid ground for heteronormativity and heterosexism in China. This may have led to the discrimination and homophobic reactions of the public toward homosexuals, further increasing the vulnerability and tendency of the victims to stay behind the closed door.

Collectivism and Shame-Based Culture

Culturally, Chinese societies are patriarchal and collectivist (Yu, 2005). Under the tradition of collectivism, individuals are collectively accountable for the glory and shame of the family (Choi & Luo, 2016). Individuals represent not only the self but also the family, the clan, and the community (Ho, 1976). To protect family honor, individual members have to obey the rules of the family (jiā fǎ) and are obligated to not bring shame to the family. The popular saying, "Don't wash your dirty linen in public" (jiā chǒu bù kě wài yáng), emphasizes that family honor and saving face are highly valued norms in Chinese societies. Intertwining with the shame-based culture rooted in Confucianism, saving face has long been an important aspect of social life in Chinese societies (Yu, 2005). This has two implications for lesbian victims in Chinese societies. First, because the family is socially and institutionally conceptualized as a heteronormative one, being a lesbian deviates from the social norm and would thus bring shame to the family. Many lesbians therefore geographically and emotionally isolate themselves from their natal family in order to maintain the face of the family while pursuing autonomy to lead their preferred intimate life (Choi & Luo, 2016). Second, because domestic violence is considered a type of shame in Chinese culture, battered women typically choose to hide their victimization to protect their family from losing face, even though hiding themselves may further intensify their sense of helplessness and isolation (Chiu, 2017). Given their particular sexual, gender, and cultural identities, seeking help would mean disclosing not only their IPV experience but also their sexual orientation, which both violate conventional norms in Chinese culture.

Chinese Familism and Norms of Marriage

The family continues to be the basic unit of Chinese society, in which adult children are still intimately tied to their parents (Pimentel, 2000). Whereas an affectionate conjugal bond based on free will emerged as the primary relationship in Western societies, "marital relationship in Chinese societies has never been as private, personalised, and sentimentalised as it has been in the West" (Xu, 1998, p. 188). Even with the rising tide of individualism in China, the centrality of the family persists.

In the Chinese patrilineal kinship system, marriage often took place to benefit the whole family rather than the individuals involved (Baker, 1979). As such, marriage is often subjected to the surveillance and control of the older generations (Chiu & Choi, 2015; Pimentel, 2000). Despite the abolishment of arranged marriage and the influence of the Western ideas of mutual and romantic love, Chinese parents have continued to take part in their adult children's mate choices and marriage decisions (Choi & Luo, 2016). Filial piety, as a core element of Chinese familism, prescribes normative intergenerational relationships that emphasize children's repayment to parents by being obedient, respectful, and responsible for providing material support and physical care when the parents age (Zhan & Montgomery, 2003). Because marriage is highly desirable for continuing the family line, children are expected "to form their own family and develop their own career" (*chéng jiā lì yè*) as a form of repayment and adherence to familial norms.

Based on this background, homosexuals in China are largely despised as disgraceful and unfilial children of their families because they have failed their familial and filial duties of getting married and having children (Liu & Choi, 2006). In order to keep up with filial standards and maintain financial security, some try to hide their sexual identity from their parents. Torn between family pressure and personal autonomy over intimacy and sexuality, some choose to enter a heterosexual marriage with a straight partner by either suppressing their homosexuality or having a homosexual partner secretly. Others choose to engage in a "nominal marriage"—a contractual "heterosexual marriage" that is formed by a female lesbian and a gay man when both of them maintain intimate relationships with their same-sex partners (Choi & Luo, 2016). It is viewed as a strategic, alternative choice for homosexual people to strive for sexual autonomy while fulfilling family duties. Although nominal marriage is not practiced by all homosexuals, it reflects the tremendous family-related pressure that some homosexuals experience. The secrecy of their sexual orientation, together with the social pressure to conform to filial gendered norms, shapes the exclusive sexuality-related vulnerability of homosexuals in China, which is often used by abusive partners to psychologically oppress and behaviorally control the victims. This is supported by the fact that only 21% of victimized lesbians seek help from family members (Tongyu, 2009). In cases in which victims' sexual identity has been exposed, some suffer from a secondary traumatization in that they are emotionally or physically abused by their parents and family members (Engebretsen, 2009). It is paradoxical that when the family might be the last resort of support for the victim, the family may further oppress the victim rather than assist her.

Gender in the Chinese Context

Heterosexual discourse that engenders individuals as being either feminine or masculine is pervasive in both Western and Chinese societies (Barlow, 1994). Women are typically stereotyped as innately nonviolent, caretaking, nurturing, and only having sex with men; those who do not enact feminine gender roles are considered unnatural, deviant, and a threat to existing gender relations (Mann, 2011). Interconnected with heterosexism, gender role stereotyping endangers female homosexuals due to the fact that their experiences are either ignored or stigmatized (Balsam, 2001). In particular, the myth of "nonviolent women" that emerged during the second wave of feminism has developed into the myth of "lesbian utopia"—that lesbian relationships are idealized as egalitarian, loving, and never violent (McLaughlin & Rozee, 2001). Even in heterosexual intimate relationships, women's aggression is considered as playful or childish and not a major issue; often, it is justified as a punitive reaction to cheating by a husband or boyfriend (Wang & Ho, 2007). In this context, when violence occurs between female intimate partners, the fight is considered a cat fight in which they cannot seriously injure each other because they are thought to not be physically strong enough to inflict serious harm (McLaughlin & Rozee, 2001). In addition, the gender bias that only men are perpetrators makes it difficult to identify perpetrators in instances of FSSIPV (Gillum & DiFulvio, 2012). Some perpetrators are aware of this potential confusion such that they intentionally use this to their advantage by playing the feminine victim role in order to avoid being arrested (Hassouneh & Glass, 2008). Because both the perpetrator and the victim are women, when the victim resists, she might be accused of mutually abusing her female partner (Renzetti, 1992). An individual may even be wrongly accused due to the misconception that the one who is abusive has to be the more masculine one (Jolly, 2004).

In the case of heterosexual discourse, however, the idealization of men and women has its own particular Chinese features. First, deriving from the classical yin and yang discourse, males and females are complementary in sexual relationships so that men are active and vigorous, and women are responsive and weak (Mann, 2011). Although images of "female red guards" and "iron ladies" were promoted during the Maoist era, women's domestic roles were revived in political discourse in the post-Mao period and independent single womanhood was hardly extolled (Goodman, 2005). Especially under the Chinese patriarchal system, single women, including lesbians, were largely stigmatized by mainstream society. Second, from 20th-century officials to communists' cadres, all sought to hold individual men and women in the country to the same standards by prescribing proper gender roles (Mann, 2011). Deviant gender expressions, especially of those "butch" or masculinized female partners in same-sex relationships, easily arouse negative judgments from the public and thus burden female homosexuals with emotional distress, which is universally considered as directly associated with IPV in same-sex relationships. This culturally and institutionally structured gender system in China has not only suppressed homosexuality but also heightened lesbian victims' vulnerability by curtailing their ability to identify IPV and seek help. The higher tolerance of some public figures with a more gender-neutral appearance may be a sign that gender roles are becoming less rigid in the contemporary era. A more inclusive social environment may lessen the stress that masculinized lesbians and their partners receive and thus conducive to creating more harmonious same-sex couple dynamics.

LOOKING TO THE FUTURE

As discussed previously, systems of the state, culture, family, and gender in China are intricately intersected to create a multiple interlocking predicament for women in abusive same-sex relationships. This implies that prevention and intervention of FFSIPV should not just target a single cause. Although China launched its first anti-domestic violence law in 2016 that protected "people living together" (gòng tóng jū zhù de rén), female victims still found difficulties in getting help due to family pressure, traditional gender ideologies, and discrimination. Legal protection asserts the rights of people in same-sex relationships, but it is only effective when victims report their plights to authorities.

In the mainstream literature based on studies in the West, FSSIPV is conceptualized as a type of violence occurring in the context in which pervasive gender role stereotyping, heterosexism, and homophobia at the societal level and imbalance power
relations at the couple level have jointly shaped the FSSIPV experiences of lesbians.
Little attention has been paid to cultural and family-level factors. Whereas romantic
love and the nuclear couple relationship and the role of the state are prominent in
Western societies, the intergenerational family may play a more substantial role in
shaping gender and sexual relations in Chinese societies. Unlike the West, the social
system in China is family-based but not individual-based. Ideologies and traditions of
collectivism, familism, and filial piety are deeply entrenched in Chinese society. Being
a lesbian in Chinese society is therefore never a choice of personal lifestyle because it
is not permitted by family, culture, or politics.

Under the hegemony of heterosexism and heteronormativity in China, stigmatization against homosexuality is based not only on sexual identity but also on marital
status. Being an unmarried childless lesbian is heavily condemned. To live up to
filial and familial norms and protect the face of the family, Chinese female homosexuals would neither expose their sexual identity nor disclose their IPV victimization. Building on the concept of the "double closet" (McClennen, 2005), battered
lesbians in the Chinese context are trapped in a "triple closet"—in the abusive intimate relationship, in the intergenerational family, and in the hegemony of heteronormativity in the society—where they are culturally, institutionally, and socially
marginalized.

On the one hand, the family continues to be an important social institution that
sets the code of conducts for individuals. On the other hand, the family is institutionalized by the state and sustained by systems of gender, marriage, and heteronormativity. It continues to serve as the primary source of support for one's career, material and
care acquisition, family formation, and childrearing. Individuals identified as lesbians
are thus positioned and structured within the patriarchal and patrilineal structure and
directly linked to the reputation of the family. For many Chinese lesbians, this means
that family is more an object that needs to be protected than a source of help and
support. Family members may even abuse the FSSIPV victim when they discover the
victim's sexual identity. It is possible that some lesbian victims suffer more psychological distress from their family than from their abusive partner, especially when coming
out and asking for help.

Advocacy

Given the characteristics of the Chinese context, tackling FSSIPV requires not only
state intervention through legal protections and law enforcement but also support
from the family and the community. Legal protection is the first step to ensure the
rights and safety of FSSIPV victims. It is of particular importance to acknowledge that
IPV exists not only in heterosexual marriages but also in same-sex intimate relationships. Current laws and ordinances regarding domestic violence should be extended
to cover same-sex intimate partners. Due to the intersecting features of FSSIPV in
China, legal protection per se is not adequate to tackle IPV in same-sex relationships.
In this regard, researchers, policymakers, and service providers should take into consideration the cultural and familial factors when examining the causes, risk factors,

and protective factors of FSSIPV and also when designing measures to intervene and prevent FSSIPV. An LGBT cultural-sensitive approach is essential for tackling discrimination and violence against homosexuals. This may include training for service providers at clinics, hospitals, and social welfare agencies, in addition to law enforcement, court personnel, and public educators, about anti-discrimination against LGBT and anti-violence. Advocacy is needed to advance the rights of people in same-sex relationships—for example, by ensuring that homosexuals are treated equally when they report to the police, seek help from social service agencies, and receive medical treatment. Strict confidentiality and the safety of FSSIPV victims should be ensured to protect them from retaliation by their perpetrators, especially in the form of outing. Victims of IPV in same-sex relationships should have the right to choose not to report their victimization to authorities so as to avoid suffering further victimization from their family members. In general, it is imperative to promote a more inclusive environment in which people living outside the hegemonic system of heterosexual marriage are respected. Public educational campaigns should aim at explaining the phenomenon of IPV in same-sex relationships and deconstructing the myths about same-sex IPV. With increased awareness, any individual has the capacity to rescue an IPV victim.

CONCLUSION

FSSIPV occurs throughout the world, and different cultures have shaped diverse understandings, perceptions, and reactions of violence in different contexts (Fernández, 2006). Yet, the literature on FSSIPV is mostly based on Western cases and the role of contextual factors has been understudied, specifically in Asian societies (Tongyu, 2009). Adopting a transnational feminist approach of intersectionality, we emphasize the importance of contextualization by outlining the distinct sociocultural and institutional factors that have shaped the experiences of battered lesbians in the Chinese context. We also advocate for an LGBT cultural-sensitive framework to tackle discrimination and violence against homosexuals. Given the paucity of official data and systematic research on FSSIPV in China, further empirical research is needed. Cross-cultural studies would help unravel the sociocultural factors that shape the diverse ways in which heteronormativity is structured and how perceptions and reactions of violence are formed in different contexts. Exploration of the impact of cultural beliefs on victims' help-seeking behaviors across countries is of particular importance. Specifically, future studies should examine the role of the family in FSSIPV because it has been overlooked in the existing literature, which is based mainly on the experiences of Western societies in which individualism, rather than familism, is prominent and prevalent.

BRIEF STORY HIGHLIGHT

To advocate for legal same-sex marriage, numerous public wedding photos have been taken in urban China in recent years. On Valentine's Day in 2009, a lesbian couple and a gay couple took wedding photos at Zhengyang Gate in the inner city of Beijing, campaigning for the public visibility of homosexual people and legal protection of

Figure 19.1 Da Na and Bu Xiu taking wedding photos on Qianmen street on Valentine's Day in Beijing.

same-sex couples. By taking photos with passers-by and doing interviews with the media, the couples attempted to reduce social discrimination against LGBT groups. Although legalization of same-sex marriage may not be sufficient to tackle FSSIPV, it is an important step to ensure the rights of homosexuals, especially when they are victimized in intimate relationships, in the family, and in society.

DISCUSSION QUESTIONS

1. If An and Mo were in a butch–femme lesbian relationship, who do you think would be the butch and who would be the aggressor? Discuss how your perception of gender affects your view of homosexuals.
2. Based on the discussion about cultural, family, gender, and political systems provided in this chapter, is coming out a necessary way out for LBGT people in China?
3. Gay pride or LGBT pride is currently gaining momentum throughout the world. In the West, it has successfully increased public awareness of LGBT issues, and it provides an avenue for LGBT people to affirm their sexual identity, equality rights, dignity, and visibility as a minority group. However, large-scale marches, protests, and public gatherings are not allowed in China. What can be done to support LGBT people and advocate for the rights of FSSIPV victims in China?

REFERENCES

Baker, H. D. (1979). *Chinese family and kinship*. London, UK: Macmillan.

Balsam, K. (2001). Nowhere to hide: Lesbian battering, homophobia, and minority stress. In E. Kaschak (Ed.), *Intimate betrayal: Domestic violence in lesbian relationships* (pp. 25–37). New York, NY: Haworth.

Barlow, T. E. (1994). Politics and protocols of Funu: (Un)making national woman. In C. K. Gilmartin, G. Hershatter, L. Rofel, & T. White (Eds.), *Engendering China: Women, culture, and the state* (pp. 339–359). Cambridge, MA: Harvard University Press.

Beijing's "happy couples" launch campaign for same-sex marriages. (2009, February 25). *The Guardian*. Retrieved from https://www.theguardian.com/world/2009/feb/25/gay-rights-china-beijing

Black, M. C., Basile, K. C., Breiding, M. J., Smith, S. G., Walters, M. L., Merrick, M. T., . . . Stevens, M.R. (2011). *The National Intimate Partner and Sexual Violence Survey (NISVS): 2010 summary report*. Atlanta, GA: National Center for Injury Prevention and Control, Centers for Disease Control and Prevention.

Briones-Robinson, R., Powers, R. A., & Socia, K. M. (2016). Sexual orientation bias crimes: Examination of reporting, perception of police bias, and differential police response. *Criminal Justice and Behavior, 43*(12), 1688–1709.

Brown, T. N., & Herman, J. (2015). *Intimate partner violence and sexual abuse among LGBT people*. Los Angeles, CA: The Williams Institute.

Cannon, C. (2015). Illusion of inclusion: The failure of the gender paradigm to account for intimate partner violence in LGBT relationships. *Partner Abuse, 6*(1), 65–77.

China bans depictions of gay people on television. (2016, March 4). *The Guardian*. Retrieved from https://www.theguardian.com/tv-and-radio/2016/mar/04/china-bans-gay-people-television-clampdown-xi-jinping-censorship

Chiu, T. Y. (2017). Migration as a multifaceted system: Intersectionality of intimate partner violence in cross-border marriages. *Violence Against Women, 23*(11), 1293–1313. doi:10.1177/1077801216659940

Chiu, T. Y., & Choi, S. Y. P. (2015). Spousal violence and in-law conflict in Asia: The case of China, Taiwan and Hong Kong. In S. Quah (Ed.), *Routledge handbook of families in Asia* (pp. 318–331). New York, NY: Routledge.

Choi, S. Y. P., & Luo, M. (2016). Performative family: Homosexuality, marriage and intergenerational dynamics in China. *British Journal of Sociology, 67*(2), 260–280.

Davis, D. S., & Friedman, S. L. (2014). Deinstitutionalizing marriage and sexuality. In D. S. Davis & S. L. Friedman (Eds.), *Wives, husbands, and lovers: Marriage and sexuality in Hong Kong, Taiwan, and urban China* (pp. 1–39). Stanford, CA: Stanford University Press.

Ellsberg, M., & Heise, L. (2005). *Researching violence against women: A practical guide for researchers and activists*. Washington, DC: World Health Organization and Program for Appropriate Technology in Health.

Engebretsen, E. L. (2009). Intimate practices, conjugal ideals: Affective ties and relationship strategies among lala (lesbian) women in contemporary Beijing. *Sexuality Research and Social Policy, 6*(3), 3–14.

Fernández, M. (2006). Cultural beliefs and domestic violence. *Annals of the New York Academy of Sciences, 1087*(1), 250–260.

French Centre for Research on Contemporary China. (2016, January 8). *Press highlights 8 January 2016*. Retrieved from http://www.cefc.com.hk/china-news/100061306

Gillum, T. L., & DiFulvio, G. (2012). "There's so much at stake": Sexual minority youth discuss dating violence. *Violence Against Women, 18*(7), 725–745.

Goldberg, N. G., & Meyer, I. H. (2013). Sexual orientation disparities in history of intimate partner violence: Results from the California Health Interview Survey. *Journal of Interpersonal Violence, 28*(5), 1109–1118.

Goodman, B. (2005). The new woman commits suicide: The press, cultural memory, and the new republic. *Journal of Asian Studies, 64*(1), 67–101.

Hamel, J., & Russell, B. (2013). The Partner Abuse State of Knowledge Project: The implications for law enforcement responses to domestic violence. In B. L. Russell (Ed.), *Perceptions of female offenders: How stereotypes and social norms affect criminal justice response* (pp. 151–180). New York, NY: Springer.

Hassouneh, D., & Glass, N. (2008). The influence of gender role stereotyping on women's experiences of female same-sex intimate partner violence. *Violence Against Women, 14*(3), 310–325.

Hattery, A. J. (2009). *Intimate partner violence.* Lanham, MD: Rowman & Littlefield.

Hester, M., & Donovan, M. (2009). Researching domestic violence in same-sex relationships—A feminist epistemological approach to survey development. *Journal of Lesbian Studies, 13*(2), 161–173.

Higgins, L. T., Zheng, M., Liu, Y., & Sun, C. H. (2002). Attitudes to marriage and sexual behaviors: A survey of gender and culture differences in China and United Kingdom. *Sex Roles, 46*(3–4), 75–89.

Ho, D. Y. F. (1976). On the concept of face. *American Journal of Sociology, 81*(4), 867–884.

Human Rights Watch. (2016). *Country summary: China.* Retrieved from https://www.hrw.org/sites/default/files/china.pdf

Jeffreys, E. (Ed.). (2006). *Sex and sexuality in China.* London, UK: Routledge.

Jolly, J. (2004, November 18). *Is violence more common in same-sex relationships?* BBC News. Retrieved from http://www.bbc.com/news/magazine-29994648

Kam, L. Y. L. (2012). *Shanghai lalas: Female tongzhi communities and politics in urban China.* Hong Kong: Hong Kong University Press.

Karmen, A. (2001). *Crime victims: An introduction to victimology* (4th ed.). Belmont, CA: Wadsworth.

Kaschak, E. (2001). *Intimate betrayal: Domestic violence in lesbian relationships.* New York, NY: Hawthorne.

Kinsey, C. A., Gebhard, H. P., Martin, E. C., & Pomeroy, B. W. (1953). *Sexual behaviour in the human female.* Philadelphia, PA: Saunders.

Kinsey, C. A., Martin, E. C., & Wardell, P. B. (1948). *Sexual behaviour in the human male.* Philadelphia, PA: Saunders.

Leonard, W., Mitchell, A., Pitts, M., Patel, S., & Fox, C. (2008). *Coming forward: The underreporting of heterosexist violence and same-sex partner abuse in Victoria.* Melbourne, Australia: Australia Research Centre in Sex, Health and Society.

Li, Y.H. (1998). *Love and sexuality of Chinese women.* Beijing: China Today Press.

Lin, L., & Chen, C. (2016, February 24). China's censors take another gay-themed Web drama offline. *The Wall Street Journal.* Retrieved from http://blogs.wsj.com/chinarealtime/2016/02/24/chinas-censors-take-another-gay-themed-web-drama-offline

Little, B., & Terrance, C. (2010). Perceptions of domestic violence in lesbian relationships: Stereotypes and gender role expectations. *Journal of Homosexuality, 57*(3), 429–440.

Liu, J. X., & Choi, K. (2006). Experiences of social discrimination among men who have sex with men in Shanghai, China. *AIDS and Behavior, 10*(1), 25–33.

Mak, W. W., Chong, E. S. K., & Kwong, M. M. F. (2010). Prevalence of same-sex intimate partner violence in Hong Kong. *Public Health, 124*(3), 149–152.

Mann, S. L. (2011). *Gender and sexuality in modern Chinese history.* New York, NY: Cambridge University Press.

McClennen, J. C. (2005). Domestic violence between same-gender partners: Recent findings and future research. *Journal of Interpersonal Violence, 20*(2), 149–154.

McLaughlin, E., & Rozee, P. (2001). Knowledge about heterosexual versus lesbian battering among lesbians. In E. Kaschak (Ed.), *Intimate betrayal: Domestic violence in lesbian relationships* (pp. 39–58). New York, NY: Hawthorne.

Messinger, A. M. (2011). Invisible victims: Same-sex IPV in the National Violence Against Women Survey. *Journal of Interpersonal Violence, 26*(11), 2228–2243.

Messinger, A. M. (2014). Marking 35 years of research on same-sex intimate partner violence: Lessons and new directions. In D. Peterson & V. R. Panfil (Eds.), *Handbook of LGBT communities, crime, and justice* (pp. 65–85). New York, NY: Springer.

National Bureau of Statistics of China. (2012). *Women and men in China.* Retrieved from https://www.unicef.cn/en/reports/women-and-men-china.

National Coalition of Anti-Violence Programs. (2016). *Lesbian, gay, bisexual, transgender, queer, and HIV-affected intimate partner violence in 2015.* New York, NY: Emily Waters.

Pattavina, A., Hirschel, D., Buzawa, E., Faggiani, D., & Bentley, H. (2007). A comparison of the police response to heterosexual versus same-sex intimate partner violence. *Violence Against Women, 13*(4), 374–394.

Pimentel, E. E. (2000). Just how do I love thee? Marital relations in urban China. *Journal of Marriage and Family, 62*(1), 32–47.

Renzetti, C. (1992). *Violent betrayal: Partner abuse in lesbian relationships.* Newbury Park, CA: Sage.

Rofel, L. (2013). Grassroots activism: Non-normative sexual politics in post-socialist China. In W.N. Sun & Y. J. Guo (Eds.), *Unequal China: The political economy and cultural politics of inequality in China* (pp. 154–168). New York, NY: Routledge.

Russell, B., & Sturgeon, J. A. D. (2019). Police evaluations of intimate partner violence in heterosexual and same-sex relationships: Do experience and training play a role? *Journal of Police and Criminal Psychology, 34*(1), 34–44.

Tongyu. (2009). *Domestic violence against homosexual and bisexual women in mainland China: Research report of "anti-domestic violence against lala in Mainland China" project.* Beijing, China: Author.

Turell, S. C. (2000). A descriptive analysis of same-sex relationship violence for a diverse sample. *Journal of Family Violence, 15*(3), 281–293.

United Nations. (2006, July 6). *In-depth study on all forms of violence against women.* New York, NY: Author.

Walters, M. L., Chen, J., & Breiding, M. J. (2013). *The National Intimate Partner and Sexual Violence Survey (NISVS): 2010 findings on victimization by sexual orientation.* Atlanta, GA: National Center for Injury Prevention and Control, Centers for Disease Control and Prevention.

Wang, X., & Ho, P. S. Y. (2007). My sassy girl: A qualitative study of women's aggression in dating relationships in Beijing. *Journal of Interpersonal Violence, 22*(5), 623–638.

Wang, X. Y., Wang, X. H., Chiu, T. Y., & Jiao, T. (2015). Research report of intimate partner violence (亲密关系中的暴力问卷调查报告). Retrieved from http://tongyu.akng.net/index.php?m=content&c=index&a=show&catid=23&id=106.

Women Coalition of HKSAR. (2007). *Survey on domestic violence in same-sex relationships.* Hong Kong: Author.

Wong, J. Y. H., Choi, E. P. H., Lo, H. H. M., Wong, W., Chio, J. H. M., Choi, A. W. M., & Fong, D. Y. T. (2017). Dating violence, quality of life and mental health in sexual minority populations: A path analysis. *Quality of Life Research, 26*(4), 959–968.

Xu, X. (1998). Convergence or divergence. *Journal of Asian and African Studies, 33*(2), 181–204.

Yu, M. M. (2005). Domestic violence in the Chinese American community. In T. D. Nguyen (Ed.), *Domestic violence in Asian American communities* (pp. 27–38). Lanham, MD: Lexington Books.

Zhan, H. J., & Montgomery, R. J. (2003). Gender and elder care in China: The influence of filial piety and structural constraints. *Gender and Society, 17*(2), 209–229.

20

Global Violence of Women in Cults

DONI WHITSETT AND NATASHA POST ROSOW ■

CASE STUDY: SARAH

Sarah was a few months old when her parents joined the Twelve Tribes of Israel, an international Bible-based sect. She knew little of the world outside the Twelve Tribes communal farm where her family lived, prayed, and worked. At age 4 years, Sarah began working at the group's retail store and caring for younger children. By age 5 years, she was caring for an infant all by herself. At age 7 years, she added work in the group's organic restaurant to her list of jobs. Although this was illegal, Sarah thought it was normal at the time. The Twelve Tribes strived for perfection and children could be beaten, often for 4–8 hours, for the tiniest infraction—dropping a pencil at school or spilling milk at meals. Sarah often cut her finger when helping her mother cook, and each time she would need to be hit with a bamboo rod. It was not just minor mistakes that brought beatings. Anything playful or imaginative was considered "frivolous" and merited punishment with the rod. Toys were prohibited. Friendships were also frowned upon. To help children and adults avoid friendships, families moved every 4 months and Sarah lost track of what state they were living in. Not that it mattered. Sarah believed that the world outside was an evil and terrifying place where nobody cared about you. Venturing out was nothing short of dangerous.

But Sarah often felt scared and alone, even inside the community. Her parents were kept busy with work and prayer. As a young child, she was left in the care of 10-year-old girls. One of these girls physically and sexually abused Sarah, but when she reported it, her mother beat Sarah on her vagina with the rod. Sarah had four siblings, but bonding between them was discouraged. Her favorite brother was sent to work at a compound in another country when he was 16 years old, and the family lost track of him entirely. Sarah struggled most with the awareness that her sole purpose on earth was to serve a man—her father first, then her future husband. As a little girl, she had to be subservient to the boys, preparing them for their future roles. Later, she would learn that there

were strict rules governing sex and marriage, and all of them were constructed to for-
bid pleasure for women. Rape and sexual abuse of girls were normal in her world. One
of Sarah's earliest memories was of being 3 years old and wishing God would make her
a boy, thinking even then "If only I could be a boy then I would be okay."

Sarah escaped the cult at age 13 years because her father chose to leave and brought
her with him. Her name and certain details of her story have been changed to protect
her identity, but The Twelve Tribes of Israel is an existing cult that still functions with
thriving communities on four continents.[1]

OVERVIEW

> We realize the importance of our voices only when we are silenced.
> —Malala Yousafzai (2013, p. 178)

Women's voices have been silenced throughout history. Nowhere is this more evident than in malevolent groups, also known as "cults," in which women and girls are
exploited and forced into submission for the pleasure of men intent on power and
control. Their agendas result in violence toward women, whose human rights and
safety are often compromised. This chapter describes the plight of women in these
groups.

Because of the secretive nature of cults, it is virtually impossible for a researcher
to gain access, and even then the objectivity of the research is questionable.[2] We usually need to rely on former member accounts to understand the nature of a particular group. Additional evidence comes from conversations with cult experts and from
the first author's professional experiences treating former members and their families for more than 25 years. Many of the examples in this chapter are drawn from the
Fundamentalist Church of Jesus Christ of Latter-Day Saints (FLDS) because it has
been highly visible in the news in recent years and there is a significant amount of
information on it.

The focus of this chapter is on North America, particularly the United States, but it
is important to remember that many cults boast international membership. The experience of women in cults, in particular, is transnational. Gender-based inequality and
unjust treatment of women and girls inside of cults mirror systemic inequality faced
by women globally, and cults by their very nature involve isolating and marginalizing
abuses of power, creating a space in which women share similar experiences regardless
of physical location.

Historically, the terms *sect* and *cult* were applied to any new religious movement.
Today, "cult" is reserved for toxic groups rather than the more benign ones. Because
the label "cult" has become an emotionally charged term, many experts prefer the
terms *high demand group* (HDG) or *high control group*. In Europe, Canada, and elsewhere, "sect" is more commonly used, and in New Zealand and Australia, these groups
are sometimes referred to as "intentional communities" (Gibson, Morgan, Woolley, &
Powis, 2011). In this chapter, we use "cult" and HDG interchangeably.

Despite the variation in terms, the cult phenomenon is truly transnational, cutting
across borders, cultures, and ethnicities. In fact, it is often the case that when a group
begins to receive negative publicity and comes to the attention of the authorities, it
moves to another country, such as in the cases of Children of God, Bhagwan Shree

Rajneesh, and the People's Temple at Jonestown (Box 20.1). In additional, cult leaders often have grandiose motivations to spread their ideas worldwide, as in the case of the Unification Church ("Moonies"), which began with Sun Myung Moon in Korea and spread throughout Asia and to the West. These are groups that perpetrate abuse and violence against women. These international cults and others like them also feature a unique kind of cultural fluidity in which the group exists in many different locations throughout the world but functions as an enclave with its own ideals and practices, operating apart from society, no matter where in the world it may be.

Accurate estimates of cultic groups and membership are difficult to obtain due to the secretive nature of the phenomenon. The best and most recent estimates from cult experts and reviews of the literature are that there are approximately 5,000 cults in the United States alone, with approximately 2 million members (Lottick, 2008), and that approximately 10–20 million people have been involved in one or more of these groups at some point in their lives (Singer, 1993). Worldwide involvement stands at approximately 1% of the global population (Kendall, 2016, p. 20). These numbers are most likely low because the groups' practice of milieu control limits disclosure, and not everyone who has or had a cult experience is aware of the fact. Note that although 1% sounds minimal, the numbers of actual people represented are in the thousands, if not millions, and when one considers the effects on families of each of these members, the numbers become even larger. We can assume that at least half of these numbers represent women, and in some groups (e.g., the polygamous cults) female members outnumber the men.

Reflecting this international phenomenon, several countries have created cult watch organizations to provide information, education, and recovery. These include a European federation of cult information organizations under French law (European Federation of Centres of Research and Information on Sectarianism); the Information Network Focus on Religious Movements founded by sociologist Eileen Barker at the London School of Economics; Info-Secte/Info-Cult in Canada; and the International Cultic Studies Association (ICSA), an American-based organization.

Box 20.1

THE JONESTOWN MASSACRE

The People's Temple came to the attention of US authorities when families lost contact with their children and asked Congress to intervene. Jones and his followers fled the country and set up a commune known as Jonestown in Guyana. In 1978, Congressman Leo J. Ryan and an investigative team flew to Guyana, where they found that some people wanted to leave Jonestown but Jones would not allow it. Ryan announced he would take anyone back to the United States who wanted to go. The plane was attacked by Temple members; five people died, including the congressman. Jones, who had become very paranoid throughout the years, then convinced his followers they were not safe and that if the government came after them, they would be tortured and the babies shot. He instructed everyone to drink Kool-Aid laced with cyanide and valium. "That day, 912 people died from the poison, 276 of whom were children" (Rosenberg, 2018).

Defining a cult is difficult given its traditional roots as simply a budding religion. An early attempt emerged from the Wingspread Conference at the University of California, Los Angeles, in 1985 (West & Langone, 1986):

A group or movement exhibiting an excessive dedication to some person, idea, or thing . . . and employing unethical manipulative techniques of persuasion and control, designed to advance the goals of the group's leaders, to the detriment of the group's members, their families, and/or the community. (p. 119)

What distinguishes an HDG from a benign group are certain characteristics identified by various experts (Singer, 1995; Tobias & Lalich, 1994). Psychologist Jay Lifton (1969) teased out the following eight criteria from his work with prisoners of war subjected to brainwashing by their Chinese captors during the Korean War: milieu control, mystical manipulation, loading the language, sacred science, demand for purity, confession, doctrine over person, and dispensing of existence. These criteria have often been used as the yardstick against which a group is measured to determine if it earns the label "cult." Appendix A defines the eight criteria. The reader is also referred to Langone's list of characteristics for a more complete picture (Tobias & Lalich, 1994). Whether or not a group is labeled a "cult" is less important than whether and how a particular individual has been harmed by it.

HISTORICAL TRENDS

Although sects/cults have been known throughout history, some of the earliest ones in the United States were founded by groups of idealistic pioneers who wanted to experiment with communal living and shared resources (Box 20.2). However, the modern emergence of the cult phenomenon in the United States dates from the 1960s and 1970s, ushered in by the desire of young people to throw off the gender and sexual conservatism of earlier decades (Kent, 2001). Idealism was sweeping the country, and the youth of America, disillusioned with the sociopolitical establishment, searched for something to believe in. Some of this disillusionment crystallized in the civil rights movement and protests against the Vietnam War. There was a fascination with all things Eastern as gurus such as Maharishi Mahesh Yogi (transcendental meditation)

Box 20.2

ONEIDA COMMUNITY

The Oneida Community was a small utopian Bible-based group founded in Oneida, New York, by J. H. Noyes in 1848. Members shared property and wives, rejecting monogamy. Noyes became autocratic, deciding who should be paired with whom. Despite financial success, their practice of "complex marriage" (free love) caused hostility with neighbors, and the community was abolished in 1881. Although the social experiment ended, its manufacturing company continued and today produces the widely known Oneida silver plate (Singer, 1995).

---

entered the American stage. The counterculture movement was in full swing; "free love" and experimentation with drugs and alternative lifestyles were the order of the day (Kent, 2001).

It was in this combination of forces that many cults were born—some Eastern or religiously based; others therapy based; a few politically based; and some an amalgam of New Age rhetoric, psychology, and religious doctrine. These early cults had members from throughout the world, and some groups moved or expanded to new countries and new continents as they grew.

This history is explored in sociologist Stephen Kent's aptly titled book, *From Slogans to Mantras* (2001). As Kent states,

> Where the late 1960s had been characterized by explosions of youthful protest over social issues, in the new decade many of those who had been protesting were turning instead to new religions or undertaking unorthodox spiritual disciplines. Gurus, swamis . . . and "enlightened souls" attracted tens of thousands of baby boomers into what often were unusual and controversial practices. (p. 1)

In contrast to those earlier large movements, the trend today is with smaller groups developing around a particular charismatic leader—a pastor, minister, rabbi, or New Age guru—who purports to have a direct connection to an Ultimate Being.

The most recent trends in cult recruitment come from the internet. A case in point is the Executive Success Program, or NXIVM, which appeals to college students focused on professional success (Box 20.3). Many of the White supremacist groups in the United States and both Western and Eastern Europe also have a presence on the internet as they often target isolated people who believe they do not belong anywhere. Another recent trend is recruitment through the wellness movement. There have been cases of cults within yoga and martial arts circles, such as Bikram Yoga, considered a cult by many people. These gateways to cults make sense given that HDGs exploit people's highest ideals—that is, to fulfill one's potential, be it physical, professional, emotional, or spiritual. This drive toward self-actualization has its roots in the United States in the human potential movement of the 1960s, which gave birth to such HDGs as Lifespring, EST, and the Forum. Some of these ideals stem from Western cultures, but their appeal has proven global in scope, and the internet allows HDGs to target individuals regardless of their physical location.

Box 20.3

NXIVM

NXIVM is a multilevel marketing group for professional development known as the Executive Success Program. Led by Keith Raniere, the group is purported to have an inner circle of female "sex slaves," primarily selected by the actress Allison Mack of television's *Smallville* fame. Women are expected to put up "collateral" of nude photos of themselves to ensure they do not disclose secret practices. The "sex slaves" are branded near the pelvic bone, without anesthesia, with the leader's initials, KR. In June 2019 Raniere was found guilty of all charges including forced labor and sex trafficking.

In the 20th century, our knowledge about the inner workings of these groups came from the first generation. These were the youth of the 1960s counterculture movement who had been seduced by the idealistic messages of charismatic leaders who exploited that idealism. Promising to end world hunger (e.g., The Forum), create world peace (e.g., Unification Church), or make everyone "sane" (e.g., Center for Feeling Therapy), this first generation was the true believers who gave up their former lives and dedicated themselves to the mission/ideology of the group. Eventually, they bore the children who, like Sarah, now comprise a large cohort coming out of cults. Known as second-generation adults (SGAs), their experience differs fundamentally from that of their parents (Funari & Henry, 2011). Whereas the first generation had previous experiences of the outside world and a pre-cult personality to fall back on, this new cohort lacks such resources. SGAs have been born or brought into a cult very young, and many factors make it particularly difficult for them to leave. They usually attended only the group's educational system, in which they were taught only what was needed to fulfill their role as the leader defined it. For female SGAs, this usually means to be obedient wives, to learn their place, not to question the will of the men, and to be sexually available (in some groups, not necessarily only to one's husband). To use an FLDS term, women and girls are taught to "keep sweet." Any skills they learn in the group are not chosen but designated by the leader. They have had little or no contact with pop culture, and common references to events that happened in mainstream society during their cult years leave them confused. Most SGAs who exit a cult have left families and friends behind. Thus, with few skills and limited education, income, and family support, they often feel like the title of a popular science fiction book, *Stranger in a Strange Land* (Heinlein, 1987). They struggle to find their own voices and to live outside in a world they have been indoctrinated to believe is sinful and evil.

Sarah was 13 years old when she escaped from the Twelve Tribes with her father. She found the "real world" to be thrilling but also overwhelming and extremely difficult to navigate. She had only learned scripture and been trained in domestic duties in the limited schooling provided on the farming compound, and she had much catching up to do. Socially, she felt isolated and confused, and for years she struggled to connect with her peers. Her clothing, her hair, her manner of speech—everything set her apart. She was excited when a group of peers in her new school invited her to play basketball but first she had to ask, "What's basketball?"

Recouping the Losses

Social media and the internet in general have provided a global forum for people who have come out of cults and want to tell their stories. However, these anecdotal accounts are often discounted as the "sour grapes" of disenfranchised members who just couldn't make the grade, who were not spiritual enough, or who failed in some other way. Some cults attempt to discredit former members by attacking them online, even creating webpages dedicated to demeaning and discrediting these individuals, their friends and family, and any entity providing assistance in separating them from the cult. Such defamatory claims also make up counter-arguments given in court by experts defending cult leaders (Robbins, 2001). Efforts to provide more evidence-based information are underway as more rigorous research has begun to enter the literature (Almendros, Gamez-Gradix, Rodriquez-Carballeira, & Carrobles, 2011; Chambers, Langone, Dole, & Grice, 1994; Goransson & Holmqvist, 2018).

Another trend in the cult field has been in regard to interventions. In the early days of modern cults in the United States, adult children were kidnapped off the streets and held against their will so they could be "de-programmed." Not only is kidnapping illegal and opens the door to prosecution but also the success rate for people leaving the cult as a result of the de-programming was only approximately 50% (Langone, 1984). In addition, the coercive nature of the intervention itself sometimes caused a rupture in family relationships that was irreparable and communication was severed forever, even if the cult-involved child exited the cult.

The new generation of interventionists, sometimes called thought reform counselors, have developed other ways to help people leave their groups. These methods are legal and more respectful of the cult-involved person because they honor his or her right to choose whether to stay or go. Furthermore, this approach is more effective in helping families remain connected so they can continue to communicate, even if the child decides to remain in the group (P. Ryan and J. Kelly, personal communication, April 1, 2016).

RECENT DEVELOPMENTS

Although both men and women are harmed by these groups, the consequences are particularly damaging for women in cults—not only in the United States but also throughout the world. The violence against women is not necessarily the kind of blatant violence of physical and sexual abuse, although this also occurs. The more pervasive violence is against their humanity, their civil and human rights—the birthright of every human being. Women in HDGs are often robbed of control over their own bodies, their sexual and reproductive rights, and their right to raise their own children. They are robbed of the right to choose their own life partner, to be educated, and to strive for their own goals. The emotional and spiritual toll cannot be overestimated.

Recently, there has been a resurgence of interest in HDGs in Western culture, with films (e.g., *Wild Wild Country* [Netflix]) and television programs (A&E series) using cults as a theme. These fascinating narratives make for good ratings, but they do not do justice to the pain and suffering of the victims/survivors.

Religious Sovereignty

The United States holds religious freedom to be sacrosanct. However, it is often difficult to balance this value with the rights of children to be safe and cared for. Occasionally, these value conflicts are brought to a head with social and legal ramifications. At the time of writing of this chapter in 2018, the issue of religious sovereignty was being questioned due to allegations of child sexual abuse (CSA) and the rights of women.

A case in point is the FLDS, a powerful splinter group of the Mormon religion (Box 20.4). Concentrated in Arizona and Utah with another large satellite group in Bountiful, British Columbia, Canada, and several smaller known outposts in Mexico, FLDS holds polygamy to be its religious right, the will of God, marrying underage girls to men often two or three times their age. The rationale

Box 20.4

FUNDAMENTALIST LATTER-DAY SAINTS

The state of Utah was founded by Mormon pioneers. In order to join the union and become a state, they had to give up their illegal practice of polygamy. Members who continued the practice were ex-communicated and formed their own community, known as the Fundamentalist Latter-Days Saints. The group became isolated and led by controlling, authoritarian, abusive leaders. The group continued for decades. At the time of this writing, the community is dissolving and struggling to redefine itself.

for polygamy is that for a man to enter the highest level of heaven, known as the Celestial Kingdom, he must have at least three wives (Dogherty, 2003, as cited in Hamilton, 2014), and the only way a woman can enter the Celestial Kingdom is through the grace of her husband. It is only recently that CSA charges have been brought against the leader, Warren Jeffs, who is currently serving a life sentence in a Texas jail for child abuse. Jeffs has 86 wives, one of whom was 12 years old when he married her. Despite his incarceration, Jeffs continues to lead from his prison cell. Nevertheless, recently there has been some pressure brought to bear on the polygamous groups. Members have been sued for food stamp fraud (Kent, 2011), and the police force in the town staffed by the FLDS has been investigated. Marci Hamilton, an attorney who has specialized in the polygamous Mormon groups, writes of the consequences of their practices:

> When underage girls are forced into marrying much older men in these communities, they are taken out of school, deprived of any means of future earning or self-support, and burdened with the expectation of bearing as many children as possible. (p. 109)

Large families come with large financial burdens, often resulting in polygamous husbands abandoning wives and children of subsequent marriages. Home schooling is provided by these women, who themselves have limited education, effectively keeping women subservient and men in control. They are kept sequestered in the community by not learning to drive or by having to share vehicles.

The FLDS also engages in human trafficking as it shuffles underage girls between Canada and the United States for sexual purposes under the banner of "marriage" (Kent, 2006; Krugel, 2017). The Blackmore family, an FLDS group in Bountiful, Canada, is notorious for this practice. Young girls are given to men by the prophet, often as rewards, or are added to the leader's own harem of wives (Bramham, 2016). Pleas and protests are silenced, if voiced at all, because girls have been socialized from birth to believe that "marriages were arranged through a revelation from God and . . . delivered through [the] prophet who was the Lord's mouthpiece on earth" (Wall, 2008, p. 1). Mothers socialize their daughters to "keep sweet," to be compliant, and to fulfill their roles. Incestuous relationships abound, with sisters marrying the same man, first cousins marrying each other, and nieces marrying their uncles. This abuse, including forced sexual encounters, has been documented in the various first-person accounts by former wives who left and testified against their leader/husband

(Kent, 2006; Musser, 2013; Wall, 2008). Similarly, in the Alamo Christian Ministries cult, Tony Alamo "married" girls as young as age 11 years (Box 20.5; Schriver, 2018). After many years of attempting to prosecute the offenders, two members of the Blackmore family have recently been convicted in these cases of child brides (Krugel, 2017). Tony Alamo was also sentenced to 175 years in prison with no possibility of parole (Schriver, 2018).

Before we conclude this discussion of the FLDS, we acknowledge the phenomenon of the Lost Boys. When a young man reaches a marriageable age, he is sent away from the community so as not to be competition for the older men. Raised in these same communities, these youth lack the education and skills to survive in mainstream society.

Another example of the value conflict between religion and human rights occurs among the Jehovah's Witnesses, a transnational group with headquarters in the United States but with members throughout the world. As of 2017, the church claimed more than 100,000 active congregations in 240 countries (Watchtower Bible and Tract Society of Pennsylvania, 2018). Their CSA rule, known as "the two witness rule," was recently brought under scrutiny by the Royal Commission in the United Kingdom and declared "outdated." This rule requires that "there must be two witnesses to an incident of abuse" ("Facts About Jehovah's Witnesses," 2017, para. 7), which not only demonstrate the obsolescence of the rule (devised more than 2,000 years ago) but also reflects the psychological naiveté of the church. In 2002, the "rule" was updated, allowing action to be taken if there are two separate accusations against the same person ("Facts About Jehovah's Witnesses," 2017). However, most CSA victims, no matter what the environment, are reluctant to come forward for many reasons. The perpetrator often threatens bodily harm to the victim and/or the victim's family and warns that they would not be believed anyway. If that is the case in the general population, how much more so for a child socialized to believe that the elder who is abusing her has been sanctioned by Jehovah himself?[3]

In the past 60 years, thousands of allegations have been leveled against elders of the Jehovah's Witnesses church worldwide, yet no reports have been filed with legal authorities (Australian Associated Press, 2015; "Facts About Jehovah's Witnesses," 2017). Although the organization claims that it handles these matters

---

Box 20.5

ALAMO CHRISTIAN MINISTRIES

Susan and Tony Alamo married in 1966 and established the Alamo Foundation. Susan's death in 1982 seems to have unraveled Tony, who began to acquire young female members as "wives." Alamo's public persona was as a celebrity promoter; he enjoyed being part of the Hollywood scene. The cult largely supported itself by manufacturing Tony's trademark jackets, which were sold in the poshest shops. Under "sweatshop"-like conditions, cult members would put the bling on the bedazzled jackets that were all the rage in the 1980s and that netted Tony a small fortune. He died in jail in 2017 at age 82 years.

internally, officials within the organization reveal that the church covers up the allegations. Efforts to help the victims have been made by former Jehovah's Witnesses who have left because of this travesty. For example, Bill Bowen runs the website silentlambs.com, a forum for these survivors to expose the abuses and to heal. Barbara Anderson (Anderson & Kelly, 2018), a researcher who worked at Jehovah's Witness headquarters in Brooklyn, New York (the Watchtower), also became frustrated and outraged by the inaction of the church and left after 40 years. She, too, runs a website and has become an outspoken critic of the church's policies. A ray of hope for justice for these survivors came in 2012 when a case was brought by one such survivor. Candace Conti won the largest jury verdict of religious sexual abuse in the United States by a single victim ($28 million). Molested at age 9 years in 1995 by a fellow congregant, Conti decided to come forward to break the silence. Unfortunately, an appeals court in 2015 reduced the award, stating that the leadership had "no duty to warn" that there was a child molester among them (Bundy, 2015).

In the United States, attorney Marci Hamilton (2012) addresses the church–state conflict. She advocates for abolishment of the statute of limitations on child abuse. She claims that the existing limits on how long a crime is open to prosecution essentially protect offenders (who can continue to abuse) and compound the harm inflicted on victims. Laws in different countries approach child abuse differently but such abuse is a problem worldwide, and cults create an environment in which crimes such as CSA often have added protection from the law.

CURRENT CONDITIONS

High demand groups have been noted to exist throughout the world, but they usually only come to the attention of the public when something sensational happens. Thus it was with the Jonestown massacre in 1978 when more than 900 people drank Kool-Aid laced with cyanide, the Waco conflagration in 1993 that claimed 80 lives, the Solar Temple suicides in Switzerland a year later, the saran gas subway attacks by the Aum Shinrikyo cult in 1995 in Japan, and the Heaven's Gate suicides in 1997 when the 38 "away team" members shed their earthly bodies to catch a ride on a spacecraft behind the Hale–Bopp comet that would take them to the Kingdom of Heaven. The most recent sensation is the NXIVM cult involving a self-proclaimed genius, an actress, and sex slaves who have been branded like cattle without anesthesia (see Box 20.3).

Sarah's former cult, The Twelve Tribes, is still very much intact and flourishing on four continents. It recently appeared in the news after authorities in Cambridge, New York, discovered child labor law infractions at one of its communities. This has also happened in Germany, where the court recently held up the removal of children from a large Twelve Tribes community in Bavaria. In the US case, the Twelve Tribes issued a statement saying that the children were not working but, rather, visiting their parents at work on the day authorities inspected the property. Former members spoke to the media about the outrageousness of that statement, noting that children are taught to lie about the work they do and to line up and file out the back door when outsiders appear.

Stories about HDGs reported in the news break through our denial that cults are not around anymore. On the contrary, they are very much present and continue to perpetrate abuses against thousands of people throughout the world on a daily basis.

Transnational Feminism

There is a growing awareness in the cult field that the dynamics of HDGs describe similar phenomena that exploit women and girls (e.g., sex trafficking, gangs, battered women, and radical terrorist groups). Indoctrination techniques are a common thread among them, and they retain their membership through fear and intimidation. Female children and women fare badly in these groups, whether because of overt violence such as sexual abuse or more subtle exploitation (e.g., subjugation). This is a transnational feminist issue, with similar ramifications impacting many different women and girls in different locations and cultural contexts. Perhaps the most extreme example in recent years is the kidnapping of 276 young Nigerian women by Boko Haram, a terrorist organization. Many of these women have been "forced into sexual slavery and trained to fight," according to Amnesty International (2015). This growing recognition of similarities has led to efforts to collaborate between cross fertilization to determine if they can learn from, and help, one another. Toward this end, the International Cultic Studies Association organized a conference in June 2017 titled "Cultic Dynamics and Radicalization," which included presentations on Islamic control and de-radicalization. Countries in Europe are also developing programs to, basically, "exit counsel" former terrorists (Boghani, 2016).

The examination of women and girls in cults brings new attention to the shared plight of women being oppressed in the same ways across a wide range of religious, cultural, ethnic, and political backgrounds. The study of cults and cult dynamics is thus rooted in the ideals of transnational feminism. The various forms of oppression are discussed next.

Sexuality and Marriage

One of the most powerful methods of control over women is through their sexuality. Power and influence increase with intimacy; thus, sexual exploitation is pervasive in cults. Lalich (1997) defines sexual exploitation as "the exercise of power for the purpose of controlling, using, or abusing another person sexually in order to satisfy the conscious or unconscious needs of the person in power, whether these needs be sexual, financial, emotional, or physical" (p. 6). It may occur in the form of a spiritual practice, nonconsensual marriage, marital rape, statutory rape, unwanted touch, or a sexualized atmosphere. As previously noted, incest runs rampant in the polygamous FLDS. The following quote by former member Debbie Palmer illustrates the results (Palmer & Perrin, 2004):

> Several of my stepsons were assigned to marry my sisters, so I also became a sister-in-law to my own stepchildren. After my mother's father was assigned to marry one of my second husband's daughters . . . I became my own great grandmother. The step-daughter became my step grandmother and I her step-mother,

so when I gave birth to two sons with her father, my own sons became my great uncles and I was their great great-great grandmother.

As with the general statistics on cults, the incidence of sexual exploitation of women is not available. However, in every workshop of former members, sexual exploitation is a common theme. Tobias and Lalich (1994) report that 40% of the women who attended one of their recovery workshops had experienced sexual abuse while in a cult. This estimate is considered to be low given the stories that psychotherapists hear from their ex-member clients. In addition, "abuse" does not always occur in the form of coercion. The more subtle forms of abuse, such as seduction, socialization, and grooming, may not be easily recognized. Although most cult leaders are men, these sexual exploits have been reported in female-headed groups as well (e.g., Elizabeth Clare Prophet, founder of Church Universal and Triumphant; Szimhart, 1995).

In the Twelve Tribes, Sarah was taught that she was born to serve, support, and "build up" men. As she entered puberty, sex was a mystery and emotional intimacy was a non-entity. There was only marriage and obedience. The night before a young woman got married, female elders would divulge the strict rules of marriage: Sex was for men to enjoy, only appropriate in the missionary position because that was considered a position that would afford his wife the least amount of pleasure, and only allowed to married couples once a week on "family night." Married couples were not allowed to show much public affection beyond holding hands or "dry kissing." Any kind of pleasure in sex would be shameful for a woman to feel. Only men were allowed to receive oral sex, which women were expected to give. Later, Sarah would explain that she grew up expecting to be raped, with her mother and other women normalizing unwanted sexual encounters and making clear that nonconsensual sex was normal—something for which young girls should be prepared.

In other cults, women are blamed for their own rape. When the daughter of Susan Alamo of the Alamo Christian Ministries cult was raped by the leader, Susan screamed pejorative names at her daughter, accusing her of "'trying to steal her man'" (Schriver, 2018, p. 8).

In some cults, celibacy is the explicit policy, but this often applies only to the members. Hypocritically, leaders may take multiple sexual partners either openly (as in the case of the polygamous groups) or secretively (as in the case of Swami Muktananda, head of Siddha Yoga) (Kent, 2012). Female targets are often seduced by being told they were specially chosen for the privilege of consorting with the leader; these sexual practices are often billed as another, higher, level of spiritual practice, designed to reach enlightenment or salvation more quickly. In the case of David Koresh's harem, the young girls were told they would be marrying Jesus Christ, and they were groomed from childhood for that honor.

David Koresh, leader of the Branch Davidians of Waco, Texas, claimed "all adult women in the group as his sexual property; he engaged in the physical abuse of children and the sexual abuse of young girls" (Kaplan, 2001, p. 496). His third wife, Michele, was the younger sister of his legal wife Rachel; she was just 12 years old when he raped her (Breault & King, 1993). He broke up marriages and created a harem after claiming to have received a message from God commanding him to form a new race of the "House of David." Girls as young as age 10 years became his "wives" (ABC News, 2003; Bunting & Willman, 1995), and mothers groomed their daughters to be the "Brides of Christ" (Breault & King, 1993). One Waco survivor, Kiri Jewell, testified before Congress that her mother took her to a hotel where Koresh was waiting (ABC News, 2003),[4] considering it an honor for her daughter to be so chosen. By cooperating, these "spiritual wives" proved their worthiness to enjoy eternal salvation. This type of grooming is not unique to the well-known cults. In a small Bible-based group in Santa Ana, California, all the women and young girls are expected to massage the feet of the leader, essentially preparing them to be his future sexual partners.

Leaders generally have no regard for legal marriages, often taking the wife of another member as another sexual conquest. If the husband complains, he is shamed by being told he is "selfish" (ex-member, personal communication, August 27, 2011). The dilution or dissolution of the "married" couple serves the leader's need for total control because to the extent that any member is attached to another, she is not attached to the leader. Some cults encourage sexual promiscuity among members, which also prevents pair bonding.

Sex has also been used for recruitment purposes. The infamous "flirty fishing" practice of the Children of God during its heyday in the 1970s brought in many new members, including diplomats. "Flirty fishing" involved female cult members, whether single or married, "flirting" and often having sex with men to bring them into the fold. In this way, female sexuality was exploited in the name of Jesus Christ because, like Koresh, the leader, David Berg, claimed to have had a vision. Having molested his own children and "married" his own underage granddaughter, he reframed incest as acceptable and his daughter apparently instructed parents to masturbate their children (Kent, 2012). Celebrities such as River Phoenix (who committed suicide), Joaquin Phoenix, and Rose McGowan grew up in this cult. Currently, this group appears to have fizzled out in the United States but still claims a presence in 91 countries (Borowik, 2016). It is still considered one of the most sexualized cults in modern history (Box 20.6).

Box 20.6

CHILDREN OF GOD

In 2005, Ricky Rodriquez, the heir apparent to lead the Children of God, searched out his former nanny, shot and killed her, and then turned the gun on himself. He left a video recording in which he stated his motivation was to seek justice and revenge for the rape and violence perpetrated on him and the other children who had been raised in the cult, which believed in sex between adults and children. Ricky himself was forced to have sex with his nanny and the granddaughter of David Berg, the leader of the cult; the granddaughter, Merry, died at age 45 years. Ricky's mother was the partner of David Berg, and his biological father was a man recruited through the group's tactic of "flirty fishing," which used women to lure men into the group. Ricky was 30 years old at the time of his death.

There is a disproportionate number of suicides among the second-generation adults (SGAs) of the Children of God that can be attributed to the complex trauma they sustained throughout their childhood. David Berg took many young girls as his child brides. Although many SGAs have come forward and reported their abuses to the Federal Bureau of Investigation, no arrests have been made. Due to the transnational nature of this group, said to operate in 91 countries, it is difficult to prosecute.

Reproduction

One of the most extreme forms of violence against women in cults is control over their reproductive rights. Whether the leader forces women to have babies or pre-vents births from happening, control over women's bodies remains in the hands of men. On one end of the continuum, women in some groups are expected to have one child per year (e.g., FLDS), but men do not feel obligated to support this large family (Hamilton, 2014). On the other end of the continuum, women are prevented from carrying pregnancies to term. For example, in one therapy cult of the 1970s that encouraged sexual relations between members, not one child was born to the 350 members, at least half of whom were women (Ayella, 1998; Mithers, 1994). Children who came with mothers were often sent away to live with relatives outside the group. More recent accounts come from Scientology, in which women are forced to have abortions (Headley, 2016). A variation on this type of control is that in some groups women are told they are not cut out to be mothers, their special talents lie elsewhere, and they are given other assignments that meet the needs of the leader rather than those of the women (ex-member, personal com-munication, May 10, 2012).

Assault on Motherhood

One of the most egregious types of violence against women is the assault on their motherhood, a transnational occurrence that happens in cults throughout the world. As "true believers," they allow their faith in the leader to override their maternal instincts to protect their children. This challenging position is exacer-bated by the fact that children in cults are often harshly disciplined, frequently to the point of physical harm. It is difficult to cope with the knowledge that one has physically abused one's child to the point of drawing blood (ABC News, 2003; Timoner, 2007). One Branch Davidian mother, who finally left with her son before the standoff, is "haunted by the spankings" she inflicted on him when he was an infant. She believed "this was God's child" and she had to discipline him harshly so he could fulfill his destiny (ABC News, 2003). Realizing that one has refused medi-cal care that would save the child's life is equally difficult to bear (Swan, 2000). Even worse is being complicit in sexual abuse, as in the case of Kiri Jewell noted previously. Likewise, it is almost unfathomable to comprehend how, during the raid on the Branch Davidians, mothers abandoned their children who had escaped, choosing instead to die with Koresh.

Sarah's mother was expected to show her love for Sarah by inflicting harsh disci-pline, beating her with the bamboo rod. She obeyed this mandate to the best of her ability, delivering harsh punishment, even when her children came to her for help, such as when Sarah reported sexual abuse at the hands of her 10-year-old caregivers. Sarah's mother in fact struggled in the group and was often "in darkness," which meant she was punished and ostracized. She was viewed as disobedient, and Sarah and her siblings were additionally beaten by other group members because "they had a bad mother." In these ways, the bond between Sarah and her mother was made tenuous.

Attachment Issues

Neuroscience research of the past few decades has taught the importance of optimal attachment experiences, or a healthy connection between a mother and child. Findings strongly suggest that the brain of a newborn develops through the relationship with his or her mother. If a child receives nurturing, empathic, maternal care, his or her brain will develop optimally. On the other hand, if a child is emotionally neglected or abused, his or her brain may be underdeveloped, leading to impaired social–emotional and cognitive functioning (Schore & Schore, 2012). Functional magnetic resonance imaging scans provide evidence that neglected children have smaller brains compared to those of children who grew up in loving homes. In addition, chronic stress in childhood puts neglected and abused children at risk for negative health and mental health outcomes as adults (Chapman, Dube, & Anda, 2007). Space does not permit an extensive discussion of all the effects that adverse childhood experiences have on the brain, but science has shown how critical early attachment can be for healthy development.

Disrupted attachment is another common theme in recovery groups. Cult leaders instinctively know that it is difficult for a woman to be both a mother to her child and a compliant "child" to the cult leader. Thus, leaders have various ways of preventing and diluting a strong mother–child attachment. Adults' time might be so overscheduled with fundraising, recruiting, and chores that they have little time or energy left for children. Or parents and children will be physically separated by either of them being sent away on missions to other countries or the children sent away to be educated in India or elsewhere. In other groups, children live in communal houses in which various adults care for them; these caregivers may rotate through and often do not want to be there. Such was the case with Sarah, who lived on a communal Twelve Tribes farm and was raised by other children tasked with her care. Other interferences are more subtle. A client of the first author remembers a time when a 2-year-old toddler was crying during an all-night Bible study session, trying to climb up on his mother's lap. The furious leader kicked the child away, contemptuously calling him a "momma's boy." The mother was unable to protest (ex-member, personal communication, August 27, 2011). Stories such as these are common; they are part of the traumatic narratives recounted by former members throughout the world, as women grieve their lost years of motherhood and children grieve their lost childhoods.

The child-rearing practices of any given group depend on the whims of the leader, and these can change from day to day. Loyalty to the leader is tested by how willing a mother is to carry out the discipline prescribed by the leader, no matter how outrageous or abusive. She essentially becomes "middle management" (Markowitz & Halperin, 1984). One cult expert recounts the story of a client who disciplined her child by putting his hand in boiling water at the insistence of the leader. This unpredictability keeps women unbalanced, in a constant state of fear, which interferes with their ability to provide the empathy and contingent caregiving that children require. Mothers or surrogate caregivers placed in such a destabilizing situation often take their frustrations out on the children, putting the latter at increased risk for child abuse. Even if a mother does not directly abuse her child, raising her children while living in such conditions can have a negative impact. One court recognized this distinction when it prohibited the Alamo children who were detained in a raid from returning to their cult biological parents, stating that the parents had failed to protect them from the severe abuses of the cult leader.

A very poignant illustration of this disrupted bond is reflected in artwork by Katharina Meredith, who was raised in the Lichtoase group, a New Age cult in Germany. Her picture consists of three panels and is titled "Disappearing Mother." In the first panel, a mother is lovingly reaching out to her child, who reaches back. In the second panel, the figure of the mother is partially grayed out. In the third panel, the mother has all but disappeared, with the child holding out her hands into empty space (Meredith, 2016).

A brief discussion is presented here about the practice of "shunning," another form of control over women by exploiting their motherhood. Shunning refers to isolation and rejection of a person who has been noncompliant. No one talks to them, and they are prohibited from engaging in communal activities. This practice is very powerful because the neural networks involved in social rejection are the same as those involved in physical pain (Kross, Berman, Mischel, Smith, & Wager, 2011). In other words, social rejection is experienced physically as well as emotionally. Thus, contrary to the children's rhyme about sticks and stones not hurting one's bones, words *do* harm. Women in cults have often been controlled by this method when they have visited their adult children who have left the group or when they have not succumbed to their husband's will (ex-member, personal communication, June 5, 2012). Recently, a woman who was ostracized from the religious community in which she was raised killed herself, her husband, and her two adult children—a murder–suicide that her friends attribute to her being shunned (Baldas, 2018).

Medical Neglect

Women and children are at risk for medical neglect, which may result in death. This is especially true when minors give birth. The risk of mortality, both for the minor and for her child, increases. Medical attention is avoided in the FLDS because polygamy and incest are felonies, so pregnancies are hidden from authorities (Kent, 2011). Because marriages are so incestuous in this group, many infants are born with genetic birth defects or condemned to live damaged and debilitating lives (Kent, 2011). Mothers have to experience the most painful life event one can endure—burying a child. To compound their grief, they are often blamed for the deformities, told that they happened as punishment for not being spiritual enough, having doubts, or not being sufficiently respectful of the elders.

Subservience

Most cultic groups are patriarchal, and women are groomed to be subservient to men, as was Sarah. The ISKCON (Hare Krishnas) group, for example, states, "Ideally the [married] woman must be completely submissive and a servant to her husband" (Daner, 1976, as cited in Kent, 2001, p. 158). In more recent times, the Quiverfull movement, which adheres to strict gender roles and a patriarchal hierarchy, is a case in point. In the Advanced Training Institute (ATI), an example of the Quiverfull movement, a woman is exhorted to be a "godly wife" by fulfilling seven basic needs, including "dressing to please her husband, having a joyful countenance and selecting clothing that draws attention to it, to honor his leadership, to make appeals, not demands, and to be grateful" (Hamilton, 2014, p. 114). In 2014, the founder of ATI, Bill Gothard, was accused of sexually assaulting women and teenage girls and removed from the faculty of ATI. Perhaps it is not surprising, given the power that men hold in these groups, that Josh Duggar, an infamous member of a Quiverfull family, admitted molesting his younger sisters as a teenager (McFarland, 2015).

One of the ways cults subjugate women is by tearing down their self-esteem. Sarah's need to be perfect caused her to never feel competent or confident, and the fact that she was given tasks totally inappropriate for her age only added to her lack of self-esteem. "I felt like such a failure when I couldn't do all those tasks perfectly," she says now.

Spiritual Violence

From the foregoing discussion, it is obvious that spiritual abuse is another type of violence inflicted on women in faith-based cults. Under the guise of some religious experience, either hallucinated or consciously made up, the exploitation of women's bodies for the sexual gratification of the leader is one of the most abhorrent consequences of cult involvement. Women who come out of these cults often feel ashamed that they were so duped to believe that having sex with the leader was for their own enlightenment or salvation rather than simply for his gratification. Working through this type of moral injury is another theme in psychotherapy offices throughout the world.

Current Reorganization

We cannot conclude this section without mentioning a sea change taking place in Hilldale, Utah, heart of the FLDS. With Warren Jeffs in jail, state officials examined the town more closely and found major abuses in terms of housing discrimination and police misconduct—not surprising given that the cult had controlled the government (Carlisle, 2018). Consequently, sweeping reforms were made that diluted the FLDS's control. Former members (known as apostates) who were previously exiled and treated like pariahs returned to Hilldale and are attempting to hold democratic elections (Sanders, 2018).

LOOKING TO THE FUTURE

As previously mentioned, various organizations attempt to bring awareness to the cult phenomenon both in the United States and abroad. Experts in the fields of mental health, sociology, psychology, exit counseling, and the law convene at the annual ICSA conferences to share information and bring their respective knowledge to bear on HDGs. In addition, local, national, and international workshops invite cult-involved families and former cult members to come together to better understand their experiences and help their loved ones. Different types of interventions, such as exit counseling, are also discussed, with the recent emphasis, as mentioned previously, on maintaining the tenuous relationship with the cult-involved loved one (P. Ryan and J. Kelly, personal communication, April 1, 2016).

More specialized services are needed to help women exiting HDGs. Tapestry Against Polygamy and Help the Child Brides are two of the better known organizations helping women who leave polygamy. Meadow Haven in Massachusetts and Wellspring in Ohio are refuges for former members of all groups to rest, recover, and process their experiences.

A major obstacle in the road to recovery exists with regard to mental health services. In general, mental health professionals are not versed in working with this population. They often minimize the effects and/or pathologize former members, not recognizing symptoms that are secondary to a cult experience. The fifth edition of the *Diagnostic and Statistical Manual of Mental Disorders* (American Psychiatric Association, 2013) acknowledges "coercive persuasion" by cult recruitment and indoctrination as a factor in dissociative disorders, which at least helps identify the etiology (p. 306).

Most women exiting cults meet the criteria for post-traumatic stress disorder and are in dire need of psychological help. In addition, they require other services including vocational training, rehabilitation, and practical help such as how to search for a job and manage money. Having spent years living in a cult in which all decisions were made for them and critical thinking was punished, they also need to be empowered to find their own voice and forge a life of their own making. Unfortunately, such services cost money, which these women do not have, and free services are limited.

An interesting point made by Mike Kropveld, executive director of Info-secte/ Info-cult, is the discrepancy between funds available for people coming out of radicalized (terrorist) groups versus funds for people coming out of cults. He believes that more funds are available to the radicalized ex-members because they pose a security threat and the issue is more clear-cut, whereas the issue of women coming out of cults is less clear and includes the question of religion, which almost always seems to be a sensitive subject (M. Kropveld, personal communication, January 6, 2017).

Another way to make inroads into these closed communities is through the government programs on which many of the women survive. As part of the requirement for receiving benefits, clients must allow home visits by caseworkers. These could be used as opportunities to connect with the women, to show concern and expose them to outside influences, which might challenge their false beliefs about "outsiders" as evil and uncaring. It is often the case that even in closed communities women are searching for a way out, as evidenced by the fact that people do escape (Musser, 2013; Wall, 2008). They just may need to know that there will be someone on the outside ready to help (M. Kropveld, personal communication, January 6, 2017). From the former member workshops, we have heard of women secretly accessing the internet (in the few cults in which computers are allowed) and searching for information and help.

The legal system needs to separate out religious belief from religious practices. However, this is easier said than done because beliefs result in behavior, as in the case of the polygamous Mormons (discussed previously). If a woman believes that the only way to get to heaven is through the good graces of her husband, she is going to "keep sweet" on the earthly plane for the longer term reward.

Opportunities for Advocacy

We have addressed the obstacles many women face in escaping from cults and getting help once they have escaped. There is also work to be done in helping prevent cults from growing in the first place. Increasing awareness, especially among vulnerable populations, is essential. College campuses are historically targeted by cults because they are sites where free thought is protected and encouraged. Unfortunately, such openness renders college students vulnerable to cult recruitment. In addition, both freshman and seniors are in states of transition, the prime time when people are searching for something to anchor them. The cult offers them a welcoming and interesting new community to join. Only later do they realize they have joined a cult, when they are trapped by conditions detailed previously in this chapter. Simply by reading this, it is hoped that you have become more educated about how cults operate, a first step to increasing awareness. An excellent way to further educate yourself and others about how to prevent joining a cult is to refer to the questions about groups in Appendix B.

Another interesting avenue for advocacy would be working to implement new policies and laws that could prevent cult leaders from exploiting and abusing members in known ways that are common throughout the world. Law professor Robin Laisure (2018) recommends using existing laws on human trafficking and applying them to criminal activity in and by cults. She argues that trafficking laws are quite strong, exist on an international scale, and are applicable against cults because traffickers and cult leaders use similar tactics to entrap and exploit their victims. These tactics include grooming, using threats and physical restraint to prevent escape, unpaid and child labor, and isolation. Trafficking is often misconstrued as an act requiring transport when "the crux of the crime of human trafficking is not the transportation of a person, but the use of force to obtain labor or service of that person" (p. 23). Such behavior occurs frequently in cults. In the United States, the Victims of Trafficking and Violence Protection Act, passed in 2000, may provide a valuable avenue for recourse for cult survivors (Laisure, 2018). Other similar laws exist internationally and may prove very useful against cults and cult leaders.

CONCLUSION

A democracy prides itself on freedom of religion and speech, codified in the United States in the First Amendment. This has made it difficult to curtail the activities of HDGs in the United States. Ironically, the 2001 attacks and subsequent events carried out by radical terrorist groups have made Americans question the boundaries of those rights. Other countries, such as Russia, China, the Netherlands, and Germany, do not have the same First Amendment limitations as the United States, where religious freedom is highly protected. In those countries, groups deemed "extremist" are not allowed to operate, and HDGs are curtailed as a result. In Russia, for example, a series of legal actions have been taken against Jehovah's Witnesses under the laws restricting "extremism," which were initially enacted to help fight terrorism (Higgins, 2017). Are we in the United States willing to curtail some of our freedoms in the interest of greater protection against terrorists? If so, then perhaps we will examine more closely the indoctrination practices of HDGs as well, with their fear inducing and mind control tactics, hiding behind the 1st amendment freedoms. Until women have a voice equal to that of men, exploitation and violence will continue.

DISCUSSION QUESTIONS

1. How do cults reinforce gender inequality?
2. What are some common experiences that are seen in almost all cults?
3. Are you aware of any organizations in your area (e.g., churches and social groups) with cult-like characteristics that concern you? What are they?
4. If you were going to educate your peers about cultic characteristics, what would you include?

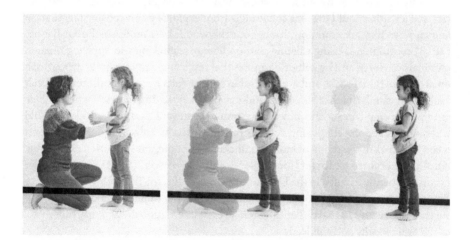

Figure 20.1 In the artist's own words: "When my parents joined the group (Lichtoase, a New Age cult in Germany) I was 10 years old. My brother was 8. We were physically separated from our parents. All the children slept in one room and the adults somewhere else. To make it worse, we were forbidden to call them *Mom* and *Dad*. We had to treat them like the other adults, hence like strangers. If we came to them because we had gotten hurt, we were turned away. Before my eyes, my mother disappeared. She turned into someone else: Her smile changed, her words changed, her manners changed. A stranger was wearing my mother's skin. I felt deeply disoriented. When I became a mother, I felt a disconnect between myself and my daughter. Sometimes the memories, the overwhelming feeling of loss and the trauma would catch up with me, and I would disappear before her eyes. I was physically there, but my mind was somewhere else, stuck in the past. It took all my strength . . . to become visible again" (Katharina Meredith).

APPENDIX A   THE EIGHT CHARACTERISTICS OF CULTS

Milieu control: The purposeful limitation of all forms of communication with the outside world. A closed system with rigid boundaries. Communication with the inner self is also controlled—that is, what is acceptable to think and feel. Control over diet, sleep cycles.

Mystical manipulation: Teaching that the group has been specially chosen to carry out a divine purpose and the recruit has been selected to play a special role in fulfilling that purpose. Uncritical faith and trust is expected.

The sacred science: The mission of the group is considered sacred, not to be questioned. The group purports to have a body of airtight evidence to support its claims.

The demand for purity: Since the Word, Idea, Mission of the group is sacred and pure, anything contaminating it must be eradicated. Anything done in the name of purity is considered moral and just, no matter how deceptive.

Confession: An expectation of baring one's innermost thoughts and feelings in order to purge oneself of doubts and impurities. Since the leader and Mission are perfect, anything that goes wrong is the fault of the member. Confession rituals pervade the group's atmosphere.

Loading the language: Thought-stopping clichés and jargon that compress the most complex of human problems into brief, highly reductive, definitive sounding phrases which are easily memorized and easily expressed.

Doctrine over person: Convincing the subject that the group and its doctrine take precedence over any individual in the group or any other teaching from outside it. Individual boundaries are obliterated.

Dispensing of existence: Teaching that all those who disagree with the philosophy of the group are doomed. Use of splitting, we/they, taken to extremes.

Source: Modified from Andres, R., & Lane, J. (1989). *Cults and consequences.* Los Angeles, CA: Commission on Cults and Missionaries.

APPENDIX B   QUESTIONS ABOUT GROUPS

Considering "joining" a group? Before you do, consider the following questions:

1. If you are invited to a dinner or lecture, do you know who is the sponsor?
2. If it is out of the city, are there means of communicating with your parents and other friends, or are you cut off from outside sources?
3. Exactly where is the retreat and how else (other than your bus) can people get there and leave?
4. If someone decides he or she wants to leave before the seminar is over, how can he or she get back home?
5. Who is the leader of the organization?
6. Is the leader open to a dialogue—can you question him or her?
7. Do you feel pressured to change your beliefs?
8. Are their values antithetical to yours?

9. Are you discouraged from questioning the motives, beliefs, or practices of the group either overtly or subtly? In other words, are you made to feel bad (ashamed, inadequate, sinful, not spiritual enough, etc.)?
10. Does the group speak in terms of "us" and "them?"
11. Are you asked to give money as part of your commitment to the group or for additional training? Are you pressured into this?
12. How does your group get its money?
13. Do you (really) know where the money goes?
14. Can you leave the group without feeling like a failure?
15. Is the organization known by any other name?
16. In the group, do you have private time? Private space?
17. Is your time overstructured? Do you have enough time to sleep?
18. Are there strange dietary restrictions? Medical restrictions?
19. Are the secrets of the group revealed only to the initiated?
20. Is there a double standard of behavior for the leader versus the members?
21. Does the group make it difficult to maintain contact with family?
22. Are you encouraged to drop friends who do not belong to the group?
23. Has the group asked you to give up your academic goals to go on a mission or other group activity that "is more important," such as eliminating world hunger.
24. Can the group give you the names of other students who have been to one of its retreats?
25. Does the organization operate on other college campuses? Which ones?
26. Why has the group chosen to recruit members by speaking to them on street corners rather than more traditional ways of recruiting?
27. Get on the internet and read what members and former members have said about their experiences in the group. Do their doubts and negative experiences resonate with you?
28. What other questions can you think of that might be helpful in determining if this is a safe group to join?

Sources: Questions are drawn from the cult literature, particularly from the following references:

Goldberg, W. (1986, March–April). *Campus Law Enforcement Journal, 16*(2).
Martin, P. (1993). *Cult proofing your kids*. Grand Rapids, MI: Zondervan.

NOTES

1. This case study is a personal account from a former member. We have attempted to be true to the original narrative, changing only those demographics that would reveal her identity.
2. In the chapter "The Children of Island Pond" in her edited book, sociologist Susan Palmer claims that the children are doing fine based on her visit to the compound. What she did not see were the children who were hidden behind curtains and in the basement because they had bruises on their bodies. Palmer's visit was

described to the first author in a therapy session by a former member who was there at the time.

3. The Watchtower claims that according to scripture, they cannot take action against an abuser when only one witness (the abused) makes an accusation, on the grounds that doing so would be in conflict with Bible principles requiring two witnesses to an act of wrongdoing (http://www.silentlambs.org/twowitnessrule.htm). An amendment to this rule allows action when two independent accusations have been made against the same accuser ("Facts About Jehovah's Witnesses," 2017).

4. This testimony given at the Congressional hearings on Waco by Kiri Jewell has been questioned by Thibodeau, who was there at the time. However, even he admits that Koresh favored girls aged 11–13 years.

REFERENCES

ABC News. (2003, April 17). Witness: The children of Waco [Television broadcast]. Primetime. New York, NY: American Broadcasting Company.

Almendros, C., Gamez-Guadix, M., Rodriquez-Carballeira, A., & Carrobles, A. (2011). Assessment of psychological abuse in manipulative groups. *International Cultic Studies Review, 2*, 61–76.

American Psychiatric Association. (2013). *Diagnostic and statistical manual of mental disorders* (5th ed.). Arlington, VA: American Psychiatric Publishing.

Amnesty International. (2015, April 14). *Nigeria: Abducted women and girls forced to join Boko Haram attacks*. Retrieved from https://www.amnesty.org/en/latest/news/2015/04/nigeria-abducted-women-and-girls-forced-to-join-boko-haram-attacks

Anderson, B., & Kelly, R. (2018.) *Barbara Anderson: Eyewitness to deceit*. New York, NY: Richard Kelly.

Australian Associated Press. (2015, August 5). Jehovah's Witness church says it will comply with mandatory reporting of child abuse. *The Guardian*. Retrieved June 14, 2018, from http://www.theguardian.com/australia-news/2015/aug/04/jehovahs-witness-church-says-it-will-comply-with-mandatory-reporting-of-child-abuse

Ayella, M. F. (1998). *Insane therapy: Portrait of a psychotherapy cult*. Philadelphia, PA: Temple University Press.

Baldas, T. (2018). Friends: Jehovah's Witnesses shunning drove Keego Harbor mom to murder-suicide. *Detroit Free Press*. Retrieved from https://www.freep.com/story/news/local/michigan/2018/02/19/keego-harbor-jehovahs-witness-mom-triple-murder-suicide/351559002

Boghani, P. (2016, March 18). "Deradicalization" is coming to American: Does it work? [Television broadcast]. *Frontline*. Retrieved from http://www.pbs.org/wgbh/frontline/article/deradicalization-is-coming-to-america-does-it-work

Borowik, C. (2016). The Family International: The emergence of a virtual new religious community. In E. V. Gallagher (Ed.), *The cult wars in historical perspective: New and minority religions* (pp. 108–120). London, UK: Routledge.

Bramham, D. (2016, November 27). More revelations about life in Bountiful expected at polygamy trial. *Vancouver Sun*. Retrieved from http://vancouversun.com/news/crime/more-revelations-about-life-in-bountiful-expected-at-polygamy-trial

Breault, M., & King, M. (1993). *Inside the cult*. New York, NY: Penguin.

Bundy, T. (2015, April 14). California court guts child abuse ruling against Jehovah's Witnesses. *Reveal.* Retrieved from https://www.revealnews.org/article/california-court-guts-child-abuse-ruling-against-jehovahs-witnesses/

Bunting, G., & Willman, D. (1995, July 20). Waco hearings open: Girl tells of forced sex. *The New York Times.*

Carlisle, N. (2018, April 17). How the FLDS controls an economy on the Utah–Arizona line as told through an auto parts store. *Salt Lake Tribune.*

Chambers, W., Langone, M., Dole, A., & Grice, J. (1994). Group Psychological Abuse Scale: A measure of cultic behavior. *Cultic Studies Journal,* 11(1), 88–117.

Chapman, D., Dube, S., & Anda, R. (2007). Adverse childhood events as risk factors for negative mental health outcomes. *Psychiatric Annals,* 37(5), 359–364.

Dogherty, J. (2003, March 13). Bound by fear: Polygamy in Arizona. *Phoenix New Times.* Retrieved from http://www.phoenixnewtimes.com/news/bound-by-fear-polygamy-in-arizona-6409119

Facts About Jehovah's Witnesses. (2017, April). *JW facts.com.* Retrieved June 14, 2018, from http://www.jwfacts.com/watchtower/paedophilia.php

Funari, L. & Henry, R. (2011). Lessons learned from SGAs about recovery and resiliency. *ICSA Today,* 2(3), 2–9.

Gibson, M., Morgan, M., Woolley, C., & Powis, T. (2011). Growing up at Centrepoint: Retrospective accounts of childhood spent at an intentional community. *Journal of Child Sexual Abuse,* 20(4), 413–434.

Goransson, M., & Holmqvist, R. (2018). Is psychological distress among former cult members related to psychological abuse in the cult? *International Journal of Cultic Studies,* 9, 43–54.

Hamilton, M. (2012). *Justice denied: What America must do to protect its children.* New York, NY: Cambridge University Press.

Hamilton, M. (2014). *God vs. the gavel: The perils of extreme religious liberty* (2nd ed.). New York, NY: Cambridge University Press.

Headley, C. (2016, December 27). *Interview by L. Remini: Leah Remini: Scientology and the aftermath* [Documentary television series]. New York, NY: A&E Television.

Heinlein, R. (1987). *Stranger in a strange land.* New York, NY: Ace. (Original work published 1961)

Higgins, A. (2017, April 4). Russia moves to ban Jehovah's Witnesses as "extremist." *The New York Times.*

Kaplan, J. (2001). The roots of religious violence in America. In B. Zablocki & T. Robbins (Eds.), *Misunderstanding cults* (pp. 478–514). Toronto, Ontario, Canada: University of Toronto Press.

Kendall, L. (2016). *Born and raised in a sect: You are not alone.* Progression.

Kent, S. (2001). *From slogans to mantras: Social protest and religious conversion in the late Vietnam era.* Syracuse, NY: Syracuse University Press.

Kent, S. (2006). A matter of principle: Fundamentalist Mormon polygamy, children, and human rights debates, *Nova Religion,* 10(1), 7–29.

Kent, S. (2011). Mormonism: Harm, human rights, and the criminalization of fundamentalist Mormon polygamy. In M. Hamilton & M. Rozell (Eds.), *Fundamentalism, politics, and the law* (pp. 163–192). New York: NY: Palgrave Macmillan.

Kent, S. (2012). Religious justifications for child sexual abuse in cults and alternative religions. *International Journal of Cultic Studies,* 3, 1–26.

Kross, E., Berman, M., Mischel, W., Smith, E., & Wager, T. (2011). Social rejection shares somatosensory representations with physical pain. *Proceedings of the National Academy of Sciences of the USA, 108*(15), 6270–6275. doi:10.1073/pnas.1102693108

Krugel, L. (2017, February 3). Two of three convicted in B.C. child bride case. *Toronto Star*. Retrieved from https://www.thestar.com/news/canada/2017/02/03/bc-judge-to-rule-in-polygamy-child-bride-case.html

Laisure, R. B. (2018). Employing trafficking laws to capture elusive leaders of destructive cults. *International Journal of Cultic Studies, 9,* 1–30.

Lalich, J. (1997). Dominance and submission: The psychosocial exploitation of women in cults. *Cultic Studies Journal, 14*(1), 1–21.

Langone, M. (1984). Deprogramming survey. *Cultic Studies Journal, 1*(1), 63–68.

Lifton, J. (1969). *Thought reform and psychology of totalism: A study of brainwashing in China.* New York, NY: Norton.

Lottick, E. (2008). Psychologist survey regarding cults. *Cultic Studies Review, 7*(1), 1–19.

Markowitz, A., & Halperin, D. A. (1984). Cults and children. *Cultic Studies Journal, 1,* 143–155.

McFarland, H. (2015). Quivering daughters: Hope and healing for the daughters of patriarchy. Book review by Lawrence Pile. *ICSA Today, 6*(2), 22–25.

Meredith, K. (2016). Disappearing mother. *ICSA Today, 7*(2), 19.

Mithers, C. L. (1994). *Therapy gone mad: The story of hundreds of patients and a generation betrayed.* Reading, MA: Addison-Wesley.

Musser, R. (2013). *The witness wore red: The 19th wife who brought polygamous cult leaders to justice.* New York, NY: Grand Central Publishing.

Palmer, D., & Perrin, D. (2004). *Keep Sweet: Children of Polygamy.* Lister, B.C.: Dave's Press, ix.

Robbins, T. (2001). Balance and fairness in the study of alternative religions. In B. Zaoblocki & T. Robbins (Eds.), *Misunderstanding cults: Searching for objectivity in a controversial field* (pp. 69–98). Toronto, Ontario, Canada: University of Toronto Press.

Rosenberg, J. (2018, June 1). *The Jonestown massacre.* ThoughtCo. Retrieved from https://www.thoughtco.com/the-jonestown-massacre-1779385

Sanders, A. (2018, May 28). From polygamy to democracy: Inside a polygamous Mormon Town. *Rolling Stone.*

Schore, J., & Schore, A. (2012). Modern attachment theory: The central role of affect regulation in development and treatment. In A. Schore (Ed.), *The science of the art of psychotherapy* (pp. 28–51). New York, NY: Norton.

Schriver, D. (2018). *Whispering in the daylight.* Knoxville. TN: University of Tennessee Press.

Singer, M. (1993, March 16). Statement of Margaret Singer to the Clinton Health Care Task Force, delivered to the White House. In M.L. Tobias & J. Lalich (Eds.), *Captive hearts, captive minds: Freedom and recovery from cults and abusive relationships* (p. 1). Alameda, CA: Hunter House.

Singer, M. (1995). *Cults in our midst: The hidden menace in our everyday lives.* San Francisco, CA: Jossey-Bass.

Swan, R. (2000). When faith fails children: Religion-based neglect: pervasive, deadly ... and legal? *The Humanist, 60*(6), 11–16.

Szimhart, J. (1995). *Lambs to the slaughter: My fourteen years with Elizabeth Clare Prophet and Church Universal Triumphant* by J. Petrangelo [Book review]. *Cultic Studies Journal, 12*(2). Retrieved from http://www.csj.org/pub_csj/csjbookreview/csjbkrev122lambs.htm

Thibodeau, D., & Whiteson, L. (1999). *A place called Waco: A survivor's story*. New York, NY: Public Affairs.

Timoner, O. (2007). *Join Us* [Film]. Pasadena, CA: Interloper Films.

Tobias, M. L., & Lalich, J. (1994). *Captive hearts, captive minds: Freedom and recovery from cults and abusive groups*. Alameda, CA: Hunter House.

Wall, E. (2008). *Stolen innocence*. New York, NY: HarperCollins.

Watchtower Bible and Tract Society of Pennsylvania. (2018). *How many of Jehovah's witnesses are there worldwide?* Retrieved from https://www.jw.org/en/jehovahs-witnesses/faq/how-many-jw-members

West, L. J., & Langone, M. D. (1986). Cultism: A conference for scholars and policy makers. *Cultic Studies Journal, 3*, 117–134.

Yousafzai, M., with Lamb, C. (2013). *I am Malala: The girl who stood up for education and was shot by the Taliban*. New York, NY: Little, Brown.

21

Leave Me Alone

Violence Against Women in Trinidad and Tobago

NIRMALA PRAKASH, MELISSA INDERA SINGH,
JENNIFER PREVOT, STEPHANIE GOPIE,
JADE VORSTER, AND PETER AVERKIOU ∎

OVERVIEW

The twin-island Republic of Trinidad and Tobago, a former colony of Great Britain with a population of approximately 1.3 million people, is multiethnic, multireligious, and multicultural. It stems from a history of Indian, Portuguese, and Chinese indentureship; African slavery; Spanish colonialism; and French influence (Republic of Trinidad and Tobago Ministry of Planning and Sustainable Development Central Statistics Office, 2011; World Bank, 2014). According to the *Trinidad & Tobago Guardian* newspaper, in 2017 more than 1,100 cases of domestic violence were reported, 43 of which resulting in murder (Dowlat, 2018). Documentation of intimate partner violence (IPV) in Trinidad and Togabo began in the colonial period, which spanned from 1845 to 1917 (Jha, 1985; Mohammed, 1994). Reported incidences of IPV, also termed domestic violence, in Trinidad and Tobago from 1995 to 2013 indicate that 5,264 people were murdered, and 442 (8.4%) of these murders were attributed to domestic violence (Seepersad, 2016). Although one in three women in Trinidad and Tobago report experiencing IPV (Doodnath, 2018), experts and researchers estimate rates of violence against women (VAW) and IPV in reality are much higher due to the culture of silences associated with DV socially, politically, and culturally—these cimres are underreported.

This chapter analyzes VAW and specifically IPV in Trinidad and Tobago. We use contextual factors of intersectionality and familial, political, and sociocultural paradigms as the lens to analyze violence as a construct within the Caribbean and specifically Trinidad and Tobago. In this chapter, *violence* is defined as the oppression from a perpetrator toward a victim. In this chapter, oppression includes broader geographical

Figure 21.1 Leave She Alone.

6 likes

helienne1 Met the future of Britain at the #nottinghillcarnival - it gives me hope! #notaskingforit

Figure 21.2 #NotAskingForIt.

(i.e., Caribbean) and sociocultural and political contexts (i.e., colonial rule, Indo-Caribbean indentureship, Afro-Caribbean slavery, and music).

Social Acceptance of Intimate Partner Violence in Music and Socialization: Trinidad Carnival

The presence of IPV is memorialized in modern Trinidadian society via lyrics of local music—calypso and soca (associated with the Afro-Trinidadian culture) and chutney (associated with the Indo-Trinidadian culture) (Sukhu, 2012). Calypso music and Carnival were brought to Trinidad and Tobago by French settlers, whereas soca music is an evolution of calypso that has African influences. Carnival, an annual event celebrated before Ash Wednesday, is similar in scope to Brazilian Carnivale or Mardi Gras in New Orleans. The creation and evolution of these festivals have followed the same trajectory. The revelry, drinking, dancing, sexuality, and full-blown camaraderie of Carnival (and Carnivale and Mardi Gras) are a final carefree celebration before fasting begins for the Catholic fasting period of Lent. The free population adapted Carnival, originally celebrated by the elite population, after the abolishment of African slavery and Indian indentured servitude. During the first hours of Carnival week, known as J'ouvert morning, Carnival participants or "revelers" apply mud, paint, and costumes to themselves and each other. The application of the mud and paint masks economic and cultural differences between the Carnival revelers, thus anonymizing racial, cultural, and socioeconomic differences of the participants. The anonymity and mixing of classes underlies the carefree mood of Carnival. Annually, Trinidad and Tobago has more than 40,000 visitors for Carnival, half of whom are from the United States (Eligon, 2011; Saro-Wiwa, 2012).

Many nationally and internationally renowned artists, including Allison Hinds, Calypso Rose, and Machel Montano, have portrayed the Caribbean history of sexuality and IPV through their music. In Hind's rendition of "Carnival Baby" (for lyrics, see http://socalyrics.weebly.com/carnival-baby.html), she sings about a woman conceived during Carnival, her mother a victim of "foul play." Note the use of the words and phrases depicting the mother's "moving and grooving" as reasons the sailor "influenced and led [her] astray." Unfortunately, by the singer's own admission, no one would believe it was "foul play." The lyrics exemplify the sociocultural acceptance of women being the cause of any foul play, or violence, that happens to them because of how women use their bodies to dance. Furthermore, one could conclude legally she has no recourse because "no one will believe it was foul play." Note the term foul play diminishes the fact that a violent act against a woman and the product of that violence, the baby, are forever branded with a derogatory reference.

In their song titled "Leave Me Alone" (for lyrics, see http://www.metrolyrics.com/leave-me-alone-lyrics-calypso-rose.html), international soca singers Machel Montano and the Calypso Queen, the mother of calypso music, Calypso Rose sang about an incidence of VAW that occurred during the 2016 Trinidad Carnival. A 30-year-old Japanese woman and musician, Asami Nagakiya, who frequently participated in Trinidad Carnival, was found strangled and raped in her yellow-bejeweled Carnival masquerade costume ("Japanese Musician," 2016). The incident made international headlines and prompted a campaign to combat VAW. According to Wilson (2016), the mayor of Trinidad's capital city, Port of Spain, responded to the murder by saying, "Women have a responsibility to ensure they are not abused during the Carnival season. It's a matter of, if she was still in her costume—I think that's what I heard—let your imagination roll" (para. 4). A national petition started by Womantra, a Trinidad-based organization, on change.org called for Mayor Raymond Tim Kee's resignation. The petition stated Mayor Tim Kee routinely blames and shames victims of abuse. His recent comments toward Japanese national Nagakiya, whose body was found under a tree on February 10, 2016, after Carnival celebrations, demonstrate his victim blaming and dismissal of VAW as an issue (Berkeley, 2016). The petition demanded the mayor's resignation and raised 10,000 signatures, successfully obtaining his resignation on February 16, 2016. As of February 1, 2018, the Asami Nagakiya murder case was still open and active, with no new leads (Doughty, 2018).

Montano and Calypso Rose released their hit single "Leave Me Alone" following Mayor Tim Kee's resignation. On Montano's YouTube channel, the song was viewed 4.3 million times within 1 year and was a staple at parties and social venues. The lyrics of "Leave Me Alone" shed light on VAW perpetrated by men. The woman in the song proclaims forcefully do not touch her, are you [men] crazy, no one should bother her while she dances, all she wants to do is safely enjoy Carnival and her attire (the Carnival costume) does not diminish that desire. Attilah Springer, a Trinidadian writer and activist, described this song as a rallying cry for women who just want to be able to enjoy their Carnival—Carnival being that space of freedom without men trying to control how much freedom women feel (Powers, 2017). In 2018, prior to the Carnival season, Trinidad and Tobago Police Service enforced a law stating offenders who perform a nonconsensual "wine" or gyration may be arrested (Mendes-Franco, 2018). A "wine" is a hip swivel performed to soca or calypso music between two people in close proximity. This close gyration pits the male torso on the female torso in a sexually explicit manner. "Wining up" on someone, described by soca artiste Kes as "thief ah wine," is socially and culturally acceptable with or without permission. "Wining up" or "theifing a wine" is an attitude and dancing style that occurs by a man without the consent of the woman dancing. Attilah Springer relayed how commonplace "theifing a wine" is with men grabbing women by the waist and forcing them to dance. According to Powers (2017), "Every single woman who engages in Carnival has had that experience" (para. 17).

Asami Nagakiya's murder also prompted the #NotAskingForIt campaign empowering women to speak up about sexual violence. According to Hosein (2017), Anya Ayoung-Chee, an internationally renowned fashion designer who won the ninth season of the television show "Project Runway," partnered with local activists and artists to design and sell hundreds of T-shirts with the phrases "Leave Me Alone" and the colloquial corollary "Leave She Alone" printed on them. Angelique V. Nixon, another activist, in partnership with Attilah Springer created the Say Something campaign calling for gender sensitivity training and the collection of data to determine rates of VAW. They spearheaded a campaign called #LifeInLeggings, in which Caribbean women talk about their experiences of street harassment or sexual abuse. In 2018, Womantra created a flowchart to describe the wining etiquette for Carnival (Loop News, 2018). In response to these social campaigns, research, and political pressure, the Gender Affairs Department of Trinidad and Tobago created a National Registry for Domestic Violence. It is important to note the swift, almost synergistic, reaction of music and Trinidadian pop culture in commenting on a political and violence

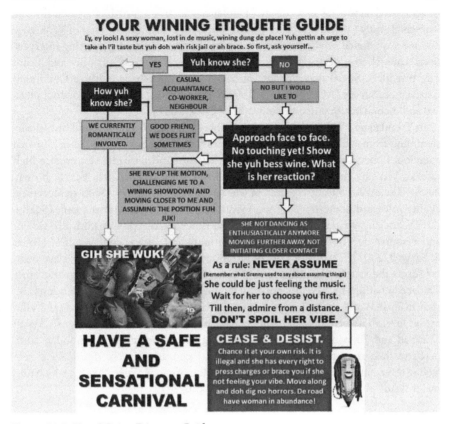

Figure 21.3 Your Wining Etiquette Guide.

problem. This synergy has occurred within calypso, soca, chutney, and reggae music across the Caribbean since colonization.

VIOLENCE AGAINST WOMEN AND INTIMATE PARTNER VIOLENCE IN TRINIDAD AND TOBAGO

The movements to combat VAW and IPV expose a deeper problem associated with VAW during Carnival. These movements show VAW and IPV are accepted, public, overt, and commonplace and harassment occurs every day in Trinidad. VAW is purposeful and rooted in familial, social, institutional, and cultural practices (Crenshaw, 1994). The sociocultural acceptance of violence began during the Caribbean's plantation paradigm, which sustained and equated Caribbean masculine identities with power and control. The criminalization of domestic violence pushed Caribbean men to alter traditions, finding ways to assert their masculinity, thereby changing the discourse of Caribbean masculine identities (Jeremiah, Gamache, & Hegamin-Younger, 2013). The transformation back is slow and arduous, with the need to modify generations of thinking and sociocultural and behavioral norms. Consistently prosecuting IPV when the police and judicial officials may not view IPV as a problem is an issue that plagues the human rights, public health, and social service arenas. Economic and sociocultural factors foster a culture of violence affecting approximately one-third of women globally (World Health Organization, 2013). Traditional views of VAW confine the experience of violence to the privacy of the relationship, putting interventions that seek to educate or reduce IPV/VAW beyond the reach of policy and health care providers. Social determinants of health and research on Adverse Childhood Experiences Survey (ACES) explain violence exposure as a determinant of poor physical and mental health outcomes in women (Black, 2011).

In Trinidad and Tobago, violence is a daily reality for women now and historically stemming from violent colonial rule. The most common form of violence is sexual coercion. Other Caribbean islands, such as Jamaica and Barbados, experience high rates of VAW by strangers (Le Franc, Samms-Vaughan, Hambleton, Fox, & Brown, 2008). The evolution of the status of women in Trinidad is slow, with stereotypical gender roles and domestic and sexual violence viewed as the woman's fault (Sukhu, 2012). Socially, spatial concentrations of violence occur when historically violent and resource-deprived countries create a foundation that encourages IPV (Riner & Saywell, 2002). The history of colonization and rule through force by slave owners forms the spatial concentrations of violence in Trinidad and Tobago and other Caribbean nations and exemplifies why theoretical models of IPV interventions created in First World countries are not transferable to the Caribbean. Disparate education levels between men and women also contribute to the high rates of VAW in Trinidad and Tobago. Women have increasing economic and social mobility compared to their male counterparts due to higher education levels, thus leaving men feeling threatened and reinforcing the degradation of gender-specific roles, which ultimately leads to VAW (Jeremiah et al., 2013; Sukhu, 2012).

CURRENT CONDITIONS

The Political Acceptance of Violence Against Women and Intimate Partner Violence in Trinidad and Tobago

> It is hereby recognised and declared that in Trinidad and Tobago there have existed and shall continue to exist without discrimination by reason of race, origin, colour, religion or sex, the following fundamental human rights and freedoms, namely: (a) the right of the individual to life, liberty, security of the person and enjoyment of property and the right not to be deprived thereof except by due process of law; (b) the right of the individual to equality before the law and the protection of the law.
> The Constitution of the Republic of Trinidad and Tobago
> —Republic of Trinidad and Tobago Ministry of the Attorney General (2018, Section 4: a, b)

Systematic discrimination against women, despite lofty ideals outlined in constitutions, is guilty of producing economic and social depression of women throughout the world, and unfortunately, Trinidad and Tobago is no exception. According to the United Nations Development Programme (2016b), Trinidad and Tobago ranks 67 on the global Gender Inequality Index, which records reproductive health, empowerment, and economic activity. Less than one-third of seats in the Trinidadian parliament are held by women (31.5%), despite the fact that 70.6% of adult women have obtained a secondary level of education compared to 68.4% of adult men (United Nations Development Programme, 2016b). Moreover, participation in the labor market by women is 52.6% compared to 73.6% for men (United Nations Development Programme, 2016b). When taken in concert with domestic violence studies, 76% of women victims of domestic violence were economically dependent on their partners as housewives in Trinidad and Tobago (Alméras & Montaño, 2007). Regarding political progress in the direction of gender equality across all aspects of life, Trinidad and Tobago, along with many countries in the Caribbean, still struggles to improve policies lessening vulnerability, economic, and social depression levels in women. In this section, we examine the past and current political climate of domestic violence, marriage, and reproductive rights in Trinidad and Tobago with respect to the well-being and vulnerability of women and propagation of IPV.

The Domestic Violence Act

Legislation for orders of protection from an abusive partner or family member became law in 1991, and it was replaced by the 1999 Domestic Violence Act. According to Lazarus-Black (2008), the 1991 act made Trinidad and Tobago "the first state in the English-speaking Caribbean to pass a comprehensive domestic violence law" (p. 42). The passage of the 1991 act produced an immediate response and manifested into thousands of applications for protection filed by women (Lazarus-Black, 2003). Domestic violence has existed throughout the history of Trinidad and Tobago, whereas societal protection by law has existed only since 1991 (Sukhu, 2012).

The Domestic Violence Act defines domestic violence as "physical, sexual, emotional or psychological or financial abuse committed by a person against a spouse, child, any other person who is a member of the household or dependent" (Republic of Trinidad and Tobago Ministry of Legal Affairs, 1999, p. 292). The act provides immediate relief and ensures "prompt and just legal remedy for victims of domestic violence" (p. 291). Protection orders are obtained from spouses, children, dependents, law enforcement, social workers, and so on. The applicant seeks the order from the court's registry at the respective magistrate's court by speaking with the Clerk of the Peace, who identifies the problem and determines whether it is a domestic violence matter or a matter for another court. Fees are associated with the filings, and roles and responsibilities of law enforcement are outlined as well as consequences of noncompliance of the protection order in the Domestic Violence Act. A first violation penalty is a maximum fine of $9,000 or a maximum of 3 months in prison, leading up to a third violation and a maximum of 5 years of imprisonment as the magistrate deems appropriate (Republic of Trinidad and Tobago Ministry of Legal Affairs, 1999). Supportive services such as shelters and hotlines are also available to some extent.

Due to the lack of legal consequences for first-time perpetrators, the effectiveness of this law is questioned. According to Amnesty International (2012), underreporting of cases of gender-based violence is linked to an inefficient justice system and inadequate police training. Further underreporting occurs due to economic dependence of the woman on her abuser causing the inability to obtain, pay for, and secure transportation throughout the procurement of the protection order. According to the World Bank (2014), more than 90% of Trinidad and Tobago's population lives in rural areas, limiting access to courts and law enforcement. Despite these factors, the Chairman of Advocates for Safe Parenthood: Improving Reproductive Equity reports that more than 18,000 applications for protection orders are filed each year (Kowlessar, 2011).

Policy and Marriage

Historical consequences of marriage laws play into the political climate of IPV in Trinidad and Tobago. Until recently, Trinidad and Tobago recognized four types of marriages—civil, Hindu, Muslim, and Orisa—and each marriage classification specified different marital ages (US Embassy in Trinidad & Tobago, n.d.). On religious grounds, children could be married in Muslim and Hindu faiths at the ages of 12 and 16 years, respectively, thus having a substantial impact on public health indicators and domestic violence rates. UNICEF (2016) reports that 8% of girls in Trinidad and Tobago are married by age 18 years. In studies conducted in the Caribbean, early marital age is associated with an increased risk of domestic violence (United Nations Development Programme, 2016a). In Jamaica, in 2008 and 2009, for example, 12% of women victims were younger than age 15 years at first marriage, 7% were aged 15–19 years, 3% were aged 20–24 years, and just 3% were aged 25 years or older (United Nations Development Programme, 2016a). Young women and girls are at a higher risk of experiencing low socioeconomic standards and subsequent violence perpetuating a culture of acceptance and generational family violence. In June 2017, laws were amended under the Miscellaneous Provisions Marriage Act eradicating marriage for all persons younger than age 18 years in all recognized forms of marriage (Republic of Trinidad and Tobago Ministry of Legal Affairs, 2017).

Policy and Reproductive Rights

Reproductive rights are critical in determining a woman's autonomy and vulnerability in society. Unsafe abortion is the major cause of maternal morbidity in Trinidad and Tobago (Martin, Hyacenth, & Suite, 2007). Abortion is illegal in Trinidad and Tobago under the Offences Against the Person Act of 3 April 1925; the act bans abortion for social and economic reasons, cases of rape or incest, and fetal indications of severe impairment(Republic of Trinidad and Tobago Ministry of the Attorney General and Legal Affairs, 2015). In addition, any person who intends to procure the miscarriage of a woman by administering to her any noxious substance, poison, or unlawfully uses any means is subject to 4 years' imprisonment (Republic of Trinidad and Tobago Ministry of the Attorney General and Legal Affairs, 2015). According to the Republic of Trinidad and Tobago Ministry of the Attorney General and Legal Affairs, a woman who "undertakes the same act with respect to herself is subject to the same penalty" (para. 56) and "any person who unlawfully supplies means to procure an abortion knowing that it is intended for that purpose is subject to two years' imprisonment" (para. 57). The law, predating Trinidad's independence, amended in the 1938

English Rex v. Bourne case, allows abortions in situations in which the woman's physical or mental health is jeopardized. Due to the law's ambiguity, medical practitioners in the public sector have admitted fear of legal ramifications and almost always withhold the option to terminate on the grounds of mental health (Martin et al., 2007). With this restriction on female reproductive rights, mortality, morbidity, and human suffering are more likely to occur, often disproportionately affecting economically disadvantaged women.

Knowledge and attitudes toward women's health are significant indicators of how long-standing conservative law and sociocultural attitudes in Trinidad and Tobago shape the climate of women's health, well-being, and resiliency to vulnerability. A 2007 study investigated the knowledge and attitudes of Trinidadians about abortions, finding 44% of respondents correctly said abortion was legal only under certain circumstances, 38% thought it was entirely illegal, 5% were not aware it was against the law at all, and 13% had no idea (Martin et al., 2007). Only 21% of respondents thought the law should provide for abortion under all circumstances (Martin et al., 2007). Half were in favor of a law broadening the circumstances under which a woman could obtain an abortion, with 29% in favor of an inflexible, restrictive law (Martin et al., 2007). Overall, the study concluded 71% of respondents were in favor of relaxing the current criminal abortion law to different degrees; 62% of women were in favor of policy reform compared to 38% of men (Martin et al., 2007). The disparity between women's and men's attitudes regarding policy reform poses challenges for the women of Trinidad and Tobago, whose government is dominated by men. Until men's attitudes toward abortion and women's reproductive rights change or more women enter into political positions, it is unlikely that the sociopolitical climate will change (Martin et al., 2007).

Despite conservative abortion laws, the Trinidadian government directly supports and sanctions the use of contraceptives. In fact, 16 health centers provide free contraception in the country. However, less than 50% of women in Trinidad and Tobago use any form of contraception (UNICEF, 2013). Uncertainty exists regarding whether the lack of contraceptive use stems from culture or religious reasons or is due to lack of accessibility; further research is needed in these areas. As in IPV reporting, accessibility is marred by economic control of the household as well as the rurality of the country. Further exacerbating accessibility issues are cultural attitudes toward sexual health and sexually transmitted diseases, which are diminished, not addressed, and/or stigmatized by religious leaders, ideologies, and cultural expressions within music and art.

LOOKING TO THE FUTURE

Gaps in research exists on the prevalence and health implications of VAW and IPV in Trinidad and Tobago so that it is not possible to form a clear consensus or theoretical model to explain the phenomenon. Most explanatory models are based on high-income countries, such as the United States, Canada, or England, where access to resources, societal views against violence, sociocultural norms, and the legislative structures do not mirror those of Caribbean nations. Moreover, in an environment in which violence is integrated into social norms, what factors protect women from acts of violence? Focused research on protective factors, rather than risk factors of VAW/

IPV, may be beneficial in the creation of a theoretical framework for health care providers in Trinidad and Tobago.

Regular collection of IPV/VAW data enables governmental, social service, and health care providers to resource, prioritize, and define their target populations, thus enabling evaluation measures. The effects of the 1999 Domestic Violence Act are unknown due to data collection shortfalls. Available data from the Inter-American Development Bank (Seepersad, 2016) reflect only sexual offenses reported and detected within each police division, which likely underestimates the actual levels of IPV due to stigma associated with reporting. Assumptions and underreporting lower prevalence rates, ultimately affects the amount of funding for and research on affects.

Recommendations for Health Care and Social Service Providers

Intimate partner violence legislation in Trinidad and Tobago is comprehensive on paper; however, in practice, reporting rates of IPV/VAW has increased slowly. Laws do not address the strongly held cultural beliefs and societal attitudes toward violence. Interventions aimed at changing social norms are needed for deep-rooted change to occur. Two evidence-based strategies have reported changes in attitudes in developing countries: small group participatory workshops and large-scale educational entertainment campaign efforts using media sources as a platform (Heise, 2011). The small group strategy, implemented in a randomized control trial in the South African program Sisters for Life in combination with an existing microfinance program, showed a reduction in IPV of 51% during a 2-year period (Kim et al., 2009). Additional small-scale community programs working with both men and women addressing sociocultural norms have also shown significant results (Kishor & Johnson, 2004).

Implementation of social services such as safe houses, support groups, and mental health resources for victims/survivors and the use of culturally competent screening tools by health care providers can hasten change in societal beliefs and the ability to reduce the prevalence of VAW/IPV. Effective interventions are guided by principles of prevention, protection, and early intervention; focus on rebuilding the lives of victims/survivors; and have a high level of accountability. Elevating advocacy and awareness of VAW/IPV addresses the silence, stigma, and shame associated with victims. Women's empowerment through education and employment opportunities helps reconnect, rebuild, and recover lives after violence.

The necessity to interrupt escalating cycles of violence and reduce stress through family therapy enables members to analyze their thoughts, behaviors, and childhood experiences while gaining tools such as accountability and anger management and changing attitudes/perspectives. The goal of family interventions is to teach members how to identify warning signs of impending violence and provide them with resources and tools to reduce prevalence and effects. Social skills training will improve the social competence of the abuser and the victim, allowing for the development of healthy differentiation among family members and the replacement of hostility with mutual respect.

Interventions aimed at changing sociocultural norms and reducing VAW/IPV are most effective when they are individualized and target specific risk factors in a community, echoing the need for better data collection in Trinidad and Tobago. Trinidad and many other Caribbean countries lack the fundamental structure of societal intervention, which is imperative in changing attitudes toward violence. With soaring violent crime rates, Trinidad and Tobago is in dire need of change to ensure women can live with legal and societal protection, health interventions, and social services. Health care providers and social welfare organizations need to employ culturally relevant and socially transformative interventions, taking the following into account:

- Abused women may make appointments but not show up.
- The batterer may accompany the abused woman and stay close during examination to monitor what is said.
- Multiple injuries can occur at a number of sites on the woman's body (areas covered by clothing).
- Sustained injuries to the neck by strangulation attempts are common; strangulation is used as a power move by the abuser.
- Aggravation of medical disorders such as diabetes or hypertension can be a sign of VAW/IPV.
- The abused woman may be shy, frightened, embarrassed, evasive, anxious, or passive.
- The abused woman may be hesitant to provide information about how she was injured.
- The abused woman may have a history of "accidents."
- Persistent injuries to their breasts, genitalia, and abdomen are common in cases of VAW/IPV.

Although not culturally normed to the Caribbean, this list reflects a starting point for Caribbean providers to craft their own unique set of screening tools.

National Policy on Gender and Development 2018: Trinidad and Tobago

Changes to political laws, policies, and attitudes toward women's health, VAW, and IPV to be congruent with international standards and nationally recognized is a needed next step. The tools and resources available to Trinidad and Tobago, as a member of the United Nations, include data collection instruments, resources, and policy language via the Convention on the Elimination of All Forms of Discrimination Against Women, the Convention on the Rights of the Child, the International Conference on Population Development Plan of Action, the Beijing Platform for Action, and the Sustainable Development Goals to aid and push for women's equality. Moreover, Trinidad and Tobago adopted the National Policy on Gender and Development in 2018 (Republic of Trinidad and Tobago Office of the Prime Minister, 2018). The policy aims to preserve the equal and inalienable rights of men, women, boys, and girls in Trinidad and Tobago as guaranteed under the constitution; provides frameworks for including gender perspectives in all activities of government and civil society; and promotes the full and equal participation of men and women in the development process (Republic of Trinidad and Tobago Office of the Prime Minister, 2018). The document, originally drafted in 2009, outlines a variety of specific goals and six strategic objectives aimed at decreasing gender disparities and improving data collection practices. The sixth strategic objective of the National Policy on Gender and Development

Act simply states "prevent, punish and eradicate gender-based violence" (p. 33) and provides the following targets:

a) Continue work toward the establishment and strengthening of the Central Registry on Gender based/Domestic Violence
b) Institutionally strengthen initiatives aimed at preventing, punishing and eradicating gender-based/domestic violence
c) Implement the management policy and plans for established safe houses, shelters, and transitions homes for victims/survivors
d) Strengthen and support bona fide organizations working on gender-based/ domestic violence
e) Train and sensitize stakeholders, including law enforcement officers and social support providers working with victims and perpetrators of gender-based violence. (p. 35)

There is great hope for the women of Trinidad and Tobago as policy and attitudes begin to embrace gender equality, the well-being of women, and ultimately the demise of VAW and IPV.

CONCLUSION

Changes in social, cultural, and political frameworks are needed to elevate the status of women in Trinidad and Tobago, educate men and women about violence and IPV, and equip people with tools to break generational cycles of violence. Institutionalized paradigms of power and control continue to erode women's sense of safety. The adverse health effects on women and children who experience violence and IPV are long-lasting and severe. Although the government of Trinidad and Tobago, the United Nations, and other regional Caribbean organizations are creating policies to combat IPV, changes in attitudes and societal stigma have a stronghold in the twin island nation. More grassroots campaigns, bold statements by pop culture, and subsequent sociocultural evolution of attitudes toward VAW and IPV are needed to create a culture of consent during Carnival. As a result of steady migration to the United States and other countries, the issue of culturally competent screening of VAW/IPV in US Caribbean communities is a concern for US health practitioners. The need for future research exists in the areas of migration, current effects of Trinidad and Tobago legislation, educational reforms, and the roles of community organizations in combating IPV.

DISCUSSION QUESTIONS

1. How can health care providers combat sociocultural norms when developing IPV interventions and tools for women in Trinidad and Tobago? In what ways would you modify these interventions/tools for use in

Caribbean American populations? For use in African continent and Indian subcontinent populations?

2. What questions could you ask to identify IPV in women from Trinidad and Tobago?

3. What health risks should providers be aware of in women from Trinidad and Tobago who may experience IPV? How can these outcomes indicate the need for further support and referrals from providers?

FURTHER READING

Deshong, H. (2015). Policing femininity, affirming masculinity: Relationship violence, control and spatial limitation. *Journal of Gender Studies, 24*(1), 85–103.

Hadeed, L. F., & El-Bassel, N. (2006). Social support among Afro-Trinidadian women experiencing intimate partner violence. *Violence Against Women, 12*(8), 740–760.

Lacey, K., West, C., Matusko, N., & Jackson, J. (2016). Prevalence and factors associated with severe physical intimate partner violence among US Black women: A comparison of African American and Caribbean Blacks. *Violence Against Women, 22*(6), 651–670.

REFERENCES

Alméras, D., & Montaño, S. (2007). *No more! The right of women to live a life free of violence in Latin America and the Caribbean.* New York, NY: United Nations.

Amnesty International. (2012). *Amnesty International report 2012: The state of the world's human rights.* Retrieved from https://www.amnestyusa.org/files/air12-report-english.pdf

Berkeley, C. (2016). *A national call for Raymond Tim Kee to resign as mayor.* Change.org. Retrieved from https://www.change.org/p/trinidad-and-tobago-a-national-call-for-raymond-tim-kee-to-resign-as-mayor

Black, M. C. (2011). Intimate partner violence and adverse health consequences: Implications for clinicians. *American Journal of Lifestyle Medicine, 5*(5), 428–439.

Crenshaw, K. (1994). Mapping the margins: Intersectionality, identity politics, and violence against women of color. In M. Fineman & R. Mykitiuk (Eds.), *The public nature of private violence* (pp. 93–118). New York, NY: Routledge.

Doodnath, A. (2018, May 1). *IDB study: 1 in 3 women victims of intimate partner violence in T&T.* Loop News. Retrieved from http://www.looptt.com/content/idb-study-1-3-women-victims-intimate-partner-violence-tt

Doughty, M. (2018, February, 1). Japan blanks carnival: Fear lingers 2 years after Asami's murder. *Trinidad and Tobago NewsDay.* Retrieved from http://newsday.co.tt/2018/02/01/japan-blanks-carnival-fear-lingers-2-years-after-asamis-murder

Dowlat, R. (2018, May 25). 100 domestic violence cases so far for 2018. *Trinidad and Tobago Guardian.* Retrieved from http://e-edition.guardian.co.tt/news/2018-05-24/100-domestic-violence-cases-so-far-2018

Eligon, J. (2011, March 9). Carnival's louder commercial beat adds dissonance. *The New York Times.* Retrieved from https://www.nytimes.com/2011/03/09/world/americas/09trinidad.html

Heise, L. (2011). *What works to prevent partner violence? An evidence overview.* London, UK: STRIVE.

Japanese musician who frequented Caribbean Carnival found strangled in Trinidad. (2016, February). *The Japan Times.* Retrieved from https://www.japantimes.co.jp/news/2016/02/12/national/crime-legal/japanese-musician-often-took-part-trinidad-carnival-found-strangled

Jeremiah, R. D., Gamache, P. E., & Hegamin-Younger, C. (2013). Beyond behavioral adjustments: How determinants of contemporary Caribbean masculinities thwart efforts to eliminate domestic violence. *International Journal of Men's Health, 12*(3), 228.

Jha, J. (1985). The 1937 disturbance in Trinidad and Tobago. *Quarterly Review of Historical Studies, 24*(2), 1–9.

Kim, J., Ferrari, G., Abramsky, T., Watts, C., Hargreaves, J., Morison, L., . . . Pronyk, P. (2009). Assessing the incremental effects of combining economic and health interventions: The IMAGE study in South Africa. *Bulletin of the World Health Organization, 87,* 824–832.

Kishor, S., & Johnson, K. (2004). *Profiling domestic violence: A multi-country study.* Calverton, MD: ORC Macro.

Kowlessar, G. (2011, January 16). "A paper can't protect anyone." *Trinidad and Tobago Guardian.* Retrieved from http://www.guardian.co.tt/news/2011/01/16/paper-can-t-protect-anyone

Lazarus-Black, M. (2003). The (heterosexual) regendering of a modern state: Criminalizing and implementing domestic violence law in Trinidad. *Law & Social Inquiry, 28*(4), 979–1008.

Lazarus-Black, M. (2008). Vanishing complainants: The place of violence in family, gender, work, and law. *Caribbean Studies, 36*(1), 25–51.

Le Franc, E., Samms-Vaughan, M., Hambleton, I., Fox, K., & Brown, D. (2008). Interpersonal violence in three Caribbean countries: Barbados, Jamaica, and Trinidad and Tobago. *Revista Panamericana de Salud Pública, 24*(6), 409–421.

Loop News. (2018, January 15). *Womantra shares Carnival "wining etiquette" guide after TTPS warning.* Retrieved from http://www.looptt.com/content/womantra-shares-carnival-wining-etiquette-guide-after-ttps-warning

Martin, C. J., Hyacenth, G., & Suite, L. S. (2007). Knowledge and perception of abortion and the abortion law in Trinidad and Tobago. *Reproductive Health Matters, 15*(29), 97–107.

Mendes-Franco, J. (2018, January 22). *Changing Trinidad & Tobago Carnival's culture starts with consent.* Global Voices. Retrieved from https://globalvoices.org/2018/01/22/changing-trinidad-tobago-carnivals-culture-starts-with-consent

Mohammed, P. (1994). *A social history of post-migrant Indians in Trinidad from 1917 to 1947: A gender perspective.* Doctoral dissertation, Institute of Social Studies, The Hague, The Netherlands.

Powers, M. (2017, February 26). "Leave me alone": Trinidad's women find a rallying cry for this year's Carnival. *The Washington Post.* Retrieved from https://www.washingtonpost.com/world/the_americas/leave-me-alone-trinidads-women-find-a-rallying-cry-for-this-years-carnival/2017/02/26/3888f116-f9e6-11e6-aa1e-5f735ee31334_story.html?noredirect=on&utm_term=.f8c5c0402e07

Republic of Trinidad and Tobago Ministry of the Attorney General. (2018). *The law and you.* Retrieved from http://www.ag.gov.tt/Features/The-Law-and-You

Republic of Trinidad and Tobago Ministry of the Attorney General and Legal Affairs. (2015, December 31). *Offences against the person act*. Retrieved from http://rgd.legalaffairs.gov.tt/Laws2/Alphabetical_List/lawspdfs/11.08.pdf

Republic of Trinidad and Tobago Ministry of Legal Affairs. (1999, October 15). *The domestic violence act, 1999*. Retrieved from http://www.ttparliament.org/legislations/a1999-27.pdf

Republic of Trinidad and Tobago Ministry of Legal Affairs. (2017, June 22). *Miscellaneous provisions (marriage) act*. Retrieved from http://www.ttparliament.org/legislations/a2017-08.pdf

Republic of Trinidad and Tobago Ministry of Planning and Sustainable Development Central Statistics Office. (2011). *2011 population and housing census preliminary count*. Retrieved from http://cso.gov.tt/media/publications-documents

Republic of Trinidad and Tobago Office of the Prime Minister. (2018). *National policy on gender and development: A green paper*. Retrieved from http://www.opm-gca.gov.tt/portals/0/Documents/National%20Gender%20Policy/NATIONAL%20POLICY%20ON%20GENDER%20AND%20DEVELOPMENT.pdf?ver=2018-03-08-134857-323

Republic of Trinidad and Tobago Office of the Prime Minister, Gender and Child Affairs. (2018). *National policy on gender and development policy*. Retrieved from http://opm-gca.gov.tt/GenderPolicy

Riner, M. E., & Saywell, R. M. (2002). Development of the social ecology model of adolescent interpersonal violence prevention (SEMAIVP). *Journal of School Health, 72*(2), 65–70.

Saro-Wiwa, N. (2012, February 16). Trinidad carnival—The Caribbean's biggest party. *The Guardian*. Retrieved from https://www.theguardian.com/travel/2012/feb/16/carnival-caribbean-trinidad-tobago

Seepersad, R. (2016). *Crime and violence in Trinidad and Tobago: IDB series on crime and violence in the Caribbean*. Retrieved from https://www.scribd.com/document/373767553/Crime-and-Violence-in-Trinidad-and-Tobago-IDB-Series-on-Crime-and-Violence-in-the-Caribbean

Sukhu, R. L. (2012). Masculinity and men's violence against known women in Trinidad—Whose responsibility? *Men and Masculinities, 16*(1), 71–92.

United Nations Development Programme. (2016a). *Caribbean human development report: Multidimensional progress: Human resilience beyond income*. Retrieved from http://hdr.undp.org/sites/default/files/undp_bb_chdr_2016.pdf

United Nations Development Programme. (2016b). *Human development for everyone*. Retrieved from http://hdr.undp.org/sites/all/themes/hdr_theme/country-notes/TTO.pdf

UNICEF. (2013). *Trends in Contraceptive Use Worldwide 2015*. Retrieved from https://www.un.org/en/development/desa/population/publications/pdf/family/trendsContraceptiveUse2015Report.pdf

UNICEF. (2016). *The state of the world's children 2016: A fair chance for every child*. Retrieved from https://www.unicef.org/publications/files/UNICEF_SOWC_2016.pdf

US Embassy in Trinidad & Tobago. (n.d.). *Getting married in Trinidad & Tobago*. Retrieved from https://tt.usembassy.gov/u-s-citizen-services/local-resources-of-u-s-citizens/getting-married-trinidad-tobago

Wilson, E. (2016, February 17). Mayor who blamed victim's "vulgar" behavior for her death resigns. *BBC Trending*. Retrieved from https://www.bbc.com/news/blogs-trending-35596675

World Bank. (2014). *Rural population (% of total)*. Retrieved from https://data.world-bank.org/indicator/SP.RUR.TOTL.ZS?view=chart

World Health Organization. (2013). *Global and regional estimates of violence against women: Prevalence and health effects of intimate partner violence and non-partner sexual violence*. Retrieved from http://apps.who.int/iris/bitstream/handle/10665/85239/9789241564625_eng.pdf;jsessionid=4C32F3280AEC8C9256F6F89392DC8E65?sequence=1

22

Peacebuilding and Gender Inclusivity

The Case of Nagorno-Karabakh

ADRINEH GREGORIAN ■

If women are better at relating and less inclined to use hardware, make sure that 50% of the peace-keepers are women.

—Galtung (1996, p. 240)

Figure 22.1 Women's March in against all forms of gender based violence, Yerevan November 2012.

CASE STUDY: NAGORNO-KARABAKH

Women play an essential role in peacemaking processes, despite the lack of their outward visibility or formal decision-making roles. One such example is that of Armenian and Azerbaijani women coming together in the early 1990s during the escalating conflict over the Soviet autonomous oblast, Nagorno-Karabakh. The oblast was a predominantly Armenian populated region nestled within the borders of the Soviet Socialist Republic of Azerbaijan. An important component of the Armenian–Azerbaijani conflict is the contrasting emotional, cultural, and historical claims that each ethnic group has to the region. However, the origins of this fault-line conflict can be traced back before the formation of the Soviet Union. Throughout history, the two ethnic groups—Christian Armenians and Muslim Azerbaijanis—coexisted under various rulers, such as the Ottoman and Russian empires. Fighting in the region has been fueled by ethnic-based political, nationalistic, and territorial issues. It is not a clash over religion but, rather, a clash over territorial entitlement (Huntington, 2011; Najafizadeh, 2013).

At the height of the Nagorno-Karabakh conflict, two women, Arzu Abdullayeva and Anahit Bayandur, heads of the International Helsinki Citizens' Assembly representing Azerbaijan and Armenia, respectively, became friends and collaborators in peacebuilding. They bonded over their agreement to help innocent people who were suffering from the effects of war and built a relationship based on mutual trust and honesty. Abdullayeva (2011) recalls, "[Bayandur] was not guided by stereotypes, she was open to new ideas and understanding" (para. 5).

Their first joint action was to visit each other's capital cities, Baku and Yerevan. In August 1992, Bayandur arrived in Baku at Abdullayeva's invitation and delivered a speech before an Azerbaijani audience. Bayandur began by calmly saying, "I came to say hello to you" (Abdullayeva, 2011, para. 6). In her speech, she explained that she had come to prove that Armenian and Azerbaijani people were not enemies—they couldn't be because they had too many things that connected them to each other. Some members of the audience were listening with respect and admiration, whereas others were waiting for an opportunity to retort. Bayandur's calm and straightforward greeting, however, prevented that from happening.

Working together, Abdullayeva and Bayandur organized the exchange of 500 prisoners of war (Abdullayeva, 2011). In 1992, they became joint recipients of the Olof Palme Peace Prize in recognition of their effort in facilitating prisoner of war exchanges and promoting dialogue (Walsh, 2014):

> To honor two women, Arzu Abdullayeva and Anahit Bayandour who, in one of the areas of a most bitter conflict, have worked for international understanding between Armenia and Azerbaijan. Their continuing work for reconciliation, hold out hope for peaceful change in the former Soviet Union. (Olof Palmes Minnesfond, 1992, para 1)

Upon Bayandur's passing in 2011, Abdullayeva wrote, "She was a wise woman and a loyal friend. I will always remember her" (para. 13).

Despite differences between the opposing groups, a women's led initiative, during the peak of violence, led to successful negotiations. To date, more than two decades after a ceasefire agreement was reached, this is the only example of successful peacebuilding throughout the conflict. This example also emphasizes the need to capitalize on the potential of Armenian and Azerbaijani women and the role they play in peacemaking in relation to Nagorno-Karabakh.

OVERVIEW

Research has shown that women in conflict carry an unequal burden of war, and their issues differ from those of men, such as widespread sexual violence used as warfare mechanisms. However, in the peacebuilding process, in which pivotal decisions are made regarding post-conflict recovery and governance, women are noticeably underrepresented, and in some cases they are completely shut out (Galtung, 1996; Plumper & Neumayer, 2006).

The lack of women in peacebuilding processes has led to the marginalization of the needs of women in conflict management and post-conflict reconstruction. Determined to address this issue, the United Nations Security Council adopted Resolution (UNSCR) 1325 on October 31, 2000, outlining the unique perils women face in conflict and the need for gender inclusivity in the peacebuilding process. UNSCR 1325 is a formal and legal document from the United Nations Security Council (2000) that mentions the unique impact of conflict on women:

> Expressing concern that civilians, particularly women and children, account for the vast majority of those adversely affected by armed conflict, including as

Figure 22.2 Environmentalist and Human Rights Activist Mariam Soukhoutyan, Yerevan May 2010.

refugees and internally displaced persons, and increasingly are targeted by combatants and armed elements, and recognizing the consequent impact this has on durable peace and reconciliation. (p. 1)

There is also special mention of the protection of women and girls from sexual and gender-based violence in armed conflict. UNSCR 1325 "calls on all parties to armed conflict to take special measures to protect women and girls from gender-based violence, particularly rape and other forms of sexual abuse, and all other forms of violence in situations of armed conflict" (p. 3). The resolution creates a legal obligation to include women in peace processes, and it also gives activists, academics, and policymakers a tool to address the distinct burdens women bear during conflicts:

Reaffirming the important role of women in the prevention and resolution of conflicts and in peace-building, and stressing the importance of their equal participation and full involvement in all efforts for the maintenance and promotion of peace and security, and the need to increase their role in decision-making with regard to conflict prevention and resolution. (p. 1)

Despite UNSCR 1325, minimal progress has been made since 2000 regarding the number of women in formal peace processes or women's access to peace talks. In addition, although follow-up Security Council resolutions have been drafted to uphold UNSCR 1325 and its reporting mechanisms, few provisions addressing women's needs have been included in subsequent peace agreements (Nduwimana, n.d.). The only visible signs of progress are the growing number of transnational feminist movements in the civil society sector promoting awareness campaigns about the differentiated impact of war on women and demonstrating the role women can play in conflict resolution. Here, there is "evidence that peace negotiations characterized by high civil society involvement are less likely to result in resumed warfare" (Diaz & Tordjman, 2012, p. 3).

The work of women's groups and organizations in conflict zones is underestimated and underresourced, yet these groups continue to be a voice of the marginalized. By examining the case of Armenia and Azerbaijan and the Nagorno-Karabakh conflict, this chapter seeks to demonstrate how women's role in peacebuilding is pivotal and should not be trivialized. Because they have differentiated needs in conflict; therefore, countries should include them in peace processes.

This chapter addresses the following questions: (1) How is the lack of gender inclusivity a global problem? (2) What are the gaps in UNSCR 1325? (3) What have the historical trends been? (4) How could gender inclusivity help in the Nagorno-Karabakh case? and (5) What should be done in the future?

As stakeholders, women's organizations have been active in civil society peace initiatives and have developed alternative political solutions to conflict. Like the example of Azerbaijani and Armenian peace activists Abdullayeva and Bayandur, women have succeeded in broaching dialogue by building trust, engaging in cross-border projects, and bringing parties across conflict lines together (Beham & Dietrich, 2013). However, countries are forgoing the opportunity to expedite peace and de-escalation of violence by not including women. Furthermore, to ensure gender inclusivity, there should be institutionalized quotas for female representation in political spaces.

Finally, because the implications of conflict affect women and men differently, gender perspectives should not be neglected in peacekeeping operations.

During the Security Council open debate on Women, Peace and Security in October 2016, it was determined that the major concerns for women have been participation and the implementation of the resolution (Peace Women, 2016). Although UNSCR 1325 was adopted unanimously by the Security Council, the global lack of gender inclusiveness in formal peace negotiations "reveals a troubling gap between the aspirations of countless global and regional commitments and the reality of peace processes" (Diaz & Tordjman, 2012, p. 1). UN Women's studies have shown that the number of women participating in peace negotiations as negotiators, mediators, and signatories remains dismal. Between 1992 and 2011, women comprised only 2% of chief mediators, 4% of witnesses and signatories, and 9% of negotiators. Women's structural exclusion from peace talks has significant consequences for issues that concern them. Women are largely only being involved as members of civil society targeting women's issues, such the protection against gender-based violence (Diaz & Tordjman, 2012).

According to the classical writings of Norwegian sociologist Johan Galtung (1996), women would bring a critical missing piece to de-escalation of violence in conflict. Galtung states,

> What upholds war? Many factors, three of them being patriarchy (rule by the male gender of the human species), the state system with its monopoly on violence, and the super-state or superpower system with the ultimate monopoly of the hegemons. Males more than females tend toward violence. (p. 12)

The overwhelming majority of global state leadership consists of men; therefore, they dictate how state systems and hegemonies are run. It is important to include women because their role will assist in bringing peace. Galtung (1996) notes,

> One approach would be to increase the space for actors to proceed nonviolently in conflict by building more nonviolent (or low violence) roles into peacekeeping . . . if women are better at relating and less inclined to use hardware, make sure that 50% of the peace-keepers are women. (p. 240)

In line with Galtung's suggestion, on a very low level, not official, there are women-led cross-border institutions using alternative spaces to raise issues.

Even when shut out of traditional patriarchal structures, such as government and military bodies, women remain active in civil society organizations. They manage, lead, and make decisions in social and cultural arenas but are mostly barred from political spaces. The situation is consistent in the cases of Armenia and Azerbaijan, in which women's inclusion in parliament, defense, security, and law enforcement is challenging. "On civil society level, women are being engaged," says peace activist Lara Aharonian, co-founder of the Women's Resource Center in Armenia, "But we need to help them transform from the grassroots level to political spaces" (L. Aharonian, personal communication, June 12, 2018). In order to transfer leadership from civil society spaces to political spaces, there must be pressure on governments to make room for women by insisting on quotas and balances.

Table 22.1 PARLIAMENTARY ELECTIONS IN ARMENIA: AN OVERVIEW

Year	Total No. of Seats	No. of Women MPs	% of Women MPs
1995	190	12	6
1999	131	4	3
2003	131	7	5
2007	131	12	9
2011	131	12	9
2014	131	14	11

MPs, members of parliament.
Source: Shahnazaryan (2015, p. 12).

As shown in Table 22.1 and 22.2, the percentage of women members of parliament in Armenia and Azerbaijan is marginal. There are many obstacles standing in the way of women in Armenia to build a political career, including lack of economic independence, lack of social capital in political networks, and traditional attitudes that promote the idea that a women's place is in the home (Shahnazaryan, 2015, p. 12). In Azerbaijan, woman's lack of participation can be attributed to "general disillusionment with the political system on the part of many women, including a large part of the educated and urban classes" (Walsh, 2015, p. 9). Quotas are important to overcome unequal opportunity and have been used to improve women's representation in the political sphere. The UN Beijing Action Plan of 1995 established a goal of 30% for women's participation in decision-making positions (United Nations, 1995), which is "understood as a critical mass to achieve transformations in decision making and procedures employing other approaches" (Buchanan et al., 2012, p. 21). Unfortunately, neither Armenia nor Azerbaijan has fulfilled this goal.

In addition to the lack of representation, women suffer from the consequences of war in different ways than men. Women are also more vulnerable to poverty and unemployment, and as health services decline, maternal mortality rises (United Nations, 1995). These are examples of how women's experiences need to be individualized and addressed; instead, they are commonly sidelined and ignored (United Nations Women, 2015).

In reference to the Nagorno-Karabakh conflict between Armenia and Azerbaijan, there are no data on rape and sexual violence during the war. No research has been

Table 22.2 PARLIAMENTARY ELECTIONS IN AZERBAIJAN: AN OVERVIEW

Year	Total No. of Seats	No. of Women MPs	% of Women MPs
1995	124	15	12.1
2000	124	13	10.48
2005	125	15	12
2010	125	20	16

MPs, members of parliament.
Source: Walsh (2015, p. 7).

conducted, and 24 years have already passed since the ceasefire. "Patriarchal closed societies are very dangerous for women," says Knarik Mkrtchyan, Coordinator of Peace Building Projects at the Women's Resource Center in Armenia, "Few women are willing to bring up the topic again because it's a huge psychological trauma on one hand, on the other hand there are no crisis centers that could help victims" (personal communication, June 20, 2018). Because of gender stereotypes, women rarely receive support from their family members and their neighborhoods, and they fear being labeled "the one who was raped during the war." Not only the rape but also the consequences of coming out as a raped woman are traumatic. The aforementioned factors pose a major challenge, and women prefer to stay silent about this issue. According to Mkrtchyan, "We sporadically hear about different cases of rape now, but the organizations do not reveal this unless the woman wants it. Confidentiality and ethical norms are very high priority in these cases" (personal communication, June 20, 2018).

Since 2000, the Security Council has passed further resolutions to address the sexual violence used as warfare. For example, Resolution 188816 was adopted unanimously in 2009 and urged the states to abstain from use of sexual violence. Resolution 182015 was adopted unanimously in 2008 in regard to sexual violence impeding international peace and security. It aims to protect women and girls from any kind of sexual violence during armed conflicts and reaffirms the provisions from UNSCR 1325. However, sexual violence is often absent from peace accords (Diaz, 2012). To impede this oversight, it is imperative that women be involved in decision-making processes to order to advocate for their issues in the peacebuilding measures.

HISTORICAL TRENDS

Although the formal inclusion of women's participation in peacebuilding has been limited, women have continued to find ways of expressing their concerns by participating in informal peace processes. Women's absence in formal peace talks is not a result of lack of experience in conflict resolution or negotiations. Instead, there has been a lack of willingness by governmental institutions to include them. Despite this, there are examples of successful peacebuilding models led by women that incorporate less militant channels, such as dialogue and unity. The cases mentioned in this section demonstrate nonviolent approaches that rely on empathy and take into account all segments of the population.

The Northern Ireland Women's Coalition was founded in 1996 by Catholic academic Monica McWilliams and Protestant social worker Pearl Sagar. The Women's Coalition was formed in reaction to the stagnant state of local politics unable to solve the decades-long conflict in Northern Ireland between the unionist—predominantly Protestant—majority and the nationalist and republican—mostly Catholic— minority. The unionists wanted to remain part of the United Kingdom, whereas the nationalists and republicans wanted to become part of the Republic of Ireland. The Women's Coalition's approach was feminist and nonsectarian, consisting of an inclusive base, bridging together women and men from all factions. The coalition soon became an influential and liberalizing force in Northern Irish politics. Talks within this coalition led to the Good Friday Agreement of 1998, bringing peace to the 30-year conflict. Two of its members, Monica McWilliams and Jane Morrice, went on to be elected to the new Northern Ireland Assembly in June 1998 (Fearon, 1999).

In 2003, Women of Liberia Mass Action for Peace began as a movement against violence and the government in an effort to end the Second Liberian Civil War. It started in the capital city, Monrovia, by mobilizing Muslim and Christian women from various classes, dressed symbolically in white, to join in nonviolent protests, including a sex strike—abstaining from as well as denying their partner sex. In this bold move, the women of Liberia challenged traditional gender norms and mechanisms of exclusion, and they succeeded in gaining access to formal political institutions. "In a country as divided as Liberia, where ethnicity and socioeconomic gaps have combined to cause the near destruction of the country, women showed that reconciliation and national unity was a feasible path for the future" (Selimovic, Brandt, Jacobson, & till Kvinna, 2012, p. 82). Their actions resulted in a peace agreement ending the 14-year civil war and also in the election of the country's first female president, Ellen Johnson Sirleaf, in January 2006 (Selimovic et al., 2012).

As mentioned previously, there have been successful outcomes concerning women's engagement in the Nagorno-Karabakh peace process. The work of Abdullayeva and Bayandur in organizing a prisoners of war exchange is the most noticeable example of women in a peacemaking role. Nevertheless, attempts continue to be made via informal meetings between civil society groups involved in local and regional peace initiatives. Their experience at the grassroots level gives them insight that exceeds that of conflict resolution specialists.

The cases of Northern Ireland, Liberia, and Nagorno-Karabakh illustrate how women participating in peacebuilding are able to transform informal power into effective outcomes. By uniting, they used their strengths to find common ground and successfully contribute to peacemaking. In addition to gaining political leadership, the actions of these women had a real impact on the negotiations taking place within traditionally male spaces of power (Selimovic et al., 2012).

RECENT DEVELOPMENTS OF NOTE

In the late 1980s, as the Soviet Union was beginning to collapse, autonomous regions throughout the former Socialist Republics were establishing their right to self-determination. As such, on February 20, 1988, the governing body of the Nagorno-Karabakh Autonomous Oblast voted to secede from the Soviet Socialist Republic of Azerbaijan and join the Soviet Socialist Republic of Armenia. This decision was not accepted by the government of Azerbaijan, and by the early 1990s, conflict between the two countries escalated into a full-scale war. On January 6, 1992, the Nagorno-Karabakh parliament formally declared independence from the new Democratic Republic of Azerbaijan, establishing itself as the Nagorno-Karabakh Republic. Later that year, Nagorno-Karabakh Armenians seized control of the geographically strategic city of Shushi and the neighboring district of Lachin, thereby creating an open road between Nagorno-Karabakh and the new Republic of Armenia (Broers, 2005; de Waal, 2003; Fischer, 2016; Klever, 2013; Saparov, 2012).

By 1994, a ceasefire agreement was reached, although fighting still persists along the border regions, with the most recent uprising being the April 2016 Four Day War. During the past two decades, the Organization for Security and Co-operation in Europe (OSCE) and the Minsk Group, with Russia, France, and the United States

Figure 22.3 Women in Black Armenia demonstration, Yerevan December 2015.

as co-chairs, have attempted to negotiate a permanent peace deal, but the dispute remains a "frozen conflict" or "no war, no peace" (OSCE, 2016).

Furthermore, no women have been represented in any of these formal or official peace-keeping initiatives and negotiations, despite the fact that both Armenia and Azerbaijan have accepted UNSCR 1325. To date, Armenian women's groups have compiled two reports on the implementation, or lack thereof, of UNSCR 1325, and Azerbaijan has not offered any (Peace Women, n.d.).

The absence of women from formal peace processes has not kept them from being active participants with vested interests. Although women are missing from governmental leadership positions, they have significant roles as leaders of nongovernmental organizations. Since the fall of the Soviet Union, women's organizations have been engaging in informal peacebuilding initiatives in an effort to temper conflict in the Caucasus region, including Armenia, Azerbaijan, and neighboring Georgia. These initiatives are a result of collaborations between local activists and international institutions aimed at promoting gender inclusivity in peacemaking. Although these efforts exist on the civil society level, they demonstrate that women play an integral role in peacemaking, peacebuilding, peacekeeping, and conflict resolution in the region.

For example, in 1994, the Trans-Caucasus Women's Dialogue brought together women from Armenia, Azerbaijan, and Georgia to participate in peace- and democracy-building training (National Peace Foundation, n.d.). In 2001, the Women for Conflict Prevention and Peace Building in the Southern Caucasus project was launched by the United Nations Development Fund for Women "to build the capacity of institutions and individuals to promote role and participation of women in the conflict prevention, conflict resolution and peace building processes in countries and in the Southern Caucasus" (Relief Web, 2001, para. 3). The 2013 Strengthening Women's Capacity for Peace-building in the South Caucasus Region project created a regional base of

Table 22.3 Hypothesis Testing, Armenia

	Force	Peace	Total
Male			
Count	142	533	675
%	21.0	79.0	100.0
Female			
Count	137	595	732
%	18.7	81.3	100.0

Source: Sarkisyan (2014, p. 24).

women activists from conflict-affected communities to work together. The objective was to "support partner NGOs from across the South Caucasus to create an enabling environment where marginalized women from conflict-affected communities can protect their rights and take active part in decision-making" (Care, 2013, p. 8).

Most recently, as a response to the Four Day War, the Armenian–Azerbaijan Civil Peace Platform was founded to bridge together citizens of Armenia and Azerbaijan and the civic institutions they represent to work alongside the OSCE Minsk Group. However, out of 19 members of the steering committee, only 5 are women; and out of the 29 members of the expert committee, only 7 are women (Armenia–Azerbaijan Civil Peace Platform, 2017).

A study by the US Agency for International Development (USAID) and the Yerevan State University Center for Gender and Leadership Studies examined gender-based differences toward the perceptions of the Nagorno-Karabakh conflict in both Armenia and Azerbaijan by analyzing the Caucasus Barometer 2011 data. The research provided insight on the average description of women and men in Armenia and Azerbaijan and determined their behavior toward the resolution of the Nagorno-Karabakh conflict (Sarkisyan, 2014). As indicated in Tables 22.3 and 22.4, data analysis shows that men in Armenia and Azerbaijan are more prone to solve the Nagorno-Karabakh conflict by the use of force, whereas women are more prone to solve the conflict peacefully. With this knowledge in mind, gender inclusivity in formal peace negotiations would better serve the process.

Table 22.4 Hypothesis Testing, Azerbaijan

	Force	Peace	Total
Male			
Count	275	287	562
%	48.9	51.1	100.0
Female			
Count	184	282	466
%	39.5	60.5	100.0

Source: Sarkisyan (2014, p. 24).

CURRENT CONDITIONS

Complex sets of interconnected problems are stalling gender inclusivity in the Nagorno-Karabakh peace process—for example, limited funding for civil society groups, preconceived gender norms of traditional patriarchal societies, lack of visibility in formal decision-making roles, and outside threats from nationalistic groups (Jocbalis, 2016). In light of these obstacles, women's groups have incorporated a transnational feminist approach by creating peace networks. "By definition, transnational feminist peace networks are means by which women extend the hand of solidarity across borders and across conflict lines to achieve just outcomes or compromises among leaders and their constituencies without resorting to violence" (Etchart, 2015, p. 715). Under the auspices of international organizations, the Armenian and Azerbaijani women's peace networks are utilizing new media platforms that transcend borders and formal political spaces in order to highlight women's voices.

The most recent comprehensive civil society peace initiative is the European Partnership for the Peaceful Settlement of the Conflict over Nagorno-Karabakh (EPNK), created and financed by the European Union in 2009. It is a consortium of five organizations: Kvinna till Kvinna (Woman to Woman) Foundation (Sweden), Conciliation Resources (United Kingdom), International Alert (United Kingdom), Conflict Management Initiative (Finland), and LINKS (United Kingdom). All have partners in Armenia, Azerbaijan, and Nagorno-Karabakh. Kvinna till Kvinna is the only organization that works on women's issues and has implemented the largest peacebuilding project conducted on a regional level. EPNK is developing a joint advocacy strategy that urges political actors involved in peace negotiations to pay special attention to key issues, such as the following (EPNK, n.d.):

Figure 22.4 Women in Black Armenia demonstration on Norther Avenue, Yerevan March 2015.

1. Increasing women's political participation in decision making through special temporary measures such as quotas;
2. Increasing women's participation in peace talks (such as their representation in the OSCE Minsk Group talks) and making gender sensitive training available to all participants involved in talks on this region;
3. Ensuring support for women who are victims of violence;
4. Protecting the human rights of IDPs [internally displaced persons] and refugees;
5. Protecting the safety of women and children living in the border areas of the conflict zones. (para. 7)

The goal of the EPNK project is to create a group of women that will be represented in the OSCE Minsk Group and that will have access to and impact on decision-making processes. The chances of this project coming to fruition, however, are lessening because of decreased funding in response to rising militarism and tension among both sides. "Funds for their meetings are becoming smaller and smaller, meaning we have less chances to meet with our Azerbaijani partners, which makes the collaboration process harder," Mkrtchyan notes (personal communication, June 20, 2018). At first, the group met four times a year in Tbilisi or Istanbul, but since 2016, it has met only twice a year. Kvinna till Kvinna used to fund study visits to Liberia, Northern Ireland, Israel, Palestine, and the Aland Islands, but it has stopped doing so due to lack of funding.

The lack of women's representation in decision-making bodies at the regional level and in negotiations, both internationally and nationally, means the consequences of war on women are not taken into consideration. In relation to this disparity, Mkrtchyan (personal communication, June 20, 2018) states, "Women's issues in conflict are not prioritized, meaning they are not perceived by the general public, most importantly by this patriarchal militarism, as equal participants of war." Unfortunately, women share in the suffering of the conflict but are not participants in any field of politics or decision-making processes (Mandl, 2011).

According to Mkrtchyan (personal communication, June 20, 2018), a gender-inclusive approach would first entail equal participation in decision-making: "It's first about quantitative equality and not just qualitative." Second, it requires gender sensitivity of policies focused on reconciliation, rehabilitation, and considering the human dimensions of the conflict. "Women are not valued in a patriarchal system," she says, "They are perceived as 'wives of the war,' whereby they support soldiers but are not equal participants." Based on discussions that Mkrtchyan has had with her Azerbaijani colleagues, they face the same issues.

Women in this region "are undervalued, not just by the general public, but also themselves," Mkrtchyan (personal communication, June 20, 2018) says, "It's the same situation in Azerbaijan. Our colleagues keep saying the same thing, 'Women are raised as servants of their husband, children, and families.' This gender socialization is a cultural norm." Because women are not "equal participants" in conflict, they lack visibility and their concerns are bypassed. Many years ago when Mkrtchyan was conducting training in Nagorno-Karabakh, the topic of pads and diapers, or lack thereof, became a major issue. During the conflict, women did not have access to soaps or clothes, much less sanitary napkins. "When they would receive pads in international humanitarian aid, they were shamed to take them," Mkrtchyan recounts.

After the Four Day War in 2016, members of the Women's Resource Center in Yerevan, including Mkrtchyan, went to Nagorno-Karabakh to assess the needs of women in light of the recent conflict. This time, the women felt less shame and requested sanitary napkins from the onset. Their basic needs were not met because female representatives were not there when humanitarian aid was organized. Mkrtchyan (personal communication, June 20, 2018) adds that this oversight is because women's experiences are not considered in conflict-related issues.

The dire situation for peace activists in Azerbaijan adds an additional layer of complexity to cross-border projects. Since independence, Azerbaijani civil society has faced harsh prosecution and arrests of political activists and their relatives (Meydan TV, 2015). In addition, social media and Skype communication is regularly under surveillance. "We have a code of ethics while working with our partners," says Mkrtchyan (personal communication, June 20, 2018), "You don't want to jeopardize your partners because there are mass prosecutions, detentions, and attacks on peace activists in Azerbaijan."

One more obstacle is that members of the group do not have many opportunities to meet because of closed boarders. Because they do not have direct access to each other's country, the only relatively reliable source of communication and perspective is mass media. Generally, mass media uses different tools to spread hate speech and manipulate public opinion. Mkrtchyan (personal communication, June 20, 2018) says, "They mostly invest in manipulation, sabotage, and hate speech, rather than bringing people together." There are some media organizations that produce independent content, but not many of them are open to the public. These organizations represent an example of groups seeking out-of-the-box approaches to circumvent nationalistic propaganda and build more transparent channels of information sharing (Atoyan & Ghahriyan, 2018).

LOOKING TO THE FUTURE

Peace movements must extend their activities across borders. Thus, they are required to be transnational in their approach, yet there is room to explore alternative methods of crossing the divide between conflicting groups. For example, according to Galtung (1996),

> Peace-making activities can be identified with the search for creative, and at the same time acceptable and sustainable, outcomes of the conflict. There is one mistake which is no longer pardonable: the single-shot "table at the top," the high table, for the "leaders." Rather, let one thousand conferences blossom, use modern communication technology to generate a visible flow of peace ideas from everywhere in society. (p. 240)

Women's groups are utilizing these modern communication technologies, primarily the internet, to connect with each other beyond borders. With regard to mass media, two categories must be considered: traditional and alternative platforms. Traditional media are sources known to propagate hate via state news outlets and social media. In Azerbaijan, freedom of expression is limited, and people are under constant surveillance. The people of Armenia experience a more free level of expression. Alternative media platforms, therefore, are positive tools that provide neutral information and create ground for the public to generate more nonjudgmental viewpoints toward the conflict and different peacebuilding efforts.

Alternative media platforms also create channels for groups to connect beyond geographical borders. Because they involve people sharing personal stories, viewers can have an overwhelming emotional response when learning about friendships that cross regional or ethnic boundaries. Filmmaking initiatives, such as Dialogue Through Film, Chai Khana, and Adami Media Prize, create discourse and combat propagandized news outlets through nonfiction storytelling. By building empathy, alternative media can play an essential role in shaping public attitudes.

Dialogue Through Film was a project from 2006 to 2014 funded by the United Kingdom and the European Union. It brought together young Armenians and Azerbaijanis from Karabakh to produce and screen documentary films (Conciliation Resources, 2012, p. 6). The concept of Dialogue Through Film was to use filmmaking to create windows for young Azerbaijanis and Karabakh Armenians to learn about media, speak directly to each other, and speak more widely to each other's society (p. 8). The mission was to showcase reflections and present-day realities of the Karabakh war through nonfiction storytelling. Public screenings were held in Armenia and Azerbaijan to promote discussion on the conflict, peace process, and resolution. In total, more than 90 films were screened for more than 3,000 people (p. 8).

Bringing together Armenians and Azerbaijanis has its challenges because participants are usually reluctant to open up and behave naturally with each other. The process of bridging groups from two sides of a conflict is very fragile: "Every step had the potential for misunderstanding" (Conciliation Resources, 2012, p. 14). Azerbaijani filmmaker Nailya Babayeva, director of the film *8th Kilometre*, recalls, "During the course of the project I learned to listen and to give away. I'm not afraid to say that I made a good friend on the Armenian side" (p. 14). Babayeva goes on to highlight the human element and collective efforts that go beyond barriers separating the two groups: "It's not right for peace building projects to divide people into Armenians and Azerbaijanis. In projects like these it's not your nationality that is the main thing, it's your common cause and your shared efforts," she says, "Whether you succeed or fail, you are in it together. It's not an individual endeavor. Everyone works together and for the whole group" (p. 14). To echo this sentiment, Armenian filmmaker Armine Martirosyan added, "Working with Azerbaijanis made me realize once again what a deeply ingrained sense of hurt we all have inside us" (p. 16).

Another organization that provides a platform for unheard voices is the women-led Chai Khana, based in Tbilisi, Georgia. Its website serves as a platform that transcends the closed borders in the region. Chai Khana translates into "tea house," but it primarily refers to a "meeting place" where people can come together to share stories and experiences. The aim of the organization is to "give voice to the under-represented across the region, amplifying their voices through dynamic human-focused storytelling" (Chai Khana, n.d., para. 1). This multimedia platform allows women, rural communities, minority groups, and conflict-affected communities in the Caucasus to share accounts through film, writing, and photography.

Finally, the Adami Media Prize for Cultural Diversity in Eastern Europe is an initiative created in 2015 to celebrate diversity and highlight voices outside of traditional institutionalized spaces. The Adami Media Prize organizers believe that by "positively showcasing diversity, the media can contribute to peaceful coexistence between different groups in society" (Adami, n.d., para. 2). It encourages filmmakers, journalists, and audiovisual media professionals in the European Union Eastern Partnership countries—Armenia, Azerbaijan, Belarus, Georgia, Moldova, and Ukraine—to promote issues ranging from migration to tolerance, and cultural diversity.

These communication outlets are especially important for the new generation of youth growing up under a "no peace, no war" status. In contrast to their parents, young Armenians and Azerbaijanis have not lived among each other and only learn about one another through the current political context, as perceived enemies. Also, in contrast to nationalistic propaganda that further polarizes the two groups, dialogue and storytelling help break these stereotypes and temper fearmongering.

Examples highlighted in this section stress the fact that gender inclusivity would help in the Nagorno-Karabakh case. When official top-down approaches fail women, civil society organizations must step in to fill the gaps. When formal negotiation tactics seem to be fruitless, out-of-the-box tools must be created to develop connections and safe spaces to share, listen, and build empathy. These steps should not be overlooked; instead, they underscore that women's inclusion in peace processes is imperative.

Advocacy

The major hurdle standing in the way of women's peace activities through civil society organizations is the lack of funding and resources. To achieve successful results, women's organizations must continue to expand their networks and support each other. Therefore, the onus is on the donor community to secure funding for capacity building and logistical support. In addition, ongoing studies should be performed to analyze peacebuilding from a gender perspective, and pressure should be placed on governments to honor UNSCR 1325 as well as uphold gender quotas in government.

CONCLUSION

As demonstrated in this chapter, women's groups and organizations have been successful at building transnational communities. The efforts of these organizations are also aiding marginalized groups in conflict zones. Therefore, their role in peacebuilding is imperative and should not be sidelined. Looking forward, there is further need to eliminate barriers to women's participation in peace processes. Civil society organizations should pressure countries to honor UNSCR 1325. More women should be placed in formal leadership roles by establishing and honoring quotas. Finally, countries should utilize the skills and knowledge of gender advisors and experts in conflict, peacekeeping missions, peace negotiations, and humanitarian crises. These are key components to overcome gender disparity and power imbalances in peacemaking processes.

DISCUSSION QUESTIONS

1. How can women's civil society organizations make a meaningful contribution toward gender equality in light of their limited resources?
2. How can the civil society sector reinforce women peace-builders and promote their agency?
3. Does the transnational feminist approach applied in the Nagorno-Karabakh case further marginalize ethnic Armenian and Azerbaijani women who do not have access to technology resources?

REFERENCES

Abdullayeva, A. (2011, September 1). *Farewell letter from Arzu Abdullayeva in memory of Anahit Bayandur*. Retrieved from http://www.1in.am/6272.html

Adami. (n.d.). *About*. Retrieved from http://archive.adamimediaprize.eu/about

Armenia–Azerbaijan Civil Peace Platform. (2017, November 3). *Members of "expert group" of Armenia–Azerbaijan Civil Peace Platform*. Retrieved from http://arm-azpeace.com/news.php?id=1880&lang=en

Atoyan, A., & Ghahriyan, S. (2018). War and peace in Karabakh: An analysis of women's perceptions. In S. Relitz (Ed.), *Obstacles and opportunities for dialogue and cooperation in protracted conflicts: Corridors proceedings* (Vol. 1, pp. 86–99). Regensburg, Germany: Leibniz Institute for East and Southeast European Studies.

Beham, M., & Dietrich, L. (2013, October). *Enhancing gender-responsive mediation: A guidance note*. Vienna, Austria: Organization for Security and Co-operation in Europe.

Broers, L. (Ed.). (2005). *The limits of leadership: Elites and societies in the Nagorno Karabakh peace process* (Accord, Issue 17). London, UK: Conciliation Resources.

Buchanan, C., Cooper, A., Griggers, C., Low, L., Manchandra, R., Peters, R., & Potter Prentice, A. (2012). *From clause to effect: Including women's rights and gender in peace agreements*. Geneva, Switzerland: Centre for Humanitarian Dialogue. Retrieved from https://www.hdcentre.org/wp-content/uploads/2016/07/24ClausereportwebFINAL-December-2012.pdf

Care. (2013, May). *Strengthening women's capacity for peace building in the south Caucasus region*. Retrieved from http://conflict.care2share.wikispaces.net/file/view/2013+CARE+Caucasus+-+Strengthening+capacity+for+peace+building_opt.pdf

Central Intelligence Agency. (2018a). *The world factbook: Armenia*. Retrieved from https://www.cia.gov/library/publications/resources/the-world-factbook/geos/am.html

Chai Khana. (n.d.). *About*. Retrieved from https://chai-khana.org/en/about

Conciliation Resources. (2012). *A handbook: Dialogue through film* [Pamphlet]. Retrieved from http://www.c-r.org/resources/dialogue-through-film-handbook

de Waal, T. (2003). *Black garden: Armenia and Azerbaijan through peace and war*. New York, NY: New York University Press.

Diaz, P. C., & Tordjman, S. (2012, October). *Women's participation in peace negotiations: Connections between presence and influence*. Retrieved from http://www.unwomen.org/~/media/headquarters/attachments/sections/library/publications/2012/10/wpssourcebook-03a-womenpeacenegotiations-en.pdf

Etchart, L. (2015). Demilitarizing the global women's peace movements and transnational networks. In R. Baksh & W. Harcourt (Eds.), *The Oxford handbook of transnational feminist movements* (pp. 702–722). New York, NY: Oxford University Press.

European Partnership for Peaceful Settlement of the Conflict over Nagorno-Karabakh. (n.d.). *Empowering Armenian and Azerbaijani women to take part in society and in peace negotiations.* Retrieved from http://www.epnk.org/project-highlights/empowering-armenian-and-azeri-women-take-part-society-and-peace-negotiations

Fearon, K. (1999). *Women's work: The story of the Northern Ireland Women's Coalition.* Belfast, Northern Ireland: Blackstaff Press. Retrieved from http://cain.ulst.ac.uk/issues/women/fearon99.htm

Fischer, S. (Ed.). (2016). *Not frozen! The unresolved conflicts over Transnistria, Abkhazia, South Ossetia and Nagorno-Karabakh in light of the crisis over Ukraine* (SWP Research Paper 9/2016). Berlin, Germany: Stiftung Wissenschaft un Politik, Deutsches Institut fur Internationale Politik un Sicherheit. Retrieved from http://nbn-resolving.de/urn:nbn:de:0168-ssoar-48891-8

Galtung, J. (1996). *Peace by peaceful means: Peace and conflict, development and civilization.* Oslo, Norway: International Peace Research Institute.

Huntington, S. P. (2011). *The clash of civilizations and the remaking of the world order.* New York, NY: Simon & Schuster.

Jocbalis, M. (2016, Spring). *Transformative gender narratives in South Caucasus: Conversations with NGO women in the Armenian–Azerbaijani conflict.* Master's thesis, Malmo University, Malmo, Sweden. Retrieved from: https://muep.mau.se/bitstream/handle/2043/21318/Jocbalis-M-DP15-v2.pdf?sequence=2

Klever, E. (2013, September 24). *The Nagorno-Karabakh conflict between Armenia and Azerbaijan: An overview of the current situation.* Brussels, Belgium. European Movement International.

Mandl, S. (2011, September). *Women in Armenia: Peace, security and democracy from a woman's rights perspective* (Desk research). Vienna, Austria: Ludwig Boltzmann Institute of Human Rights.

Meydan TV. (2015, August 5). *Arzu Abdullayeva: The most painful times of the past 20 years.* Retrieved from https://www.meydan.tv/en/site/society/7345/Arzu-Abdullayeva-"The-most-painful-times-of-the-past-20-years".htm

Najafizadeh, M. (2013). Ethnic conflict and forced displacement: Narratives of Azerbaijani IDP and refugee women from the Nagorno-Karabakh War. *Journal of International Women's Studies, 14*(1), 161–183. Retrieved from http://vc.bridgew.edu/jiws/vol14/iss1/10

National Peace Foundation. (n.d.). *Transcaucasus women's dialogue.* Retrieved from https://www.mott.org/grants/national-peace-foundation-transcaucasus-womens-dialogue-199800109

Nduwimana, F. (n.d). *United Nations Security Council Resolution 1325 (2000) on women, peace and security: Understanding the implications, fulfilling the obligations.* Retrieved from http://www.un.org/womenwatch/osagi/cdrom/documents/Background_Paper_Africa.pdf

Olof Palmes Minnesfond. (1992). *1992–Arzu Abdullayeva and Anahit Bayandour.* Retrieved from http://www.palmefonden.se/1992-arzu-abdullayeva-och-anahit-bayandour-2

Organization for Security and Economic Cooperation. (2016, December 8). *Joint statement by the heads of delegation of the OSCE Minsk Group co-chair countries.* Retrieved from https://www.osce.org/mg/287531

Peace Women. (n.d.). *Country/region profile of: Azerbaijan.* Retrieved from http://www.peacewomen.org/profile/country-region-profile-azerbaijan

Peace Women. (2016, October 25). *Security Council open debate on women peace and security.* Retrieved from http://www.peacewomen.org/security-council/security-council-open-debate-women-peace-and-security-october-2016

Plumper, T., & Neumayer, E. (2006, Summer). The unequal burden of war: The effect of armed conflict on the gender gap in life expectancy. *International Organization, 60,* 723–754.

Relief Web. (2001, October 12). *UNIFEM: Women for Conflict Prevention and Peace Building in the Southern Caucasus.* Retrieved from https://reliefweb.int/report/georgia/unifem-women-conflict-prevention-and-peace-building-southern-caucasus

Saparov, A. (2012). Why autonomy? The making of Nagorno-Karabakh autonomous region 1918–1925. *Europe-Asia Studies,* 64(2), 281–323. Retrieved from http://dx.doi.org/10.1080/09668136.2011.642583

Sarkisyan, A. (2014). *Security issues from gender perspectives: Nagorno-Karabakh through the eyes of Armenian and Azerbaijani women.* Yerevan, Armenia: Yerevan State University Center for Gender and Leadership Studies.

Selimovic, J. M., Brandt, Å. N., Jacobson, A. S., & till Kvinna, K. (2012). *Equal Power–Lasting Peace. Obstacles for women's participation in peace processes.* Stockholm, Sweden: Kvinna till Kvinna Foundation.

Shahnazaryan, G. (2015, March 30). Women's political participation in Armenia: Institutional and cultural factors. *Caucasus Analytical Digest, 71,* 9–13. Retrieved from http://www.css.ethz.ch/content/dam/ethz/special-interest/gess/cis/center-for-securities-studies/pdfs/CAD-71.pdf

United Nations. (1995). *Beijing declaration and platform for action.* Retrieved from http://www.un.org/womenwatch/daw/beijing/pdf/BDPfA%20E.pdf

United Nations Security Council. (2000, October 31). *Resolution 1325.* Retrieved from https://documents-dds-ny.un.org/doc/UNDOC/GEN/N00/720/18/PDF/N0072018.pdf?OpenElement

United Nations Women. (2015). *Infographic: Women and armed conflict.* Retrieved from http://www.unwomen.org/en/digital-library/multimedia/2015/10/infographic-women-armed-conflict

Walsh, S. (2014, October 9). *Nagorno-Karabakh: A gender inclusive approach to peace.* Retrieved from https://www.opendemocracy.net/od-russia/sinead-walsh/nagornokarabakh-gender-inclusive-approach-to-peace

Walsh, S. (2015, March 30). Representation, reform and resistance: Broadening our understanding of women in politics in Azerbaijan. *Caucasus Analytical Digest, 71,* 6–8. Retrieved from http://www.css.ethz.ch/content/dam/ethz/special-interest/gess/cis/center-for-securities-studies/pdfs/CAD-71.pdf

23

The US Military–Prostitution Complex, Patriarchy, and Masculinity

A Transnational Feminist Perspective of the Sexual Global Exploitation of Women

EUGENIA L. WEISS AND ANNALISA ENRILE ▪

AUTHORS' NOTE

From a critical and self-reflective lens, both authors are academic women from the West. Eugenia, a middle-class half Jewish/Latina immigrant from Chile to the United States, with a son serving in the US Army, brings a particular lived experience and bias to what is included in this chapter and how concepts are expressed. Similarly, Annalisa, also middle class, was raised in a military family (her father was in the Navy) in the military city of San Diego, California. Furthermore, Annalisa's background as a Pilipino-American woman, human rights activist has allowed her to interview those in the Philippines most affected by the US military bases that dominated the country in the past. We mention this as a reflexive position and in full transparency to the reader, that we consider ourselves coming from privileged positions and this may color our perceptions and views of the content that we have chosen to present in this chapter and the manner in which these are represented. Thus, we aspire to proceed with humility and with the aim of objectivity, yet we are influenced by our own experiences and those of the women whom we know. The personal is political, and although we would like to be purely objective, we acknowledge that especially in this type of endeavor, few things are.

This chapter also contains a stance on language because we have selected to not use the terms "sex worker" and "sex work" to denote prostitution. Although there is the assertion that sex work is a form of empowerment and indicates choice, as material and

Third World feminists, we believe any objectification, commodification, and commercialization of women's bodies represents an unequal power balance that minimizes or completely erases any notions of choice (Kotiswaran, 2011). Furthermore, the literature on the military–prostitution complex is based on the concept of women's exploitation and the use of a woman's body for power (Raymond, 2013). Overs (2009) notes that there are other aspects of "work," such as self-esteem, mastery, and stigma, that the "sex work" stance does not address. As such, the terms "prostitute/prostitution" and "commercial sexual exploitation" are used intentionally in this chapter.

CASE STUDY: CHONG SUN FRANCE

On December 4, 1987, Chong Sun France was convicted of second degree murder and felonious child abuse of her son, Moses Krystowski, and sentenced to twenty years imprisonment. The difficult circumstances of Chong's life, however, actually began back in South Korea. Chong Sun France grew up in rural poverty in Sosan. Her father was rarely employed and her family had to live in a tent. While a teenager, she began working as a maid to help support the family but stopped when she was molested by her employer. When Chong Sun found that a friend of hers had met and married a well off foreign soldier while working in the military camptowns, she decided to follow her example. Chong Sun went to a camptown called Ahnjongri and worked [as a prostitute] in the clubs. She eventually met and married Danny France, an American soldier, and came to the U.S. in 1980. Although she had hoped to bring her family over, her husband became abusive and the marriage ended in divorce. Like many other Korean G.I. brides, the lack of language skills and legal help led to her losing custody of her child. Chong Sun later met another American, whom she married, and they had two children. Again, both physical and emotional abuse occurred but this time, determined not to lose her children, Chong Sun fled the state with her 2 year old son Moses and 6 month old daughter, Esther. Chong Sun moved to Jacksonville, North Carolina, the site of the large marine base Camp Lejeune, and a whole neighborhood of bars that served the soldiers. A friend had told her that she could find work there, and she did, as a bartender near the motel where she was staying. During the hours she had to work, Chong put her two children to sleep in bed, turned on the television, and locked the door. Chong did not have any friends or family in Jacksonville, nor the money to hire a babysitter while she went to work. On May 28, 1987, Chong returned home from work to find her son, Moses dead, the television and dresser toppled over on him. She attempted to call her former husband, knocked on the doors of another tenant and the motel owner, and then called the police. She cleaned up the room, fearful that a social worker might take her daughter away if the room was in disarray. When the police arrived, Chong said the death of her son was accidental. But in grief, she also screamed, "I killed my son." Chong was arrested and charged with second degree murder. The court transcripts make clear that bias and misunderstanding were imbedded in Chong Sun France's case, starting with the police officers' actions upon their arrival and throughout the trial. One officer described Chong at her arrest as "sick," "crazed," "hateful"

and "very hysterical." Although the officers and both prosecuting and defending attorneys stated that Chong's English was impossible to understand, no
court interpreter was provided. The prosecution concluded that Chong had
asphyxiated Moses by slamming him inside the dresser drawer and then tried
to make it look like an accident, but simple forensic tests which might have
clarified the situation were never done like x-rays of the boy's body. The court
did not have sufficient evidence to prove the alleged murder, but it found her
guilty based on an assessment of the "kind of" mother and woman she was
presumed to be—a club woman, an absconding wife, an irresponsible mother
leaving her children home alone—an immigrant who could barely speak in
her own defense. In the end, Chong Sun France was convicted and sent to the
Correctional Institution for Women in Raleigh, North Carolina with a twenty
year sentence. An appeal was attempted, but rejected. In Jacksonville there
is a small community of Korean Americans. However, as in Korea, there is
little social contact between the Korean women who work in the bar areas
or former club women who are now married to soldiers, and the rest of the
Korean community. When the local community heard of Chong Sun France's
unfair conviction and sentence, though, it was moved to rally to her defense.
Then the NYC Rainbow Church, made up of Korean women mostly married to former G.I.s, became involved and a Free Chong Sun France campaign was started. Groups across the country and in South Korea became
involved, sending petitions and letters to the North Carolina governor, who
finally called a special hearing to reassess the case and trial. On December 31,
1992, after 6 years in prison, Chong Sun France was given clemency and was
released. Now living in New York, she works to help other Korean women at
the Community Center.

> —Reproduced from "The Case of Chong Sun France" in a
> documentary titled *The Women Outside: Korean Women and
> the U.S. Military* by Takagi and Park (1995, pp. 13–14)

OVERVIEW

The case study sets the stage for the rest of the chapter as an illustration of a former
prostitute and survivor of the South Korean "camptowns" (*kijich'on* prostitution) that
sexually served US military personnel during the Korean War and how her life trajectory was very much shaped by the course of institutionalized prostitution sponsored by the Korean government and supported by the American military. In this
chapter, a transnational feminist and gender analysis is provided in a global context of
inequalities under political, economic, and patriarchal power perspectives. As Cynthia
Enloe (2014) notes, "Conducting a feminist gender analysis requires investigating
power: What forms does power take? Who wields it? . . . For what ends?" (pp. 8–
9). From a radical feminist lens, the pursuit of gender equality is achieved through
elevating female ideals and curtailing the patriarchal frameworks and power that
frame the pillars of our society (Gilman, 1898) while also assuming a transnational
post-colonialism approach (Mohanty, 1984) that challenges the second-class status of
women in a global context. Through an exploration of US military bases abroad and the
associated institutional prostitution practices/policies (i.e., the military–prostitution

complex), this chapter examines the impact of US military power, both historically and currently, on women's rights. Military culture is hypermasculine and patriarchal in nature, and it is considered to espouse a sexist masculine-warrior type of ideology and ethos (Dunivin, 1994; Sasson-Levy, 2003). Military male domination has been suggested to play a significant role in the development of the global sex industry and sex trafficking (Jeffreys, 2009).

This chapter attempts to tie issues of gender, power, hypermasculinity, and militarism to the impact on so-called "Third World" women and prostitution. Linking topics necessitates the use of broad strokes in terms of the coverage of subject matter and excludes definitions of gender beyond binary constructs. The focus is exclusively on women and girls as victims/survivors, as opposed to men or boys. Rape of civilian women and girls as a weapon of war (the use of sexual violence to achieve military and war objectives) is also not discussed, although there are arguably overlaps with the topics presented here. In addition, the issue of women in the US military and the prevalence of sexual assault and harassment perpetrated on them by male service members is beyond the scope of this chapter. For more in-depth coverage of military sexual trauma, the reader is referred to Zaleski (2015, 2018). Despite the aforementioned limitations, the intersections of dominant ideologies embodied by the military that function to maintain transnational masculinity and patriarchal systems are highlighted. Advocacy is also promoted through the networks of resistance throughout the world that can build true agency in women and their allies to combat dysfunctional narratives and practices that serve to maintain the status quo in oppressive gender relations and the unequal distribution of power.

The topics of prostitution, global sex tourism, and human sex trafficking have deep roots and linkage to the US military–prostitution complex. Red light districts evolved from so-called "rest and relaxation" or "restoration" (R&R) locations where the military would send their men on leave (vacation) or to recuperate from an injury as well as in neighborhoods in close proximity to US military bases (Sturdivant & Stoltzfus, 1992). For instance, red light districts proliferated throughout central Luzon in the Philippines, where the largest Pacific Fleet of the United States was housed as well as the largest Marine training grounds. This was also the case in Okinawa, Japan, and in Thailand. In Vietnam, during the Vietnam War, red light districts were located closer to the front lines (Sturdivant & Stoltzfus, 1992). When the US military started to devolve, close bases, and streamline its overseas deployments, these red light districts transitioned into major tourism areas, particularly for sex tourism (Jeffreys, 2009). In many of these areas, it was mostly retired military who opened the bars and clubs that comprised the districts (A. Balawan, personal communication, March 12, 2018). Because the US military was located throughout the Asia Pacific region, these ubiquitous red light districts were co-located with them. Whether by plan or by sheer convenience, as the US military expanded its reach, it inevitably created the US military–prostitution complex that is thriving even today in these areas.

According to Jeffreys (2009), "In its sheer scale, military prostitution can be seen as kick-starting a crucial aspect of the globalization of prostitution, the sexual exploitation of a sexual proletariat of women and children from poor countries by [mostly] members of rich westernized nations" (p. 107). In this chapter, and in alignment with Raymond (2013), prostitution (selling sex for money) is viewed as a form of violence against women, a commodification of women, based on a radical feminist argument that conservative versus liberal perspectives of sexuality fail to capture that prostitution is a "stronghold of sexualized male dominance" (pp. xvi–xvii). Raymond offers the following take on conservative versus liberal viewpoints that skirt challenging the status quo:

> In the liberal view, prostitution is a woman's choice; in the conservative view, prostitution is her determined behavior. In the liberal view, prostitution is a woman's economic necessity; in the conservative view, prostitution is a man's natural need. In the liberal view, prostitution is a female sexual liberation; in the conservative view, prostitution is female sexual perversion. In the liberal view, prostitution is a woman's basic human right; in the conservative view, prostitution is her essential moral failing. (p. xvii)

Furthermore, according to Raymond (2013), the concept that women "choose" prostitution as a voluntary option is one that must consider the "choosing" as being highly dependent on the context of other options. For example, there is the argument that because as many as 73% of prostitutes have experienced past sexual trauma, they are not really able to operate within the context of choice (Lutnick et al., 2015). Similarly, because the average age at which prostitutes first "begin" or their first experience being commercially sexually exploited is 13 years in the United States, 14 years in Canada, and one would assume even lower in developing countries, the same rationale for considering all minors sexually trafficked may be applied here (Development Services Group, 2014). In addition, the notion of "voluntary sex work" (and sex migrant work) is a cover for the sexual exploitation of women by neocolonial and supposed human rights defenders who claim that prostitution is enabling economic opportunities for women and allows for their sexual freedom and agency as espoused by liberal feminists (Denfeld, 1995). Raymond notes the following:

> Some women enter the sex industry because they have been forced, coerced or deceived. Others enter [by personal "choice"] because offenders abuse their vulnerabilities including past and present sexual abuse, poverty and economic disadvantage, marginalization, and loss of self, and use predatory recruitment tactics that can include peer or family pressure. Those who enter the industry knowing that they will engage in prostitution often have no idea of the conditions that await them. No matter whether women experience forced entry or initial "choice," they are still used and used up by an industry that exploits them to the hilt. (p. 19)

Mohanty (2003) brings to light the fact that Western feminist discourse and political praxis are not "homogenous in its goals, interests or analyses" (p. 17). However, Mohanty cautions through a transnational and postcolonial feminist lens that Western (White, middle-class) or "First World" feminists (both radical and liberal) make sweeping assumptions and US/Eurocentric judgments about women in the Third World (typically characterized as non-Western, underdeveloped, and economically dependent nations that can also include minorities or people of color in the United States). Furthermore, First World/Third World dichotomies (or social categories) only serve to reinforce problematic hierarchies of privilege and institutional power structures of the West (White, middle-class, United States and Western Europe). Therefore, although these terms are admittedly inadequate and yet commonly utilized,

they require a critical lens and deconstructing in order to avoid paternalistic categories and narratives associated with Western cultural imperialism. Mohanty adds that
feminists in developing countries or "Third World feminists" "run the risk of marginalization or ghettoization from both mainstream (right and left) and Western feminist
discourses" (p. 17). One of the main points from Mohanty's writings is that women in
the Third World or from any other world are not a "coherent group." She states,

> Women are constituted as women through the complex interaction between
> class, culture, religion and other ideological institutions and frameworks. They
> are not "women"—a coherent group solely on the basis of a particular economic
> system or policy. Such reductive cross-cultural comparisons result in the coloni-
> zation of the specifics of daily existence and the complexities of political inter-
> ests that women of different social classes and cultures represent and mobilize.
> (p. 30)

Thus, from Mohanty's perspective, the notion of "sisterhood" must not be based on
gender alone but also must include geographical location, sociohistorical context, and
geo-economics and politics. Lila Abu-Lughod (2013) takes the notion of colonialism and Western stereotypes further when discussing poor Middle East and South
and Southeast Asian Muslim women in her book, *Do Muslim Women Need Saving?*
Abu-Lughod notes that Western powers have directly shaped circumstances for these
women and that we, as Westerners, should examine our own responsibilities (e.g.,
power rivalries, global economies, and the international War on Terror) when examining global conditions for such women. She notes that "we do not stand outside the
world, overlooking a sea of poor, benighted people living under the shadow—or the
veil—of oppressive cultures; we are part of that world" (p. 49). Abu-Lughod references Enloe's work, *Globalization and Militarism* (2007), when she states that "militarization always has hidden consequences for women; these surely have more force
than 'culture' or 'tradition'" (p. 53). In addition, Abu-Lughod criticizes the work of
Kristof and WuDunn (2009), who focus on women's oppressive stories from Africa,
Asia, and the Middle East and immigrant enclaves in Europe, in that she believes
that the authors trivialize the seriousness of gender and women's issues in the United
States and Europe (both White middle-class and those considered minorities or people of color). In this vein, Abu-Lughod notes that although Kristof and WuDunn have
good intentions, women's problems are situated as being "over there" and thus this
promotes a sense of "othering."

The Military–Prostitution Complex

The United States as an "empire" (Lutz, 2009) has more military installations outside of its boundaries than any other nation in the world, with an estimated 800 bases
in approximately 70 countries, including US territories, as well as smaller confirmed
and unconfirmed security cooperatives or "lily pads" (Vine, 2015). Even where there
are no formal bases, there are treaties such as Visiting Forces Agreements or Status of
Forces Agreements that enable the US military to enjoy rights in different countries
(Velasco, 2015). Even these types of agreements may exacerbate commercial sexual
exploitation. Prostitutes in the Philippines report the phenomenon of "akyat barco"

(climbing the ship/boat) wherein they are "sent for" and take a small boat directly to the US Navy ships, which are not allowed to dock directly (A. Balawan, personal communication, March 12, 2018). This assumes a collusion between the military and the local pimps because there is no way the women would be able to gain entrance to the ships without being let on them.

Raymond (2013) states that there is a historical context for the role of US colonialism and the promotion of prostitution, particularly in developing countries, and calls this the "military–prostitution complex" (p. xvi). Raymond provides the example of the prior military bases in the Philippines located in the cities of Olongapo and Angeles City during the Philippine–American War (1899–1902) that set the stage for prostitution around other bases throughout the world and influenced the current sex industry in the Philippines among other places. The military–prostitution complex is an institutionalized system in that under General Arthur MacArthur Jr., for example, during the U.S. occupation of the Philippines, there was a government sponsored "certification" from a health and sexually transmitted disease (STD) or venereal disease (VD) perspective of Filipinas and others to "sexually service" U.S. male military personnel (Raymond, 2013). These pink health certificates were posted on bulletin boards inside the base so that "unhealthy" women could be identified. This is not to suggest that local prostitution did not exist prior to US occupation but, rather, that the military–prostitution complex intensified the effects of the development of the modern sex industry (Raymond, 2013).

During World War II, the Imperial Japanese Army initially used Japanese women and girls sold by their families to brothels, but they also "recruited" (coerced, kidnapped, or deceived) an estimated 100,000–200,000 Asian women and girls, mostly from Korea, the Philippines, China, Indonesia, Malaysia, and even the Netherlands, to sexually service Japanese soldiers in government-established brothels. These girls and women were euphemistically called "comfort women," and post-World War II, during the American military occupation in Japan, the comfort women were passed on to the US military to service the male American troops (Raymond, 2013; Tanaka, 2002). The United States set up "comfort stations" in Japan through the Japanese Recreation and Amusement Association, which helped establish this system in order "to protect the chastity of Japanese women" (deter the rape of civilians or the development of romantic relationships) and "prevent pollution of the race" from the American occupation troops (Schaller, 1997, as cited in Raymond, 2013, p. 156). The organized sexual slavery of Southeast Asian women by Japan, which has been recognized as wartime sexual slavery and a violation of human rights, and later sponsored by the US military through the provision of prophylactic stations, penicillin for the women, and forced inspections for STDs in the women speaks to the American role in not only patronizing prostitution but also the collusion of organized sex slave abuse (Tanaka, 2002). In the spring of 1946, General Douglas MacArthur (the son of General Arthur MacArthur), who was in charge of the US administration of the occupation in Japan, was allegedly pressured by military chaplains to end the use of comfort women by male American troops (Raymond, 2013). The US military–prostitution complex was continued in the Philippines post-World War II and later in South Korea (during the Korean War) and the Vietnam War. It was not until 2005 that patronizing prostitution anywhere in the world by US service members was criminalized under Article 138-4 of the Uniform Code of Military Justice (the US military's criminal law); however, enforcement of this rule is another issue (Raymond, 2013). The US military is often considered a subculture of American society that is based on hierarchal and patriarchal organizational structures and "comprised of [a set of] values, beliefs, traditions, norms, perceptions, and behaviors" (Coll, Weiss, & Metal, 2013, p. 23). According to Moe (2018), who writes about military culture and service member deployment in the continental United States, and abroad,

> Much of our understanding of military culture in the research is based on norms, traditions, and values that are inculcated through training and more evident in garrison life. However, it is on deployment where these norms, traditions, and values are interpreted and sometimes challenged and rejected in areas ranging from uniform standards to rules regarding personal morality. (p. 118)

HISTORICAL TRENDS

According to Jeffreys (2009), the bolstering of aggressive masculinity and violence in warfare has been tied to sexual exploitation and prostitution "in its many forms to comfort and entertain soldiers, to pump them up, to maintain their military aggression, [and] is pervasive across militaries and conflict zones" (p. 109). In the West, feminist concern with regard to military prostitution dates back to the United Kingdom's Contagious Diseases Acts of the 1860s (Jeffreys, 1985, 2009). The acts by the state were created to protect British servicemen from VD/STDs, whereby "women in designated areas near camps and ports who were suspected of prostitution could be arrested, examined and locked up in 'lock' hospitals if found to be infected" (p. 108). Feminist Josephine Butler claimed that these acts were a violation of women's rights; later, in the 1980s, Cynthia Enloe furthered this work through the theory of "militarization" as it pertains to the "othering" of women, where women are utilized to sexually serve war-ready militaries (Jeffreys, 2009). There is debate about the distinctions among circumstances of "sexual slavery" as more severe forms of sexual exploitation versus prostitution. In the former, women are kidnapped, forced, deceived, and/or uncompensated financially or even killed after sexual abuse. Tanaka (2002) recommends examining this issue of sexual slavery versus prostitution as one of "continuities." Jeffreys (2009) notes that the use of so-called comfort women in Japan by the military during and post-World War II occurred in the context of colonization and war but not as part of an organized genocidal campaign, whereas different versions of "rape camp" prostitution were created by the Nazis in Europe, where Jewish girls and women in concentration camps and those imprisoned in ghettos were forced into brothels to sexually serve German soldiers and others, and by Bosnian Serb militias that kidnapped non-Serb and Bosnian (Bosnian Muslim and Croatian) women and girls and brought them into rape camps with severe consequences, including murder (MacKinnon, 2006). Both of these circumstances, the Jewish Holocaust and Bosnian genocide, occurred in the context of genocide and ethnic cleansing (this is not meant to diminish the brutal consequences of what the comfort women in Japan or the camptown women in Korea or others have endured; rather, it is meant to note the contextual differences).

The US military involvement in militarized prostitution is typically not included in the discussion of rape camps or military sexual slavery, although similarities or, as Tanaka (2002) suggests, continuities do exist; however, the differences are often in terms of degrees of violence perpetrated on the women (Jeffreys, 2009). It is noteworthy that sex crimes such as rape have been committed by American service members abroad, but these are not necessarily cases of institutionalized military prostitution but, rather, sexual assaults by "bad apples" on civilian women near US military installations. For example, between 1945 and 2011, there were approximately 350 reported cases of rapes and sexual assaults perpetrated by American male military personnel in Okinawa, Japan, of girls as young as age 12 years, as documented by the group Okinawa Women Act Against Military Violence (Vine, 2015; Women for General Security, n.d.). On the other hand, the Mai Lay massacre and rape of civilian women and children as young as age 10 years during the Vietnam War in 1968 by American forces have been suggested to be a result of serious failure in military leadership rather than acts conducted by misfits (Levesque, 2018). Although considered a horrific and the most significant war crime perpetrated by American troops during the Vietnam War (347–504 unarmed women, children, and old men were slaughtered, and 20 women and girls were raped), of all the military officers from My Lai brought to trial, only one was convicted and served a 3-year prison sentence (Levesque, 2018).

During the Korean War (1950–1953), camptowns or small cities surrounding the US military bases were created and coordinated by national and local South Korean governments and businesses. In camptowns, poor Korean girls (often orphans) and women (widows) served in clubs and bars as "servers," "waitresses," and "dancers" or "entertainers"—in other words, as sex providers for the R&R of male American military personnel (Moon, 1997). The case study presented at the beginning of this chapter is from a documentary titled *The Women Outside: Korean Women and the U.S. Military* by Takagi and Park (1995). The film and its accompanying narrative demonstrate through this real-life testimonial how the life trajectory of Chong Sun France, a former military prostitute and survivor of the Korean camptowns, was very much influenced by the US military–prostitution complex. Although Chong Sun France married a US service member, this is not to imply that all of the women in the camptowns sought escape from sexual exploitation by marrying American service members (or to be "rescued" by them) because this represents only one example of the experiences of the many women who were exposed and exploited by both the Korean and American governments. In their testimonials, many victims/survivors report incidents of rape, violence, and abuse at the hands of US military personnel and others. Moon (1997) notes that sex services were regulated by the Korean Ministry of Health and Social Affairs as well as the US military in that the women in the clubs were "registered" and had weekly medical examinations for STDs and other communicable diseases. According to Vine (2015), it is "easy to condemn GIs for taking advantage of an often exploitative sex industry in places like South Korea" (p. 181). Although Vine does not excuse the behavior of individual military members, he notes that the US military created camptowns with little options for other forms of recreation and that the American military espouses a patriarchal and sexist culture that also reflects the attitudes of US society as a whole. In addition, Vine cautions against making generalizations about men in the military being rapists; rather, he states,

> Men are not naturally rapists, and the majority of men in the military—whatever their degree of obedience—do not commit sexual assaults. But across societies, certain conditions enable rape and make sexual assault more likely. These are the conditions generally found in the U.S. military and on bases worldwide.

This is an environment where females are considered inferior; where women are frequently reduced to sex objects in camptowns, in pornography, and in USO [United Service Organization] shows; and where men are trained and encouraged to enact a masculinity centered on demonstrating one's strength and dominance over others who are considered weaker, inferior, and deserving of being dominated. (pp. 189-190)

Enloe (1988) posits that the military–prostitution complex (or the institutionalization of prostitution by the US military) takes from existing societal gender norms and further intensifies the cultural meanings of being a "man" and a "soldier." This involves the use of power over inferior or weaker others (i.e., women) and represents a "militarized masculinity." Vine (2015) adds that the hierarchical attitudes are fundamental to military training and that dehumanizing others is required in order to be able to kill other human beings, and thus "institutionalized military prostitution provides one important source for this dehumanization of women and the militarized masculinity that helps to perpetuate it" (p. 182). Furthermore, there is another dynamic in terms of differences in race and ethnicity and the US societal negative stereotypes and often discriminatory attitudes toward people of color and those considered from the Third World, in that "in places where there is an ethnic difference between GIs and sex workers, military prostitution can also reinforce societal beliefs about supposed racial and ethnic superiority, and the naturalness of some people serving and others being serviced" (Vine, 2015, pp. 182–183). This idea was supported by the rationale that war and conflict brought out aggressions in soldiers that they would take out on Third World women in order to "save" the sensibilities of the (mostly) White wives they left behind at home (Stur, 2011).

The institutionalization of military prostitution occurred in a similar manner in the Philippines after it was occupied by the United States post-World War II (Farr, 2004; Jeffreys, 2009) and during the Vietnam War. In addition, according to Vine (2015),

Thailand's Pattaya Beach became one of the world's largest red-light districts. It was a favored spot for R&R, or some called it, I&I, intoxication and intercourse. When the military withdrew from South Vietnam, it left behind an estimated seven hundred thousand sex workers. (p. 166)

Taiwan also served as a destination for R&R during the Vietnam War. The Taiwanese government accepted American service member sex tourism as a way to promote national economic and political interests, particularly to further its relationship with the United States as an ally (Cheng, 2009; Wang, 1989). Power relations were further highlighted by Yen (2014) as building upon Foucault's (1978) notion of a human body (in this case, women's bodies) representing a field of definition and intervention in power and politics. Yen also notes the power disparities between the American service members and the Taiwanese prostitutes in relation to "gender, region, race, class, ethnicity [and] or sexuality" (p. 777). According to news reports and documentation from the Taiwanese Department of Health, under the "request" and "instruction" of the US military, the Taiwanese government set up medical clinics to address women's health to prevent the spread of VD to the servicemen, and the Taipei City Health Bureau inspected and patrolled the bars (Yen, 2014).

Furthermore, whenever and wherever military bases closed, the base towns relocated to other US military bases in Guam, Hawaii, Okinawa, and Germany, for instance. Jeffreys (2009) finds a direct link between military prostitution and the industrialization of prostitution and sex trafficking throughout the world and concludes that "after military prostitution caused the industrialization of prostitution in a country, local women and girls became the raw materials of the global sex industry, not only prostituted within local and sex tourism industries at home but trafficked into prostitution worldwide" (p. 119). Although Jeffreys posits that the military–prostitution complex was a causal factor, we suggest that it is an associated factor and one of many others, such as advances in technology and globalization, that have exacerbated the industrialization of prostitution and sex trafficking worldwide. Furthermore, women's groups such as Gabriela Philippines have reported the fine lines between the sex industry and sex trafficking, especially with the growing demand for increasingly younger girls (Lindio-McGovern, 2007). In addition, Vine (2015) suggests that male American service members' experiences in camptown-style prostitution, the objectification of women, and the masculine-oriented climate cannot be ignored in the context of military sexual trauma—that is, the sexual assault and harassment of women serving in the military perpetrated by fellow servicemen.

RECENT DEVELOPMENTS OF NOTE

Commercialized sex areas or zones continue to exist near US bases worldwide (including in Germany, Japan, and South Korea), as do red-light districts situated near US domestic bases (Vine, 2017). Vine notes that during the 1990s, with the improvement of the South Korean economy, Korean women working in the sex industry (i.e., camptowns) were mostly replaced with a majority of Filipina and some Russian and former Soviet Republic women and that the camptowns continue to be a booming business contributing to the local and national economics (the Korean government offers the E-6 "entertainers" visa to import women and provides mandatory HIV testing and STD tests on a regular basis). In addition, in the 1990s, with the deployment of United Nations peacekeeping forces and reconstruction activities in countries such as Cambodia, Haiti, Rwanda, Sierra Leone, Guinea, Kosovo, and Liberia, there were reports of women and girls being forced into prostitution and being sexually abused by so-called peacekeepers (Farr, 2004; Harrington, 2005). Jeffreys (2009) notes that the nongovernmental organization Refugees International has found that the "behavior of peacekeepers has much in common with sex tourism. In both cases, men from richer countries find themselves free to play with the sexual exploitation of economically desperate girls, many very young, in poor countries" (p. 122).

Even during the United States' continued military involvement in a highly conservative setting, namely the Middle East and specifically Afghanistan and Iraq, there have been reports of US military personnel and private defense contractors visiting brothels and engaged in sex with trafficking victims. Chandrasekaran (2007), an embedded journalist, reports that during the American occupation in Iraq following the toppling of Saddam Hussein, in 2003 and 2004, the Coalition of Provisional Authority (CPA) run by the US military, allied forces (Britain, Poland, Australia, Spain, and Italy), and private defense firms (e.g., contractors such as Halliburton) established a 7-square-mile American enclave in central Baghdad; Hussein's palace housed the headquarters of CPA operations. According to Chandrasekaran, this post-conflict reconstruction effort in Iraq, dubbed the Emerald City in the Green Zone (secure area), was a "fanta-syland" where military rules and Iraqi customs did not necessarily apply to its inhabit-ants, which were mostly Western White civilian men and military service members. Chandrasekaran notes the following about the "sex starved" men in the Green Zone and their interests in seeking out prostitutes:

> There were prostitutes in Baghdad but you could not drive into town to get laid like in Saigon. There was a persistent rumor of a brothel "whorehouse" in the Green Zone but CPA staffers said it was a military thing. Only soldiers knew the location. (p. xx)

Schwellenbach and Leonnig (2010) reported on how US defense contractors were allegedly involved in soliciting prostitutes and victims of sex trafficking in Iraq and Afghanistan but that there was no enforcement of the US criminal policy that forbids government contractors to engage in sex trafficking in war zones or solicit prostitutes because many of them are victims of the global sex trade. This policy was enacted fol-lowing an incident that occurred approximately 10 years earlier involving employees of US defense contractor DynCorp International, who were accused of but never pros-ecuted for "buying and selling women throughout Eastern Europe" (Schwellenbach & Leonnig, 2010, para. 8). In 2006, the US Commander in Iraq confirmed that private defense contractors and subcontractors were engaged in human labor trafficking on American bases and were "ordered to end abuses" (Sly, 2006). In addition, US service members who have deployed to combat zones and bases in the Middle East and other regions, even those within the ranks of leadership, have also been frequent users of pornography (Myers, 2016).

CURRENT CONDITIONS

In 2017, the US Department of Defense (Defense Manpower Data Center, 2017) reported that official troop numbers included more than 50,000 service mem-bers and civilian employees in the Middle East and Central Asia, with 25,910 military personnel in Afghanistan, Iraq, and Syria (against the Islamic State). These numbers differed from the original Pentagon figures, which were lower because the Pentagon did not account for those deployed as special operations, in support of contingency operations, in temporary assignments, or in overlapping rotations (Woody, 2017). The lack of clarity and transparency in public access to this type of information is evi-dent when visiting the Defense Manpower Data Center website (https://www.dmdc. osd.mil/appj/dwp/dwp_reports.jsp).

Although the United States has had an overall military force reduction in recent years, according to Vine (2015) there are two reasons for the acquisition and maintenance of American military bases overseas since World War II that still apply today:

They are "redundancy"—the more bases, the safer the nation—and "strategic denial"—preventing supposed enemies from using a territory by denying them access—both of which hold that even if the military has little interest in using a base or territory, it should acquire as many as possible for every possible contingency and almost never cede its acquisitions. (p. 383)

According to Vine (2015), the presence of American bases and defense contractors in the Middle East is a continued strategy in the pursuit for global power and founded on American corporate economic interests that include the rich resources of the region, such as petroleum. Furthermore, the current buildup and maintenance of bases in Africa and the Middle East, including countries such as Egypt, Djibouti, Ethiopia, Kenya, Pakistan, Iraq, Afghanistan, Egypt, Saudi Arabia, Kuwait, Bahrain, Qatar, United Arab Emirates, Oman, and others (except Iran), are examples of America asserting "influence and [to] dominate far-off lands, resources and markets" (p. 43).

Given the historical evidence of the comfort women in Japan, the camptowns in Korea, and the many other accounts throughout the world regarding the role of US military bases and the sex industry, it is safe to surmise as others have (Enloe, 2007; Jeffreys, 2009; Moon, 1997; Tanaka, 2002) that the presence of military installations throughout the world and even those that exist today in the continental United States promotes the sexual exploitation of women and contributes to trafficking and sex tourism. Furthermore, there is a direct link between American imperialistic practices and policies, militarism, and sexual violence toward women and girls in the global sphere, and the perpetuation of such violence continues as a legacy beyond the life of the military base.

Perhaps nothing is more exemplary of this legacy than the social cost of what is left behind—the children of US military. Although the fathering of children is not a new phenomenon, the United States chose to recognize its responsibility for children in Asia fathered after 1950 due to the intense engagement of the military during that time. During the late 1980s, there were an estimated 2,000 Amerasians in Korea, 1,500 in Japan, 1,000 in Taiwan, 5,000 in Thailand, 1,000 in Laos, and 25,000 combined in Vietnam and the Philippines (Gage, 2007). Many of these children experienced stigma, hardship, and hatred in their home countries (Nwadiora & McAdoo, 1996). The United States passed the Amerasian Immigration Act of 1982, which provided support for these children, allowing them to immigrate to the United States (based on specific criteria) (Montes, 1994). However, Japan, the Philippines, and Taiwan were excluded (Gage, 2007). One reason for exclusion was that lawmakers believed that Amerasian children were more accepted in these countries and did not experience discrimination. A number of testimonies proved this was not true, with many examples of unjust and unsafe treatment (Gage, 2007). Another reason that was given, specific to the Philippines, was that the mothers' of the children were prostitutes and because prostitution is illegal in the Philippines, the appeal for inclusion of the Philippines could not be made in court (Gage, 2007; Kolby, 1995). To date, there has not been any movement for the inclusion of Japan, the Philippines, or Taiwan, despite the fact that the US military continues to take up considerable territory in these three countries either through formal bases or Visiting Forces Agreements, thus establishing the US military–prostitution complex well into the 21st century.

LOOKING TO THE FUTURE

Although the US government denies or downplays its militarization and pursuit of global domination (imperialism), many Americans and others who are affected by the American military presence in their countries are not as "enthusiastic" about US interference in so many nations of the world (Johnson, 2004) because the extension of this global power results in many negative and even unintended consequences. Johnson aptly describes the US presidency and government as a "military juggernaut intent on world domination" (p. 4). As we look toward the future, women—regardless of social and economic status, race/ethnicity, or nationality—can empower themselves to take action through various grassroots network organizations (as a form of resistance) to attempt to stop or at least curtail US militarism (and militarism in general) and encourage diplomacy and peace in international affairs. One such organization is the Women for General Security (www.genuinesecurity.org), which works transnationally and whose vision is a

> world of genuine security based on justice and respect for others across race, class, gender and national boundaries. We strategize for economic planning that meets people's needs, especially women and children. We work toward the creation of a society free of militarism, violence, and all forms of sexual exploitation, and for the safety, well-being, and long-term sustainability of our communities. (para. 1)

This organization represents the US contingency of the International Women's Network against Militarism (http://iwnam.org). Another organization, Women's Action for New Directions (https://www.wand.org), mobilizes women to become politically involved, resist militarism, and "disarm patriarchy."

CONCLUSION

Although it was not possible to cover all the complexities associated with this topic, this chapter attempted to link militarism with the impact of oppressive patriarchal and masculine ideologies and practices that prostituted women abroad have experienced through a transnational feminist and gendered lens. It also discussed how these facets of domination have converged into the current-day sex industry, sex tourism, and the promotion of international sex trafficking. Furthermore, the chapter noted that the presence of US military bases abroad reflects the extension of global powers and imperialism by the American government.

DISCUSSION QUESTIONS

1. What is the military–prostitution complex and how has it contributed to the promotion of sexual exploitation of women worldwide?
2. What is a transnational feminist perspective on American imperialism and the global sex industry?
3. Who were the "comfort women" of Japan, and how was the use of them a form of sex slavery and sex trafficking?

Figure 23.1 The live statue art commemoration of the comfort women in Japan by Yoshiko Shimada, titled "On Becoming a Statue of a Japanese Comfort Woman" (2012), outside the Embassy of Japan in London.
Source: Reproduced from "Japanese Artist to Commemorate 'Comfort Women.'" (2018, February 16). *Rafu Shimpo, Los Angeles Japanese Daily News.* Retrieved from https://www. rafu.com/2018/02/japanese-artist-to-commemorate-comfort-women

REFERENCES

Abu-Lughod, L. (2013). *Do Muslim women need saving?* Cambridge, MA: Harvard University Press.

Chandrasekaran, R. (2007). *Imperial life in the Emerald City: Inside Iraq's Green Zone.* New York, NY: Vintage.

Cheng, C. (2009). *On the post-war tourism of Taiwan and its effect on tourism exchange (1956–1987).* Taoyuan City, Taiwan: Graduate Institute of History, National Central University.

Coll, J. E., Weiss, E. L, & Metal, M. (2013). Military culture and diversity. In A. Rubin, E. L. Weiss, & J. E. Coll (Eds.), *Handbook of military social work* (pp. 21–34). Hoboken, NJ: Wiley.

Defense Manpower Data Center. (2017). *DMDC website location report 1703.* Washington, DC: Author.

Denfeld, R. (1995). *The new Victorians: A young woman's challenge to the old feminist order.* St. Leonards, New South Wales, Australia: Allen & Unwin.

Development Services Group. (2014). *Commercial sexual exploitation of children/ sex trafficking* [Literature review]. Washington, DC: Office of Juvenile Justice and Delinquency Prevention. Retrieved from https://www.ojjdp.gov/mpg/litreviews/ CSECSexTrafficking.pdf

Dunivin, K. O. (1994). Military culture: Change and continuity. *Armed Forces & Society, 20*(4), 531–547.

Enloe, C. (1988). Beyond "Rambo": Women and the varieties of militarized masculinity. In E. Isaakson (Ed.), *Women and the military system* (pp. 71–93). New York, NY: St. Martin's.

Enloe, C. (2007). *Globalization and militarism.* New York, NY: Rowman & Littlefield.

Enloe, C. (2014). *Bananas, beaches and bases: Making sense of international politics* (2nd ed.). Los Angeles, CA: University of California Press.

Farr, K. (2004). *Sex trafficking: The global market in women and children.* New York, NY: Worth.

Foucault, M. (1978). *Discipline and punish: The birth of the prison.* New York, NY: Pantheon.

Gage, S. J. L. (2007). The Amerasian problem: Blood, duty, and race. *International Relations, 21*(1), 86–102.

Gilman, C. P. (1898). *Women and economics.* Boston, MA: Small & Maynard.

Harrington, C. (2005). The politics of rescue: Peacekeeping and anti-trafficking programmes in Bosnia-Herzegovina and Kosovo. *International Feminist Journal of Politics, 7*(2), 175–206.

Jeffreys, S. (1985). *The spinster and her enemies: Feminism and sexuality 1880–1930.* London, UK: Women's Press.

Jeffreys, S. (2009). *The industrial vagina: The political economy of the global sex trade.* New York, NY: Routledge.

Johnson, C. A. (2004). *The sorrows of empire: Militarism, secrecy and the end of the republic.* New York, NY: Holt.

Kolby, E. (1995). Moral responsibility to Filipino Amerasians: Potential immigration and child support alternatives. *Asian American Law Journal, 2,* 61.

Kotiswaran, P. (2011). *Dangerous sex, invisible labor: Sex work and the law in India.* Princeton, NJ: Princeton University Press.

Kristof, N. D., & WuDunn, S. (2009). *Half the sky: Turning oppression into opportunity for women worldwide.* New York, NY: Vintage.

Levesque, C. J. (2018, March 18). The truth behind My Lai. *The New York Times.* Retrieved from https://www.nytimes.com/2018/03/16/opinion/the-truth-behind-my-lai.html

Lindio-McGovern, L. (2007). Neo-liberal globalization in the Philippines: Its impact on Filipino women and their forms of resistance. *Journal of Developing Societies, 23*(1–2), 15–35.

Lutnick, A., Harris, J., Lorvick, J., Cheng, H., Wenger, L. D., Bourgois, P., & Kral, A. H. (2015). Examining the associations between sex trade involvement, rape, and symptomatology of sexual abuse trauma. *Journal of Interpersonal Violence, 30*(11), 1847–1863.

Lutz, C. (2009). *The bases of empire: The global struggle against military posts.* London, UK: Pluto Press.

MacKinnon, C. (2006). *Are women human? And other international dialogues.* Cambridge, MA: Belknap.

Moe, J. (2018). Preparation for deployment and life during deployment. In E. L. Weiss & C. A. Castro (Eds.), *American military life in the 21st century: Social, cultural, and economic issues and trends* (pp. 117–129). Santa Barbara, CA: ABC-CLIO.

Mohanty, C. T. (1984). Under Western eyes: Feminist scholarship and colonial discourse. *Boundary, 12*(3), 333–358.

Mohanty, C. T. (2003). *Feminism without borders: Decolonizing theory, practicing solidarity.* Durham, NC: Duke University Press.

Montes, M. B. (1994). U.S. recognition of its obligation to Filipino Amerasian children under international law. *Hastings Law Journal, 46,* 1621.

Moon, K. S. (1997). *Sex among allies: Military prostitution in U.S.–Korea relations.* New York, NY: Columbia University Press.

Myers, M. (2016, March 8). Strike group boss watched porn for hours on Navy computer: Report. *Navy Times.* Retrieved from https://www.navytimes.com/story/military/2016/03/08/strike-group-boss-watched-porn-hours-navy-computer-report/81510180

Nwadiora, E., & McAdoo, H. (1996). Acculturative stress among Amerasian refugees: Gender and racial differences. *Adolescence, 31*(122), 477.

Overs, C. (2009, March 12–14). *"Ain't I a woman"—A global dialogue between sex worker rights movement and the Stop the Violence Against Women movement Bangkok, Thailand.* Melbourne, Australia: The Paulo Longo Research Initiative, Department of Epidemiology and Preventative Medicine. Monash University, Alfred Hospital Campus.

Raymond, J. G. (2013). *Not a choice, not a job: Exposing myths about prostitution and the global sex trade.* Washington, DC: Potomac Books.

Sasson-Levy, O. (2003). Feminism and military gender practices: Israeli women soldiers in "masculine" roles. *Sociological Inquiry, 73*(3), 440–465.

Schwellenbach, N., & Leonnig, C. (2010, July 18). U.S. policy a paper tiger against sex trade in war zones. *Washington Post.* Retrieved from http://www.washingtonpost.com/wp-dyn/content/article/2010/07/17/AR2010071701401.html?noredirect=on

Sly, L. (2006, April 24). Iraq war contractors ordered to end abuses. *Chicago Tribune.* Retrieved from http://articles.chicagotribune.com/2006-04-24/news/0604240221_1_orders-promise-harsh-actions-iraq-from-impoverished-countries-return-passports

Stur, H. M. (2011). *Beyond combat: Women and gender in the Vietnam War era.* New York, NY. Cambridge University Press.

Sturdivant, S. P., & Stoltzfus, B. (1992). *Let the good times roll: Prostitution and the U.S. military in Asia.* New York, NY: New Press.

Takagi, J. T., & Park, H. (1995). *The women outside: Korean women and the U.S. military: Documentary study guide.* New York, NY: Third World Newsreel Publication. Retrieved from http://www.twn.org/catalog/guides/Women-Outside-Study-Guide.pdf

Tanaka, Y. (2002). *Japan's comfort women: Sexual slavery and prostitution during World War II and the U.S. occupation.* London, UK: Routledge.

Velasco, M. A. M. (2015). The Visiting Forces Agreement (VFA) in the Philippines: Insights on issues of sovereignty, security and foreign policy. *Asia Pacific Journal of Multidisciplinary Research, 3*(4), 82–89.

Vine, D. (2015). *Base nation: How U.S. military bases abroad harm America and the world.* New York, NY: Metropolitan Books.

Wang, C. (1989). The political transition and social campaign in Taiwan. *Taiwan: A Radical Quarterly in Social Studies, 2*(1), 71–116.

Women for General Security. (n.d.). *Okinawa women act against military violence.* Retrieved from http://www.genuinesecurity.org/partners/okinawa.html

Woody, C. (2017, November 28). There's confusion about US troop levels in the Middle East, and Trump may keep it that way. *Business Insider.* Retrieved from http://www.businessinsider.com/how-many-us-troops-are-in-middle-east-confusion-trump-2017-11

Yen, J. (2014). The body matters: Nationalism and American sex tourism in postcolonial Taiwan. *Journal of Research in Gender Studies, 4*(1), 777–787.

Zaleski, K. L. (2015). *Understanding and treating military sexual trauma.* New York, NY: Springer.

Zaleski, K. L. (2018). *Understanding and treating military sexual trauma* (2nd ed.). New York, NY: Springer.

Tables, figures, and boxes are indicated by *t, f,* and *b* following the page number
For the benefit of digital users, indexed terms that span two pages (e.g., 52–53) may, on occasion, appear on only one of those pages.